a cluster is 2, 4, 8, 16, etc sectors, smallest 4 sectors, 1 clusters - 2h (128M) hard drives

IDE (common 16 sector   done

IDE - integrated device electronics   SCSI - small compu
                                        - best in networ

FAT - File Allocation table
    - has room for 64h entries, fat-16 FAT-24
    - FFFFH - end of file   0000H - free   FFF7H - BAD
    - tell whats full, empty, bad, good on the disk

Boot strap loader	FAT	Boot Directory

0003	0004
0002	FFFF
0001	0002
0000	batch 403

↑
BIOS - Basic
    I/O
    system

        can only hold so many / much   DSDD 5¼ - 122 names

                                        hard drives - 244 names

Boot sector is used to load DOS   sector - 512 byte

- all FM, MFM, use BLL

- fastest access time - 7ms
    average 12ms - 14ms

The refresh rate of a video display is the number of times per second that the image is displayed

A pair of disk tracks (top and bottom) is not called a cycle, but is called a cylinder

# of memory locations that are reserved to store video images with a certain resolution, is 1 X 2   ex 640 X 480 resolution

            memory = 640 X 480 = 307,200

R+B = Magenta

G+B = Cyan
            higher intensity
R+G = yellow or brown   regular intensity

VRAM - can update or send new data at all times, even when printing on screen
has 2 ports

in the computers memory you have 160h of memory for video but 32h is for video Bios Rom and only 128h for sending out or in from the video card
- for 1M video card, it is seperated into 8 parts

RGB
    000 - black   110 - brown
    001 - Blue   111 - white
    010 - Green   60 Hz vertical scanning
    100 - Red   15,750 Hz horizontal rate
    011 - Cyan
    101 - magenta

                                        # of lines 15,750/60

0-15 → normal colors

16-31 - grey scale n shades of gray

32-255 - various shades of the colors - default palet

<u>monitors</u>

TTL — CGA (0-5v) Red video, Green video, Blue video, Hi intensity — 16 colors only

Analog — VGA, SVGA, EGA, XGA, SVGA (0-.7v) infinite number of colors are able
to be displayed

— .28 dot pitch — buy nothing higher in monitors

Microprocessors and Peripherals

Hardware, Software, Interfacing, and Applications

Second Edition

Barry B. Brey

DeVry Institute of Technology
Columbus, Ohio

Merrill, an imprint of
Macmillan Publishing Company
New York

Maxwell Macmillan Canada
Toronto

Maxwell Macmillan International Publishing Group
New York   Oxford   Singapore   Sydney

Cover photo courtesy of Intel Corporation

This book was set in Times Roman
Administrative Editor: Stephen Helba
Production Coordinator: Anne Daly
Art Coordinator: Pete Robison
Cover Designer: Cathy Watterson

Photo credits: Page 3, Amdaul Corporation; page 4, Digital Equipment Corporation; pages 8, 12, Hewlett-Packard, Inc.; pages 10, 11, Intel Corporation; page 388, Apple, Inc.

Macmillan Publishing Company
866 Third Avenue, New York, New York 10022

Maxwell Macmillan Canada, Inc.
1200 Eglington Avenue East, Suite 200
Don Mills, Ontario M3C 3N1

Library of Congress Catalog Card Number: 87-63189
International Standard Book Number: 0-675-20884-X
Printed in the United States of America
4   5   6   7   8   9 — 92

To my daughter, Brenda

MERRILL'S INTERNATIONAL SERIES IN ELECTRICAL AND ELECTRONICS TECHNOLOGY

Preface

The second edition of *Microprocessor/Hardware Interfacing and Applications* has been retitled *Microprocessors and Peripherals: Hardware, Software, Interfacing, and Applications* to reflect the increased coverage of peripherals. The text can be used in a one- or two-term course towards a two- or four-year engineering technology degree, a computer science degree, or an electrical engineering degree. It is also readily usable by the practicing technologist or engineer who desires updating in the field of microprocessor interfacing and peripheral devices.

The new edition uses many of the successful features of the first edition and incorporates a number of key changes:

- Chapters 11 and 12 are new and are devoted to disk memory and printers
- Learning objectives have been added to the beginning of each chapter
- A point-by-point summary is now used at the end of each chapter

This text assumes that the reader has a sound understanding of digital electronics and at least a programming course, preferably in assembly language programming for the 6800 or the 8085A microprocessor. Appendices are provided so that the reader can learn how each 6800 or 8085A instruction operates if no previous programming course has been taken.

The text contains many example applications that make it extremely useful for self-study or classroom study. In addition, each chapter contains an objectives list so the reader can decide if the chapter will provide the major information required, a numerical summary so that the chapter information can be easily reviewed, and a glossary listing the new terms in each chapter. Ample end-of-chapter questions and problems provide the reader with the opportunity to test out the information learned in the chapter.

Chapter 1 compares and contrasts the mainframe computer system with the microprocessor and introduces the reader to the text's terminology. It also describes how software and hardware relate to a total system design approach.

Chapter 2 introduces the architecture of the microprocessor by describing the internal operation of each functional unit. It offers information on a wide variety of available microprocessors and describes commonly used microprocessor system buses such as the STD-BUS.

Chapters 3 and 4 detail the Motorola and Intel series of microprocessors. A knowledge of both is worthwhile, but the text is written so that the 8085A is used mainly throughout with some applications of the 6800 such as I/O interfacing and interrupts.

Chapter 5 introduces memory interfacing. It examines how memory devices operate, explains address decoding, and provides the design methodology for both static and dynamic memory systems.

Chapters 6 and 7 provide the foundation in I/O interfacing principles that are built upon in the remaining chapters of the text. Some of these include: programmable interface components, keyboards, displays, solenoid-operated devices, analog-to-digital converters, digital-to-analog converters, and stepper motors.

Chapter 8 offers precise coverage of interrupt structures and interrupt processed I/O. It compares interrupt structures of the commonly available microprocessors and includes a discussion of a real time clock, a priority interrupt controller, and a printer queue.

Chapter 9 introduces digital communications, with information on both serial and parallel techniques using standard interface components. It introduces the RS-232C, the IEEE-488, current loops, FSK and PSK data transmission, and MODEMs.

Chapter 10 details direct memory access (DMA), which, although heavily used in industry, is all but ignored in most textbooks. It compares DMA structures of different microprocessors and DMA controllers. An application of DMA is presented in the form of a CRT controller. New in this edition is a coverage of video technology and also video display terminals.

Chapter 11 completely covers disk memory systems from the floppy disk to the hard disk. It also introduces magnetic bubble memory and optical disk memory. The 8272A floppy disk controller is studied and interfaced to the 8085A.

Chapter 12 details printers and printer interfaces. The RS-232C printer interface and Centronics printer interface are presented and interfaced to the microprocessor. A complete schematic and the software for a dot matrix printer is also presented.

Chapters 13 and 14 deal strictly with applications. Here the microprocessor is used in a complete system and all of the hardware and software are provided and discussed.

Appendices are provided for the Z80 microprocessor, the 8085A instruction set, the 6800 instruction set, data sheets, and selected answers to the old-numbered questions and problems in the text.

Acknowledgments

With gratitude, I wish to acknowledge the assistance of the following reviewers: John Blankenship, of DeVry Institute of Technology in Atlanta; Ramakant A. Gayakwad, DeVry Institute of Technology in Los Angeles; John L. Morgan, DeVry Institute of Technology in Dallas; Ralph Folger of Hudson Valley Community College (N.Y.); David Hata, Portland Community College (Oregon); Peter Holsberg, Mercer County Community College (N.J.); Eldon W. Husband, University of Houston at Clear Lake City.

A special thank you is given to David Leitch, of DeVry Institute of Technology—Columbus, whose figure-by-figure and word-by-word checking of the galley proofs has been invaluable.

Contents

1
Introduction to Microprocessors

2
Microprocessor Architecture

3

The 8085A, 8086, and 8088 Microprocessors   43

4

The MC6800, MC6809, and MC68000 Microprocessors   77

5

Memory Interface   99

6
Basic Input/Output Interface Circuitry   143

7
Input/Output Systems   181

8
Interrupt Processed I/O   219

9

Microprocessor-Based Communications   255

10

Direct Memory Access   291

11

Disk Memory Systems   333

12
Printers

13
8085A Application Examples

14
MC6800 Application Examples

Appendices

Index

1

Introduction to Microprocessors

Upon completion of this chapter, you will be able to

1 Describe the history of computers and explain their evolution into microprocessors.

2 Show how the 4-bit microprocessor evolved into the 8-bit microprocessor and cite the reasons for this evolution.

3 List the steps required to develop software for a system.

4 List the steps used to develop the hardware for a system.

5 Explain what equipment is used for the tasks of both software and hardware development.

Almost all forms of consumer, industrial, and military electronics equipment use micro-processors. Thus all electronics professionals need a firm grasp of microprocessor hardware interfacing.

To provide some insight into this exploding field, chapter 1 introduces you to the past, present, and possible future of the computer and the microprocessor.

1–1 MAINFRAME COMPUTER SYSTEMS

The first electronic digital computer systems, built in the late 1940s, were developed to solve complex scientific problems. These systems were massive and power hungry, with relatively low speeds and small memories. It's hard to believe they are related to the efficient mainframe computers of today.

It was in the early 1950s, when the business applications of computers were realized, that the boom began. Computers could handle vast amounts of information at relatively high speeds, making them ideal for accounting and record handling in large businesses. Drawbacks to their use were their expense and the significant space they required.

Since these beginnings, the large mainframe computer systems have made continuous and tremendous strides. The areas of improvement are all-encompassing. For example, memory size and speed increased significantly with the advent of the integrated circuit. Whereas the old machines ran at a few thousand operations per second, systems now accomplish well over ten million operations per second. Data transfer has become much more efficient through new methods of ''human interface,'' through printers for hardcopy and CRT terminals for softcopy.

Modernizing changes were due largely to the expansion of knowledge about digital technology. Progress in vacuum tubes, diode switching logic, small- and medium-scale integration, and large- and very-large-scale integration followed closely.

Memory is a good example of how this progress was achieved. In the beginning, memory consisted of two vacuum tubes that were required to store one binary bit of information. Today billions of bits can be stored in the area once occupied by a vacuum tube. Even more amazing is that power consumption is less than that required for the filament in a vacuum tube. No wonder the field has exploded.

The programming environment has changed, too. In the early days, a programmer had to communicate with the machine in *its* own language, machine language. This cumbersome method required hours just to be able to print a list of numbers. Now the programmer enters commands in a pseudo-English language, and a device called a *compiler* translates it into a fairly efficient machine-language program. Without these strides in communication, we would still be working on a program to generate the telephone company's monthly bills!

The large mainframe computer (see figure 1–1) solves problems for both the business and scientific communities. Today they handle data processing and accounting for most companies, model all types of business ventures, solve extremely complex scientific problems, and help design many products. One additional area of use is the dedicated task application: processes such as automated board testing, system testing, production line control, and products such as microwave ovens, automobile emission control systems,

FIGURE 1-1 A typical large mainframe computer system.

SOURCE: Courtesy of Amdaul Corporation.

CRT terminals, and printers. Some of these applications have given way to smaller computer systems as they have been developed. (Few large computer systems are included in dedicated task functions because of their cost.)

To be sure, the large mainframe computer will remain vital to businesses because of its massive storage capacity and speed. The future certainly also holds new language development, possibly an English-language compiler, so that anyone can direct large systems easily. The most significant changes will probably come in this area of human interface. Even now, ''networking'' (talking to the large system through a smaller computer) is becoming commonplace because of the time it saves the computer. As you can imagine, the new trend is toward small computer systems for a variety of tasks, including networking or data entry into large computer systems.

MINICOMPUTER SYSTEMS 1–2

As the previous section indicates, the cost and size of the mainframe computer made it impossible to use in certain dedicated task applications. To overcome this situation, the industry developed a scaled-down version, dubbed the *minicomputer*. The main differences between the mainframe computer and the minicomputer are word size and processing speed. Mainframes typically can manipulate 32-bit binary numbers, while minicomputers typically manipulate 16-bit binary numbers. The logic circuitry incorporated in the minicomputer also reduces its speed.

FIGURE 1–2 The VAX-11/730 minicomputer system, foreground; the
VAX-11/750 (left); the VAX-11/780 (right); and the VAX-11/782 (rear).
SOURCE: Photo courtesy of Digital Equipment Corporation.

Minicomputers, such as the VAX-11 in figure 1–2, typically handle such applications as board testing, system testing, automation, networking, and a variety of other fairly complex tasks. As technology advanced, minicomputers became more powerful and compact. Today, minicomputers are performing, at greater speeds, tasks as complex as those performed by the early mainframe computers.

Eventually, the minicomputer will undoubtedly be replaced by the superminicomputer. In fact, there is significant evidence that this is occurring today: the DEC PDP-11 is now made with the LSI-11 microprocessor; the TI 990 minicomputer uses the TMS-9900 microprocessor; and this list continues as manufacturers flock to microprocessors.

The superminicomputer, with the structure, speed, and capacity of the current mainframe computer, will probably perform local area network control and file management functions in the future.

1–3 THE MICROPROCESSOR-BASED MICROCOMPUTER

In the beginning, microprocessor fabrication mainly used small- and medium-scale integrated circuits. These circuits typically consisted of a 4-bit arithmetic unit, a control read-only memory (CROM), and some simple control logic. The arithmetic unit was capable of incrementing and decrementing a number and performing binary coded decimal addition. The control read-only memory held microcode, which directed the arithmetic unit and hardware attached to the system through the control logic circuitry. The control logic directed the control read-only memory by providing a memory address and various other control signals for the system. These early microprocessors were employed in devices such as cash registers, calculators, and a variety of other fundamental digital systems.

The first integration of these devices into single-component microprocessors was the four-function calculator. In fact, today's calculator chips have retained much from their early medium-scale integrated circuit beginnings. They are still binary coded decimal processors, using programmable logic arrays to direct and control the calculator.

The current microprocessor has evolved in several areas. The arithmetic unit has been modified into an arithmetic and logic unit, functioning with both binary and binary coded decimal numbers. Register arrays incorporated into the microprocessor allow for more efficient programming. Finally, a special form of memory, the *last-in, first-out stack,* permits more orderly handling of subroutines.

The Early Microprocessors

The first integrated microprocessor was a 4-bit processor designed to handle a *nibble* (4 bits) of data. These early microprocessors were implemented using PMOS technology, which made them slow and fairly awkward to interface to standard TTL logic circuitry. Instructions were executed in about 20 μs, extremely slow by today's standards.

The Intel 4004, the first microprocessor, was designed for a few limited applications. It could only address 4K nibbles of memory, which severely limited its program and data storage capabilities. (A *K* is 1024 bits.) Some of the early Intel 4004 applications were games, test equipment, and other simple digital systems.

The next phase of development for the microprocessor was the Intel 8008, a more powerful version of the Intel 4004. The 8008 could manipulate an entire byte (generally 8 bits) of data, making it more flexible in application. The amount of program storage space was increased from 4K nibbles to 16K bytes, which allowed for more powerful software-based systems. Since most data handled in computer applications are eight bits wide, the 8008 saw much more application than the earlier 4004 microprocessor. The relatively low speed of the 8008, which was capable of only about fifty thousand operations per second, created problems and limited its application.

N-Channel MOSFET Breakthrough

In the early 1970s, MOSFET integrated circuit technology experienced a breakthrough with the then-new N-channel technology. N-channel technology was faster than P-channel technology, which led to its quick rise in popularity. It also worked from a positive power supply, making it easier to interface to TTL logic circuitry.

Intel announced and sampled the Intel 8080 microprocessor in late 1973. It was constructed from NMOS logic, which allowed it to outperform the earlier 8008 by a factor of ten. The 8080 microprocessor could execute 500,000 operations per second and address 64K bytes of memory. It also maintained an upward software compatibility with the 8008; all of the 8008 instructions will function on the 8080. Since then, the 8080 has become an extremely widely used and applied microprocessor.

Other integrated circuit manufacturers began producing a wide variety of microprocessors but never seemed to narrow the lead of the Intel 8080. Examples of other early microprocessors are National Semiconductor's IMP-4 and SC/MP, Rockwell International's PPS-4 and PPS-8, Motorola's MC6800, and Fairchild's F-8. Most microprocessors used either N- or P-channel MOSFET technology, some used CMOS technology, and still others used TTL and IIL technologies. Today there are basically three types of microprocessors in production: the general-purpose microprocessor, the single-component microcomputer, and the bit-slice microprocessor. Bit-slice microprocessors can be cascaded to allow functioning systems with word widths from 4 bits to 200 bits.

Single-Component Microcomputer

In the mid 1970s, a new form of microprocessor entered the marketplace, the single-component microcomputer. This device contained a processor, read-only memory for program storage, read/write memory for data storage, input/output connections for interfacing to the outside world, and (in some) a timer/events counter. Two of the single-component microcomputers are the Intel 8048 and the Motorola 6805R2. This new breed of microcomputer allowed many systems to be built with one integrated circuit. Some applications currently include microwave ovens, washing machines, CRT terminals, and printers.

This device is found in an increasing number of applications and deserves more discussion. Unfortunately, more coverage at this time would be impossible without first developing an understanding or a good general knowledge of microprocessor interfacing. The transition to this device is extremely easy once interfacing and programming have been mastered.

Modern Microprocessors

Currently the mainstays of the modern microprocessor are the 8- and 16-bit versions of microprocessors. The current heavyweights in this area are the Intel 8085A and the Intel 8088. The 8085A is an 8-bit microprocessor; the 8088 is a 16-bit microprocessor, handling data transfers 8 bits at a time. The main reason for Intel Corporation's success is its ability to maintain programming and hardware compatibility with earlier products and to provide a wide range of peripheral interface components. Other current-technology microprocessors available are the Intel 8086, Zilog Z8000 and the Motorola MC68000. These current-technology microprocessors have few differences in the instruction sets, architecture, and memory structures. The main ingredient for success seems to be an upward compatibility from one generation to the next and a wide variety of hardware interface components.

Microprocessors of the Future

The future may bring 32-bit architectures with essentially the same speed and throughput as modern mainframe computer systems. In fact, Intel has released such a system, the 80386, which is even called a *micromainframe*! Future architectures will include space for massive program and data storage with capacity for machine and human interface. This text will emphasize the importance of interfacing, which will continue to be an important function of the computer engineer.

THE SOFTWARE DEVELOPMENT TASK 1—4

Software design for the modern microprocessor-based system has become too complex to be accomplished efficiently by a single individual. A team of software specialists is generally required for implementing most designs in a reasonable amount of time.

The software specialist has changed over the years. At one time a programmer needed little knowledge of hardware; today the specialist develops the software to replace once-standard hardware circuitry such as counters and multiplexers. Developing modern micro-processor-based software requires in-depth understanding of digital hardware circuitry.

The technique of software development has changed tremendously over the years. At one time the programmer developed software using an assembly language program that accepted information in symbolic machine language and converted it into binary machine code. This, of course, still required many hours and was little improvement over writing a program in binary machine language. The only real advantages of the assembler were that it reduced coding errors and was self-documenting.

Today more high-level languages are being used in the development task to generate programs for microprocessor-based systems. PASCAL and C language, both fairly efficient generators of binary machine language, are two high-level languages in current use. Unfortunately, high-level languages cannot generate all the machine language required.

Hardware interface control usually involves considerable binary bit manipulation, for which most higher-level languages have little capacity. The assembler, which allows the programmer to manipulate the data more efficiently at the bit level, is still applicable in this area and may remain so for quite a few more years. Another limitation of the high-level languages, which is sometimes overlooked, is the fact that the machine code generated by these languages is not as efficient as code developed by an experienced programmer. In many cases coding efficiency is not critical, except in hardware interface. An example of critical code is the software used to time an event, such as the length of time the magnatron in a microwave oven remains on to defrost an item of food. Since each instruction and the time it takes to execute are important, an assembler would be used to generate this type of code.

Modular Programming

The modular approach is an efficient method for developing system software. A *module,* or small portion of an entire system, allows a programmer to concentrate on one area of the program at a time. This allows the programmer to develop, test, and debug small portions of the total program. The software manager assigns the modules to the programmers most qualified to develop each, thus making the most effective use of the programming staff.

Once all modules have become operational, the manager links them together to form the system program. This seems to be the most sensible and often-used approach to software development. Its main drawback is the interface between software modules. Sometimes data flow among modules is not exactly as predicted, causing problems that are fairly hard to detect and correct.

Built-in Diagnostic Tests

In today's sophisticated microprocessor-based systems, it is often difficult or impossible for the technician to enter a program for the purpose of system testing. System test or diagnostic programs must be included whenever a system's software is developed. If a fault is detected, the software should indicate the fault by lighting LED indicators or displaying a particular code number on the screen of the CRT, if one is available.

This diagnostic software must be able to test the system RAM and ROM and also exercise the hardware. *RAM testing* involves running a functional test or a static test of the memory whenever power is first applied to the system. ROMs and their programs can be tested by running a checksum on their contents, by exclusive-ORing all of the bytes of data on the ROM together and checking against the correct checksum stored on the ROM. The hardware testing is system dependent. To test a printer, the printer can print all of the characters; to test a CRT terminal, the software can display all of the characters on the screen. A more complete discussion of this type of testing is included in chapters 5 and 6.

Software Development Tools

The software development aide is a critical portion of the software development function. A typical software development aide, as pictured in figure 1–3, should contain several CRT terminals for program module entry, a shared disk for module storage, a printer for hardcopy documentation, a ROM programmer to place the developed software on a ROM, and, finally, some method of connection to the actual hardware circuitry of the system. The aide is tied to the hardware during system testing so that part of the developed software or the entire system can be tested on the actual hardware. This aide must also be able to link modules together, assemble symbolic code, compile high-level languages, and debug faulty software.

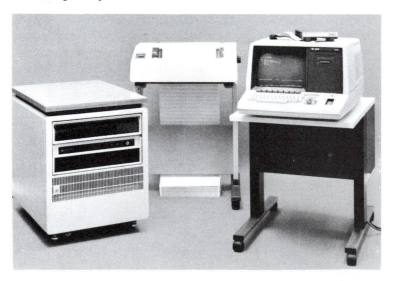

FIGURE 1–3   The 64000 logic development system.
SOURCE: Courtesy of Hewlett-Packard, Inc.

The Development Task

To use the software development aide, the software specialist creates the program module through the CRT terminal. Once the module is operational, it is saved on the disk for later use in developing the entire system program. Once all modules have been developed, the software manager links them together, tests them as a system, and debugs any faults that appear.

After testing is completed, the final step in the development process is *emulation:* either running the program in a different computer system or actually connecting the prototype model of the hardware to the software development system. The latter is the best possible test, since it actually tests or exercises the hardware and the software together as a unit.

During software analysis, the software development aide should be capable of indicating faults as they occur to the programmer. At times, this may be difficult, and in certain cases a short program must be written to test every aspect of the program module under development. To test a subroutine that would add together ten different numbers, for example, one would write a short program that uses the subroutine. This short program is called a *software driver,* since it is specifically written to test the subroutine. It is interesting to note that software drivers are often longer and more involved than the software under test.

Once the entire system is debugged and emulated, it can be burned or programmed into an EPROM. Since most development systems incorporate an EPROM programmer, this is usually a very easy task. Once the EPROMs are programmed, the final test is executed by placing them into the prototype model and running the system. Hardware testing usually requires fairly sophisticated test equipment, which will be discussed in the next section.

THE HARDWARE DEVELOPMENT TASK 1–5

Hardware design methodology differs from software design methodology; hardware design requires that components be found to implement the desired system. The first and most obvious task is to select a microprocessor for the system. This is often the first step, but can be premature if a microprocessor that cannot adequately handle the hardware is selected. The first item to examine is the type of hardware interface components that have been chosen or designed; then the most applicable microprocessor for the task can be selected.

Since the software may be developed by a separate team of individuals, they receive the hardware specifications at this point. After analyzing the hardware specifications, the software team estimates the amount of ROM space required for program storage and the amount of RAM space required for data storage. Once this information is available, it is possible to develop a complete logic diagram for the hardware. From it, a prototype can be built and tested as thoroughly as possible while the software is developed and debugged.

Microprocessor Trainers

If the microprocessor selected for use in a system is foreign to the engineering staff, time is allocated to training, commonly by microprocessor trainers produced by the microprocessor manufacturers. Figure 1–4 illustrates the 8086A-based SDK-86 trainer from Intel. In some cases, training may include seminars to introduce the engineering staff to the new microprocessor.

A typical microprocessor training system contains a keyboard, a grouping of alphanumeric displays, a serial interface for a CRT terminal, and software located in a ROM. The keyboard allows access to the microprocessor and its hardware interface components, which are usually provided on the training aide. The displays allow the user to scan through the memory, display the contents of the internal registers, and single-step through a program. The single-step feature allows the user to learn the operation of the microprocessor. The trainer enables the user to develop a proficiency with both the hardware and the software. It is not intended as a system-designing tool, since most aides are fairly limited. This is one of the most effective methods for mastering a new microprocessor, since the unit can be taken home in most cases.

In-Circuit Emulators

In a discussion of hardware development aides, it is important to mention the in-circuit emulator. An *in-circuit emulator,* such as the one included in the illustration of figure 1–5, allows the engineer to plug the hardware into the software development system for complete testing with the actual software to be used in the completed system. One other important feature is that the hardware can often be tested before the system software has been completed, identifying simple hardware faults that may not normally surface until final testing. In most applications, the software development station will contain the software until both the software and the hardware have been completely debugged and appear to be functional.

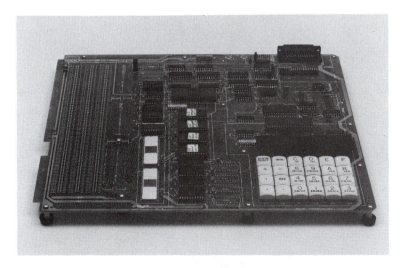

FIGURE 1–4   The SDK-86 Intel 8086-based microprocessor training aide.

SOURCE: Courtesy of Intel Corporation.

FIGURE 1–5   A personal development system that includes an in-circuit emulator.

SOURCE: Courtesy of Intel Corporation.

Data Analyzers

Another important tool for the hardware engineer is the *digital data analyzer*, which is essentially a multichannel digital storage oscilloscope. Most modern data analyzers can capture data in increments of time in nanoseconds (ns). This allows the designer to view timing changes with unprecedented accuracy.

The *logic,* or *data, analyzer* stores a snapshot of many digital signals over a specific period of time, allowing the user to view very complex timing without the problem of synchronization associated with the analog oscilloscope. Figure 1–6 shows a 16-channel digital logic analyzer. This is possible because most data analyzers contain some form of storage element. This *storage element,* or *memory,* can be used to sample a period of time and save it for later comparisons. In fact, the analyzer can take a snapshot of a complex set of timing waveforms and automatically compare the contents of its internal memory with a new set of waveforms. This feature can be used to accomplish a very efficient automatic test.

Synchronization in data analyzers is accomplished by externally triggering on key binary bit patterns. This allows the user to search an incoming data stream for a particular binary bit pattern. Once the analyzer triggers, it begins storing data in an internal memory that can be viewed by the user at any time.

Data are viewable in many different formats: binary, octal, hexadecimal, ASCII, and as waveforms on the face of the CRT. Some newer data analyzers will display 48 different waveforms at one time. Another display mode that is sometimes useful is the mapped mode. *Mapped-mode operation* causes the screen to be filled with dots representing bits of information stored in the memory. This map will normally contain a pattern that, in some

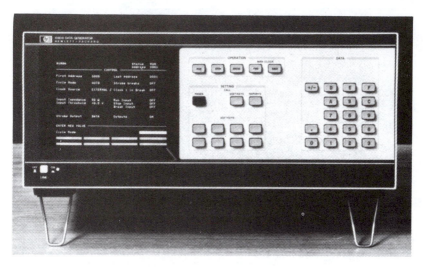

FIGURE 1–6 The 8182A data analyzer.

SOURCE: Courtesy of Hewlett-Packard, Inc.

cases, can be used to test a system. If the software were to hang up in an infinite loop, this would become apparent on the CRT screen.

Data analyzers are also, in some cases, capable of performing signature analysis. Signature analysis is normally used by a technician to test a faulty digital system. A data stream normally has a unique binary bit pattern, called its *signature*. If this pattern is known, the technician can determine whether a product is functioning properly by comparing the measured signature with a predetermined signature. If there is no match, the technician must then locate the faulty component.

Another important role of the data analyzer is in production testing. Since it contains memory, it can be used to test a newly manufactured system by comparing known data from a good system with the data sampled from the newly manufactured system. Since most data analyzers will automatically indicate a data match, virtually anyone can learn to handle automated testing in this manner.

Summary

1   The mainframe computer system is a large computer that performs operations at rates of more than 10 million per second. It is also a device that accesses massive amounts of data in billions of memory locations.

2   The minicomputer system is a scaled-down mainframe computer that performs complex tasks such as process control and local area network control.

3   The microprocessor is a miniaturized version of a minicomputer that is fabricated on a single integrated circuit. Microprocessors are found in three forms: the general-purpose microprocessor, the microcomputer, and the bit-slice microprocessor.

4 The microcomputer is an integrated circuit that contains a microprocessor, read-only memory, RAM, and I/O connections.

5 The major technology breakthrough that ushered in the age of the microprocessor was the advent of NMOS logic. NMOS logic circuitry allowed the microprocessor to function at a rate 20 times faster than PMOS logic and also allowed it to be easily interfaced to TTL logic circuitry.

6 Software development consists of using a high-level language to program the system with assembly language, which is used to provide any binary bit manipulation software required.

7 Modular programming allows the system to be broken into software modules that can be developed by programmers. This allows the system to be developed by many programmers at one time.

8 Software development is accomplished on logic development systems such as the HP64000. The system contains a CRT terminal for data entry, a disk memory for module storage, a printer for hardcopy, programming languages, and an editor.

9 Hardware development is accomplished by using a development station that allows the completed hardware to be attached so that it can be tested with the software. This task is called emulation.

10 Data analyzers are often used for testing the hardware. The data analyzer is actually a multichannel oscilloscope that can store up to 48 different waveforms. These stored waveforms are displayed in binary, octal, ASCII, hexadecimal, and machine language, as well as in timing diagram form.

Glossary

Assembler   A program that converts symbolic machine language into binary machine language.

Byte   Generally, a grouping of eight binary bits.

Compiler   A program that converts or translates a high-level language into binary machine language.

Computer   A machine that can receive, transmit, store, and manipulate information.

Data analyzer   A multichannel digital oscilloscope that can process information and display it in many different forms.

Diagnostics   Programs that have been expressly written to test the memory or the system hardware.

Emulator   A device that can imitate either partially or completely the operation of a given microprocessor.

Hard copy   The printed output of a computer.

Hardware   A computer system's electronic circuitry.

Interpreter   A computer program that generates a pseudocoded or tokenized language that is not machine language. BASIC is often this type of system.

Large-scale integration   A microcircuit containing between one hundred and one thousand logic elements.

Logic analyzer   See Data analyzer.

Machine language   The binary bit patterns that direct a computer's operation.

Mainframe computer   A large computer system designed for general-purpose data processing.

Medium-scale integration   A microcircuit containing between 11 and 99 logic elements.

Microcomputer   A computer system integrated on one integrated circuit or a small computer system based on a microprocessor.

Minicomputer   A scaled-down mainframe computer system.

MIPS   Millions of instructions per second.

Modular programming   A type of programming that divides the software design task into modules that are easy to develop and debug.

Nibble   Generally, a grouping of four binary bits.

Program   A grouping of instructions that direct the operation of a computer system.

Signature   A unique number that indicates the data contained in a serial stream of digital data.

Signature analyzer   A device that can accumulate binary bits of information in order to develop a signature of the data.

Small-scale integration   A microcircuit containing ten or fewer logic elements.

Soft copy   The displayed output of a computer system on a CRT terminal.

Software   A set of instructions, written by a programmer, that directs the computer in the manipulation of data.

Very-large-scale integration   A microcircuit containing over one thousand logic elements.

Questions and Problems

1   Contrast the main differences between a microprocessor and a mainframe computer system.

2   In what situation would an assembler be preferred to a compiler?

3   In what situation would a compiler be preferred to an assembler?

4   What major breakthrough allowed microprocessors to function at a faster rate?

5   List two different commonly used high-level languages.

6   What is the first step in hardware development?

7   What is the significance of the software module in software development?

8   Why are diagnostics used in a microprocessor-based system?

9   Outline the steps that are normally followed in the software development task.

10   List the component parts of a software development system.

11   List four applications for microprocessors.

12   List an application suitable for a 4-bit microprocessor.

13   List an application suitable for an 8-bit microprocessor.

14   Will the world ever see a 128-bit microprocessor? Explain your answer.

15   Define MIPS.

2

Microprocessor Architecture

Upon completion of this chapter, you will be able to

1 Identify and describe the components of a computer system.

2 List the buses in a computer system and explain their purpose.

3 Show how a multiplexed address/data bus is demultiplexed.

4 Draw the circuit required to buffer both a unidirectional and a bidirectional bus.

5 Explain how a microprocessor is automatically reset whenever DC power is applied.

6 Describe the methods employed to address data in a microprocessor.

7 Compare the STD and the S100 buses.

Before we can discuss a particular microprocessor, it is a good idea to examine computer architecture in general. This provides a context for understanding the architecture of a particular microprocessor.

This chapter discusses the component parts of the microprocessor as well as the ancillary components in the microprocessor-based system. It also contrasts, in brief, some of the features found in modern microprocessors, including the various types in production and the instructions available to the programmer.

2–1 GENERAL COMPUTER ARCHITECTURE

The block diagram of a computer system, illustrated in figure 2–1, depicts the typical layout for almost all bus-oriented digital computer systems. The central unit controls the flow of information between itself and the memory or input/output equipment. This central unit is called the *central processing unit* (CPU) in a mainframe or minicomputer and the *microprocessing unit* (MPU) or μp in a microcomputer.

The CPU communicates with the memory and the I/O through a few control lines attached to each unit. These control lines basically control the reading and writing of information and comprise the computer system's *control bus*. In addition to the control bus, there exists a group of wires, the *system data bus,* that conveys the information to and from memory and I/O. A third set of connections, the *address bus,* points to a specific memory location or to a unique I/O device.

Through these three buses, the central unit manipulates information in the memory and passes information between itself and an external device. All bus-oriented digital computer systems use the same three buses to process information. The data bus carries the information; the address bus points to the location of the information; and the control bus controls the direction, flow, origin, and destination of the data. In fact, most computer system functioning is similar, allowing a detailed description of interfacing to be presented without undue detail about a specific microprocessor.

2–2 THE MPU

Data transfer, arithmetic and logic operations, and decision making are the three main functions shared by all MPUs. The main differences between an MPU and a CPU are the speed at which these three basic functions can be performed and the binary bit size of the

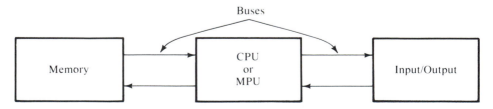

FIGURE 2–1   The basic block diagram of an electronic digital computer system.

data. Data size, or width, in some of the newer microprocessors has equaled that of many mainframe computer systems. The CPU in a mainframe computer system is about one hundred times faster than the typical microprocessor. If this appears to be a minor difference, imagine a single day's worth of data processing taking one hundred days on a microprocessor based computer system. It should be fairly clear why mainframe computer systems are still in use and will probably continue to be for quite some time.

Data Transfer Operations

Data transfer is the most important function of the MPU, since it spends at least 95 percent of its time transferring data. Data transfers can follow many different paths in most microprocessors. The most common path is between the microprocessor and the memory in the system, since fetching instructions for a program demands a lot of time. The rest of the time, data are transferred between the microprocessor and the I/O and passed around inside the processor itself. Most microprocessors include a scratch pad memory, or register array, for this last purpose.

Arithmetic and Logic Operations

About 4 percent of the MPU's time is spent on simple arithmetic and logic operations. The arithmetic function that is most often performed is addition. Through the addition operation, the microprocessor can subtract, by first complementing a number and adding it to a second number to generate a difference. This complement in most microprocessors is a 2's complement, so that one is actually performing 2's complement addition to obtain the difference. The main advantage of the 2's complement method—as compared to the 1's complement method—is the fact that a negative zero cannot occur, and signed numbers present no major problem in the 2's complement system. Therefore, most processors are capable of adding and subtracting (by adding).

Many of the newer microprocessors are also capable of multiplication and division. These operations are actually performed by shifting and adding for multiplication and by shifting, comparing, and subtracting for division.

Microprocessors can also perform some basic logic operations. These operations often include logical multiplication (AND), logical addition (INCLUSIVE-OR), inversion (NOT), EXCLUSIVE-OR, and various forms or shifting and rotating. The most commonly used logic operation is the AND function, which is used to mask, or clear to zero, a portion of a binary number. In fact, complete bit control over a binary quantity is possible by using the AND function to clear bits to zero; the OR function to set bits to ones; and the EXCLUSIVE-OR function to complement or invert bits. Some microprocessors actually have a special TEST or BIT TEST instruction, which may be used to test bits in the accumulator. This instruction usually performs the AND operation without changing the number under test.

Decision-making Operations

The least-used, but nonetheless important, function of the MPU is its ability to make some form of decision. All of the decisions that a microprocessor is capable of performing are based upon numerical tests. For example, a number can be tested and the result can indicate a negative quantity. The microprocessor can make a decision based upon this negative result by modifying its instruction flow. Instruction flow modification is accomplished by a form of conditional branch or conditional jump instruction. Other commonly testable conditions are positive, zero, not zero, carry after an addition, borrow after a subtraction, parity even, parity odd, overflow and equality.

The Mainframe Computer Versus the Microprocessor

What arithmetic operations can a mainframe computer system perform that a microprocessor cannot directly accomplish? One is floating point arithmetic, which can only be performed through software or by using a floating point arithmetic processor, which is actually a special-purpose microprocessor. Such a device is interfaced to the microprocessor in chapter 7.

Basic Microprocessor Architecture

The diagram in figure 2–2 represents the general architecture of many of the microprocessors that are available today. The internal architecture is composed of an instruction register, an arithmetic and logic unit (ALU), a register array, and a control circuit that coordinates the operation of the microprocessor.

   The control logic causes the microprocessor to perform its two main functions, the *fetch,* or *acquisition,* and *execution* phases of operation. The fetch phase causes the microprocessor to send the address of the next instruction to be executed out of the device through the address bus. The control logic then causes the memory to read information from the addressed location by sending a MEMORY READ signal out through the control bus. Data is fetched into an internal register called an *I,* or *instruction register,* which holds the instruction while the control logic decodes it and begins executing it. One other very important event occurs during the fetch sequence: the program counter is incre-

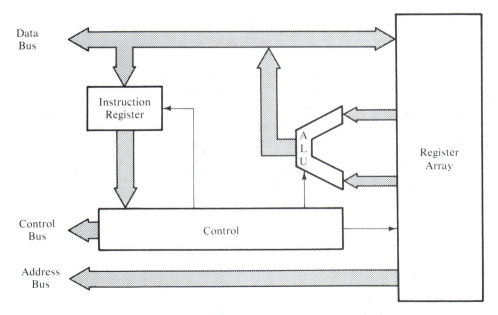

FIGURE 2–2   The internal representation of a microprocessor.

mented so that the next fetch phase will fetch the next sequential instruction from the memory. This is the basic sequence of events required to fetch an instruction from the memory and to begin executing it.

The program counter is a register located within the register array that is used by the microprocessor to track the program. Each memory location in a computer system is numbered so that the program counter can address the next step in a program. In this fashion, the program counter counts up through the program to locate each subsequent step or instruction.

The ALU is responsible for performing the arithmetic and logic operations inside the microprocessor. The control logic directs the operation of the ALU and causes it to perform an arithmetic or logic operation on data from the memory or the register array. The result of this operation is passed back to the memory or the register array to complete the operation.

The register array contains one or more general-purpose registers, at least one accumulator that holds the result from the ALU, a program counter that keeps track of which instruction is to be executed next, and, in almost all cases, a stack pointer register responsible for tracking the last-in, first-out stack memory.

MEMORY 2-3

The memory in a computer system stores the data and instructions of the programs. Instructions are stored in the computer system's memory for quick access. The calculator normally cannot store its instructions in memory, so it requires the operator's memory to enter a sequence of instructions through the keyboard. In the computer, the operator must still enter the instructions, but when they have been stored in the memory, the computer can go through them at a very high rate of speed. It can also use the same sequence of instructions with many different sets of data over and over again. The calculator would require the operator to reenter the entire program with each new set of data. This stored program concept has led to the tremendous processing power of the modern computer.

Program Storage

In microprocessor-based systems, the program and system diagnostics are customarily stored in a read-only memory (ROM). Various forms of ROMs have been developed over the years for this purpose. The ROM must be programmed at the factory while it is being manufactured; the PROM is programmed by burning open fusible links; the EPROM is programmed electrically and erased with ultraviolet light; and the EEPROM and EAROM are programmed and erased electrically.

In most systems the ROM stores the program and diagnostics, while the PROM or EPROM is used to develop the prototype system. The role of the EEPROM and EAROM is to store important data for extended periods of time. This long-term storage is not subject to power failures and is also reprogrammable by the user of the system. These features make it extremely useful for storing tax tables in electronic cash registers, tab positions in CRT terminals, and similar features in other types of equipment.

Data Storage

Data are commonly stored in semiconductor RAM, which is fabricated from bipolar transistors or MOSFETs. The most common type is the NMOS memory, which can access data in 100 ns or less. NMOS memory is available in two forms: the dynamic form (DRAM), which requires periodic refreshing; and the static form (SRAM), which retains data as long as power is applied. Since dynamic memory requires additional circuitry to accomplish refreshing, it is normally used only in memory systems of over 64K bytes in size.

2–4 INPUT/OUTPUT

The main purpose of the input/output block (figure 2–1) is to allow the microprocessor to communicate directly with people or with another computer or machine. The most familiar types of I/O equipment are CRT terminals and printers. Other forms include indicator lamps, switches of all types, solenoids, relays, disk systems, and speakers.

Typical microprocessor I/O equipment includes the analog-to-digital converter, digital-to-analog converter, photosensitive device, and the microphone. In fact, any device that responds to an electrical signal or produces an electrical signal can be, and often is, used as an I/O device in a microprocessor-based system.

2–5 BUS STRUCTURES

The Address Bus

Address buses are present and basically the same in all microprocessors. They are incorporated into the system to address the memory and the I/O equipment. Address buses in various microprocessors differ only in width. The most common number of address connections available today is 16, with some of the newer microprocessors containing either 20 or 24 connections. Most address buses are three-state connections, which will go to their high-impedance state at some time during normal microprocessor operation.

In some cases the address bus connections are shared or multiplexed with other buses or signals at the microprocessor. In microprocessors where the address bus is multiplexed, the manufacturer provides a signal to demultiplex the bus. Figure 2–3 illustrates the Intel 8085A, which has a multiplexed address/data bus.

In the 8085A, the processor sends out the least significant half of the memory address on the address/data bus, along with the address latch enable (ALE) signal. The 74LS373 transparent octal latch captures this portion of the address (A_0-A_7) and holds it until the processor sends out another address along with ALE. The gate (G) input to the latch causes it to accept data when high and to remember or capture data when low. This latch will also provide additional drive capability to the address pins.

In many microprocessors today, the address bus and other output pins are capable of driving only one standard TTL unit load. This will, in many systems, be insufficient to drive the system bus, so that additional buffering is often required.

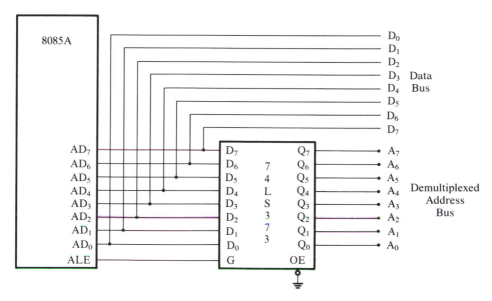

FIGURE 2–3   The Intel 8085A microprocessor with a circuit to demultiplex its address/data bus.

The Address Bus Buffers

Figure 2–4 illustrates how the address bus connections on the Motorola MC6800 can be buffered to provide additional drive. This circuit uses two 74LS244 octal three-state buffers to provide additional drive capability to the address bus. Before the addition of these buffers, the MC6800 was capable of driving one standard TTL unit load or five low-power Schottky-clamped TTL unit loads. With the addition of these buffers, it can now drive twenty standard TTL unit loads or about one hundred low-power Schottky-clamped TTL unit loads.

The BUSEN connection allows the buffered outputs to be floated or placed in their high impedance state during some of the processor's operations. Besides providing additional drive, the buffered outputs present a lower output impedance to the bus than do the original pins on the MC6800. This impedance is nearly the same as the characteristic impedance of the bus itself, which helps to eliminate noise that might otherwise be generated.

In most single board systems, excluding the very large single board or multiple board systems, output buffers are not normally required because of the relatively short buses and light loading. Under most circumstances, buffers are present only when driving heavy TTL loads or more than ten MOSFET loads.

If additional buffers are required, as in figure 2–4, propagation delay times of these buffers must be taken into account when developing a system. For example, with the address bus, the propagation delay time of the buffer is subtracted from the access time allowed to the memory by the microprocessor. If, in addition to the buffers on the address bus, buffering is added to the data bus, time allowed to access memory is decreased by the sum of both propagation delay times. It is important to consider these delay times when

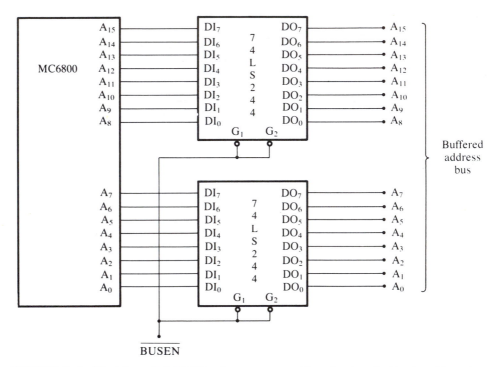

FIGURE 2–4   The Motorola MC6800 microprocessor with a circuit to buffer the address bus.

using memory or I/O devices with access times that are nearly equal to the time allotted by the microprocessor.

Data Bus

The data bus is typically a bidirectional bus that may, in some processors, also be multiplexed with some other information. If an external buffer is required on this bus, it takes the form of a bidirectional bus buffer or bus transceiver. The circuit of figure 2–5 illustrates the Intel 8088, which contains a multiplexed bidirectional data bus. In this diagram, an octal latch demultiplexes the address/data bus, and an octal bus transceiver buffers the data bus. The $\overline{RD}$ signal from the processor is an active low signal that changes the direction of data flow through the bus transceiver. When this signal is active, data will flow toward the microprocessor. The $\overline{RD}$ signal becomes active only when the processor anticipates data from the memory or the I/O. During a write to I/O or memory, the $\overline{RD}$ pin is inactive, allowing data to flow out to the system through the bus transceivers.

The $\overline{BUSEN}$ connection is used during a direct memory access or bus request operation in the system. In a direct memory access operation, these buses are normally placed in their high-impedance state. $\overline{BUSEN}$ accomplishes this by disabling the buffers whenever a logic one occurs.

Control Bus

The control bus is one of the most important buses in the system, since it actually controls the memory and I/O equipment. Each microprocessor in production today has a slightly

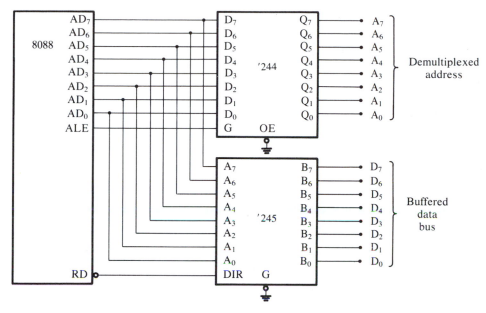

FIGURE 2–5 The Intel 8088 microprocessor with a circuit to buffer the data bus and demultiplex the address/data bus.

different control bus configuration. The most important control bus signals are the read and write signals, since these are the basic functions of the memory and the input/output circuitry.

In some microprocessors these are actually separate lines; in others, they are incorporated into a single control line. The Intel 8080A uses $\overline{\text{MEMR}}$, $\overline{\text{MEMW}}$, $\overline{\text{IOR}}$, and $\overline{\text{IOW}}$ to control memory and I/O; the Commodore (formerly MOS Technology) 6502 uses R/$\overline{\text{W}}$ and phase two of the clock; the Intel 8085A uses $\overline{\text{RD}}$, $\overline{\text{WR}}$, and IO/$\overline{\text{M}}$; and the Motorola MC6800 uses VMA, R/$\overline{\text{W}}$, and phase two of the clock (E). Although many different control signals are in use, they all essentially indicate read and write.

I/O Control

There are two different techniques for handling the control of I/O devices, which examining the control signals of different microprocessors will illustrate. One of these techniques is the *memory-mapped I/O,* in which I/O devices are treated as memory. In fact, with regard to software and hardware control signals, the I/O is indeed memory.

The other technique is *isolated I/O* or *I/O-mapped I/O,* in which the I/O device is a separate I/O device. That is, the I/O device has a unique I/O address, not a memory address. Processors that use this type of I/O have special instructions, IN and OUT, to transfer data to and from this separate I/O space. Both techniques have advantages and disadvantages.

In the memory-mapped I/O scheme, there are two basic control signals: read and write. In the isolated I/O scheme, there are four basic control signals: memory read, memory write, I/O read, and I/O write. The main advantage of the memory-mapped I/O system is that it requires only two control signals to function. The isolated I/O scheme requires four, but it does not require any of the memory space to function. Which one of these schemes is better? It depends upon the application and the microprocessor chosen.

In addition to these basic memory and I/O control signals, there are special inputs and outputs, such as interrupt control, direct memory access control, ready, reset, and various other processor-dependent control signals. This chapter will not discuss in detail processor-dependent control signals, only those that apply to all microprocessors in general. The reader will find more information on the Intel control signals in chapter 3, the Motorola control signals in chapter 4, and the Zilog control signals in the Appendix on the Z80.

Interrupts

The interrupt input on most microprocessors will, when placed at its active level, interrupt the program and CALL up a subroutine from the memory. The purpose of this subroutine is to service the interrupt, and it is for this reason that this type of subroutine is called an *interrupt service subroutine*. Interrupts handle extremely slow external I/O devices, such as keyboards, in order to improve the performance of the microprocessor based system. They also free microprocessor execution time in applications such as real time clocks. This discussion will be expanded in chapter 8.

Direct Memory Access

The hold, or bus request, input on many microprocessors facilitates the I/O technique of *direct memory access*. The main function of this input is to cause the microprocessor to relinquish control of the memory and I/O by disconnecting itself from the address, data, and control buses. Once the processor is disconnected, another processor takes over the memory and I/O space. This is useful in systems where more than one controller or processor must gain access to the memory and I/O. This input, along with acknowledgment outputs, will be discussed in chapter 10.

Reset

The reset input on most microprocessors allows the microprocessor to be initialized whenever power is applied or at the discretion of the operator. Power on clearing is normally accomplished by using a simple RC circuit, as illustrated in figure 2–6. Whenever Vcc, or 5 V, is applied, the capacitor, which is initially discharged, begins to charge toward 5 V. This takes some time because the RC time constant of the circuit allows the microproces-

FIGURE 2–6   The reset circuitry for a Commodore 6502 microprocessor.

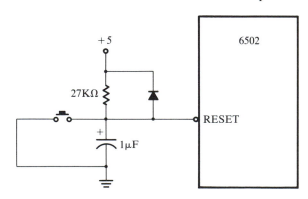

sor ample time to feel a logic zero on its reset pin while Vcc is applied to reset itself. The push button switch allows the operator to reset the microprocessor whenever it might be required. Upon resetting, many microprocessors are internally initialized, so that they function at a predefined memory location fetching an instruction. This reset location, in some microprocessors a vector, is very important because it is at this location that the system program must begin. In the case of a vector, the vector points to the beginning of the system software.

Wait States

The READY or MRDY pin provided on many microprocessors indicates to the microprocessor that the memory and/or the I/O circuitry is ready to function. If a slow memory device—a device with a longer-than-normal access time—is to be connected to the microprocessor, the ready input causes the microprocessor to enter into waiting states. Wait states are multiples of the system clock pulses and cause the system to allow more time for the memory to access data. Because of the wide range of timing among microprocessors, the best source of information about the operation and timing of this pin is the literature provided by the manufacturer, including, in some cases, the circuit recommended to cause wait states.

Bus Timing

Bus timing is extremely important to the hardware engineer, who mainly concentrates on the timing required to achieve a particular result. Some of these times are memory access time, read or write pulse widths, memory cycle time, clock pulse width, and clock period. Most of these timing signals will be discussed in greater detail in chapters 3 and 4.

Clock Period

The clocking period will be discussed at this point, since it does not depend on understanding memory and I/O interfacing. There are normally two discrete limits to the clocking period that are determined by the internal structure of the microprocessor and must be observed for proper operation: The shortest clocking period depends on the type of logic family that comprises the microprocessor and is caused by internal *propagation delay times*. The longest allowable clocking period is determined by the fact that most microprocessors use dynamic storage in their register arrays. Dynamic registers require periodic refreshing to maintain the integrity of the data stored in them. If the clocking period is longer than that recommended by the manufacturer, the integrity of the data stored internally is lost.

The clock waveform or waveforms are normally generated by a crystal controlled oscillator that is incorporated into the microprocessor or available as an ancillary component from the manufacturer. The system hardware generally governs the operating period within the constraints allowed by the manufacturer.

Bus Contention

Since memory components have one pin that controls reading and writing of data, why do some microprocessors provide two control signals for the memory? These signals prevent what is often referred to as *bus conflict* or *bus contention*.

A bus contention occurs whenever the bus is driven from two points at the same time.

This condition does not damage any of the devices connected to the bus, but it may cause a temporary loss of data at a critical point in the microprocessor timing. To prevent this conflict, it is important to use all of the supplied control signals when interfacing memory and/or I/O devices. Bus contention is illustrated further in chapters 5 and 6, which discuss memory and I/O interface.

2-6 A COMPARISON OF TYPICAL MICROPROCESSORS

Four-bit Microprocessors

The TMS 1000 (Texas Instruments) dominates the 4-bit microprocessor market. In large quantities, its price has dropped to less than one dollar, with applications in such systems as microwave ovens, washing machines, and dishwashers.

Eight-bit Microprocessors

The area of heaviest competition and application is the 8-bit microprocessor. In comparing 8-bit microprocessors, one finds that their function and application are about the same. For example, virtually all 8-bit microprocessors have a 16-bit address bus. Some microprocessors share a portion of the address bus connections with the data bus, and others share the data bus connections with information about microprocessor function. In every case the data bus is 8 bits in width, and it is always bidirectional. There is little variation in speed among microprocessors; all operate within a range between 1 μs and 0.20 μs.

Eight-bit microprocessors differ most in availability of ancillary components. Some microprocessor manufacturers supply a wide variety of interface components, while others provide virtually none. Microprocessor interfacing is simplified when most of the intricate design work has already been accomplished by the manufacturer. The more successful microprocessors have a vast line of interface components.

Another feature that is often overlooked in comparing microprocessors is the interrupt structure of the processor. Interrupt inputs vary from one to up to five. In all cases the interrupt scheme can be expanded by adding external hardware, but in small systems requiring only a few interrupt inputs, it is useful to have a processor with more than one such input. Most modern applications of the microprocessor can be improved by using one or more interrupts to speed information processing. Therefore, this is an important aspect of selecting the right microprocessor to do the job.

Sixteen-bit Microprocessors

Variation in 16-bit architectures is greater than in standard 8-bit architectures. One significant variation is the width of the data bus. The data bus is either 8 or 16 bits in width, which presents a problem in selecting a particular 16-bit microprocessor. The 8-bit bus architecture is appropriate for the user who has invested time and money in 8-bit peripherals. Designing a system by eliminating the need to develop new memory and I/O interfaces significantly reduces the expense.

The 16-bit microprocessor that employs an 8-bit data bus preserves this investment and allows a significant increase in performance due to the internal 16-bit architecture. All 16-bit microprocessors incorporate instructions for multiplication, division, and block data manipulation, thus reducing software coding time. These new instructions reduce the time required to develop a new system and correspondingly reduce the development cost.

The user who requires more speed selects a 16-bit data bus version of the 16-bit microprocessor or possibly a 32-bit microprocessor. The 32-bit microprocessor is normally reserved for high-technology applications and may eventually replace the smaller mainframe computer systems.

Bit-Slice Microprocessors

Bit-slice technology is appropriate only when an application requires extremely high speed, very wide word widths, or a tailored instruction set. Since the instruction set of the bit-slice microprocessor is more basic than the fixed word width microprocessor, it requires more time for software development. A typical fixed word width microprocessor, such as the Intel 8085A, has a few hundred instructions; the bit-slice processor may contain tens of thousands of instructions. Developing a bit slice technology system requires significant increases in cost and training time.

Single-Component Microcomputers

Single-component microcomputers, available from various manufacturers, are useful in less-complex applications. Each single component microcomputer contains a microprocessor, ROM or EPROM for program storage, and RAM for data storage. In most cases, they also contain connections for input and output operations. Often small- and medium-sized systems can be implemented by using one of these processors and very few other components. This, of course, decreases the expense of development time for both hardware and software. In addition, the fewer components in a system, the easier it is for the field service technician to maintain.

Microprocessor Selection

As the previous discussion suggests, it is difficult to select a microprocessor for an application without first researching the hardware aspects of the system to be designed. Once the hardware is specified, software to implement the system is analyzed for proper processor operation. If the application requires complex arithmetic operations, a 16-bit microprocessor is appropriate. If the application requires simple arithmetic and many string manipulations, an 8-bit microprocessor is chosen. Its application in the system dictates the choice of microprocessor.

Table 2-1 lists some of the available microprocessors, including package size, address bus width, data bus width, basic processor word size, and special features.

A COMPARISON OF MICROPROCESSOR INSTRUCTION SETS 2-7

Figure 2-7 illustrates the internal structure of a variety of microprocessors. All include an accumulator, an index register or pointer, some general-purpose registers, a stack pointer, and a program counter. The number of internal registers varies widely, but generally, the more registers a microprocessor contains, the more flexible it becomes. It is easier to write efficient software—in terms of memory utilization, speed, and cost—with a larger number of internal registers.

TABLE 2-1 A comparison of microprocessors.

Part	Manufacturer	Type	Word Bit Size	Address Bus Width	Number of Pins	Speed	Clock	Date
2901	Advanced Micro Devices	Bit Slice	4	Varies	40	0.115	9	1975
6502	Commodore	MPU	8	16	40	3	1	1975
mN602	Data General	MPU	16	16	40	2.4	8.3	1979
T-11	Digital Equipment Corp.	MPU	16	16	40	1.2	7.5	1982
F8	Fairchild	MPU	8	16	40	2	2	1974
4040	Intel	MPU	4	13	24	12.3	2	1974
8048	Intel	Single Chip	8	12	40	6	2.5	1977
8080	Intel	MPU	8	16	40	2	2	1973
8085	Intel	MPU	8	16	40	1.3	3	1976
8086	Intel	MPU	16	20	40	0.4	5	1978
8088	Intel	MPU	16	20	40	0.4	5	1979
80188	Intel	MPU	16	20	68	0.4	5	1982
80186	Intel	MPU	16	20	68	0.4	5	1982
80286	Intel	MPU	16	32	128	0.4	5	1983
80386	Intel	MPU	32	32	128	0.2	10	1984
iAPX-432	Intel	MPU	32	32	64	0.4	8	1981
6100	Intersil	MPU	12	15	40	5	2.5	1974
3870	MOSTEK	Single Chip	8	12	40	2	4	1977
6800	Motorola	MPU	8	16	40	2	1	1974
6805	Motorola	Single Chip	8	8	28	2	4	1979
6809	Motorola	MPU	8	16	40	1.5	2	1979
68000	Motorola	MPU	16	24	64	0.6	8	1980
68008	Motorola	MPU	16	20	48	0.6	8	1981
68010	Motorola	MPU	16	24	64	0.6	8	1982
68020	Motorola	MPU	32	32	128	0.3	12	1983
16016	National Semiconductor	MPU	16	24	48	0.4	6	1983
1802	RCA	MPU	8	16	40	5	3.2	1978
PPS-4	Rockwell	MPU	4	10	40	8.3	4	1974
2650	Signetics	MPU	8	15	40	1.5	3	1975
TMS1000	Texas Instruments	MPU	4	9	28	15	0.4	1974
TMS9900	Texas Instruments	MPU	16	16	64	4.7	3	1976
Z80	Zilog	MPU	8	16	40	1.6	2.5	1976
Z8001	Zilog	MPU	16	16	48	0.4	4	1981

NOTE: Clock = CPU clock frequency in megahertz (MHz).
Speed = shortest instruction execution time in microseconds (μs)

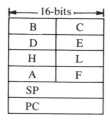

16-bits

B	C
D	E
H	L
A	F
SP	
PC	

8085A

16-bits

AX	AH	AL	Accumulator
BX	BH	BL	Base
CX	CH	CL	Count
DX	DH	DL	Data
	FH	FL	Flags
	SP		Stack pointer
	BP		Base pointer
	SI		Source index
	DI		Destination index
	IP		Instruction pointer
	CS		Code segment
	DS		Data segment
	SS		Stack segment
	ES		Extra segment

8086, 8088

16-bits

A	B
X	
SP	
PC	
	CCR

MC6800

16-bits

D	A	B
	DPR	CCR
	X	
	Y	
	U	
	S	
	PC	

MC6809

32-bits

D_0	
D_1	
D_2	
D_3	
D_4	
D_5	
D_6	
D_7	
A_0	
A_1	
A_2	
A_3	
A_4	
A_5	
A_6	
SSP (A_7')	
USP (A_7)	
	SR

MC68000

16-bits — 16-bits

B	C	B'	C'
D	E	D'	E'
H	L	H'	L'
A	F	A'	F'
SP			
IX			
IY			
PC			
	I		

Z80

FIGURE 2–7 The internal programming models or structures for the 8085A, 8086, 8088, MC6800, MC6809, MC68000, and the Z80 microprocessors.

Base Page Addressing

Some microprocessors, with a limited number of internal registers, use a portion of the memory as an extension of the internal register structure. This extension is called a *base page* or *scratch pad memory*.

The base page, which is usually 256 bytes in length, is usually located at the beginning of the memory system. This extension of the internal register array (addressed by the numbers 00 through FF) effectively increases the amount of register storage from a few bytes to more than 256 bytes. The only disadvantage of this type of addressing is that it normally takes more time to reference memory than it does to reference an internal register. This means each base page instruction takes less room to store in a program, but it may take longer to execute.

In the MC6809 microprocessor, the base page can be located in any area of the memory through a base page pointer register. This is a tremendous asset in processing large quantities of data, since more than one set of base page registers is available.

Indexed Addressing

Index registers, or pointers, are a very important portion of the makeup of the internal register structure. The pointer or pointers reference lists of data in the microcomputer's memory system. Without this ability, programming would be cumbersome, if not impossible. Many programs require at least two index registers or pointers, since it is often necessary to manipulate two sets of information at one time. If fewer than two are available, problems of this nature are much more difficult to solve.

Relative Addressing

Another form of addressing often found in microprocessors is relative addressing. In most cases, this form of addressing is not essential, but when it is available, it reduces the number of bytes required to implement a particular task. The major problem of relative addressing is that it is difficult to determine the displacement when one is coding with binary machine language. If an assembler is to be used for program development, however, this presents no problem.

Displacement is a number that indicates how far away from the location of the next instruction the address or data is located. For example, to refer to a byte of information that is four bytes after the next instruction, one uses a displacement of four.

The main advantage of relative addressing is that the data are addressed by their distance from the instruction and not by their memory addresses. This means that the program and data may be placed anywhere in the memory without changing the operand addresses located with the instructions. This means that the software is *relocatable*.

Indirect Addressing

Less common is *indirect addressing,* in which an indirect instruction allows the programmer to refer to a byte of data through a location stored in another memory location or register. For example, if memory location 12 contains a 6 and the instruction loads the accumulator indirectly from 12, the contents of location 6 are actually placed in the accumulator.

Indirectly addressing memory through another memory location has its application, but little in the type of software normally associated with hardware control. It is most useful for implementing jump tables in systems such as interpreters and more complex software.

Immediate Addressing

Immediate addressing loads an internal register or a memory location with the data that immediately follow the up-code in the memory. In most cases, many arithmetic and logic instructions are available in this form. Immediate addressing is useful whenever a program deals with constants. The data can be stored with the instruction, allowing the program to be written more easily.

Variable Length Instructions

All microprocessors are able to address a byte or word of data in the memory directly by using different-length instructions. Some use a 3-byte-long instruction; others address a base page of memory by a 2-byte-long instruction.

Input/Output Techniques

Input/output techniques are available in the memory mapped I/O scheme and the isolated I/O scheme. In the *memory-mapped* scheme, all instructions that deal with the memory are available to handle data transfer to or from the I/O equipment. In the *isolated,* or I/O-mapped, I/O scheme, two instructions, input and output, handle I/O transfer. Though the isolated I/O technique of transfer sounds cumbersome, in many cases it is at least as efficient as memory-mapped I/O. Also, if the machine has isolated I/O, it can also accomplish memory-mapped I/O; but a machine designed without isolated I/O can never accomplish isolated I/O.

Stacks

Stack memory schemes are basically the same in all microprocessors: they store data and *return addresses* from subroutines without regard to memory address. They perform these functions through a special register, the *stack pointer,* which tracks the stack automatically. When the stack pointer register is initialized in a program, the processor maintains the stack if proper syntax is followed.

Many microprocessors require that data be placed on the stack and retrieved from the stack in pairs of bytes. Some microprocessors store and retrieve single bytes of data, and others store both single- and double-byte numbers on their stacks.

Another major consideration for the programmer is the direction of the data flow to and from the stack. Since the stack is a last-in, first-out memory, the data are reversed in order by the stack. For example, if a 4 followed by a 2 is placed onto the stack, the 2 followed by the 4 is extracted from the stack.

Complex Instructions

Some of the complex instructions available on newer microprocessors include multiplication, division, translation, and various forms of character string manipulation. Certain microprocessors perform ASCII arithmetic, which is often quite useful. As the need for newer and more complicated instructions arises, manufacturers will develop new microprocessors to meet industry demand.

2–8 MICROCOMPUTER SYSTEM BUSES

Two common bus standards, the IEEE-696/S100 BUS and the STD-BUS, have gained wide acceptance throughout the industry. These standards define the pin configurations and card sizes of microcomputer interface printed circuit boards. The S100 standard is a 100-pin standard, and the STD-BUS is a 56-pin standard. Both are adaptable to a wide variety of 8-bit microprocessors, and the S100 standard is also adaptable to the newer 16-bit microprocessors.

The IEEE-696/S100 Bus Standard

MITS, Inc., developed the S100 bus for their Altair 8800 microcomputer system in 1974. It soon became the de facto standard, with a large number of other microcomputer manufacturers adopting it as their system bus. Since that time about one hundred manufacturers have been producing boards for this bus. S100 boards can accomplish most tasks from providing additional memory to synthesizing speech.

In 1978, a committee of the Institute of Electrical and Electronics Engineers (IEEE) drafted a proposal making the S100 bus a standard bus for microcomputer systems. Some of the changes from the original bus included a wider data bus of 16 bits, a wider memory address bus of 24 bits, and extended direct memory access control.

The most current version of the IEEE-696/S100 standard is illustrated in table 2–2. The standard requires three power supply voltages on the bus. These voltages are $+8$ V, -16 V, and $+16$ V. These supply voltages generate $+5$ V, -5 V, $+12$ V, and -12 V, which are developed by local regulators on each plug-in printed circuit board. The

TABLE 2–2 The IEEE-696/S100 bus standard pin assignments.

Pin No.	Signal	Description
1	$+8$ V	Power supply input for the $+5$ V regulators. Must be between $+7$ V and $+25$ V, with an average of no more than $+11$ V.
2	$+16$ V	Power supply input for the $+12$ V regulators. Must be between $+14.5$ V and $+35$ V with an average of no more than $+21.5$ V.
3	XRDY	XRDY must be true along with RDY (pin 72) to indicate that the bus is ready.
4	$\overline{\text{VI0}}$	Vectored interrupt line 0.
5	$\overline{\text{VI1}}$	Vectored interrupt line 1.
6	$\overline{\text{VI2}}$	Vectored interrupt line 2.
7	$\overline{\text{VI3}}$	Vectored interrupt line 3.
8	$\overline{\text{VI4}}$	Vectored interrupt line 4.
9	$\overline{\text{VI5}}$	Vectored interrupt line 5.
10	$\overline{\text{VI6}}$	Vectored interrupt line 6.
11	$\overline{\text{VI7}}$	Vectored interrupt line 7.
12	$\overline{\text{NMI}}$	Nonmaskable interrupt input.
13	$\overline{\text{PWRFAIL}}$	Power failure signal.

TABLE 2–2 *(continued)*

Pin No.	Signal	Description
14	$\overline{\text{DMA3}}$	Direct memory access address bit 3.
15	A18	Address bit position 18.
16	A16	Address bit position 16.
17	A17	Address bit position 17.
18	$\overline{\text{SDSB}}$	The status bit disable control bit.
19	$\overline{\text{CDSB}}$	The control signal disable control bit.
20	GND	Signal ground.
21	—	Not defined at this time.
22	$\overline{\text{ADSB}}$	The control signal that disables the address bus.
23	$\overline{\text{DODSB}}$	The control signal that disables the data output bus.
24	φ	Status valid strobe signal.
25	$\overline{\text{pSTVAL}}$	Status bits valid strobe.
26	pHLDA	The hold acknowledge signal used to acknowledge a direct memory access.
27	—	Not defined at this time.
28	—	Not defined at this time.
29	A5	Address bit position 5.
30	A4	Address bit position 4.
31	A3	Address bit position 3.
32	A15	Address bit position 15.
33	A12	Address bit position 12.
34	A9	Address bit position 9.
35	DO1	Data output bus bit position 1 or bidirectional data bus bit 1.
36	DO0	Data output bus bit position 0 or bidirectional data bus bit 0.
37	A10	Address bit position 10.
38	DO4	Data output bus bit position 4 or bidirectional data bus bit 4.
39	DO5	Data output bus bit position 5 or bidirectional data bus bit 5.
40	DO6	Data output bus bit position 6 or bidirectional data bus bit 6.
41	DI2	Data input bus bit position 2 or bidirectional data bus bit 10.
42	DI3	Data input bus bit position 3 or bidirectional data bus bit 11.
43	DI7	Data input bus bit position 7 or bidirectional data bus bit 15.
44	sM1	The status bit that indicates the current bus cycle is an op-code fetch.
45	sOUT	The status bit that indicates the current bus cycle is an output.
46	sINP	The status bit that indicates the current bus cycle is an input.
47	sMEMR	The status bit that indicates the current bus cycle is a memory read.

TABLE 2–2   *(continued)*

Pin No.	Signal	Description
48	sHLTA	The status bit that indicates the processor is currently halted.
49	CLOCK	A 2-MHz squarewave.
50	GND	Signal ground.
51	+8 V	See pin 1.
52	−16 V	See pin 2 except for the polarity.
53	$\overline{\text{GND}}$	Signal ground.
54	$\overline{\text{SLAVE CLR}}$	Used to reset bus slave devices.
55	$\overline{\text{DMA0}}$	Direct memory access address bit 0.
56	$\overline{\text{DMA1}}$	Direct memory access address bit 1.
57	$\overline{\text{DMA2}}$	Direct memory access address bit 2.
58	$\overline{\text{sXTRQ}}$	The status bit that requests 16-bit slaves to assert $\overline{\text{SIXTN}}$.
59	A19	Address bit position 19.
60	$\overline{\text{SIXTN}}$	The signal asserted by 16-bit slaves in response to the $\overline{\text{sXTRQ}}$ signal.
61	A20	Address bit position 20.
62	A21	Address bit position 21.
63	A22	Address bit position 22.
64	A23	Address bit position 23.
65	—	Not defined at this time.
66	—	Not defined at this time.
67	$\overline{\text{PHANTOM}}$	A signal that disables the normal slave devices and enables the phantom slave devices.
68	MWRT	Memory write control signal derived from the logical combination of $\overline{\text{pWR}}$ and sOUT.
69	—	Not defined at this time.
70	GND	Signal ground.
71	—	Not defined at this time.
72	RDY	See pin 3.
73	$\overline{\text{INT}}$	Main processor interrupt input.
74	$\overline{\text{HOLD}}$	Used to request a direct memory access.
75	$\overline{\text{RESET}}$	Used to reset bus master devices.
76	pSYNC	This control signal identifies BS1.
77	$\overline{\text{pWR}}$	Indicates the presence of valid data on the data output bus or the bidirectional data bus.
78	pDBIN	Indicates that the bus master is waiting for data on its input data bus or bidirectional data bus.
79	A0	Address bit position 0.
80	A1	Address bit position 1.
81	A2	Address bit position 2.
82	A6	Address bit position 6.
83	A7	Address bit position 7.
84	A8	Address bit position 8.
85	A13	Address bit position 13.
86	A14	Address bit position 14.
87	A11	Address bit position 11.
88	DO2	Data output bus bit position 2 or bidirectional data bus bit 2.

34

TABLE 2–2   *(continued)*

Pin No.	Signal	Description
89	DO3	Data output bus bit position 3 or bidirectional data bus bit 3.
90	DO7	Data output bus bit position 7 or bidirectional data bus bit 7.
91	DI4	Data input bus bit position 4 or bidirectional data bus bit 12.
92	DI5	Data input bus bit position 5 or bidirectional data bus bit 13.
93	DI6	Data input bus bit position 6 or bidirectional data bus bit 14.
94	DI1	Data input bus bit position 1 or bidirectional data bus bit 9.
95	DI0	Data input bus bit position 0 or bidirectional data bus bit 8.
96	sINTA	The signal that identifies an interrupt acknowledge.
97	$\overline{\text{sWO}}$	The status bit that identifies a write bus cycle.
98	$\overline{\text{ERROR}}$	The bus signal that indicates a bus error in the current bus cycle.
99	$\overline{\text{POC}}$	Used to initialize all devices whenever power is applied to the system.
100	GND	Signal ground.

standard limits the current from each of these power supplies on each board to no more than 1 A.

This bus allows up to eight vectored interrupt inputs, greatly extending the computational power of the bus and microcomputer system. In addition to these vectored interrupt inputs, there are provisions to allow up to 16 direct memory access devices to function in the system. The data bus connections are provided for unidirectional or bidirectional capabilities of 8 or 16 bits in width. The address bus has been widened so that the microprocessor can directly address up to 16 megabytes of system memory, as opposed to the original 64K bytes of memory. The control signals are flexible to allow most microprocessors to adapt well to this bus.

The STD-BUS

The STD-BUS was developed in 1978 as a low-cost original equipment manufacturer (OEM) microcomputer system bus. Most of the 8-bit microprocessors adapt well to this bus, but the 16-bit microprocessor, excluding the Intel 8088, cannot use it. Figure 2–8 illustrates both the S100 bus card and the STD-BUS card for comparison. As the figure demonstrates, the S100 bus card is much larger than the STD-BUS card, so that it is often more useful for microcomputer implementation.

Table 2–3 presents the STD-BUS pin configuration as a comparison with the S100 bus of table 2–2. The STD-BUS was designed to implement the Z80, 8080, 8085, 8088,

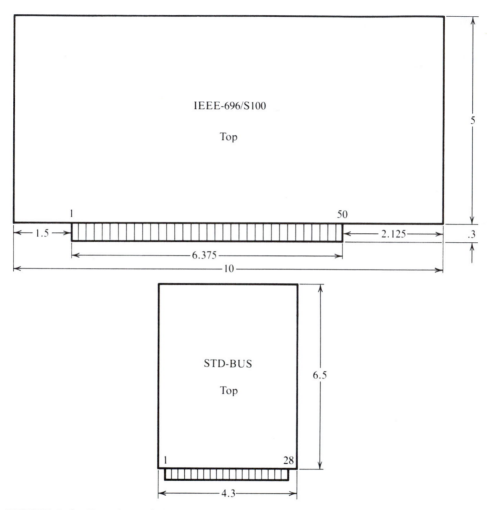

FIGURE 2–8   Top views of the IEEE-696/S100 and STD-BUS printed circuit plug boards.

MC6800, and the MC6809. The S100 bus is capable of supporting the aforementioned microprocessors and 6502, Z8000, MC68000, and both the 8086 and 8088.

Bus Considerations

It is very important to understand both the IEEE-696/S100 BUS and the STD-BUS, since they find wide application in industry and are similar to other buses. Some important considerations to take into account in designing a card for either bus standard follow.

Bus Drivers   The bus drivers for both buses require that the driver is capable of being three-stated, sinking at least 24 mA of current at no more than 0.5 V and sourcing at least 2 mA of current at no fewer than 2.4 V. These requirements are easily achieved today with devices such as the 74LS240 and 74LS244 octal bus drivers. The bus receivers should exhibit some hysteresis to help eliminate any noise picked up on the buses.

TABLE 2–3 The STD-BUS pin connections.

Pin No.	Signal	Description
1	+5 V	Regulated +5 V into the board.
2	+5 V	Regulated +5 V into the board.
3	GND	Signal ground.
4	GND	Signal ground.
5	−5 V	Regulated −5 V into the board.
6	−5 V	Regulated −5 V into the board.
7	D3	Bidirectional data bus bit 3.
8	D7	Bidirectional data bus bit 7.
9	D2	Bidirectional data bus bit 2.
10	D6	Bidirectional data bus bit 6.
11	D1	Bidirectional data bus bit 1.
12	D5	Bidirectional data bus bit 5.
13	D0	Bidirectional data bus bit 0.
14	D4	Bidirectional data bus bit 4.
15	A7	Address bit position 7.
16	A15	Address bit position 15.
17	A6	Address bit position 6.
18	A14	Address bit position 14.
19	A5	Address bit position 5.
20	A13	Address bit position 13.
21	A4	Address bit position 4.
22	A12	Address bit position 12.
23	A3	Address bit position 3.
24	A11	Address bit position 11.
25	A2	Address bit position 2.
26	A10	Address bit position 10.
27	A1	Address bit position 1.
28	A9	Address bit position 9.
29	A0	Address bit position 0.
30	A8	Address bit position 8.
31	$\overline{\text{WR}}$	Write strobe to memory or I/O.
32	$\overline{\text{RD}}$	Read strobe to memory or I/O.
33	$\overline{\text{IORQ}}$	Input/output selection bit.
34	$\overline{\text{MEMRQ}}$	Memory selection bit.
35	$\overline{\text{IOEXP}}$	Input/output expansion bit.
36	$\overline{\text{MEMEX}}$	Memory expansion bit.
37	$\overline{\text{REFRESH}}$	Signal that indicates a refresh address is present on the address bus.
38	$\overline{\text{MCSYNC}}$	Machine cycle sync signal.
39	$\overline{\text{STATUS 1}}$	CPU status signal one.
40	$\overline{\text{STATUS 0}}$	CPU status signal zero.
41	$\overline{\text{BUSAK}}$	Bus acknowledge signal.
42	$\overline{\text{BUSRQ}}$	Bus request signal.
43	$\overline{\text{INTAK}}$	Interrupt acknowledge signal.
44	$\overline{\text{INTRQ}}$	Interrupt request signal.
45	$\overline{\text{WAITRQ}}$	Wait request signal.
46	$\overline{\text{NMIRQ}}$	Nonmaskable interrupt request signal.

TABLE 2–3   *(continued)*

Pin No.	Signal	Description
47	$\overline{\text{SYSRESET}}$	System reset signal.
48	$\overline{\text{PBRESET}}$	Operator pushbutton reset signal.
49	$\overline{\text{CLOCK}}$	System clock.
50	$\overline{\text{CNTRL}}$	AUX timing.
51	PCO	Daisy chain output
52	PCI	Daisy chain input.
53	AUXGND	AUX signal ground.
54	AUXGND	AUX signal ground.
55	AUX + V	+ 12 V power supply input.
56	AUX − V	− 12 V power supply input.

Power Supply Decoupling   It is also extremely important to decouple each board from the power distribution network by using a *ferrite bead* and a capacitive decoupling network. Each component on the board should also be decoupled from the local power distribution grid if it is subject to generating switching transients. Totem pole output TTL logic gates, for example, generate switching transients and should therefore be bypassed, using a 0.01–0.1 μF capacitor placed as closely as possible to their power supply input pins. Most NMOS devices must also be bypassed, since they have output circuitry that can also generate switching transients.

Component Placement   Component placement on the board itself is also critical in some instances. All devices should be placed as close as possible to the bus connections to reduce lead lengths. This procedure reduces the amount of noise generated on the bus which can be coupled into other printed circuit cards in the system.

Standard Waveforms

The waveforms pictured in figure 2–9 illustrate the standard set of memory read and memory write waveforms available in the S100 bus system. Each of these waveform sets is divided into bus states or clocking periods. During bus state one (BS1), the memory address and status information are placed on the bus by the microprocessor. At bus state two (BS2), the control signals for the memory appear on the system bus. During bus state three (BS3), the data are written into memory or extracted from the memory by the microprocessor. Since each of these bus states is 500 ns in length, the S100 system is capable of one bus transfer every 1.5 μs. The standard clock frequency for the S100 standard is defined in the specification as a 2-MHz clock. Timing on the STD-BUS is almost identical to the S100 bus since they are based on similar microprocessors. The S100 bus was based on or designed around the Intel 8080, and the STD-BUS was designed around the Zilog Z80, which has signals almost identical to the 8080's.

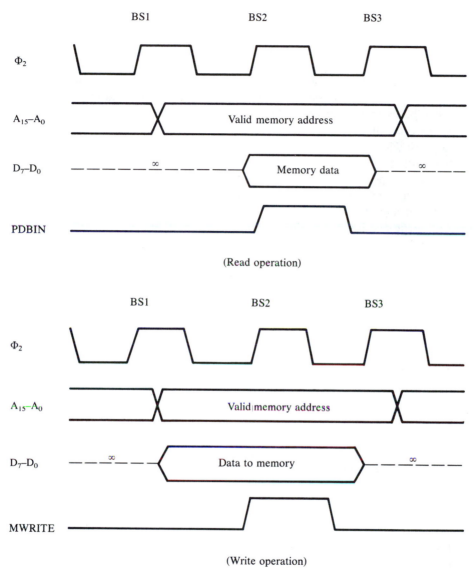

(Read operation)

(Write operation)

FIGURE 2–9 IEEE-696/S100 bus read and write timing diagrams.

Other Bus Standards

Other bus standards, such as the Q-bus (Motorola) and the Multibus (Intel), have been developed by various microcomputer manufacturers. Since they are used by very few microcomputer systems, they will not be discussed here. A comparison of the S100 bus or the STD-BUS with almost any of these buses reveals basically the same set of connections and timing.

Summary

1 A computer system is composed of three main sections: the microprocessing unit (MPU) or central processing unit (CPU), the memory, and the I/O.

2 Three buses interconnect the CPU or MPU with the memory and the I/O: the address bus, the data bus, and the control bus. The address bus supplies the memory with the address of the data or the I/O device with its address. The data bus is used to transfer the data between the MPU and the memory or I/O. The control bus provides the memory and I/O with a read or a write signal.

3 The MPU performs three basic operations: data transfer, arithmetic and logic, and decisions. Data transfers occur between the MPU and the I/O and memory. Arithmetic and logic operations include: addition, subtraction, AND, OR, EX-CLUSIVE-OR, and invert. Decisions are based on numerical facts such as: zero, carry, and parity.

4 The memory in a computer system stores the program and the data used by the program.

5 I/O allows the microprocessor to communicate to humans or machines.

6 The address/data bus is demultiplexed with an octal latch that receives its clock pulse from the ALE pin on the 8085A microprocessor.

7 The 74LS244 is a bus buffer that is often used to buffer a unidirectional bus.

8 The 74LS245 is a bidirectional bus buffer whose direction is controlled with the $\overline{\text{RD}}$ signal from the microprocessor.

9 A bus contention occurs whenever the bus is driven simultaneously from two or more sources and is prevented by using the $\overline{\text{RD}}$ signal from the microprocessor.

10 The reset signal for the microprocessor is provided with an RC time constant that ensures the reset pin is a logic zero long enough for the microprocessor to reset whenever power is applied to the system.

11 Many addressing modes are available, some of which are: base, indexed, relative, indirect, and immediate.

12 Two common microcomputer buses are the IEEE-696/S100 and the STD-BUS. The main difference between these buses is that the STD-BUS requires a regulated power supply into the board, while the S100 bus contains local regulation on each card.

Glossary

Address bus   A group of wires that carries an address to the memory and to the input/output devices in a computer system.

ALU   Arithmetic and Logic Unit. It performs all of the microprocessor's arithmetic and logic operations.

Base page   Generally the first 256 bytes of the memory, which are used as a scratch pad.

Bus contention Also called a *bus conflict*, this occurs whenever two or more devices drive any bus at the same time.

Control bus A group of wires that controls the memory and input/output devices in a computer system.

CPU Central Processing Unit. Controls the memory and the input/output equipment in a computer system.

Data bus A group of wires used by the microprocessor to transfer data to and from memory and I/O.

Decoupling capacitor A capacitor that decouples an integrated circuit from the power supply. This is normally required to prevent problems with power supply transients.

DMA Direct Memory Access. An input/output technique that transfers data directly into or out of the memory without the intervention of the microprocessor.

EAROM Electrically Alterable Read-Only Memory. Can be programmed and erased while resident in a computer system; it will retain data even after the power has been removed from the system.

EEPROM Electrically Erasable Programmable Read-Only Memory (see EAROM).

EPROM Erasable Programmable Read-Only Memory. Can be programmed electrically, but must be erased under an ultraviolet lamp.

Ferrite bead A small inductor that is often used in decoupling circuitry.

LIFO Last-In, First-Out memory. Stores and retrieves data in the order indicated.

Interrupt An input/output technique by which the hardware in the system can call a subroutine in the computer's memory.

MPU MicroProcessing Unit.

NOVRAM A nonvolatile RAM (see EAROM).

OEM Original Equipment Manufacturer.

Parity A count of the number of ones in a binary number, expressed as even or odd.

PROM Programmable Read-Only Memory. Programmed by burning open small fusible links.

Propagation delay The time required for a signal to move from one point to another, usually through a logic element.

RAM Random Access Memory. Can be written into or read from in an equal amount of time.

ROM Read-Only Memory. Programmed by the manufacturer and cannot be written into or erased by the user.

Stack A portion of the memory commonly used to store data and return addresses for subroutines in a computer.

Wait condition When a microprocessor has stopped executing instructions and is waiting for information from a slow device.

Questions and Problems

1 What three main components comprise all digital computer systems?
2 What are the three functions of the MPU?
3 What are the two functions of the memory in a computer system?

4 What useful task is performed by the input/output equipment in a computer system?

5 Programs are often stored in which type of memory?

6 Where would the use of an EAROM be desirable?

7 What is a transparent latch?

8 Output pins on most microprocessors are capable of driving how many standard TTL unit loads?

9 Explain why propagation delay times can normally be ignored in microprocessor based systems.

10 What is a bus transceiver?

11 How is an input/output device treated in a system that uses a memory-mapped I/O?

12 Interrupts are particularly useful in handling which type of external input/output devices?

13 Whenever a HOLD is asserted in a microprocessor, which events will occur?

14 Explain how the circuit in figure 2–6 functions.

15 Contrast the IEEE-696/S100 bus standard with the STD-BUS standard.

16 Local regulation would be used with which one of the bus standards mentioned in question 15?

17 Describe the significance of power supply decoupling.

18 How does the hysteresis of a bus receiver reduce noise problems?

3

The 8085A, 8086, and 8088 Microprocessors

Upon completion of this chapter, you will be able to

1 Describe the function of each pin of the 8085A, 8086, and 8088 microprocessors.
2 Provide the 8085A, 8086, and 8088 with a clock signal.
3 Buffer the basic buses of the 8085A, 8086, and 8088 microprocessors.
4 Generate the $\overline{\text{MEMR}}$, $\overline{\text{MEMW}}$, $\overline{\text{IOR}}$, and $\overline{\text{IOW}}$ signals that are sometimes found in an 8085A-based system.
5 Reset the 8085A, 8086, and 8088 microprocessors, describe which internal registers are cleared or set, and indicate the address of the first instruction after a reset.
6 Detail the operation of the read and write timing of the 8085A, 8086, and 8088 microprocessors.
7 Determine the execution time of an 8085A instruction.
8 Describe how a logic analyzer is used to test a microprocessor.

This chapter provides hardware detail on the 8085A, 8086, and 8088 to enable the reader to use any of these microprocessors throughout the rest of this text. The student is advised to concentrate on the 8085A; after it is mastered, the 8086 and 8088 can be studied.

Most of the discussion emphasizes the 8085A, with references to the 8086 and 8088 for comparison. The Intel user's manuals can provide additional detail on these microprocessors.

3–1 PINOUTS

Figure 3–1 illustrates the 8085A, 8086, and 8088 microprocessor pinouts. All three microprocessors are packaged in 40-pin integrated circuits requiring a single 5V power supply for proper operation. The 8085A uses a maximum of 170 mA of current, the 8086 uses a maximum of 360 mA, and the 8088 uses a maximum of 340 mA.

Drive Capabilities

All three microprocessors can provide 2.0 mA of sink current and 400 μA of source current at any of the output pin connections. This is enough current to drive one 74XXX TTL unit load, one 74SXXX TTL unit load, five 74LSXXX TTL unit loads, or about ten NMOS, CMOS and 74HCXXX unit loads. Table 3–1 illustrates the sink and source current requirements for all of these logic types. Normally no more than ten MOS loads are connected because each MOS input places a fairly large amount of capacitance on an output connection, and this degrades the bus signals.

TABLE 3–1 Unit loading of various logic families.

Family	Type	Sink Current	Source Current
TTL	74XXX	1.6 mA	40 μA
TTL	74LSXXX	0.39 mA	20 μA
TTL	74SXXX	2.0 mA	50 μA
CMOS	74HCXXX	10 μA	10 μA
CMOS	CDXXX	10 μA	10 μA
NMOS	—	10 μA	10 μA

Input Loading

Input connections sink and source a maximum of only 10 μA of current. In addition, they present approximately 10 pF of capacitance. Input voltages are directly TTL compatible and therefore present no problem when interfacing to standard TTL logic circuitry.

Noise Immunity

The system noise immunity for any of these microprocessors is about 350 mV, due to a derated logic zero output voltage of 0.45 V maximum. Some systems require special attention when interfacing external circuitry to these microprocessors. If a higher noise immunity is desired, it can be achieved by adding buffers to all of the output connections.

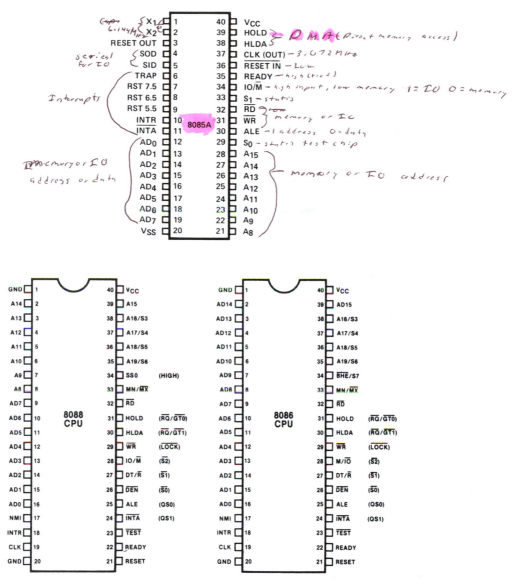

FIGURE 3–1 Pin diagrams or pinouts of the Intel 8085A, 8086, and 8088 microprocessors.

SOURCE: Reprinted by permission of Intel Corporation, Copyright 1978 and 1981.

CLOCK CIRCUITRY 3–2

The 8085A contains an internal oscillator that, in most cases, generates the basic timing for this microprocessor. The 8086 and 8088 require the addition of an external clock generator to provide their basic timing.

8085A Clock Circuitry

Under normal operation, a crystal of either 6.0 MHz or 6.144 MHz is attached to the X1 and X2 inputs of the 8085A, as pictured in figure 3–2(a). The crystal frequency is internally divided by two to produce the basic microprocessor timing and the clock out signal from the clock out pin. Permissible crystal frequencies for the 8085A range between 1.0 MHz and 6.2 MHz for reliable operation. If a frequency is chosen outside of this range, Intel does not guarantee proper operation.

Figures 3–2(b) and 3–2(c) illustrate two other less commonly used methods for obtaining a microprocessor clock signal for the 8085A. The main disadvantage of the RC or LC timing network is its lack of accuracy and stability. In most cases, the microprocessor clock times external events; since it must be fairly accurate, a crystal clock is generally used.

An external clock input may be found in a system that already has a TTL-compatible clock waveform present. This clock waveform can and often does drive the microprocessor, as illustrated in figure 3–2(d).

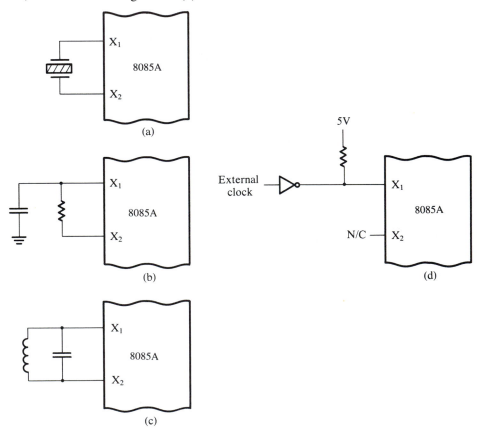

FIGURE 3–2 Methods of obtaining a clock for the Intel 8085A microprocessor: (a) crystal, (b) RC timing, (c) LC timing, (d) external clock.

8086 and 8088 Clock Circuitry

The 8086 and 8088 require an external clock generator or an external TTL-compatible clock for operation. In most applications, the 8284A clock generator supplies the clock waveform and provides synchronization for the READY and RESET inputs to these microprocessors. Figure 3–3 illustrates the 8284A clock generator attached to the clock inputs of either an 8086 or an 8088. The 8284A divides the crystal frequency by three for

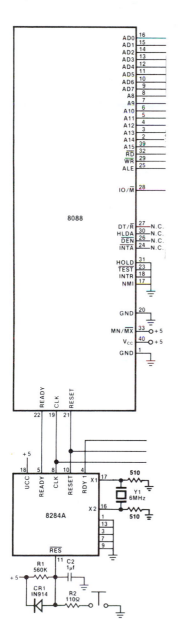

FIGURE 3–3 Obtaining the clock for the Intel 8086/8088 microprocessor using the Intel 8284A clock generator.

SOURCE Reprinted by permission of Intel Corporation, Copyright 1981.

the clock input to the microprocessor and develops a peripheral clock signal one-sixth the crystal frequency. The 8086 and 8088 both typically use a clock frequency of 5.0 MHz, so that a 15-MHz crystal is attached to the 8284A to achieve this clock frequency.

3–3 ADDRESS BUS CONNECTIONS

The 8085A, 8086, and 8088 all use a multiplexed address bus. The 8085A multiplexes the least significant half of its 16-bit address bus with the data bus. The 8086 multiplexes all 20 of its address bus connections with the data bus and some status information. The 8088 is a cross between the 8085A and the 8086 in the way that its address bus is multiplexed. The least significant 8 bits of the 20 bits of the address bus are multiplexed with the data bus, and the most significant 4 bits are multiplexed with status information. Refer to figure 3–4 for a more detailed view of this bus in all three microprocessors.

The 8085A can address 64K of memory and 256 different I/O devices through its address bus. Both the 8086 and the 8088 can directly address 1024K bytes of memory and 64K different I/O devices. The 8088 directly addresses bytes of memory, and the 8086 can directly address either bytes or 16-bit words of memory. 8086/8088 memory is organized as sixteen 64K byte banks of memory.

3–4 DATA BUS CONNECTIONS

The data bus connections in all three microprocessors are multiplexed with other address information. This is allowable since data flow on this bus only after the memory is given sufficient time to access data. The overall effect of this multiplexed bus has been to reduce the total number of pin connections on these microprocessors. The 8085A and 8088 multiplex the data bus with the least significant half of the address bus, and the 8086 multiplexes its 16-bit data bus with the least significant 16 bits of the address bus.

The address latch enable (ALE) signal in all three cases allows the address bus information to be separated from the data bus information for use in the system. Figure 3–5 illustrates all three processors and the methods used to demultiplex this information. The data bus in these schematics actually still contains memory addressing information, but since it is not used for data, it can be ignored.

Figure 3–6 depicts a method that is sometimes required for buffering the data bus, since the 8088 and 8086 are often used in a large system.

The data bus buffer's direction of data flow is controlled by the microprocessor's Data Transmit/Receive (DT/$\overline{\text{R}}$) signal. Normally the direction of data flow is out of the microprocessor through the bus buffers unless a read is occurring. In this case, the DT/$\overline{\text{R}}$ signal becomes a logic zero for a read and switches the direction of the data flow through the data bus buffers into the microprocessor. The data enable ($\overline{\text{DEN}}$) connection from the 8088 becomes active only when the data bus is to be used by the processor. At all other times, this output is inactive, keeping the 8256 bus transceiver in its high impedance state.

Buffers decrease the amount of time allowed for memory access by 10–20 ns. If this

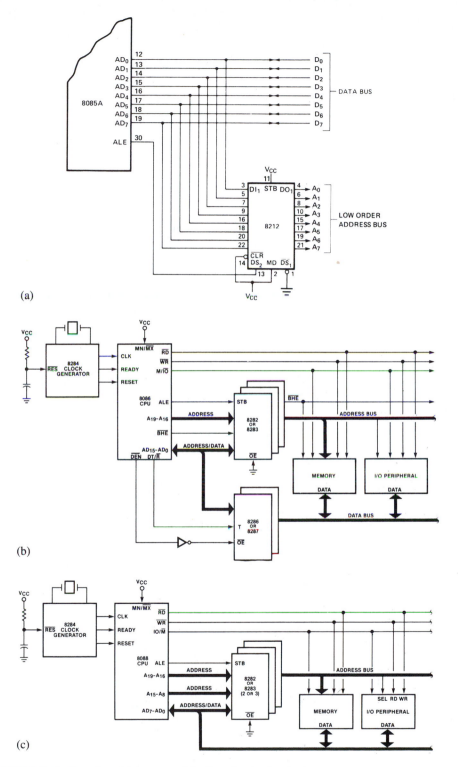

FIGURE 3–4 Bus demultiplexers and buffers for the Intel microprocessors: (a) demultiplexing the 8085A address/data bus, (b) demultiplexing and buffering the 8086 address and data buses, (c) demultiplexing the 8088 address/data bus.

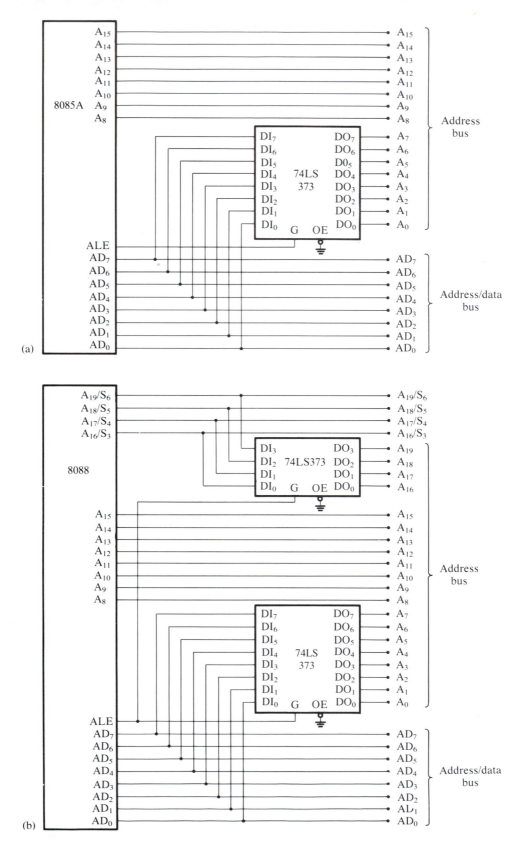

FIGURE 3–5 (a) 8085A and (b) 8088 address/data and address buses.

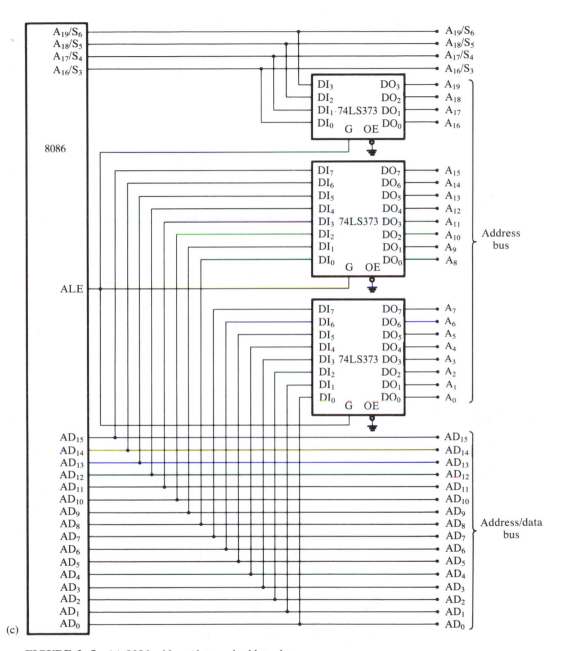

(c)

FIGURE 3-5 (c) 8086 address/data and address buses.

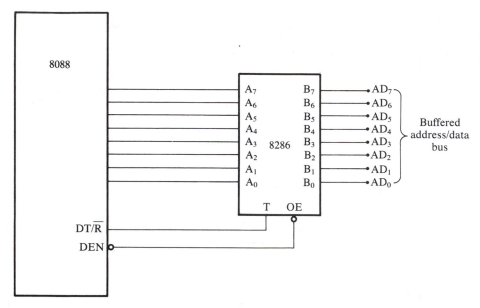

FIGURE 3–6 The 8088 connected to an 8286 octal bus transceiver to create a buffered address/data bus.

degree of reduction is objectionable, the 74S series TTL circuits (which have a shorter propagation delay time) reduce the time below 10 ns.

3–5 CONTROL BUS CONNECTIONS

The control bus structures of the 8085A and the 8086 and 8088 in the minimum mode are almost identical when comparing major control signals that accomplish memory and I/O references. In the maximum mode, which requires an external bus controller, the 8086 and 8088 resemble the now-obsolete 8080A. Maximum mode operation allows the 8086 and the 8088 to function in a very large system. Minimum mode operation allows these processors to be used in a smaller dedicated task application. Table 3–2 contrasts the control signals of the 8085A, 8086, and 8088.

In the minimum mode the HOLD and HLDA signals cause and acknowledge a direct memory access (see chapters 8–10).

The $\overline{WR}$ pin is identical in all three cases and times the writing of data to either memory or an I/O device.

The IO/$\overline{M}$ signal is present on all three microprocessors, but it is inverted on the 8086. The 8085A and the 8088, which are 8-bit data bus microprocessors, use the same IO/$\overline{M}$ signal; the 8-bit peripherals designed for the 8085A also function without additional circuitry with the 8088.

Figure 3-7 illustrates the 8085A connected to a 3-to-8 line decoder that generates the four control signals: $\overline{MEMR}$ (memory read), $\overline{MEMW}$ (memory write), $\overline{IOR}$ (I/O read), and $\overline{IOW}$ (I/O write). These control signals appear elsewhere in this book and are, in

TABLE 3–2 A comparison of the control signals for the 8085A and the 8086/8088.

Signal	8085A	8086/8088
ALE	Used to latch A0 through A7.	Used to latch A0 through A7 in the 8088 and A0 through A15 in the 8086.
$\overline{WR}$	Write strobe to the bus.	Write strobe to the bus.
$\overline{RD}$	Read strobe to the bus.	Read strobe to the bus.
HOLD	Input used to request a DMA.	Input used to request a DMA.
HLDA	Output used to acknowledge a DMA.	Output used to acknowledge a DMA.
$\overline{DEN}$	—	Used to enable the system data bus if external bus buffers are present.
DT/$\overline{R}$	—	Used to change the direction of data flow through external data bus buffers if present.
IO/$\overline{M}$	Indicates an I/O or memory operation.	Indicates an I/O or memory operation in the 8088 only.
$\overline{IO}$/M	—	Indicates an I/O or memory operation in the 8086 only.
INTR	Interrupt request.	Interrupt request.
$\overline{INTA}$	Acknowledges the INTR.	Acknowledges the INTR.
NMI	(TRAP) on the 8085 is a nonmaskable interrupt input.	Is a nonmaskable interrupt input.
RST 7.5 RST 6.5 RST 5.5	Maskable interrupt inputs.	—
READY	Indicates the bus is ready for a transfer.	Indicates the bus is ready for a transfer.
RESET	RESET causes program execution from 0000H.	Causes program execution from FFFF0H.
MN/$\overline{MX}$	—	Selects minimum or maximum mode operation.

certain cases, an important change from the standard control bus signals, $\overline{RD}$ (read), $\overline{WR}$ (write), and IO/$\overline{M}$ (I/O or memory).

The DT/$\overline{R}$ and $\overline{DEN}$ signals are only present on the 8086 and the 8088 and control external data bus buffers when the system requires them. DT/$\overline{R}$ controls the direction of the data flow, and $\overline{DEN}$ enables or disables the external buffers. These buffers are normally disabled for a direct memory access.

The $\overline{RD}$ signal, which appears on all three microprocessors for all modes of operation, times the transfer of data into the microprocessor from an external memory or I/O device.

ALE is used to demultiplex the address/data bus and appears in the first clocking period of every bus transfer machine cycle. A *bus transfer machine cycle* is one in which data actually flow into or out of the microprocessor through the data bus. It is important to note

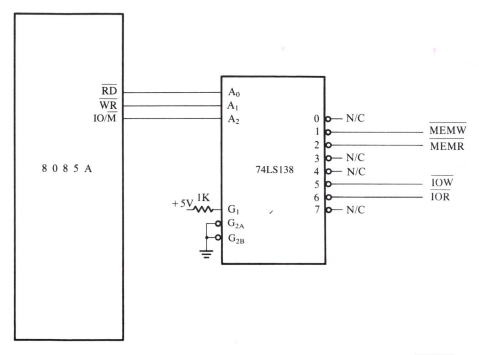

FIGURE 3–7 The 8085A configured to generate the four system control signals $\overline{\text{MEMW}}$, $\overline{\text{MEMR}}$, $\overline{\text{IOW}}$, and $\overline{\text{IOR}}$.

that there are some machine cycles that do nothing. During these do-nothing cycles, called *bus idle,* or *passive,* cycles, the bus is idle and can be used for some other operation.

In the 8088 an additional minimum mode control signal, $\overline{\text{SS0}}$, has been provided. $\overline{\text{SS0}}$, with the DT/$\overline{\text{R}}$ and IO/$\overline{\text{M}}$ signals, can be decoded to indicate the type of machine cycle that the microprocessor is currently executing (as pictured in table 3–3).

In maximum mode operation, both the 8086 and the 8088 require an additional component to function. The 8288 bus controller is needed to generate an expanded set of system control signals. Figure 3–8 compares a minimum mode system with a maximum mode system.

The major difference between these two systems is the memory and I/O control sig-

TABLE 3–3 8086 and 8088 machine cycle types.

IO/$\overline{\text{M}}$	DT/$\overline{\text{R}}$	$\overline{\text{SS0}}$	Function
0	0	0	Code access
0	0	1	Memory read
0	1	0	Memory write
0	1	1	Passive
1	0	0	Interrupt acknowledge
1	0	1	I/O read
1	1	0	I/O write
1	1	1	Halt

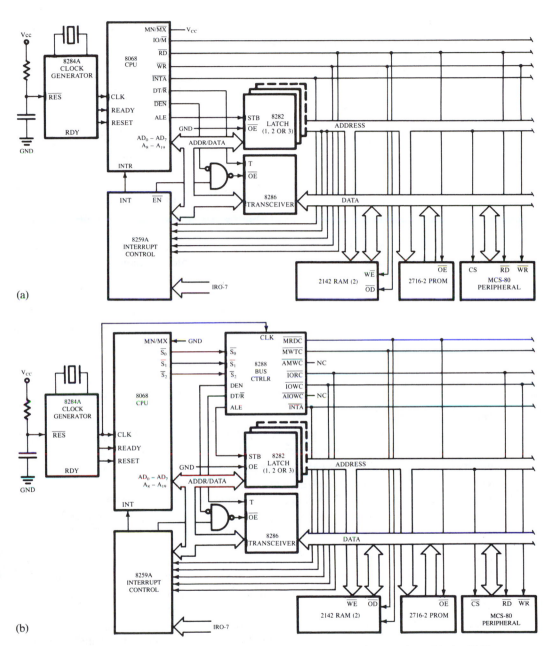

FIGURE 3–8 (a) The 8088 connected to a system in minimum mode operation, (b) the 8088 connected to a system in maximum mode operation.

SOURCE: Reprinted by permission of Intel Corporation, Copyright 1981.

nals. In the minimum mode system, $\overline{\text{RD}}$ and $\overline{\text{WR}}$ are used to control both the I/O and the memory. In the maximum mode system, four new control signals have been developed for this purpose by the 8288 bus controller. $\overline{\text{MRDC}}$ and $\overline{\text{MWTC}}$ control the memory, and

$\overline{\text{IORC}}$ and $\overline{\text{IOWC}}$ control the I/O devices. Notice that these signals perform the same functions as the signals developed in figure 3–7 for the 8085A.

The advanced memory and I/O write signals $\overline{\text{AMWC}}$ and $\overline{\text{AIOWC}}$ are not connected in this example but do find application if the memory or I/O device needs more time to accomplish a write. These advanced signals are issued to allow an external device to begin an early access.

TABLE 3–4   Segment register selection.

S4	S3	Function
0	0	Alternate data
0	1	Stack
1	0	Code
1	1	Data

In addition to the new signals generated by the bus controller, four status signals have also been provided. The S3 and S4 status bits indicate which segment register forms the current memory address, as indicated in table 3–4. S5 is exactly the same as the PSW interrupt enable bit, and S6 is always zero.

The $\overline{\text{INTA}}$ signal is used as a strobe whenever an interrupt takes effect. It is used in the 8086 and 8088 to read the interrupt vector from the external hardware and in the 8085 to read a RST or a CALL instruction from the external hardware.

3–6 RESET

The 8085A Reset

The 8085A is reset by placing a logic zero on the active low $\overline{\text{RESET IN}}$ pin. This input must be held at a logic zero level for at least 10 ms after the power supply connection to Vcc has reached 5 V; if it is not held low for this length of time, Intel does not guarantee a reset. In addition to the reset input, Intel provides a RESET OUT connection to reset other devices in a system. Table 3–5 illustrates the internal circuits initialized by the $\overline{\text{RESET IN}}$ signal. It is important to note that the program counter is cleared to zero on a reset. This causes the instruction at memory location zero to be executed after a $\overline{\text{RESET IN}}$.

The 8086 and 8088 Reset

The 8086 and the 8088 are reset by placing a logic one on the active high RESET pin. This pin must be held at this level for at least four clocking periods, except after power on, where it must be held for 50 μs to guarantee a reset. Table 3–6 illustrates the internal effect of a reset. The first instruction executed after a reset is a location FFFF0 because the code segment register is set to an FFFF and the instruction pointer is cleared to a zero.

A Typical Power-On-Clearing Circuit

The output of the power-on-clearing circuit (see figure 3–9) is connected to the active low reset input of an 8085A or to the $\overline{\text{RES}}$ input of the 8284A clock generator of the 8086 or 8088 system. The 8284A clock generator contains a circuit that inverts this signal and generates the RESET input for the 8086 or 8088.

TABLE 3–5 The effect of the 8085A RESET IN signal.

Circuit	Reset/Set
Program counter	Reset
Instruction register	Reset
INTE flip-flop	Reset
RST 7.5 flip-flop	Reset
TRAP flip-flop	Reset
SOD flip-flop	Reset
Machine state flip-flop	Reset
Machine cycle flip-flop	Reset
Internally latched flip-flops for HOLD, INTR, and READY	Reset
RST 5.5 mask	Set
RST 6.5 mask	Set
RST 7.5 mask	Set

TABLE 3–6 The effect of the 8086 and 8088 RESET signal.

Circuit	Condition
Flags	Cleared
Instruction pointer	0000
Code segment register	FFFF
Data segment register	0000
Stack segment register	0000
Extra segment register	0000
Queue	Empty

BUS TIMING 3–7

If the 8085A is operated with a 3 MHz clock, it takes 1 μs to transfer a byte of information to or from the I/O or the memory. It takes the 8085A three of its clocking cycles to transfer a byte of information. The 8086 and 8088 require four clocking periods to accomplish the transfer of a byte for the 8088, or 16 bits for the 8086. It would seem that these microprocessors are slower than the 8085A, but this is not the case since the clocking period is typically 200 ns. At this rate a bus transfer occurs in 800 ns, rather than the 1 μs rate for the 8085A.

8085A Read Timing

Figure 3–10 pictures the basic read timing diagrams for the 8085A. It also illustrates the AC timing characteristics for these waveforms. The read timing diagram is divided into clocking states (labeled T1, T2, and T3). These three states comprise one 8085A bus cycle.

During clocking state T1 the memory address or an I/O port number is issued to the system. During this state the microprocessor also sends out the ALE signal to demultiplex the address/data bus. It is important to note that ALE becomes a logic one before the

FIGURE 3–9 A typical power-on-clearing circuit for a microprocessor.

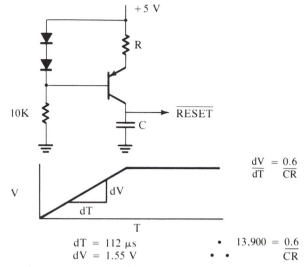

$$\frac{dV}{dT} = \frac{0.6}{CR}$$

dT = 112 μs
dV = 1.55 V

$$\bullet \quad 13,900 = \frac{0.6}{CR}$$

address is available, which means that a positive edge triggered latch cannot demultiplex this information. Instead, most systems use a positive gated transparent latch.

During timing state T2 the read control signal $\overline{RD}$ is sent to the system. In this state the 8085A also samples the READY input to see whether a wait state is required for the current bus transfer. This state allows the memory time to access data and to accomplish some internal operations.

Data are transferred through the data bus connections during state T3 and the microprocessor samples or reads the data present on the data bus at this time. These data come either from a memory device or an external input device.

8085A Read Control Signal Timing

In the 8085A the amount of time allowed for the memory or the I/O to access data is TAD time, which amounts to 575 ns at the highest allowable clocking rate. Most memory devices have an access time of 450 ns or less, making them compatible with the 8085A.

Another critical time in most memory devices is TRD time in the 8085A timing diagram. The 8085A allows 300 ns for the memory device to respond from the leading edge, one-to-zero transition, of the $\overline{RD}$ signal. Most memory devices require a minimum of 150 ns to interface easily with the 8085A.

The last timing interval of importance to memory or I/O interface is the turn-off delay time of the memory device's output buffers. Most memory devices have a turn-off delay time no greater than 120 ns. Examining the timing diagram for the 8085A shows the allowable turn-off time TRAE, which is 150 ns, will leave a 30-ns margin.

8085A Write Timing

Figure 3–11 illustrates the basic write timing for the 8085A microprocessor. The trailing edge (zero-to-one transition) of the write pulse $\overline{WR}$ is usually the portion of the waveform that causes a write to occur and is a reference in RAM memory timing diagrams.

The data are valid on the data bus 450 ns before the trailing edge of the $\overline{WR}$ strobe in the 8085A. These same data are valid only 100 ns after the trailing edge of $\overline{WR}$. Fortunately the data hold time requirement in most memory devices is 0 ns, so that this time presents no problem when selecting a RAM. The duration of time that data must be present before the trailing edge of WR varies from RAM to RAM.

Minimum Mode 8086 and 8088 Read Timing

Figure 3–12 illustrates the basic read timing diagram and the AC characteristics for the 8086 and 8088 microprocessors. These microprocessors differ from the 8085A in that it takes four clock states for a bus cycle, as opposed to three for the 8085A.

State T1 provides the system with the ALE pulse and memory address on both the

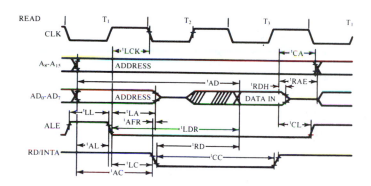

8085AH, 8085AH-2: (T_A = 0°C to 70°C, V_{CC} = 5V ±10%, V_{SS} = OV)*
8085AH-1: (T_A = 0°C to 70°C, V_{CC} = 5V ±5%, V_{SS} = OV)

Symbol	Parameter	8085AH[2] (Final) Min.	8085AH[2] (Final) Max.	8085AH-2[2] (Final) Min.	8085AH-2[2] (Final) Max.	8085AH-1 (Preliminary) Min.	8085AH-1 (Preliminary) Max.	Units
t_{CYC}	CLK Cycle Period	320	2000	200	2000	167	2000	ns
t_1	CLK Low Time (Standard CLK Loading)	80		40		20		ns
t_2	CLK High Time (Standard CLK Loading)	120		70		50		ns
t_r, t_f	CLK Rise and Fall Time		30		30		30	ns
t_{XKR}	X_1 Rising to CLK Rising	25	120	25	100	20	100	ns
t_{XKF}	X_1 Rising to CLK Falling	30	150	30	110	25	110	ns
t_{AC}	A_{8-15} Valid to Leading Edge of Control[1]	270		115		70		ns
t_{ACL}	A_{0-7} Valid to Leading Edge of Control	240		115		60		ns
t_{AD}	A_{0-15} Valid to Valid Data In		575		350		225	ns
t_{AFR}	Address Float After Leading Edge of READ (INTA)		0		0		0	ns
t_{AL}	A_{8-15} Valid Before Trailing Edge of ALE [1]	115		50		25		ns

*Note: For Extended Temperature EXPRESS use M8085AH Electricals Parameters.

FIGURE 3–10 The 8085A read timing diagram and AC characteristics.

SOURCE: Reprinted by permission of Intel Corporation, Copyright 1983.

Symbol	Parameter	8085AH[2] (Final)		8085AH-2[2] (Final)		8085AH-1 (Preliminary)		Units
		Min.	Max.	Min.	Max.	Min.	Max.	
t_{ALL}	A_{0-7} Valid Before Trailing Edge of ALE	90		50		25		ns
t_{ARY}	READY Valid from Address Valid		220		100		40	ns
t_{CA}	Address (A_{8-15}) Valid After Control	120		60		30		ns
t_{CC}	Width of Control Low ($\overline{RD}$, $\overline{WR}$, $\overline{INTA}$) Edge of ALE	400		230		150		ns
t_{CL}	Trailing Edge of Control to Leading Edge of ALE	50		25		0		ns
t_{DW}	Data Valid to Trailing Edge of $\overline{WRITE}$	420		230		140		ns
t_{HABE}	HLDA to Bus Enable		210		150		150	ns
t_{HABF}	Bus Float After HLDA		210		150		150	ns
t_{HACK}	HLDA Valid to Trailing Edge of CLK	110		40		0		ns
t_{HDH}	HOLD Hold Time	0		0		0		ns
t_{HDS}	HOLD Setup Time to Trailing Edge of CLK	170		120		120		ns
t_{INH}	INTR Hold Time	0		0		0		ns
t_{INS}	INTR, RST, and TRAP Setup Time to Falling Edge of CLK	160		150		150		ns
t_{LA}	Address Hold Time After ALE	100		50		20		ns
t_{LC}	Trailing Edge of ALE to Leading Edge of Control	130		60		25		ns
t_{LCK}	ALE Low During CLK High	100		50		15		ns
t_{LDR}	ALE to Valid Data During Read		460		270		175	ns
t_{LDW}	ALE to Valid Data During Write		200		120		110	ns
t_{LL}	ALE Width	140		80		50		ns
t_{LRY}	ALE to READY Stable		110		30		10	ns
t_{RAE}	Trailing Edge of $\overline{READ}$ to Re-Enabling of Address	150		90		50		ns
t_{RD}	$\overline{READ}$ (or $\overline{INTA}$) to Valid Data		300		150		75	ns
t_{RV}	Control Trailing Edge to Leading Edge of Next Control	400		220		160		ns
t_{RDH}	Data Hold Time After $\overline{READ}$ $\overline{INTA}$	0		0		0		ns
t_{RYH}	READY Hold Time	0		0		5		ns
t_{RYS}	READY Setup Time to Leading Edge of CLK	110		100		100		ns
t_{WD}	Data Valid After Trailing Edge of $\overline{WRITE}$	100		60		30		ns
t_{WDL}	LEADING Edge of $\overline{WRITE}$ to Data Valid		40		20		30	ns

FIGURE 3–10 continued

WRITE

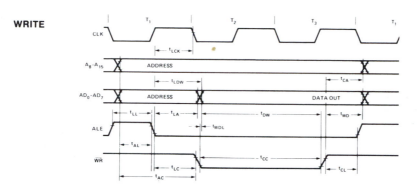

FIGURE 3–11   The 8085A write timing diagram.

BUS TIMING—MINIMUM MODE SYSTEM

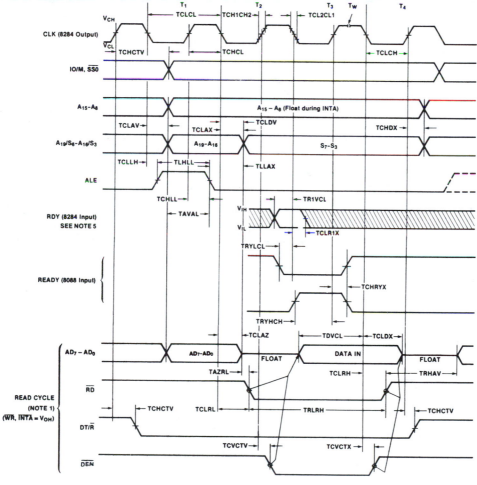

FIGURE 3–12   The 8086 read timing diagram and AC characteristics.

(8086: T_A = 0°C to 70°C, V_{CC} = 5V ± 10%)
(8086-1: T_A = 0°C to 70°C, V_{CC} = 5V ± 5%)
(8086-2: T_A = 0°C to 70°C, V_{CC} = 5V ± 5%)

MINIMUM COMPLEXITY SYSTEM TIMING REQUIREMENTS

Symbol	Parameter	8086		8086-1 (Preliminary)		8086-2		Units
		Min.	Max.	Min.	Max.	Min.	Max.	
TCLCL	CLK Cycle Period	200	500	100	500	125	500	ns
TCLCH	CLK Low Time	118		53		68		ns
TCHCL	CLK High Time	69		39		44		ns
TCH1CH2	CLK Rise Time		10		10		10	ns
TCL2CL1	CLK Fall Time		10		10		10	ns
TDVCL	Data in Setup Time	30		5		20		ns
TCLDX	Data in Hold Time	10		10		10		ns
TR1VCL	RDY Setup Time into 8284A (See Notes 1, 2)	35		35		35		ns
TCLR1X	RDY Hold Time into 8284A (See Notes 1, 2)	0		0		0		ns
TRYHCH	READY Setup Time into 8086	118		53		68		ns
TCHRYX	READY Hold Time into 8086	30		20		20		ns
TRYLCL	READY Inactive to CLK (See Note 3)	−8		−10		−8		ns
THVCH	HOLD Setup Time	35		20		20		ns
TINVCH	INTR, NMI, TEST Setup Time (See Note 2)	30		15		15		ns
TILIH	Input Rise Time (Except CLK)		20		20		20	ns
TIHIL	Input Fall Time (Except CLK)		12		12		12	ns

FIGURE 3–12 continued

address bus and the address/data bus. In addition to ALE, DT/$\overline{R}$ becomes a logic zero for data received.

In state T2, the $\overline{RD}$ signal is issued to the memory or I/O to begin a memory or I/O read. The $\overline{DEN}$ signal is also activated during this clock cycle, activating the external data bus buffer.

States T3 and T4 provide time for the information to be read from the external memory or I/O device. The data bus is sampled by the microprocessor in the middle of T3 and on into T4. This is required by the increased speed of these processors.

Minimum Mode 8086 and 8088 Read Control Signal Timing

The access times allowed for the memory and I/O devices are understandably shorter for these microprocessors than for the 8085A because of the increased clock frequency. The

TIMING RESPONSES

Symbol	Parameter	8086		8086-1 (Preliminary)		8086-2		Units
		Min.	Max.	Min.	Max.	Min.	Max.	
TCLAV	Address Valid Delay	10	110	10	50	10	60	ns
TCLAX	Address Hold Time	10		10		10		ns
TCLAZ	Address Float Delay	TCLAX	80	10	40	TCLAX	50	ns
TLHLL	ALE Width	TCLCH−20		TCLCH−10		TCLCH-10		ns
TCLLH	ALE Active Delay		80		40		50	ns
TCHLL	ALE Inactive Delay		85		45		55	ns
TLLAX	Address Hold Time to ALE Inactive	TCHCL−10		TCHCL−10		TCHCL−10		ns
TCLDV	Data Valid Delay	10	110	10	50	10	60	ns
TCHDX	Data Hold Time	10		10		10		ns
TWHDX	Data Hold Time After WR	TCLCH−30		TCLCH−25		TCLCH−30		ns
TCVCTV	Control Active Delay 1	10	110	10	50	10	70	ns
TCHCTV	Control Active Delay 2	10	110	10	45	10	60	ns
TCVCTX	Control Inactive Delay	10	110	10	50	10	70	ns
TAZRL	Address Float to READ Active	0		0		0		ns
TCLRL	RD Active Delay	10	165	10	70	10	100	ns
TCLRH	RD Inactive Delay	10	150	10	60	10	80	ns
TRHAV	RD Inactive to Next Address Active	TCLCL−45		TCLCL−35		TCLCL−40		ns
TCLHAV	HLDA Valid Delay	10	160	10	60	10	100	ns
TRLRH	RD Width	2TCLCL−75		2TCLCL−40		2TCLCL−50		ns
TWLWH	WR Width	2TCLCL−60		2TCLCL−35		2TCLCL−40		ns
TAVAL	Address Valid to ALE Low	TCLCH−60		TCLCH−35		TCLCH−40		ns
TOLOH	Output Rise Time		20		20		20	ns
TOHOL	Output Fall Time		12		12		12	ns

NOTES:
1. Signal at 8284A shown for reference only.
2. Setup requirement for asynchronous signal only to guarantee recognition at next CLK.
3. Applies only to T2 state. (8 ns into T3).

FIGURE 3–12   continued

time allowed to the memory or I/O by the 8086 or 8088 microprocessor is approximately 460 ns at the highest allowable clocking frequency. Since the access time is barely longer than 450 ns, some problems may occur in interfacing standard 450 ns memory. A margin of about 20 ns must be maintained between the actual access time of the memory component and the access time allowed to the memory component by the processor. If not, reliable operation is doubtful. In this case, it is wise to choose a memory component with an access time of less than 450 ns.

These processors allow the memory 285 ns of time to be enabled from the $\overline{RD}$ strobe signal; the 8085A allows 300 ns. Any of these is adequate, since most memory devices require 150 ns or less from the $\overline{RD}$ strobe.

The 8086 and 8088 allow the memory output buffers TRHAV time, or 255 ns, to turn off or three-state. Most memory devices require only 120 ns.

Minimum Mode 8086 and 8088 Write Timing

Figure 3–13 illustrates the basic write timing for the 8086 and 8088 microprocessors, which differs little from that of the 8085A. The main difference is the extra clocking state T4, which allows more writing time to the memory.

The only significant differences in read and write timing are the logic level of the DT/$\overline{R}$ signal and the activation of the $\overline{WR}$ strobe instead of the $\overline{RD}$ strobe. The data are valid at

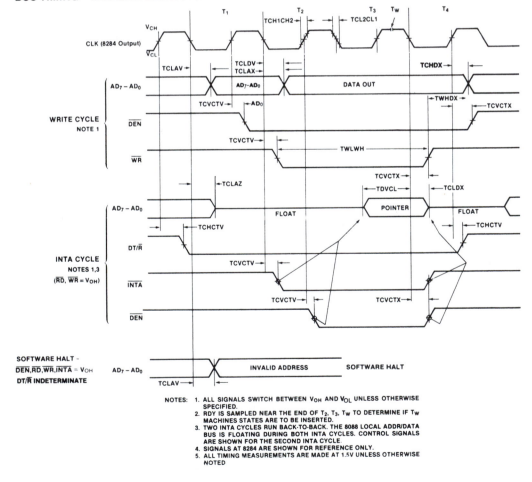

FIGURE 3–13 The 8086 write timing diagram.

SOURCE: Reprinted by permission of Intel Corporation, Copyright 1983.

the data bus for 340 ns before the trailing edge of the $\overline{WR}$ strobe and 39 ns after the trailing edge. These times present no major problem in interfacing, since the data hold time on a memory component is usually 0 ns. The data setup time, of course, will vary from one memory component to another.

MAXIMUM MODE 8086/8088 OPERATION 3–8

In the maximum mode the 8284 bus controller develops the control bus signals discussed earlier. The timing for these control signals is illustrated in figure 3–14 and is almost identical to the timing in the minimum mode illustrated in the last section.

New signals that are used for systems with multiple processors on the system bus have replaced the HOLD and HLDA connections on the 8086 and 8088. The $\overline{RG/GT0}$ and RQ/GT1 interface either the 8089 I/O coprocessor or the 8087 arithmetic coprocessor to the microprocessor. Since these request/grant signal lines are synchronous control lines, all processors and coprocessors must be referenced to the same system clock.

Another connection provided in maximum mode is the $\overline{LOCK}$ connection. This output is used with the 8289 bus arbiter in shared bus systems to lock the bus so that an instruction can be completely executed without intervention from the arbiter. The lock is induced under software control by prefixing an instruction with the lock prefix.

Finally, there are two outputs to track the internal queue, if required. The QS1 and QS0 pins indicate the condition of the internal FIFO or queue register after the indicated activity occurs. Table 3–7 illustrates the bit decoding pattern for these two status signals.

TABLE 3–7   Queue status.

QS1	QS0	Function
0	0	No operation
0	1	First byte of op-code
1	0	Empty queue
1	1	Subsequent byte

INTERRUPTS 3–9

8085A Interrupts

The 8085A microprocessor has a very powerful interrupt structure capable of handling five different external interrupting devices. One of these inputs is nonmaskable while the other four are maskable. They all have a fixed priority scheme, which is presented in table 3–8, where level 1 is the highest and 5 the lowest.

Each of the interrupt inputs, except INTR, causes the 8085A to generate internally a 1-byte CALL instruction called a *RESTART*. The addresses for these restarts are listed in the table with the type of triggering required to activate each of the interrupt inputs.

Whenever the 8085A accepts an interrupt, all future interrupts are disabled except TRAP, the nonmaskable interrupt. Unless the interrupt service subroutine reenables the interrupts before a return occurs, no more interrupts can ever take effect.

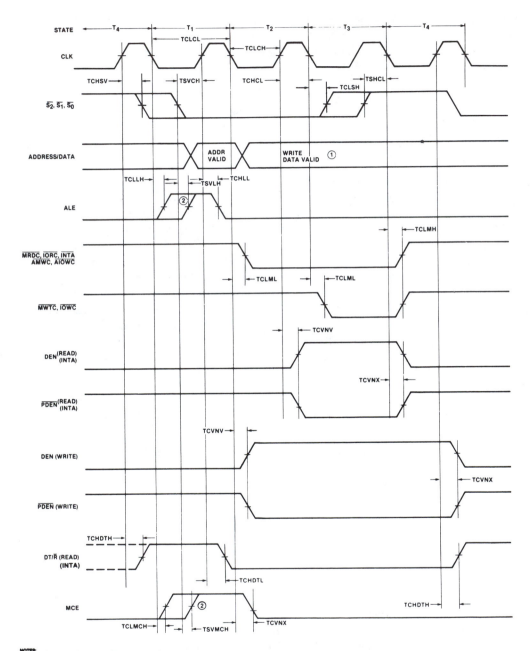

FIGURE 3–14 The timing diagram of the 8288 Bus Controller.

SOURCE: Reprinted by permission of Intel Corporation, Copyright 1983.

TABLE 3–8 8085A interrupt information.

Name	Priority	Address	Sensitivity
TRAP	1	24H	Rising edge and high level
RST 7.5	2	3CH	Rising edge
RST 6.5	3	34H	High level
RST 5.5	4	2CH	High level
INTR	5	*	High level

NOTE: *The address CALLed by this input is determined by the external hardware.

The INTR input is internally decoded to produce a pulse on the $\overline{INTA}$ output whenever it is accepted. This strobe occurs in lieu of an internally generated input and is used to fetch a RESTART or CALL instruction from external hardware. Figure 3–15 pictures a simple circuit for gating an RST 5 into the microprocessor in response to an INTR pulse.

8086 and 8088 Interrupts

The interrupt structure of the 8086 and 8088 is more powerful than that of the 8085A because it has many more levels of interrupts. The 8086 and 8088 have two hardware interrupt inputs, a nonmaskable interrupt input (NMI) and INTR, which is similar to the INTR interrupt input of the 8085A.

The NMI input is always active; whenever it is pulsed high, it causes an interrupt to the interrupt service subroutine pointed to by Vector 2. When this interrupt is accepted, it disables the INTR pin, pushes the contents of the flag register onto the stack, and calls the interrupt service subroutine.

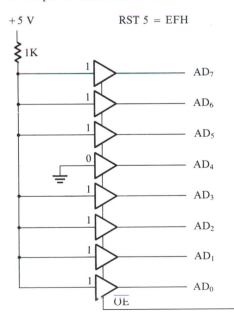

FIGURE 3–15 A circuit that will force a RST 5 onto the data bus in response to an interrupt request.

An interrupt vector is a 4-byte-long entry into a table in memory locations 00000H through 003FFH. Two values are stored in this table at each active interrupt vector: the instruction pointer (IP) in the first 2 bytes, followed by the code segment (CS) register. Intel reserves interrupt vectors 5 through 31 for use in present and future Intel products; these should not be used if an Intel product will ever be connected to the 8086 or 8088. Table 3–9 illustrates the interrupt vectors.

TABLE 3–9   8086/8088 interrupt vector table.

SOURCE: (Reprinted by permission of Intel Corporation, copyright 1981)

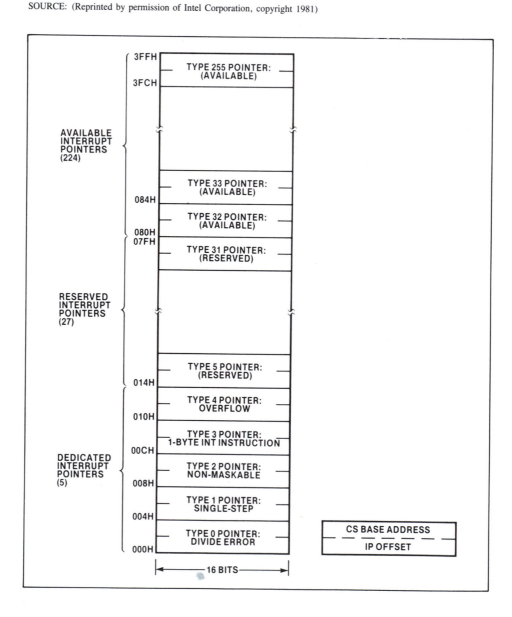

The INTR interrupt input is level sensitive and must be held active until recognized by the microprocessor. It works in the same manner that the INTR pin functions on the 8085A. When accepted, the $\overline{INTA}$ output or acknowledge signal pulses twice. During the first pulse, the processor locks out all other arbiters in the system, so that the bus is not accessed by another processor. During the second pulse of the $\overline{INTA}$ pin, the external hardware must provide an 8-bit interrupt vector to the microprocessor. The vector is applied to the least significant half of the data bus during the second pulse of $\overline{INTA}$. Figure 3–16 pictures a simple circuit for causing an interrupt vector 128 base ten to the data bus.

DIRECT MEMORY ACCESS CONNECTIONS 3–10

The 8085A uses the same type of control signals for DMA as the 8086 or 8088 in minimum mode. The HOLD input and the HLDA output are used to gain access to the microprocessor buses for a DMA.

When the HOLD input is accepted by the microprocessor, it relinquishes control of the memory and I/O connected to its buses by floating the address bus, data bus, and control bus to their high-impedance state. This effectively disconnects the microprocessor from the system.

Once the microprocessor has three-stated its buses, the external device is signaled through the HLDA output. HLDA indicates that the microprocessor has indeed released the memory and I/O for external usage. Once HLDA is active, the external device gains complete control of the microprocessor's address and I/O space. The external device is then free to manipulate the I/O circuitry and the memory.

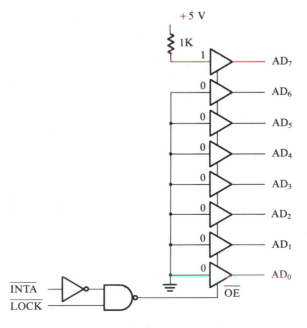

FIGURE 3–16 A circuit that will force interrupt vector 128 onto the 8086 or 8088 data bus in response to an interrupt request.

3–11 MISCELLANEOUS 8085A PIN CONNECTIONS

SID and SOD

The SID and SOD connections on the 8085A are used as 1-bit I/O ports. Serial input data (SID) can be sampled by executing the RIM instruction. This leaves the value of the SID pin in the sign bit position of the accumulator after a RIM instruction.

Serial output data (SOD) are controlled by placing the desired level in the sign bit of the accumulator and a logic one in the next bit position. When the SIM instruction is executed, the content of the sign bit is latched into the SOD pin.

S0 and S1

S0 and S1 are two status bits provided on the 8085A. These bits indicate, in conjunction with the IO/$\overline{\text{M}}$ signal, the current type of machine cycle, as listed in table 3–10.

TABLE 3–10 8085A machine cycle status.

IO/$\overline{\text{M}}$	S1	S0	Status
0	0	0	Halt
0	0	1	Memory write
0	1	0	Memory read
0	1	1	Op-code fetch
1	0	0	Halt
1	0	1	I/O write
1	1	0	I/O read
1	1	1	Interrupt acknowledge

READY

The READY input slows the microprocessor so that a slower memory or I/O device can be used in the system. In normal operation, this pin is held at a logic one level.

If the READY pin is held at a logic zero level, the microprocessor will wait for an indefinite period of time. This waiting period is measured in multiples of the processor clock. When the pin is returned to its logic one state, all processing continues in the normal mode.

This pin can cause single step operation and implement the run/stop function. Figure 3–17 illustrates its use in the run/stop function on an 8085A microprocessor.

3–12 MISCELLANEOUS 8086 AND 8088 PIN CONNECTIONS

The $\overline{\text{TEST}}$ input is tested by the WAIT instruction. If the $\overline{\text{TEST}}$ pin is a logic one, or inactive, the $\overline{\text{WAIT}}$ instruction will cause the microprocessor to stop executing instructions until the $\overline{\text{TEST}}$ pin is grounded. Although in most applications this pin is grounded, it has interesting uses.

The $\overline{\text{BHE}}$ signal, present only on the 8086, indicates which byte in the memory is to be selected by the microprocessor. This signal is combined with address bit A0 to select a whole word, upper byte, lower byte, or no byte of information. Table 3–11 illustrates the logical combinations of A0 and $\overline{\text{BHE}}$.

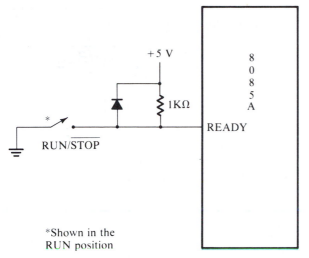

FIGURE 3–17 A circuit that will allow the 8085A to be stopped at any instant in time without the loss of data.

*Shown in the RUN position

BHE	A0	Function
0	0	Whole word
0	1	Upper byte
1	0	Lower byte
1	1	None

TABLE 3–11 Memory byte selection.

INSTRUCTION TIMING 3–13

To calculate the time required to execute a program or wasted in a delay loop, it is necessary to know the execution times for each instruction. The times for the 8085A are illustrated in table 3–12 as clock cycle times. To determine the time required to execute an instruction, multiply the number of clock cycles by the basic clock cycle time of the microprocessor. For example, if it takes seven clock cycles to execute a MVI A,02 at a clock cycle time of 0.333 μs, then it takes the 8085A 2.333 μs to execute this instruction.

The table illustrates that a few instructions require either 7 or 11 clock cycles to execute (7/11). For example, with JNC DOG, it takes 11 cycles on no carry and 7 cycles on a carry condition.

MICROPROCESSOR TESTING WITH A LOGIC ANALYZER 3–14

The logic analyzer is extremely useful in microprocessor testing. In fact, it is the only device that can be used to effectively view the timing of a processor functioning in a system. It is even possible to view the program execution path or track with the logic analyzer, which is extremely useful in debugging complicated software.

TABLE 3–12 Instruction execution times for the 8080/8085A microprocessor.

(Reprinted by permission of Intel Corporation, copyright 1983)

8080A/8085A INSTRUCTION SET INDEX

Instruction		Code	Bytes	T States 8085A	T States 8080A	Machine Cycles
ACI	DATA	CE data	2	7	7	F R
ADC	REG	1000 1SSS	1	4	4	F
ADC	M	8E	1	7	7	F R
ADD	REG	1000 0SSS	1	4	4	F
ADD	M	86	1	7	7	F R
ADI	DATA	C6 data	2	7	7	F R
ANA	REG	1010 0SSS	1	4	4	F
ANA	M	A6	1	7	7	F R
ANI	DATA	E6 data	2	7	7	F R
CALL	LABEL	CD addr	3	18	17	S R R W W*
CC	LABEL	DC addr	3	9/18	11/17	S R•/S R R W W*
CM	LABEL	FC addr	3	9/18	11/17	S R•/S R R W W*
CMA		2F	1	4	4	F
CMC		3F	1	4	4	F
CMP	REG	1011 1SSS	1	4	4	F
CMP	M	BE	1	7	7	F R
CNC	LABEL	D4 addr	3	9/18	11/17	S R•/S R R W W*
CNZ	LABEL	C4 addr	3	9/18	11/17	S R•/S R R W W*
CP	LABEL	F4 addr	3	9/18	11/17	S R•/S R R W W*
CPE	LABEL	EC addr	3	9/18	11/17	S R•/S R R W W*
CPI	DATA	FE data	2	7	7	F R
CPO	LABEL	E4 addr	3	9/18	11/17	S R•/S R R W W*
CZ	LABEL	CC addr	3	9/18	11/17	S R•/S R R W W*
DAA		27	1	4	4	F
DAD	RP	00RP 1001	1	10	10	F B B
DCR	REG	00SS S101	1	4	5	F*
DCR	M	35	1	10	10	F R W
DCX	RP	00RP 1011	1	6	5	S*
DI		F3	1	4	4	F
EI		FB	1	4	4	F
HLT		76	1	5	7	F B
IN	PORT	D8 data	2	10	10	F R I
INR	REG	00SS S100	1	4	5	F*
INR	M	34	1	10	10	F R W
INX	RP	00RP 0011	1	6	5	S*
JC	LABEL	DA addr	3	7/10	10	F R/F R R†
JM	LABEL	FA addr	3	7/10	10	F R/F R R†
JMP	LABEL	C3 addr	3	10	10	F R R
JNC	LABEL	D2 addr	3	7/10	10	F R/F R R†
JNZ	LABEL	C2 addr	3	7/10	10'	F R/F R R†
JP	LABEL	F2 addr	3	7/10	10	F R/F R R†
JPE	LABEL	EA addr	3	7/10	10	F R/F R R†
JPO	LABEL	E2 addr	3	7/10	10	F R/F R R†
JZ	LABEL	CA addr	3	7/10	10	F R/F R R†
LDA	ADDR	3A addr	3	13	13	F R R R
LDAX	RP	000X 1010	1	7	7	F R
LHLD	ADDR	2A addr	3	16	16	F R R R R

Instruction		Code	Bytes	T States 8085A	T States 8080A	Machine Cycles
LXI	RP,DATA16	00RP 0001 data16	3	10	10	F R R
MOV	REG,REG	01DD DSSS	1	4	5	F*
MOV	M,REG	0111 0SSS	1	7	7	F W
MOV	REG,M	01DD D110	1	7	7	F R
MVI	REG,DATA	00DD D110 data	2	7	7	F R
MVI	M,DATA	36 data	2	10	10	F R W
NOP		00	1	4	4	F
ORA	REG	1011 0SSS	1	4	4	F
ORA	M	B6	1	7	7	F R
ORI	DATA	F6 data	2	7	7	F R
OUT	PORT	D3 data	2	10	10	F R O
PCHL		E9	1	6	5	S*
POP	RP	11RP 0001	1	10	10	F R R
PUSH	RP	11RP 0101	1	12	11	S W W*
RAL		17	1	4	4	F
RAR		1F	1	4	4	F
RC		D8	1	6/12	5/11	S/S R R*
RET		C9	1	10	10	F R R
RIM (8085A only)		20	1	4	–	F
RLC		07	1	4	4	F
RM		F8	1	6/12	5/11	S/S R R*
RNC		D0	1	6/12	5/11	S/S R R*
RNZ		C0	1	6/12	5/11	S/S R R*
RP		F0	1	6/12	5/11	S/S R R*
RPE		E8	1	6/12	5/11	S/S R R*
RPO		E0	1	6/12	5/11	S/S R R*
RRC		0F	1	4	4	F
RST	N	11XX X111	1	12	11	S W W*
RZ		C8	1	6/12	5/11	S/S R R*
SBB	REG	1001 1SSS	1	4	4	F
SBB	M	9E	1	7	7	F R
SBI	DATA	DE data	2	7	7	F R
SHLD	ADDR	22 addr	3	16	16	F R R W W
SIM (8085A only)		30	1	4	–	F
SPHL		F9	1	6	5	S*
STA	ADDR	32 addr	3	13	13	F R R W
STAX	RP	000X 0010	1	7	7	F W
STC		37	1	4	4	F
SUB	REG	1001 0SSS	1	4	4	F
SUB	M	96	1	7	7	F R
SUI	DATA	D6 data	2	7	7	F R
XCHG		EB	1	4	4	F
XRA	REG	1010 1SSS	1	4	4	F
XRA	M	AE	1	7	7	F R
XRI	DATA	EE data	2	7	7	F R
XTHL		E3	1	16	18	F R R W W

Machine cycle types:

F	Four clock period instr fetch
S	Six clock period instr fetch
R	Memory read
I	I/O read
W	Memory write
O	I/O write
B	Bus idle
X	Variable or optional binary digit
DDD	Binary digits identifying a destination register
SSS	Binary digits identifying a source register
RP	Register Pair

B = 000, C = 001, D = 010 Memory = 110
E = 011, H = 100, L = 101 A = 111

BC = 00, HL = 10
DE = 01, SP = 11

*Five clock period instruction fetch with 8080A.

†The longer machine cycle sequence applies regardless of condition evaluation with 8080A.

•An extra READ cycle (R) will occur for this condition with 8080A.

*All mnemonics copyrighted ⊙Intel Corporation 1976.

Instruction Tracking with the Logic Analyzer

The op-codes of an instruction can be stored with the memory addresses in the memory of the logic analyzer for later viewing as hexadecimal op-codes. In some newer analyzers, it is even possible to store the mnemonics of these op-codes in the memory of the analyzer and to display a symbolic listing. This, of course, would not be a program listing; it would be a dynamic listing of the instructions as actually executed in the system.

To track the op-codes in an operating system with a logic analyzer, three signal components must be connected to the analyzer. The data input connection for the analyzer is connected to the address/data bus in order to view the op-codes as they are fetched. In addition to data, a logic analyzer needs a clock signal to acquire the information from the data bus. In the case of the 8085A, a clock signal must be provided when S1 and S0 are both high at the same time that $\overline{RD}$ is a logic zero. The clock input must be set so that it is active on the zero-to-one transition of the $\overline{RD}$ strobe. The circuitry required to generate this clock is illustrated in figure 3–18.

In addition to the data and clock inputs, the analyzer must also be triggered at the proper point. This is accomplished by using the beginning address of the software under test. Many analyzers have a set of 16 trigger qualifying inputs that can be attached to the address bus for the purpose.

Once the analyzer is triggered, it stores the op-codes for each subsequent memory location until its internal memory is full. At this time, the listing of the op-codes is displayed and checked.

In many cases it is desirable to display not only the instruction, but also the data as they leave or enter the processor. In this case, the circuit of figure 3–18 is modified into the circuit of figure 3–19. This change would capture each byte of data written to or read from the memory or the I/O equipment in the system.

Displaying the Timing Diagram of the Microprocessor

If the hardware or its timing in a system is suspect, the logic analyzer can display the complete timing diagram or a portion of it. To display the complete timing diagram, a logic analyzer capable of displaying more than 16 channels of information is necessary.

To display the timing diagram, the clock input to the analyzer is normally connected to the clock of the microprocessor under test; if desired, it can also be set to internal clocking. The problem with this is that there may be an anomaly in the timing diagram.

The data inputs are connected to the $\overline{RD}$ and $\overline{WR}$ signals and a few of the data and address bus connections to provide a timing diagram for the system that can detect timing problems.

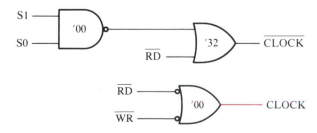

FIGURE 3–18 The circuitry required to generate an op-code acquisition clock for a logic analyzer.

FIGURE 3–19 The circuit required to generate a clock for ac-quisitioning all data bus transfers.

Summary

1   The 8085A, 8086, and 8088 microprocessors are capable of driving ten MOS, five 74LSXXX, one 74SXXX, or one 74XXX unit load without external buffers. If more loads are driven, external buffering is required.

2   The 8085A microprocessor normally operates with either a 6.0-MHz or 6.144-MHz crystal, producing an internal operating frequency of either 3.0 MHz or 3.072 MHz.

3   The 8086 and 8088 require the 8284A clock generator and a 15-MHz crystal to achieve their normal operating frequency of 5.0 MHz.

4   The 8085A is fully buffered with a 74LS373, a 74LS244, and a 74LS245; the 8086 is fully buffered with three 74LS373s and two 74LS245s; and the 8088 is fully buffered with two 74LS373s, a 74LS244, and a 74LS245.

5   Some 8085A-based systems require the IO/$\overline{M}$, $\overline{RD}$, and $\overline{WR}$ signals for control and some require $\overline{MEMR}$, $\overline{MEMW}$, $\overline{IOR}$, and $\overline{IOW}$, which are derived from IO/$\overline{M}$, $\overline{RD}$, and $\overline{WR}$.

6   Resetting the 8085A causes it to begin executing software from memory location 0000H and resetting the 8086 or 8088 causes execution from location FFFF0H.

7   The 8085A allows the memory 575 ns to access data once in every three clocks and the 8086 or 8088 allows 460 ns once in every four clocks. This means that standard 450 ns memory interfaces to the 8085A without any problem, whereas problems are encountered with the 8086 and 8088.

8   The 8085A has five interrupt inputs and the 8086 and 8088 have two interrupt inputs. These microprocessors have two basic types of interrupts: maskable and nonmaskable.

9   The SID and SOD pins on the 8085A are used for serial data or as 1-bit I/O ports.

10   READY is used to stop all processing from one clock period to an infinite number of clocking periods.

11   Instructions all require a fixed amount of time to execute. Because the clock is controlled by a crystal, these execution times are very accurate and can be used to time events.

12   Logic analyzers are extremely useful in testing a microprocessor because they can capture the microprocessor's timing from its buses as it executes a program. This allows software to be debugged on the fly, and it also allows the hardware's timing signals to be viewed as the system executes.

Glossary

Access time   The time required to access data in a memory device.

Bus cycle   A grouping of clock states used to access the memory or I/O through the microprocessor buses.

Clock cycle time One clocking period.

Clock state One clocking period.

DMA Direct Memory Access. A technique to transfer data directly to or from the memory or an external device.

FIFO First In, First Out. A type of memory in which the first piece of information in is the first to come out.

Instruction cycle The time required to fetch and execute one machine language instruction.

Interrupt A technique whereby the hardware can initiate a subroutine CALL.

Machine cycle A grouping of clock periods used to perform a task, such as op-code fetch.

Nonmaskable interrupt An interrupt input that cannot be disabled or turned off.

Queue See FIFO.

Single step The ability to execute a program one bus cycle or one instruction at a time.

Wait state A period of time equal to one clocking period caused by the READY input pin.

Questions and Problems

1 What is the noise immunity for the Intel series of microprocessors?

2 What is the maximum number of MOS loads that can be connected to the microprocessor?

3 How many low-power Schottky TTL unit loads can be connected to an output pin safely?

4 What is the maximum clock frequency allowable for the 8085A?

5 What is the clock cycle time whenever a 4-MHz crystal is attached to the 8085A?

6 An RC circuit can generate the clock for an 8085A. Why is it not normally used in place of a crystal?

7 By what factor will the 8284A clock generator divide the crystal frequency?

8 How many bytes of memory can the 8085A address directly?

9 How many bytes of memory can the 8088 address directly?

10 What is the purpose of the ALE signal?

11 Whenever the data bus is buffered, will the memory access time increase or decrease?

12 What is the purpose of the $\overline{\text{RD}}$ signal?

13 What is the purpose of the $\overline{\text{WR}}$ signal?

14 Which edge of the $\overline{\text{WR}}$ strobe can write the information to the memory or an I/O device?

15 What is the purpose of the DT/$\overline{\text{R}}$ and $\overline{\text{DEN}}$ signals in the 8088 microprocessor?

16 What do status bits generally indicate?

17 When the 8085A microprocessor is RESET, it begins executing the program stored at which memory location?

18 When the 8088 microprocessor is RESET, it begins executing the program stored at which memory location?

19 What memory access time does the 8085A allow if operated at its maximum clock frequency?

20 Which memory access time does the 8086 allow if operated at its maximum clock frequency?

21 List each interrupt input pin for the 8085A and indicate each interrupt vector location.

22 Redraw the diagram illustrated in figure 3–15 so that the 8085A will respond to a RST 3 instruction.

23 Redraw the diagram illustrated in figure 3–16 so that the 8088 will respond to interrupt vector 100 decimal.

24 Which 8085A interrupt inputs are level sensitive?

25 Describe what happens to the buses during a HOLD.

26 Which Intel microprocessor has the ability to accomplish serial I/O directly?

27 List two results that the READY input can accomplish.

28 Given the following 8085A sequence of instructions, determine how many clock cycles are required to execute it.

```
                MVI   A,10H
        LOOP:   DCR   A
                JNZ   LOOP
```

29 How many microseconds are required to execute the sequence of instructions in question 28 if the 8085A clock cycle time equals 1 μs?

30 What would be the maximum execution time for the instructions in question 28 if the number moved into the accumulator could be changed? (Assume a 1 μs clock period.)

31 Why would a logic analyzer be a good software debugging tool?

32 Would it be possible to use the ALE signal as a clock pulse to the logic analyzer? If so, explain which information could be captured for the 8085A microprocessor.

4

The MC6800, MC6809, and MC68000 Microprocessors

Upon completion of this chapter, you will be able to

1 Describe the function of each pin of the MC6800, the MC6809, and the MC68000.
2 Provide a clock to the MC6800, the MC6809, and the MC68000.
3 Buffer the buses of the MC6800, the MC6809, and the MC68000.
4 Explain the operation of the MC6800 during a read or write.
5 State the effect of resetting the MC6800, the MC6809, and the MC68000.
6 Describe the operation of the MC6800, the MC6809, and the MC68000 during an interrupt request.
7 Determine the amount of time required to execute an MC6800 instruction.
8 Show how the logic analyzer is used to test a microprocessor based system.

This chapter introduces the current line of Motorola microprocessors. It is important to learn the operation and interfacing of either the MC6800 or MC6809 microprocessor first, since the remainder of this text emphasizes them. Once you learn them, transition to the MC68000 or any other microprocessor manufactured by any of the IC houses is easy. For example, the 8085A is also covered in some detail.

Whichever microprocessor you choose to study, you will find subsequent chapters interesting and useful.

4–1   PINOUTS

Figure 4–1 illustrates the MC6800, MC6809, and MC68000 microprocessors' pinouts. The MC6800 and MC6809 are both packaged in 40-pin dual in-line packages; the MC68000 is integrated into a 64-pin dual in-line package. All three devices operate from a single 5V power supply with power dissipations of less than 1.5 W.

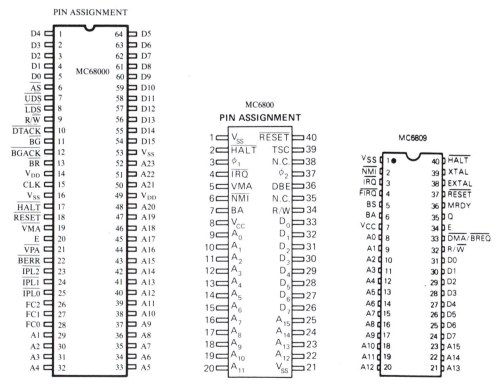

FIGURE 4–1   Pin diagrams or pinouts of the Motorola MC6800, MC6809, and MC68000 microprocessors.

SOURCE: Courtesy of Motorola, Inc.

Output Loading

The MC6800 and MC6809 microprocessors are capable of providing 1.6 mA of sink current and 400 μA of source current at any of the output pins. This current will drive one 74XXX TTL unit load, four 74LSXXX TTL unit loads, or about ten NMOS, 74HCXXX, or CMOS unit loads. Only ten NMOS or CMOS unit loads may be connected because each MOS input places a fairly large amount of capacitance on an output connection. Too much bus capacitance will degrade the timing signals issued by the microprocessor, causing performance problems. To prevent this, MOS loads are limited to ten or less. Refer to table 3–1 in chapter 3 for a detailed look at unit loading.

The MC68000 is capable of sinking 1.6 mA on the HALT pin, 3.2 mA on the address pins, and about 5.0 mA on the data bus connections. With this device, more TTL components can be driven directly from the output pins of the microprocessor. This means that a larger system may be connected directly to the MC68000 without the addition of external bus buffers. Since the source current at these outputs remains at 400 μA, the maximum number of MOS loads remains at 10 or less.

It is interesting to note that the MC6800 and MC6809 microprocessors will not drive a 74SXXX-series TTL load. This limitation can be overcome by using a 74ASXXX-series gate or a FAST gate from Fairchild.

Input Loading

Input connections on all three microprocessors sink and source a maximum of 2.5 μA of current and present about 10 pF of capacitance. In addition to low loading, they are also compatible with the standard TTL voltage levels.

Noise Immunity

The system noise immunity in any of the Motorola processors is about 400 mV and is directly compatible with standard TTL noise immunities. In systems that contain heavy capacitive loads, long bus connections, or excessive current loads, bus buffers at the output connections are recommended. With additional buffering, it is possible to connect up to 100 MOS or 74LSXXX TTL unit loads to an output connection. Most buffers, especially bus buffers, contain an enhanced pullup network that has been designed to drive capacitive loads.

CLOCK CIRCUITRY 4–2

The MC6809 contains an internal clock generator that, in most cases, generates the basic timing for the microprocessor. The MC6800 and the MC68000 both require the addition of an external clock generator to provide their basic timing.

MC6809 Clock Circuitry

Under normal operation, a crystal with a frequency of 8 MHz would be attached between the EXTAL and XTAL input pins of the MC6809 (as pictured in figure 4–2). The crystal

FIGURE 4–2   The MC6809
clock generation circuitry.

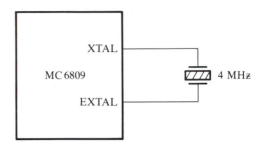

is internally divided by a factor of four to produce the 2-MHz basic operating frequency. The range of allowable crystal frequencies is between 8.0 MHz and about 400 kHz for reliable operation. If an operating frequency outside this range is chosen, Motorola will not guarantee the proper operation of the MC6809.

In addition to a crystal, the MC6809 may be driven from an external TTL source by grounding the XTAL pin and connecting the external TTL clock signal to the EXTAL connection. This method of operation is used in multiple processor systems, where one timing source drives all of the processors.

MC6800 and MC68000 Clock Circuitry

The MC6800 and the MC68000 require an external clock generator for proper operation. The MC6875 clock generator, as illustrated in figure 4–3, can generate the required multiphase clock inputs for the MC6800. The MC68000 requires a TTL-compatible clock input of up to 8.0 MHz for proper operation. A circuit that can be used to generate this clock is illustrated in figure 4–4.

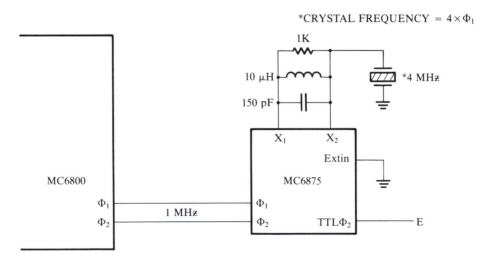

FIGURE 4–3   The MC6875 clock generator connected to the MC6800 microprocessor.

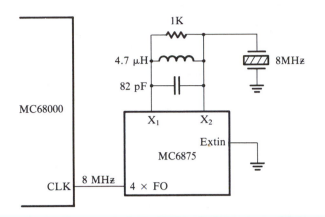

FIGURE 4–4 The MC68000 clock generation circuitry.

ADDRESS AND DATA BUS CONNECTIONS 4–3

The Address Bus

Both the MC6800 and the MC6809 contain 16 pins that have been dedicated to addressing the memory and I/O. This feature allows either of these microprocessors to address 64K bytes of memory and I/O space directly.

The MC68000 contains 23 address connections, which allow it to access an astounding 16M bytes of memory and I/O directly. This is equal to eight million 16-bit words of memory information. In addition to the number of address connections present, the amount of drive current available is triple that of the MC6800 or MC6809.

The Data Bus

The data bus of the MC6800 and MC6809 microprocessors is 8 bits wide; the MC68000 uses a 16-bit data bus. This bus, in all three cases, is a bidirectional, three-state bus that passes information out of, or into, the microprocessor.

As with the address bus, the data bus on the MC68000 possesses an enhanced drive capability. This capability allows the microprocessor to be structured into a larger system before bus buffering is required.

MC68000 Bus Buffering

Figure 4–5 illustrates the inclusion of a set of data and address bus buffers for the MC68000 microprocessor. The $\overline{AS}$, or address strobe, output is connected to the enable ($\overline{G}$) input on the address buffers. The $\overline{AS}$ signal becomes a logic zero whenever the address bus contains a valid memory address. In this circuit, $\overline{AS}$ switches the three-state buffers to their *enabled,* or on, condition.

The bidirectional bus transceivers, which are connected to the data bus, are controlled by the R/$\overline{W}$ control signal. Since the R/$\overline{W}$ signal selects the direction of data flow on the data bus, it is usable as a directional control input to the transceivers. During a memory or I/O read, R/$\overline{W}$ is high and causes the data to flow in from the data bus; during a memory or I/O write, this line is low and causes the data to flow out to the memory and I/O.

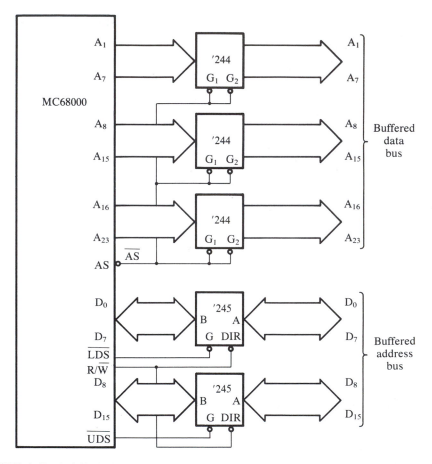

FIGURE 4–5 A fully buffered MC68000 microprocessor.

4–4 CONTROL BUS CONNECTIONS

The control bus structures of the MC6800, MC6809, and the MC68000 are almost identical when only the major control signals are examined. If the MC6800 and MC6809 are compared, they differ only in the way that direct memory access I/O is controlled. Comparing all three demonstrates many more differences. Table 4–1 contrasts these differences.

The Basic Memory and I/O Control Signals

All three microprocessors use the $R/\overline{W}$ signal to command the memory or I/O to read or write data. In the MC68000 this signal also works in conjunction with the $\overline{LDS}$ and $\overline{UDS}$ data strobes, which indicate how the microprocessor will react with the data bus during the current bus cycle. Table 4–2 illustrates how the MC68000 interprets the data bus for each combination of the $R/\overline{W}$, $\overline{LDS}$, and $\overline{UDS}$ signals.

TABLE 4–1 Comparative control signals.

MC6800/MC6809	MC68000	Function
R/$\overline{\text{W}}$	R/$\overline{\text{W}}$	Controls reading or writing to memory or I/O
VMA	$\overline{\text{AS}}$, $\overline{\text{VMA}}$	Valid memory address present on the address bus
φ2,E	$\overline{\text{UDS}}$, $\overline{\text{LDS}}$, $\overline{\text{E}}$	Enables data bus so that no contention can occur
$\overline{\text{NMI}}$	LEVEL 7	Nonmaskable interrupt
$\overline{\text{IRQ}}$, $\overline{\text{FIRQ}}$	LEVEL 0–6 TRAPS	Maskable interrupts
$\overline{\text{MRDY}}$	$\overline{\text{DTACK}}$	Slow memory control
$\overline{\text{DMA/BREQ}}$,BA BS,DBE,TSC	$\overline{\text{BR}}$, $\overline{\text{BG}}$ BGACK	DMA control and bus arbitration

TABLE 4–2 MC68000 bus control strobes.

$\overline{\text{UDS}}$	$\overline{\text{LDS}}$	R/$\overline{\text{W}}$	Function
0	0	0	Valid data bus (bits 0-15)
0	0	1	Valid data bus (bits 0-15)
0	1	0	Bits 8–15 appear on both halves of bus
0	1	1	Bits 8–15 appear on upper half of bus. Lower half contains unknown information
1	0	0	Bits 0–7 appear on both halves of bus
1	0	1	Bits 0–7 appear on lower half of bus. Upper half contains unknown information
1	1	X	Data bus contains unknown information

In addition to these three control signals, the $\overline{\text{VMA}}$ and $\overline{\text{E}}$ signals are also present on all three microprocessors. The $\overline{\text{VMA}}$ signal indicates that the address bus contains a "valid memory address"; the $\overline{\text{E}}$ signal, or *enable*, is used to enable the memory or I/O device. The $\overline{\text{E}}$ signal is actually not present on the MC6800, but it is the phase-two TTL output of the clock generator circuitry. The MC68000 contains $\overline{\text{VMA}}$ and $\overline{\text{E}}$ so that MC6800 peripherals are compatible with the MC68000.

Additional MC6809 Control Signals

The MC6809 has several other control signals that are not present on the MC6800. These include BS, $\overline{\text{FIRQ}}$, MRDY, and $\overline{\text{DMA/BREQ}}$. The BA and BS signals indicate the present state of the MC6809, as illustrated in table 4–3.

The MRDY signal extends the access time provided for the memory by extending the current read or write cycle. The extension may be anything from one clocking period up to 10 μs in duration. This is most useful if a slower external device is to be interfaced to the MC6809. An example is an analog-to-digital converter, as illustrated for the 8085A in chapter 6.

TABLE 4–3 BA and BS processor state signals.

BA	BS	Processor State
0	0	Normal
0	1	Interrupt or reset acknowledge
1	0	Sync acknowledge
1	1	Halt/bus grant acknowledge

The $\overline{\text{DMA}}/\overline{\text{BREQ}}$ input is used for a direct memory access or bus arbitration; it is covered, along with the $\overline{\text{FIRQ}}$ input, later in this chapter.

Additional MC68000 Control Signals

The advanced architecture of the MC68000 microprocessor includes some additional control pins, such as $\overline{\text{BGACK}}$, $\overline{\text{VPA}}$, $\overline{\text{DTACK}}$, $\overline{\text{BERR}}$, $\overline{\text{BR}}$, $\overline{\text{BG}}$, $\overline{\text{IPL0}}$, $\overline{\text{IPL1}}$, $\overline{\text{IPL2}}$, FC0, FC1, and FC2. These pins control such features as interrupts and direct memory access or bus arbitration.

The FC0, FC1, and FC2 signals indicate the status of the MC68000 as depicted in table 4–4.

FC0, FC1, and FC2 are used to indicate the mode of operation, either supervisor or user. In the supervisor state, the MC68000 can control an external memory management device and system software. This capacity provides security, since the memory management unit and system software cannot be accessed by the normal user. The access requires a shift to the supervisor state, which is a privileged state.

The $\overline{\text{BERR}}$ input signal informs the processor of a bus error and is provided by the external hardware. The type of hardware most likely to generate this signal is a memory parity checking circuit. If a parity error is detected, this signal becomes active, and the processor executes an exception sequence or an interrupt. This sequence reads the user-supplied bus error handling subroutine's address from memory location $00008. Control is then transferred to this error-handling subroutine for a possible repeat of the bus cycle.

The $\overline{\text{BR}}$, $\overline{\text{BG}}$, and $\overline{\text{BGACK}}$ signals are used when more than one MC68000 or a DMA controller is connected in a system. $\overline{\text{BR}}$ is an input that requests the use of the bus. $\overline{\text{BG}}$ is an output that indicates that the MC68000 will release bus control at the end of the current cycle. The $\overline{\text{BGACK}}$ input indicates that some other device has become the bus master. These signals are discussed in greater detail in the section on bus arbitration.

TABLE 4–4 MC68000 bus function control signals.

FC2	FC1	FC0	Cycle Type
0	0	0	Undefined
0	0	1	User data
0	1	0	User program
0	1	1	Undefined
1	0	0	Undefined
1	0	1	Supervisor data
1	1	0	Supervisor program
1	1	1	Interrupt acknowledge

The $\overline{\text{VPA}}$ input is activated whenever an external MC6800 peripheral device is addressed. This is provided so that the wealth of MC6800 8-bit peripheral devices can function with the MC68000. It also signals the processor to use automatic vectoring for an interrupt, as described in the interrupt section of this chapter.

RESET OR RESTART 4—5

If the MC6800 or MC6809 microprocessors are reset, they look at memory location $FFFE for the restart vector. The restart vector holds the starting address of the system program.

Resetting or restarting the MC68000 is completely different because two vectors apply to this function. When the MC68000 is first powered up, locations zero through three must contain the supervisor stack pointer (SSP). Locations four through seven must contain the location of the first instruction to be executed after a reset. These vectors are used only during a power up sequence.

The RESET instruction in the MC68000 will not cause the reset vectors to be called. This instruction will only cause the $\overline{\text{RESET}}$ output pin to become active for 124 clocking periods after it has been executed. This instruction and the resulting signal on the $\overline{\text{RESET}}$ pin are only used for reinitializing the external peripheral components in the system. It has absolutely no effect on the internal registers of the MC68000.

If repowering the processor is desirable, it can be accomplished by using the reset vectors stored in the vector table and by placing a logic zero on the $\overline{\text{RESET}}$ pin.

BUS TIMING 4—6

The standard operating frequency for the MC6800 and the MC6809 is 1 MHz. At this rate they are capable of transferring one byte of information per clocking period or one byte every microsecond. The MC68000 works with an internal clock frequency of 8 MHz and can transfer one byte of data every 500 ns since the internal timing is set up so that four external clock pulses are required for a bus transfer.

MC6800 Read and Write Timing

Figure 4–6 illustrates the basic read and write timing diagrams of the MC6800 microprocessor and its AC characteristics. In the MC6800 timing diagrams, the address is presented to memory and I/O during the logic zero portion of the phase two clock. When the phase two clock becomes a logic one, data are transferred into the processor or sent out from it.

The time allowed for a memory access (Tacc) is equal to 540 ns worst case. In other words, the memory, plus the time delay introduced by buffers, should have an access time of no longer than 540 ns. In addition to this time constraint, it is also important to note that data must be held for 10 ns minimum after the phase two clock returns to the logic zero level. If the phase two clock is used as an enable (or E) signal, the amount of time required to enable the memory device must not exceed 350 ns. Since the output buffers in a memory device typically take 120 ns to enable, this is generally ample time.

MAXIMUM RATINGS

Rating	Symbol	Value	Unit
Supply Voltage	V_{CC}	-0.3 to +7.0	Vdc
Input Voltage	V_{in}	-0.3 to +7.0	Vdc
Operating Temperature Range—T_L to T_H MC6800, MC68A00, MC68B00 MC6800C, MC68A00C MC6800BQCS, MC6800CQCS	T_A	 0 to +70 -40 to +85 -55 to +125	°C
Storage Temperature Range	T_{stg}	-55 to +150	°C
Thermal Resistance Plastic Package Ceramic Package	θ_{JA}	 70 50	°C/W

ELECTRICAL CHARACTERISTICS (V_{CC} = 5.0 V, · 5%, V_{SS} = 0, T_A = T_L to T_H unless otherwise noted)

Characteristic		Symbol	Min	Typ	Max	Unit
Input High Voltage	Logic	V_{IH}	V_{SS} + 2.0	—	V_{CC}	Vdc
	$\phi1,\phi2$	V_{IHC}	V_{CC} - 0.6	—	V_{CC} + 0.3	
Input Low Voltage	Logic	V_{IL}	V_{SS} - 0.3	—	V_{SS} + 0.8	Vdc
	$\phi1,\phi2$	V_{ILC}	V_{SS} - 0.3	—	V_{SS} + 0.4	
Input Leakage Current		I_{in}				µAdc
(V_{in} = 0 to 5.25 V, V_{CC} = max)	Logic*		—	1.0	2.5	
(V_{in} = 0 to 5.25 V, V_{CC} = 0.0 V)	$\phi1,\phi2$		—	—	100	
Three-State (Off State) Input Current	D0–D7	I_{TSI}	—	2.0	10	µAdc
(V_{in} = 0.4 to 2.4 V, V_{CC} = max)	A0–A15, R/$\overline{W}$		—	—	100	
Output High Voltage		V_{OH}				Vdc
(I_{Load} = -205 µAdc, V_{CC} = min)	D0–D7		V_{SS} + 2.4	—	—	
(I_{Load} = -145 µAdc, V_{CC} = min)	A0–A15, R/$\overline{W}$, VMA		V_{SS} + 2.4	—	—	
(I_{Load} = -100 µAdc, V_{CC} = min)	BA		V_{SS} + 2.4	—	—	
Output Low Voltage (I_{Load} = 1.6 mAdc, V_{CC} = min)		V_{OL}	—	—	V_{SS} + 0.4	Vdc
Power Dissipation		P_D	—	0.5	1.0	W
Capacitance		C_{in}				pF
(V_{in} = 0, T_A = 25°C, f = 1.0 MHz)	$\phi1$		—	25	35	
	$\phi2$		—	45	70	
	D0–D7		—	10	12.5	
	Logic Inputs		—	6.5	10	
	A0–A15, R/$\overline{W}$, VMA	C_{out}	—	—	12	pF

CLOCK TIMING (V_{CC} = 5.0 V, · 5%, V_{SS} = 0, T_A = T_L to T_H unless otherwise noted)

Characteristics		Symbol	Min	Typ	Max	Unit
Frequency of Operation	MC6800	f	0.1	—	1.0	MHz
	MC68A00		0.1	—	1.5	
	MC68B00		0.1	—	2.0	
Cycle Time (Figure 1)	MC6800	t_{cyc}	1.000	—	10	µs
	MC68A00		0.666	—	10	
	MC68B00		0.500	—	10	
Clock Pulse Width	$\phi1,\phi2$ — MC6800	$PW_{\phi H}$	400	—	9500	ns
(Measured at V_{CC} - 0.6 V)	$\phi1,\phi2$ — MC68A00		230	—	9500	
	$\phi1,\phi2$ — MC68B00		180	—	9500	
Total $\phi1$ and $\phi2$ Up Time	MC6800	t_{ut}	900	—	—	ns
	MC68A00		600	—	—	
	MC68B00		440	—	—	
Rise and Fall Times		$t_{\phi r}, t_{\phi f}$	—	—	100	ns
(Measured between V_{SS} + 0.4 and V_{CC} - 0.6)						
Delay Time or Clock Separation (Figure 1)		t_d				ns
(Measured at V_{OV} = V_{SS} + 0.6 V @ t_r = t_f ≤ 100 ns)			0	—	9100	
(Measured at V_{OV} = V_{SS} + 1.0 V @ t_r = t_f ≤ 35 ns)			0	—	9100	

FIGURE 4–6 The read and write timing diagrams and characteristics of the MC6800 microprocessor.

SOURCE: Courtesy of Motorola, Inc.

READ/WRITE TIMING (Reference Figures 2 through 6)

Characteristic	Symbol	MC6800			MC68A00			MC68B00			Unit
		Min	Typ	Max	Min	Typ	Max	Min	Typ	Max	
Address Delay	t_{AD}										ns
C = 90 pF		–	–	270	–	–	180	–	–	150	
C = 30 pF		–	–	250	–	–	165	–	–	135	
Peripheral Read Access Time $t_{ac} = t_{ut} - (t_{AD} + t_{DSR})$	t_{acc}	–	–	530	–	–	360	–	–	250	ns
Data Setup Time (Read)	t_{DSR}	100	–	–	60	–	–	40	–	–	ns
Input Data Hold Time	t_H	10	–	–	10	–	–	10	–	–	ns
Output Data Hold Time	t_H	10	25	–	10	25	–	10	25	–	ns
Address Hold Time (Address, R/W̄, VMA)	t_{AH}	30	50	–	30	50	–	30	50	–	ns
Enable High Time for DBE Input	t_{EH}	450	–	–	280	–	–	220	–	–	ns
Data Delay Time (Write)	t_{DDW}	–	–	225	–	–	200	–	–	160	ns
Processor Controls											
Processor Control Setup Time	t_{PCS}	200	–	–	140	–	–	110	–	–	ns
Processor Control Rise and Fall Time	t_{PCr}, t_{PCf}	–	–	100	–	–	100	–	–	100	ns
Bus Available Delay	t_{BA}	–	–	250	–	–	165	–	–	135	ns
Three-State Delay	t_{TSD}	–	–	270	–	–	270	–	–	220	ns
Data Bus Enable Down Time During φ1 Up Time	t_{DBE}	150	–	–	120	–	–	75	–	–	ns
Data Bus Enable Rise and Fall Times	t_{DBEr}, t_{DBEf}	–	–	25	–	–	25	–	–	25	ns

CLOCK TIMING WAVEFORM

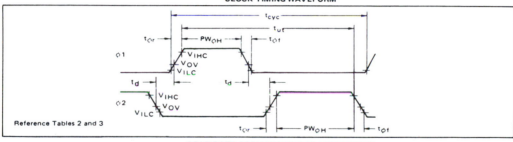

Reference Tables 2 and 3

READ DATA FROM MEMORY OR PERIPHERALS

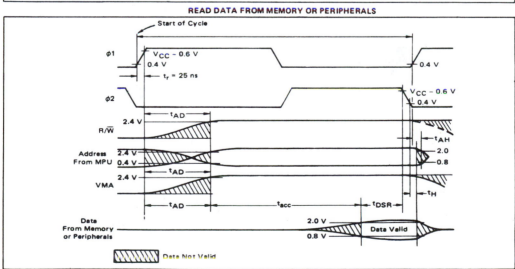

FIGURE 4–6 *continued*

WRITE IN MEMORY OR PERIPHERALS

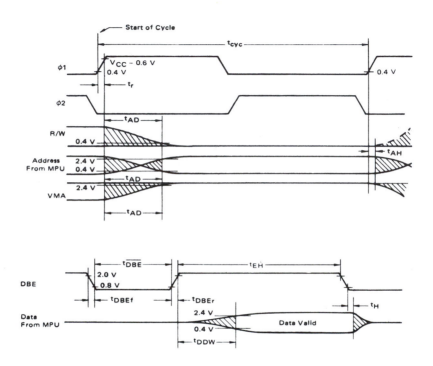

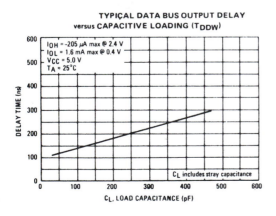

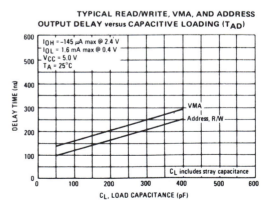

FIGURE 4-6 *continued*

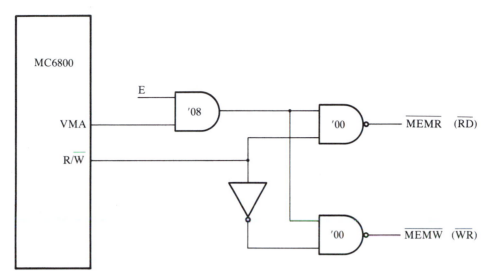

* E is the phase 2 TTL CLOCK

FIGURE 4–7   Using the MC6800 to generate the $\overline{\text{MEMR}}$ and $\overline{\text{MEMW}}$ control signals.

MC6800 Memory Read and Write Signals

The circuit depicted in figure 4–7 allows the MC6800 or MC6809 to be used with most of this text. It also allows it to be used, without effort, with most of the industrywide standard memory components, such as the TMS4016 RAM, 2716 EPROM, and others.

By combining the phase two TTL signal or E signal with the VMA output and the R/$\overline{\text{W}}$ signal, we obtain the $\overline{\text{MEMR}}$ or $\overline{\text{RD}}$ and $\overline{\text{MEMW}}$ or $\overline{\text{WR}}$ control signals that are used throughout this book. These pulses are approximately 500 ns in width and are compatible with many standard memory components. Since the 680XX series microprocessors do not support isolated I/O, no attempt has been made to develop the I/O control signals $\overline{\text{IOR}}$ and $\overline{\text{IOW}}$. For I/O control and its application, refer to the section in chapter 6 on memory-mapped I/O.

MC68000 Read and Write Timing

Figure 4–8 illustrates the timing diagrams for the MC68000 microprocessor. The MC68000 will transfer one word, or 16 bits, of information every 500 ns, since it operates at a basic clock frequency of 8 MHz. The amount of access time allowed to the memory component attached to the MC68000 is approximately 290 ns. This means that higher-speed memory components must be selected for use with this processor.

The $\overline{\text{AS}}$, or address strobe, signal activates a memory component. It is normal to use this signal to supply the MC68000 with its $\overline{\text{DTACK}}$ signal in systems that contain memory that can access data within 290 ns.

The MC6809 MRDY and the MC68000 $\overline{\text{DTACK}}$

The MRDY connection on the MC6809 prolongs the processor bus cycle for low-speed memory or I/O devices. This input can be held at a logic zero level for up to 10 μs for these slower devices. If held longer than 10 μs, Motorola will not guarantee the validity of the data stored in the MC6809 internal register array.

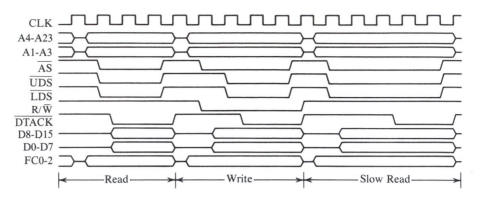

FIGURE 4–8   Basic read and write timing for the MC68000 microprocessor.
SOURCE: Courtesy of Motorola, Inc.

The $\overline{\text{DTACK}}$ input, or *data acknowledge,* of the MC68000 can serve about the same purpose as the MRDY input of the MC6809. The difference is that the MRDY input is an optional feature that can be ignored by connecting it to a logic one, while the $\overline{\text{DTACK}}$ input must be used.

During a read operation, for example, the MC68000 sends out the control signals and waits for the external device (usually memory) to send the $\overline{\text{DTACK}}$ signal back to the microprocessor. In fact, if the $\overline{\text{DTACK}}$ signal does not occur, the system waits just as it does with MRDY. Once the processor accepts the information, the $\overline{\text{DTACK}}$ signal must be returned to its inactive state before another bus cycle can occur. Without this timing, the MC68000 will not function.

4–7   MC6809 AND MC68000 BUS ARBITRATION (DMA)

MC6809 Bus Arbitration

The MC6809 microprocessor has an input labeled $\overline{\text{DMA}}/\overline{\text{BREQ}}$ that requests access to the MC6809 system bus. When this pin is active, the microprocessor releases control of the system bus by three-stating the address, data, and control buses. This allows an external device to access the memory and I/O connected to the MC6809 directly.

The BA and BS signals grant or acknowledge the bus request when they are both at logic one levels. This same level also indicates that the microprocessor may be halted.

MC68000 Bus Arbitration

If more than one microprocessor or similar device is to function on the same bus system, a need for bus arbitration arises. The set of connections described in this segment determines which device will control the bus so that no conflict can occur. Bus conflicts will almost always result in a loss of data.

The $\overline{\text{BR}}$, or *bus request* signal, is an input to the MC68000 that asks for or requests the system bus. If the MC68000 is at the end of its current bus cycle, it will grant the bus request by sending out the $\overline{\text{BG}}$, or *bus grant* signal. Once the requesting device notices the

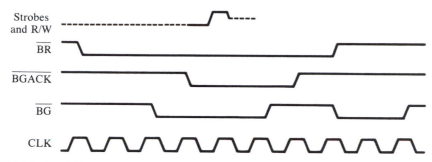

FIGURE 4–9   MC68000 bus arbitration timing.

SOURCE: Courtesy of Motorola, Inc.

$\overline{BG}$ signal, it returns a $\overline{BGACK}$, or *bus grant acknowledge* signal, back to the MC68000 to indicate that it has taken over the system buses.

This arbitration dialog is normally carried out between the MC68000 and an external DMA controller. During the bus grant, the MC68000 relinquishes control of the system by floating the address, data, and control bus. This of course will allow the external device to gain complete control over the system buses. The typical three-wire handshake is illustrated in the timing diagram of figure 4–9.

INTERRUPT STRUCTURES   4–8

MC6800 Interrupt Structure

The MC6800 microprocessor has two hardware interrupts and one software interrupt that are vectored through the top part of the memory. Table 4–5 illustrates the interrupt vectors for the MC6800 microprocessor. These vectors contain the location of the software that will be executed in response to these input signals.

MC6809 Interrupt Structure

The MC6809 microprocessor has three hardware interrupts and three software interrupts that are vectored through the top portion of the memory. A new hardware interrupt, labeled $\overline{FIRQ}$, has been added to the $\overline{IRQ}$ and $\overline{NMI}$ inputs of the MC6800. The only difference between the new interrupt and the two old interrupts is that the $\overline{FIRQ}$ input will only store the program counter and the status register on the stack. The $\overline{IRQ}$ and $\overline{NMI}$ inputs place all of the internal registers, except the hardware stack pointer, on the stack.

Table 4–6 illustrates the vector locations for the interrupt inputs to the MC6809.

TABLE 4–5   MC6800 interrupt vectors.

Vector Location	Signal
$FFFE, $FFFF	Reset
$FFFC, $FFFD	$\overline{NMI}$
$FFFA, $FFFB	SWI
$FFF8, $FFF9	$\overline{IRQ}$

TABLE 4–6   MC6809 interrupt vectors.

Vector Location	Signal
$FFFE, $FFFF	Reset
$FFFC, $FFFD	$\overline{\text{NMI}}$
$FFFA, $FFFB	SWI
$FFF8, $FFF9	$\overline{\text{IRQ}}$
$FFF6, $FFF7	$\overline{\text{FIRQ}}$
$FFF4, $FFF5	SWI2
$FFF2, $FFF3	SWI3
$FFF0, $FFF1	Reserved

MC68000 Interrupt Structure

The interrupt structure for the MC68000 is quite different from the structure for the MC6800 and MC6809. A complete listing of the many different interrupts appears in table 4–7.

TABLE 4–7   MC68000 interrupt vectors.

Vector Number	Address	Assignment
0	00000	Reset initial SSP
	00004	Reset initial PC
2	00008	Bus error
3	0000C	Address error
4	00010	Illegal instruction
5	00014	Divide by zero
6	00018	CHK instruction
7	0001C	TRAPV instruction
8	00020	Privilege violation
9	00024	Trace
10	00028	Line 1010 emulator
11	0002C	Line 1111 emulator
12–23	00030–0005F	Reserved by Motorola
24	00060	Spurious interrupt
25	00064	Level 1 interrupt
26	00068	Level 2 interrupt
27	0006C	Level 3 interrupt
28	00070	Level 4 interrupt
29	00074	Level 5 interrupt
30	00078	Level 6 interrupt
31	0007C	Level 7 interrupt
32–47	00080–000BF	TRAP instruction vectors
48–63	000C0–000FF	Reserved by Motorola
64–255	00100–003FF	USER interrupt vectors

This vector table occupies the first 1024 bytes of memory or first 512 words of memory. Seven of these vectors are used for external interrupts; the remaining vectors are used for reset, for various Motorola system functions, and for TRAPS.

TRAPS are used by the system program to call up error handling routines; they may also be used as short form subroutine jumps if so desired. The TRAP number references a vector in the vector table that indicates the address of the TRAP subroutine.

External interrupts are caused by applying the interrupt device number, one through seven binary, on the three interrupt inputs $\overline{IPL0}$, $\overline{IPL1}$, and $\overline{IPL2}$. Level seven has the highest priority; level one has the lowest. A one binary on these three pins indicates that no interrupt is being requested. These interrupts reference the seven vectors listed in table 4–7 if the $\overline{VPA}$ input is asserted.

If desired, the external hardware may apply the interrupt vector location by not asserting the $\overline{VPA}$ input. If an external interrupt vector is supplied through the least significant 8 bits of the data bus, a vector to any of the 256 possible table entries can occur. This is useful if multiple interrupt processed I/O devices exist at each interrupt priority level.

Masking various interrupt levels is accomplished through the status register and the three bits assigned to perform this function. Interrupts are prohibited if the masks are the same priority level or greater than the currently requested interrupt level. The level seven interrupt cannot be inhibited or masked by the mask bits. It is equivalent to the $\overline{NMI}$ interrupt input on the MC6800 and MC6809.

INSTRUCTION TIMING 4–9

This section includes a list of the instructions and the number of clock cycles required to execute them. Only the MC6800 instructions are provided in this chapter. They are given to allow the student to calculate some of the time delays required for homework problems or outside development. The complete instruction set for the MC6800 is listed in table 4–8. To calculate the amount of time required to execute an instruction, multiply the number of instruction cycles by 1 μs. This is, of course, for the standard 1-MHz version of the MC6800.

THE MC6800 AND THE LOGIC ANALYZER 4–10

The logic analyzer is an extremely useful device in microprocessor testing. In fact, it is the only device that can be used to view the timing of a microprocessor while it is functioning in a system. It is even possible to view the program execution path or track with the logic analyzer, which can be extremely useful in debugging complicated software.

Instruction Tracking with the Logic Analyzer

The op-codes of an instruction can be stored with the memory addresses in the memory of the logic analyzer for later viewing as hexadecimal op-codes. In some of the newer logic analyzers, it is even possible to view this information in mnemonic form as a listing on the

TABLE 4–8 MC6800 instruction timing.

	(Dual Operand)	ACCX	Immediate	Direct	Extended	Indexed	Implied	Relative
ABA		•	•	•	•	•	2	•
ADC	x	•	2	3	4	5	•	•
ADD	x	•	2	3	4	5	•	•
AND	x	•	2	3	4	5	•	•
ASL		2	•	•	6	7	•	•
ASR		2	•	•	6	7	•	•
BCC		•	•	•	•	•	•	4
BCS		•	•	•	•	•	•	4
BEA		•	•	•	•	•	•	4
BGE		•	•	•	•	•	•	4
BGT		•	•	•	•	•	•	4
BHI		•	•	•	•	•	•	4
BIT	x	•	2	3	4	5	•	•
BLE		•	•	•	•	•	•	4
BLS		•	•	•	•	•	•	4
BLT		•	•	•	•	•	•	4
BMI		•	•	•	•	•	•	4
BNE		•	•	•	•	•	•	4
BPL		•	•	•	•	•	•	4
BRA		•	•	•	•	•	•	4
BSR		•	•	•	•	•	•	8
BVC		•	•	•	•	•	•	4
BVS		•	•	•	•	•	•	4
CBA		•	•	•	•	•	2	•
CLC		•	•	•	•	•	2	•
CLI		•	•	•	•	•	2	•
CLR		2	•	•	6	7	•	•
CLV		•	•	•	•	•	2	•
CMP	x	•	2	3	4	5	•	•
COM		2	•	•	6	7	•	•
CPX		•	3	4	5	6	•	•
DAA		•	•	•	•	•	2	•
DEC		2	•	•	6	7	•	•
DES		•	•	•	•	•	4	•
DEX		•	•	•	•	•	4	•
EOR	x	•	2	3	4	5	•	•

	(Dual Operand)	ACCX	Immediate	Direct	Extended	Indexed	Implied
INC		2	•	•	6	7	•
INS		•	•	•	•	•	4
INX		•	•	•	•	•	4
JMP		•	•	•	3	4	•
JSR		•	•	•	9	8	•
LDA	x	•	2	3	4	5	•
LDS		•	3	4	5	6	•
LDX		•	3	4	5	6	•
LSR		2	•	•	6	7	•
NEG		2	•	•	6	7	•
NOP		•	•	•	•	•	2
ORA	x	•	2	3	4	5	•
PSH		•	•	•	•	•	4
PUL		•	•	•	•	•	4
ROL		2	•	•	6	7	•
ROR		2	•	•	6	7	•
RTI		•	•	•	•	•	10
RTS		•	•	•	•	•	5
SBA		•	•	•	•	•	2
SBC	x	•	2	3	4	5	•
SEC		•	•	•	•	•	2
SEI		•	•	•	•	•	2
SEV		•	•	•	•	•	2
STA	x	•	•	4	5	6	•
STS		•	•	5	6	7	•
STX		•	•	5	6	7	•
SUB	x	•	2	3	4	5	•
SWI		•	•	•	•	•	12
TAB		•	•	•	•	•	2
TAP		•	•	•	•	•	2
TBA		•	•	•	•	•	2
TPA		•	•	•	•	•	2
TST		2	•	•	6	7	•
TSX		•	•	•	•	•	4
TSX		•	•	•	•	•	4
WAI		•	•	•	•	•	9

NOTE: Interrupt time is 12 cycles from the end of the instruction being executed, except following a WAI instruction. Then it is 4 cycles.

SOURCE: Courtesy of Motorola, Inc.

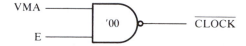

VMA ————
'00   ——— $\overline{\text{CLOCK}}$
E ————

FIGURE 4–10 Circuitry required to generate a clock pulse for the logic analyzer.

screen of the analyzer. This, of course, is not a listing of the program; it is a dynamic listing of the instructions as they are actually executed in the system.

To track the program in an operating system with a logic analyzer, three signal components must be connected to the analyzer. The data input connections for the analyzer are connected to the MC6800 data bus, allowing the instructions and data to be displayed as they appear on the data bus. In addition to the data, a logic analyzer needs a clock signal to acquire the information from the data bus. This signal is obtained by logically combining the VMA signal with phase two of the clock. It is important that the analyzer clock is set on the negative edge of the output of the circuit in figure 4–10.

In addition to the data and clock inputs, the analyzer must also be triggered at the proper point by using the beginning address of the software under test as a trigger. Many analyzers have a 16-channel trigger-producing circuit for this purpose.

Once the analyzer is triggered, it stores the information from the data bus in its internal memory until it is full. At this time the listing of the program can be viewed and checked for errors.

Displaying the Timing Diagram of the MC6800

To test the entire system, it is a good idea to view the timing of the microprocessor on the logic analyzer. To display the complete timing diagram, you need an analyzer capable of displaying more than 24 signals at one time. In many cases the analyzer may have only 8 or 16 channels. If this is the case, you have to be more selective with the signals viewed on the analyzer.

To display the timing diagram for the MC6800, you may want to use the internal clock set to sample the information at the rate of every 20–50 ns. This procedure generates a fairly accurate timing diagram. The data inputs may consist of the VMA, R/W, and the clock signal, plus a few data bus bits and a few address bus bits. This will not display a complete timing diagram, but at least you can determine if the memory or I/O is functioning properly.

Summary

1 The MC6800 and the MC6809 are capable of driving one 74XXX, four 74LSXXX, and ten 74HCXXX, CMSO, or NMOS loads. The MC68000 can drive many more loads because of its increased drive current.

2 The MC6809 has an internal clock generator that functions with an 8.0-MHz crystal attached to the XTAL and EXTAL pins to produce a 2.0-MHz internal clock frequency. Both the MC6800 and the MC68000 require an external clock generator. The MC6800 requires a 1.0-MHz clock and the MC68000 requires an 8.0-MHz clock.

3 The MC6800 and MC6809 both address 64K bytes of memory with a 16-bit

address bus. The MC68000 addresses 16M bytes of memory with a 23-bit address bus.

4 The MC6800 and MC6809 use a R/$\overline{\text{W}}$, $\overline{\text{VMA}}$, and an E signal to control the memory and I/O. A read or a write operation is indicated with the R/$\overline{\text{W}}$ signal and the $\overline{\text{VMA}}$ (valid memory address) and E (enable) are used to enable the memory or I/O.

5 Both the MC6800 and MC6809 reset to the memory location addressed by the reset vector (FFFE—FFFF). The MC68000 resets to the location addressed by its reset vector (000004—000008).

6 The MC6800 allows 540 ns for the memory to access data. The MC68000 allows 290 ns. With the MC68000, standard memory are too slow to operate without wait states.

7 The $\overline{\text{DTACK}}$ signal is used to adjust the speed of the MC68000 so that it is possible to access memory that operates at any speed. The MC68000 waits until $\overline{\text{DTACK}}$ returns to continue executing software so that slower memory can be accessed.

8 The MC6800 contains two hardware interrupt inputs ($\overline{\text{NMI}}$ and $\overline{\text{IRQ}}$), the MC6809 contains three hardware interrupt inputs ($\overline{\text{NMI}}$, $\overline{\text{IRQ}}$, and $\overline{\text{FIRQ}}$), and the MC68000 contains three interrupt inputs that can be used to access any of 256 different interrupt vectors.

9 The exact time required to execute an instruction can be determined by multiplying the clock cycle time by the number of clock cycles required to execute a given instruction.

10 The logic analyzer is a tool that can be used to capture the timing diagram of the microprocessor as it executes software.

Glossary

Access time   The amount of time required by a memory component to access or retrieve information.

Bus arbitration   An access technique used when more than one bus controller or microprocessor exists on the same memory and I/O bus structure.

Bus cycle   Whenever information is moved out of or into the microprocessor through its bus.

Direct memory access (DMA)   A computer's ability to store or retrieve information directly from the memory without the intervention of the microprocessor.

Instruction cycle   Equal to one clocking period in the MC6800, MC6809, and MC68000.

Interrupt   An I/O technique that allows a slower external I/O device to interrupt the instruction flow of the microprocessor. This is accomplished through a hardware subroutine jump.

Memory management   A technique whereby available memory space can be increased to an unlimited amount.

Parity A technique used to check for the validity of data.

Pinout The pictorial view of an integrated circuit defining each pin connection.

Read cycle The time required for the microprocessor to read data from the memory or an I/O device.

Sink current The amount of current available at an output whenever that output is a logic zero.

Source current The amount of current available at an output whenever that output is a logic one.

Transceiver A digital device that can either drive a bus line or receive data from a bus line.

Vector A number stored in the memory that is used to point to another location in the memory.

Write cycle The time required for the microprocessor to write information to a memory or an I/O device.

Questions and Problems

1 List the number of pin connections on the MC6800, the MC6809, and the MC68000.

2 How many TTL unit loads can the MC6800 or MC6809 microprocessor directly drive?

3 How many TTL unit loads can the MC68000 microprocessor directly drive? Explain your answer.

4 What is the noise immunity for the MC6800, MC6809, and MC68000?

5 Which crystal frequency would be selected to operate the MC6800 at 1 MHz?

6 Which crystal frequency would be selected to operate the MC6809 at 1 MHz?

7 How many memory locations can the MC6800 or MC6809 directly address?

8 How many memory locations can the MC68000 directly address?

9 How many data bus connections are available on the MC68000 microprocessor?

10 Which MC6800 bus is a bidirectional bus?

11 What is the purpose of the $\overline{AS}$ pin on the MC68000?

12 What is the purpose of the $\overline{LDS}$ and $\overline{UDS}$ strobes on the MC68000?

13 The $\overline{BERR}$ signal on the MC68000 indicates which condition?

14 Which three signals control a DMA action on the MC68000 microprocessor?

15 Which signals control the DMA action of the MC6809 microprocessor?

16 Where must the RESET vector be stored in the MC6800 or MC6809 microprocessor?

17 Where must the RESET vector be stored in the MC68000 microprocessor?

18 How much time is allowed for memory access in a MC6800 based system?

19 How much time is allowed for memory access in a MC68000 based system?

20 Explain the operation of the circuit in figure 4–7.

21 What is the purpose of the $\overline{DTACK}$ signal in the MC68000 microprocessor?

22 List the types of interrupts available for the MC6800 microprocessor.

23 List the types of interrupts available for the MC6809 microprocessor.

24 List the types of interrupts available for the MC68000 microprocessor.

25 What is the difference between the $\overline{\text{FIRQ}}$ and the $\overline{\text{IRQ}}$ inputs on the MC6809?

26 Which MC68000 interrupt input level has the highest priority?

27 How long does it take the MC6800 to execute the LDAA instruction if a clock frequency of 1 MHz has been selected?

28 Given the following MC6800 program, determine how long it takes to execute if a 1-MHz clock is used.

```
          LDAA  #$10
    LOOP  DECA
          BNE   LOOP
```

29 The logic analyzer can monitor the instruction flow in a subroutine or a program. Write a short program to test I/O location $C000.

30 If you were to use the internal clock on the logic analyzer and you set it for a 1 μs sample rate, what would you view on the screen if the data bus were connected to the analyzer's data inputs?

5

Memory Interface

Upon completion of this chapter, you will be able to

1 Explain the operation of the ROM, EPROM, SRAM, and DRAM and indicate the function of all of the control inputs to these devices.
2 Decode the memory address to select ROM or RAM, using integrated decoders or PROMs.
3 Populate a memory with ROM and RAM at any location by either completely specifying the addresses or incompletely specifying the addresses.
4 Interface memory to the STD-BUS.
5 Explain the operation of a discrete DRAM controller.
6 Design memory systems for microprocessors.

This chapter introduces memory interfacing, a portion of microprocessor system design that develops an understanding of decoding. Decoding is extremely important because it is used in both memory and I/O interfacing.

This chapter provides a detailed study of the various types of memory devices, including ROM, EPROM, SRAM, and DRAM. Since these devices will be included in most future systems, a complete understanding of them is an asset.

In addition, decoding of completely and incompletely specified memory address is presented. These techniques and their proper application will almost always reduce the overall cost of a memory system.

5-1 CHARACTERISTICS OF MEMORY DEVICES

The ROM, or read-only memory, and the RAM, or random access read and write memory, are the two general categories of memory devices in common use today. Both types have many of the same features, including address connections, data bus connections, and similar control connections. The read-only memory is commonly used to store programs and long-term data nonvolatilely; the semiconductor random access memory stores temporary data, since it is a volatile memory.

Read Only Memory (ROM)

Read only memory can be subdivided into many different categories, such as the PROM, EPROM, EAROM, and EEPROM. The ROM is a device that is mask-programmed at the factory by the manufacturer in the last phase of fabrication. It is most often used in large production runs because the manufacturer charges thousands of dollars for the initial mask.

The PROM is a field-programmable device programmed by a machine called a *PROM burner* or *PROM programmer*. The PROM type of ROM is programmed by burning open small fuses located inside the integrated circuit; hence its name. Since a fuse is burned open during programming, this device may be programmed only once.

The EPROM has an advantage over the PROM because it can be erased. The EPROM is erased by exposing it to a high-intensity ultraviolet light for approximately 6–40 minutes, depending upon the type of EPROM. When programmed, fuses are not burned as with the PROM; instead, an electrical charge is trapped in an insulated gate region. This trapped or programmed charge will be held for many years in this gate region. The charge is erasable through a quartz crystal window using ultraviolet light, which causes a photocurrent to flow, neutralizing the trapped charge. The main problems with the EPROM are that it takes a considerable amount of time to erase, and it must be removed from the equipment for erasing.

The EAROM or EEPROM is a device that can be programmed and erased electrically. It is often called a *read-mostly memory* (RMM) since it is often used to store data for extended periods of time. It typically requires about 4 to 10 ms to erase and another 4 to 10 ms to write new information, giving it a clear advantage over the EPROM. Its main disadvantage is the fact that it can be erased and reprogrammed only about ten thousand times.

Random Access Memory (RAM)

Random access memory can be divided into two major categories, the *static RAM* (SRAM) and the *dynamic RAM* (DRAM). Static random access memory is capable of storing information statically for as long as power is applied to the device. Dynamic memory will store information only for a few milliseconds before it is lost. A few milliseconds of time may not seem like much, but in this amount of time a microprocessor is able to accomplish quite a few tasks.

When dynamic memory is used in a system, additional circuitry is required to refresh the information periodically. When a DRAM is refreshed, the data from a group of memory locations is read and rewritten. If a memory system is small, static devices are used because of the additional cost of the refreshing circuitry. The breakeven point seems to be at about 16K bytes of memory. Memory systems containing more than 16K bytes will generally be dynamic; systems containing less memory will be static.

Memory Size

The device illustrated in figure 5–1 is a 2K-byte EPROM. Notice that 11 of the pin connections are used for memory addressing, 8 for data output connections, 3 for control, and 2 for the power supply connections. This particular EPROM is very commonly used today because of the single 5-V power supply requirement, its byte-sized capacity, and the ease at which it is interfaced to most commonly available microprocessors. Additional standard EPROMs along with their memory size include: 2708 (1K × 8), 2732 (4K × 8), 2764 (8K × 8), 27128 (16K × 8), 27256 (32K × 8) and the 27512 (64K × 8).

How do you determine how much memory is available in a device with 11 address

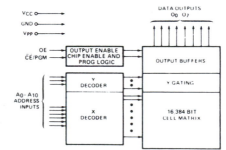

FIGURE 5–1   The pinout of the Intel 2716 2K × 8 EPROM.

SOURCE: Reprinted by permission of Intel Corporation. Copyright 1979.

connections? The number of locations on the memory device can be computed by raising 2 to a power equal to the number of address connections, as illustrated in example 5–1.

EXAMPLE 5–1

$$2^{11} = 2048 \text{ or } 2K \text{ locations}$$

In the same way, you can determine how much memory can be addressed or connected to a microprocessor if the number of address connections is known. The Intel 8085A has 16 address connections; it is capable of directly addressing 2^{16}, or 65,536, different memory locations.

Figure 5–2 illustrates the 4564 dynamic RAM, which is capable of storing 64K bits of information. Notice that it has been integrated into a 16-pin integrated circuit. It appears that the manufacturer has made a mistake, or example 5–1 is incorrect. Sixteen address connections are required to address this amount of memory, and only 16 pins are available. To help reduce the size of the component, the manufacturer has elected to multiplex the address connections so that only 8 pins are actually needed to address this amount of memory. Multiplexed address connections have been in use since the early 1970s. To use this device, the $\overline{\text{CAS}}$ (or *column address strobe*) and $\overline{\text{RAS}}$ (or *row address strobe*) inputs strobe the address into internal address registers, where it is held to address the memory array.

Memory Data Connections

In figure 5–2 you will notice that the device uses separate pins for input and output data. This is one method, called *separate I/O,* of connecting a memory device to a system that has two data buses—one for input data and one for output data. Today very few microprocessor-based systems use two buses; instead, they use bidirectional data buses and memory devices that are capable of functioning with a bidirectional bus.

The 4564 can be used as a bidirectional device by connecting its input and output data pins. This connection effectively produces a bidirectional bus, since the data output pin is normally at its high-impedance state. It is important that devices connected in this manner

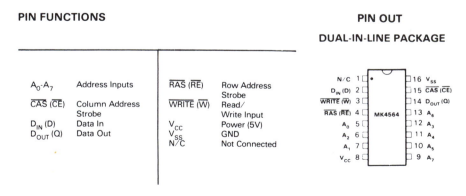

FIGURE 5–2   The pinout for the MK4564 64K $\times$ 1 dynamic RAM.
SOURCE: Courtesy of MOSTEK, Inc.

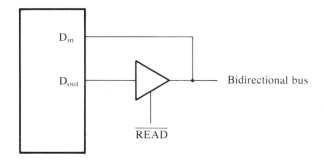

FIGURE 5–3 Connecting a memory device that contains separate I/O pins as a common I/O memory device.

have three-state output connections. Additional drive can be obtained by connecting a three-state buffer between the data output connection and the bidirectional bus if needed, as illustrated in figure 5–3. The $\overline{READ}$ signal is activated to drive the bus with data from this device.

Memory Control

The control connections on memory devices are nearly the same for all devices. Figure 5–1 used two pins for its control, the $\overline{OE}$ and $\overline{CE}$ pins. $\overline{OE}$, or *output enable,* causes the internal three-state output buffers to drive the output pins, provided that $\overline{CE}$, or *chip enable,* has also been activated. All memory devices have some form of chip enable or chip selection logic. Even the circuit in figure 5–2 has this logic, but it is hidden in the function of the $\overline{CAS}$ pin. Normally a memory device will contain either a $\overline{CE}$ or a $\overline{CS}$ pin for control and, at times, $\overline{S}$.

Some devices, such as the one shown in figure 5–4, have multiple-chip enable logic. Whenever more than one chip enable pin is present, it aids the hardware designer in interfacing the device to a microprocessor. When multiple chip selection pins exist, all must be activated to enable the memory component. In figure 5–4, $\overline{CS1}$ and $\overline{CS2}$ must both be grounded and CS3 must be pulled up to a logic one to select the device. Once selected, data will appear at the output connections within a short period of time.

Another control pin found on RAM memory devices is the $\overline{W}$, $\overline{WE}$, or R/$\overline{W}$ pin. Figure 5–5 pictures the TMS4016 static RAM, which contains a $\overline{W}$ pin and a $\overline{G}$ (gate or enable) pin. Both pins can facilitate the device's connection to a bidirectional data bus. This memory has been organized as a bytewide memory device with 2048 memory locations. The $\overline{W}$, or *write enable,* pin causes a write into this memory component.

As we have seen in this section, memory devices are nearly all alike in function and application. More detail will be provided later, along with the design methodology for their connection to microprocessors.

TIMING CONSIDERATIONS OF MEMORY DEVICES 5–2

To interface a memory device to a microprocessor, you must have a thorough understanding of the memory device itself. Operation of a memory component can only be understood by reading the timing diagrams provided by the manufacturer. Along with the timing diagram is a listing of electrical characteristics that describe the times required to

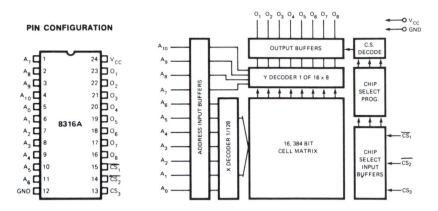

PIN CONFIGURATION

BLOCK DIAGRAM

A.C. CHARACTERISTICS $T_A = 0°C$ to $+70°C$, $V_{CC} = +5V \pm 5\%$ unless otherwise specified

SYMBOL	PARAMETER	LIMITS			UNIT
		MIN.	TYP.[1]	MAX.	
t_A	Address to Output Delay Time		400	850	nS
t_{CO}	Chip Select to Output Enable Delay Time			300	nS
t_{DF}	Chip Deselect to Output Data Float Delay Time	0		300	nS

CONDITIONS OF TEST FOR A.C. CHARACTERISTICS

Output Load . . . 1 TTL Gate, and $C_{LOAD} = 100$ pF
Input Pulse Levels . . . . 0.8 to 2.0V
Input Pulse Rise and Fall Times . (10% to 90%) 20 nS
Timing Measurement Reference Level
Input 1.5V
Output . . . . 0.45V to 2.2V

CAPACITANCE [2] $T_A = 25°C$, f = 1 MHz

SYMBOL	TEST	LIMITS	
		TYP.	MAX.
C_{IN}	All Pins Except Pin Under Test Tied to AC Ground	4 pF	10 pF
C_{OUT}	All Pins Except Pin Under Test Tied to AC Ground	8 pF	15 pF

(2) This parameter is periodically sampled and is not 100% tested.

A.C. WAVEFORMS

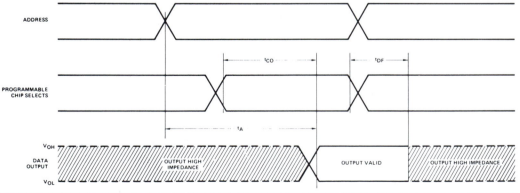

FIGURE 5–4 The 8316 ROM, which contains multiple chip enable inputs.

SOURCE: Reprinted by permission of Intel Corporation. Copyright 1978.

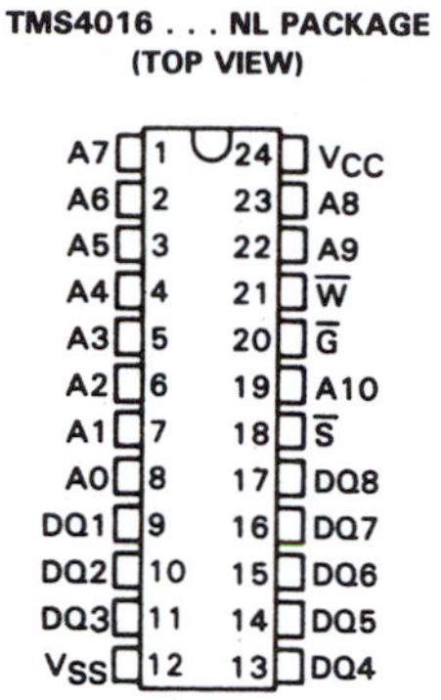

TMS4016 . . . NL PACKAGE
(TOP VIEW)
A7 1 24 VCC
A6 2 23 A8
A5 3 22 A9
A4 4 21 W̄
A3 5 20 Ḡ
A2 6 19 A10
A1 7 18 S̄
A0 8 17 DQ8
DQ1 9 16 DQ7
DQ2 10 15 DQ6
DQ3 11 14 DQ5
VSS 12 13 DQ4

PIN NOMENCLATURE	
A0 – A10	Addresses
DQ1 – DQ8	Data In/Data Out
$\overline{G}$	Output Enable
$\overline{S}$	Chip Select
V_{CC}	+5-V Supply
V_{SS}	Ground
$\overline{W}$	Write Enable

FIGURE 5–5 The pinout of the TMS4016, 2 K × 8 static RAM (SRAM). (Courtesy of Texas Instruments Incorporated)

control and utilize the device. You must understand these times and the timing diagram to ensure a device's proper operation with a particular microprocessor. It is important to note that not all memory components are compatible with all microprocessors.

Basic Timing Diagrams

A few words about timing diagrams before looking deeply into one of them: Notice in figure 5–6 that the address connections are not shown individually but as a composite waveform of all the address inputs. This arrangement has been chosen to conserve space and to make it easier to understand the waveforms.

The only thing that a composite waveform can indicate is a change in bit patterns. This is viewed as an *X*, or *crossover point,* on the timing diagrams. Another common practice on timing diagrams is to show a line halfway between a logic one and a logic zero for a high-impedance condition. It does *not* indicate that the voltage level is 2.5 V. This type of

Address
Valid address
X or change
Data
Valid data
∞
∞

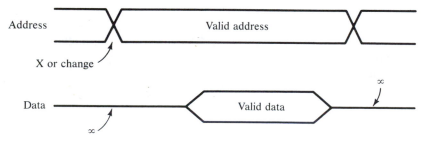

FIGURE 5–6 Interpreting general memory timing diagrams.

waveform most often appears on data output connections from memory devices and microprocessors.

EPROM Timing

A complete set of timing diagrams for the 2716 EPROM is provided in figure 5–7, along with its electrical characteristics. Refer to this figure for the following discussion of read timing, which applies to all memory devices.

The first change that occurs when reading information from a memory device is the application of the memory address. This application triggers an external decoder that generates the $\overline{CE}$ input to the memory. After this step, the microprocessor issues the read signal, which causes the $\overline{OE}$ input to become logic zero. The memory then, in a short period of time, begins to drive the data bus with information for the microprocessor.

Access time, the amount of time required to access information, varies considerably from memory device to memory device. In the memory device in figure 5–7, it takes 450 ns for data to be accessed from the address inputs or the $\overline{CE}$ input. (This is by definition the access time for a memory component.) Since the $\overline{CE}$ input is developed by an external memory address decoder, the decoder propagation delay time is added to the access time of the memory device. How long it takes the data to be accessed would then be 450 ns plus the decoder's propagation delay time.

Another critical time is the period required for the output buffers to be activated. The output buffers are enabled by the application of a logic zero to the $\overline{OE}$ connection of this memory device. The electrical characteristics indicate that this procedure requires 120 ns. The $\overline{OE}$ connection prevents bus conflicts or contentions in microprocessors that use a multiplexed data bus. In microprocessors without a multiplexed data bus, this pin can be treated as an additional chip enable input. Whenever more than one chip enable is present, all must be placed at their active levels to obtain information at the output of the memory.

To summarize, the microprocessor sends a memory address, which is decoded by an external decoder, to the memory. The output of the decoder activates the $\overline{CE}$ input and starts to access data inside the memory component. Finally, the microprocessor sends out some form of memory read signal, which activates $\overline{OE}$ and causes the memory to apply data to the data bus.

Static RAM Timing

Figure 5–8 illustrates the timing diagram and specifications for the 2114, 1K by 4, SRAM. You will notice that the timing diagram is very similar to the one for the 2716 EPROM with one exception: the $\overline{WE}$ input replaces the $\overline{OE}$ input. The number of address inputs is reduced by one pin because this device contains only 1024 memory locations (instead of the 2048 memory locations in the 2716). The 2716 has eight output connections; the 2114, because of a change in internal organization, only has four. The I/O pins input data to the memory and also extract data from the memory. These are common I/O pins, which are present on quite a few RAM memory devices.

In figure 5–8(a), you will notice that only the address information, the $\overline{CS}$ (or *chip selection*) information, and the data output information are provided. It is understood that $\overline{WE}$ (write enable) input is at its inactive level because a read operation is being illustrated. The microprocessor outputs a memory address to the address pins, and an external

A.C. Characteristics

Symbol	Parameter	2716 Limits			2716-1 Limits			2716-2 Limits			Unit	Test Conditions
		Min	Typ[4]	Max	Min	Typ[4]	Max	Min	Typ[4]	Max		
t_{ACC}	Address to Output Delay			450			350			390	ns	$\overline{CE} = \overline{OE} = V_{IL}$
t_{CE}	$\overline{CE}$ to Output Delay			450			350			390	ns	$\overline{OE} = V_{IL}$
t_{OE}	Output Enable to Output Delay			120			120			120	ns	$\overline{CE} = V_{IL}$
t_{DF}	Output Enable High to Output Float	0		100	0		100	0		100	ns	$\overline{CE} = V_{IL}$
t_{OH}	Address to Output Hold	0			0			0			ns	$\overline{CE} = \overline{OE} = V_{IL}$

Capacitance[5] $T_A = 25°C$, $f = 1$ MHz

Symbol	Parameter	Typ.	Max.	Unit	Conditions
C_{IN}	Input Capacitance	4	6	pF	$V_{IN} = 0V$
C_{OUT}	Output Capacitance	8	12	pF	$V_{OUT} = 0V$

A.C. Test Conditions:

Output Load: 1 TTL gate and $C_L = 100$ pF
Input Rise and Fall Times: ≤ 20 ns
Input Pulse Levels: 0.8V to 2.2V
Timing Measurement Reference Level:
   Inputs   1V and 2V
   Outputs   0.8V and 2V

A.C. WAVEFORMS

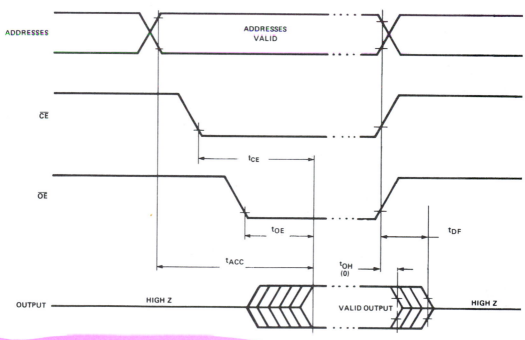

FIGURE 5-7   The timing diagram and AC characteristics for the Intel 2716 EPROM.
SOURCE: Reprinted by permission of Intel Corporation. Copyright 1978.

107

decoder generates a logic zero for the $\overline{CS}$ pin. Then, after some prescribed access time, data will appear at the I/O pins.

One significant change to note is that the access time for various versions of the 2114 RAM is much shorter than the access time for the 2716 EPROM, as denoted in figure 5–7. This reduction in access time is required in a system that uses a multiplexed data bus since the bus is not available for use until some time after the memory address is sent out to the memory. This decrease in access time allows the read signal to be combined logically with the memory address to activate the $\overline{CS}$ input for the RAM. This procedure is necessary to avoid a bus conflict with this type of RAM because it has no $\overline{OE}$ connection.

Figure 5–8(b) illustrates the write timing for the 2114 RAM. Here, unlike in figure 5–

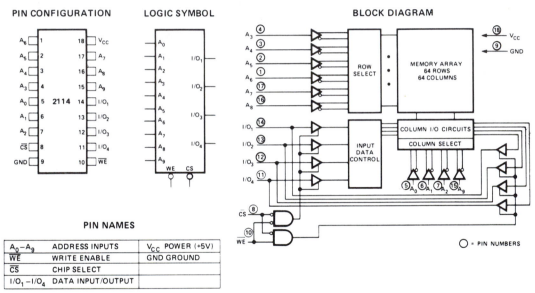

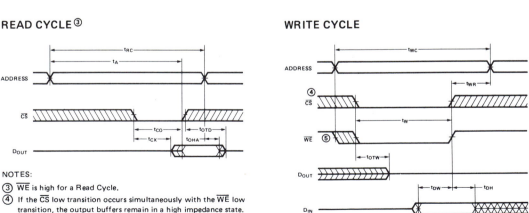

NOTES:

③ $\overline{WE}$ is high for a Read Cycle.

④ If the $\overline{CS}$ low transition occurs simultaneously with the $\overline{WE}$ low transition, the output buffers remain in a high impedance state.

⑤ $\overline{WE}$ must be high during all address transitions.

FIGURE 5–8 (a) The Intel 2114 1K × 4 static RAM pinout, timing, and AC characteristics.

SOURCE: Reprinted by permission of Intel Corporation. Copyright 1978.

A.C. CHARACTERISTICS $T_A = 0°C$ to $70°C$, $V_{CC} = 5V \pm 5\%$, unless otherwise noted.

READ CYCLE [1]

SYMBOL	PARAMETER	2114-2, 2114L2 Min.	2114-2, 2114L2 Max.	2114-3, 2114L3 Min.	2114-3, 2114L3 Max.	2114, 2114L Min.	2114, 2114L Max.	UNIT
t_{RC}	Read Cycle Time	200		300		450		ns
t_A	Access Time		200		300		450	ns
t_{CO}	Chip Selection to Output Valid		70		100		120	ns
t_{CX}	Chip Selection to Output Active	20		20		20		ns
t_{OTD}	Output 3-state from Deselection		60		80		100	ns
t_{OHA}	Output Hold from Address Change	50		50		50		ns

WRITE CYCLE [2]

SYMBOL	PARAMETER	2114-2, 2114L2 Min.	2114-2, 2114L2 Max.	2114-3, 2114L3 Min.	2114-3, 2114L3 Max.	2114, 2114L Min.	2114, 2114L Max.	UNIT
t_{WC}	Write Cycle Time	200		300		450		ns
t_W	Write Time	120		150		200		ns
t_{WR}	Write Release Time	0		0		0		ns
t_{OTW}	Output 3-state from Write		60		80		100	ns
t_{DW}	Data to Write Time Overlap	120		150		200		ns
t_{DH}	Data Hold From Write Time	0		0		0		ns

NOTES:

1. A Read occurs during the overlap of a low $\overline{CS}$ and a high $\overline{WE}$.
2. A Write occurs during the overlap of a low $\overline{CS}$ and a low $\overline{WE}$.

FIGURE 5–8 (b)

8(a), the $\overline{WE}$ signal is illustrated because it is used by the memory to accomplish a memory write. In some memory devices, this pin is labeled $R/\overline{W}$, or $\overline{W}$, and has exactly the same function as $\overline{WE}$.

For the microprocessor to write information into the 2114, it first sends out a memory address that is decoded to enable the device. The write signal that follows indicates that the data to be written into the memory are available on the data bus.

The time required to write information is normally equal to or less than that required to read information. In the case of the 2114, the period required to write information is about 200 ns from the $\overline{WE}$ signal; the time required to read information is about 450 ns.

Memory Cells

Figure 5–9 illustrates the 4116 dynamic RAM. Dynamic RAMs differ from static RAMs in that they require periodic refreshing. A static RAM stores information for an indefinite amount of time; a dynamic RAM stores information for only a few milliseconds, due to the internal structure of the dynamic RAM.

Figure 5–10(a) illustrates a basic static RAM memory element or cell; figure 5–10(b) illustrates a basic dynamic cell. These illustrations show that the DRAM cell requires only

FUNCTIONAL DIAGRAM

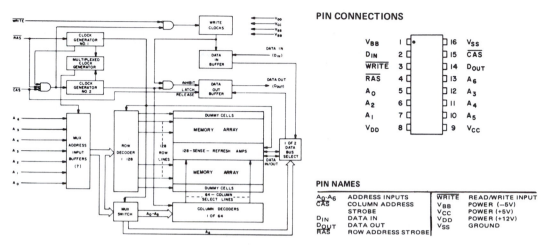

FIGURE 5–9 The MK4116 16K × 1 dynamic RAM.

SOURCE: Courtesy of MOSTEK, Inc.

half the transistors of the SRAM cell. Although this suggests that a DRAM can accommodate twice as much memory as the SRAM, many more than twice as many DRAM cells can be placed in the same area. The DRAM cell dissipates much less power than the SRAM cell. Power is dissipated in a DRAM cell only when data is written, read, or refreshed, which allows it to be physically smaller.

Again referring to figure 5–9, notice that there are only seven pins devoted to memory

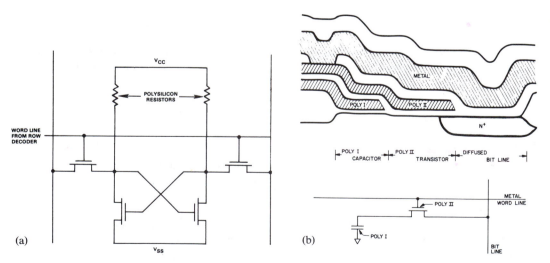

FIGURE 5–10 RAM Memory Cells: (a) the MK4108 static memory cell, (b) the MK4116 dynamic memory cell.

SOURCE: Courtesy of MOSTEK, Inc.

addressing. How is this possible when this memory device has 16K bits of information stored inside? It's possible because the address pins are used for 14 bits of address information that are strobed or multiplexed into the seven pins, seven bits at a time. A much more detailed discussion of DRAM and its timing is presented in a later section of this chapter.

EEPROM Timing

The last memory device to be discussed is the 2816 EEPROM in figure 5–11, which is receiving wide application because of its nonvolatility. This device is often called a *nonvolatile RAM* (NOVRAM). It can be written and erased electrically without losing information when disconnected from the power supply. The 2816 EEPROM is very useful for storing information that is changed only occasionally.

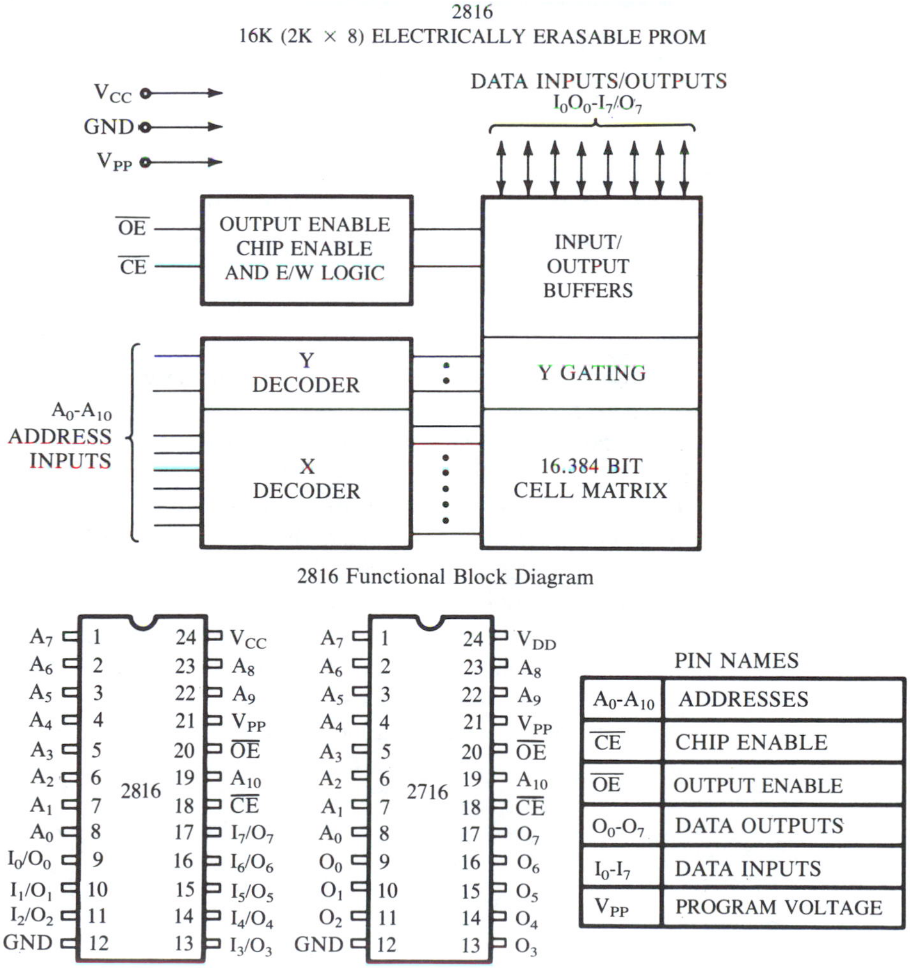

2816
16K (2K × 8) ELECTRICALLY ERASABLE PROM

2816 Functional Block Diagram

	PIN NAMES	
A_0-A_{10}	ADDRESSES	
$\overline{CE}$	CHIP ENABLE	
$\overline{OE}$	OUTPUT ENABLE	
O_0-O_7	DATA OUTPUTS	
I_0-I_7	DATA INPUTS	
V_{PP}	PROGRAM VOLTAGE	

FIGURE 5–11 The Intel 2816 2K × 8 EEPROM.

SOURCE: Reprinted by permission of Intel Corporation, Copyright 1982.

In the past a battery was required with standard RAM to create a nonvolatile RAM. The main timing difference between EEPROM and RAM is that erasure or writing takes much more time in the EEPROM. The 2816, for example, requires 10 ms to write or to erase information. This may seem to be too much time, but if data are written only occasionally, it presents no problem in most systems.

Another difference is that the 2816 requires a 21-V power supply for programming, so that a system incorporating this device requires an additional power supply.

This type of memory usually includes applications such as tab positioning on CRT terminals and sales tax look-up tables in electronic cash registers. In fact, the 2816 may eventually replace other forms of ROM since a change in software can be accomplished in the machinery without removing the integrated circuits from the system. The software can even be changed remotely through a telephone line or a data link to the manufacturer.

5–3 ADDRESS DECODING

An *address decoder* is a device or digital circuit that indicates that a particular area of memory is being addressed, or pointed to, by the microprocessor. In other words, an address decoder is a simple combinational logic circuit used to decode the memory address. Most address decoders have one or more outputs that become active for a particular area of memory.

The Basic Address Decoder

The circuit of figure 5–12 uses a simple 4-input NAND gate as a memory address decoder. The output of the NAND gate is active low, so that its output becomes a logic zero only when all of the inputs are pulled high. In this example, a microprocessor with a 16-bit address bus is connected to the NAND gate. The output of the NAND gate will go low whenever the microprocessor addresses a memory location that begins with an A hexadecimal. As example 5–2 indicates, the first four bits of the address bus are decoded by the NAND gate, with the remaining bits illustrated as *X*s, called *don't cares,* because as far as this circuit is concerned we are not interested in their logic levels. If all zeros are inserted for the don't cares, we can locate the lowest-numbered memory location decoded by the circuit. In this case the lowest-numbered memory address decoded is A000H. Notice that a capital letter *H* following a number denotes a hexadecimal quantity. With some microprocessors, a dollar sign ($) preceding the number indicates a hexadecimal quantity.

EXAMPLE 5–2

A15	A14	A13	A12	A11	A10	A9	A8		A7	A6	A5	A4		A3	A2	A1	A0	
1	0	1	0	X	X	X	X		X	X	X	X		X	X	X	X	(A X X X H)
					or													
1	0	1	0	0	0	0	0		0	0	0	0		0	0	0	0	(A 0 0 0 H)
					to													
1	0	1	0	1	1	1	1		1	1	1	1		1	1	1	1	(A F F F H)

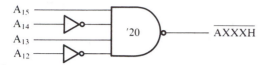

FIGURE 5–12 Basic circuit for decoding an address beginning with an A hexadecimal.

The highest location decoded by the decoder can be determined by substituting all logic ones for the don't cares. In this case, the highest location decoded is AFFFH. This decoder will produce a logic zero at its output for any memory location between A000H and AFFFH. We have decoded a 4K-byte segment of the microprocessor's address space. It is very important to remember that 1000H is equal to 4K and that 400H is equal to 1K. This relationship makes developing memory address decoding circuitry easier.

Let's suppose that a particular application requires a 2K-byte segment of ROM using the 2716 EPROM. The engineering department has indicated only that this device must function at memory locations 2000H through and including 27FFH. The first step (see example 5–3) is to write down both extremes of the memory locations in binary. The binary representations indicate that the right-hand 11 address bits, A0 through A10, change from all zeros to all ones within this area of memory; the left-hand 5 address bits, A11 through A15, remain the same. In fact, if you were to compare the next-lowest and the next-highest binary memory addresses, 1FFFH and 2800H, you would notice that the first five bits would change. In other words, the first five bits of the address are unique to this area of memory.

EXAMPLE 5–3

A15	A14	A13	A12	A11	A10	A9	A8	A7	A6	A5	A4	A3	A2	A1	A0	
0	0	1	0	0	0	0	0	0	0	0	0	0	0	0	0	or 2000H
							to									
0	0	1	0	0	1	1	1	1	1	1	1	1	1	1	1	or 27FFH

Since the output of this circuit must generate a logic zero to ground the enable input of the 2716, a truth table, table 5–1, is developed. From the truth table we can write a Boolean logic expression for the logic zero output. The expression for this range of addresses is depicted in equation 5–1. This expression can be implemented with a five-input OR gate if one is available.

$$A15 + A14 + \overline{A13} + A12 + A11 = \overline{2000\text{H to } 27\text{FFH}} \qquad \textbf{5–1}$$

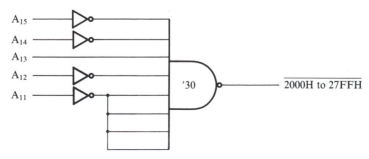

FIGURE 5–13 A circuit to implement equation 5–2.

TABLE 5–1   2000H to 27FFH
address decoder truth table.

A15	A14	A13	A12	A11	Out
0	0	0	0	0	1
0	0	0	0	1	1
0	0	0	1	0	1
0	0	0	1	1	1
0	0	1	0	0	0
0	0	1	0	1	1
0	0	1	1	0	1
0	0	1	1	1	1
0	1	0	0	0	1
0	1	0	0	1	1
0	1	0	1	0	1
0	1	0	1	1	1
0	1	1	0	0	1
0	1	1	0	1	1
0	1	1	1	0	1
0	1	1	1	1	1
1	0	0	0	0	1
1	0	0	0	1	1
1	0	0	1	0	1
1	0	0	1	1	1
1	0	1	0	0	1
1	0	1	0	1	1
1	0	1	1	0	1
1	0	1	1	1	1
1	1	0	0	0	1
1	1	0	0	1	1
1	1	0	1	0	1
1	1	0	1	1	1
1	1	1	0	0	1
1	1	1	0	1	1
1	1	1	1	0	1
1	1	1	1	1	1

Since only a five-or-more-input NAND gate is available, DeMorgan's theorem is used on the left-hand side of equation 5–1 to convert it to NAND gate form as shown in equation 5–2. Figure 5–13 illustrates this Boolean expression

$$\overline{\overline{A15} \cdot \overline{A14} \cdot A13 \cdot \overline{A12} \cdot \overline{A11}} = \overline{2000\text{H to }27\text{FFH}} \qquad \textbf{5–2}$$

implemented with an eight-input NAND gate (the 74LS30 eight-input NAND) and inverters (the 74LS04 hex inverter).

Integrated Decoder Circuits

In most applications, more than one memory device is usually required for system operation. It would be extremely wasteful to use an eight-input NAND gate for each memory device. To avoid such waste, a decoder, selected from the variety in production by the IC houses, is used.

An extensive search for the ideal decoder suggests that for many applications the 74LS138 or Intel 8205 3-to-8 line decoder is ideal. In fact, after examining many pieces of microprocessor based equipment, it appears that the entire industry has also discovered this device. The most useful features of this device are the multiple enable inputs.

Figure 5–14 depicts this decoder along with a truth table describing its operation. This decoder has active low outputs that become active only when all of the enable inputs are at their active levels. Whenever this device is enabled, the 3-bit binary number present at the address inputs causes one of the output pins to become active.

Using Decoder Circuits

Suppose that a given system requires eight EPROMs of the 2716-type to function at memory addresses 0000H through 3FFFH. This can be accomplished by using eight

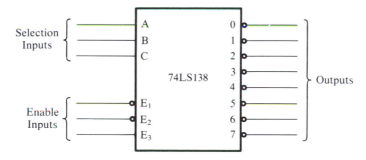

Inputs						Outputs							
Enable			Select										
$\overline{E_1}$	$\overline{E_2}$	E_3	C	B	A	$\overline{0}$	$\overline{1}$	$\overline{2}$	$\overline{3}$	$\overline{4}$	$\overline{5}$	$\overline{6}$	$\overline{7}$
1	X	X	X	X	X	1	1	1	1	1	1	1	1
X	1	X	X	X	X	1	1	1	1	1	1	1	1
X	X	0	X	X	X	1	1	1	1	1	1	1	1
0	0	1	0	0	0	0	1	1	1	1	1	1	1
0	0	1	0	0	1	1	0	1	1	1	1	1	1
0	0	1	0	1	0	1	1	0	1	1	1	1	1
0	0	1	0	1	1	1	1	1	0	1	1	1	1
0	0	1	1	0	0	1	1	1	1	0	1	1	1
0	0	1	1	0	1	1	1	1	1	1	0	1	1
0	0	1	1	1	0	1	1	1	1	1	1	0	1
0	0	1	1	1	1	1	1	1	1	1	1	1	0

FIGURE 5–14 The 74LS138 3-to-8 line decoder and truth table.

8-input NAND gates and a multitude of inverters; or it can be accomplished with one 74LS138 decoder. Sounds hard to believe, doesn't it?

The first step in designing this interface is to write the binary address with A10 through A0 as don't cares, as illustrated in example 5–4. We don't care about these address bits since the memory devices themselves internally decode these address bit positions. Remember that the 2716 has 11 address pins.

EXAMPLE 5–4

A15 A14 A13 A12 A11 A10 A9 A8 A7 A6 A5 A4 A3 A2 A1 A0	
0 0 0 0 0 X X X X X X X X X X X	or 0000H
	to
0 0 1 1 1 X X X X X X X X X X X	or 3FFFH

Observe that A15 and A14 are the only binary bit positions in this range of addresses that remain unchanged. These two bits enable the 74LS138 decoder. The next three address bit positions (A13, A12, and A11) do change; in fact, they change or vary through every binary combination from 000 to 111. These three bits are ideal candidates for the address inputs of the decoder. The completed circuit is illustrated in figure 5–15.

Notice that only the 74LS138 decoder and eight EPROMs appear in the complete circuit. Again, this is by far the most efficient method of decoding memory addresses that

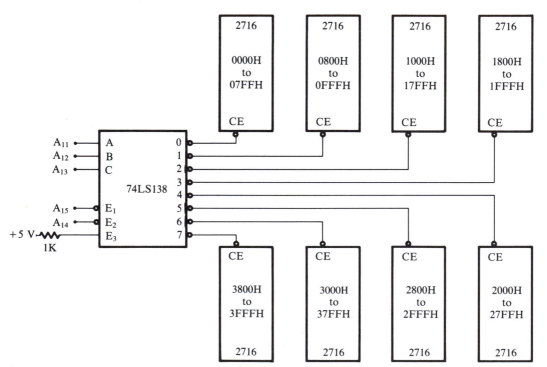

FIGURE 5–15 A circuit that will select one of the eight EPROMs if the correct address appears on the inputs of the 74LS138 3-to-8 line decoder.

the author has encountered. It is an effective approach even if only one or two devices are to be selected or enabled with their outputs.

The rule followed in industry today is to minimize the component count. The fewer integrated circuits in a system, the easier and more reliable it is to maintain or trouble-shoot.

PROM Decoders

Another device that may be found as a memory address decoder is the TTL bipolar PROM. For example, the 74S288 PROM, which has five address inputs and eight outputs, can be used in the same way the 74LS138 was used in figure 5–15. The only difference is that each of the PROM's 32 memory locations must be programmed with the correct output bit patterns to enable the eight memory devices. This is a much costlier approach to memory device selection, but one that is used occasionally. Its main advantage is that the decoded address range can be changed at some point in the future by changing the PROM—not by rewiring the circuit. Figure 5–16 illustrates the 74S288, which selects eight 2716 EPROMs, and the contents of the PROM.

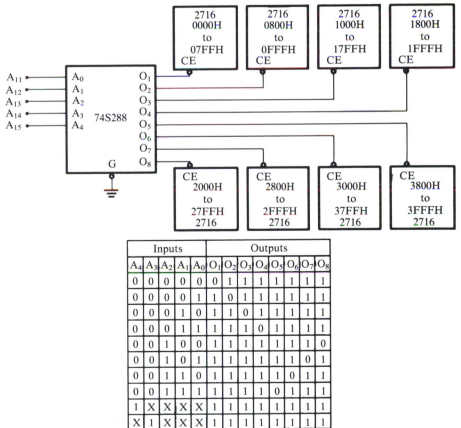

Inputs					Outputs							
A_4	A_3	A_2	A_1	A_0	O_1	O_2	O_3	O_4	O_5	O_6	O_7	O_8
0	0	0	0	0	0	1	1	1	1	1	1	1
0	0	0	0	1	1	0	1	1	1	1	1	1
0	0	0	1	0	1	1	0	1	1	1	1	1
0	0	0	1	1	1	1	1	0	1	1	1	1
0	0	1	0	0	1	1	1	1	1	1	1	0
0	0	1	0	1	1	1	1	1	1	1	0	1
0	0	1	1	0	1	1	1	1	1	0	1	1
0	0	1	1	1	1	1	1	1	0	1	1	1
1	X	X	X	X	1	1	1	1	1	1	1	1
X	1	X	X	X	1	1	1	1	1	1	1	1

FIGURE 5–16 A circuit that will select one of the eight EPROMs if the correct address appears on the inputs of the 74S288 PROM decoder.

5—4 STATIC MEMORY SYSTEMS

Static memory systems are found in applications requiring only a small amount of RAM for implementation. Because ROM is always static, the principles in this section apply to the ROM section in any system. The first step in developing any system memory is the memory map. A *memory map* illustrates which segments are to be used for RAM, and, in some cases, where the I/O resides.

Memory Maps

Figure 5–17 illustrates a typical memory map of a small system. This particular system requires 12K bytes of memory for program storage in ROM and 4K bytes of memory for data storage in RAM. The segments for both types of memory were arbitrarily chosen for this example problem.

As illustrated in figure 5–17, ROM1 resides at memory locations 0000H through 0FFFH; ROM2 resides at memory locations 1000H through 1FFFH; and ROM3 resides at memory locations 2000H through 2FFFH. RAM1 resides at memory 6000H through 67FFH, and RAM2 resides at memory locations 6800H through 6FFFH. The ROM and RAM in this system are contiguous by themselves, but not together as a unit. In most

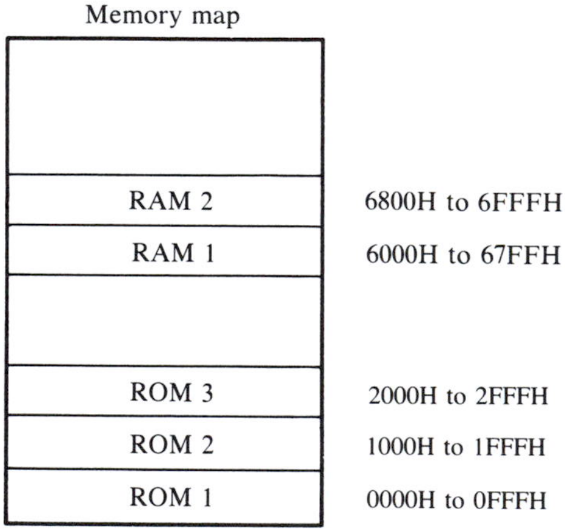

FIGURE 5–17 The memory map of a small memory system consisting of two segments of RAM and three segments of EPROM.

Memory map

RAM 2	6800H to 6FFFH
RAM 1	6000H to 67FFH
ROM 3	2000H to 2FFFH
ROM 2	1000H to 1FFFH
ROM 1	0000H to 0FFFH

	A_{15} A_{14} A_{13} A_{12}	A_{11} A_{10} A_9 A_8	A_7 A_6 A_5 A_4	A_3 A_2 A_1 A_0
ROM	0 0 0 0	X X X X	X X X X	X X X X
		to		
ROM	0 0 1 0	X X X X	X X X X	X X X X
RAM	0 1 1 0	X X X X	X X X X	X X X X
		to		
RAM	0 1 1 0	X X X X	X X X X	X X X X

cases it may not be necessary to construct a memory that is contiguous, but for this example it is assumed to be a system requirement.

Once the memory has been mapped, the ROM and RAM boundary addresses are written in binary, so that a decoder can be selected for the system. This is illustrated at the bottom of the figure. In both cases, the address bits that are internally decoded by the memory devices are drawn as don't cares. The remaining address bit positions must be decoded by an external memory address decoder to select or enable the memory devices at the appropriate time. Since these ROM and RAM sections have different numbers of address bits to be externally decoded, two decoders are required for this application.

Multiple Memory Device Decoders

The circuit depicted in figure 5–18 shows the result using two 3-to-8 line (74LS138) decoders. The first decoder, which is connected to the four most significant address bit positions, generates signals whenever the microprocessor addresses data in the bottom half of the memory. Each one of the eight outputs will become active for a 4K-byte segment of the memory.

In this application, the first three 4K-byte segments are used for ROM1, ROM2, and ROM3, which are connected to the first three outputs. Output zero will go low for memory addresses 0000H through 0FFFH; output one will go low for memory addresses 1000H through 1FFFH; and output two will go low for memory addresses 2000H through 2FFFH.

In addition to these three connections to the ROMs, you will notice that the $\overline{\text{MEMR}}$ signal is also connected to their $\overline{\text{OE}}$ pins. This synchronizes the transfer of data from the ROMs to the microprocessor. More detail on where the $\overline{\text{MEMR}}$ signal comes from and how it is generated is provided in chapters 3 and 4.

Output six of the first decoder enables the second decoder whenever the microprocessor points to a memory location 6XXXH. The second decoder then generates an output for the two RAM devices because it decodes address bit A11.

Output zero, of the second decoder, becomes active whenever addresses 6000H through 67FFH are sent out of the microprocessor. Output one becomes active whenever the microprocessor presents memory addresses 6800H through 6FFFH. These outputs select or enable the two RAM devices.

In addition to selection inputs, the RAMs also contain a $\overline{\text{W}}$ connection and a $\overline{\text{G}}$ connection. These inputs control the application of data to the memory and also control when data are sent to the microprocessor from the memory. $\overline{\text{MEMW}}$ causes the write to occur, and $\overline{\text{MEMR}}$ causes the read to occur.

Since the number of integrated circuits used in a system is important, the circuit in figure 5–18 is redesigned, using a TTL PROM for memory address decoding rather than two 74LS138 decoders. By reducing the number of integrated circuits used in a system, we improve its reliability, reduce its power consumption, reduce its size, and make it easier for a technician to troubleshoot for faults.

Figure 5–19 illustrates the same system, using the 3624A PROM in place of the two 74LS138 decoders. This PROM is organized as a 512-byte memory device and can be used in almost any memory decoder circuit.

To understand how the outputs of the PROM function, peruse table 5–2, which illus-

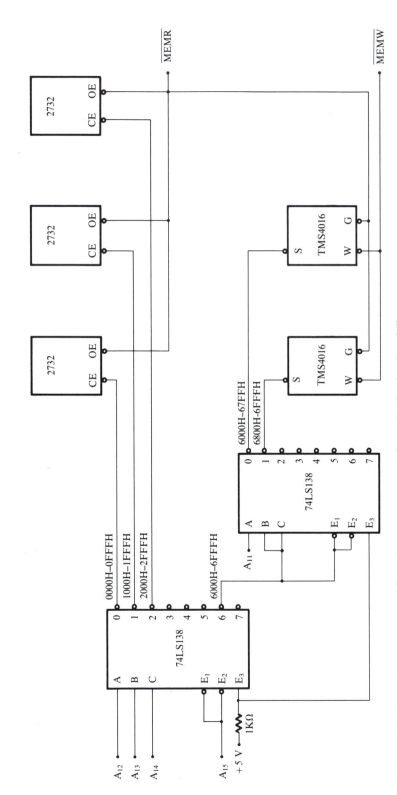

FIGURE 5–18 A circuit constructed from the memory map of figure 5–17 using 3-to-8 line decoders for memory address selection.

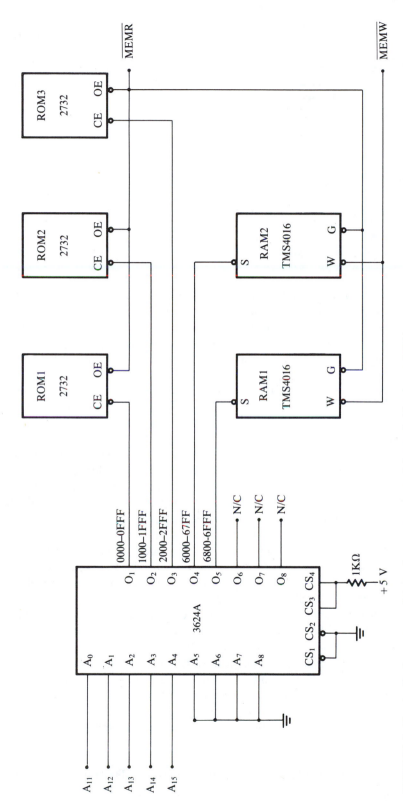

FIGURE 5-19 A circuit constructed from the memory map of figure 5-17 using a 3624A PROM decoder for memory address selection.

121

TABLE 5–2   The 3624A programmed logic for the circuit of Figure 5–19.

PROM Inputs									PROM Outputs							
A8	A7	A6	A5	A4	A3	A2	A1	A0	08	07	06	05	04	03	02	01
0	0	0	0	0	0	0	0	0	X	X	X	1	1	1	1	0
0	0	0	0	0	0	0	0	1	X	X	X	1	1	1	1	0
0	0	0	0	0	0	0	1	0	X	X	X	1	1	1	0	1
0	0	0	0	0	0	0	1	1	X	X	X	1	1	1	0	1
0	0	0	0	0	0	1	0	0	X	X	X	1	1	0	1	1
0	0	0	0	0	0	1	0	1	X	X	X	1	1	0	1	1
0	0	0	0	0	1	1	0	0	X	X	X	1	0	1	1	1
0	0	0	0	0	1	1	0	1	X	X	X	0	1	1	1	1
(All other combinations)									X	X	X	1	1	1	1	1

trates the data stored on this PROM. For example, the first output of the PROM (01) will become active whenever the memory address begins with four zeros. This occurs whenever memory addresses 0000H through 0FFFH appear on the address bus. Output two becomes active whenever 00001 binary appears on the address bus. The remaining bit patterns are easily calculated by looking at the truth table and writing down the binary bit patterns for these outputs.

The main advantage of using the PROM to decode the memory address is the reduction in component count. The main disadvantage is that a PROM must be programmed, which requires special equipment and time. These advantages and disadvantages are weighed during system development.

Another option that deserves investigation is *incompletely specified* memory address decoding. Up until now, we have been using all of the memory address bits to select a memory device. This is applicable only in a system that will eventually contain every memory location. Most applications do not use the entire memory; therefore, the technique covered in the first portion of this section is useful only in a handful of applications.

This time, suppose that the system memory will contain only three 4K-byte ROMs and two 2K-byte RAMs. This assumption makes memory address decoding a lot simpler, since we do not need to decode all of the bits of the memory address to select five different devices. In fact, to select five different devices, we need have available only a 3-bit binary address, since it offers eight different combinations.

Starting with the memory map as we did earlier, we can segment it into eight different sections. Each section can be a memory device. In this example, five of the eight sections are used for memory, as illustrated in figure 5–20.

ROM1 is enabled whenever the memory address begins with 000, ROM2 whenever the memory address begins with 001, and so forth. The three most significant address bit positions are connected to a 3-to-8 line decoder (as illustrated in figure 5–21) to produce the required chip selection outputs for the memory devices.

Output zero of the decoder becomes active for memory addresses 0000H through 1FFFH, which is not 4K bytes of memory. This would seem to create a problem when connecting a 4K-byte memory device to this output, but it doesn't. The memory device will respond to locations 0000H through 0FFFH or locations 1000H through 1FFFH. In

Memory map

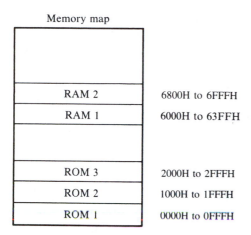

RAM 2	6800H to 6FFFH
RAM 1	6000H to 63FFH
ROM 3	2000H to 2FFFH
ROM 2	1000H to 1FFFH
ROM 1	0000H to 0FFFH

FIGURE 5–20 A memory map for an incompletely specified memory system.

other words, the data in the ROM will appear at the outputs twice in this range of memory. ROM1 is said to *overlay*, or shadow, 8K bytes of memory, of which only 4K bytes will be used. If the program is written to function in memory locations 0000H through 0FFFH, that is exactly where it will function. The fact that it also appears at locations 1000H through 1FFFH is not important, since this area of memory is never addressed by the program.

The remaining ROMs also overlay 8K bytes of memory each, again creating no problem for the programmer developing the software for the system. Address assignments for

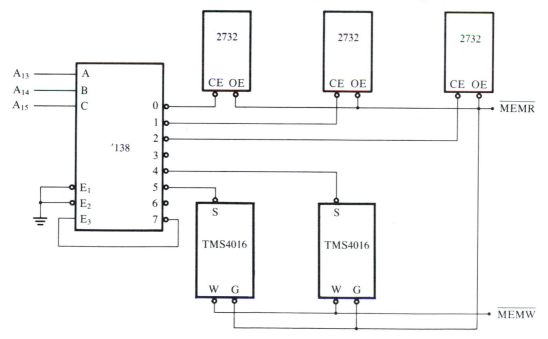

FIGURE 5–21 A circuit that can be used to implement the memory map of figure 5–20.

the ROMs can be: ROM1 (0000H–0FFFH), ROM2 (3000H–3FFFH), and ROM3 (4000H–4FFFH). Notice that the ROM storage is not contiguous storage, which can present a slight problem in developing the software for the system. To bypass this difficulty, the program is required to jump or branch from memory location 0FFFH to memory location 3000H for a continuation of the program.

Each of the RAM devices also overlays an 8K-byte block of the memory and appears four times in the block. Again, this does not present a problem, since the memory can be made contiguous by proper selection of the memory addresses. The RAMs can reside at locations 9800H through 9FFFH for RAM1 and A000H through A7FFH for RAM2. This is contiguous memory that will function perfectly.

As far as simplicity is concerned, this last implementation is by far the best for a small system since it only requires one decoder. Output seven, which is never active under normal usage, is a pullup for active high input E3. This practice saves the cost of the resistor and is common. This procedure reduces the total cost of the system. The connection may cause a problem in a system that has not been completely debugged if this area of memory is addressed. If this area of memory is addressed by the processor, it can lock out all of the memory.

A word on memory access times at this point is appropriate. The propagation delay time through the 74LS138 decoder is approximately 22 ns, and the propagation delay time through the 2364A PROM is approximately 70 ns. Comparing these two times, which subtracts from the time allowed by the microprocessor for the memory to access data, indicates that it is wise to use the decoder instead of the PROM.

For example, if the microprocessor allows 575 ns of time for the memory to access data, and the memory device itself requires 450 ns to access the data, the system has a 125-ns *margin:* the decoder can use up to 125 ns of time before the system becomes inoperative. In this case, using the decoder or the PROM creates no problem; but if the memory access time is longer or the time allowed by the processor is shorter, the PROM cannot decode the address. The margin should always be at least 20 ns or longer.

STD-BUS Memory Interface

The next example problem, illustrated in figure 5–22, depicts a buffered printed circuit card for use in the STD-BUS system. Notice that all connections into or out of this card are buffered; that is, inputs represent one LS unit load and outputs are buffered to drive a considerable number of unit loads. The 12 least significant address inputs are buffered through two 74LS244 octal bus buffers, and the remaining address bits are connected to a dual 2-to-4 line decoder.

The microprocessor in the STD-BUS system sends out a memory address along with the $\overline{\text{MEMEX}}$ signal and the $\overline{\text{MEMRQ}}$ signal. For normal memory operation the $\overline{\text{MEMEX}}$ signal is a logic one and the $\overline{\text{MEMRQ}}$ signal is a logic zero. The $\overline{\text{MEMEX}}$ signal is applied to the $\overline{\text{1G}}$ input of the decoder, which causes the two most significant address bits to be decoded and produce a logic zero on one of the four $\overline{\text{1Y}}$ outputs of the decoder. The strapping provided at these outputs selects the 16K block of memory at which the board will function: 0 (0000H–3FFFH); 4 (4000H–7FFFH); 8 (8000H–BFFFH); and C (C000H–FFFFH). The diagram illustrates that the strapping has connected this board to function at memory locations 0000H through 3FFFH. The output of the strap is connected

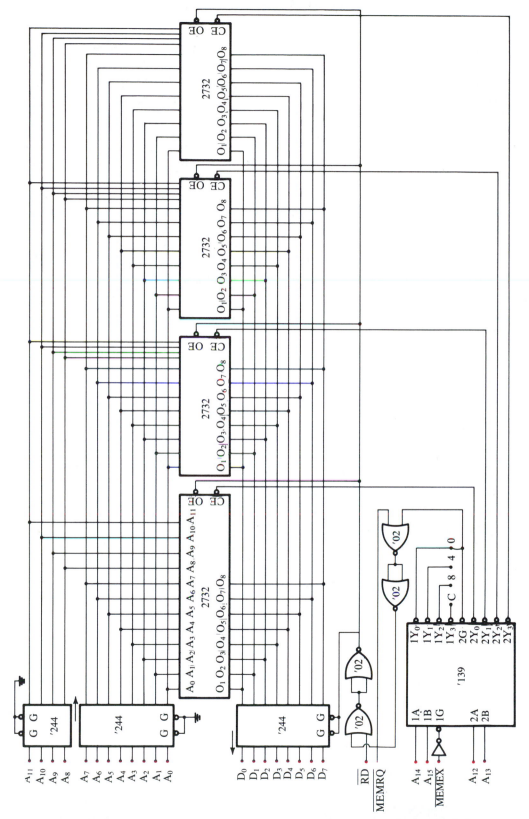

FIGURE 5-22 A fully buffered 16K × 8 EPROM printed circuit card for the STD-BUS standard microcomputer bus.

to two points in the circuit: one enables or selects the other half of the decoder through $\overline{2G}$; the other point gates the $\overline{MEMRQ}$ signal through, to be combined with the $\overline{RD}$ strobe.

The second section of the decoder, if enabled, decodes address bits A13 and A12 to select one of the four EPROMs. The outputs of this decoder function as follows: $\overline{2Y0}$ for memory addresses 0000H through 0FFFH, $\overline{2Y1}$ for memory addresses 1000H through 1FFFH, $\overline{2Y2}$ for memory addresses 2000H through 2FFFH, and $\overline{2Y3}$ for memory addresses 3000H through 3FFFH. In this example, the decoding scheme reduces the access time by about 44 ns, which is the time required for the address to propagate (1) through the top portion of the decoder, (2) down through the strap, and (3) through the bottom section of the decoder.

Once the appropriate EPROM is selected by the decoder, the microprocessor issues a $\overline{RD}$ signal so that the data can be read from the memory without a bus conflict. The $\overline{RD}$ signal is gated through to the $\overline{OE}$ connection on each EPROM and also to the active low gate input of the data bus buffer (74LS244). If the board is enabled by the proper or selected range of addresses, data are applied to the data bus by the data bus buffers.

This particular board has been implemented with a minimal number of integrated circuits to make maintenance easier and to increase the reliability of the board. Some important portions of this board do not appear in the schematic diagram and are worth mentioning at this point.

Power supply inputs and decoupling are not shown but are extremely critical to the proper operation of this board. A general rule of thumb to follow when decoupling ICs from the power supply is that each totem pole output requires about 2000 pF of capacitance for proper operation. The capacitors are required since totem pole outputs generate noise at the power supply connections that can be coupled into another device in the system. It is also important not to lump this capacitance together at one point. It should be distributed about the board in smaller 0.1- or 0.01-μF capacitors.

5–5 DYNAMIC MEMORY SYSTEMS

Dynamic memory is normally used whenever the amount of RAM required for the system is 16K bytes or larger. The main disadvantage of dynamic memory is that it must be periodically refreshed or rewritten since it can retain stored data for only a few milliseconds.

Refreshing is typically accomplished by either the microprocessor, through some internal hardware (as in the Zilog Z80), or through an external dynamic RAM controller. *Pseudo static RAM* devices, or PSRAM, are now becoming available with most of the refreshing logic built into the memory device. Until they become commonly available, it will be the circuit designer's responsibility to connect the dynamic devices up to large systems. This section will focus on the standard dynamic RAM.

64K-Bit Dynamic RAM
The 4564, illustrated in figure 5–2, is a typical dynamic RAM used in many newer applications. This device is organized as a 64K-by-1-bit memory device; therefore, eight such devices are required to develop a 64K-byte DRAM memory.

Several problems arise when attempting to use one of these devices. With most DRAMs an address multiplexer must be incorporated into the system to provide the address at the proper time. Since refreshing must be accomplished for all memory locations, a refresh counter may be required. Also, an external refresh logic circuit must be provided to accomplish refresh timing for the DRAM.

The Address Multiplexer

The address can be multiplexed using two 74157-quad 2-to-1 line multiplexers, as illustrated in figure 5–23. In this circuit the least significant portion of the memory address is presented to the DRAM until $\overline{RAS}$ goes high, when the most significant portion of the address is presented. This occurs because the S input to the 74157 selects the B inputs when it becomes a logic one and the A inputs when it becomes a logic zero.

The output pins on the multiplexer are connected to the memory address pins of the 4564 through 33-Ω resistors that dampen the amount of negative undershoot on these pins. If only one of a set of eight MK4564s is in use, these resistors are optional.

The Refresh Counter

The refresh counter can be a discrete counter located in the microprocessor, as in the Z80 microprocessor; in a DRAM controller; or built into the memory, as with the PSRAM. The counter for this type of DRAM must be a 7-bit binary counter. The internal structure of the DRAM requires 128 refresh cycles because it is organized with 128 rows of memory and each row must be refreshed during a read or a write. The counter, located on the

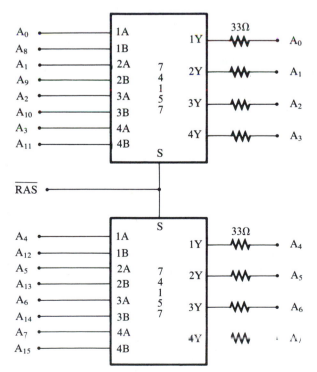

FIGURE 5–23 A circuit used to multiplex the address inputs to a dynamic RAM.

circuit board with the 4564, will most likely be used in a system employing this type of DRAM. The counter is connected to the DRAM during a refresh cycle and incremented at the end of the refresh period.

Control Signal Timing

The external logic required to operate the DRAM must contain some form of time delay to generate the $\overline{\text{CAS}}$ signal from the $\overline{\text{RAS}}$ signal. This can be accomplished by using a TTL delay line or by developing an external timing circuit. The delay line technique may or may not be used, since it is a fairly expensive piece of hardware.

Hidden Refresh

Since most microprocessors require more time to fetch and decode an op-code than to read from memory, this is the ideal time to refresh a dynamic memory. In some cases there is actually enough time for refreshing after a read or a write. This type of refresh is called a *hidden refresh* because it takes no additional time from the microprocessor to accomplish it. Another method of refreshing memory requires that the READY input to the micro-processor be controlled to cause a WAIT state, during which time the external circuit refreshes the memory. This text will discuss and develop the hidden refresh technique because of its efficiency and wide application.

Dynamic RAM Timing

Figure 5–24 illustrates the timing for the 4564 dynamic RAM. The row address is applied to the address connections by the $\overline{\text{RAS}}$, or row address strobe, signal. This strobe enters the row address into an internal latch, where it is held during a memory cycle. After tRCD time, which is quite critical, from a 30 ns minimum to a 65 ns maximum, the column address and the $\overline{\text{CAS}}$ (column address strobe) must be applied. This strobe sends the column address into an internal register where it is also held for the current memory cycle. $\overline{\text{CAS}}$ performs one other important task: it causes the memory device to begin to access data.

If the read signal is applied during the current cycle, the contents of the selected location appear at the output pin within 150 ns after the $\overline{\text{RAS}}$ input becomes a logic zero. The data at the output pin remain valid and stable until the $\overline{\text{CAS}}$ pin returns to a logic one. The time required for the output buffer to return to its high-impedance state is 40 ns from the trailing edge of the $\overline{\text{CAS}}$ signal.

The main difference between a read cycle and a write cycle is the level of the write input. This input must be placed low before $\overline{\text{CAS}}$ goes high and must remain low for at least 45 ns before $\overline{\text{CAS}}$ goes high to cause a memory write.

A refresh cycle may be accomplished at any time after a read or a write. The cycle itself is accomplished by placing a logic zero on the $\overline{\text{RAS}}$ pin of this dynamic memory. This refresh pulse must be at least 150 ns in width and must not occur until $\overline{\text{RAS}}$ has been high for at least 100 ns.

One other timing requirement is that the refresh pulse must return to a logic one at least 100 ns before $\overline{\text{RAS}}$ again becomes a logic zero. As you can see, refresh timing is critical; it will be discussed further in the next section.

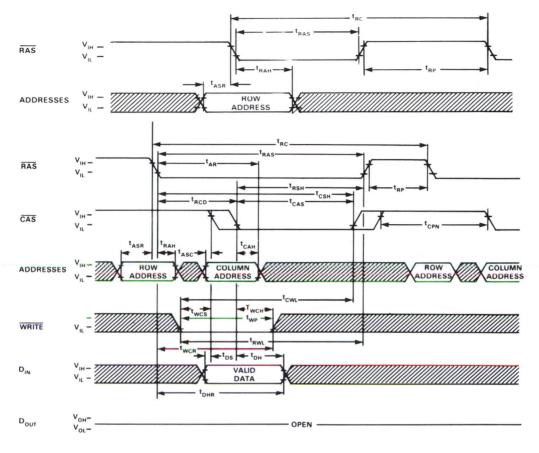

READ CYCLE

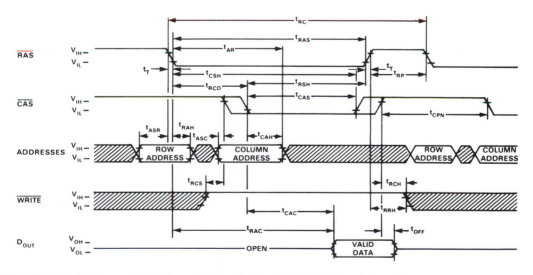

FIGURE 5–24 Timing and AC characteristics for the MK4564 64K × 1 dynamic RAM.
SOURCE: Courtesy of MOSTEK, Inc.

1. All voltages referenced to V_{SS}.
2. I_{CC} is dependent on output loading and cycle rates. Specified values are obtained with the output open. Only one MK4564 is active.
3. An initial pause of 500 μs is required after power-up followed by any 8 $\overline{RAS}$ cycles before proper device operation is achieved. Note that $\overline{RAS}$ may be cycled during the initial pause.
4. AC characteristics assume t_T = 5 ns.
5. V_{IH} min. and V_{IL} max. are reference levels for measuring timing of input signals. Transition times are measured between V_{IH} and V_{IL}.
6. The minimum specifications are used only to indicate cycle time at which proper operation over the full temperature range ($0°C \leq T_A \leq 70°C$) is assured.
7. Load = 2 TTL loads and 50 pF.
8. Assumes that $t_{RCD} \leq t_{RCD}$ (max). If t_{RCD} is greater than the maximum recommended value shown in this table, t_{RAC} will increase by the amount that t_{RCD} exceeds the value shown.
9. Assumes that $t_{RCD} \geq t_{RCD}$ (max).
10. t_{OFF} max defines the time at which the output achieves the open circuit condition and is not referenced to V_{OH} or V_{OL}.
11. Operation within the t_{RCD} (max) limit insures that t_{RAC} (max) can be met. t_{RCD} (max) is specified as a reference point only; if t_{RCD} is greater than the specified t_{RCD} (max) limit, then access time is controlled exclusively by t_{CAC}.
12. Either t_{RRH} or t_{RCH} must be satisfied for a read cycle.
13. These parameters are referenced to $\overline{CAS}$ leading edge in early write cycles and to $\overline{WRITE}$ leading edge in delayed write or read-modify-write cycles.
14. t_{WCS}, t_{CWD}, and t_{RWD} are restrictive operating parameters in READ/WRITE and READ/MODIFY/WRITE cycles only. If $t_{WCS} \geq t_{WCS}$ (min) the cycle is an EARLY WRITE cycle and the data output will remain open circuit throughout the entire cycle. If $t_{CWD} \geq t_{CWD}$ (min) and $t_{RWD} \geq t_{RWD}$ (min) the cycle is a READ/WRITE and the data output will contain data read from the selected cell. If neither of the above conditions are met the condition of the data out (at access time and until $\overline{CAS}$ goes back to V_{IH}) is indeterminate.
15. In addition to meeting the transition rate specification, all input signals must transmit between V_{IH} and V_{IL} (or between V_{IL} and V_{IH}) in a monotonic manner.
16. Effective capacitance calculated from the equation $C = I \frac{\Delta t}{\Delta V}$ with ΔV = 3 volts and power supply at nominal level.
17. $\overline{CAS}$ = V_{IH} to disable D_{OUT}.
18. Includes the DC level and all instantaneous signal excursions.
19. $\overline{WRITE}$ = don't care. Data out depends on the state of $\overline{CAS}$. If $\overline{CAS}$ = V_{IH}, data output is high impedance. If $\overline{CAS}$ = V_{IL}, the data output will contain data from the last valid read cycle.

ELECTRICAL CHARACTERISTICS AND RECOMMENDED AC OPERATING CONDITIONS
(3,4,5,15) ($0°C \leq T_A \leq 70°C$), V_{CC} = 5.0V $\pm$ 10%

| SYMBOL | | PARAMETER | MK4564-15 | | MK4564-20 | | MK4528-25 | | UNITS | NOTES |
STD	ALT		MIN	MAX	MIN	MAX	MIN	MAX		
t_{RELREL}	t_{RC}	Random read or write cycle time	260		345		425		ns	6,7
t_{RELREL} (RMW)	t_{RMW}	Read modify write cycle time	310		405		490		ns	6,7
t_{RELREL} (PC)	t_{PC}	Page mode cycle time	155		200		240		ns	6,7
t_{RELQV}	t_{RAC}	Access time from $\overline{RAS}$		150		200		250	ns	7,8
t_{CELQV}	t_{CAC}	Access time from $\overline{CAS}$		85		115		145	ns	7,9
t_{CEHQZ}	t_{OFF}	Output buffer turn-off delay	0	40	0	50	0	60	ns	10
t_T	t_T	Transition time (rise and fall)	3	50	3	50	3	50	ns	5,15
t_{REHREL}	t_{RP}	$\overline{RAS}$ precharge time	100		135		165		ns	
t_{RELREH}	t_{RAS}	$\overline{RAS}$ pulse width	150	10,000	200	10,000	250	10,000	ns	
t_{CELREH}	t_{RSH}	$\overline{RAS}$ hold time	85		115		145		ns	
t_{RELCEH}	t_{CSH}	$\overline{CAS}$ hold time	150		200		250		ns	
t_{CELCEH}	t_{CAS}	$\overline{CAS}$ pulse width	85	10,000	115	10,000	145	10,000	ns	
t_{RELCEL}	t_{RCD}	$\overline{RAS}$ to $\overline{CAS}$ delay time	30	65	35	85	45	105	ns	11
t_{REHWX}	t_{RRH}	Read command hold time referenced to $\overline{RAS}$	20		25		30		ns	12
t_{AVREL}	t_{ASR}	Row address set-up time	0		0		0		ns	
t_{RELAX}	t_{RAH}	Row address hold time	20		25		30		ns	
t_{AVCEL}	t_{ASC}	Column address set-up time	0		0		0		ns	
t_{CELAX}	t_{CAH}	Column address hold time	30		40		50		ns	
$t_{RELA(C)X}$	t_{AR}	Column address hold time referenced to $\overline{RAS}$	100		130		160		ns	

FIGURE 5-24 *continued*

ELECTRICAL CHARACTERISTICS AND RECOMMENDED AC OPERATING CONDITIONS (Continued)
(3,4,5,15) (0°C $\leq T_A \leq$ 70°C), V_{CC} = 5.0V $\pm$ 10%

SYMBOL			MK4564-15		MK4564-20		MK4528-25			
STD	ALT	PARAMETER	MIN	MAX	MIN	MAX	MIN	MAX	UNITS	NOTES
t_{WHCEL}	t_{RCS}	Read command set-up time	0		0		0		ns	
t_{CEHWX}	t_{RCH}	Read command hold time referenced to $\overline{CAS}$	0		0		0		ns	12
t_{CELWX}	t_{WCH}	Write command hold time	45		55		70		ns	
t_{RELWX}	t_{WCR}	Write command hold time referenced to $\overline{RAS}$	115		150		185		ns	
t_{WLWH}	t_{WP}	Write command pulse width	35		45		55		ns	
t_{WLREH}	t_{RWL}	Write command to $\overline{RAS}$ lead time	45		55		65		ns	
t_{WLCEH}	t_{CWL}	Write command to $\overline{CAS}$ lead time	45		55		65		ns	
t_{DVCEL}	t_{DS}	Data-in set-up time	0		0		0		ns	13
t_{CELDX}	t_{DH}	Data-in hold time	45		55		70		ns	13
t_{RELDX}	t_{DHR}	Data-in hold time referenced to $\overline{RAS}$	115		150		190		ns	
t_{CEHCEL} (PC)	t_{CP}	$\overline{CAS}$ precharge time (for page-mode cycle only)	60		75		85		ns	
t_{RVRV}	t_{REF}	Refresh Period		2		2		2	ms	
t_{WLCEL}	t_{WCS}	$\overline{WRITE}$ command set-up time	–10		–10		–10		ns	14
t_{CELWL}	t_{CWD}	$\overline{CAS}$ to $\overline{WRITE}$ delay	55		80		100		ns	14
t_{RELWL}	t_{RWD}	$\overline{RAS}$ to $\overline{WRITE}$ delay	120		165		205		ns	14
t_{CEHCEL}	t_{CPN}	$\overline{CAS}$ precharge time	30		35		45		ns	

AC ELECTRICAL CHARACTERISTICS
(0°C $\leq T_A \leq$ 70°C) (V_{CC} = 5.0V $\pm$ 10%)

SYM	PARAMETER	MAX	UNITS	NOTES
C_{I1}	Input Capacitance (A_0 - A_7), D_{IN}	10	pF	16
C_{I2}	Input Capacitance RAS, CAS	10	pF	16
C_{I3}	Input Capacitance $\overline{WRITE}$	20	pF	16
C_O	Output Capacitance (D_{OUT})	14	pF	16,17

FIGURE 5–24 *continued*

128K-Byte Dynamic Memory Interface

The circuit illustrated in figure 5–25 presents a typical 128K-byte dynamic memory system for use with the Intel 8088 microprocessor. The array itself contains sixteen 4564 DRAMS, for a total of 128K bytes of storage. The data in and data out pins are connected to a pair of 8216 bidirectional bus transceivers that interface the data connections to the 8088 data bus. The normal direction of data flow through these transceivers is into the memory array. The array drives the 8088 data bus only when the appropriate memory address is present with the $\overline{RD}$ or read signal.

The address bus is connected to a pair of 74157 multiplexers controlled by $\overline{RAS}$. RAS determines whether A0 through A7 or A8 through A15 are connected to the memory array through a second set of multiplexers. This second set selects a memory address or a refresh address from a 7-bit refresh counter. The refresh count is applied to the array during the refresh period, as controlled by the $\overline{RFSH}$ signal. At the end of a refresh period, the counter is incremented by the positive transition of the $\overline{RFSH}$ signal. The remaining four address connections are attached to the 74LS138 decoder, which enables the appropriate bank or segment of dynamic RAMs.

In the diagram, the decoder is hard-wired to select memory locations 00000H through 1FFFFH or the first 128K bytes of memory. Other connections are possible, allowing the user to select any area of the 1M-byte memory space.

The timing for this memory interface is developed in the circuit of figure 5–26. This circuit contains a crystal controlled clock that generates a 25-MHz clock pulse train that is applied to the clock input of the 74S163 binary synchronous counter. This counter is cleared to zero whenever the microprocessor requests a memory cycle.

Since the most significant two bits of the counter are connected to an OR gate, $\overline{RAS}$ is generated for four clocking periods after the memory request. This and the other signals generated by the timing circuit are illustrated in figure 5–27.

The falling edge of $\overline{RAS}$ causes the Q output of the JK flip-flop to become a logic one, in turn causing $\overline{CAS}$ to become a logic zero. The time between the falling edge of $\overline{RAS}$ and the falling edge of $\overline{CAS}$ is approximately 25–35 ns, which is well within specifications for this device. $\overline{CAS}$ is returned to a logic one at the end of the current memory cycle when the $\overline{RD}$ or $\overline{WR}$ pulse, which caused the cycle, returns to a logic one. This return is accomplished through the asynchronous $\overline{SET}$ input of the JK flip-flop.

The refresh ($\overline{RFSH}$) signal is generated when the counter's outputs are 10XX binary, about 140 ns after $\overline{RAS}$ returns to a logic one. When the counter reaches a count of 1100 binary, it stops counting and remains in this state until the next $\overline{RD}$ or $\overline{WR}$ arrives from the 8088.

Since a memory cycle occurs, at most, once every 800 ns, all timing requirements for refreshing, reading, and writing for this memory are easily met. The type of refreshing employed is called *hidden refresh,* since a refresh occurs with every read or write and does not require any extra time from the microprocessor.

There is only one problem that can arise with this type of refreshing. If the microprocessor is halted, no memory read or write cycle occurs and the information stored in the memory is lost. A halt instruction or a DMA of long duration can cause the loss of data. It is necessary to include a circuit to detect this condition if the program is halted by the microprocessor. Since the halt instruction is seldom used in practice, this type of circuitry is not included in the previous dynamic memory interface.

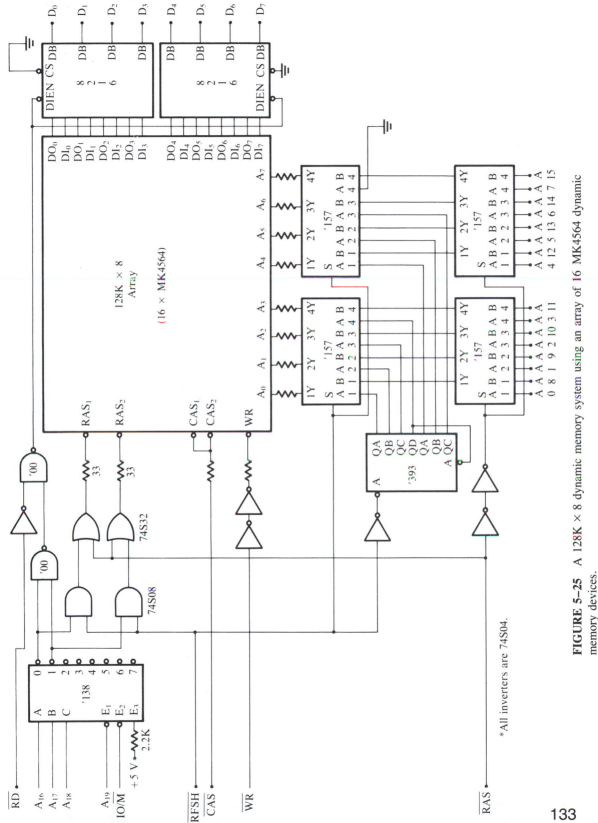

FIGURE 5–25 A 128K × 8 dynamic memory system using an array of 16 MK4564 dynamic memory devices.

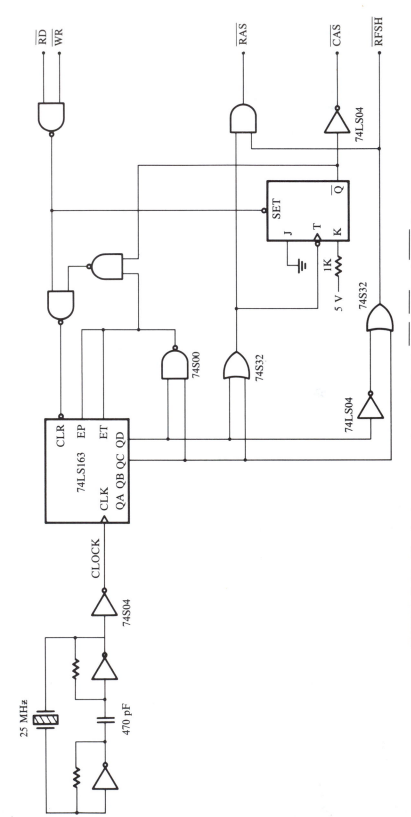

FIGURE 5–26 The circuit to generate the control signals $\overline{RAS}$, $\overline{CAS}$, and $\overline{RFSH}$ for the schematic of figure 5–25.

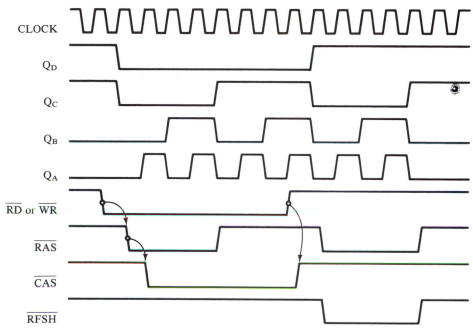

FIGURE 5–27   The signal timing diagram for the circuit of figure 5–26.

MEMORY TESTING 5–6

An important portion of system design and repair is the ability to test a memory component. Memory testing involves determining whether a memory device and/or the memory selection logic is functioning properly. Memory testing software is found in many cases today in the system program. Many systems perform a memory self-test every time that power is applied to the system. Self tests will normally test the RAM and the ROM in a system. The self-test software is stored at the very beginning of the system program at the microprocessor's reset location. In addition to the self-test program, maintenance software is often included to perform a more complex test of the memory. Most self-test software is often called *static* testing, whereas most maintenance test software is called *dynamic* testing.

ROM Self-Testing

How can a ROM be tested in a system? It is actually very simple. The ROM contains a known set of data that can be checked numerically either by adding or exclusively-ORing all of the bytes together and checking the result. The result is stored in one of the memory locations on the ROM for this purpose. This procedure will not catch every possible ROM failure, but it will catch a majority of them. Figure 5–28 illustrates the flowchart for a typical ROM self-test program. If an error is detected, the system program is aborted and some type of error indication is presented to the operator. In a system that includes a CRT terminal, a number may appear on the screen. If no visual display for the operator is

FIGURE 5–28 The flowchart for a ROM self-test subroutine.

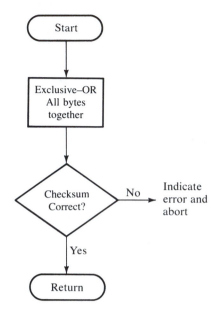

FIGURE 5–29 The flowchart for a functional RAM test subroutine.

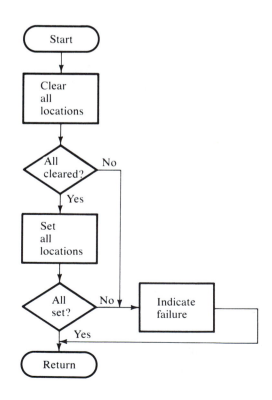

present, an error code can be displayed on a set of LED indicators for the repairperson. This code indicates that a ROM is faulty; in fact, it can indicate which ROM is faulty.

RAM Self-Testing

RAM self-testing in a system is not much more complicated than ROM testing. The only major difference is that the RAM doesn't have a known set of data when power is applied. The data are provided by the test routine.

One simple static test of the system RAM is to test whether or not each memory location is capable of storing ones and zeros. The test program can set all of the bits of the RAM and test them to see if they are actually set. If that checks, the program can then clear all of the bits and check to see if they cleared. If both tests are passed, chances are excellent that all of the RAM is good. A flowchart for a RAM test is provided in figure 5–29. It is important to set or clear all of the bits before checking. Sometimes a memory cell will remember the information for a few hundred microseconds, giving the memory time to forget, if it is faulty. As with the ROM, if the RAM fails the test, there is some type of indication for the operator or repairperson.

Fully Testing a RAM for Maintenance

In many cases the static testing described for self-testing RAMs finds the faulty component. It always finds the bad or burned-out memory cell. Other errors that occur in memory devices are not revealed by static testing. Sometimes internally generated noise changes the contents of a memory cell. This type of change can be detected only by the appropriate test sequence.

Dynamic testing most often consists of storing data into some of the memory locations. Once these data are stored, the software attempts to disrupt them by writing to other locations in the memory. If noise were to cause any of the original locations to change, the component might malfunction occasionally at some future time.

Checkerboard Testing

Another dynamic test is the *checkerboard test,* which stores alternate ones and zeros into each location in the memory. After this is accomplished, the program checks the memory to see if any change has occurred. The next step is to complement one location and test the rest. Next, complement the next location and test the rest. This procedure is repeated until every memory location is complemented and tested. At the end of this sequence, the program begins again, complementing the first location and testing the next. A flowchart for this type of dynamic test is illustrated by figure 5–30.

Memory Decoder Testing

In some cases the memory devices are functional but appear to be bad because of a decoder failure. Figure 5–31 shows a 74LS138 4-to-8 line decoder that is connected to a memory array. A flowchart for the test program is pictured in figure 5–32, along with the waveforms that are generated at the output pins of the decoder. These outputs can be checked on an oscilloscope or, more easily, tested with a digital logic probe. If the waveforms are present, the decoder is probably functioning properly and the memory indeed is bad.

FIGURE 5–30 The flowchart for a checkerboard RAM test.

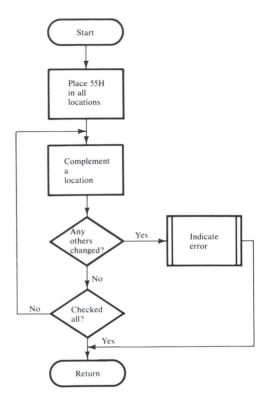

FIGURE 5–31 A decoder circuit that decodes 1K blocks of the memory address from 8000H through 9FFFH.

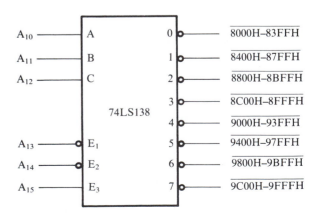

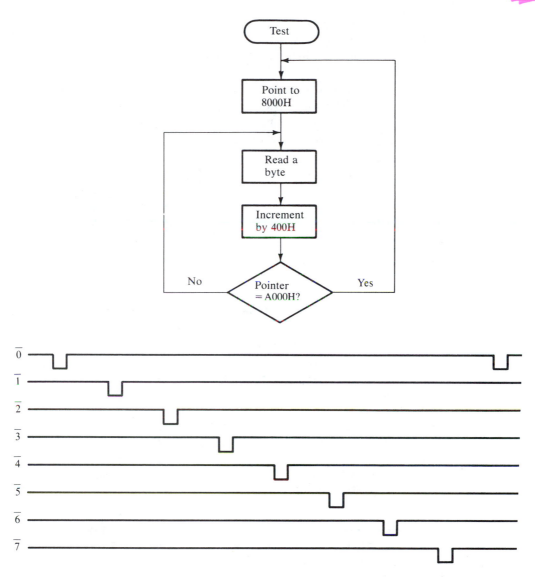

FIGURE 5–32 The flowchart of the test program and output waveforms for the decoder in figure 5–31.

Summary

1   Various types of read-only memory devices are available to the memory system
    designer. The ROM is a factory-programmed device, the PROM is field-
    programmable, the EPROM is field-programmable and erasable, and the
    EEPROM is programmable and erasable in the system.

2 Two types of RAM (read/write) memory devices are available: the SRAM (static RAM) which retains data for as long as power is applied, and the DRAM (dynamic RAM) which retains data for a few milliseconds before it must be refreshed.

3 The number of address connections on a memory device determines the number of locations contained within the device. The number of locations is determined by raising two to a power equal to the number of address pins.

4 Memory contains two types of data output connections: common I/O, which means that data flow into or out of these connections, or separate I/O, which means there is a separate pin for input data and separate pin for output data.

5 The most important timing specification for a memory device is its access time, which is the amount of time it takes the memory device to locate the data from the application of the memory address. In modern memory, this access time is equal to 450 ns or less.

6 The address decoder is a device that takes the memory address from the microprocessor and decodes a unique range of addresses that are used to select a memory device.

7 The 74LS138 3-to-8 line decoder is commonly used to decode memory address ranges because of the number of input connections on the device.

8 The PROM is often used to decode memory address ranges because it at times can replace more than one integrated decoder and it also allows the address ranges to be changed by simply replacing the PROM at a later date.

9 The memory map is a pictorial diagram of the memory that is used to develop the memory decoder circuitry.

10 Memory is completely decoded whenever the memory device exists at only the locations available on the device and incompletely decoded when the device exists in a larger area of memory. For example, if a $2K \times 8$ memory device is decoded in 2K of memory, it is completely decoded; if it exists in 4K of memory it is incompletely decoded.

11 A DRAM interface requires an address multiplexer because the DRAM memory component has multiplexed address inputs. For example, the MK4564 has eight address connections that are used to enter a 16-bit address into the memory device. In order to accomplish this, a multiplexer is used to select eight bits of the address at one time and another eight bits of the address at another.

12 The refresh counter is a binary counter that is used to keep track of the refresh address for DRAMs. If the DRAM contains 128 rows of memory to be refreshed, then the refresh counter is a 7-bit counter.

13 The $\overline{CAS}$ DRAM memory connection is used to strobe the column address into the memory and also used to select the memory device. The $\overline{RAS}$ input is used to strobe the row address into the memory and instigate a refresh of rows.

14 Timing for a DRAM memory interface is normally obtained from a high-frequency oscillator. The oscillator is used to develop the timing signals required to read, write, and refresh the DRAM.

Glossary

Access time   The time required for a memory component to produce the addressed information at its output pins.

Address decoder   A device that decodes the memory address presented on the address bus by the microprocessor to selected memory devices.

Common I/O   The same pin on a memory device is used to input and output data.

Completely specified   When memory devices populate the entire memory space and the decoder treats it accordingly, the memory is said to be completely specified.

Contiguous memory   A block of memory in which one location touches the next location without any gaps.

Dynamic memory testing   A memory test designed to cause errors to occur inside the memory device, if possible.

Dynamic RAM (DRAM)   A memory device that stores information for a brief period of time, usually only about 2 ms.

Hidden refresh   A technique in which a memory refresh requires none of the microprocessor's time. It is hidden within the op-code fetch in many cases.

Incompletely specified   A memory that will never be completely filled; some of the address bits are ignored by the address decoder.

Memory map   A drawing of the proposed structure of the memory system.

Nonvolatile   A memory device that is able to retain data whenever the power is removed from the system.

Refresh   The act of periodically rewriting information in a dynamic RAM.

Separate I/O   A data connection in which there is a separate pin for input data and a separate pin for output data.

Static memory testing   A memory-testing technique that checks each location for functionality.

Static RAM   A device that stores information as long as the power is applied to the system.

Volatile   A device that loses data whenever power is removed from the system.

Questions and Problems

1   List three commonly available types of read only memory.
2   Describe the difference between static and dynamic memory.
3   How many address pins would be found on a nonmultiplexed 16K-memory device?
4   Why do some memory devices have more than one chip enable or chip select input?
5   What is a bus contention or conflict?
6   Which connection present on most memory devices can be used to prevent a bus contention?

7 Describe the difference between common and separate I/O as it applies to memory.

8 Explain the term *memory access time*.

9 Why is the dynamic RAM so much more dense than the static RAM?

10 Why is an EEPROM called a *read mostly memory?*

11 Develop the circuitry required to select an EPROM for memory locations 3000H through 3FFFH.

12 Why aren't NAND gates normally used as decoders?

13 Find a better decoder than the 74LS138. At least *try* to find a better decoder.

14 What is meant by the term *contiguous memory?*

15 Develop a memory system using six 2716 EPROMs located in a contiguous block of memory from location 5000H through memory location 7FFFH.

16 Develop a memory system using two 2716 EPROMs and three 2732 EPROMs located in memory location 0000H through and including memory location 3FFFH.

17 Develop a memory system using four 2732 EPROMs for program storage at memory locations C000H through FFFFH and three 4016 RAMs at memory locations 0000H through 17FFH.

18 Develop a memory system that uses one 2716 EPROM and one 4016 RAM. Locate them anywhere you wish. (HINT: Use incompletely specified decoding.)

19 Develop a memory system that uses two 2716 EPROMs, three 2732 EPROMs, and one 4016 RAM. Locate them anywhere you wish.

20 Why is it important to minimize the number of integrated circuits used in a design?

21 Why is it important to bypass integrated circuits?

22 Why is a resistor connected in series with various pins in a dynamic memory interface?

23 What is the purpose of the $\overline{\text{RAS}}$ input on a dynamic RAM?

24 What is hidden refresh? Why would it be used in a memory system?

25 The decoder in the circuit of figure 5–25 could be used to select any bank of memory up to which memory location?

26 The 74S163 illustrated in figure 5–26 will count up to which binary count?

27 Once the counter of figure 5–26 has been cleared it cannot be cleared again until what occurs?

28 What problem may occur in the operation of the circuit in figure 5–25?

29 Develop a ROM test program from the flowchart of figure 5–28. This program must test a 2K-byte ROM, beginning at location zero. The checksum is stored at the last location of this ROM.

30 From the flowchart of figure 5–29 develop a program that will test a 1K-byte RAM residing at locations 1000H through 13FFH.

31 Develop the software required to test the decoders of figure 5–18.

6

Basic Input/Output Interface Circuitry

Upon completion of this chapter, you will be able to

1 Describe the operation of simple input and output devices such as switches and indicators.
2 Describe the interface between the microprocessor and the outside world.
3 Select an I/O device by decoding the memory mapped or isolated I/O port number.
4 Describe the operation of the 8155 and MC6821 peripheral interface adapters.
5 Interface the 8155 and the MC6821 to the microprocessor.
6 Develop the software required to initialize and program the 8155 and the MC6821.
7 Describe strobed operation of the peripheral interface adapter.

This chapter introduces the basic input/output interface circuitry found in most applications. As stated previously, I/O interfacing is a very important portion of microprocessor design. A complete understanding is critically important for success in this field.

Basic interface components, along with their connection to the microprocessor, are described in this chapter. These basics are then used as a foundation for learning more complex I/O systems in the next and subsequent chapters of this text.

6-1 SIMPLE INPUT/OUTPUT DEVICES

Simple input/output devices that are commonly found in most systems include switches, numeric displays, relays, and solenoids. Most of these are very easy to understand but may require some circuit detail for their proper interfacing. This section will cover all of these devices. Solenoids and relays will be covered again in other sections of this chapter, since they require some software and hardware to interface properly.

Switches

Almost all switches in use today are single pole, single throw toggle or push button switches. In the past, digital electronic circuitry used the single pole, double throw switch because of *contact bounce*. Contact bouncing (see figure 6-1) occurs in any mechanical switch and produces many connections or contacts when thrown. They bounce in the same way that a hammer bounces when dropped on a hard surface, and this can cause serious problems in most digital systems.

The circuits of figures 6-2(a) and 6-2(b) illustrate two different types of contact bounce eliminators. These circuits are required to debounce mechanical switch contacts if a microprocessor does not read the switches. Their major disadvantage is the type of switch required and the additional circuitry needed to debounce the switches.

Today the switch and accompanying resistor, pictured in figure 6-2(c), are all that are required to connect a switch to a microprocessor-based digital system. The contact bounce is handled by software inside the microprocessor. In certain instances the pullup resistor may actually be incorporated inside the microprocessor interface circuit.

LED Displays

The display devices in common use today vary considerably from those of the past. One of the most common is the simple light-emitting diode, or *LED*. Figure 6-3 illustrates a typical digital-to-LED interface. Notice that a standard TTL component drives the LED. Most single LEDs require approximately 10 mA of current flow to be illuminated at full brilliance. Since the forward voltage drop across an LED is approximately 1.65 V, the value of the current limiting resistor would be 330 Ω in this example.

FIGURE 6-1 Contact bounce occurs when a switch is closed and may also occur when it is opened.

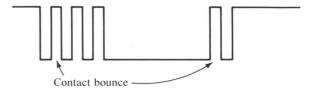

Contact bounce

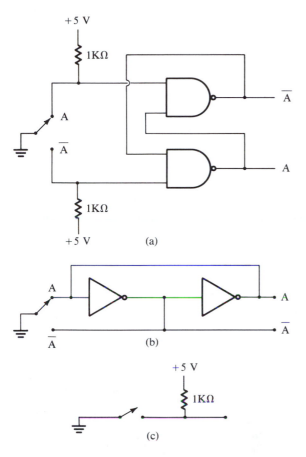

(a)

(b)

(c)

FIGURE 6–2 Switch interface circuitry: (a) a SPDT switch connected to a NAND gate contact bounce eliminator, (b) a SPDT switch connected to an inverter contact bounce eliminator, (c) a SPST switch setup to be connected to a microprocessor based system with software contact bounce elimination.

A standard TTL component is used instead of a low-power Schottky TTL device because the low-power Schottky device is not capable of sinking the required amount of current. The standard TTL gate can safely sink 16 mA of current; the low-power Schottky TTL device can sink only 4 mA of current. Whenever any digital circuit is to be interfaced to an LED, make sure that it will be capable of sinking enough drive current. The logic 1 output from a gate will supply only 400 μA of current, so never use this logic level.

Figure 6–4 illustrates a common anode seven-segment LED display whose internal

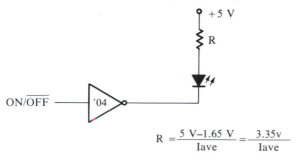

$$R = \frac{5 \text{ V} - 1.65 \text{ V}}{\text{Iave}} = \frac{3.35 \text{v}}{\text{Iave}}$$

FIGURE 6–3 A single light emitting diode (LED) connected to an inverter driver.

FIGURE 6–4 A seven-segment
common anode LED display.

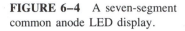

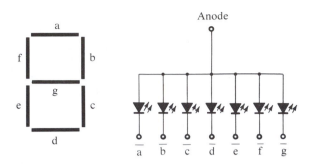

structure is nothing more than a single LED for each of the lettered segments. Drivers for
this device can be the same as those indicated in figure 6–3. In many cases displays are
multiplexed and may require much more current. In such cases, you are most likely to find
high-current drivers such as transistors or Darlington pairs used in place of the TTL logic
gate drivers.

Fluorescent Displays

Fluorescent display devices, such as the one pictured in figure 6–5, have become more
popular in recent years because they have a higher intensity than the seven-segment LED
displays and can be filtered to a wider variety of colors. The only disadvantages of the
fluorescent display (in comparison to the LED display) are its requirements for a filament
voltage, a negative grid voltage, and a drive voltage of 15–30 V, and its much shorter life
span. This type of display emits a blue-green light instead of the characteristic red light
emitted by most LEDs.

The fluorescent display is operated by applying a 15–30 V signal to each anode that is
to be illuminated. At the same time, the grid voltage must be changed from a negative
voltage to a slightly positive voltage. This procedure causes the tube to begin conduction,
and the electrons that strike the anode excite it into producing light.

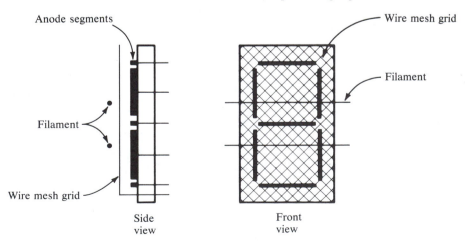

FIGURE 6–5 A seven-segment fluorescent display tube.

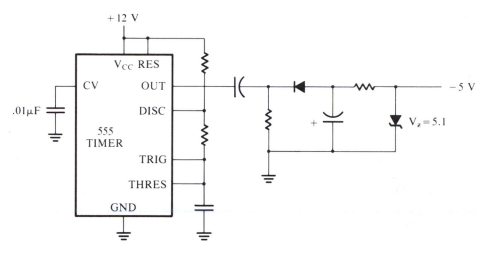

FIGURE 6–6 A charge pump and oscillator that can provide a low current negative supply voltage.

The Negative Grid Supply

Since the fluorescent display device requires a negative grid supply voltage to turn a segment on and off, the interface circuit must contain a negative power supply. When one is available, this presents no problem in the design of the display; when it is not, it can involve additional cost. To minimize the added cost, a charge pump can supply this negative voltage.

A *charge pump,* as illustrated in figure 6–6, is an oscillator followed by a differentiator, which produces positive and negative pulses. The negative pulses can be rectified and regulated to produce a negative DC voltage. In most cases the amount of current available from this type of supply is small. For this application the grid current is very small, making it an ideal candidate for a charge pump.

Anode Switch

Figure 6–7 illustrates a typical anode driver for a fluorescent display. This driver happens to be a PNP transistor that has been made TTL-compatible with an NPN transistor. A

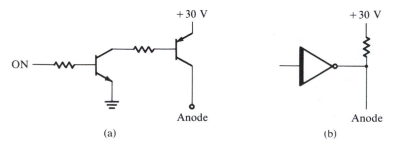

FIGURE 6–7 (a) An anode driver using discrete transistor logic, (b) an anode driver using a high-voltage open collector TTL inverter and a current-limiting resistor.

logic one applied to the base of the NPN transistor causes it to saturate. This in turn causes base current to flow in the PNP transistor, which also saturates. The 30 V applied by the PNP transistor to the anode cause the segment to light.

Liquid Crystal Displays

The last type of display device to be discussed is the liquid crystal display, or LCD. This type of device is more common in calculators and digital watches than in other areas because it is commonly available in only these formats. It has the advantage of being highly visible in bright light where other devices are extremely difficult to see. It also uses an extremely low amount of power, which makes it ideal for most applications.

This type of display is by far the hardest to use, since it requires AC excitation voltages rather than DC excitation voltages. These AC voltages must be between 30 Hz and 1000 Hz and are normally TTL logic levels. Figure 6–8 depicts the internal structure of the LCD and the required excitation waveforms. The electrostatic field developed between the electrodes aligns the liquid crystal molecules, which allow light to pass through the material to the mirror below. Since the mirror is exposed to light, it reflects more light than the surrounding area and appears to light up. This type of display is a *reflective LCD*.

Another type of LCD, the *absorption* type, absorbs light when a voltage is placed across its electrodes. A piece of black paper behind it absorbs most of the light, so it appears to darken. This type is most often found in digital watches and other consumer products.

Relays and Solenoids

The last types of simple input/output devices to be discussed are the relay and solenoid. Relays are used primarily to switch many different voltages at one time or to switch very high voltages. Applications for solenoids include moving mechanical devices such as printing characters on printers.

Figure 6–9 shows how a typical solenoid or relay is interfaced to a digital system. In most cases the Darlington pair illustrated is prepackaged in one three-terminal transistor-like device. Notice that the circuit requires very few components to implement, since in most cases the Darlington pair has sufficient gain to allow a direct TTL connection to its input. If not, an external pullup or helper resistor can provide increased bias current sufficient to activate the device. This resistor can allow a current flow of up to I_{SINK} of the TTL device.

6–2 THE INTERFACE POINT

What is the *interface point?* It is the point at which a TTL-compatible input or output device releases or accepts data. An input device releases data to the microprocessor, and an output device accepts data from the microprocessor. All input and output devices require the same basic interface circuitry.

The Basic Input Interface

Most microprocessors accept data from an input device through the data bus connections and therefore require some form of switch to connect this data to the bus at the appropriate

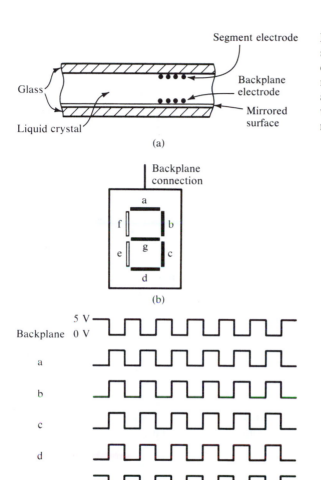

Segment electrode
Backplane electrode
Mirrored surface
Glass
Liquid crystal

(a)

Backplane connection

(b)

5 V
Backplane 0 V

a

b

c

d

e

f

g

(c)

FIGURE 6–8 (a) The internal structure of a reflective liquid crystal display (LCD), (b) the segment and backplane connections of an LCD, (c) the TTL-compatible waveforms required to display the number three.

time. The most effective digital switch available is the three-state buffer. Figure 6–10 illustrates a set of eight buffers, the 74LS244 octal buffer, connected to an 8-bit TTL-compatible input device. Examples of TTL-compatible input devices are binary switches, the output of an analog-to-digital converter, and many other types of peripheral interface components.

The decoder selects the device by producing a logic zero at its output, which enables (turns on) the three-state buffers. In most microprocessors, this strobe is normally active for about 300–1000 ns.

Once enabled, these buffers connect the data from the input device to the microproces-

FIGURE 6–9 A DC solenoid
and its Darlington pair driver.

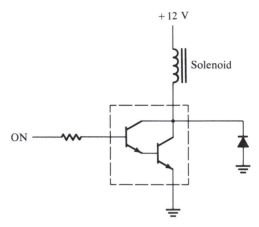

sor's data bus for processing. The device decoder, as discussed in the next section, indicates that the microprocessor has executed an input instruction.

All input devices must either use this circuit or have a similar circuit built into them. In many cases the decoder is an external circuit and the three-state buffers are internal to the I/O circuit.

The Basic Output Interface

Whenever data are sent out of the microprocessor to an external output device, they appear on the data bus for only a brief period of time. It is during this window that the external device must capture the information. In almost all instances, the external output device uses some form of latch to grab onto and hold the data bus information.

Figure 6–11 illustrates a typical output interface circuit. A device decoder generates a strobe pulse that provides a clock pulse for the 74LS374 octal latch in this circuit. For

FIGURE 6–10 A typical TTL-compatible input interface circuit illustrating the three-state bus buffers that drive the microprocessor bus.

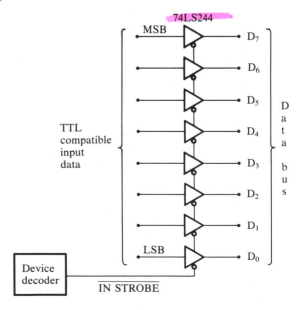

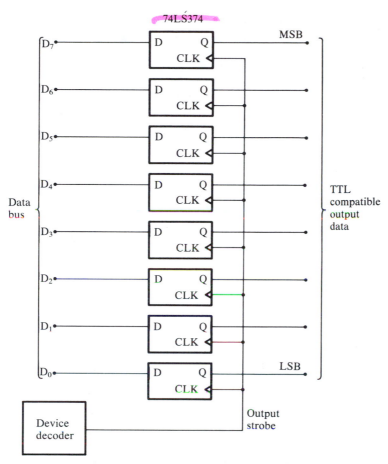

FIGURE 6-11 A typical TTL-compatible output interface illustrating the data latches required to capture the data bus information for the external circuitry.

more complete details on this timing, refer to the section on *memory write* in chapters 3 and 4. Additional information on this strobe is provided in the next section. Information from the data bus, which has been applied to the D inputs of the latch, is held for the external TTL-compatible device. Notice that the clock pulse input is a positive edge triggered input to the latch.

In most microprocessors, information is available to the external device for only a microsecond or less without the external latch. Suppose you were required to display a binary number on eight LEDs. If the latch were not present, the information might flash on the displays for a microsecond, hardly enough time to observe the number. As you can imagine, without this latch few devices can be effectively connected to the processor.

As with the input circuitry, the decoder is usually a separate circuit and the latches are often built into the external device. In fact, it is difficult to find a microprocessor peripheral component that doesn't contain a latch for the output data. Some devices contain a latch for the input data, as well.

6–3 INPUT/OUTPUT DEVICE SELECTION

Memory mapped I/O and isolated I/O are the two basic input/output schemes in use today. Memory mapped I/O treats the input/output device as if it were a location in the memory. Isolated I/O treats it separately from the memory. Both schemes are usable in most applications, since it is rare that the entire memory is used for program and data storage. Intel and Zilog microprocessors use either isolated I/O or memory mapped I/O; Motorola microprocessors can only use memory mapped I/O.

The Memory Mapped I/O Decoder

Suppose that eight different I/O devices are required for a particular application, and the memory mapped I/O technique is to be employed. Since we have decided to use this scheme, we must first set aside a portion of memory for the input/output devices. Figure 6–12 illustrates the proposed memory and input/output maps for this system. Maps are a useful method of looking at a memory and I/O structure before the appropriate decoders are designed.

Memory locations CF00H through CFFFH, a page in the memory, are employed for the input/output area. You may argue that this is a lot of memory for eight input/output devices, unless you consider the entire memory. Only a very small portion of the available memory is used for I/O. We typically do this to reduce the number of address bits that must be decoded to produce the device selection strobes.

$$\text{1100 \quad 1111 \quad 0000 \quad 0000 \quad or \quad CF00H}$$
$$\text{to}$$
$$\text{1100 \quad 1111 \quad 1111 \quad 1111 \quad or \quad CFFFH}$$

After examining this I/O address range, it is apparent that CFXXH, which is common to all of the I/O devices, is the bit pattern that must be decoded.

An eight-input NAND gate would most likely be used to decode this address range and develop the page selection strobe ($\overline{\text{PAGE CF}}$). This strobe would enable a decoder to

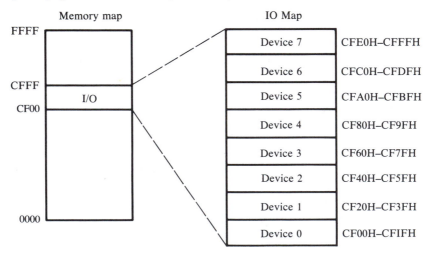

FIGURE 6–12   An example memory and I/O map for memory mapped I/O page CFXX.

select one of the eight different I/O devices. The page selection logic and the page decoder appear in figure 6–13.

The most significant eight address connections are decoded to produce the page selection strobe, but we still have eight address bits to decode to select the eight different I/O devices. A 3-to-8 line decoder develops the device strobes because we plan to connect only eight devices in this region of memory.

Five of the eight remaining address bits can be ignored, since they are not needed to produce the strobes. It is decided to use A7, A6, and A5 for the decoder inputs; but any of the remaining eight address bits can be used for this purpose.

Each location that is decoded overlays 32 different I/O device addresses. Ouput zero of the decoder is active for locations CF00H through CF1FH or for 32 different addresses. As with memory, this presents no problem since the program can be written to use only one of these locations. The same is true about the remaining seven outputs.

Isolated I/O Decoder

Figure 6-14 depicts the memory and input/output maps for a microprocessor capable of using isolated I/O. With this technique, the entire memory is always available for the system. The I/O map can be viewed as a miniature memory for the purpose of I/O device selection and control.

In this example, the input/output devices exist at I/O port locations 80H through 9FH. This arrangement leaves a large space in the I/O map for other input/output devices that may also be included in the system at a later time.

The I/O port or device number appears on a microprocessor that uses isolated I/O on the address bus in the same manner that a memory address appears. The only difference is that the port number, an 8-bit number, appears twice on the 8085A address bus. Example 6–1 shows the binary bit pattern present on the address bus for I/O port number 7AH.

EXAMPLE 6–1 $\boxed{0111 \quad 1010 \quad 0111 \quad 1010 = \text{7A7AH}}$

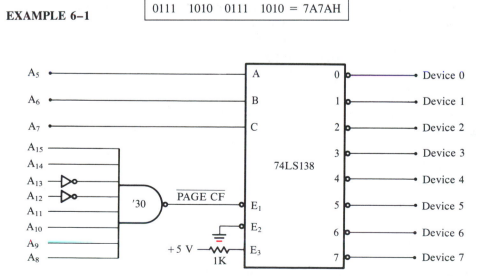

FIGURE 6–13 The memory mapped I/O port decoder for the map illustrated in figure 6–12.

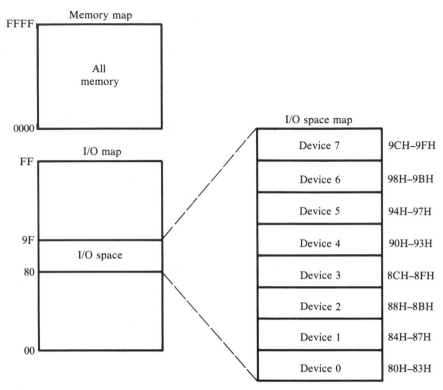

FIGURE 6–14   An example memory map and I/O map for an isolated I/O system.

The circuit in figure 6–15 illustrates the way port numbers 80H through 9FH can be decoded. In this example the most significant half of the address bus enables the 3-to-8 line decoder. The most significant half is normally used with the 8085A because it is not multiplexed. The Z80 has its port number appear on the least significant part of the address bus. If this processor is to be interfaced, you must use that half of the address bus. The 8086 and 8088 use a 16-bit port number, which appears on the least significant 16 address bus connections.

FIGURE 6–15   The isolated I/O port decoder for the I/O map illustrated in figure 6–14.

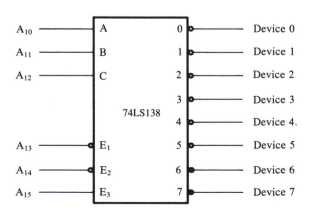

Once the decoder is enabled, its outputs become active as dictated by address connections A12, A11, and A10. The choice of these address connections is arbitrary; other connections could be selected.

Output zero becomes a logic zero for the instructions IN 80H through an IN 83H or for an OUT 80H through an OUT 83H. These I/O port locations overlay four different port addresses. This procedure, of course, presents no problem in almost all systems since the program is written for only one location.

A Comparison of Isolated and Memory-Mapped I/O Decoders

Comparing the circuits of figures 6–13 and 6–15, we notice that both decoders appear to be decoding a memory address. This is true; without completing the timing required to accomplish either memory-mapped or isolated I/O, this is all they accomplish. These circuits develop signals that can be used only to select an input/output device; they do not generate the strobes required to transfer any of the data.

Memory-Mapped I/O Strobe Generation

Figure 6–16 illustrates a circuit that generates eight different memory-mapped I/O input strobes. If you compare this circuit with the circuit of figure 6–13, you see two changes: the page select strobe is changed to page D4H and the $\overline{\text{MEMR}}$ (memory read) signal is attached to an enable input. This decoder will now function only for a memory read from page D4H. It also develops one of the eight different input strobe signals for this page of I/O. Each of the input strobes becomes a logic zero for a period of time equal to the $\overline{\text{MEMR}}$ signal, and this is when the processor expects to receive information from the external device.

If output strobes are required in a system, the circuit of figure 6–16 can be modified to produce them by replacing the $\overline{\text{MEMR}}$ signal with the $\overline{\text{MEMW}}$ signal. This change en-

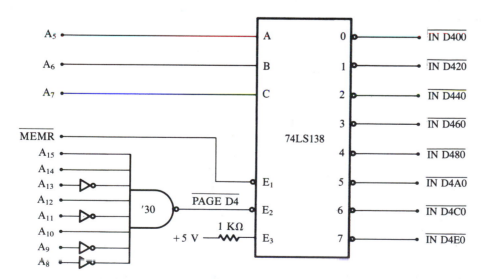

FIGURE 6–16 A circuit that will develop eight different memory mapped I/O strobes. These signals will only go low for a read from the indicated ranges of memory.

ables the decoder for a memory write into the selected page. At this time the microprocessor has data available for the external device.

Isolated I/O Strobe Generation

The circuit in figure 6–17 shows how a decoder can be used in an isolated I/O scheme to generate both input and output strobes. The decoder in this circuit is enabled only for I/O port numbers 00H through 3FH and only at the time of an I/O read or an I/O write. Once enabled, input C selects outputs 0 through 3 for an input instruction and outputs 4 through 7 for an output instruction. This circuit will generate four input strobes and four output strobes.

After examining both I/O schemes, it appears that the amount of circuitry required to implement isolated I/O is much less than with memory-mapped I/O. Whether or not isolated I/O is used depends on the microprocessor, the type of hardware control software needed in a system, and the circuit designer's preference.

6–4 THE PERIPHERAL INTERFACE ADAPTER (PIA)

A peripheral interface adapter contains two or three parallel I/O ports or locations that can be programmed to handle input or output data. Some of these adapters also contain either RAM or ROM memory. Still others contain a timer or programmable modulus counter that can generate a variety of different signals. The timer is also used to count external events in some applications.

These devices allow almost any TTL-compatible input or output device to be interfaced to the microprocessor. They contain the basic input and output circuitry discussed previously in this chapter. In addition to the basic I/O circuitry, PIAs contain a handshaking or synchronization mechanism that is typically used with asynchronous external I/O devices to synchronize them with the microprocessor.

This section will discuss two different types of PIAs: one contains I/O ports, memory,

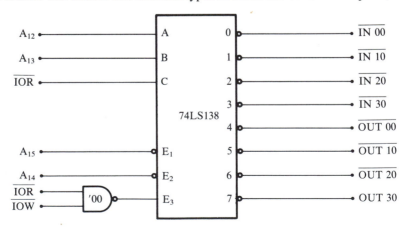

FIGURE 6–17 A circuit that will generate four isolated I/O output strobes and four isolated I/O input strobes.

and a timer; the other contains I/O ports alone. The 8155 is discussed because of its ease in interfacing to a multiplexed bus microprocessor, and the MC6821 because of its wide application with the MC6800. Granted, there are many other PIA components on the market today, but these two devices are representative of all of them.

A Typical Port Pin Connection

Figure 6–18 illustrates the typical circuit for a bidirectional parallel port pin. Bidirectional port pins are programmable as inputs or outputs, or, if the application requires it, they can be used as truly bidirectional I/O lines.

The RD port and WR port signals are developed by the internal control logic of the adapter. These signals become active only when the device is enabled and the correct I/O address is present to select this particular bit of the port.

The $\overline{OUT}$ and $\overline{IN}$ signals are also developed internally and are used to program the port pin as either an input or an output. If the port pin is programmed as an output, $\overline{OUT}$ is a logic zero and $\overline{IN}$ is a logic one. In this mode, the signal from the three-state buffer, which is connected to the Q output of the flip-flop, is passed through to the port pin. The data are held in an internal latch for this port pin and remain there until new information is outputted to the pin.

In the input mode, $\overline{OUT}$ is a logic one and $\overline{IN}$ is a logic zero. This causes the buffer, which has been connected to the flip-flop, to be disabled and allows the RD port signal to pass through to the other three-state buffer. So whenever data are read from this port pin, the RD port strobe goes high, causing the control input to the buffer to become zero when reading the port pin. Once the data are read, it is often held in an internal latch for the microprocessor.

The 8155 Combination I/O, RAM, and Timer

Peripheral interface adapters are available for multiplexed data buses or standard nonmultiplexed data buses. The multiplexed bus version is normally set up to work with isolated I/O, and the nonmultiplexed version works with either isolated or memory-mapped I/O.

The 8155, which is designed to work with isolated I/O and a multiplexed address/data bus, is illustrated in figure 6–19. The 8155 contains two 8-bit bidirectional I/O ports, one 6-bit multipurpose I/O port, 256 bytes of RAM, and a 14-bit programmable modulus counter or timer. The timer is capable of producing either a square wave or a pulse at its output.

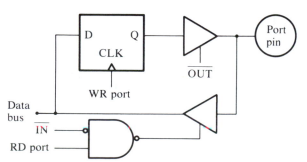

FIGURE 6–18 A typical internal representation of a programmable bidirectional PIA port pin connection.

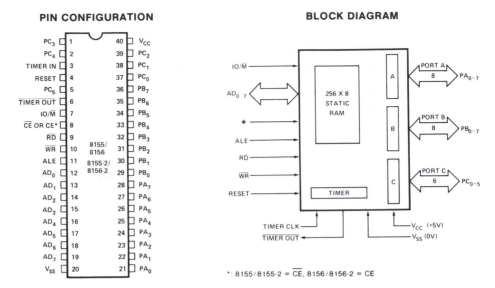

FIGURE 6–19   The block diagram and pinout of the 8155/8156 combination RAM, I/O, and timer integrated circuit.

SOURCE: Reprinted by permission of Intel Corporation, Copyright 1983.

8155 Selection

Devices are selected through the active low $\overline{CE}$ input of the 8155, which controls both the I/O and memory selection. If an active high CE is required, the 8156 can be used, since it is identical to the 8155 except in the logic level of the selection input. The selection of I/O or memory is controlled by the IO/$\overline{M}$ control signal present on some of the microprocessors designed for isolated I/O. Since both the I/O space and the memory space are enabled by $\overline{CE}$, much of the following text will discuss device selection.

Table 6–1 indicates the internal I/O ports or I/O addresses for the 8155. This device contains six different usable I/O port addresses. The most significant five bits of the port address are don't cares and enable the device through an external decoder. These don't

TABLE 6–1   8155 I/O port assignments.

A15	A14	A13	A12	Port Address A11 or	A10	A9	A8	
A7	A6	A5	A4	A3	A2	A1	A0	Selected Device
X	X	X	X	X	0	0	0	Command/Status
X	X	X	X	X	0	0	1	Port A
X	X	X	X	X	0	1	0	Port B
X	X	X	X	X	0	1	1	Port C
X	X	X	X	X	1	0	0	LSB of timer
X	X	X	X	X	1	0	1	MSB of timer

cares are often fixed at some logic level by the external decoder. The external decoder generates the $\overline{CE}$ signal for the 8155 by decoding these five address bits.

A simple decoder is connected to the $\overline{CE}$ input in the circuit of figure 6–20. This decoder has fixed both the I/O port addresses and the addresses of the internal memory. The internal memory overlays memory addresses A000H through BFFFH because the decoder enables the 8155 for any memory operation whose address begins with a 101 binary. The IO/$\overline{M}$ signal, which controls the selection of I/O or memory, is at a logic zero level to generate a memory reference, so the internal memory is activated whenever an address occurs with this bit pattern. Since there are only 256 bytes of RAM, the actual range of addresses may be A000H through A0FFH or any one of 32 possible ranges. The choice of the actual address range depends on the system and preoption of the system designer.

$$\text{MEMORY} = \text{101X XXXX XXXX XXXX} = \text{A000H to BFFFH}$$
$$\text{I/O} = \text{101X XXXX} = \text{A0H to BFH}$$

The I/O overlays I/O addresses A0H through BFH. Any time that the first three bits of the address bus contain a 101 binary, the decoder's output activates the 8155. If, at the same time, the IO/$\overline{M}$ signal is a logic one, an I/O device is activated. Notice that the I/O and the memory address spaces are not independent of each other with this integrated circuit. Because of this, exercise care in planning the I/O port numbers and the memory addresses.

The I/O addresses also overlay a large portion of the I/O address space, and the actual values may be A0H through A5H, A8H through ADH, B0H through B5H, or B8H through BDH. Again, the choice of the actual I/O port numbers is the preoption of the system designer.

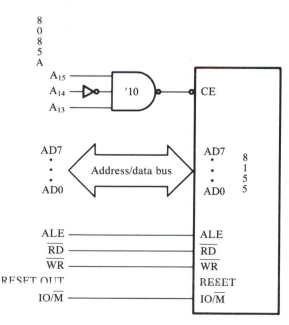

FIGURE 6–20 An example decoder and interconnection diagram from the 8155 to the 8085A microprocessor.

8155 Command Register

The 8155 is a programmable I/O device that must be programmed for normal operation so that the I/O pins can be controlled and the timer can be set with a count and started if needed. The command register, which accomplishes the programming, is the internal register that directs the operation of the 8155. Bits 7 and 6 of the command register, as illustrated in table 6–2, program the operation of the internal timer; bits 5 and 4 control the interrupts; bits 3 and 2 control the operation of port C; and bits 1 and 0 control the operation of ports B and A.

Port C can be programmed to operate in two alternate modes that will be discussed later in this section. Once the correct bit pattern for the command register is determined, it is loaded into the accumulator and sent out to the command register with an OUT instruction. Programming the command register normally occurs at the system reset location or whenever a change in operation is required.

TABLE 6–2   8155 command register bit assignments.

Command Register
7 | 6 | 5 | 4 | 3 | 2 | 1 | 0

Bit Positions	Function
7 and 6	Program the operation of the Timer 0 0 = Timer NOP 0 1 = Stop timer 1 0 = Stop timer after terminal count 1 1 = Start timer
5	Programs the port B interrupt function 0 = Disable interrupt port B 1 = Enable interrupt port B
4	Programs the port A interrupt function 0 = Disable interrupt port A 1 = Enable interrupt port A
3 and 2	Program the operation of port C 0 0 = Input 0 1 = ALT mode 3 1 0 = ALT mode 4 1 1 = Output
1	Programs the operation of port B 0 = Input 1 = Output
0	Programs the operation of port A 0 = Input 1 = Output

The Timer

The internal timer must normally be loaded with the correct count before it is started or reprogrammed during a program. If it isn't, the timer will still operate, but its first counting sequence will be random. Loading is accomplished by sending the least significant eight bits of the count to I/O port number XXXX X100 and the most significant portion, along with the mode bits M2 and M1, to I/O port number XXXX X101. The timer ports and the bit patterns for M1 and M2 are illustrated in table 6–3. Once the timer is loaded with the count and mode, it may be started by storing a new command in the command/status register of the 8155. If the timer is being reprogrammed for a different count or mode of operation, it must be stopped and restarted to generate the new output. If you skip this step, the count will not change.

The timer count can range in value from 2H to 3FFFH and can generate a squarewave or pulse. The duration of the pulse output is equal to one input clock period, while the square wave is symmetrical.

For example, if the timer is programmed to divide by 7 as a square wave, the output is high for four input clock periods and low for three. If pulse mode is selected, the output remains a logic one until the seventh clock pulse. At this time, it becomes a logic zero for one clocking period.

Figure 6–21 illustrates the waveforms obtained at the output of the timer for each of the four different modes of operation. For this illustration, a count of five is chosen so that the outputs can be observed for an odd count. In addition, the input to the timer is drawn so that the outputs can be referenced to the input clock pulse, which is normally obtained from the CLK OUT pin of the 8085A microprocessor.

8155 Reset

Whenever the 8155 is reset by applying a logic one to the active high RESET pin, it is programmed so that the three I/O ports are set up as inputs, the output latches are cleared, and the timer is stopped. The contents of the internal memory will not be modified by a RESET.

8155 Example Problem

To help you gain a complete understanding of the 8155, figure 6–22 illustrates an example circuit programmed to function as indicated.

First the I/O port numbers to be used in this example must be determined. The decoder, connected to the $\overline{\text{CE}}$ pin of the 8155, enables the device whenever the first three address bits are high. The I/O ports then have addresses 111X X000 through 111X X101, so that they overlay ports E0H through F5H and also F0H through F5H. The port numbers used in this example are E0H through E5H. (See table 6–3.)

When gathering the information from the illustration, notice that port A is an output port, ports B and C are input ports, and the timer must be programmed to divide by 1500. Also notice that the timer must produce a continuous squarewave at 2000 Hz. Since the count must be programmed into the timer before it is started, this is the first step of the initialization dialog. Once the count and mode are programmed, the timer may be started and the remaining I/O port functions may be programmed. The initialization dialog is normally placed at the RESET location in the system's memory or location 0000H for the 8085A.

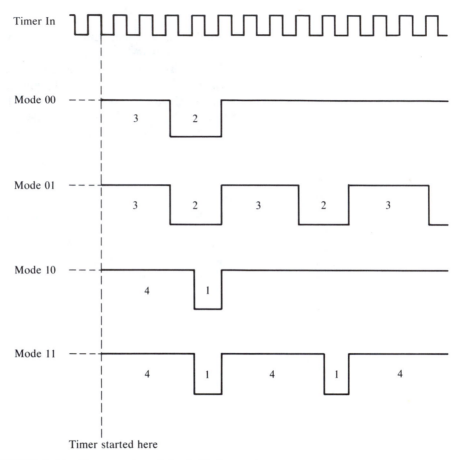

FIGURE 6–21   The operation of the 8155 timer using a count of five.

```
                    ;8155 initialization dialog for the 8085A
                    ;
                    ;this software must be executed before any
                    ;8155 operation can be performed
                    ;
0000  3EDC          RESET:    MVI   A,0DCH
0002  D3E4                    OUT   0E4H          ;set LSB of count
0004  3E45                    MVI   A,45H
0006  D3E5                    OUT   0E5H          ;set mode and MSB of count
0008  3EC1                    MVI   A,11000001B
000A  D3E0                    OUT   0E0H          ;program command register
```

When the 8155 is programmed as illustrated, it will continue to function in this fashion until it is reprogrammed or RESET.

Handshaking with the 8155

The ALT3 and ALT4 modes operation for port C provide handshaking for external I/O devices, including printers that indicate when they are ready for the next character and keyboards that indicate that they have a character available for the microprocessor.

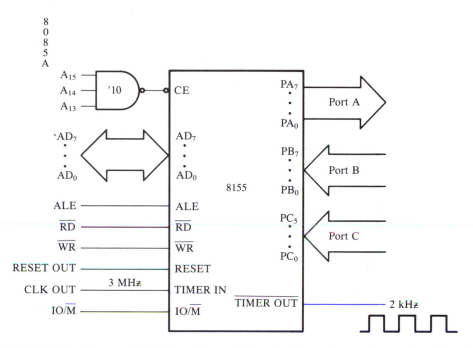

FIGURE 6–22 An example 8155 interface with Port A designated as an output, Ports B and C designated as inputs, and the timer set up to divide the clock by 1500.

Handshaking is a term that describes a communications protocol between two separate digital systems. This handshake, in many cases, is accomplished through two wires or signal lines. You and an automobile exhibit a type of handshake every time you start the car. You turn the ignition key and the starter begins to turn the engine. In response, the

TABLE 6–3 8155 timer ports.

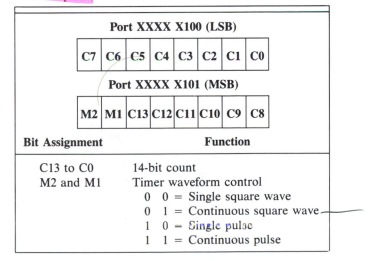

Port XXXX X100 (LSB)							
C7	C6	C5	C4	C3	C2	C1	C0
Port XXXX X101 (MSB)							
M2	M1	C13	C12	C11	C10	C9	C8

Bit Assignment	Function
C13 to C0	14-bit count
M2 and M1	Timer waveform control
	0 0 = Single square wave
	0 1 = Continuous square wave
	1 0 = Single pulse
	1 1 = Continuous pulse

engine starts and signals you by making some noise; this is the other signal path in the handshake. One signal goes from you to the engine through the starter and the other goes from the engine to you through the sound of the engine's starting. If either of these signals is lost, you cannot be sure the automobile has started.

Handshaking synchronizes a device such as a printer to the microprocessor. This synchronization is accomplished, in many cases, with a pair of wires and some software. A wire from the microprocessor signals the printer that data are being sent to the printer. The printer, when ready to receive more data, sends a signal back to the microprocessor. This ''handshake'' between the microprocessor and printer synchronizes their operation. The microprocessor waits for the ready signal from the printer before sending another byte of information.

Alternate Modes of Operation

Table 6–4 lists the pin assignments for port C whenever it is programmed for either alternate modes ALT3 or ALT4. Notice that the port C pins take on a meaning other than as input or output pins.

The $\overline{STB}$, or strobe signal, strobes data into or out of a port; the BF, or buffer full signal, indicates whether or not data are present inside the I/O port; and INTR, or interrupt request, becomes a one after the arrival of the $\overline{STB}$ signal. INTR causes an interrupt to occur in a microprocessor. Interrupts will be discussed in detail in chapter 8.

8155 Strobed Input Operation

Strobed input operation of the 8155 is illustrated in figure 6–23(a). The strobe input, which comes from the external device, causes the data to be held in an internal latch, forces the buffer full flag (BF) high, and forces the INTR signal high. The software provided by the user tests BF to determine if data have been strobed into the port by the $\overline{STB}$ signal.

When BF is detected high, the software reads or inputs data from this port. The data are then transferred into the accumulator of the microprocessor, and the buffer full flag is cleared by the 8155. Buffer full is cleared whenever the data are read from the port.

8155 Strobed Output Operation

Strobed output operation is pictured in the timing diagram of figure 6–23(b). The order of operation for strobed output is the reverse of strobed input. The data are first written into the port by the microprocessor, which causes the data to be held in an internal latch, clears INTR, and forces buffer full (BF) high.

TABLE 6–4 8155 port C alternate modes ALT3 and ALT4.

Pin #	ALT3 Pin Name	ALT4 Pin Name
PC0	Port A INTR	Port A INTR
PC1	Port A BF	Port A BF
PC2	Port A $\overline{STB}$	Port A $\overline{STB}$
PC3	Output pin	Port B INTR
PC4	Output pin	Port B BF
PC5	Output pin	Port B $\overline{STB}$

a. Strobed Input Mode

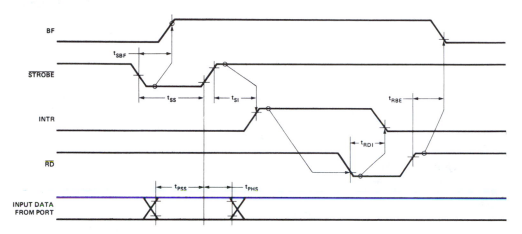

b. Strobed Output Mode

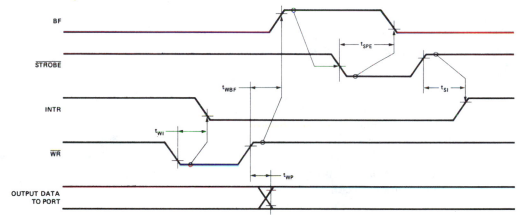

FIGURE 6–23 (a) Timing diagrams for strobed input operation of the 8155, (b) timing diagrams for strobed output operation of the 8155.

SOURCE: Reprinted by permission of Intel Corporation. Copyright 1983.

Buffer full indicates to the external device that data are present in the port. The external device responds by sending a strobe to the port, which indicates that it has received the information. The strobe then forces buffer full low and also sets the INTR signal.

The software associated with this port checks the buffer full flag to determine if the external device has removed the data from the port. If not, the software waits for the buffer full flag to be cleared by the external strobe signal. This type of operation is useful with the printer interface discussed earlier in the text.

8155 Keyboard Interface

The circuit of figure 6–24 indicates the way a keyboard may be connected to the 8155 by using the strobed input mode of operation for port A.

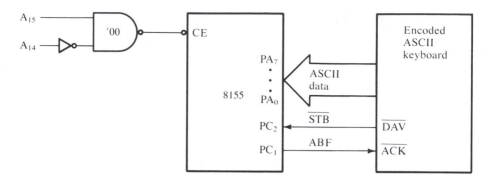

FIGURE 6–24 An example of the 8155 connected to an ASCII encoded keyboard using strobed input operation.

Whenever a key is depressed on the keyboard, ASCII data are presented to port A, along with a 1.5-μs pulse from $\overline{\text{DAV}}$, or data available. The $\overline{\text{DAV}}$ pulse, connected to the strobe input of port A, stores the ASCII character in port A and forces the buffer full flag high.

The buffer full flag must be detected by the software to determine if a key on the keyboard is depressed. Detection is accomplished by polling the BF flag bit, as illustrated in the software for this example. Once the keystroke is detected, the data are input to the microprocessor, clearing the buffer full flag.

The buffer full then indicates to the keyboard that the data are accepted. The keyboard looks for the negative edge of BF to acknowledge the receipt of the ASCII character.

8155 Status Register Bit Assignment

Table 6–5 illustrates the contents of the accumulator after data are input or read from the 8155 status register. The bits in the register indicate the current conditions of the timer, interrupts, and buffer full signals. This register is important in developing the software polling for the keyboard.

A brief explanation of each of the status register bit positions follows:

TIM Whenever the internal timer reaches its terminal count, this bit position becomes a logic one. For example, if the timer is programmed to divide by ten, this bit becomes a logic one on the tenth clock pulse.

IEB Whenever this bit position is a logic one, it indicates that the port B interrupt has been enabled through the command register.

BBF The port B buffer full flag (BBF) indicates that data have been strobed into the port

TABLE 6–5 8155 status register bit assignment.

Accumulator After Status Read							
X	T I M	I E B	B B F	I R B	I E A	A B F	I R A

B latch for an input operation or that data have been extracted from the port for an output operation.

IRB The *interrupt request bit* reflects the condition of the port B INTR pin.

IEA This position indicates that interrupt port A has been enabled using the command register. Whenever this bit position is a logic one, it indicates that the port B interrupt has been enabled through the command register.

ABF The port A buffer full flag (ABF) indicates that data have been strobed into port A for an input operation or extracted from port A for an output operation.

IRA This position reflects the condition of the port A INTR signal.

The Keyboard Software

To develop the software for this keyboard, the port A buffer full flag must be located. This flag bit is located in the status register of the 8155 and can be examined by inputting the status register at port number XXXX X000. In this example, figure 6–24, the I/O port assignment is 10XX X000 (80H) for the command/status register.

```
                         ;8155 initialization dialog
                         ;
0000  3E04      INIT:    MVI   A,00000100B      ;select ALT3
0002  D380               OUT   80H              ;Port A = Input
                         ;
0100                     ORG   100H
                         ;
                         ;INKEY subroutine
                         ;
0100  DB80      INKEY:   IN    80H              ;get status word
0102  E602               ANI   2                ;isolate ABF
0104  CA0001             JZ    INKEY            ;if no data
0107  DB81               IN    81H              ;get data
0109  C9                 RET                    ;return
```

The INKEY subroutine provides the necessary software to read an ASCII coded character from the keyboard. The status word is input and ABF is checked or polled to see whether data have been strobed into port A from the keyboard; if not, the subroutine begins again. It continues to repeat until a character finally arrives from the keyboard. Once a character is strobed into port A, the subroutine detects ABF and inputs the data to the accumulator. It then returns to the program that called it with the ASCII data in the accumulator.

The MC6821 Peripheral Interface Adapter (PIA)

Figure 6–25 depicts the block diagram and pinout of the MC6821 peripheral interface adapter (PIA), which is fairly popular in systems that utilize memory-mapped I/O. It contains two 8-bit bidirectional programmable parallel I/O ports that may be programmed as any combination of inputs and outputs. For example, the MC6821 can be programmed so that it functions with 12 output pins and 4 input pins.

In addition to the two 8-bit I/O ports or peripheral data registers, the MC6821 contains two data direction registers, which program the direction of data flow in the two I/O ports. They also control two control registers, which direct the operation of the MC6821.

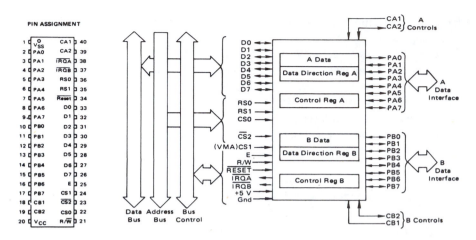

FIGURE 6–25   The pinout and block diagram of the MC6821 PIA.

SOURCE: Courtesy of Motorola, Inc.

Selection

The MC6821 is selected by the chip selection inputs CS0, CS1, and $\overline{CS2}$, and the enable input E or phase two clock. For the MC6821 to perform an operation, all chip enable and selection pins must be active.

For example, if information is to be written into the PIA, $\overline{CS2}$ and R/$\overline{W}$ are grounded. CS0 and CS1 are placed at a logic one. The data from the microprocessor's data bus are then written into the PIA on E or phase two of the clock.

In addition, the internal registers must also be selected. This selection is accomplished through two external register selection pins, RS0 and RS1, and two internal bits in control registers A and B. Normally the RS0 and RS1 pins are connected to two of the address bus connections from the microprocessor so that the I/O port address selects the desired register. Table 6–6 indicates which registers are selected with RS0 and RS1.

The control registers, as illustrated in table 6–7(a) through 6–7(e), select either the DDR or the peripheral data register and the function of several pins on the MC6821. The DDR access bit, bit 2 in both registers, selects the DDR for the respective port whenever it is a zero. If the DDR access bit is a one, it selects the peripheral data register. The remaining bits control the interrupt requests and the function of the CA2, CB2, CA1, and CB1 handshaking or control pins.

If the control register is read by the microprocessor, interrupt status bits CRA6, CRA7, CRB6, and CRB7 are the only bits that convey information. More information regarding interrupt operation of this device appears in chapter 8.

MC6821 Reset

Whenever the MC6821 is reset by applying a logic zero on the active low $\overline{RESET}$ input, all of the internal registers are cleared. This procedure programs peripheral registers A and B as input devices. It also disables $\overline{IRQA}$ and $\overline{IRQB}$.

TABLE 6-6 MC6821 register selection bits.

RS1	RS0	CRA-2	CRB-2	Function
0	0	1	X	Peripheral register A
0	0	0	X	Data direction register A
0	1	X	X	Control register A
1	0	X	1	Peripheral register B
1	0	X	0	Data direction register B
1	1	X	X	Control register B

TABLE 6-7 (a) MC6821 Control register bit assignment.

					Control Register A			
7	6	5	4	3	2	1	0	
IRQA1	IRQA2	CA2 Control			CRA-2	CA1 Control		

					Control Register B			
7	6	5	4	3	2	1	0	
IRQB1	IRQB2	CB2 Control			CRB-2	CB1 Control		

TABLE 6-7 (b) MC6821 control inputs CA1 and CB1.

CRA-1 (CRB-1)	CRA-0 (CRB-0)	Interrupt Input CA1 (CB-1)	Interrupt Flag CRA-7 (CRB-7)	MPU Interrupt Request $\overline{IRQA}$ ($\overline{IRQB}$)
0	0	↓ Active	Set high on ↓ of CA1 (CB1)	Disabled — $\overline{IRQ}$ remains high
0	1	↓ Active	Set high on ↓ of CA1 (CB1)	Goes low when the interrupt flag bit CRA-7 (CRB-7) goes high
1	0	↑ Active	Set high on ↑ of CA1 (CB1)	Disabled — $\overline{IRQ}$ remains high
1	1	↑ Active	Set high on ↑ of CA1 (CB1)	Goes low when the interrupt flag bit CRA-7 (CRB-7) goes high

NOTES: 1. ↑ indicates positive transition (low to high)
2. ↓ indicates negative transition (high to low)
3. The Interrupt flag bit CRA-7 is cleared by an MPU Read of the A Data Register, and CRB-7 is cleared by an MPU Read of the B Data Register.
4. If CRA-0 (CRB-0) is low when an interrupt occurs (Interrupt disabled) and is later brought high, $\overline{IRQA}$ ($\overline{IRQB}$) occurs after CRA-0 (CRB-0) is written to a "one".

TABLE 6–7 (c) Control of CA2 and CB2 as interrupt inputs.

CRA-5 (CRB-5)	CRA-4 (CRB-4)	CRA-3 (CRB-3)	Interrupt Input CA2 (CB-2)	Interrupt Flag CRA-6 (CRB-6)	MPU Interrupt Request $\overline{\text{IRQA}}$ ($\overline{\text{IRQB}}$)
0	0	0	↓ Active	Set high on ↓ of CA2 (CB2)	Disabled — $\overline{\text{IRQ}}$ remains high
0	0	1	↓ Active	Set high on ↓ of CA2 (CB2)	Goes low when the interrupt flag bit CRA-6 (CRB-6) goes high
0	1	0	↑ Active	Set high on ↑ of CA2 (CB2)	Disabled — $\overline{\text{IRQ}}$ remains high
0	1	1	↑ Active	Set high on ↑ of CA2 (CB2)	Goes low when the interrupt flag bit CRA-6 (CRB-6) goes high

NOTES:
1. ↑ indicates positive transition (low to high)
2. ↓ indicates negative transition (high to low)
3. The Interrupt flag bit CRA-6 is cleared by an MPU Read of the A Data Register, and CRB-6 is cleared by an MPU Read of the B Data Register.
4. If CRA-3 (CRB-3) is low when an interrupt occurs (Interrupt disabled) and is later brought high, $\overline{\text{IRQA}}$ ($\overline{\text{IRQB}}$) occurs after CRA-3 (CRB-3) is written to a "one".

TABLE 6–7 (d) Control of CA2 as an output.

CRA-5	CRA-4	CRA-3	CA2 Cleared	Set
1	0	0	Low on negative transition of E after an MPU Read "A" Data operation.	High when the interrupt flag bit CRA-7 is set by an active transition of the CA1 signal.
1	0	1	Low on negative transition of E after an MPU Read "A" Data operation.	High on the negative edge of the first "E" pulse which occurs during a deselect.
1	1	0	Low when CRA-3 goes low as a result of an MPU Write to Control Register "A".	Always low as long as CRA-3 is low. Will go high on an MPU Write to Control Register "A" that changes CRA-3 to "one".
1	1	1	Always high as long as CRA-3 is high. Will be cleared on an MPU Write to Control Register "A" that clears CRA-3 to a "zero".	High when CRA-3 goes high as a result of an MPU Write to Control Register "A".

(Courtesy of Motorola, Inc.)

TABLE 6–7   (e) Control of CB2 as an output.

| | | | CB2 | |
CRB-5	CRB-4	CRB-3	Cleared	Set
1	0	0	Low on negative transition of first E pulse following an MPU Write "B" Data Register operaton.	High when the interrupt flag bit CRB-7 is set by an active transition of the CB1 signal.
1	0	1	Low on the positive transition of the first E pulse after an MPU Write "B" Data Register operation.	High on the positive edge of the first "E" pulse following an "E" pulse which occurred while the part was deselected.
1	1	0	Low when CRB-3 goes low as a result of an MPU Write in Control Register "B".	Always low as long as CRB-3 is low. Will go high on an MPU Write in Control Register "B" that changes CRB-3 to "one".
1	1	1	Always high as long as CRB-3 is high. Will be cleared when an MPU Write Control Register "B" results in clearing CRB-3 to "zero".	High when CRB-3 goes high as a result of an MPU Write into Control Register "B".

(Courtesy of Motorola, Inc.)

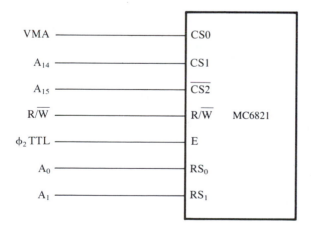

FIGURE 6–26   A typical MC6821 interface to a MC6800 or MC6809 microprocessor.

MC6821 Interface

The MC6821 is specifically designed to function with Motorola microprocessors, but it can also be used with other microprocessors. A typical interface for the MC6821 is illustrated in figure 6–26. VMA, which becomes a logic one for a valid memory address, activates CS0; address bus connections A14 and A15 complete the selection of this device. In other words, the device is selected for valid memory locations $4000 through $7FFF, or one-fourth of the available memory ($=hexadecimal).

Address bits A0 and A1 determine which internal register is selected for the data transfer: $4000 selects data direction register A or port A, $4001 control register A, $4002 data direction register B or port B, and $4003 control register B.

The phase 2 ($\phi2$) TTL connection, or E, times the transfer to or from the MC6821, while the R/$\overline{\text{W}}$ signal selects the direction of the transfer.

MC6821 Interfaced to an 8085A

Figure 6–27 pictures the MC6821 wired to function as an 8085A memory-mapped or isolated I/O peripheral device. S1 provides an advanced write signal for the proper operation and the NAND gate enables the MC6821 at the appropriate time in the 8085A timing. Interchanging the $\overline{\text{MEMR}}$ and $\overline{\text{MEMW}}$ with the $\overline{\text{IOR}}$ and $\overline{\text{IOW}}$ signals selects either memory-mapped operation or isolated I/O operation.

The only problem with this interface is the timing required by the 8085A on a read operation. The 8085 requires information within 300 ns from the $\overline{\text{MEMR}}$ signal, and the MC6821 provides the information within 320 ns. This mismatch can be corrected in two different ways: the clock frequency of the 8085A can be reduced slightly from its maximum; or a higher speed version of the PIA, the MC68A21, can be substituted.

As an isolated I/O device, ports 60H through 63H can be used; as a memory mapped I/O device, address 6000H through 6003H can be used. The memory mapped version requires an overlay area from location 6000H through 7FFFH, and the isolated I/O version requires an overlay area from port 60H through 7FH.

MC6821 Keyboard Interface

This time the keyboard interface described with figure 6–24 is connected to an MC6821 and an MC6800 microprocessor (figure 6–28). The memory space decoded by the chip select inputs is from location $8000 through $BFFF.

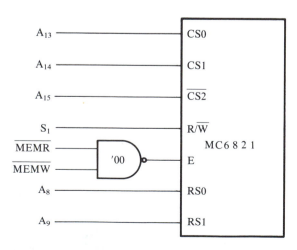

FIGURE 6–27 A typical MC6821 interface to an 8085A microprocessor.

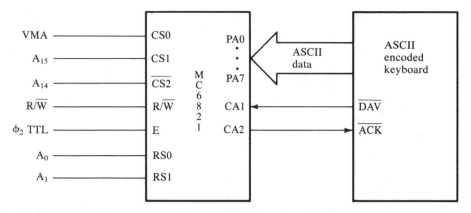

FIGURE 6–28   An MC6800 microprocessor interfaced to an ASCII encoded keyboard through an MC6821 PIA.

Initialization Dialog

The first step that must be accomplished is initialization of the MC6821 at the reset location, which is pointed to by the reset vector of the MC6800. Looking at table 6–7, we can determine the correct bit pattern for the command register for this application. The following initialization dialog would program both the command register for the MC6821 and the data direction register.

```
                    *Initialization dialog
                    *
0000  7F8001        RESET:   CLR   $8001   select DDR
0003  7F8000                 CLR   $8000   program (A) as input
0006  862C                   LDAA  #$2C    set control pattern
0008  B78001                 STAA  $8001   select DDR
```

The data direction register is selected for port A. Next, port A is programmed as an input port. This is not necessary when the MC6821 is RESET; it is illustrated for an application in which this is not the case. Next, the control register is loaded with a $2C that disables interrupts, programs pin CA1 as a negative edge triggered input for $\overline{\text{DAV}}$, programs pin CA2 as a negative going output for the $\overline{\text{ACK}}$, and allows access to peripheral data register A.

Keyboard Input Subroutine

Finally, a subroutine must be written to poll or check bit position seven of CRA to determine when data are available at port A. The return occurs whenever data are detected and the data are found in accumulator B after the return.

```
                    *INKEY subroutine
                    *
0100  7D8001        INKEY    TST   $8001   test CRA 7
0103  2AFD                   BPL   INKEY   if CRA 7 = 0
0105  F68000                 LDAB  $8000   get data from port A
0108  39                     RTS           return
```

When both examples are compared in this section of the text, it is apparent that the initialization dialog for the MC6821 (11 bytes) is longer than for the 8155 (4 bytes). The subroutines in both examples are approximately equivalent in length. The subroutine for the 8155 takes 11 bytes of memory, and the subroutine for the MC6821 takes 10 bytes. Which of the two devices and their respective microprocessors is more suitable depends on the application at hand.

6–5 SOLENOID-OPERATED DEVICES

Many output devices use a solenoid or relay to accomplish some form of work. For example, a dot matrix printer uses seven or nine solenoids to print information on the paper and may also use a solenoid to advance the paper to the next line. Another example is a point-of-sales terminal (POS), which uses a solenoid to open the cash drawer, advance paper, print information on its ticket printer, and—if equipped with a coin changer—return the correct denominations of coins for change.

Solenoid Interface
Solenoids usually demand a considerable amount of current from the controlling source. Since the controlling source is often a microprocessor, some form of buffer or current

FIGURE 6–29   (a) A typical TTL-compatible Darlington solenoid driver using a helper resistor, (b) an optically isolated TTL-compatible solenoid driver.

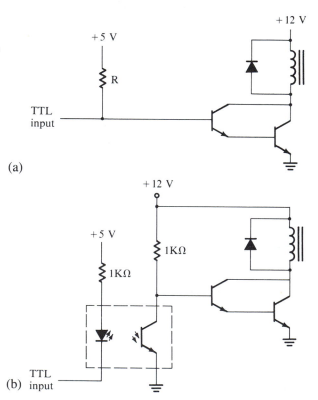

driver must be connected between the microprocessor's output circuitry and the solenoid. Figure 6–29 depicts a Darlington driver and an optical coupler that is used for isolation between the microprocessor and the solenoid's DC power supply.

The source current available for the Darlington pair from most output ports is about 400 μA. If more current is required, an external pullup resistor can be included to increase the amount of source current for the Darlington pair. This can increase the current to 400 μA plus the sink current handling capability of the output port.

For example, the amount of available source current for the Darlington pair can be boosted to 2.4 mA for an 8155 output pin. This equals the sink current of the output pin plus the source current (400 μA).

Darlington Driver

The circuit illustrated in figure 6–29(a) uses a Darlington pair with a gain of 2000 minimum and a solenoid that requires 2 A of current. Without an external resistor, the Darlington pair can only drive a solenoid requiring 800 mA of current. In this case a pullup resistor to boost the drive current to the required 1.0 mA is required. At an output voltage of 1.4 V, the resistor must supply 600 μA of current, which, in addition to the 400 μA of current from the port, is 1.0 mA. This means that with a voltage drop of 3.6 V, the difference between 1.4 and 5 V, across the resistor, a current of 600 μA must flow. In this case the calculated value would be 6K Ω. Since 6K is not a standard resistor value, a 5.6K ohm resistor is used.

Does this create a problem with the current sinking capability of the I/O port? The amount of sink current that will flow in this circuit is 5.6K divided by the supply voltage of 5 V. This amount of current does not exceed the 2 mA sink capability, so the circuit will function properly.

Optical Isolation

The optical isolator depicted in figure 6–29 (b) separates the power supplies of the microprocessor and the external solenoid. In many cases this is desirable because of the large fluctuation in load currents found at the solenoids. This fluctuation can be coupled back to the logic power supply, causing major problems in the reliability of the microprocessor-based system.

8155 Solenoid Software

Figure 6–30 illustrates a solenoid attached to the 8155 PIA. The I/O port number for this solenoid is decoded as 61H, which is bit position 7 of port A.

In this example the timer is used to generate the required amount of time delay for the solenoid. In practice this may be done, or a simple software time delay subroutine can be used.

The solenoid selected for this application requires an activation time of 4 ms for proper operation. To accomplish this, the timer develops the required amount of delay. Since the clock cycle time of the 8085A is 0.333 μs with a 6-MHz crystal, the timer count has to be 12,000 or 2E18H. The subroutine for activating the solenoid for this amount of time follows:

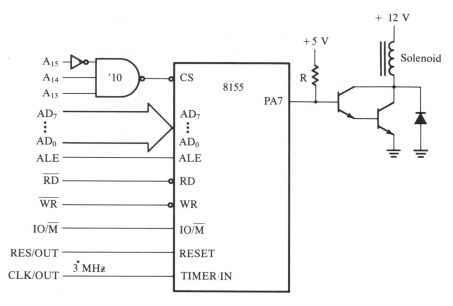

FIGURE 6–30   An 8085A microprocessor interfaced to a solenoid through the 8155 PIA.

```
0000  3E43      SOLE:   MVI   A,01000011B   ;stop timer
0002  D360              OUT   60H
0004  DB60              IN    60H           ;clear TC flag bit
0006  3E18              MVI   A,18H         ;load time delay count
0008  D364              OUT   64H
000A  3E6E              MVI   A,6EH
000C  D365              OUT   65H
000E  3E80              MVI   A,80H         ;activate solenoid
0010  D361              OUT   61H
0012  3EC3              MVI   A,11000011B   ;start timer
0014  D360              OUT   60H
0016  DB60      TEST:   IN    60H           ;get 8155 status
0018  E640              ANI   40H           ;isolate TC flag bit
001A  CA1600            JZ    TEST          ;if delay not timed out
001D  3E00              MVI   A,0           ;deactivate solenoid
001F  D361              OUT   61H
0021  C9                RET
```

This subroutine stops the timer to ensure that it is not already counting and then clears the terminal count flag. the TC flag has to be cleared since it is latched high whenever a TC is reached. In this application there is no method of knowing whether or not this flag is cleared. The act of reading the status register in the 8155 will always clear the TC flag.

The remaining portion of this subroutine loads the timer, fires the solenoid, and waits for it to time out. Polling tests the TC flag bit in the status register. Once a TC is detected, the solenoid is deenergized and a return from the subroutine occurs.

MC6821 Solenoid Software

The MC6800 and the MC6821 are illustrated in figure 6–31 driving a solenoid that is connected to a pin on the PIA. Memory locations $E000 through $E003 are decoded to control this interface.

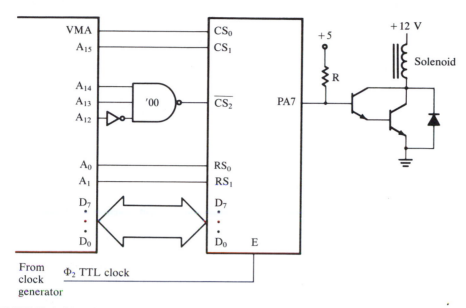

FIGURE 6–31 The MC6800 microprocessor interfaced to a solenoid through an MC6821 PIA.

Unlike the 8155, the MC6821 does not contain a timer; a timer either must be added to the system or a software time delay must be utilized. The latter technique is chosen for this application.

```
0000  8680      SOLE    LDAA  #$80   turn solenoid on
0002  B7E001            STAA  $E001
0005  861E              LDAA  #$1E   count A = 30
0007  C632      LOOP1   LDAB  #$32   count B = 50
0009  5A        LOOP2   DECB
000A  26FD              BNE   LOOP2  waits 300 us
000C  4A                DECA
000D  26F8              BNE   LOOP1  waits 9 ms
000F  7FE001            CLR   $E001  turn solenoid off
0012  39                RTS
```

This subroutine wastes 9 ms between the time the solenoid is turned on and off. The technique uses two nested time delay loops, with the inner loop wasting 300 μs of time. (The outer loop goes through the inner loop 30 times, so that the total delay is 30 times 300 μs, or 9 ms.) This is the time required to ensure the proper operation of the solenoid. Refer to chapter 4 for the information required to calculate this time delay sequence.

AC Solenoid

In certain applications it may be necessary to control an AC relay or solenoid, and a different interface must be used. In most cases isolation is more important when interfacing to an AC solenoid than to a DC solenoid, so an optical isolator is more likely to be used. Isolation is more important when AC control is considered, since a shorted TRIAC

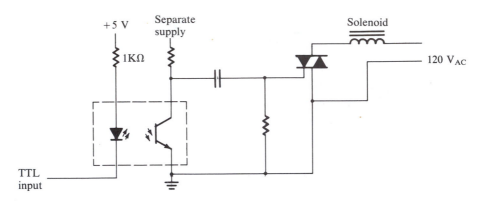

FIGURE 6–32   An optically coupled interface to an AC solenoid.

can apply 115 VAC to the logic circuitry. If this happens most of it is destroyed, and a fire may even result.

A simple circuit for interfacing an AC solenoid is illustrated in figure 6–32. An optically isolated TRIAC is connected to the output of a port pin. This TRIAC in turn controls a larger power TRIAC, since most optically isolated TRIACs cannot handle a large amount of current. To activate the solenoid: (1) a logic zero is placed on the input of the optically isolated TRIAC, (2) causing it to conduct, and (3) in turn causing the power TRIAC to conduct, which (4) activates the solenoid.

Summary

1   Switches tend to bounce when thrown and must be debounced by either a digital circuit or by the microprocessor and some software.

2   Light-emitting diodes (LEDs) are used to indicate events in a microprocessor-based system. A typical LED requires 10 mA of current to illuminate. A set of 7 LEDs can be grouped together to form a 7-segment LED display.

3   The fluorescent display is a numeric display characterized by a blue-green color.

4   Liquid crystal displays (LCD) are the most efficient because they require very little current to display numbers. Their big disadvantage is that they require an AC drive signal.

5   The basic input interface is a set of eight three-state buffers that apply TTL-compatible input data to the microprocessor's data bus whenever the IN instruction is executed.

6   The basic output interface is a set of eight D-type flip-flops that capture the data on the data bus for an external device whenever the OUT instruction is executed.

7   Two types of I/O systems are available: memory-mapped I/O and isolated I/O. With memory-mapped I/O, a portion of the system memory is used as I/O. With isolated I/O, a separate set of instructions (IN and OUT) are used to access a separate set of addresses that are used for I/O.

8 The 8155 peripheral interface adapter is a device that contains 256 bytes of RAM, two 8-bit I/O ports, one 6-bit I/O port, and a 14-bit programmable timer or counter. Each I/O port is programmed as input or output, and in two additional modes that are used for strobed input and strobed output operation.

9 The timer located within the 8155 is programmed to produce either squarewaves or pulses at the timer output. The duration of these signals is determined by the count that is programmed into the timer. For example, a count of 10 will cause the output to have a repetition rate equal to one-tenth of the input rate.

10 8155 strobed input operation allows data to be strobed into one of the 8-bit I/O ports. Whenever this happens the 8155 activates its buffer full (BF) signal to indicate that some external device has placed data in the port for the microprocessor.

11 Strobed output operation of the 8155 is similar to strobed input except buffer full (BF) becomes a logic one to indicate that the microprocessor has stored data in the port for an external device.

12 The MC6821 peripheral interface adapter is a device that contains two 8-bit fully programmable I/O ports. Each of the pins of these two ports is programmable as inputs or as outputs, so it is possible to have 12 bits of inputs and 4 bits of outputs, for example.

Glossary

ASCII code An alphanumeric code used with almost all microprocessor-based computer systems.

Command register A register that controls a programmable I/O device.

Contact bounce Whenever a mechanical contact is made, a switch will physically bounce, which produces erroneous pulses.

Contact bounce eliminator A circuit that removes or eliminates the electrical contact bounces.

8155 A programmable I/O device that contains three separate I/O ports, 256 bytes of RAM, and a programmable 14-bit modulus counter.

Fluorescent display A device that emits a blue-green light.

Handshaking The act of synchronizing the microprocessor with an external circuit through software or hardware.

Initialization dialog A program that initializes all of the programmable I/O devices in a system.

LED Light-Emitting Diode. Emits light whenever a small current is passed through it.

Liquid crystal display A device that displays information by either blocking or passing light.

MC6821 A programmable interface adapter that contains two I/O ports and handshaking signals for the two ports.

Page An area of memory equal to 256 bytes.

Peripheral interface adapter A circuit that connects an external device to the microprocessor.

Port Another name for the I/O memory address or isolated I/O location.

Status The condition of an I/O device.

Timer A programmable modulus counter.

Questions and Problems

1 Describe the operation of the contact bounce eliminator of figure 6–1(b).

2 What is a disadvantage of the fluorescent numeric display?

3 All input devices require which type of circuitry for proper operation?

4 All output devices require which type of circuitry for proper operation?

5 How is the strobe produced in I/O circuitry?

6 Compare isolated I/O with memory-mapped I/O.

7 What is a page of memory?

8 What is one advantage of isolated I/O?

9 What is one advantage of memory-mapped I/O?

10 Develop a decoder that will generate a logic one for page EDH.

11 Develop a decoder that will generate a logic one for isolated I/O ports AXH.

12 Design a circuit that will develop eight I/O strobes at memory-mapped I/O locations 10XXH. Make certain to label the address ranges of your output strobes.

13 Design a circuit that will generate 16 I/O strobes at isolated I/O addresses 9XH. Make certain to label the strobes.

14 Compare the 8155 and MC6821 programmable interface components.

15 Interface an 8155 to function at isolated I/O space CXH.

16 How many 8155s can be interfaced to a single microprocessor?

17 Interface an MC6821 to function at page $7X.

18 How many 6821s can be interfaced to a single microprocessor?

19 Develop initialization dialog for the 8155 in problem 15 if ports A and C were to function as inputs, port B as an output, and the timer were to produce a series of pulses at 1/374 of the input rate.

20 Develop the initialization dialog for the MC6821 in problem 17 if port A is to function as a simple input device and port B is to function as a simple output device.

21 Develop a decoder that will enable the 8155 for I/O ports 6XH and memory address 2000H through 2FFFH.

22 Explain the way the control register in the MC6821 selects either the DDR or port register.

23 Describe the operation of the buffer full flag for the strobed input mode of operation of the 8155.

24 Which two MC6821 pins select an internal register?

25 Connect seven solenoids to an output port of the 8155 and develop the hardware and software to control these seven 10-ms solenoids. Your subroutine should fire the solenoids in the pattern passed to it in the accumulator register.

26 Connect seven solenoids to the MC6821 and develop the hardware and software to operate them for 10 ms. The parameter controlling which solenoids are to be activated is passed to the subroutine through accumulator B.

7

Input/Output Systems

Upon completion of this chapter, you will be able to

1 Interface keyboards to the microprocessor using either a keyboard encoder or I/O ports and develop the software for the interface.

2 Interface 7-segment display devices to the microprocessor using multiplexed techniques and develop the software for the interface.

3 Connect analog and digital data to the microprocessor through digital-to-analog and analog-to-digital converters.

4 Control a stepper motor from the microprocessor.

5 Interface an EEPROM to the microprocessor.

6 Expand memory using paging.

7 Use and interface the Am9512 arithmetic processor.

This chapter uses the PIA, introduced in the last chapter, in many common applications. These include keyboards, displays, digital-to-analog converters, analog-to-digital converters, arithmetic processors, EEPROMs, and stepper motors. All of these systems are component portions of larger systems. Understanding them makes developing a large system much easier.

In addition, this chapter develops a scheme for expanding the memory in a system. This technique has become known as *memory management*. With this technique it is possible to extend the available memory in any microprocessor to an unlimited amount.

7−1   KEYBOARDS

Keyboards are interfaced in two different ways in most microprocessor-based systems. The first method uses a keyboard encoder that detects keystrokes, converts the keystrokes into ASCII code, and signals the microprocessor that information is available. The second method requires an input port and an output port, which are used with some software to multiplex the keys in a keyboard matrix.

Keyboard Encoder

The AY-5-2376, a typical keyboard encoder, is illustrated in figure 7−1. The keys are attached to the encoder through an 11-by-8 keyboard matrix, which allows 88 keys to be connected to the encoder.

The encoder, under normal operation, scans the keyboard matrix for a key closure. Once the closure is detected, the internal circuitry addresses a ROM, which provides the ASCII address of the key at the data output connections. This information is not considered valid until the AY-5-2376 generates the output strobe signal after time is allowed for the key switch to stop bouncing.

The RC circuit connected to pin 19 of the AY-5-2376 is used to set the contact bounce time for the keyswitches connected to the matrix. If the resistor is 680 KΩ and the capacitor is .004 μF, then the delay time for debouncing is 1.5 ms. The RC network attached to pins 2, 3, and 40 provide the internal clock for the AY-5-2376 which is used to scan the keyboard. R of 100 KΩ and C of 30 pF is used to create an internally recommended clock rate of 50 KHz. Pin 6 is used to select even or odd parity. If it is grounded, even parity is selected and if pulled high, odd parity. Finally, pin 20 is used to select the type of strobe found at the data strobe output pin. If this is grounded, the strobe is active low and if pulled high, it is active high.

In addition to the 88 key switches connected in the keyboard matrix, two additional switch connections accomplish the shift and the control functions. These additional inputs select different ASCII codes for the key switches. The internal ROM is a 264-word read only memory, which provides three sets of ASCII codes, depending upon the conditions of shift and control.

Keyboard Encoder to 8155 Interface

Figure 7−2 pictures the AY-5-2376 connected to an 8155 peripheral interface adapter. The strobe output, which becomes active after a valid keystroke, strobes the keyboard

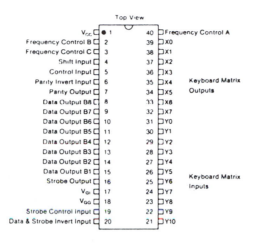

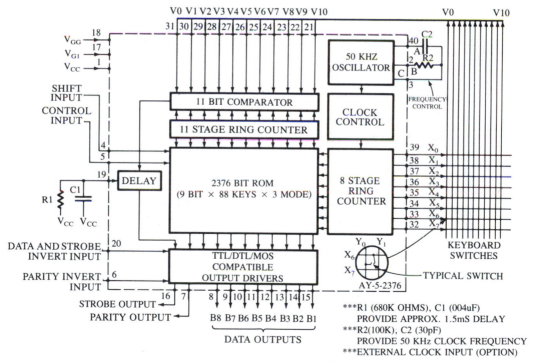

FIGURE 7–1 The pinout and block diagram of the AY-5-2376 keyboard encoder.

SOURCE: Courtesy of General Instruments, Inc.

data into the I/O port for use by the microprocessor. Once the software detects this event, data are input to the microprocessor and the I/O port is again ready for another byte of information from the keyboard.

The subroutine that is used to test the AY-5-2376 for data follows:

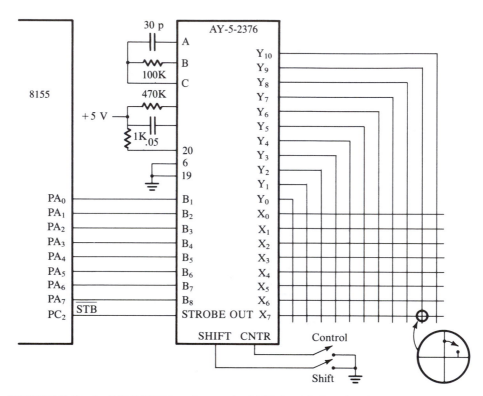

FIGURE 7-2 An AY-5-2376 interface to the 8155 through Port A using the strobed input mode of operation.

```
                    ;Subroutine that checks the keyboard encoder for
                    ;data. If data are found, it returns with the data in
                    ;the accumulator. If data are not found, it waits
                    ;for the data.
                    ;
                    ;The accumulator and flags are destroyed
                    ;
0100                            ORG     100H
0100 DB00           INKEY:      IN      STATUS          ;get buffer full flag
0102 E602                       ANI     2               ;isolate ABF
0104 CA0001                     JZ      INKEY           ;if no data
0107 DB01                       IN      PORTA           ;input ASCII data
0109 C9                         RET                     ;return
```

Hexadecimal Keypad Interface

The keyboard encoder is used only when a full keyboard is connected to the microprocessor. Most applications do not require a complete keyboard, so this circuit is not found. In its place you would probably find the circuit illustrated in figure 7–3 with a small keyboard matrix of 16 keys.

For this interface to fit many different types of parallel interface adapters, the diagram identifies only port A and port B.

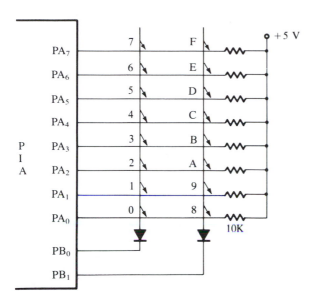

FIGURE 7–3 A hexadecimal keypad connected to Port A of a PIA.

This keyboard is organized as a 2-by-8-bit matrix. Port A must be programmed as an input port, while the two bits used in port B must be programmed as outputs. This is accomplished with the initialization dialog discussed in the last chapter and with the subroutines for this circuit.

The subroutines that will scan the keyboard must be capable of selecting a column of eight keys, detecting if any of the eight keys is depressed, debouncing the keystroke, and providing a code to identify the key's location. The flowchart provided in figure 7–4 illustrates this sequence of events.

This flowchart can be broken into three basic parts: wait for a key release, wait for a key depression, and calculate the key code. The software must wait for a release before finding a key because there is no way to tell when the software will be called. It might be called while the prior keystroke is still active, which would cause the software to detect many keystrokes for one.

Once the software has waited and found that the key is released, it searches for a closed keyswitch. Notice that once a key is found, a time delay is entered to debounce it. It is again checked; if still valid it is a good key and the software calculates the key code. If it is not closed after the time delay then noise may have triggered the time delay and it is ignored.

8085A Keypad Software

When developing the software for the 8085A keypad interface, binary bit patterns 0000 0010 and 0000 0001 are chosen as codes to select the columns, and binary bit patterns 0000 0000 and 0000 1000 are chosen as an indicator for the first key in the selected column.

The time required for debouncing the keys depends upon the type of push button switches selected for the keyboard. In general, push button switches will stop bouncing after 10–20 ms.

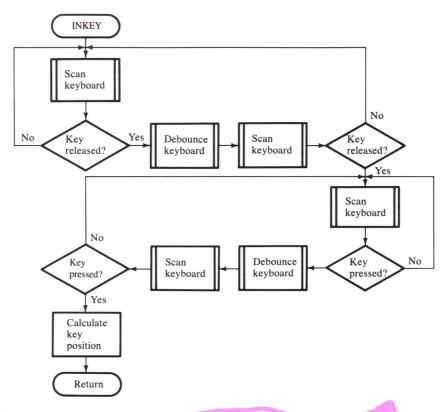

FIGURE 7–4   The flowchart for scanning the keyboard illustrated in figure 7–3.

The 8155 is initialized by programming the command register so that port A is an input port and port B is an output port. The initialization dialog is placed at the start of the system software at the reset location.

```
                  ;initialization dialog for the 8155
                  ;keyboard interface
                  ;
0000  3E02        RESET:   MVI   A,00000010B   ;set port A = input
0002  D310                 OUT   COMMAND       ;set port B = output
```

After the 8155 is initialized, it can be controlled to scan the keyboard. The INKEY subroutine that scans this keyboard follows:

```
                  ;8085A assembly language version
                  ;
                  ;subroutine to detect a keystroke and return
                  ;with the key code in the C-register.
                  ;
                  ;all registers except HL are destroyed
                  ;uses the SCAN and DELAY subroutines
2000                       ORG   2000H
                  ;
                  ;check for key release
                  ;
2000  CD2F20      INKEY:   CALL  SCAN          ;check all keys
```

```
2003  C20020              JNZ    INKEY      ;if key is depressed
2006  CD2520              CALL   DELAY      ;debounce
2009  CD2F20              CALL   SCAN       ;check all keys
200C  C20020              JNZ    INKEY      ;if key is depressed
                          ;
                          ;check for a key
                          ;
200F  CD2F20      LOOP:   CALL   SCAN       ;check all keys
2012  CA0F20              JZ     LOOP       ;if no key depressed
2015  CD2520              CALL   DELAY      ;debounce
2018  CD2F20              CALL   SCAN       ;check all keys
201B  CA0F20              JZ     LOOP       ;if no key depressed
                          ;
                          ;determine key code
                          ;
201E  0D                  DCR    C
201F  0F          LOOP1:  RRC               ;locate row
2020  0C                  INR    C          ;modify key code
2021  DA1F20              JC     LOOP1      ;if not found
2024  C9                  RET               ;return
```

The first portion in the 8085A version of the keyboard software checks whether the previous key has been released. This check is necessary because the software that uses this subroutine may call it before the keyboard operator has had time to remove a finger from the button. If the key is released, the second part of the subroutine searches for another key closure. Once a key closure is detected, the subroutine searches the binary bit pattern for the closed contact; as it does, it modifies the key code in the C-register. When the code of the keystroke has finally been calculated, a return occurs with C equal to the key's code number.

```
                          ;time delay subroutine (20 ms)
                          ;
2025  112006      DELAY:  LXI    D,1568     ;load count
2028  1B          DELAY1: DCX    D          ;decrement count
2029  7A                  MOV    A,D        ;test DE for a 0
202A  B3                  ORA    E
202B  C22820              JNZ    DELAY1     ;if DE not 0
202E  C9                  RET
```

The amount of time used for the contact debounce delay is left up to the user, since it varies with different switches. The count 1568 in the DELAY subroutine is chosen for a 20-ms time delay for this example.

```
                          ;keyboard scanning subroutine
                          ;modifies B and C, destroys A and F
                          ;return zero = no keystroke
                          ;return not zero = keystroke
202F  7A          SCAN:   MOV    A,2        ;select a column
2030  0E00                MVI    C,0        ;set row starting code
2032  D312                OUT    PORTB
2034  DB11                IN     PORTA      ;check rows
2036  FEFF                CPI    0FFH
2038  C0                  RNZ               ;return on key
2039  3E01                MVI    A,1        ;select next column
203B  D312                OUT    PORTB
203D  DB11                IN     PORTA      ;check rows
203F  FEFF                CPI    0FFH
2041  0E08                MVI    C,8
2043  C9                  RET               ;return
```

The keyboard scanning subroutine selects a column by modifying the data at port B. Once a column of eight keys is selected, port A is input and checked for a keystroke. If one or more bits are logic zeros at this time, it indicates that a key is depressed and the subroutine returns with the accumulator containing the row bit pattern. If no key is depressed, the column selection bit pattern and the row-beginning key code are modified and the next column of eight keys is checked.

6800 Keypad Software

To implement the hex keypad with the MC6800 and MC6821 PIA, the PIA must first be programmed or initialized at the reset location for the system program. The dialog that follows programs port A as an input port and port B as an output port.

```
                        *6821 hex keypad initialization dialog
                        *
0000  7F8001   RESET    CLR    CRA          select port A DDR
0003  7F8000            CLR    PORTA        port A = input
0006  7F8003            CLR    CRB          select port B DDR
0009  86FF              LDAA   #$FF         port B = output
000B  B78002            STAA   PORTB
000E  8604              LDAA   #$04         select port A DR
0010  B78001            STAA   CRA
0013  B78003            STAA   CRB          select port B DR
```

The keypad scanning subroutine, which follows, checks to see whether a key is released. This is done because the software jumping to this subroutine may execute in a very short period of time. If it jumps to the subroutine before the operator releases the key, multiple keystrokes are entered into the system. Once the key is released, the INKEY subroutine detects which key has been pressed and returns with the code of the key in accumulator B.

```
                        *6800 assembly language version
                        *subroutine to detect a keystroke and
                        *return with the key code in accumulator B
                        *
                        *wait for key release
                        *
0100  BD2000   INKEY    JSR    SCAN         check all keys
0103  26FB              BNE    INKEY        if key is depressed
0105  BD1000            JSR    DELAY        debounce
0108  BD2000            JSR    SCAN         check all keys
010B  26F3              BNE    INKEY        if key is depressed
                        *
                        *wait for new key
                        *
010D  BD2000   LOOP     JSR    SCAN         check all keys
0110  27FB              BEQ    LOOP         if no key depressed
0112  BD1000            JSR    DELAY        debounce
0115  BD2000            JSR    SCAN         check all keys
0118  27F3              BEQ    LOOP         if no key depressed
                        *
                        *determine key code
                        *
011A  5A                DECB
011B  44       LOOP1    LSRA                locate key
011C  5C                INCB                modify key code
011D  25FC              BCS    LOOP1        if no key
011F  39                RTS                 return
```

The time delay subroutine uses nested loops to achieve a time delay of 20 ms. This time delay is required to debounce the mechanical key switches in the keyboard matrix.

```
                    *20 ms time delay subroutine
                    *
1000  8614          DELAY    LDAA  #$14          load count
1002  C6A5          DELAY1   LDAB  #$A5
1004  5A            DELAY2   DECB                decrement count B
1005  26FD                   BNE   DELAY2        if count B not zero
1007  4A                     DECA                decrement count A
1008  26F8                   BNE   DELAYL1       if count A not zero
100A  39                     RTS                 return
```

The SCAN subroutine selects a column of eight keys and determines whether or not a key is depressed. If a key is detected, a return equal occurs; if no key is detected, a return not equal occurs.

```
                    *check for any key subroutine
                    *
                    *return equal = no keystroke
                    *return not equal = keystroke
                    *
2000  8602          SCAN     LDAA  #$02          select column
2002  B78002                 STAA  PORTB
2005  5F                     CLRB                set key code
2006  B68000                 LDAA  PORTA         check keys
2009  81FF                   CMPA  #$FF
200B  260C                   BNE   RET           if keystroke
200C  8601                   LDAA  #$01          select column
200D  B78002                 STAA  PORTB
2010  C608                   LDAB  #$08          set key code
2012  B68000                 LDAA  PORTA         check keys
2015  81FF                   CMPA  #$FF
2017  39            RET      RTS                 return
```

MULTIPLEXED DISPLAYS 7—2

Display devices are normally multiplexed to reduce the component count in a microprocessor-based system. In microprocessors, the seven-segment code is developed with software to further reduce the amount of external hardware required in the system.

BCD to Seven-Segment Code Conversion

Code conversion from binary coded decimal to seven-segment code is usually done via a table lookup subroutine. The BCD coded number forms the address of the seven-segment coded character stored in a table in the memory. This method of code conversion is widely used because of its speed and relatively low cost. Table 7–1 illustrates the typical lookup table for a common anode seven-segment display. The display and driver circuitry is pictured in figure 7–5. When a logic one is applied to the base of the segment driver, it becomes forward biased. This sinks current for the cathode of the display, which then lights.

TABLE 7–1 Common anode seven-segment lookup table.

Address	X	a	b	c	d	e	f	g	Displayed Data
				Data					
TABLE	0	1	1	1	1	1	1	0	0
TABLE+1	0	0	1	1	0	0	0	0	1
TABLE+2	0	1	1	0	1	1	0	1	2
TABLE+3	0	1	1	1	1	0	0	1	3
TABLE+4	0	0	1	1	0	0	1	1	4
TABLE+5	0	1	0	1	1	0	1	1	5
TABLE+6	0	1	0	1	1	1	1	1	6
TABLE+7	0	1	1	1	0	0	0	0	7
TABLE+8	0	1	1	1	1	1	1	1	8
TABLE+9	0	1	1	1	1	0	1	1	9

The load resistors (RL) for the segment drivers are chosen by using the amount of segment current required to illuminate a segment and VCC minus the drop across the LED. Here each segment requires 10 mA of current and the voltage across RL is 3.0 V. Using Ohm's law determines that the value of RL is 300 Ω. The base resistor (Rb) is determined by finding the base current (in this example, 100 μA, or the emitter current of 10 mA divided by the gain of the transistor, or 100) and the voltage applied to the segment input minus the emitter-base voltage drop. Here the voltage applied is the minimum TTL logic one voltage of 2.4 V minus 0.7 V or 1.7 V. The value of Rb is 1.7 V/100 μA or 17 KΩ.

FIGURE 7–5 A seven-segment LED display illustrating the segment drivers.

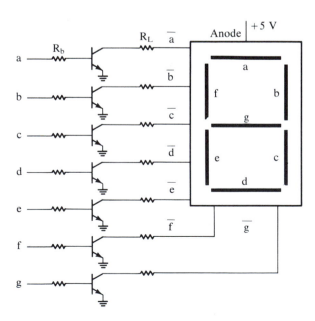

8085A Table Lookup Software

Software to convert the unpacked or single BCD digit in the accumulator of an 8085A into a seven-segment coded number follows:

```
                        ;8085A assembly language version
                        ;
                        ;subroutine to convert the contents of
                        ;the accumulator to 7-segment code.
                        ;HL is destroyed
                        ;refer to table 7-1
                        ;
0000  E60F      CONVERT:    ANI   0FH        ;mask left nibble
0002  210010                LXI   H,TABLE    ;point to lookup table
0005  85                    ADD   L          ;add BCD to address (HL)
0006  6F                    MOV   L,A
0007  7C                    MOV   A,H
0008  CE00                  ACI   0
000A  67                    MOV   H,A
000B  7E                    MOV   A,M        ;get 7-segment data
000C  C9                    RET
```

6800 Table Lookup Software

Software to convert the contents of accumulator B in the MC6800 from a single unpacked BCD digit into seven-segment code follows:

```
                    *6800 assembly language version
                    *
                    *subroutine to convert the contents of
                    *accumulator B to 7-segment code.
                    *X is destroyed
                    *refer to table 7-1
                    *
0000  C40F      CONVERT   ANDB #$04      mask left nibble
0002  CE1000              LDX  #TABLE    get table address
0005  FF2000              STX  TEMP      save address
0008  FB2001              ADDB TEMP + 1
000B  F72001              STAB TEMP + 1
000E  2403                BCC  CONV1
0010  7C2000              INC  TEMP
0013  FE2000    CONV1     LDX  TEMP      get address
0016  E600                LDAB X         get code
0018  39                  RTS
```

Location TEMP in the above software is two bytes of memory somewhere in the base page. This reduces the length of this subroutine. The extra work allows this subroutine to be stored in a ROM. If a ROM will not be used, the subroutine can be shortened considerably.

Multiple-Digit Display

The table lookup technique for code conversion, along with other software, multiplexes the two-digit display illustrated in figure 7–6. Port A supplies both displays with seven-segment code through a set of drivers, and port B selects either digit zero or digit one. Again, the type of peripheral interface adapter is not specified, so that any can be utilized.

Port A provides seven-segment data for both displays through a set of current amplifiers. These amplifiers are required to provide enough drive current for the displays, which

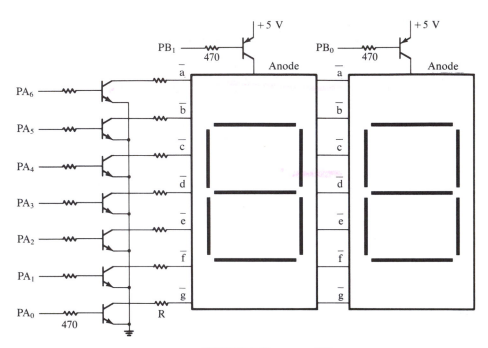

FIGURE 7–6   A two-digit multiplexed seven-segment LED display.

typically require 10 mA per segment. Since this is a two-digit multiplexed display, each display segment requires twice this amount of current to remain illuminated at normal intensity. A three-digit display requires three times the current, and so forth.

The software developed to drive the displays will make one pass only; that is, it will display each digit only once. It is the responsibility of the software using this subroutine to call it continually to maintain a constantly displayed number. If you wish to do quite a bit of processing between calls, it is important to blank the displays to prevent damage. The displays may be blanked by turning off both displays.

Figure 7–7 illustrates the flowchart for the DISP subroutine. Port B selects the digit that displays the information at port A. The two "digit" selection pins at port B are connected to transistor switches that select a digit. These switches must be capable of passing the current from all seven segments in the selected display. In this circuit, that amounts to 140 mA peak for each seven-segment display, with an average current of 70 mA.

The subroutine that causes the 1-ms time delay is not illustrated but can be developed in the same manner as the DELAY subroutine in the section on keyboards. The DELAY subroutine is included to reduce the switching time to the displays. Without it, RF is generated and propagated from the displays, causing a problem with the Federal Communications Commission (FCC).

8085 Version of the Display Software

Before the display can be used, the 8155 must be programmed. In this application, ports A and B must be programmed as output ports for the display. As with the prior software, the initialization dialog is found at the reset location.

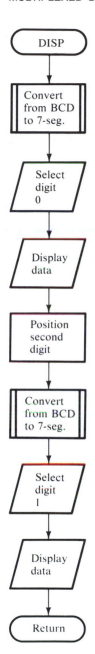

FIGURE 7–7 A flowchart of the subroutine required to multiplex the two LED displays pictured in figure 7–6.

```
                    ;8155 initialization dialog
                    ;
0000  3E03   RESET:    MVI   A,00000011B   ;program ports A & B
0002  D310            OUT   COMMAND        ;as output ports
```

Once the 8155 is programmed, the DISP subroutine can be used whenever data are to be displayed on the two-digit display.

```
                         ;8085 assembly language version
                         ;subroutine to display the packed BCD number
                         ;in the accumulator on the two-digit display
                         ;
0100                     ORG   100H
0100  F5        DISP:    PUSH  PSW             ;save BCD
0101  CDXXXX             CALL  CONVERT         ;convert to 7-segment code
0104  D311               OUT   PORTA           ;send data
0106  3E02               MVI   A,2             ;select digit 0
0108  D312               OUT   PORTB
010A  CDXXXX             CALL  DELAY           ;wait 1 ms
010D  F1                 POP   PSW             ;get BCD
010E  0F                 RRC                   ;position next digit
010F  0F                 RRC
0110  0F                 RRC
0111  0F                 RRC
0112  CDXXXX             CALL  CONVERT         ;convert to 7-segment code
0115  D311               OUT   PORTA           ;send data
0117  3E01               MVI   A,1             ;select digit 1
0119  D312               OUT   PORTB           ;select digit 1
011B  CDXXXX             CALL  DELAY           ;wait 1 ms
011E  C9                 RET
```

6800 Version of the Display Software

Before the display can be used, the MC6821 must be programmed. In this application ports A and B must be programmed as output ports for the display. As with the prior software, the initialization dialog is found at the reset location. Steps 3 and 4 are only required if the MC6821 is not reset. This may be the case in some systems, so it may be better to include these steps as a matter of practice.

```
                         *6821 initialization dialog
                         *
1000  7F8001    RESET    CLR   CRA             select DDR A
1003  7F8003             CLR   CRB             select DDR B
1006  86FF               LDAA  #$FF            set to output
1008  B78000             STAA  DDRA            program port A
100B  B78002             STAA  DDRB            program port B
100E  8604               LDAA  #$04
1010  B78001             STAA  CRA             select DR A
1013  B78003             STAA  CRB             select DR B
```

After the MC6821 is programmed, the DISP subroutine can be used whenever data are to be displayed on the two-digit display.

```
                         *6800 assembly language version
                         *subroutine that takes the packed BCD
                         *number from acc B and displays it on
                         *the display
                         *
1200  37        DISP     PSHB                  save BCD
1201  BD0000             JSR   CONVERT         convert
1204  F78000             STAB  PORTA           send data
```

```
1207  C602        LDAB  #$02      select digit 0
1209  F78002      STAB  PORTB
120C  BDXXXX      JSR   DELAY     wait 1 ms
120F  33          PULB            get BCD
1210  54          LSRB            position
1211  54          LSRB
1212  54          LSRB
1213  54          LSRB
1214  BD0000      JSR   CONVERT   convert
1217  F78000      STAB  PORTA
121A  C601        LDAB  #$01      select digit
121C  F78002      STAB  PORTB
121F  BDXXXX      JSR   DELAY     wait 1 ms
1222  39          RTS
```

DIGITAL-TO-ANALOG AND ANALOG-TO-DIGITAL CONVERTERS   7–3

Many microprocessor-based systems require the generation or reception of analog voltages. With the many types of prepackaged digital-to-analog and analog-to-digital converters available today, this is a simple task. In fact, some of the newer microprocessors are manufactured with built-in analog-to-digital converters.

Eight-Bit Digital-to-Analog Converters

Figure 7–8 illustrates a microprocessor-compatible 8-bit digital-to-analog converter. This particular device will generate an output voltage of 0–2.55 V in steps of 0.01 V, with a full-scale accuracy of plus or minus 0.6 percent. The output settles, or becomes valid, within 1.5 μs after a new 8-bit code is strobed into its internal latch.

Memory-Mapped Connections of the AD558 DAC

Figure 7–9 pictures the AD558 DAC connected to a microprocessor as a memory-mapped I/O device. $\overline{CE}$ is connected to the active low write signal from the microprocessor, and $\overline{CS}$ is connected to the output of a simple address decoder. The data bus from the microprocessor is joined to the data bus connections. Any time that the microprocessor writes information into a memory location decoded by the decoder, the contents of the data bus

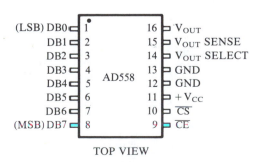

TOP VIEW

FIGURE 7–8 The AD558 microprocessor-compatible 8-bit digital to analog converter.

SOURCE: Courtesy of Analog Devices, Inc.

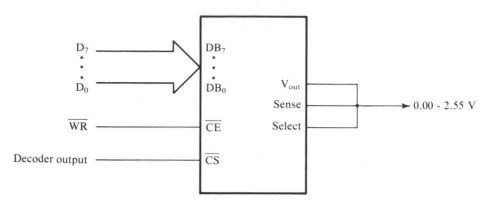

FIGURE 7–9 The AD558 digital-to-analog converter connected to a microprocessor data bus and control signals.

are latched into the DAC. This procedure generates an analog output voltage that is proportional to the digital input in about 1.5 μs.

Eight-Bit Analog-to-Digital Converters

Analog-to-digital converters in data acquisition systems monitor external analog voltages. Figure 7–10 pictures the AD7574 8-bit analog-to-digital converter, which functions with a single 5-V power supply and is directly compatible with virtually all microprocessors. It converts the analog input into an 8-bit digital output within 15 μs.

AD7574 ADC

The AD7574 is controlled through two connections to the microprocessor, $\overline{RD}$ and $\overline{CS}$. The $\overline{RD}$ input, on the zero-to-one transition, clears the converter and begins a new conversion; on the one-to-zero transition, data appear on the output pins if $\overline{CS}$ is also active. $\overline{CS}$ blocks data from appearing at the output connections and a busy signal on the $\overline{BUSY}$ pin but doesn't prevent the converter from being internally reset. Because of this, extreme care must be taken in the use of this device.

8085A to ADC Interface

Figure 7–11 pictures an INTEL 8085A connected to the AD7574 ADC, using the READY input for slowing the microprocessor to match the speed of this converter. When-

FIGURE 7–10 The AD7574 8-bit microprocessor compatible analog to digital converter.

SOURCE: Courtesy of Analog Devices, Inc.

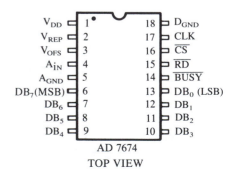

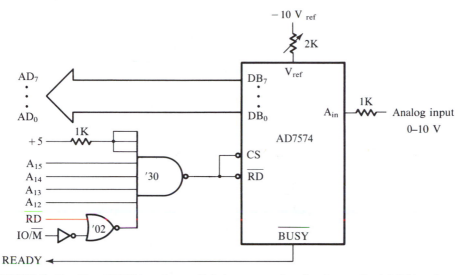

FIGURE 7–11 The AD7574 analog-to-digital converter interfaced to an Intel 8085A microprocessor.

ever data are read from I/O device FXH with an IN FXH instruction, the output of the decoder forces $\overline{RD}$ and $\overline{CS}$ on the converter to become active. This initiates a conversion and causes the $\overline{BUSY}$ signal to become a logic zero during the conversion process. The logic zero on the $\overline{BUSY}$ output causes the 8085A to enter into WAIT states because of the zero presented at its READY input. The $\overline{BUSY}$ line remains a logic zero until the converter finishes converting the analog input to digital. When $\overline{BUSY}$ returns to a logic one, it allows the 8085A to continue executing instructions. To ensure that the converted data are fresh, the first IN FXH is ignored.

MC6800 to ADC Interface

The MC6800 must be interfaced to the AD7574 differently, since it does not possess a READY input or any comparable input. An example of a possible connection is pictured in figure 7–12. In this example the $\overline{CS}$ pin is grounded and the converter is controlled from its $\overline{RD}$ input.

When the MC6800 reads data from memory location \$EFXX, the $\overline{RD}$ pin on the converter becomes a logic zero, forcing data to be read from the converter. After the $\overline{RD}$ returns to a logic one, the converter is reset and takes another sample of the analog input data. The only problem that arises with this interface is that the first ADC read contains old information and 15 μs must be allowed for the converter to complete a conversion.

```
*subroutine to read a number from the
*AD7574 and return the result in acc A
*6800 clock = 1 MHz
*
1000  B6EF00    ADC    LDAA EF00    start conversion
1003  36               PSHA         wait 16 us
1004  32               PULA
```

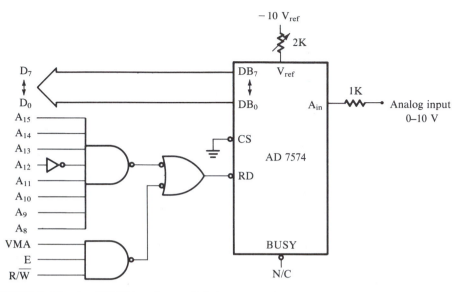

FIGURE 7–12   An AD7574 analog-to-digital converter interfaced to a Motorola MC6800 or MC6809 microprocessor.

```
1005 36              PSHA
1006 32              PULA
1007 B6EF00          LDAA EF00      read data
100A 39              RTS
```

7–4 STEPPER MOTORS

Stepper motors are digital motors that are becoming extremely common in "low torque" digital applications. They are precisely positionable in either a closed or open loop control system with a minimum of circuitry. Some stepper motors can be positioned to within a degree or less of the required position.

A typical schematic representation of a stepper motor is depicted in figure 7–13. This motor has four separate windings to control its relative position. Currents through the coils generate magnetic fields to position the rotor. The rotor is a permanent magnet that is positioned by the magnetic fields generated in the field coils. Once the rotor is moved to its final position, the magnetic fields from these coils keep the rotor at that position. In the example shown, the rotor moves in a clockwise direction.

The Current Driver

Generating the field currents requires a current driver. Figure 7–14 is a schematic diagram of a typical current driver for one of the four stepper motor coils. The driver is capable of generating a current flow through the coil and of reducing the amount of current for holding the coil at a particular position. Moving the rotor requires more current than holding it at a constant position requires.

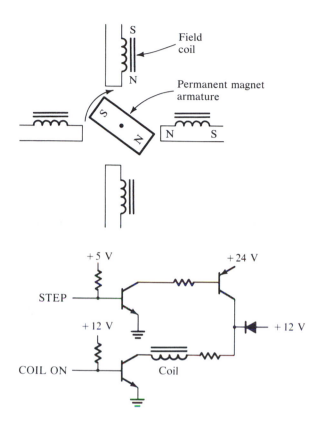

FIGURE 7-13 The internal representation of a stepper motor.

FIGURE 7-14 A typical stepper coil driver. STEP causes 24 V to be applied to the coil, and COIL ON determines whether or not current flows through the coil.

The direction of rotation is determined by the pattern of current flows through the coils in a sequence. This sequence determines the speed and direction of the rotation. The STEP input is provided by the software that controls the stepper motor and causes the current through the coils to increase so that a step occurs.

Stepper Control

The control of a stepper motor requires four separate current drivers and one step control signal. If the step interval is equal to 1.8 degrees, 200 steps or pulses are required to rotate the rotor through one revolution. By sending the drivers the binary bit patterns illustrated in table 7–2, the direction and speed of the rotor can be easily controlled. This bit pattern causes two of the four stepper motor coils to be energized at a time. Moving the bit patterns in the directions indicated rotates the magnetic field inside the motor. The faster a pattern is moved, the faster the motor turns.

It is also possible to half-step the armature in the stepper motor by modifying the bit pattern sent to the four field coils. Table 7–3 illustrates the patterns required to half-step a stepper. Notice that there are eight different codes per rotation instead of four as in Table 7–2, for twice the resolution.

Software to control the stepper motor is required to control both the direction of rotation and the number of steps to be rotated. It must also have the ability to remember the current position of the rotor. Software for controlling the stepper and interface of figure

TABLE 7–2 Stepper motor control bit patterns.

Counterclockwise Pattern				Clockwise Pattern			
0	0	1	1	1	1	0	0
0	1	1	0	0	1	1	0
1	1	0	0	0	0	1	1
1	0	0	1	1	0	0	1

TABLE 7–3 Stepper motor bit patterns for a half-step.

Counterclockwise Pattern	Clockwise Pattern
0 0 1 1	1 1 0 0
0 0 1 0	0 1 0 0
0 1 1 0	0 1 1 0
0 1 0 0	0 0 1 0
1 1 0 0	0 0 1 1
1 0 0 0	0 0 0 1
1 0 0 1	1 0 0 1
0 0 0 1	1 0 0 0

FIGURE 7–15 An interface from TTL-compatible circuitry to a four-coil stepper motor.

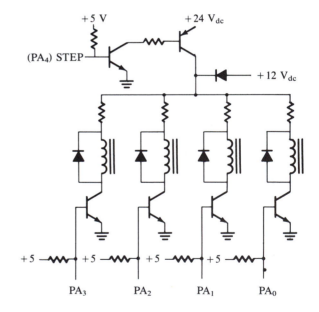

200

7–15 has been developed for both the Intel 8085A and the Motorola 6800. A flowchart illustrates this subroutine in figure 7–16. In both cases, memory location LOC indicates the current bit pattern of the previous data sent to the stepper motor. It is this bit pattern that must be modified to cause the proper direction of rotation. The B register in both cases represents both the direction of rotation and the number of steps to be rotated. If B contains a positive number, the rotation is in the clockwise direction; if negative, the rotation is in the counterclockwise direction.

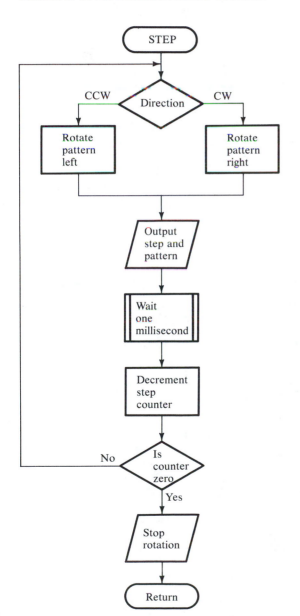

FIGURE 7–16 The flowchart of a subroutine that will control the direction of rotation and the number of steps for the stepper motor interface of figure 7–15.

```
                         ;8085 assembly language version
                         ;subroutine to control a stepper motor
                         ;B = number of steps and direction
                         ;CW = + and CCW = -
                         ;
      1000                        ORG    1000H
                         ;
                         ;test for direction
                         ;
      1000 78            STEP:    MOV    A,B      ;get direction
      1001 87                     ADD    A        ;direction to carry
      1002 3A2A10                 LDA    LOC      ;get prior location
      1005 DA1E10                 JC     STEP2    ;counterclockwise?
      1008 0F                     RRC             ;setup for clockwise
                         ;
                         ;rotate stepper
                         ;
      1009 322A10        STEP1:   STA    LOC      ;save new position
      100C F610                   ORI    10H      ;setup step bit
      100E D301                   OUT    PORTA    ;start rotation
      1010 CDXXXX                 CALL   DELAY    ;wait 1 ms
      1013 78                     MOV    A,B      ;get count
      1014 E67F                   ANI    7FH      ;remove sign bit
      1016 3D                     DCR    A        ;decrement count
      1017 CA2210                 JZ     STEP3    ;if done
      101A 05                     DCR    B        ;decrement count
      101B C30010                 JMP    STEP     ;move another step
                         ;
                         ;setup for counterclockwise
                         ;
      101E 07            STEP2:   RLC
      101F C30910                 JMP    STEP1    ;go step motor
                         ;
                         ;stop rotation and end subroutine
                         ;
      1022 3A2A10        STEP3:   LDA    LOC      ;get location
      1025 E60F                   ANI    0FH      ;clear STEP
      1027 D301                   OUT    PORTA    ;stop rotation
      1029 C9                     RET
                         ;
      102A 33            LOC:     DB     33H      ;initial position
                         *6800 assembly language version
                         *subroutine to control a stepper motor
                         *Acc B = number of steps and direction
                         *CW = + and CCW = -
                         *
                         *test for direction
                         *
      1000 B6102F        STEP:    LDDA   LOC      get direction
      1003 5D                     TSTB   A        direction to carry
      1005 2B19                   BMI    STEP2    counterclockwise?
      1007 44                     LSRA            setup new position
      1008 2402                   BCC    STEP1    if no carry
```

```
100A  3B80                        ADDA  #$80       adjust result
100C  B7102F      STEP1           STAA  LOC        save new position
100F  8A10                        ORAA  #$10       set STEP
1011  B78000                      STAA  PORTA      start rotation
1014  BDXXXX                      JSR   DELAY      wait 1 ms
1017  17                          TBA              get count
1018  847F                        ANDA  #$7F       strip sign
101A  4A                          DECA             decrement count
101B  2700                        BEQ   STEP3      if count 0
101D  5A                          DECB             decrement count
101E  20E1                        BRA   STEP       move another step
                  *
                  *if counterclockwise
                  *
1020  48          STEP2           ASLA             setup new position
1021  24E9                        BCC   STEP1      no carry
1023  4C                          INCA             adjust
1024  20E6                        BRA   STEP1      go rotate
                  *
                  *finish subroutine
                  *
1026  B6102F      STEP3           LDAA  LOC        get position
1029  840F                        ANDA  #$0F       clear STEP
102B  B78000                      STAA  PORTA      stop rotation
102E  39                          RTS
                  *
102F  33          LOC             FCB   #$33       initial value
```

Positional Feedback

The position of the stepper motor may or may not be critical to a particular application. For example, if paper is being fed in a printer with the stepper motor, the position is not important. Feeding one line of paper may merely mean that the stepper must be pulsed 20 times for each line of paper. Pulsing it 10 times would move the paper one-half of a line.

On the other hand, if the stepper positions the dot matrix print head in a printer, positional feedback may indeed be important. One method of obtaining this feedback is to sense a home position. In printers, the home position is normally the left-hand margin of the page. This is most often accomplished with an optical device that includes an LED and a phototransistor. When the head is homed, the beam of light is broken, which can be sensed with the hardware and software.

Once this home position is known, the printer software can step over the required steps to any printing position without any further feedback. Errors can occur without further feedback, but with today's modern stepper motors, they happen very rarely.

EEPROM INTERFACE 7–5

The EEPROM, as discussed in the chapter on memory systems, is a device capable of retaining information once the power has been removed. This feature is very useful in many applications where entering setup information into a system is tedious. This device allows this type of data to be stored for an extended period of time without the application of system power. It is not suited for all applications, since it has a limited life span of only 10,000 write and erase cycles per byte.

Unfortunately this device is not as easy to interface to a microprocessor as a ROM or RAM because it requires much more time to write or erase information. It also requires a special 21-V pulse to accomplish the erase or write.

2816 EEPROM

Figure 7–17 illustrates the pinout of the 2816 2K-byte EEPROM from Intel. This device is similar to the 2716 EPROM that was interfaced in the chapter on memory. About the only difference is that it contains I/O pins rather than output pins. The I/O pins read information and program data, when required.

Programming and erasing take 10 ms per byte. They are accomplished by applying the data to be stored in a location on the I/O pins, the address on the address pins, and a 21-V pulse on the programming pin. This programming pulse must be present for 9–15 ms.

Basic High-Speed Interface

Figure 7–18 illustrates the basic circuitry required to program or read the EEPROM without a large investment in hardware or software. The 8155 programs the device by

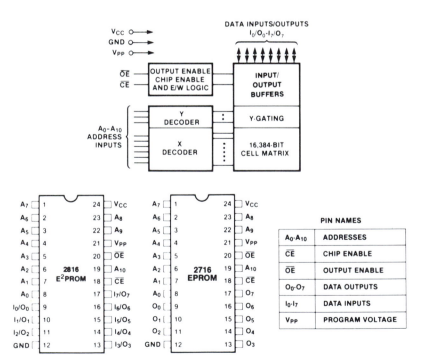

FIGURE 7–17   The pinout and internal block diagram of the Intel 2816 EEPROM.
SOURCE: Reprinted by permission of Intel Corporation, Copyright 1982.

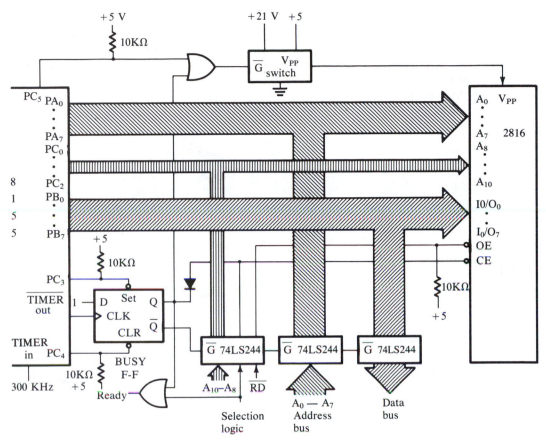

FIGURE 7-18 The circuit required to program the 2816 EEPROM and to read it in a system.

timing the basic sequence and applying the programming pulse. It also provides the data and address for the purpose of programming the 2816.

The system progresses at full speed while programming or erasing a byte in the EEPROM. The only time that any delay in accessing the 2816 is observed is when a read is attempted as the device is being programmed. If this occurs, the processor READY line is pulled low, causing it to wait until the current programming is completed.

The 8155

Ports A, B, and C of the 8155 are programmed as input devices until a program cycle begins. Then port A and a portion of C supply the address to the 2816, and port B supplies the data. The busy flip-flop develops the READY signal for the system, controls the buffer, and allows the V_{PP} switch to be activated.

The timer within the 8155 develops a 10-ms programming pulse for the EEPROM. In this example it doesn't directly generate the pulse; it sets the busy flip-flop, which ends the programming or erase sequence.

The Generation of the Programming Pulse

The programming pulse is generated from the output of the busy flip-flop, which is turned on by the software at the beginning of a write cycle and PC4. Once activated, PC5 and the switch apply a 21-V pulse to the V_{PP} pin of the EEPROM. At the end of the timing sequence, the output of the timer sets the busy flip-flop, which ends the application of the programming pulse to V_{PP}. This interface assumes that 21 V is available in the system. If it is not, some type of switching regulator that will develop approximately 15 mA of current can be included.

The Software

The software for this application can be broken down into three portions: initialization dialog, a programming subroutine or erase subroutine, and a polling subroutine.

The polling subroutine tests the timer's terminal count bit to determine whether or not a byte is programmed or erased.

```
0000  DB80        POLL:    IN    STATUS        ;get 8155 status
0002  E640                 ANI   40H           ;isolate TC flag
0004  C9                   RET
```

As you can see, this is a very short subroutine, which returns zero if TC is not reached. If the TC is reached, a return not zero occurs and is tested if the system program is to access the 2816.

The initialization dialog is required to set up the 8155 ports so that all ports are input ports. In addition, the busy flip-flop must be set initially so that data can be read from the EEPROM until a programming sequence or erase sequence is required.

```
0005  3E4C        INIT:    MVI   A,01001100B   ;program 8155
0007  D380                 OUT   COMMAND       ;stop timer
0009  3E7F                 MVI   A,7FH         ;set busy flip-flop
000B  D383                 OUT   PORTC
000D  DB80                 IN    STATUS        ;clear TC flag
000F  3EFF                 MVI   A,0FFH        ;deactivate set
0011  D383                 OUT   PORTC
0013  3E00                 MVI   A,00000000B   ;all ports input
0015  D380                 OUT   COMMAND
0017  C9                   RET
```

The programming subroutine and erase subroutine must be capable of sending the address to the EEPROM, as well as the data to be programmed into it. This is accomplished by sending some parameters to these subroutines through register B for the programmed data and the DE pair for the address of the data. Erasure is obtained by programming all ones into a location.

This subroutine must also be able to clear the busy flip-flop and program the timer for the 10-ms pulse that sets the busy flip-flop at the end of the programming sequence.

```
                           ;
                           ;this subroutine will program a byte in the
                           ;B-register at the address indicated by DE.
                           ;
0018  CD2300      PROG:    CALL  SETUP         ;address byte
001B  CD3400               CALL  TIME          ;start timer
```

```
001E  78                MOV   A,B         ;get data
001F  CD4100            CALL  VPP         ;start programming
0022  C9                RET
                      ;
                      ;setup address and programming pulse
                      ;
0023  3E0F    SETUP:    MVI   A,0FH       ;setup ports as output
0025  D380              OUT   COMMAND
0027  3EEF              MVI   A,0EFH      ;clear busy flip-flop
0029  D383              OUT   PORTC
002B  7B                MOV   A,E         ;send address
002C  D381              OUT   PORTA
002E  7A                MOV   A,D
002F  F6F8              ORI   0F8H
0031  D383              OUT   PORTC
0033  C9                RET
                      ;
                      ;start timer
                      ;
0034  3EB8    TIME:     MVI   A,0B8H      ;program timer
0036  D384              OUT   TIMEL
0038  3E8B              MVI   A,8BH       ;single pulse mode
003A  D385              OUT   TIMEH
003C  3ECF              MVI   A,0CFH      ;start timer
003E  D380              OUT   COMMAND
0040  C9                RET
                      ;
                      ;send data and activate Vpp
                      ;
0041  D382    VPP:      OUT   PORTB       ;send data
0043  7A                MOV   A,D         ;get address
0044  E6DF              ANI   0DFH        ;enable Vpp
0046  D383              OUT   PORTC
0048  C9                RET
```

MEMORY EXPANSION TECHNIQUES 7–6

There are many techniques for expanding the amount of available space in a memory system. They all seem to hinge on about the same technique, memory bank selection. To expand a memory system, all that is required is the addition of some extra memory address pins and a more sophisticated software operating system.

In most cases only a part of the memory system is expandable, as illustrated in the diagram of figure 7–19. In this system the bottom 16K bytes of memory are common to all additional blocks of memory. Only the memory devices above location 3FFFH have additional address inputs. For this reason, many blocks are illustrated for this portion of the memory system. It would be easy to add 8 address bits to any 8-bit microprocessor by adding an 8-bit output port for this purpose. This expands or allows 256 additional blocks of memory to be added, probably enough for most computer systems using an 8-bit microprocessor.

The Hardware

The hardware required for the bank selection is merely a simple 8-bit output port or device that uses either memory mapped or isolated I/O techniques. Figure 7–20 illustrates a

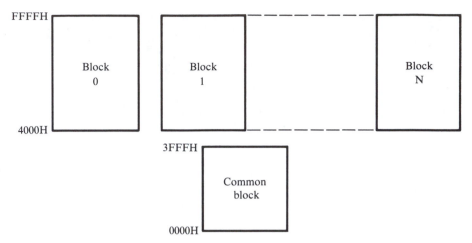

FIGURE 7–19 One possible system configuration for expanding the size of a system memory.

74LS374 latch used as an additional address register for memory banks. This gives the system a 24-bit memory address instead of the original 16 bits.

For isolated I/O port, number 3FH specifies which bank of memory is to be used for locations 4000H through FFFFH. In memory mapped I/O, the address location used to change banks is 3FXXH.

The Software

The bottom portion of this memory system probably contains system software in a read-

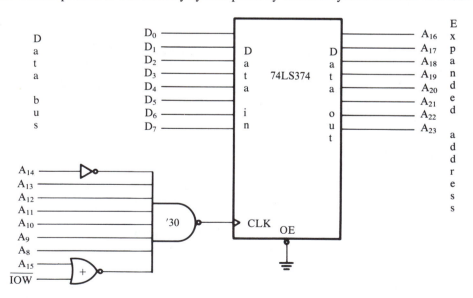

FIGURE 7–20 Address bus expansion latch and the decoder logic for I/O port 3F or memory-mapped location 3FXX, if $\overline{\text{IOW}}$ is changed to $\overline{\text{WR}}$.

only memory. This software comprises the operating system for the computer and may also contain a high-level language, such as an assembler or compiler. It also contains a subroutine to handle memory management for the multiple banks of memory.

A system might include several CRT terminals that share the same basic system. This arrangement would reduce total system costs, since the software could allocate banks of memory to each different CRT terminal. The allocation could be accomplished dynamically. This scheme of memory utilization assigns only the required amount of memory to each CRT terminal or user.

This is only one of many possibilities for bank selection logic. Most microprocessor manufacturers provide some form of memory management component that will essentially accomplish this type of memory management and bank selection for the user.

ARITHMETIC PROCESSORS $7-7$

With the microprocessor used for high-level language compilation, it is often desirable to include an arithmetic processor in the system. Most manufacturers make such a device, which is often capable of accomplishing most floating point arithmetic operations. Since most higher-level languages use this type of arithmetic, a separate dedicated processor can be advantageously applied. Software required to perform this type of arithmetic is extremely long and very slow. This even applies to the newer microprocessors, which contain at least a fixed point multiply and a divide instruction.

The Am9512 Floating Point Processor

The Am9512 floating point processor, illustrated in figure 7–21, is capable of both 32- and 64-bit floating point arithmetic. The operations that it can perform include addition, subtraction, multiplication, and division.

Execution times range from 4 clocking periods to 4,560 clocking periods. If a 2-MHz clock is used, that equates to 2–2280 μs. If software is developed to accomplish these operations, it takes quite a bit longer.

Table 7–4 illustrates the complete instruction set for this device, along with the binary op-codes required to perform the indicated tasks. The most significant bit (X) controls the SVREQ pin (discussed under the topic of pin descriptions later in this section). TOS, or *top of stack,* describes the position of data on an internal stack that holds the data for the arithmetic operation of the Am9512. In addition to the references to TOS in table 7–4, you will also notice NOS. NOS, or *next on stack,* refers to the position on the stack that is POPed out of the Am9512. More discussion of TOS and NOS appears later in this text with the description of the internal stack.

Pin Descriptions

CLK   an external clock input of up to 2 MHz.

RESET   clears the END, ERR, and SVREQ output pins.

C/$\overline{\text{D}}$ defines whether a read or write will occur to the command/status register or the internal data stack.

END   an output that indicates the end of the current operation. This output remains high after the end of an operation until an $\overline{\text{EACK}}$.

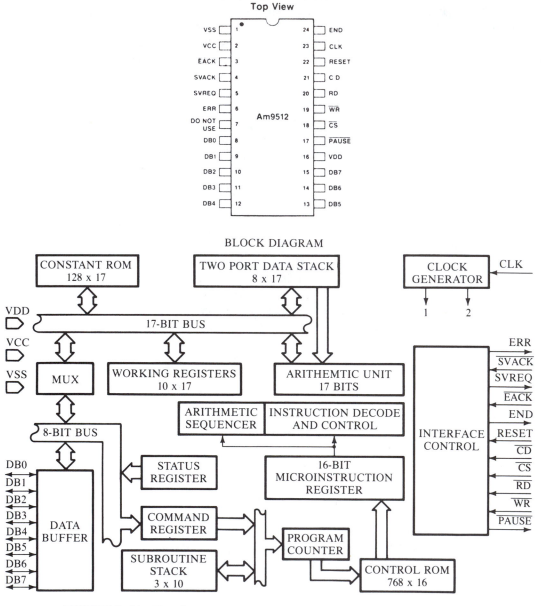

FIGURE 7–21 The pinout and internal block diagram of the Am9512 arithmetic processor.

$\overline{\text{EACK}}$ this input acknowledges an END operation by clearing the END output.

SVREQ   this output is essentially the same as END, except that it can be selectively
controlled by the eighth bit position in a command.

TABLE 7-4 Am9512 commands.

7	6	5	4	3	2	1	0	Mnemonic	Description
X	0	0	0	0	0	0	1	SADD	Single precision addition NOS = NOS + TOS
X	0	0	0	0	0	1	0	SSUB	Single precision subtraction NOS = NOS − TOS
X	0	0	0	0	0	1	1	SMUL	Single precision multiply NOS = NOS × TOS
X	0	0	0	0	1	0	0	SDIV	Single precision divide NOS = NOS/TOS
X	0	0	0	0	1	0	1	CHSS	Single precision sign change TOS = −TOS
X	0	0	0	0	1	1	0	PTOS	Single precision push
X	0	0	0	0	1	1	1	POPS	Single precision pop
X	0	0	0	1	0	0	0	XCHG	Single precision exchange Swap TOS with NOS
X	0	1	0	1	1	0	1	CHSD	Double precision sign change TOS = −TOS
X	0	1	0	1	1	1	0	PTOD	Double precision push
X	0	1	0	1	1	1	1	POPD	Double precision pop
X	0	0	0	0	0	0	0	CLR	Clear status
X	0	1	0	1	0	0	1	DADD	Double precision addition NOS = NOS + TOS
X	0	1	0	1	0	1	0	DSUB	Double precision subtraction NOS = NOS − TOS
X	0	1	0	1	0	1	1	DMUL	Double precision multiply NOS = NOS × TOS
X	0	1	0	1	1	0	0	DDIV	Double precision divide NOS = NOS/TOS

$\overline{\text{SVACK}}$ clears SVREQ.

ERR   indicates that the current command has resulted in an error. Some error conditions that are indicated are: divide by zero, exponent overflow, and exponent underflow. Reading the status register clears this error indicator.

PAUSE   this output is used for synchronization with some microprocessors. In an 8085A-based system, it is connected to the READY pin.

Basic Operation

The Am9512 operates on the data entered into its internal data stack. For this reason, it must be loaded with both operands before an operation can be executed properly. The operands must be placed on the stack with the least significant byte first. This stack can hold up to four single-precision or two double-precision numbers. The first number placed on the internal stack ends up as the TOS, and the second number ends up as the NOS. A logic zero placed on the C/$\overline{\text{D}}$ pin indicates data entry or extraction from the stack.

Floating Point Data Formats

Table 7–5 illustrates the data format for both the single- and double-precision floating point numbers. Each type of number has two portions, a mantissa and an exponent. The left-hand bit of both types of data contains the sign bit of the mantissa. If the sign bit is a one, a negative number is contained in the mantissa; if zero, a positive number is contained. Positive and negative numbers differ in sign bit only; the mantissa always contains the magnitude of the number, as described in the following text.

$$2^{exp} \text{ X mantissa = floating point number} \qquad \textbf{7–1}$$

The next portion of both words contains the exponent of the number. The single precision number contains an 8-bit exponent stored in excess 127 notation. That is, an exponent of 4 is actually stored as an unsigned number equal to 131, or 1000 0011 binary. An exponent of -100 is represented as a 27, or 0001 1011 binary. With a double-precision number, the exponent is an 11-bit binary number expressed in excess 1023 notation.

The mantissa is either a 24-bit normalized number for single precision or a 53-bit normalized number for double precision. Each actually contains one less bit, but an implied bit of one is assumed outside of the stored quantity. All mantissas are represented as numbers in the following true magnitude form: 1.XXX, where XXX is the number stored as the mantissa and the one is implied.

EXAMPLE 7–1

Represent a 42 decimal in single-precision FPF.
Binary = 101010
Normalized floating point form = 1.0101×2^5
(s)   (exp)   (mantissa)
FPF = 0   10000100   01010000000000000000000

In example 7–1, the original decimal number 42 is converted to a binary number. This number is then normalized to produce a 1.0101. The exponent of 2 indicated is a 5, since the *radix* is moved five places to the left during normalization. Finally, this floating point number is formed into a 32-bit number that is compatible with the Am9512. To store a zero in this form, all bits of the number are made zero, including the sign bit, exponent, and the mantissa.

The 8085A Interface

Figure 7–22 illustrates the basic interface to an 8085A microprocessor. The only external

TABLE 7–5 Floating point word formats.

Single Precision		
31	30 — 23	22 — 0
S	Exponent	Mantissa

Double Precision		
63	62 — 52	51 — 0
S	Exponent	Mantissa

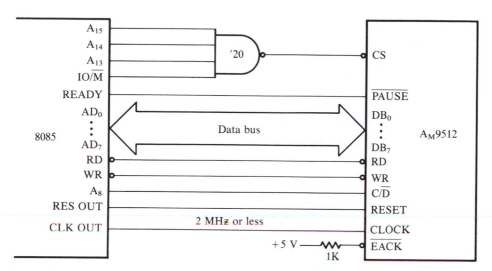

FIGURE 7–22 An Am9512 arithmetic processor interfaced to an Intel 8085A microprocessor.

hardware required is the port or device decoder. In this case a simple four-input NAND gate decodes a port number. Address bit position A8 is connected to the C/$\overline{\text{D}}$ input to select command or data.

The port number decoded by this example is EXH. The software illustrated later in this section uses port E0H for data and port E1H for command and status. As you can see, the interface circuitry required is very simple.

The Am9512 Status Register
Before the software for this application can be developed, the status word of the Am9512 must be examined. The bit pattern for this register is shown in table 7–6 and a description of each bit follows:

BIT7 (BUSY) indicates that a command is being processed by the Am9512 when high. A zero condition indicates that the device is idle.

BIT6 (SIGN) indicates the sign of the result.

BIT5 (ZERO) indicates that the result is a zero.

BIT3 (DIVIDE EXCEPTION) indicates that an attempt to divide by zero has occurred.

BIT2 (EXPONENT UNDERFLOW) indicates that an exponent underflow has occurred.

BIT1 (EXPONENT OVERFLOW) indicates that an exponent overflow has occurred.

TABLE 7–6 Am9512 status register.

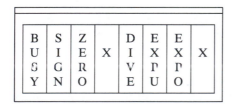

B U S Y	S I G N	Z E R O	X	D I V E	E X P U	E X P O	X

The Am9512 Control Software

The control software for the Am9512 consists of subroutines to test the status register, load and unload the internal data stack, and start an operation.

The first subroutine to be illustrated tests the Am9512 to determine whether an operation is complete. A return from this subroutine will only occur for a completed operation, with the type of return indicating whether any errors have occurred. Return zero means no errors, and return not zero means that an error has occurred.

```
                    ;status polling software
                    ;
0000  DBE1    STAT:     IN    0E1H          ;read status
0002  B7                ORA   A             ;test accumulator
0003  FA0000            JM    STAT          ;if busy
0006  E60E              ANI   0EH           ;isolate errors
0008  C9                RET
```

The next subroutine developed loads the 4-byte-long single-precision number, pointed to by the HL pair, into the Am9512. It is assumed that the least significant byte is stored in the lowest numbered memory location.

```
                    ;this subroutine loads a single precision
                    ;number into the Am9512 from the memory
                    ;location addressed by HL
                    ;
0009  0604    LOAD:     MVI   B,4           ;load counter
000B  7E                MOV   A,M           ;get a byte
000C  D3E0              OUT   0E0H          ;send it
000E  23                INX   H             ;point to next byte
000F  05                DCR   B             ;decrement count
0010  C20B00            JNZ   LOAD+2        ;if not done
0013  C9                RET
```

The next subroutine removes the answer from the Am9512. It again is assumed to be a single-precision number that is to be extracted from the floating point processor. The HL pair points to the location in memory where the answer is to be stored.

```
                    ;subroutine to extract the answer from
                    ;the Am9512 and save it in memory at the
                    ;location addressed by HL
                    ;
0014  0604    UNLOAD:   MVI   B,4           ;load counter
0016  DBE0              IN    0E0H          ;get byte
0018  77                MOV   M,A           ;save byte
0019  23                INX   H             ;point next
001A  05                DCR   B             ;decrement count
001B  C21600            JNZ   UNLOAD+2      ;if not done
001E  C9                RET
```

The next step is an example problem. Another subroutine is written to use the three prior subroutines to multiply two single-precision numbers together. The numbers are stored at locations NUMB1 and NUMB2, and the answer is stored at location ANS. If an error is detected as a result of this multiplication, a return not zero occurs. If the answer is correct, a return zero occurs.

```
                        ; subroutine to multiply NUMB1 times NUMB2
                        ;and store the result at ANS
                        ;
001F  3E00    MULT:     MVI   A,0            ;clear command
0021  D3E1              OUT   0E1H
0023  213900            LXI   H,NUMB1        ;address data
0026  CD0900            CALL  LOAD           ;load multiplicand
0029  CD0900            CALL  LOAD           ;load multiplier
002C  3E03              MVI   A,3            ;SMUL command
002E  D3E1              OUT   0E1H
0030  CD0000            CALL  STAT           ;time out command
0033  F5                PUSH  PSW            ;save errors
0034  CD1400            CALL  UNLOAD         ;save product
0037  F1                POP   PSW            ;get errors
0038  C9                RET
                        ;
0039          NUMB1:    DS    4
003D          NUMB2:    DS    4
0041          ANS:      DS    4
```

This appears to be a lot of software just to multiply two numbers together, but if you look at the normal floating point software of approximately six hundred bytes, you form a different opinion. This is just one of many operations that can be performed by the floating point processor.

Summary

1 The keyboard encoder is a device that scans a keyboard, returns the ASCII code with parity when a key is pressed, and sends a strobe to the keyboard interface indicating a valid character is available.

2 Key switches bounce for 10–20 ms, which means that they must be debounced by the software or keyboard encoder. Debouncing is accomplished by testing for a closed switch and then waiting for 20 ms to see if the switch is still closed. If it is closed, it is a valid key closure.

3 Keyboard-scanning software waits for a release, checks for a key after the release, and then calculates the position of the key switch.

4 Multiplexed displays share a single set of I/O ports for many digits of display.

5 Seven-segment code for displays is obtained by finding the code in a lookup table.

6 Whenever displays are multiplexed, the nominal segment current is multiplied by the number of display digits to determine the peak segment current. For example, if the nominal current is 10 mA per segment and it is a six-digit display, the peak segment current is 60 mA.

7   The AD558 digital-to-analog converter requires 1.5 μs to convert an 8-bit binary number to an analog voltage.

8   The AD7574 analog-to-digital converter requires 15 μs to convert from an analog voltage to an 8-bit binary number. The converter is started by pulsing the $\overline{RD}$ pin and then it can be read in 15 μs. The $\overline{BUSY}$ pin indicates that the converter is actively converting an analog voltage.

9   A stepper motor is a device whose armature is moved in discrete steps by applying current to one or two field coils at a time.

10   The stepper motor can be full-stepped or half-stepped for greater resolution.

11   Generally, a holding voltage is applied to the stepper coils so that the shaft connected to the armature remains stationary after the armature stops moving.

12   The 2816 EEPROM is a device that functions as a read only memory with an access time of 450 ns, and as a device that can be erased and rewritten in the circuit. It requires 10 ms of time to erase and rewrite a location in the EEPROM with a 21-V programming pulse.

13   Memory is expanded beyond 64K bytes by using an I/O port to extend the memory address range of the microprocessor. With this technique, only a portion of the memory is expanded in most cases.

14   The Am9512 arithmetic processor is a device that is capable of floating point arithmetic operations such as multiplication and division.

15   Floating point numbers contain a sign bit that indicates the sign of the fractional part, an exponent that indicates the relative position of the binary point, and a fractional part that is always a binary number (n) with a value $1 > n <= 0.1$.

Glossary

Analog-to-digital converter   A device that converts an analog voltage into a binary or binary coded decimal number that is proportional to the voltage.

Digital-to-analog converter   A device that converts a binary or binary coded decimal number into an analog voltage proportional to the number.

Exponent   In floating point numbers, it is the binary power of two that indicates the relative position of the radix point.

Floating point number   A number that is stored with a mantissa and an exponent. It typically is capable of storing hundreds of bits of information in only 4–8 bytes of memory.

Floating point processor   A device that computes the answers to many floating point arithmetic operations.

Mantissa   The normalized fractional portion of a floating point number.

Memory bank   An additional area of memory allowed by an additional set of address pins controlled by the I/O structure.

Multiplex   To share either a wire or a circuit with more than one signal.

Radix   The base of a number: radix two is the same as base two.

Stepper motor   A digital motor that is controlled by pulses.

Switching supply A power supply that is operated class C to reduce the power consumption and heat dissipation.

Table lookup A programming technique that draws data from a prestored table in the memory.

Questions and Problems

1 Interface an AY-5-2376 to an 8155 and develop a subroutine that will take data from the keyboard encoder and return with it in the accumulator.

2 Interface an AY-5-2376 to a 6821 and develop the subroutine required to take data from the keyboard encoder and return with it in accumulator B.

3 Modify the circuit of figure 7–4 so that 32 keys can be scanned. After this is accomplished, develop a subroutine to scan all 32 keys.

4 Develop a subroutine for the 8085A that will waste exactly 1.9 ms of time. Assume that the system clock frequency is 3 MHz. (Refer to chapter 3.)

5 Develop a subroutine for the 6800 that will waste exactly 7.8 ms of time. Assume that the system clock frequency is 1.0 MHz. (Refer to chapter 4.)

6 Interface two ADCs and one DAC converter to the microprocessor of your choice and develop the software to receive data from both ADCs and to send the sum of the data out of the DAC. Make sure to scale the sum by a factor of 50 percent, so that it can be sent without distortion.

7 Write a program using the subroutines developed for the stepper motor in this chapter that will rotate the motor in the clockwise direction at the rate of 60 RPM.

8 Write a program using the subroutines developed for the stepper motor in this chapter that will rotate the motor one step per second for 150 steps in the clockwise direction and then reset the motor in the counterclockwise direction to its starting point.

9 Using the subroutines provided in the chapter, what is the maximum rotational rate of the stepper motor? (Give the answer in RPMs.)

10 Develop an EEPROM memory system that contains 4K bytes of memory.

11 How much time would be required to program all 4096 bytes of memory?

12 Where would memory bank selection prove useful?

13 What problems do you foresee with software-selectable memory bank locations? Should protection be included in this type of scheme for memory management?

14 Develop the software required to divide one single-precision number by another. Use the subroutines provided in the chapter.

15 Develop the subroutines required to multiply two double-precision numbers together.

16 Most math books contain the required algorithm for calculating the sine of a number using a series. Look up this series expansion and develop the software to generate the sine of a number.

8

Interrupt
Processed I/O

Upon completion of this chapter, you will be able to

1 Define and explain the term *interrupt.*
2 Write interrupt service subroutines.
3 Describe the interrupt structure of the 8085A, Z80, MC6800, and MC6809.
4 Connect the 8085A so that it can call an interrupt service subroutine at any memory location.
5 Explain the operation of the 8085A instructions: EI, DI, RIM, and SIM.
6 Use the 8259A to expand the interrupt structure of the 8085A microprocessor.
7 Explain the software required to implement a real-time clock.
8 Explain the software and hardware used to implement a print spooler or queue.

Interrupts are extremely important microprocessor hardware. The interrupt allows an external system to gain the attention of the microprocessor through an interruption. The currently executing program can be interrupted by the external system through this technique.

The interrupt feature may at first glance seem unimportant, but it is used extensively. It attends to the needs of any low-speed external device because the only time that the microprocessor "knows" of the existence of the device is during an interrupt. This frees up a tremendous amount of computer time.

8–1 INTRODUCTION TO INTERRUPTS

An *interrupt* is a hardware-initiated subroutine call or jump that interrupts the currently executing program. Normally, subroutines are called with the software; with an interrupt, an external device can demand the attention of the microprocessor by calling a subroutine through the interrupt structure of the microprocessor. There are usually pin connections on the microprocessor that, when activated, cause an interrupt to occur.

A good example of the usefulness of an interrupt is the keyboard interface discussed in chapter 7. To read data from the keyboard, the microprocessor devotes all of its time to scanning the keyboard for a key switch closure. It scans the keyboard for as long as it takes the operator to strike a key.

If the keyboard uses an interrupt whenever a key switch is closed, the processing time utilized by the keyboard interface is reduced to a minimum. This is because with an interrupt, the only time that the microprocessor pays attention to the keyboard is when a key is actually depressed. Therefore, the microprocessor can accomplish useful tasks while the operator is contemplating the next keystroke.

The Interrupt Service Subroutine

The software used in response to the interrupt signal from the hardware is called an *interrupt service subroutine*. In the prior example, the act of typing on a key causes an interrupt. This interrupt then summons the interrupt service subroutine that determines exactly which key has caused the interrupt.

The interrupt service subroutine differs only slightly from a standard subroutine. It usually includes an instruction that reenables future interrupts and other instructions that save the contents of any register used within the interrupt service subroutine.

It is often the responsibility of the interrupt service subroutine to acknowledge the interrupt or to signal that the interrupt has been accepted. In some microprocessors, this is handled internally and is not the responsibility of the software. This acknowledgment usually occurs when the data are transferred to or from the interrupting device and is often a function of the external hardware.

Faults

The main problem with an interrupt-driven I/O is the fact that an interrupt can occur at any instant in time, which can cause system errors that are very hard to detect. Troubleshooting in a faulty system is difficult because of the apparent randomness of the interrupt. This difficulty can be overcome by developing proper diagnostic software to aid the technician in the repair of a faulty system. Also, additional external hardware can be provided for fault detection.

Types of Interrupts

Two basic types of interrupt inputs exist on various microprocessors, the *maskable* and the *nonmaskable* interrupt inputs. The nonmaskable interrupt input is always active and therefore handles critical events such as power failures and system restarts. The maskable interrupt input is more useful because it can be turned on and off with the software to fit a particular application. Microprocessors may include one or both of these inputs, and a few include many interrupt inputs to handle complicated control applications.

Microprocessor Interrupt Connections

Figure 8–1 illustrates the interrupt connections of four commonly used microprocessors: the 8085A, MC6800, MC6809, and Z80. The MC6800, MC6809, and Z80 contain a pin labeled NMI for nonmaskable interrupt; the 8085A contains a TRAP pin that performs the same function. The MC6800 and the Z80 have one maskable interrupt, the MC6809 has two maskable interrupts, and the 8085A has four maskable interrupt inputs. It appears that the 8085A has a more powerful hardware interrupt structure than the MC6800, MC6809, and the Z80. The inclusion of these additional interrupt pins reduces the external hardware overhead required for a multiple interrupt implementation. The more powerful interrupt structure of the Z80 will be discussed in section 8–4.

8085A INTERRUPT STRUCTURE 8–2

The 8085A has four interrupt control instructions: EI (enable interrupts), DI (disable interrupts), RIM (read interrupt masks), and SIM (set interrupt masks). The EI instruction turns on all of the unmasked interrupt pins; DI turns off all except the TRAP, which can never be deactivated. This task is accomplished by controlling the logic state of an internal interrupt enable flip-flop. EI sets it and DI clears it.

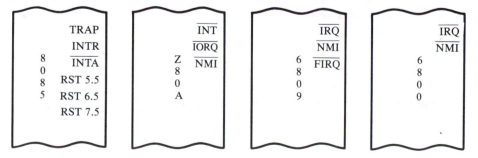

FIGURE 8–1 The interrupt pin connection of four common microprocessors: the Intel 8085A, Zilog Z80, and Motorola MC6800 and MC6809.

TABLE 8–1 Accumulator bit pattern before a SIM.

7	6	5	4	3	2	1	0
SOD	SOE	X	R7.5	MSE	M7.5	M6.5	M5.5

The SIM Instruction

The bit pattern that must be placed in the accumulator of the 8085A before a SIM instruction is executed is listed in table 8–1. The SIM instruction performs three separate tasks in the 8085A. SIM can control the SOD (serial output data) pin, reset the internal RST 7.5 interrupt request flip-flop, and mask any of the RST pins.

The SOD pin is controlled by placing a logic one in the SOE (SOD enable) bit of the accumulator and the desired logic level to be transferred to the SOD latch in the SOD bit. This is followed by the SIM instruction, which causes SOD to change to whatever was present in the SOD position of the accumulator.

The R7.5 bit, when placed high, will clear any interrupt request that may be pending on the internal RST 7.5 interrupt-request flip-flop. The RST 7.5 input is an edge-triggered input; in certain applications, it may be necessary to ignore a request on this pin. Figure 8–2 illustrates the internal RST 7.5 interrupt-request flip-flop, the logic circuitry for masking, and the EI and DI instructions. The TRAP flip-flop is cleared whenever the processor accepts it or at the time of a reset. The RST 7.5 flip-flop is cleared by the SIM instruction whenever it is accepted or at the time of a reset.

The remaining four bits of the SIM control word mask the RST interrupt inputs. To modify these masks, a one is placed in the MSE (mask set enable) bit position; and the appropriate masks are placed in the M7.5, M6.5, and M5.5 bit positions. A logic zero turns on the corresponding RST input and a logic one turns it off. The conditions of these masks are only valid if the interrupt structure is enabled by the EI instruction.

The RIM Instruction

Table 8–2 illustrates the bit pattern found in the accumulator after the RIM instruction is executed. This bit pattern indicates (1) the logic level of the SID (serial input data) pin; (2) which RST interrupts are pending; (3) the state of the internal interrupt enable flip-flop, which is controlled by EI and DI; and (4) the logic levels of the masks.

RIM is most often used to allow a particular interrupt mask to be set or cleared without affecting the other masks. In the example illustrated, the RST 7.5 interrupt input is enabled without affecting the RST 6.5 or RST 5.5 masks.

TABLE 8–2 Accumulator bit pattern after a RIM.

7	6	5	4	3	2	1	0
SID	I7.5	I6.5	I5.5	IE	M7.5	M6.5	M5.5

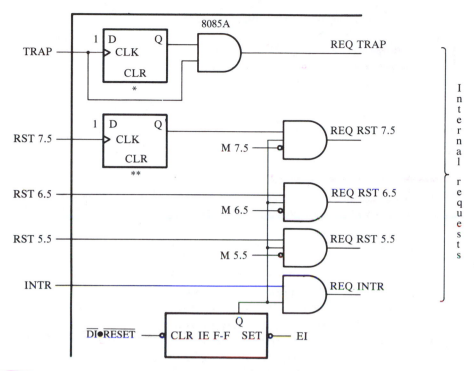

FIGURE 8–2   The internal representation of the Intel 8085A interrupt structure.

*The TRAP flip-flop is cleared on a RESET and when it's accepted by the microprocessor.
**The RST 7.5 flip-flop is cleared on a RESET, when it's accepted by the microprocessor, or with the SIM instruction.

```
                     RIM              ;read masks
2000  E603           ANI    03H       ;clear all except M6.5 & M5.5
2002  F608           ORI    08H       ;set MSE
                     SIM              ;modify masks
```

The Interrupt Inputs

Table 8–3 indicates the locations of the subroutines called by the interrupt inputs, the sensitivity of these inputs, and their priority levels. It is important to note that the RST

TABLE 8-3   Interrupt addresses for the 8085A.

Pin Name	Priority	Subroutine	Sensitivity
TRAP	1	0024H	Rising edge and high level
RST 7.5	2	003CH	Rising edge
RST 6.5	3	0034H	High level
RST 5.5	4	002CH	High level
INTR	5	*	High level

NOTE: This input does not have a decoded subroutine address.

locations are only four bytes in length and normally contain a PUSH PSW and a JMP to the interrupt service subroutine.

The TRAP input is both positive-edge sensitive and level sensitive for use in power failure detection circuitry. The RST 7.5 input is positive-edge sensitive for any application requiring this type of sensitivity. The RST 6.5, RST 5.5, and INTR inputs are level sensitive; they must be held at their active levels until they are recognized at the end of the current instruction. The time required to recognize these three inputs varies with different instructions and clock speeds of the 8085A. It is also important to note that the HOLD input causes an interrupt to be delayed until after the HOLD condition has ended.

The INTR Input and INTA Output

The INTR input does not call an interrupt service subroutine directly. Instead, the 8085A issues an INTA pulse when this input is acknowledged, as illustrated in figure 8–3. It is the designer's responsibility to add hardware that will force an instruction onto the data bus in response to the INTA output of the 8085A. For most applications, a RST 1 through RST 7 is forced onto the data bus; on occasion, a CALL instruction is. (Note that the RST 0 instruction is normally used for a software and hardware RESET.) Figure 8–4 pictures the application of a RST 5 in response to an INTR interrupt request. The RST 5 instruction, an EFH, is hardwired to the inputs of the eight three-state buffers. Whenever the INTR input is placed at the logic one level requesting an interrupt, the microprocessor responds with an INTA pulse. This procedure enables the buffers and applies the EFH or RST 5 op-code on the data bus. The microprocessor responds by executing the RST 5 or it calls the subroutine that begins at memory location 28H.

TRAP Input

The TRAP interrupt input, as mentioned, is nonmaskable. One word of caution about the use of this interrupt: TRAP will disable other interrupt inputs whenever it is accepted, which may cause problems in systems with more than one interrupt. If TRAP is used with other interrupts, the following software is normally added to the end of the TRAP interrupt service subroutine.

```
2023 F5          TRAP:     PUSH PSW
2024 C5                    PUSH B
                            .
                            .
2025 C1                    POP  B
2026 20                    RIM              ;read masks
2027 E608                  ANI  08H         ;isolate IE
2029 CA202D                JZ   TRAPO       ;if zero end
202C FB                    EI
202D F1          TRAPO:    POP  PSW
202E C9                    RET
```

In this software the IE bit indicates the state of the interrupt-enable flip-flop prior to acceptance of the TRAP interrupt. If IE were a logic one, then interrupts would be reenabled, and if IE were a logic zero, then interrupts would remain disabled.

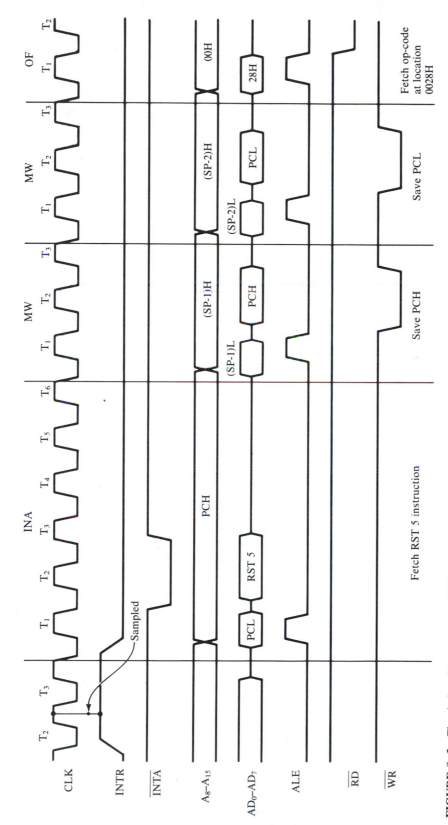

FIGURE 8–3 The timing diagram for an INTR showing the RST 5 instruction in response to the interrupt.

FIGURE 8–4 A circuit that will cause a RST 5 instruction to be gated onto the 8085A data bus in response to an INTR.

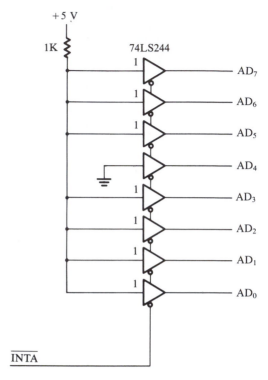

8–3 MC6800 AND MC6809 INTERRUPT STRUCTURE

The MC6809 has three interrupt inputs: one is a nonmaskable interrupt input, $\overline{\text{NMI}}$, and the others are maskable interrupts, $\overline{\text{IRQ}}$ and $\overline{\text{FIRQ}}$. The MC6800 has all the same inputs except the $\overline{\text{FIRQ}}$. The $\overline{\text{NMI}}$ input causes the MC6809 to look to memory locations $FFFC and $FFFD for the address of the interrupt service subroutine. The $\overline{\text{IRQ}}$ input uses $FFF8 and $FFF9, and the $\overline{\text{FIRQ}}$ input uses $FFF6 and $FFF7 for their service subroutine vectors.

When the interrupt input is accepted by the MC6809 or MC6800, it automatically saves the contents of all internal registers on the stack and looks to the appropriate interrupt vector for the starting location of the interrupt service subroutine. The exception to this rule is the $\overline{\text{FIRQ}}$, or *fast interrupt request* input, which saves only the contents of the program counter and condition code register.

At the end of the interrupt service subroutine, a special return instruction (RTI) reloads the registers saved on the stack and returns to the program that was interrupted. This return instruction is different from RTS, which does not restore any register except for the program counter. An extra flag bit in the status register indicates whether the interrupt is a $\overline{\text{FIRQ}}$ or normal interrupt for the MC6809. This is examined by RTI to determine which registers must be unloaded from the stack.

In the MC6800 the $\overline{\text{IRQ}}$ interrupt input is enabled by the CLI instruction and disabled by the SEI instruction. These instructions control the interrupt enable bit (I) in the condition code register, which in turn controls whether or not the interrupt is accepted by the microprocessor.

In the MC6809, the (I) and (F) interrupt masks are controlled by the ORCC instruction, which sets or disables them, and the ANDCC instruction, which clears or enables these bits. The (F) condition code bit controls the $\overline{\text{FIRQ}}$ input, and the (I) condition code bit controls the $\overline{\text{IRQ}}$ input.

Z80 INTERRUPT STRUCTURE 8–4

The Z80 has two interrupt inputs, the nonmaskable interrupt input ($\overline{\text{NMI}}$) and the maskable interrupt input ($\overline{\text{INT}}$). The nonmaskable interrupt input CALLs the interrupt service subroutine, which must reside beginning at location 0066H in the memory. Refer to Appendix A on the Z80 for their timing.

Maskable Interrupt

The maskable interrupt input can be used in three different ways by the Z80. The first mode of operation, *mode 0,* is identical to the method used by the INTR pin on the 8085A. The only difference is that to generate $\overline{\text{INTA}}$, the $\overline{\text{IORQ}}$ signal must be logically combined with the M1 signal (as illustrated in figure 8–5). This circuit inserts a RST 4 instruction in response to the $\overline{\text{INT}}$ request. It does this because the RST 4 instruction, an E7H, is

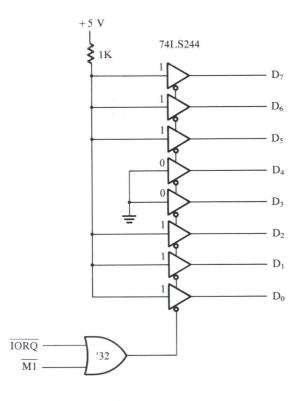

FIGURE 8–5 · A circuit that will cause a RST 4 instruction to be gated onto the Z80 data bus in response to an $\overline{\text{INT}}$.

hardwired to the buffer inputs. When the processor acknowledges the $\overline{\text{INT}}$ input, the buffers gate this op-code onto the data bus for execution by the microprocessor.

A second method, or *mode 1,* causes the Z80 to respond to the $\overline{\text{INT}}$ input with a RST 7. This is useful in a small system that requires only one maskable interrupt input. It does not require any additional hardware for implementation.

The third mode of operation, *mode 2,* for the $\overline{\text{INT}}$ input is by far the most powerful. This mode allows multiple interrupt inputs for larger systems. When the Z80 responds to this type of interrupt, it reads the least significant portion of the interrupt service subroutine address from the data bus, as illustrated in figure 8–6. This portion of the vector address is combined with the most significant portion, which is stored in a special internal Z80 register called the *I register.* This allows the interrupt service subroutine to be stored anywhere in the Z80 memory address space.

Interrupt Control Instructions

The EI instruction enables the $\overline{\text{INT}}$ pin, and the DI instruction disables it. This is exactly the same as in the 8085A microprocessor. In addition to these two instructions, three more interrupt control instructions are found in the instruction set. IM 0 selects the first mode, IM 1 selects the second, and IM 2 selects the third and most powerful mode. The interrupt vector location is specified by the LD I,A instruction, which copies the contents of the accumulator into the interrupt vector register. This register, along with the 8 bits of address information fetched during an interrupt acknowledge, forms the interrupt vector address for mode 2 operation.

FIGURE 8–6   This circuit will cause a CALL to memory location XX97H to occur in response to the INT input. The XX portion of the address is stored in the I register.

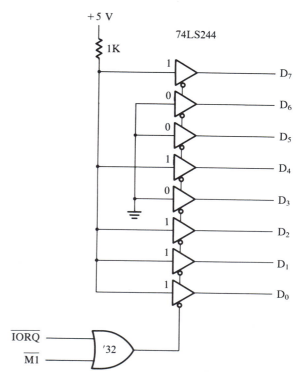

Most interrupt inputs are level sensitive and must be held high until accepted by the microprocessor. The 8085A RST 7.5 and TRAP inputs are exceptions, since they are edge-triggered inputs. To ensure that the interrupt is accepted, a simple latch to accomplish this synchronization may be required. Figure 8–7 illustrates this latch. In certain circumstances the latch is built into the external interrupt device.

The clock input to the D-type latch is a positive edge-sensitive input that is pulsed to request an interrupt. The Q output is connected directly to the positive level-sensitive interrupt input of the microprocessor, or the $\overline{Q}$ is connected to the negative level-sensitive input of the microprocessor. When the microprocessor acknowledges the acceptance of the interrupt through either an $\overline{INTA}$ signal or the act of controlling the interrupting I/O device, the flip-flop is reset to clear the interrupt request.

Real-Time Clock

An application of a simple interrupt is a real-time clock. The clock discussed here is a time-of-day clock that receives its timing signal from the AC power line. Real-time clocks serve this purpose and clock events in real time.

Clock Hardware

Figure 8–8 illustrates the hardware required to cause a periodic interrupt on the RST 7.5 edge-triggered interrupt input of an 8085A microprocessor. A 6.3-V AC signal from the power transformer is rectified and waveshaped by a Schmitt trigger amplifier to produce 60 positive edges per second at the RST 7.5 input. Rectification is accomplished by the clamping diode located within the Schmitt trigger input circuit. The Schmitt trigger is used instead of an inverter because of the rise time requirement of the RST 7.5 input. This guarantees that the interrupt service subroutine, which keeps correct time, will be called exactly 60 times per second.

Clock Software

The time for the real-time clock is kept in four RAM memory locations that contain the binary coded decimal time of day. The first location functions as a divide-by-60, or MOD-60, counter to produce 1-s timing pulses for the remainder of the clock. The seconds and minutes locations are also modulus-60 counters, which produce 1-h pulses for the modulus-24-hour counter.

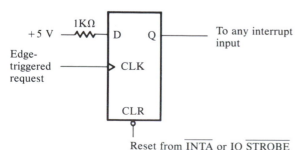

FIGURE 8–7 A method for converting a level sensitive interrupt input into an edge triggered interrupt input.

FIGURE 8–8 A 60-Hz interrupt
input for a real time clock.

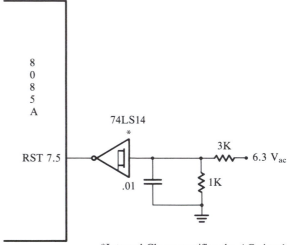

*Internal Clamp rectifies the AC signal.

```
4000  00        TIME:   DB    0           ;1/60 seconds counter
4001  00                DB    0           ;seconds counter
4002  00                DB    0           ;minutes counter
4003  00                DB    0           ;hours counter
```

Update Subroutine

Since there are four counters that must be periodically updated, it is wise to develop a
subroutine to handle any one of them. This subroutine must be supplied with the modulus
of the counter to be updated and its location in the memory. For this example, the HL pair
holds the address of the counter, and the B register holds the modulus of the counter to be
incremented. B dictates to the subroutine when a counter will be cleared. This information
is supplied by the calling program or, in this case, the interrupt service subroutine.

```
                        ;this subroutine increments the contents of the
                        ;memory location indexed by the HL pair.
                        ;B indicates the maximum count plus one of
                        ;this counter.
                        ;
4004  7E        UPDATE: MOV   A,M          ;get counter
4005  C601              ADI   1            ;increment it
4007  27                DAA                ;make result BCD
4008  77                MOV   M,A          ;save counter
4009  90                SUB   B            ;check for TC
400A  C0                RNZ
400B  77                MOV   M,A          ;clear count
400C  23                INX   H            ;address next counter
400D  C9                RET
```

In the UPDATE subroutine the counter is incremented, and a return not zero occurs if
it does not reach its terminal count. If the terminal count is reached, the counter is cleared
to zero and the pointer in the HL pair is incremented to the next counter's address. A
return zero indicates that the next counter should be incremented because of the overflow,
and a return not zero indicates that the next and subsequent counters contain the correct
time.

Clock Initialization

The interrupt service subroutine is called 60 times per second if the RST 7.5 interrupt is unmasked and enabled at the RESET location in the system. This initialization sequence follows:

```
0000  3E0B          RESET:   MVI   A,00001011B   ;unmask RST 7.5
                             SIM
0002  FB                     EI
```

Clock Interrupt Service Subroutine

The interrupt service subroutine itself, as depicted by the flowchart in figure 8–9, must correctly update the BCD clock located in the RAM.

This is accomplished by updating the 1/60-seconds counter each time an interrupt occurs. If this counter overflows, as it does once per second, the seconds counter is updated. The seconds counter overflows once per minute; at this time the minutes counter is updated, and so forth.

```
3000  F5            RST75:   PUSH  PSW            ;save registers
3001  E5                     PUSH  H
3002  C5                     PUSH  B
3003  0660                   MVI   B,60H          ;load modulus
3005  210040                 LXI   H,TIME         ;point to clock
3008  CD0440                  CALL  UPDATE         ;increment 1/60 counter
300B  C21F30                 JNZ   DONE
300E  CD0440                 CALL  UPDATE         ;increment seconds
3011  C21F30                 JNZ   DONE
3014  CD0440                 CALL  UPDATE         ;increment minutes
3017  C21F30                 JNZ   DONE
301A  0624                   MVI   B,24H          ;load new modulus
301C  CD0440                 CALL  UPDATE         ;increment hours
301F  C1            DONE:    POP   B              ;restore registers
3020  E1                     POP   H
3021  F1                     POP   PSW
3022  FB                     EI                   ;enable future interrupts
3023  C9                     RET
```

A system using this type of clock would seem to become very inefficient, since the program or system would be interrupted 60 times per second. This is not the case, since this interrupt consumes less than 0.5 percent of the microprocessor's processing time. In most cases this loss can readily be acceptable for the total system. The interrupt can easily be modified to include the day, month, and year without increasing significantly the time used by the interrupt service subroutine.

One possible pitfall of this type of clock is that another interrupting device may require more time than 1/60 second. If this occurs, the result is a subsequent loss of the correct time. Exercise care in using this clock with other interrupts.

INTERRUPT PRIORITY SCHEMES   8–6

On numerous occasions the one or two interrupt inputs provided on most microprocessors prove to be too few. The one exception is the 8085A, which has five of these interrupt

FIGURE 8–9 The flowchart of
the interrupt service subroutine
that keeps time in the real-time
clock circuit of figure 8–8.

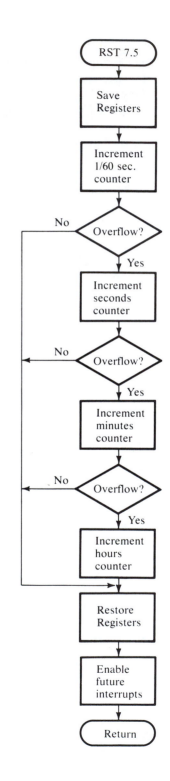

inputs. Expanding the number of interrupt inputs is relatively simple because most manufacturers provide an interrupt expansion component.

The Daisy Chain

One interrupt expansion circuit in use is the daisy chain. Figure 8–10 depicts a typical four-channel daisy chain interrupt system. The interrupt request signal from any of the four channels clears the accompanying interrupt request flip-flop, whose output is then logically combined with the outputs of the other three flip-flops to produce an interrupt request signal for the microprocessor. When acknowledging the interrupt, the microprocessor returns an acknowledgment signal through the daisy chain to the nearest requesting device. This acknowledgment signal clears the request, sets the Q output of the flip-flop,

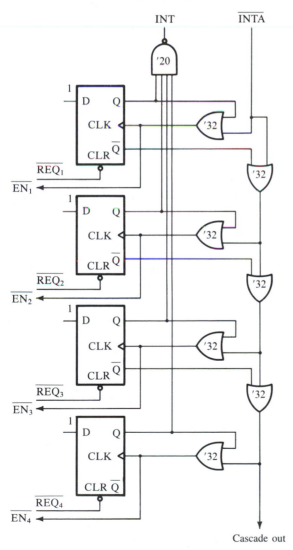

FIGURE 8–10 A daisy-chained interrupt expansion circuit.

Cascade out

FIGURE 8–11 A circuit for causing multiple RST interrupts in an 8085A or Z80 based system.

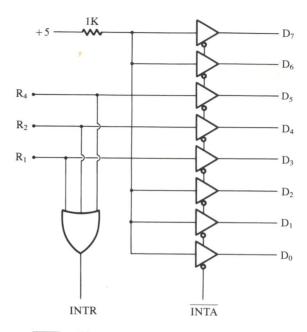

and enables the interrupting device. The $\overline{ENX}$ outputs go low for only about 25 ns in this circuit and may therefore need to be latched by the requesting device.

The main shortcoming of this system is that all interrupts remain active at all times, and the priority scheme is fixed. The device nearest the interrupt-acknowledge output of the microprocessor, $\overline{REQ1}$, is the one with the highest priority.

Restart Priority

Another priority scheme in the Intel or Zilog processors involves using the restart instructions. The circuit in figure 8–11 can be used to expand the interrupt capabilities of these microprocessors easily by causing the microprocessor to execute different restart instructions. The processor accomplishes this by gating the RST instructions onto the data bus for various interrupt input conditions.

Request-inputs R1, R2, and R4 cause the microprocessor to execute RST1, RST2, and RST4, respectively. If more than one of these interrupt inputs occurs at a time, different restart subroutines are called. For example, if the R1 and R2 inputs are active at the same time, a RST3 instruction is issued to the microprocessor. The RST3 service subroutine resolves priority between these two request signals. See table 8–4 for the complete list of RST instructions called by this technique.

This technique is relatively simple but can be used only for the Intel and Zilog 8-bit microprocessors. It also has the limitation of being expandable to only three external interrupts.

Priority Encoder

The priority encoder is the most useful type of interrupt-expanding device available today. It may be purchased in IC form and used as desired, or it may be included within an interrupt controller provided by the manufacturer. Generally, expansion through this type

TABLE 8–4 Vector locations for figure 8–11.

R4	R2	R1	RST Instruction
0	0	0	None
0	0	1	RST 1
0	1	0	RST 2
0	1	1	RST 3
1	0	0	RST 4
1	0	1	RST 5
1	1	0	RST 6
1	1	1	RST 7

of device is limited to no fewer than 64 external interrupting devices. A microprocessor-based system with so many interrupt-processed I/O devices is extremely rare.

The 8259A Interrupt Controller
a zero on A0 for OCW3 and OCW3 when turned on the interrupts are mashed off

Figure 8–12 illustrates the Intel 8259A programmable interrupt controller, which allows the user to expand the interrupt capabilities of an Intel or Zilog microprocessor to eight or more interrupt inputs. It permits the use of the RST instructions; if required, it inserts

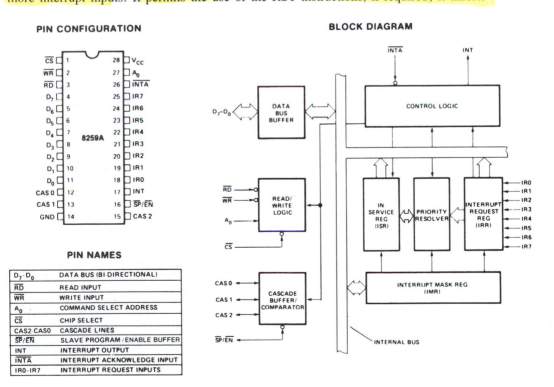

FIGURE 8–12 The pinout and block diagram of the 8259A programmable interrupt controller.

SOURCE: Reprinted by permission of Intel Corporation. Copyright 1983.

CALL instructions in response to an interrupt. This device also allows the user to select the type of priority scheme desired for the interrupt inputs.

8259A Initialization

To use the interrupt controller in a system, four separate command words are used in the initialization process. Figure 8–13 illustrates these four command words, ICW1 through ICW4.

ICW1   indicates whether or not ICW4 is needed, which is discussed further below. It also indicates whether there is a single device or more than one device in the system.

    IC4   indicates whether ICW4 is needed.

    SNGL   indicates whether this is a single 8259A or whether more than one exists in the system.

    ADI   indicates whether the CALL address interrupt vectors are to be four or eight bytes in length.

    LTIM   selects level or edge triggering for the eight interrupt request inputs.

    A7, A6, and A5   specify part of the address of the second byte of the CALL instruction. (See tables 8–5 and 8–6 for more detail on these bits.)

ICW2   specifies the third byte of the CALL instruction for the 8085A microprocessor. If the 8086 or 8088 is in use, it specifies the interrupt vector.

ICW3   used in a cascaded system only. This initialization command word selects master or slave operation and indicates the slave ID or which slaves are present in the system to the master.

ICW4   normally used in buffered mode. *Buffered mode* is a mode of operation in a system where the data bus contains bidirectional bus buffers. These buffers must be controlled during an interrupt by the 8259A to pass the instruction or vector to the microprocessor. The $\overline{EP}/\overline{EN}$ pin provides this control function to the data bus buffers.

    μPM   selects which microprocessor is in use with the 8259A.

    AEOI   controls the automatic end of interrupt operation. If activated, the last $\overline{INTA}$ pulse automatically internally acknowledges the interrupt request. If not acti-

TABLE 8–5   Second byte of a CALL if vectors are placed four bytes apart.

IR	Interval = 4							
	D7	D6	D5	D4	D3	D2	D1	D0
7	A7	A6	A5	1	1	1	0	0
6	A7	A6	A5	1	1	0	0	0
5	A7	A6	A5	1	0	1	0	0
4	A7	A6	A5	1	0	0	0	0
3	A7	A6	A5	0	1	1	0	0
2	A7	A6	A5	0	1	0	0	0
1	A7	A6	A5	0	0	1	0	0
0	A7	A6	A5	0	0	0	0	0

(Reprinted by permission of Intel Corporation, copyright 1983)

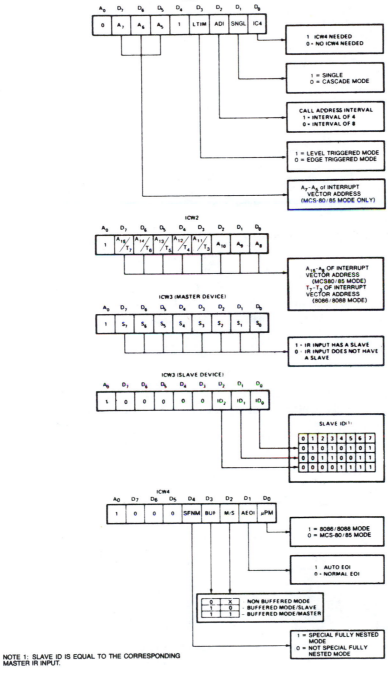

FIGURE 8–13 The four initialization command words for the 8259A programmable interrupt controller.

SOURCE: Reprinted by permission of Intel Corporation. Copyright 1983.

TABLE 8–6 Second byte of a CALL if vectors are placed eight bytes apart.

IR	Interval = 8							
	D7	**D6**	**D5**	**D4**	**D3**	**D2**	**D1**	**D0**
7	A7	A6	1	1	1	0	0	0
6	A7	A6	1	1	0	0	0	0
5	A7	A6	1	0	1	0	0	0
4	A7	A6	1	0	0	0	0	0
3	A7	A6	0	1	1	0	0	0
2	A7	A6	0	1	0	0	0	0
1	A7	A6	0	0	1	0	0	0
0	A7	A6	0	0	0	0	0	0

(Reprinted by permission of Intel Corporation, copyright 1983)

vated, the interrupt service subroutine must clear the interrupt request through an operation command, as described later in this section.

M/S   selects master/slave operation. This is used only if the system contains multiple 8259As. The master releases the CALL instruction, and the slave device releases the second and third bytes of the CALL to the 8085A.

BUF   used in a large system to enable the buffer control signal $\overline{EP/EN}$.

SFNM   selects the specially nested mode of operation for the 8259A. This mode is used in a large buffered system with multiple 8259As.

Initialization Example

Figure 8–14 depicts an 8259A attached to an 8085A microprocessor. In this case, it expands the interrupt inputs with eight additional interrupt request inputs. The 8259A

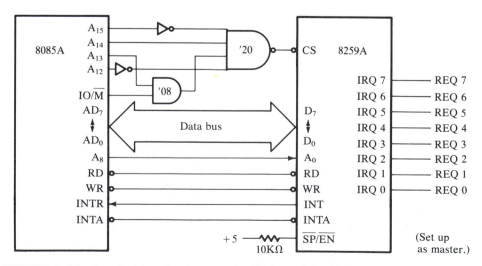

FIGURE 8–14   A typical interface between the 8085A and the 8259A programmable interrupt controller.

TABLE 8–7 Interrupt vectors for figure 8–14.

Interrupt Pin	Vector Location
IR0	0800H
IR1	0804H
IR2	0808H
IR3	080CH
IR4	0810H
IR5	0814H
IR6	0818H
IR7	081CH

is decoded to respond to I/O port numbers 6XH. In this example, it is assumed that this device and its interrupt inputs are to CALL the subroutines that begin in an interrupt vector table at memory location 0800H. Each vector is to be four bytes in length. Table 8–7 pictures the interrupts and the interrupt vector locations.

To create a system with these vector locations, the 8259A must be initialized. The ICWs, or initialization command words, discussed earlier accomplish the programming. Only ICW1 and ICW2 are normally programmed, unless the 8086 is used or there is more than one 8259A present.

```
                    ;this sequence of instructions will initialize
                    ;the 8259A so that the interrupt vector table
                    ;begins at 0800H.
                    ;
4000  3E16  INIT:   MVI   A,00010110B ;setup ICW1
4002  D360          OUT   60H
4004  3E08          MVI   A,00001000B ;setup ICW2
4006  D361          OUT   61H
```

This initialization dialog programs the 8259A so that its interrupt inputs are edge sensitive, the vector interval is four bytes, and the vector table begins at location 0800H. From this point forward, a positive edge on any of the interrupt inputs will CALL a subroutine from the vector table.

8259A Operation Command Words

In addition to the initialization commands, it is necessary to program the operation of the 8259A through three separate command words (as pictured in figure 8–15).

Operation command word OCW1 controls the eight interrupt inputs to the 8259A. To mask (1) a channel inhibits it, or prevents an interrupt. To clear a mask (0) enables, or turns on, the corresponding interrupt input.

OCW2 controls the operation of the internal interrupt priority system.

L2, L1, and L0 signals that set the lowest priority interrupt input. If 010 is selected, IR2 has the lowest priority and IR3 has the highest. These bits are also used with the EOI bit specifically to clear one of the interrupt requests.

EOI clears the interrupt request with the highest priority from the interrupt service subroutine.

SL used with the L2, L1, and L0 bits to clear a specific interrupt request.

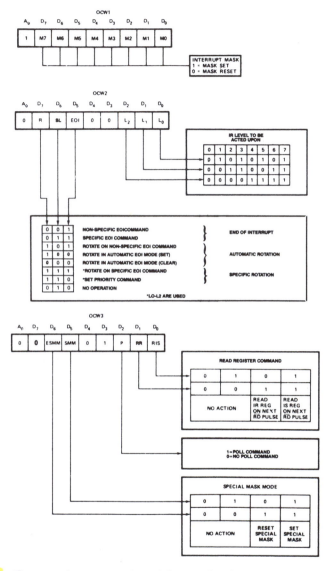

FIGURE 8–15   The operation command word formats for the 8259A programmable interrupt controller.

SOURCE: Reprinted by permission of Intel Corporation. Copyright 1983.

> **R**   causes an automatic priority rotation. The most recently serviced interrupt becomes the lowest priority input.

OCW3   accomplishes the following functions:

> **RIS and RR**   select which register is read on the next $\overline{\text{RD}}$ pulse. The IR register indicates which interrupts are pending, and the IS register indicates which interrupts are masked. These registers are illustrated in figure 8–16 with the Poll register.

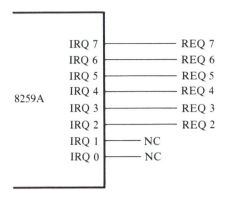

FIGURE 8–16 This interface is identical to the one pictured in figure 8–14, except that two of the eight interrupt inputs are not connected.

P   if active, it causes the next read ($\overline{RD}$) to read the highest interrupt input currently requesting service.

SMM and ESMM   control the operation of the special mask mode. When an interrupt is accepted in normal mode, all lower-priority interrupts are disabled. In a case in which a lower-level interrupt is to take effect, the special mask mode is used. This mode allows all other interrupts to take effect when enabled.

More programming is required to operate the interrupt controller pictured in figure 8–16. You will notice that not all of the interrupt inputs are actually connected to an external device. These unused inputs should be turned off, or masked. In addition to masking the unused inputs, a rotating priority scheme is employed for the remaining inputs. The remainder of the initialization dialog follows:

```
4008  3E03          MVI   A,00000011B  ;setup OCW1
400A  D361          OUT   61H
400C  3E82          MVI   A,10000010B  ;setup OCW2
400E  D360          OUT   60H
```

From this point forward, the 8259A will function as an interrupt vectoring device.

Interrupt Acknowledge with the 8259A

To acknowledge an interrupt, the interrupt controller must be written into, using one of the OCWs described in the preceding paragraphs. Suppose that the IRQ7 input has just taken effect and at this point we are in that interrupt service subroutine. To acknowledge this, we can use OCW2 and the nonspecific end of an interrupt or OCW2 and the specific end of an interrupt. With the nonspecific end of interrupt, it is assumed that it is the latest interrupt, and with the specific EOI we must specify which interrupt. The software illustrated below uses the specific EOI to end the IRQ7 interrupt. It is found at the very end of the IRQ7 interrupt service subroutine.

```
                    ;these instructions form the very end of
                    ;the IRQ7 interrupt service subroutine
                    ;
4200  3EC7   ACK:      MVI   A,11000111B  ;acknowledge IRQ7
4202  D360             OUT   60H
4204  FB               EI                 ;enable future interrupts
4205  C9               RET
```

Polled Interrupts

Still another method of handling multiple-interrupt inputs is a polling scheme. This type of interrupt system is adaptable to any microprocessor and uses relatively inexpensive hardware.

Figure 8–17 pictures the schematic diagram of a simple but effective polling scheme. This particular system contains eight interrupt inputs connected to one of the microprocessor's interrupt request inputs. The eight interrupt request lines are connected to a NAND gate, where they are logically combined to produce a logic zero at its output when no request is active. If one or more requests occur, the output of the NAND gate becomes a logic one. (This may or may not be the correct logic level for a particular application, but it can be inverted to produce the correct level.) The eight request lines also connect to an 8-bit input device. This allows the user to determine, through software, which input has caused the interrupt and to assign priority if more than one occurs at the same time.

```
                      ;polling interrupt response subroutine
                      ;
2000  DB10            POLL:    IN     PORT          ;input interrupt requests
2002  210E20                   LXI    H,TABLE-2     ;address jump table
2005  07              LOOP:    RLC                  ;check interrupt bit
2006  23                       INX    H             ;address next vector
2007  23                       INX    H
2008  DA0520                   JC     LOOP          ;if not found
200B  7E                       MOV    A,M           ;get vector address
200C  23                       INX    H
200D  66                       MOV    H,M
200E  6F                       MOV    L,A
200F  E9                       PCHL                 ;jump to vector address
                      ;
                      ;interrupt vector table
                      ;
2010  0022            TABLE:   DW     I7            ;highest priority
2012  0023                     DW     I6
```

FIGURE 8–17 A circuit for causing an interrupt allowing the system to look at the interrupting inputs.

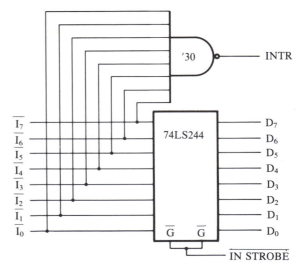

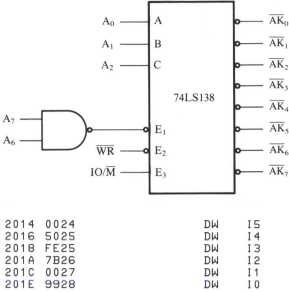

FIGURE 8–18 A circuit that
will generate eight different interrupt-acknowledge pulses for the
interrupting devices. (Refer to
table 8–8 for additional detail on
these signals.)

```
2014  0024          DW    I5
2016  5025          DW    I4
2018  FE25          DW    I3
201A  7B26          DW    I2
201C  0027          DW    I1
201E  9928          DW    I0
```

To acknowledge the request, the interrupt service subroutine sends a signal to the requesting device. This signal can clear the appropriate interrupt request in addition to transferring the data. Figure 8–18 illustrates a simple logic circuit that can be used for the request and the data strobe. If A2, A1, and A0 contain 111 at the time of the OUT instruction, the 74LS138 sends the strobe to interrupt device number seven (AK7). If an input device is in use, an IN instruction is used in place of the OUT. Table 8–8 illustrates the I/O port numbers used with this circuit to develop these strobes.

INTERRUPT-DRIVEN FIFO 8–7

In many applications the data are input or output at a relatively low speed and throughput can be drastically increased by an interrupt. In the example of a printer interface, the speed of the printer itself is relatively low when compared to the microprocessor. It may

TABLE 8–8 Acknowledge strobe ports for figure 8–18.

Port Number		Acknowledge Signal
11XX	X000	$\overline{AK0}$
11XX	X001	$\overline{AK1}$
11XX	X010	$\overline{AK2}$
11XX	X011	$\overline{AK3}$
11XX	X100	$\overline{AK4}$
11XX	X101	$\overline{AK5}$
11XX	X110	$\overline{AK6}$
11XX	X111	$\overline{AK7}$

be able to print an average of 50 characters per second, while the microprocessor can send it information at the rate of about ten thousand characters per second.

In this application the throughput of the computer can be enhanced greatly if an interrupt occurs every time that the printer requires a character to be printed. The only time that the computer has to communicate with the printer is at the time of an interrupt, freeing the microprocessor for more useful tasks.

Centronics Printer Interface

The Centronics parallel printer interface is very commonly used today. Figure 8–19 illustrates the timing diagram for this interface. All of the signals are TTL logic levels, so no special level translation is required between the printer and the computer system.

The $\overline{ACK}$ and $\overline{STROBE}$ signals comprise the control structure of this simple-to-use interface. The acknowledge signal ($\overline{ACK}$) is an output from the printer to the computer indicating that a character has been received and the printer is ready for the next character.

The $\overline{STROBE}$ signal comes from the computer and tells the printer that data are available on the data connections.

In an interrupt-processed system, the $\overline{ACK}$ signal causes an interrupt, and the $\overline{STROBE}$ signal is developed by the PIA whenever a character is transmitted to the printer.

8085A Interface

Figure 8–20 depicts a Centronics-type printer interface connected to an 8155 and 8085A. Port A is set up to send the data to the printer as a strobed output port.

The $\overline{STROBE}$ signal for the printer is developed from an output pin on port C. The $\overline{ACK}$ signal from the printer is connected to the $\overline{STB}$ input for port A. In strobed output operation, the $\overline{STB}$ input causes the INTR output of the 8155 to become a logic one. In this case, an interrupt is requested when the printer acknowledges receipt of an ASCII character.

The 8155 in this application is selected whenever the four most significant address connections are at a logic one condition. This means that the 8155 turns on for I/O port

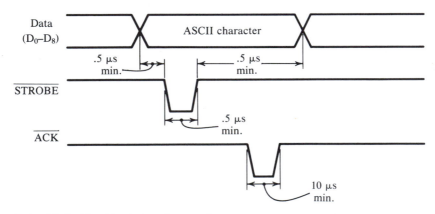

FIGURE 8–19   The timing diagram for the Centronics-type printer interface.

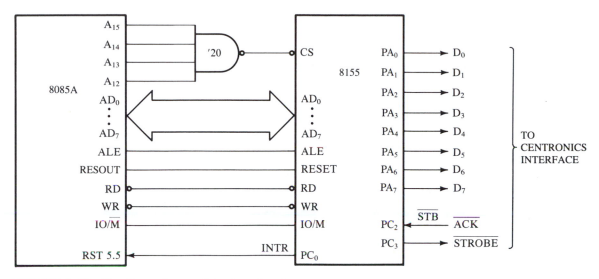

FIGURE 8–20   The Centronics parallel printer interface connected to an 8085A microprocessor through an 8155 PIA.

numbers FXH. The software featured later in this section uses ports F0H through F5H for the control of this interface.

MC6800 Interface

See figure 8–21 for a schematic diagram of the MC6800-to-Centronics printer interface. This interface uses the MC6821 to generate an interrupt pulse for the microprocessor along with the data and handshaking for the printer. The MC6821 responds to memory addresses $EXXX in this example. Addresses $E000 through $E003 are actually used in the software.

Port A is programmed as an output device to transmit data to the printer. Pin CA1 is connected to the $\overline{ACK}$ signal from the printer to request an interrupt through the $\overline{IRQA}$ pin. Pin CA2 sends the $\overline{STROBE}$ signal to the printer whenever data are being transmitted.

The Queue or FIFO

In the type of application just described it is customary to use a FIFO or queue to store the data to be sent to the printer. The length of the queue will probably be at least one line in length, or it might be up to several pages. A *queue* or *FIFO* is a special arrangement of the cyclical memory whereby data are addressed through two pointers, an input pointer and an output pointer. It's a cyclical memory, since the same area of memory is used over and over by the system, just as the stack uses the same area of memory. In the case of a printer interface, the input pointer is addressed through a subroutine and the output pointer is addressed by the interrupt service subroutine. Since this type of memory system is completely managed by the software, its cost is relatively low.

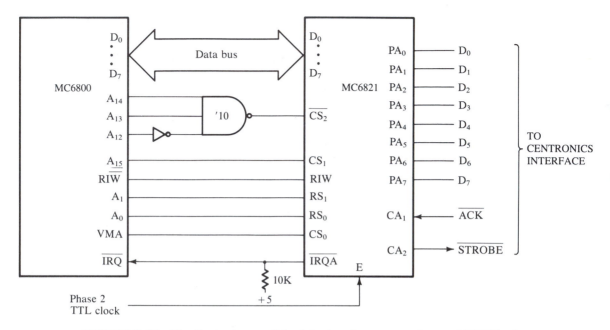

FIGURE 8–21   The Centronics parallel printer interface connected to an MC6800 microprocessor through the MC6821 PIA.

256-Byte Queue

A 256-byte queue uses 256 bytes (a small portion of the computer memory) for a queue, plus two bytes of additional memory for the input and output pointers. In the MC6800 software, two bytes per pointer reduce the amount of software. Note that a 256-byte queue is capable of storing only 255 bytes of data; one byte is lost because of the full and empty conditions. The queue is depicted in figure 8–22. In this example, if the queue is empty the pointers are equal; if it is full, the input pointer is one less than the output pointer.

FIGURE 8–22   A symbolic presentation of the 256-byte queue or FIFO memory.

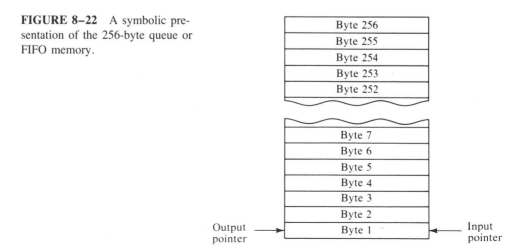

Initialization Dialog

The initialization dialog is rather short, since all that is to be accomplished is programming the PIA. The dialog required for both the MC6800 and the 8085A interfaces follows:

```
                        *initialization dialog (MC6800)
                        *
0000  7FE001      INIT      CLR   $E001           select DDR A
0003  86FF                  LDAA  #$FF            setup A as output
0005  B7E000                STAA  $E000
0008  86FD                  LDAA  #$FD            program pins
000A  B7E001                STAA  $E001           CA1 and CA2

                        ;initialization dialog (8085A)
                        ;
0000  3E15        INIT:     MVI   A,15H           ;program ports
0002  D3F0                  OUT   OF0H            ;and enable interrupt
0004  3EFF                  MVI   A,OFFH          ;set STROBE high
0006  D3F3                  OUT   OF3H
```

Queue Software

Subroutines to control the storing and removing of data must be capable of checking the full and empty conditions of the queue. They must also be able to modify the pointer and handle the method of storage required for this type of memory system. The flowchart for this subroutine is depicted in figure 8–23 and the actual subroutines for both the 8085A and MC6800 follow:

```
                        ;input subroutine (8085A)
                        ;
2000  F5          INPUT:    PUSH  PSW             ;save data
2001  3A0011      INP:      LDA   POINTI          ;get input pointer
2004  6F                    MOV   L,A
2005  3A0111                LDA   POINTO          ;get output pointer
2008  3D                    DCR   A
2009  BD                    CMP   L               ;test for full
200A  CA0120                JZ    INP             ;if full
200D  2610                  MVI   H,PAGE          ;set page address
200F  F1                    POP   PSW             ;get data
2010  77                    MOV   M,A             ;save data in queue
2011  7D                    MOV   A,L             ;increment input pointer
2012  3C                    INR   A
2013  320011                STA   POINTI          ;save input pointer
2016  C9                    RET

                        *input subroutine (MC6800)
                        *
2000  36          INPUT     PSHA                  ;save data
2001  B61101      INP       LDAA  POINTI+1        ;get input pointer
2004  4C                    INCA                  ;setup pointer
2005  B11103                CMPA  POINTO+1        ;test for full
2008  27F7                  BEQ   INP             ;if full
200A  FE1100                LDX   POINTI          ;get input pointer
200D  32                    PULA                  ;get data
200E  A700                  STAA  X               ;save data
2010  7C1101                INC   POINTI+1        ;increment input pointer
2013  39                    RTS
```

FIGURE 8–23 A flowchart of
the INPUT subroutine used to fill
the queue.

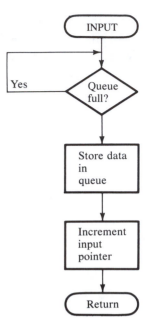

The INPUT subroutine stores information into the queue without pause until the queue
is full. When it is full, the subroutine enters into a wait loop until the external interrupting
device interrupts this wait loop and extracts data from the queue. (It would be nice to use
a HLT (8085A) or a WAI (MC6800), but the subroutine is shorter with a loop.) When data
are extracted from the queue, the output pointer is incremented.

The OUTP subroutine is called by the interrupt service subroutine and one of two
results occurs. If the queue is empty, a return zero occurs from the OUTP subroutine that
must be used by the interrupt service subroutine to disable interrupts. If data are transmitted normally and the queue is not empty, the interrupt service subroutine must allow
future interrupts to occur. The flowchart for the OUTP subroutine is illustrated in figure
8–24.

```
          ;output subroutine (8085A)
          ;
          ;return zero = empty
          ;return not zero = not empty
          ;
2017 3A0111   OUTP:   LDA   POINTO      ;get output pointer
201A 7D               MOV   A,L         ;save pointer
201B 3A0011           LDA   POINTI      ;get input pointer
201E BD               CMP   L           ;test for empty
201F C8               RZ                ;return if empty
2020 2610             MVI   H,PAGE      ;address queue
2022 7E               MOV   A,M         ;get data
2023 D3F1             OUT   0F1H        ;send it to printer
2025 97               SUB   A           ;send STROBE
2026 D3F3             OUT   0F3H
2028 2F               CMA
2029 D3F3             OUT   0F3H
202B 7D               MOV   A,L         ;get output pointer
202C 3C               INR   A           ;increment pointer
```

```
202D  320111          STA    POINTO        ;save output pointer
2030  3E01            MVI    A,1           ;setup return not zero
2032  B7              ORA    A
2033  C9              RET

                *output subroutine (MC6800)
                *
                *return zero = empty
                *return not zero = not empty
                *
2014  FE1102  OUTP:   LDX    POINTO        load output pointer
2017  BC1100          CPX    POINTI        test for empty
201A  2711            BEQ    OUTE          if empty
201C  A600            LDAA   X             get data
201E  B7E000          STAA   $E000         send it to printer
2021  8605            LDAA   #$05          send STROBE
2023  B7E001          STAA   $E001
2026  86FD            LDAA   #$FD
2028  B7E001          STAA   $E001
202B  7C1103          INC    POINTO+1      increment output pointer
202E  8601            LDAA   #$01          set return not zero
2030  39      OUTE    RTS
```

Likewise, after the INPUT routine is called for the first time, the interrupts must be enabled to allow the interrupt structure to operate and transmit the data to the printer.

The TRANS subroutine sends a string of information to the printer through the queue. The string starting point must be placed in the HL pair for the 8085A and the index

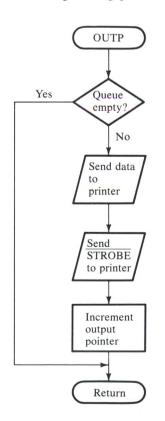

FIGURE 8–24 A flowchart of the OUTP subroutine used to extract data from the queue and print it.

FIGURE 8–25 A flowchart for
the TRANS subroutine used to
transmit data through the queue to
the printer.

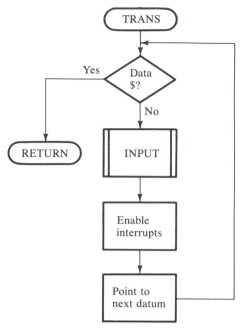

register for the MC6800 before this subroutine is called. The string must always terminate
with a "$". This works somewhat like the print string subroutine in a CP/M-based
system. *CP/M* is an acronym for control program microprocessor; this system is found in
many business computers and is also becoming popular for home and hobby computers.
According to some sources, it is the most popular operating system in use today. Figure
8–25 illustrates the flowchart for the transmission subroutine.

```
              ;transmit subroutine (8085A)
              ;
2034  7E        TRANS:   MOV   A,M            ;get a byte of data
2035  FE24               CPI   '$'            ;test for $
2037  C8                 RZ                   ;if finished
2038  E5                 PUSH  H              ;save HL
2039  CD0020             CALL  INPUT          ;save it in queue
203C  3E0E               MVI   A,0EH          ;enable RST 5.5
203E  30                 SIM
203F  FB                 EI                   ;enable interrupts
2040  E1                 POP   H              ;restore HL
2041  23                 INX   H              ;address next data
2042  C33420             JMP   TRANS

              *transmit subroutine (MC6800)
              *
2031  A600      TRANS    LDAA  X              get data
2033  8124               CMPA  #$24           test for $
2035  270E               BEQ   TRANE          if finished
2037  FF1104             STX   TEMP           save pointer
203A  BD2000             JSR   INPUT          save data in queue
203D  0E                 CLI                  enable interrupt
203E  FE1104             LDX   TEMP           get address
2041  08                 INX                  address next
2042  20ED               BRA   TRANS          send next
2044  39        TRANE    RTS
```

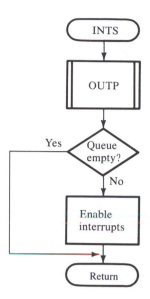

FIGURE 8–26 A flowchart that illustrates the operation of the interrupt service (INTS) subroutine for the queue.

The INTS subroutine is used whenever the printer interrupts the microprocessor. This subroutine is flowcharted in figure 8–26. INTS causes a transfer of data through the OUTP subroutine described earlier. If the queue happens to be empty, a return zero from the OUTP subroutine occurs and the interrupt service subroutine is exited through OFF.

```
                    ;INTS subroutine (8085A)
                    ;
     2045 E5        INTS:     PUSH H              ;save registers
     2046 F5                  PUSH PSW
     2047 CD1720              CALL OUTP           ;print character
     204A CA4E20              JZ   OFF            ;empty
     204D FB                  EI                  ;enable interrupts
     204E F1        OFF:      POP  PSW            ;restore registers
     204F E1                  POP  H
     2050 C9                  RET

                    *INTS subroutine (MC6800)
                    *
     2045 BD2014    INTS      JSR  OUTP           print character
     2048 2700                BEQ  OFF            if empty
     204A OE                  CLI                 enable interrupts
     204B B6E000    OFF       LDAA $E000          clear interrupt
     204E 39                  RTS
```

As can be perceived through the above software, this application requires a little software overhead; it is worth it, however, since the processor continues at full speed at least until the queue fills up. This would give about 4.5 s of additional computing time every time that the printer is accessed; depending upon the application, it can be extremely important.

Summary

1 An interrupt is a hardware-initiated subroutine call or jump that interrupts the currently executing program.

2 The interrupt service subroutine is the subroutine called by the interrupt. This subroutine usually accomplishes some form of I/O operation before returning to the program that was interrupted at the point of the interruption.

3 There are two basic types of interrupts: nonmaskable and maskable. The nonmaskable interrupt is always active; the maskable interrupt can be turned on and off with software.

4 The 8085A microprocessor has four internally decoded interrupt inputs: TRAP, RST 7.5, RST 6.5, and RST 5.5; and one externally decoded interrupt input: INTR.

5 The 8085A interrupt structure is controlled by four instructions: DI (disable interrupts), EI (enable interrupts), RIM (read interrupt masks), and SIM (set interrupt masks).

6 The SIM instruction allows the 8085A to set or clear interrupt mask bits, reset the RST 7.5 flip-flop, and send serial data to the SOD pin.

7 The RIM instruction allows the 8085A to read the following information: serial data from the SID pin, the interrupt pins (RST 7.5, RST 6.5, and RST 5.5), the interrupt-enable flip-flop (IE), and the status of the interrupt masks (M7.5, M6.5, and M5.5).

8 The MC6800 has two interrupt inputs: $\overline{IRQ}$ and $\overline{NMI}$. $\overline{IRQ}$ is a maskable interrupt input that vectors through memory locations $FFF8 and $FFF9. NMI is a nonmaskable interrupt input that vectors through memory locations $FFFC and $FFFD.

9 The MC6809 has the $\overline{IRQ}$ and $\overline{NMI}$ inputs plus a new maskable interrupt input $\overline{FIRQ}$ (fast interrupt request) which vectors through memory locations $FFF6 and $FFF7.

10 The Z80 microprocessor has two interrupt inputs: $\overline{INT}$ and $\overline{NMI}$. The $\overline{NMI}$ input is nonmaskable and calls the subroutine that begins at memory location 0066H. The maskable interrupt ($\overline{INT}$) has three modes of operation (modes 0, 1, and 2). Mode 0 operation inserts a RST 4 instruction, mode 1 inserts a RST 7 instruction, and mode 2 functions as the 8085 INTR input.

11 The daisy chain is a scheme that is used to connect multiple interrupting devices to a single interrupt input.

12 The 8259A is a programmable priority interrupt controller that has eight interrupt inputs that are connected to a single interrupt input.

13 The Centronics printer interface is used to send parallel data to a printer. The $\overline{STB}$ signal is used to send data into the printer and the $\overline{ACK}$ signal indicates that the printer has printed the data.

14 A queue is a first-in, first-out (FIFO) memory that is used to buffer high-speed devices with low-speed devices.

Glossary

Daisy chain   A method of asynchronously coupling and directing a serial signal. In many cases it is used for directing the interrupt-acknowledge signal.

FIFO   A memory that stores information on a first-in, first-out basis.

Interrupt   Breaking into a program through the use of an external signal from the hardware, which jumps to an interrupt service subroutine.

Interrupt acknowledge   A hardware signal that indicates that an interrupt input has been accepted by the microprocessor.

Interrupt service subroutine   A subroutine used by the external hardware to accomplish a task.

Interrupt vector   A location or two in the memory or microprocessor that points the way to an interrupt service subroutine.

Maskable interrupt   An interrupt input that can be turned off or deactivated.

Nonmaskable interrupt   An interrupt input that can never be disabled or turned off.

Polling   The act of looking at several interrupt signal lines to determine which are active.

Priority   The order in which multiple interrupt inputs are processed.

Programmable interrupt controller   A device that is capable of recognizing multiple interrupt inputs and directing the response to these interrupts.

Queue   A memory that stores information on a first-in, first-out basis.

Real time   Time as it actually occurs.

Real-time clock   A device that keeps track of "real time."

Restart   A special one-byte call instruction in the 8080A, 8085A, and Z80 microprocessors.

Terminal count   The state in a modulus counter equal to the modulus. A modulus ten counter's terminal count is a ten.

Questions and Problems

1   What is an interrupt?

2   What is an interrupt service subroutine?

3   Why must interrupts be enabled in the interrupt service subroutine of an 8085A microprocessor?

4   Which special instruction ends an interrupt service subroutine in the MC6809?

5   List three applications in which an interrupt would prove useful.

6   Which three functions are performed by the SIM instruction of the 8085A microprocessor?

7   List what the RIM instruction allows you to determine about the 8085A microprocessor.

8   Which instructions control the maskable interrupt input of the MC6809?

9   Where would a nonmaskable interrupt be useful?

10   Interface a simple push button to a microprocessor as an interrupt input. Develop

the software required to allow this button to operate and store zeros in memory locations 1000H through 1FFFH when pressed.

11   For the 8085A, develop software that will turn off interrupt input RST 6.5 without affecting the other interrupt inputs.

12   Interface a four-key keypad to the microprocessor, using interrupt processing. The system must detect a keystroke; debounce it; and store the data 0,1,2, or 3 into memory location 70H, and a zero, to be used as a flag, in memory location 71H.

13   Write the software required to detect a keystroke with the system in problem 12.

14   Using programmable timers (as discussed in a previous chapter), cause a periodic interrupt once every second. The interrupt service subroutine should update a binary counter in memory locations 1000H and 1001H to be used as a timer.

15   Write the initialization dialog for an 8259A so that it will refer to an interrupt vector table located at memory location 1000H. This table should contain eight spaces for each vector entry. You are also required to select a rotating priority scheme.

16   Modify the INPUT subroutine in this chapter to function with a 2048-byte queue at locations 1000H through 17FFH.

17   Develop a polled interrupt scheme for the 6800 microprocessor that contains two interrupt inputs. Give these interrupts equal priority in your software.

18   Determine exactly how many bytes per second can be transferred to an I/O device using the 8085A microprocessor. (Refer to chapter 3.)

19   Determine exactly how many bytes per second can be transferred to an I/O device using the 6800 microprocessor. (Refer to chapter 4.)

20   Would an interrupt service subroutine reduce the maximum transfer rate of the microprocessor? Explain your answer.

9

Microprocessor-Based Communications

Upon completion of this chapter, you will be able to

1 Show the difference between asynchronous and synchronous serial data.

2 Define the terms Baud rate, start bit, mark, space, stop, parity, simplex, half duplex, and full duplex as they apply to data communications.

3 Interface the 8251A to the 8085A microprocessor and develop the software to initialize it and operate it in either synchronous or asynchronous modes.

4 Interface the 6850 to the MC6800 microprocessor and develop the software to initialize and operate it.

5 Describe the RS-232C standard and indicate what components are used to generate and detect RS-232C logic levels.

6 Describe the operation of the 20-mA current loop.

7 Explain the difference between FSK and PSK.

8 Indicate how a modem is controlled with the 8251A and the 6850.

9 Explain the function of the talker and listener in the IEEE-488 bus.

This chapter introduces digital communications from the microprocessor's viewpoint. It doesn't go into lengthy detail on the methods of modulation or the protocols normally associated in the data communications environment. It enables you to make the transition from the purely digital environment to the communications environment.

This chapter develops an understanding of serial and parallel data communications. It then describes some of the many communications interface standards that convey this information to its destination. Many of the more common communications interface standards are explained with a technique or device that will generate the standard form of data communications.

9-1 INTRODUCTION TO DIGITAL COMMUNICATIONS

Serial and parallel data transfer are the two basic methods of communicating digital information between microprocessors and peripheral equipment. Both techniques are in widespread use throughout the industry and each has its advantages and disadvantages.

Serial Data Transfer

Serial data transfer is commonly used whenever digital information must be relayed over a relatively long distance. The data are often transferred through the telephone wires or over the airwaves via some form of radio carrier. The main reason for long-distance serial transfer is the reduction in the number of wires required to carry the information. Unfortunately, the speed at which these data can be transferred serially is normally limited to, at present, no more than 4,800 bits per second over commercial voice-grade telephone equipment. Leased service is available for rates of 9,600 bits per second. In theory a voice-grade channel can carry up to about 20,000 bits per second. Higher speeds are attainable if special digital communications links are leased from the telephone company.

Parallel Data Transfer

Parallel transmission of data is used for short distances where the speed of information transfer is critical. This form of data communication is found in newer types of computer peripheral equipment with transfer speeds of up to one million characters per second. This equipment includes printers, disk drives, and various other forms of peripheral components.

Asynchronous Serial Data

Serial data are transferred in either the asynchronous or synchronous form. In *asynchronous transmission*, sometimes referred to as *start-stop transmission*, start and stop bit intervals are transmitted with each byte of information for the purpose of synchronization. No clock waveform is transmitted with asynchronous data, since the start and stop bits are used for synchronization.

In *synchronous data transmission*, synchronization is effected by transmitting a synchronization character or two, followed by a large block of data. In addition to the sync characters, a clock waveform must also be transmitted. Therefore, synchronization occurs for a block of data in a synchronous system and for each piece of data in an asynchronous system.

FIGURE 9–1 Asynchronous, or start-stop, serial data.

Figure 9–1 illustrates the typical format used for transmitting data asynchronously. Each piece of information is preceded by a start bit that is at a logic zero or, by definition, a *space*. This is followed by data bits that comprise the information that is always transmitted with the least significant bit first. The stop bit, or bits in some older systems, follows the data and is always at the logic one level or, by definition, a *mark*.

Baud Rate

The speed at which serial data are transferred is referred to as the *baud rate*. The baud rate is arrived at by taking the reciprocal of the bit time interval for most applications. Refer to the section on PSK (phase shift keying) for a different definition of baud rate as it applies to that form of data. For example, a bit time of 9.09 ms would have a rate of 110 baud, except for PSK. If the serial message consists of a start bit, eight data bits, and two stop bits, a system working at this rate would be capable of transferring ten bytes of data per second.

Table 9–1 illustrates some commonly used baud rates, along with the number of stop bits and data bits, type of transmission, and the normal application of each rate. Note that all of the baud rates listed are multiples, except 110 baud, which is used for communications between electromechanical teletypewriters (which are quickly disappearing). The only systems employing two stop bits or 1.5 stop bits were designed for mechanical devices. The extra time allowed by additional stops was required for mechanical synchronization in these devices. All other systems use one stop bit.

Synchronous Serial Data

In synchronous transmission, data are transmitted with clock pulses, so it is not necessary

TABLE 9–1 Commonly used baud rates.

Baud	Data Bits	Stop Bits	Type	Application
110	5	1.5	Asynchronous	Baudot TTY
110	7 + P*	2	Asynchronous	ASCII TTY
300	7 + P	1	Asynchronous	FSK MODEM
600	7 + P	1	Asynchronous	FSK MODEM
1200	Variable	–	Synchronous	PSK MODEM
2400	Variable	–	Synchronous	PSK MODEM
4800	Variable	–	Synchronous	PSK MODEM
9600	Variable	–	Synchronous	PSK MODEM

NOTE: *P = Parity   TTY = Teletypewriter
MODEM = MOdulator/DEModulator

to send synchronization bits along with the data, as with the asynchronous system. Synchronization can be accomplished by transmitting sync information periodically.

For example, transferring 100 bytes of information by asynchronous methods would take 1000 bit times. This assumes that one start and one stop bit per byte of data is being transmitted. In a synchronous system that sends one sync byte before the start of transmission and an end-of-message character at the end of transmission, it requires only 816 bit times. If information is transmitted for any extended period of time, synchronous communication is obviously much more efficient.

Since this synchronous communication can take many forms, many computer manufacturers have developed standard communications protocols, such as *BISYNC* (binary synchronous communications), *SDLC* (serial data link control), and *HDLC* (high-level data link control). These types of protocols are illustrated in figure 9–2. BISYNC is a byte-oriented protocol; SDLC and HDLC are both bit-oriented protocols.

9–2 SERIAL COMMUNICATIONS INTERFACE ADAPTERS

There are two basic types of interface adapters for use with serial communications: the universal asynchronous receiver/transmitter (*UART*) and the universal synchronous receiver/transmitter (*USRT*). These devices are made by almost all of the integrated circuit manufacturers and are easily interfaced to the microprocessor. Some manufacturers have actually combined the synchronous and asynchronous functions into the same component and coined it a *USART,* or universal synchronous/asynchronous receiver/transmitter. This book will deal with the two most common microprocessor-compatible communications interface adapters, the 8251A from Intel and the MC6850 from Motorola.

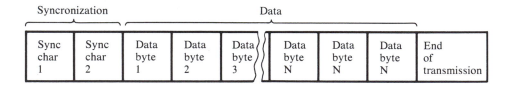

Bisync data format

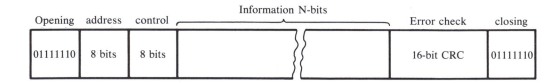

HDLC/SDLC data format

FIGURE 9–2 Two forms of synchronous serial communications protocols.

Transmission

Data are transmitted from the UART in the serial asynchronous form described in section 9–1. This is accomplished by loading the parallel information into a shift register along with the start, parity, and stop bits. This information is then shifted out of the shift register at the desired baud rate. Figure 9–3 illustrates a simple circuit that transmits seven data bits along with even parity, one start bit, and one stop bit.

Reception

Data are received by a UART through a shift register that is clocked at the desired baud rate. The only aspect of its operation that is hard to understand is that it must determine the correct starting point. This determination is made by searching the incoming data stream for a start bit.

To determine the location of the start bit, this circuit must detect a negative edge. Once it finds a negative edge, the circuit takes one more sample of the incoming signal, which is exactly in the middle of the start bit. If the second sample is a logic zero, a start bit has been detected; if not, operation returns to detecting a negative edge. A circuit for detecting this is illustrated in figure 9–4.

Once a valid start is detected, a shift register is clocked at the desired baud rate for eight clock periods. This shifts the seven data bits and the parity bit into the shift register. The outputs of the shift register now contain the parallel message. After receiving the last stop bit, a signal indicating that data have been received is sent to the computer.

THE 8251A COMMUNICATIONS INTERFACE ADAPTER   9–3

The 8251A communications interface adapter is a combination synchronous/asynchronous receiver/transmitter that is directly compatible with the Intel and Zilog families of

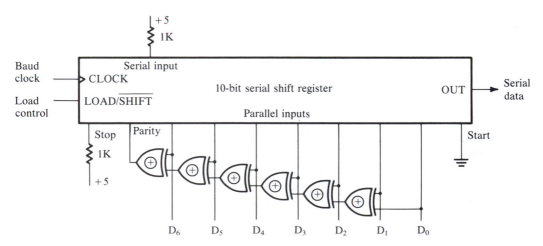

FIGURE 9–3 A circuit that will generate a serial asynchronous message with one stop bit, a parity bit, and a start bit.

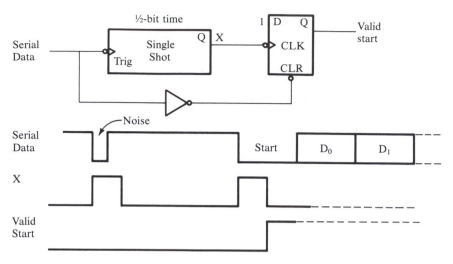

FIGURE 9–4 A logic circuit that will detect a valid start bit.

microprocessors. Figure 9–5 illustrates the pinout and block diagram of this interface component.

In the asynchronous mode of operation, this device is able to transmit and receive information at baud rates of up to 19,200. This ability makes it usable for just about any application that requires asynchronous serial data. It can also send and detect a break, detect parity, frame and overrun errors, and transmit and receive at different baud rates.

In the synchronous mode of operation, the 8251A can automatically insert one or two sync characters, making it useful for any byte-oriented synchronous communications system. It will also transmit and receive data at rates of up to 64,000 baud in this mode. If synchronization is lost, the device automatically enters the hunt mode of operation and searches for the next sync character or character pair to reestablish synchronization.

8251A Hardware Interface

Looking at the block diagram and pinout of the 8251A in figure 9–5, you will notice that the connections have been designed for implementation with an Intel-based microprocessor. Figure 9–6 depicts an 8251A interfaced to an 8085A microprocessor so that it functions at I/O port locations D0H and D1H.

The C/$\overline{\text{D}}$ connection selects the internal command/status or data register for both the receiver and the transmitter. C/$\overline{\text{D}}$ is connected to address connection A8 for the purpose of register selection. Port D0H therefore will specify the data register, and port D1H, the command/status register.

The $\overline{\text{CS}}$ pin is connected to a port decoder that decodes port number D0H and D1H for selecting the 8251A. Once this device is selected and the command/status or data register is specified with C/$\overline{\text{D}}$, a $\overline{\text{RD}}$ or $\overline{\text{WR}}$ signal from the 8085A transfers data to or from the 8251A.

The clock input (CLK) is normally connected to the clock output of the 8085A or any other source that is minimally 30 times the desired baud rate. This input does not determine the baud rate; it is used only for internal timing.

PIN CONFIGURATION

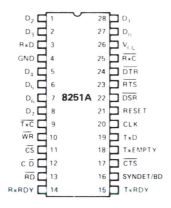

PIN NAMES

D_7/D_0	Data Bus (8 bits)
C/D	Control or Data is to be Written or Read
RD	Read Data Command
WR	Write Data or Control Command
CS	Chip Enable
CLK	Clock Pulse (TTL)
RESET	Reset
TxC	Transmitter Clock
TxD	Transmitter Data
RxC	Receiver Clock
RxD	Receiver Data
RxRDY	Receiver Ready (has character for 8080)
TxRDY	Transmitter Ready (ready for char from 8080)
DSR	Data Set Ready
DTR	Data Terminal Ready
SYNDET/BD	Sync Detect/ Break Detect
RTS	Request to Send Data
CTS	Clear to Send Data
TxE	Trnsmitter Empty
V_{CC}	+5 Volt Supply
GND	Ground

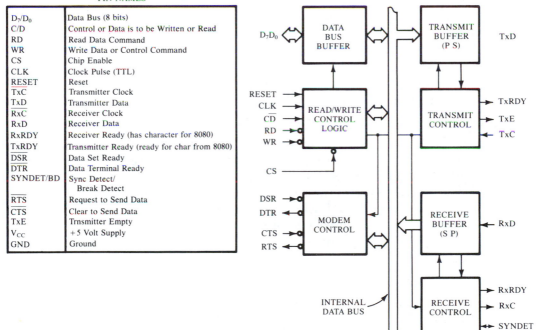

FIGURE 9–5 The pinout and block diagram of the 8251A programmable communications interface adapter.

SOURCE: Reprinted by permission of Intel Corporation. Copyright 1983.

The baud rate of this device is determined by the $\overline{TxC}$ input for the transmitter and the $\overline{RxC}$ input for the receiver. The hardware designer has the option of using a 1X, 16X, or 64X multiplier for this input. In other words, a 19,200-Hz clock can generate 19,200 baud at 1X, 1200 baud at 16X, or 300 baud at 64X.

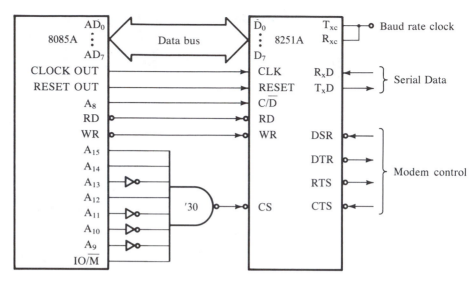

FIGURE 9–6 An 8251A programmable communications interface adapter interfaced to the 8085A.

The $\overline{\text{DSR}}$, $\overline{\text{DTR}}$, $\overline{\text{RTS}}$, and $\overline{\text{CTS}}$ pins are discussed in the section on modems, since these are modem control pins. If no modem is to be used with the 8251A, these pins can be used as simple input and output bits.

8251A RESET

The RESET input of the 8251A does not reset reliably in many 8251As. In order to ensure that the 8251A is reset after the application of power, program the command register with a 00H, 00H, 00H, and a 40H. The first three 00s sent to the command register internally set it up so that it is ready to receive a command. The 40H is a command that causes the 8251A to reset properly. The software that follows is used to reset the 8251A after the application of power or at any time that it must be reprogrammed.

```
0000  3E           RESET:   MVI   A,0               ;clear A
0002  D311                  OUT   COMMAND
0004  D311                  OUT   COMMAND
0006  D311                  OUT   COMMAND
0008  3E40                  MVI   A,40H             ;reset command
000A  D311                  OUT   COMMAND
```

8251A Initialization

When power is first applied or the 8251A is RESET, it expects to receive a mode instruction word through the command register. The mode instruction word specifies how the 8251A is to react to future commands and data transfers. Table 9–2 pictures the mode instruction word format for asynchronous operation. Bit positions B2 and B1 select the clock rate multiplier discussed previously. L2 and L1 program the 8251A to transmit and receive either five, six, seven, or eight data bits. Position PEN enables the internal parity generation and detection circuitry, and EP selects even or odd parity if PEN is active. Bits

7	6	5	4	3	2	1	0
S2	S1	EP	PEN	L2	L1	B2	B1

Binary Code	S2, S1 Stop Bits	L2, L1 Data Bits	B2, B1 Baud Rate
0 0	–	5	–
0 1	1	6	1X
1 0	1.5	7	16X
1 1	2	8	64X

TABLE 9–2 Mode instruction word format.

S2 and S1 select the number of stop bits to be used by the USART; this is normally 1 but may be 1.5 for Baudot code or 2 for ASCII coded teletypewriter communications.

The short sequence of instructions that follows will program the 8251A to function at a baud rate multiplier of 16X, a character length of eight bits with odd parity, and one stop bit.

```
0100  3E5E      SETUP:    MVI   A,01011110B  ; setup the 8251A
0102  D3D1                OUT   0D1H
0104  3E15                MVI   A,00010101B  ;enable receiver
0106  D3D1                OUT   0D1H         ;and transmitter
```

Once this device is initialized with the mode instruction word, it will not accept another until it is reset by the hardware or the software. In this example, the next time the command register is written into it, it is to control the 8251A, not to initialize it.

Command/Status Register

The command register bit format is pictured in table 9–3; it is used to command the 8251A after initialization. Note that this format is used for both asynchronous and synchronous operation. To transmit and receive information, both the TxEN and RxE bits

TABLE 9–3 8251A command register.

7	6	5	4	3	2	1	0
EH	IR	RTS	ERN	SBRK	RxE	DTR	TxEN

Bit Name	Function
EH	Enter hunt mode (synchronous operation)
IR	Internal reset
RTS	Written to the $\overline{\text{RTS}}$ pin (inverted)
ER	Resets parity, overrun, and framing errors
SBRK	Send a break character (asynchronous operation)
RxE	Enables the receiver
DTR	Written to the $\overline{\text{DTR}}$ pin (inverted)
TxEN	Enables the transmitter

TABLE 9–4   8251A status register.

7	6	5	4	3	2	1	0
DSR	SYNDET	FE	OE	PE	TxE	RxRDY	TxRDY

Bit Name	Function
DSR	Reads the $\overline{\text{DSR}}$ pins (inverted)
SYNDET	SYNC character detection (synchronous operation)
FE	Framing error
OE	Overrun error
PE	Parity error
TxE	Transmitter empty
RxRDY	Receiver ready
TxRDY	Transmitter ready

must be made active and sent out to the command register (see the previous initialization dialog). The other bits are active or inactive, depending upon the utilization requirements of this device.

Table 9–4 pictures the status register bit pattern of the 8251A. This register is read through the command/status register port number, and it indicates the condition of the 8251A. Notice that three types of errors are detected by this integrated circuit. (In practice, these error flags must be reset through the software reset bit of the command register before the reception software can safely continue.)

FE   a framing error should not occur under normal operation since it indicates that the received data are missing a stop bit or have an incorrect number of stop bits. This error normally occurs if the data are being received at the wrong baud rate or if the receiver or transmitter frequencies are out of tolerance.

OE   an overrun error occurs if the data are not removed from the internal data holding register before the next complete piece of information is received. Again, under normal operation this error should not occur. If it does, there is most likely a mistake in the software.

PE   a parity error occurs if the received data are determined to contain incorrect parity. This occurs occasionally because of noise on the transmission line; it is the programmer's responsibility, through the software, to indicate an error or somehow plead for a retransmission of the erroneous byte of data.

Data Transfer Software

The data transfer software for the 8251A is extremely simple to write, as illustrated below:

```
                    ;subroutine that sends memory data addressed
                    ;by HL
                    ;
                    ;the accumulator and flags destroyed
                    ;
0200  DBD1          SEND:    IN     0D1H          ;get status
0202  0F                     RRC                  ;TxRDY to carry
```

```
0203 D20002              JNC   SEND        ;if not ready
0206 7E                  MOV   A,M         ;get data
0207 D3D0                OUT   0D0H        ;send data
0209 C9                  RET
```

In the SEND subroutine, the TxRDY bit is tested until it indicates that the transmitter is ready to receive another byte of information for transmission. The TxEMPTY bit is not used because it indicates that all bits of data have been completely transmitted. The TxRDY bit indicates that a byte is currently being transmitted and that the internal data holding register is ready for the next byte. This transmitter is buffered so that it can transmit one byte while holding a second byte for the transmitter. This increases the throughput of the system slightly by reducing the time required to poll the USART for the first and second transmitted pieces of information. It is important to note that the $\overline{CTS}$ pin must be grounded to transmit data.

```
                         ;subroutine to receive a byte of information
                         ;from the 8251A and store it in memory addressed
                         ;by HL
                         ;
                         ;the accumulator and flags destroyed
                         ;
0300 DBD1     GET:       IN    0D1H        ;get status
0302 E602                ANI   2           ;isolate RxRDY
0304 CA0003              JZ    GET         ;if not ready
0307 DBD1                IN    0D1H        ;get status
0309 E638                ANI   38H         ;isolate errors
030B C2XXXX              JNZ   ERROR       ;if an error
030E DBD0                IN    0D0H        ;get data
0310 77                  MOV   M,A         ;save data
0311 C9                  RET
```

The GET subroutine tests the RxRDY bit to determine whether or not the USART has received a piece of data. If data have not been received, the RxRDY bit is a logic zero, causing the subroutine to loop back to GET. If data are available, RxRDY is a logic one, causing the subroutine to test for error conditions. If an error occurs, a branch is made to a user-defined error-handling routine. In many cases, ERROR places a question mark in the location indicated by the HL pair or asks for a retransmission. If no error has occurred, the data are read from the USART and stored in the location indexed by the HL pair.

Interrupts with the 8251A

To use interrupts, the previously described software can be disregarded in favor of hardware connections to the 8085A (as illustrated in figure 9–7). For a transmitter interrupt, the TxRDY pin is connected to RST 5.5; the RxRDY pin is connected to the RST 6.5 pin for a receiver interrupt. Interrupt service subroutines are called each time the transmitter is ready for another byte of information and each time the receiver contains a byte of information for the computer.

Synchronous Operation

With synchronous operation, the mode instruction word format changes to the one depicted in table 9–5. Here the right two-bit positions must both be at the logic zero level to

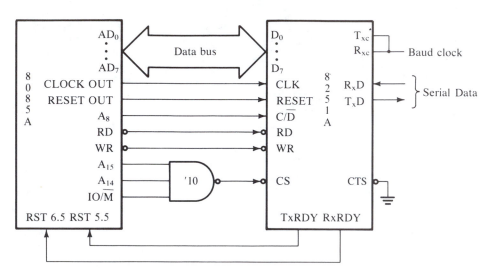

FIGURE 9–7 The 8251A programmable communications interface adapter connected to an 8085A as an interrupt-processed I/O device.

specify synchronous operation. L2 and L1 still specify the number of bits to be transmitted per character, and PEN and EP still control the parity. ESD and SCS are unique to synchronous operation and determine whether sync detect (SD) is an input or an output pin and also whether there is to be a single or double sync character. Once this word is sent to the 8251A, it must be immediately followed by the one- or two-sync characters to be used for synchronization. In other words, this initialization procedure is one to two bytes longer than for asynchronous operation.

The clock inputs for both the receiver and transmitter have no multiplier for synchronous operation: the multiplier is always 1X. Also, it should be noted that synchronous communication is allowed to proceed at a maximum baud rate of 64K.

TABLE 9–5 Synchronous mode instruction format.

7	6	5	4	3	2	1	0
SCS	ESD	EP	PEN	L2	L1	0	0

Bit Name	Function
SCS	Single character SYNC operation
ESD	External SYNC detect (0 = output 1 = input)
EP	Even parity
PEN	Parity enable
L2, L1	Refer to table 9–2 for the bit pattern

Synchronous Transmission

In synchronous transmission the one- or two-sync characters are sent out to the USART using the SEND subroutine listed earlier in the text. This device will automatically send sync characters only at the end of transmitting a block of information; it is up to the user to send them prior to the transmission. The number of bytes sent between sync characters depends upon the type of protocol selected for the system.

Synchronous Reception

To achieve synchronization, an enter hunt command is issued to the 8251A prior to the reception of any information. Once synchronization is achieved, data may then be received in the normal fashion.

```
                    ;synchronous initialization dialog
                    ;
0400  3E00   SETUP:   MVI   A,0              ;reset the 8251A
0402  D3D1            OUT   0D1H
0404  D3D1            OUT   0D1H
0406  D3D1            OUT   0D1H
0408  3E40            MVI   A,40H
040A  D3D1            OUT   0D1H
040C  3E1C            MVI   A,00011100B      ;mode instruction
040E  D3D1            OUT   0D1H
0410  3E7E            MVI   A,SYNC1          ;setup sync 1
0412  D3D1            OUT   0D1H
0414  3E7F            MVI   A,SYNC2          ;setup sync 2
0416  D3D1            OUT   0D1H
0418  3E15            MVI   A,00010101B      ;enable 8251A
041A  D3D1            OUT   0D1H
```

A subroutine for asynchronous reception first commands the 8251A to enter the hunt mode to search for the sync characters. Once the sync characters are detected, the subroutine then receives data in the same fashion as in the GET subroutine.

```
                    ;synchronous reception subroutine
                    ;receives a block of data and stores
                    ;it in the memory block addressed by HL
                    ;
                    ;accumulator and flags destroyed
                    ;
0500  3E95   GETS:    MVI   A,10010101B  ;enter hunt mode
0502  D3D1            OUT   0D1H
0504  DBD1   GETS1:   IN    0D1H         ;get status
0506  E640            ANI   40H          ;isolate SYNDET
0508  CA0405          JZ    GETS1        ;if not in sync
050B  DBD1   GETS2:   IN    0D1H         ;get status
050D  E602            ANI   2            ;isolate RxRDY
050F  CA0B05          JZ    GETS2        ;if not ready
0512  DBD1            IN    0D1H         ;test errors
0514  E638            ANI   38H
0516  C2XXXX          JNZ   ERROR
0519  DBD0            IN    0D0H         ;get data
051B  77              MOV   M,A          ;save data
051C  23              INX   H
051D  FE04            CPI   EOT          ;test for EOT
051F  C20405          JNZ   GETS1        ;not end of transmission
0522  C9              RET
```

9–4   THE MC6850 COMMUNICATIONS INTERFACE ADAPTER

The Motorola MC6850 asynchronous communications interface adapter (ACIA), unlike the Intel 8251A, is meant to be used for asynchronous data only. This of course presents no drawback to asynchronous communication.

The MC6850 Pinout and Basic Description

Figure 9–8 illustrates the pinout and block diagram of the ACIA. This device is capable of transmitting and receiving serial data at baud rates of up to 19,200. It is directly compatible with just about any microprocessor that is currently being manufactured, but was specifically designed for use with the MC6800 or MC6809 microprocessors.

The clock inputs, R_x and T_x, control the baud rates of the receiver and transmitter sections and are usually tied together. The ACIA, like the 8251A, is programmable, since

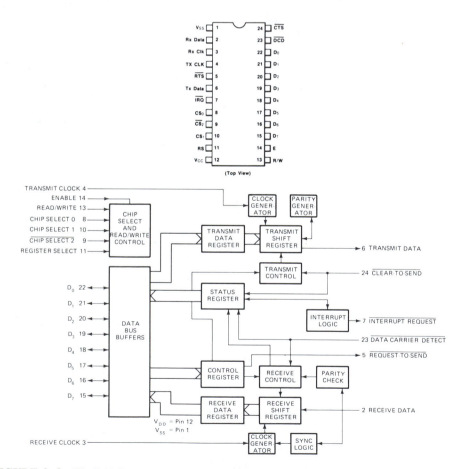

FIGURE 9–8   The MC6850 ACIA pinout and block diagram.

SOURCE: Courtesy of Motorola, Inc.

its baud rate is selectable to some extent by the software. Pin RS, the register selection pin, is used in the same manner as the C/$\overline{\text{D}}$ pin on the 8251A, except that the logic levels for selection are inverted. A logic zero selects the control/status register, and a logic one selects the data register.

Modem control is accomplished through the $\overline{\text{RTS}}$, $\overline{\text{CTS}}$, and $\overline{\text{DCD}}$ pins of the ACIA. Although these connections do not completely conform to standard modem control inputs, they can easily be used for this purpose. Modem control will be discussed in the section on modems.

Programming the ACIA

Programming is accomplished by sending an 8-bit number out to the ACIA control register. Table 9–6 illustrates the bit pattern required for this control register.

Bit positions CR0 and CR1 select the appropriate baud rate multiplier and can also reset the device. For example, if the input clock frequency is 19,200 Hz, divide-by-1 would cause operation at 19,200 baud; divide-by-16 would cause operation at 1200 baud; and divide-by-64 would cause operation at 300 baud. The ACIA is reset to clear any error indications in the status register. These error indicators are discussed in a later section.

Bits CR2, CR3, and CR4 determine the format of the character that will be transmitted

TABLE 9–6   The 6850 ACIA control register.

Control Register							
CR7	CR6	CR5	CR4	CR3	CR2	CR1	CR0

CR1	CR0	Function
0	0	÷ 1
0	1	÷ 16
1	0	÷ 64
1	1	Reset

CR4	CR3	CR2	Function
0	0	0	7 bits, even parity, and 2 stops
0	0	1	7 bits, odd parity, and 2 stops
0	1	0	7 bits, even parity, and 1 stop
0	1	1	7 bits, odd parity, and 1 stop
1	0	0	8 bits, no parity, and 2 stops
1	0	1	8 bits, no parity, and 1 stop
1	1	0	8 bits, even parity, and 1 stop
1	1	1	8 bits, odd parity, and 1 stop

CR6	CR5	Function
0	0	$\overline{\text{RTS}}$ = 0, Transmit interrupt disabled
0	1	$\overline{\text{RTS}}$ = 0, Transmit interrupt enabled
1	0	$\overline{\text{RTS}}$ = 1, Transmit interrupt disabled
1	1	$\overline{\text{RTS}}$ = 1, Transmit interrupt disabled and transmits a break on transmit data output.

and received by the ACIA. For example, if all three bits are programmed as zeros, seven data bits with even parity and two stop bits are transmitted and received.

CR5 and CR6 control the transmitter interrupt and the $\overline{\text{RTS}}$ pin and determine whether or not a break character is transmitted. A *break* is, by definition, a space that is transmitted for at least two consecutive character times.

CR7 or RIE enables the $\overline{\text{IRQ}}$ pin for the receiver section of the ACIA. An interrupt occurs for a received byte of data, an overrun error, or a positive transition on the $\overline{\text{DCD}}$ pin connection.

ACIA Status

The status register, as illustrated in table 9–7, is read by selecting the device and placing a logic zero on the RS pin. This register indicates error conditions, the condition of some of the modem control pins, and the general operating condition of the ACIA.

RDRF indicates that data are available for the microprocessor, which must remove the data before the next character is received. If not, the OVRN bit will become active, indicating an overrun error. Other errors detected by the receiver are framing error (FE) and parity error (PE). The framing error indicates that a character is received with an incorrect number of stop bits, and PE indicates that the received data contain the wrong parity.

The $\overline{\text{IRQ}}$ status bit indicates that the input buffer is full, there is an overrun error, or there is a positive transition on the $\overline{\text{DCD}}$ pin. If the external interrupt pin is connected to the microprocessor's interrupt input, the software checks the status word to determine the cause of the interrupt request.

The remaining bit positions indicate the external conditions of the $\overline{\text{DCD}}$ and $\overline{\text{CTS}}$ modem control input pins.

The MC6850 Hardware Interface

Figure 9–9 pictures the MC6850 ACIA connected to an MC6800 microprocessor. The ACIA is located at I/O locations $E0X0 and $E0X1, as decoded by the page decoder.

TABLE 9–7   ACIA status register.

7	6	5	4	3	2	1	0
IRQ	PE	RO	FE	$\overline{\text{CTS}}$	DCD	TDRE	RDRF

Pin Name	Function
IRQ	Interrupt request
PE	Parity error
RO	Overrun error
FE	Framing error
$\overline{\text{CTS}}$	$\overline{\text{CTS}}$ pin
$\overline{\text{DCD}}$	$\overline{\text{DCD}}$ pin
TDRE	Transmitter empty
RDRF	Receiver full

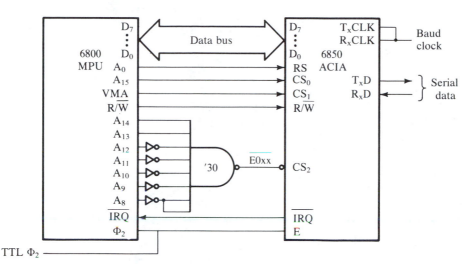

FIGURE 9–9   The Motorola MC6850 ACIA interfaced to the MC6800 microprocessor.

For this example, the interrupt input is connected from the MC6850 to the MC6800 to demonstrate an interrupt processing subroutine. The remaining pin connections to the MC6850 are fairly straightforward and will not be discussed here.

ACIA Software Example

In this example the clock input to the ACIA is generated by an external source at a frequency of 4800 Hz. The desired baud rate is 300, so the initialization dialog must set the internal divider to 16 to obtain this baud rate. It is also desired that the ACIA send and receive seven data bits with even parity and two stop bits.

```
                        *initialization dialog
                        *
0500  8603      START   LDAA  #$03          reset the ACIA
0502  B7E000            STAA  $E000
0505  86A1              LDAA  #$A1          setup ACIA
0507  B7E000            STAA  $E000
```

The Interrupt Service Subroutine

The interrupt service subroutine must determine whether the receiver or the transmitter caused the interrupt. It must also determine if the interrupt is caused by an error and, if so, take the appropriate action.

This interrupt service subroutine stores received data at location $D000 and a logic zero at location $D001. The zero at $D001 is a flag to the system software indicating that a byte of data has been received. The data stored at memory location $D002 are transmitted by the interrupt service subroutine, and a zero is placed at location $D003 as a flag.

```
                        *interrupt service subroutine for the ACIA
                        *
050A  B6E000    INTER   LDAA  $E000         get status
050D  2B0A              BMI   RECV          if receiver
050F  B6D000            LDAA  $D000         get data
```

```
0512 B7E000              STAA  $E000          send data
0515 7FD003              CLR   $D003          clear flag
0518 38                  RTI
                 *
0519 8570       RECV     BITA  #$70           test error bits
051B 2655                BNE   ERR            if an error
051D B6E001              LDAA  $E001          get data
0520 B7D000              STAA  $D000          save data
0523 7FD001              CLR   $D001          clear flag
0526 38                  RTI
```

Location ERR in the interrupt service subroutine determines which type of error has occurred and takes corrective action, depending upon the system using the ACIA. The only procedure that occurs in all forms of error handling subroutines is a reset to clear the error flags.

9–5 THE RS-232C INTERFACE STANDARD

The EIA RS-232C interface standard is used almost universally for the interconnection of terminal equipment that receives or transmits serial asynchronous data. This standard specifies the pin connections and connector to be employed in this type of application and also the logic levels and protocol used.

Logic Levels

The standard specifies that the logic one level must be no less than -3.0 V and no greater than -25 V; the logic zero level must be no less than $+3.0$V and no greater than $+25$ V. Note that this is negative logic. In addition to voltage levels, the standard specifies that the receiver and transmitter be able to sustain a short circuit to any of these levels for an indefinite period of time. In other words, this particular standard is largely immune to operator abuse.

Since no logic level rides on a zero volt potential, this system is also fairly immune to ground loop problems that often arise in interconnecting terminal equipment. Ground loop currents often flow, causing noise on the ground connection that affects the normal zero volt logic zero level.

Line Characteristics

The transmission line type normally employed is a twisted pair of shielded wire with a line capacitance of no more than 1200 pF and no less than 300 pF. In practice a 300-pF or 330-pF capacitor is often added to the terminal equipment's transmit pin to ensure that the lower capacitance limit is met.

The standard also specifies that the line length be limited to 50 meters if the user expects to receive the same information that was transmitted. If longer line lengths are needed, EIA has other standards that allow line lengths of up to seven miles.

Connectors

Figure 9–10 depicts the connector specified by EIA for this interface standard. Also listed are the pin definitions for each of the 25 pin connections. In many cases pins 1, 2, 3, and 7 are the only pins that are interconnected between the terminal equipment and computer or modem. Pin 1 is a protective ground that connects the chassis of the equipment together for safety.

In practice, when connecting CRT terminals to computer systems, pins 2 and 3 are twisted in the cable so that transmit is connected to receive. When printers and modems are connected with this standard, the transmit pin (pin 2) is connected on both ends, transmit to transmit. It is best to check the interface wiring diagram before connecting a piece of equipment using this standard.

Drivers and Receivers

Figure 9–11(a) illustrates the typical line driver and figure 9–11(b) the typical line receiver. These devices convert from standard TTL logic levels to RS-232C levels or RS-232C to TTL. Both are 4-channel devices that typically send and receive plus and minus 12-V signals. In some applications, to reduce the cost of power supply, +5 V and −12 V are used. In both cases the noise immunity is the difference between the power supply voltage and the 3-V minimum level set by EIA.

If required, the standard input voltage thresholds may be modified by connecting a resistor between the control pin, illustrated in figure 9–11(b), and ground; or between the control pin and one of the power supplies. In most cases this pin is left disconnected to provide the standard plus and minus 3-V thresholds.

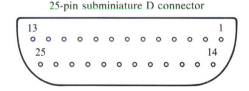

25-pin subminiature D connector

1 – Protective ground	2 – Transmit data
3 – Receive data	4 – RTS
5 – CTS	6 – DSR
7 – Signal ground	8 – Received line signal detector
9 – Test	10 – Test
11 – No assignment	12 – Secondary received line signal detector
13 – Secondary CTS	14 – Secondary transmit data
15 – Transmit signal timing	16 – Secondary received data
17 – Receiver signal timing	18 – No assignment
19 – Secondary RTS	20 – DTR
21 – Signal quality detector	22 – Ring indicator
23 – Data signal rate select	24 – Transmit signal timing
25 – No assignment	

FIGURE 9–10 The EIA RS-232C interface standard connector and pin assignments.

FIGURE 9–11 RS-232C receiver and transmitter: (a) the MC1488 TTL to RS-232C line driver, (b) the MC1489 RS-232C to TTL line receiver.

SOURCE: Courtesy of Motorola, Inc.

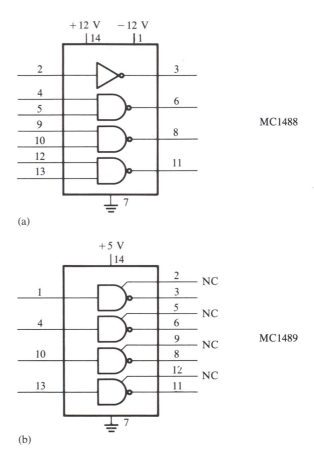

9–6 CURRENT LOOPS

Current loops find their application with electromechanical devices such as teletypewriters. The most common form of current loop is the 20-mA current loop; a 60-mA loop is also used by some manufacturers of terminal equipment.

Cable length with a current loop is limited to approximately 2000–3000 feet. This limit is mainly due to IR losses in the cable. Data transmission rates are also limited to no more than 150 baud.

Two types of loops find widespread application: one causes current to flow for a mark and no current for a space and is called a *neutral system*. The other allows current to flow in opposite directions for the space and mark and is called a *polar system*.

Figure 9–12 illustrates both the transmitter and receiver for a 20-mA neutral system: 20mA of current flows for a mark and no current flows for a space. These circuits translate from TTL voltage levels to current loop levels. This circuitry may not be found in electromechanical applications. In its place a driver may be only a resistor and a series contact, while the receiver may be a solenoid coil.

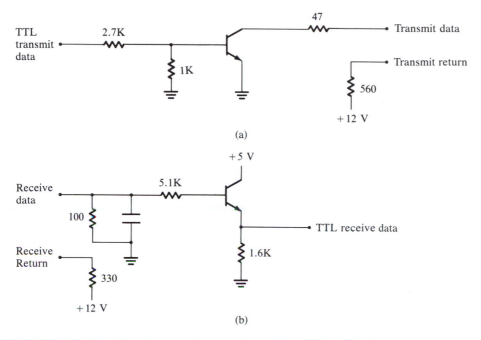

FIGURE 9–12   Two 20-mA current loop translators: (a) a TTL-to-20-mA current loop translator, (b) a 20-mA current loop-to-TTL translator.

This system of serial communications is not very common, mainly because of the low operating speed due to the electromechanical devices that are normally attached to it.

DATA TRANSMISSION METHODS 9–7

There are two basic modulation methods employed in data communications: *frequency shift keying (FSK)* and *phase shift keying (PSK)*. FSK is used in low-cost, low-speed applications; PSK is used in high-speed data communications. PSK is more efficient but costs quite a bit more to generate and detect. Figure 9–13 illustrates the waveforms that are obtained from both types of transmissions.

FSK Generation
FSK is extremely easy to generate digitally by microprocessor. All the microprocessor has to do is generate one frequency for a mark and a second frequency for a space by switching two external frequencies or by developing software to generate the two frequencies.

There are two bands of common frequencies in use for FSK digital communications. The low band uses 1070 Hz for a space and 1270 Hz for a mark. The high band uses 2025 Hz for a space and 2225 Hz for a mark. These two bands allow simultaneous two-way or full duplex communications over the same pair of wires. FSK is typically used in data communications schemes where the data transmission rate is 300 baud or less. On occa-

FIGURE 9–13 Frequency shift keying (FSK) and phase shift keying (PSK) data formats.

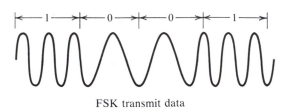

FSK transmit data

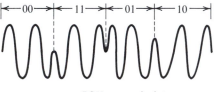

PSK transmit data

sion this technique is employed for simplex, or one-way only, communications at baud rates of up to 1200.

Figure 9–14 illustrates a simple system for generating FSK by using a multiplexer. When a logic one is applied to the control input, a 2225-Hz tone is presented at the output; when a logic zero is applied, a 2025-Hz tone appears. In practice this output must be converted to a sine wave for transmission.

FSK Detection

FSK detection is usually accomplished with a phase-locked loop or a similar device, such as a tone decoder. Figure 9–15 illustrates a tone-decoding phase-locked loop that can demodulate the incoming FSK signal to produce a TTL-compatible signal. This signal is sampled by the microprocessor to develop an intelligent data word. The phase-locked loop is allowed to free run halfway between the logic zero and logic one frequency. The internal phase detector's output can then provide a digital wave corresponding to the two different input frequencies.

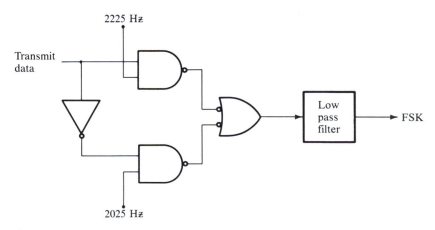

FIGURE 9–14 A circuit that can be used to generate FSK serial data.

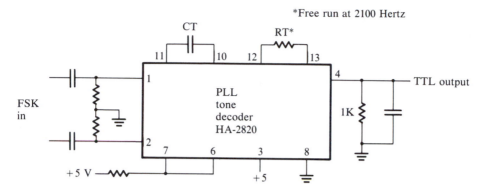

FIGURE 9–15 An FSK detector using a phase-locked loop tone decoder.

PSK

PSK is more commonly used for commercial digital communications because of the speed at which this type of communication can be carried out. In a PSK system two bits (a *DIBIT*) or three bits (a *TRIBIT*) are encoded in the phase angle of the transmitted signal. In other words, during one bit period, it is possible to send either two bits or three bits of information. This effectively doubles or triples the baud rate. Remember that the baud rate indicates the number of pieces of data transmitted per second, not the frequency of the transmitted signal. In this case the bit rate and the baud rate are different.

In a DIBIT system, four phase angles, 0, 90, 180, and 270 degrees, can be transmitted: 0 degrees can represent a 00, 90 degrees a 01, 180 degrees a 10, and 270 degrees an 11. In the TRIBIT system, 45, 135, 225, and 315 degrees are used, in addition to the previous phase angles, to allow three bits to be encoded at one time.

At the receiver the clock signal that is transmitted along with the data is compared to the data to reveal the phase angle. This phase angle reconstructs the original DIBIT or TRIBIT of data.

Using this type of modulation it is possible to communicate over standard telephone lines at rates of up to 3600 baud. Rates of 9600 baud are obtainable if specially compensated telephone lines are leased from the telephone company.

MODEMS 9–8

A *modem* is a device that translates a synchronous or asynchronous digital data stream into an FSK or a PSK signal for use on telephone lines or other media. It will also, in most cases, simultaneously receive data in FSK form or PSK form and convert the data back into synchronous or an asynchronous data stream. The word *modem* itself is an acronym of MOdulator/DEModulator.

Typical Modem Connection

Modems are normally connected to a computer or terminal equipment through an RS-232C interface connection. The Type D asynchronous modem interface, as specified by

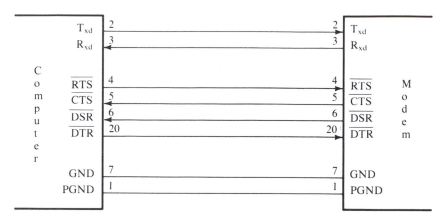

FIGURE 9–16 A typical modem-to-computer interconnection diagram.

EIA, is the most common and easiest to understand and will be discussed for this reason. Figure 9–16 illustrates a typical interface between an asynchronous modem and a computer system.

Pin Functions

Pin 1 Protective ground must be connected from the frames of both the modem and the computer to earth ground.

Pin 2 The transmit data pin is an output from the computer or terminal that supplies data for the modem. This pin is an input pin on the modem labeled *transmit*.

Pin 3 The receive data connection presents data to the computer from the modem and is an output pin at the modem.

Pin 4 The $\overline{\text{RTS}}$, or request to send, connection is an input to the modem that must be at the logic zero state to enable the modem to transmit data.

Pin 5 Clear to send, or $\overline{\text{CTS}}$, is a signal from the modem that indicates its transmitter's condition. A logic zero indicates that the modem is ready to transmit.

Pin 6 $\overline{\text{DSR}}$, or data set ready, indicates that the modem is connected to a communications channel and ready to transmit or receive data when a logic zero is present.

Pin 7 Signal ground.

Pin 17 The receiver signal element connection, which is not shown in figure 9–16, is used in synchronous communications to time or clock the reception of data. The one-to-zero transition on this output pin indicates the center of a bit of information at pin 3.

Pin 20 Data terminal ready, or $\overline{\text{DTR}}$, is an input to the modem that causes it either to connect or disconnect itself from the communications channel. If a logic zero, communication is allowed to proceed; if a logic one, the modem disconnects.

Pin 22 The ring indicator, which is not depicted in figure 9–16, indicates that the modem is receiving a ring signal. This enables automatic answering circuitry present in some modems' interfaces.

Pin 24 The transmitter signal element, which is not shown in figure 9–16, is provided to the modem for synchronous data communications. The one-to-zero transition must coincide with the center of the transmitted data bit applied to pin 2.

The Modem Handshake

Modem control software has to test the condition of the $\overline{\text{CTS}}$ and $\overline{\text{DSR}}$ signals before transmitting information to the modem. The modem also has to be conditioned by the computer by applying a logic zero on the modem connections $\overline{\text{DTR}}$ and $\overline{\text{RTS}}$.

If one of the two communications interface adapters discussed earlier in this chapter is used, most of the modem control is already accomplished by these devices. For example, the Intel 8251A has all four of the pin connections required for modem control, while the Motorola MC6850 contains only some of the connections.

8251A Modem Control

Figure 9–17 depicts the 8251A connected to a modem. Notice the inclusion of RS-232C line drivers and receivers for both the control and data connections to the modem.

When the 8251A is operated, it checks to see whether the $\overline{\text{CTS}}$ input is at a logic zero; if it is, the TxRDY pin becomes a logic one if the transmitter has been enabled. Before the modem can be used, the condition of the $\overline{\text{DSR}}$ must be checked by inputting the status word and testing the DSR bit position. If both pins are active, data transmission can be allowed.

Before the actual transmission occurs, the modem must be conditioned by the 8251A. This is accomplished by activating both the $\overline{\text{DTR}}$ and $\overline{\text{RTS}}$ connections to the modem. $\overline{\text{DTR}}$ is a signal to the modem that indicates that the 8251A has been powered up and is ready to send or receive data. The $\overline{\text{RTS}}$ signal to the modem requests that the modem send data. This signal is important if the modem is operated in simplex mode.

In the *simplex* mode, only the transmission or reception of information can occur at any instant in time. To send data, the 8251A requests that the modem turn the line around for transmission through the $\overline{\text{RTS}}$ signal. It then waits for the modem to signal that it is clear to send information ($\overline{\text{CTS}}$).

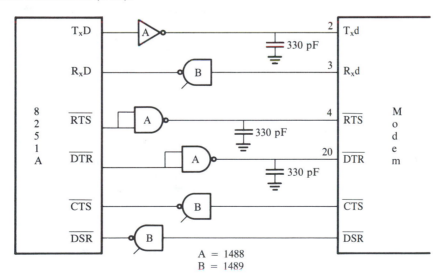

FIGURE 9–17 The 8251A programmable communications interface adapter connected to a MODEM.

If *full duplex* operation is used, as it often is, the $\overline{\text{RTS}}$ and $\overline{\text{CTS}}$ signals really don't have much meaning. $\overline{\text{RTS}}$ and $\overline{\text{CTS}}$ remain at logic zero levels after power is applied to the system.

MC6850 Modem Control

Figure 9–18 illustrates the MC6850 ACIA interfaced to a modem. Control of the modem is accomplished through the $\overline{\text{CTS}}$, $\overline{\text{RTS}}$, and $\overline{\text{DCD}}$ pins on the MC6850. The $\overline{\text{DSR}}$ and $\overline{\text{DTR}}$ signals are not tested or controlled by this device and are controlled externally.

The $\overline{\text{DTR}}$ signal to the modem can be provided by the power supply. When the system is turned on, this pin becomes a logic zero if connected to the output of an inverter, but only if the inverter's input is connected to 5 V. The $\overline{\text{DSR}}$ signal can be tested with a 1-bit input device, or it can be ignored because the modem does not receive or indicate that it is ready to send data through the $\overline{\text{CTS}}$ connection.

The $\overline{\text{RTS}}$ signal from the ACIA conditions the modem for a transmission. It requests that the modem allow a data transmission. If the modem will allow transmission, the $\overline{\text{CTS}}$ signal is at a logic zero level. Otherwise, the ACIA must wait until the modem is clear to send data.

Some modems have an output signal that becomes active if a received carrier is detected. This output is connected to the $\overline{\text{DCD}}$ input of the ACIA. If the carrier is lost—if the telephone line is disconnected—the $\overline{\text{DCD}}$ input goes to a logic one, possibly causing an interrupt.

9–9 IEEE-488 GENERAL PURPOSE INSTRUMENTATION BUS (GPIB)

The IEEE-488 parallel data transfer standard was developed by the Hewlett-Packard Corporation for use in their instruments. It was adopted as a general purpose instrumentation

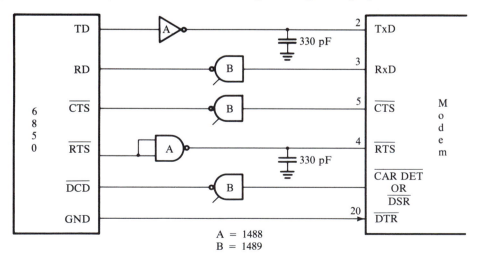

FIGURE 9–18   The MC6850 ACIA connected to a MODEM.

bus (GPIB) by IEEE in 1975. This standard is like the RS-232C standard because it defines the pin connections, protocol, and standard messages for communications.

IEEE-488 allows 8-bit parallel bidirectional communications among as many as 15 devices. These devices must be separated by no more than 2 m per device or 20 m total, whichever is less. Data transfer rates are allowable at up to one million bytes per second. The interface itself consists of eight bidirectional data lines, three handshaking connections, and five interface management connections.

Data Connections

The data connections may be open collector or three-state logic. In most applications these lines use three-state bidirectional data transceivers, as described in earlier chapters, since they increase the usable frequency range of the bus. The frequency range is increased because a three-state driver contains a low impedance pullup network that charges the line capacitance more quickly. This reduction in zero-to-one transition time allows higher data transmission rates. The data pins are labeled DI01 through DI08, where DI01 is the least significant bit position. The actual pin numbers are illustrated in figure 9–19.

Handshaking Connections

The IEEE-488 interface standard uses a three-wire handshake to accomplish data transfer.

DAV   The DAV, or data available, indicates the availability or validity of data on the data bus connections.

NRFD   The NRFD connection, or not ready for data pin, indicates the readiness of the device or devices connected to the bus to receive data.

NDAC   The NDAC, or not data accepted, indicates the condition of acceptance by the devices connected to the bus.

Pin	Function
1	DI01
2	DI02
3	DI03
4	DI04
5	EOI
6	DAV
7	NFRD
8	NDAC
9	IFC
10	SRQ
11	ATN
12	SHIELD
13	DI05
14	DI06
15	DI07
16	DI08
17	REN
18–23	Wire grounding pairs for pins 6–11
24–	Signal ground

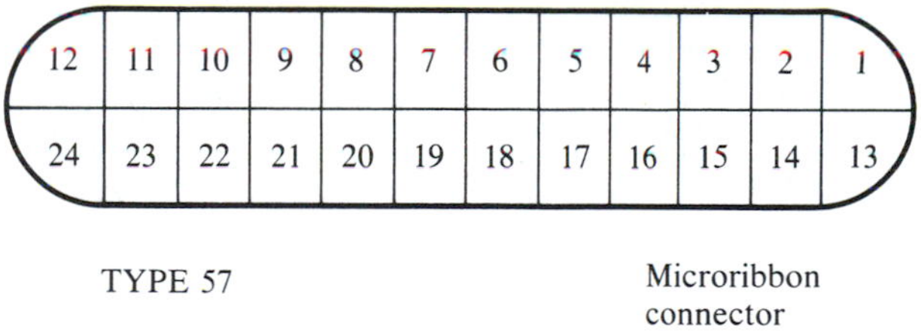

TYPE 57

Microribbon connector

FIGURE 9–19   The IEEE-488 bus connector and connector pin assignments.

The Handshake

Figure 9–20 illustrates the data bus and three handshaking connections to demonstrate the normal handshake that occurs on this bus. When the talker or sending device has information to be placed on the bus, it checks to determine if all devices are ready (NRFD = 1). If they are ready, it places the data on the data bus connections and issues a logic one on the DAV connection to indicate that the bus contains valid data. To complete the handshake, the talker waits for a response from all of the listeners by sampling the NDAC line. When all the devices connected to the bus have received the information, a logic one appears on NDAC to signal the end of the transfer.

Interface Management Connections

These connections, IFC, ATN, SRQ, REN, and EOI, manage the flow of information through the GPIB:

IFC IFC, or interface clear, clears the interface; that is, all of the devices connected to the GPIB.

ATN The ATN, or attention, line indicates how the data on the data lines are to be interpreted. When ATN is true, the current talker is disabled so that a new device can take over the bus.

SRQ The SRQ, or service request, line indicates that a device connected on the bus needs attention and is requesting an interruption of current events on the bus.

REN The remote enable connection, in conjunction with other messages, selects remote or local control of the device.

EOI EOI, or end or identify, ends a sequence of events or identifies the device during polling.

Interface Functions

Any device connected to the GPIB can assume any one of three identities: the listener, the talker, or the controller. Some devices on the bus can even change their function in midstream, allowing multiple control points on the same bus.

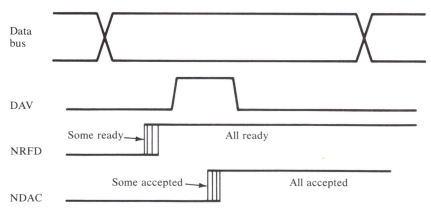

FIGURE 9–20 The IEEE-488 three-wire handshake.

The Listener   The *listener* is a device that receives data or status information over the bus from other devices in the system. Examples of such devices include printers, disk systems, display devices, and signal generators.

Each listener in a system responds only when addressed. In fact, many listeners can be made receptive at the same time to receive data from a common source. A listener also responds to a variety of other signals in a system.

The Talker   The *talker* is a device that can provide parallel data or status information to the bus and is used for devices that send information to a computer system. Devices that are often equipped with this interface function include multimeters, frequency counters, disk drives, and data analyzers.

Each talker in a system responds to a unique address or device location that allows the bus controller to select different talkers. Only one talker is allowed to send data down the bus at a time. It also responds to a variety of commands from the GPIB controller.

The Controller   The *controller* function is the most complicated, since it must be capable of commanding the various talkers and listeners connected to the bus. It must be capable of sending addresses and commands to any or all talkers and listeners on the bus and of conducting polls to see which devices are active.

Provisions have been made so that more than one controller may exist on the GPIB at one time. This is allowed if only one is active at any given moment. Switches between multiple controllers are accomplished through the ATN signal line.

Typical Small GPIB System

The block diagram in figure 9–21 illustrates a small instrumentation system connected to a microprocessor. Device one is the microprocessor, which can command the other devices connected to the bus because it can control, talk, and listen. Device two is a printer, which can accept information from the microprocessor to be printed; therefore, it is a listen-only device. Device three is a frequency counter, which is a talk-only component.

This simple system can monitor the frequency of an external system, and the microprocessor can print a listing at various periods of time. The microprocessor can also perform a statistical analysis on this information and print it in addition to the readings.

System Controller Communications

Suppose that the controller wishes to read data from the frequency counter to compile a report. It accomplishes this task by commanding the counter to talk by placing the address of the counter on the bus with the my talk address (MTA) command. The counter is now enabled to send data through the bus to a listener or listeners. If a printed report is to be compiled at the same time, the controller commands the printer, as well as the microprocessor, to begin listening. This procedure is accomplished by addressing them with the my listening address (MLA) command. After all of the devices are programmed by the controller, communications between the counter and the microprocessor and printer proceed unhindered.

The 8291A GPIB Talker/Listener

Figure 9–22 illustrates the pinout and block diagram of the 8291A talker/listener. This device is used with a microprocessor to enact the talk-only, listen-only or the talker/

FIGURE 9–21 The block diagram of a small IEEE-488 general purpose instrumentation bus system.

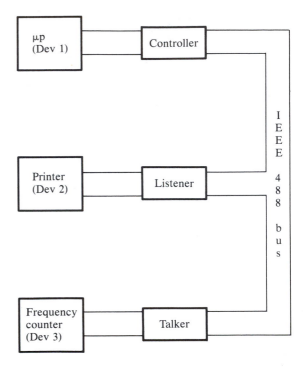

listener function (illustrated in the block diagram of figure 9–21). This device is capable of implementing the complete system handshaking, extended addressing, and automatic handling of many functions.

Figure 9–23 pictures the 8291A connected to a set of buffers that drive the bus. The only external circuitry required to accomplish this is a set of transceivers for the data bus connections and control pins NRFD, NADC, DAV, and EOI.

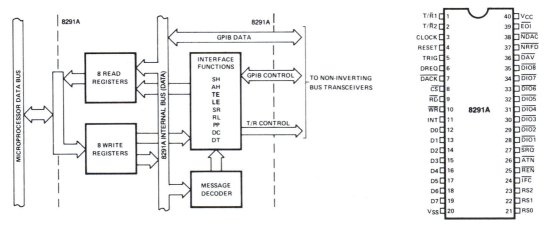

FIGURE 9–22 The 8291A IEEE-488/GPIB talker/listener pinout and block diagram

SOURCE: Reprinted by permission of Intel Corporation. Copyright 1983.

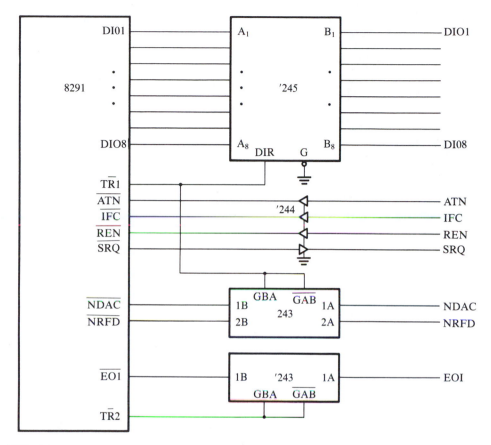

FIGURE 9–23 The 8291A talker/listener interfaced to the IEEE-488 bus through a series of external bus buffers.

The 8292 GPIB Controller

Figure 9–24 pictures the pinout and the block diagram of the 8291A, 8292 GPIB system. The 8292 controller provides the command protocol to enable and disable the various talkers and listeners connected to the bus. It also contains the logic required to pass control to another controller that may or may not be controlling the bus. The controller can also poll the devices in the system to determine which are active.

Summary

1   Asynchronous serial data are transmitted with a start bit, data bits, often a parity bit, and one or two stop bits. The start and stop bits are used to synchronize the reception of the data.

2   Synchronous serial data are transmitted with a clock and contain no start or stop

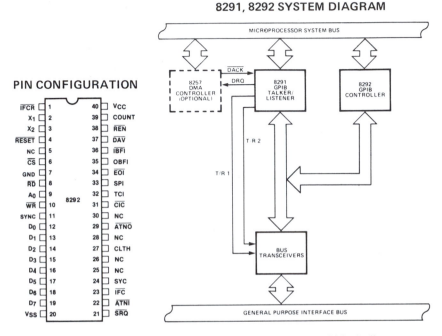

FIGURE 9–24 The 8292 IEEE-488/GPIB bus controller pinout and block diagram.

SOURCE: Reprinted by permission of Intel Corporation. Copyright 1983.

bits for synchronization, which means that more bits of information can be transmitted per second using the same clocking rate.

3   A UART is a universal asynchronous receiver/transmitter that converts parallel-to-asynchronous serial data and asynchronous serial data to parallel. The UART internally uses a shift register to accomplish this data conversion.

4   The 8251A is a programmable universal synchronous/asynchronous receiver/transmitter (USART) that converts between serial synchronous or asynchronous and parallel data.

5   The 8251A USART is reset with a series of outputs to its command register. The data output consists of the following four bytes: 00, 00, 00, and 04.

6   Once the 8251A is reset, it is programmed by sending it a mode instruction word which selects either synchronous or asynchronous operation. With asynchronous operation, the number of stop bits, data bits, type of parity, and clock rate multiplier are selected. With synchronous operation the number of sync characters (one or two) are selected along with the operation of the type of parity, number of data bits, and the operation of synchronization detection. After the mode of operation is selected, the command register is programmed.

7   The 8251A detects three types of receiver errors: (1) parity error, (2) overrun error, and (3) framing error. A parity error occurs if the wrong parity is received, an overrun error occurs when the data are not removed from the 8251A

before the next character is received, and a framing error occurs if the stop bit or bits are missing.

8   The 6850 ACIA is an asynchronous communications interface adapter that converts between serial asynchronous data and parallel data. It is programmable with the following features: number of data bits, type of parity, number of stop bits, and clock rate multiplier.

9   The $\overline{\text{IRQ}}$ output pin of the 6850 is programmable so that it interrupts the microprocessor if the receiver has data, if the transmitter has data, or both.

10   The RS-232C interface standard is a serial standard that supports both synchronous and asynchronous data and also allows a modem to be controlled in either full- or half-duplex operation.

11   A current loop uses current flows in either one direction (unipolar) or two directions (bipolar) to send and receive serial data.

12   A modem is a modulator/demodulator that converts between serial digital data and either FSK (frequency shift keying) or PSK (phase shift keying). FSK encodes data as two distinct audio tones and PSK encodes data in the phase angle of a tone.

13   Modem handshaking is accomplished with the $\overline{\text{CTS}}$, $\overline{\text{DSR}}$, $\overline{\text{DTR}}$, and $\overline{\text{RTS}}$ signals. The $\overline{\text{DSR}}$ signal indicates that the modem is operational, the $\overline{\text{DTR}}$ signal indicates that the computer is operational, the $\overline{\text{RTS}}$ signal requests that the modem is made ready to transmit data, and the $\overline{\text{CTS}}$ signal indicates that the modem is ready to transmit data.

14   The IEEE-488 GPIB (general purpose instrumentation bus) is used to transfer parallel data between a microprocessor and peripherals. The microprocessor (or bus master) contains a controller and peripherals contain either a talker, a listener, or both.

Glossary

ACIA   Asynchronous Communications Interface Adapter. A device that receives and transmits asynchronous serial data.

Asynchronous communications   These forms of digital communications are carried out by converting parallel information into serial information with the synchronizing bits START and STOP.

Baud rate   The number of data bits and synchronizing bits transmitted per second in an FSK digital communications system. In a PSK system, the baud rate represents the number of pieces of information per second. This can be two or three times the bit rate.

BISYNC   A synchronous, byte-oriented communications protocol using two synchronization bytes.

DIBIT   A pair of bits used to select one of four different phase angles in a PSK communications system.

Full duplex   A system in which data can be transmitted and received at the same time.

FSK   Frequency Shift Keying. A transmission technique whereby data are encoded as two distinct transmitting frequencies, one for each logic level.

GPIB   General Purpose Instrumentation Bus. Often used to interconnect parallel components to a microcomputer system.

Half-duplex   A system where data are transmitted and received in both directions, but only one direction at a time.

IEEE-488   A parallel interface standard accepted by the Institute of Electrical and Electronic Engineers (see GPIB).

Listener   A device that receives information on the GPIB.

Modem   An acronym for MOdulator/DEModulator. A communications device that sends and receives modulated digital data.

Parity   A count of the number of ones, expressed as even or odd.

Programmable communications interface adapter   A programmable device that generates and receives serial data in the asynchronous or synchronous mode.

Protocol   A standard method of rules that dictates the way data are transferred.

PSK   Phase Shift Keying. A transmission technique whereby data are encoded in phase angles of the transmitted signal.

RS-232C   A serial interface standard developed by the Electronics Industries Association.

SDLC   Serial Data Link Control. A bit-oriented communications protocol.

Simplex   Data communicated in one direction.

Synchronous communications   Communications that include a clock pulse for synchronization.

Talker   A device that sends data on the GPIB.

TRIBIT   Three bits of information that select eight different phase angles in a PSK communications system.

UART   Universal Asynchronous Receiver/Transmitter. A device that converts parallel data to serial data and serial data to parallel data.

USART   Universal Synchronous/Asynchronous Receiver/Transmitter. A device that can communicate by using either asynchronous or synchronous serial data.

USRT   Universal Synchronous Receiver/Transmitter. A device that receives and transmits synchronous serial data.

Questions and Problems

1   Describe the basic difference between synchronous and asynchronous digital communications.

2   If an asynchronous communications signal contains eight bits of data, one start bit, and two stop bits and each bit time is 9.09 ms, what is the baud rate?

3   Asynchronous data normally have how many stop bits?

4   Sync bytes are used with which type of communication?

5   Asynchronous serial data communications normally occur at baud rates up to which maximum baud rate?

6   Contrast the command structures of the MC6850 and 8251A communications interface adapters.

7   Develop the software required to program the 8251A to function asynchronously with seven data bits, two stop bits, even parity, and a clock-divide-by rate of 16.

8   Develop the software to program the MC6850 to function with seven data bits, two stop bits, even parity, and a clock-divide-by rate of 16.

9   How many pin connections exist on the RS-232C interface connector?

10   If a cable has 10 pF of capacitance per meter, what is the longest cable that can be used with RS-232C? (Assume that the driver contains a 300-pF capacitive load.)

11   In a system that uses +12 V and −5 V to power the RS-232C interface, what is the noise immunity of this interface?

12   Why do you suppose that the RS-232C interface standard has been short-circuit- and open-circuit-proofed?

13   What is the main disadvantage of a current loop interface?

14   What is a polar current loop?

15   Explain how FSK data are generated.

16   Explain how PSK data are formed if two bits are used to select each phase.

17   Which type of transmission would normally find its place in synchronous communications environments?

18   Describe the purpose of each of the following modem interconnections: $\overline{DSR}$, $\overline{DTR}$, $\overline{RTS}$, and $\overline{CTS}$.

19   Which modem signal lines must be checked by data terminal or computer before communications can proceed?

20   Which data terminal or computer signal lines must be checked by the modem before communications can proceed?

21   What is the main difference between the interconnections of the modem and data terminal in synchronous and asynchronous systems?

22   Develop the software required to control a modem using the MC6850.

23   Develop the software required to control a modem using the 8251A.

24   Explain the function of a GPIB.

25   Describe the ways the three handshaking signals are applied in the IEEE-488 GPIB.

10

Direct Memory Access

Upon completion of this chapter, you will be able to

1 Describe DMA (direct memory access).
2 Explain why $\overline{\text{IOR}}$, $\overline{\text{IOW}}$, $\overline{\text{MEMR}}$, and $\overline{\text{MEMW}}$ are needed for a DMA action.
3 Program the 8275–5 DMA controller.
4 Define various terms as they apply to video technology.
5 Explain the function of the blocks in the block diagram of a monitor.
6 Describe how CRTs are refreshed.

Direct memory access is probably one of the most difficult I/O techniques to understand, but it is worth the extra effort because of its extreme power in a processor-based system. This technique is usable for data transfer at extremely high speeds and may, in some cases, be the only technique that can be used.

This chapter introduces the DMA structure of the microprocessor and discusses an application of the technique, CRT screen refreshing, which must occur at a very high rate of speed. CRT screen refreshing is one of the most common examples of this I/O technique.

10-1 INTRODUCTION TO DIRECT MEMORY ACCESS

Direct memory access (DMA) is used whenever data transfer rates exceed the capability of a software transfer. For instance, a typical microprocessor is able to transfer about ten thousand bytes of data per second with a program. This, of course, includes the time it takes to get the information from the memory, send it to an I/O device, and increment a pointer for the next byte. If the required data transfer rates are much faster, a new technique must be found to effect the transfer. The new technique, DMA, is a method whereby the external device goes directly into the memory and either extracts or stores information. The only limitation to the speed of this type of transfer is the speed of the memory system and the speed of the DMA controller.

This I/O technique is found in any system that requires a high data transfer rate. Two common examples are the CRT terminal for screen refreshing and a disk drive for data transfer.

In the CRT terminal, the electron beam moves across the screen at a tremendous rate and requires data at the rate of one character in about every 750 ns maximum. You might think that the microprocessor would have very little processing time with transfer at this rate. It has, because there are times (during retrace and so forth) when the processor is free to do other tasks.

In a disk drive a common data transfer rate is 250,000 bits of information per second. Since over 30,000 bytes of data must be transferred per second, this is also a good application for DMA. Disk drives that are able to store information in double and quad densities are even better candidates for DMA transfers because of their speed.

The Microprocessor DMA Structure

The two connections on almost all microprocessors that are used for controlling the DMA transfer are the HOLD and HLDA pins. The HOLD input requests a DMA cycle. This input causes the microprocessor to suspend operations and to disconnect itself from the data, address, and control buses. This disconnection is accomplished by three-stating or floating these buses. Once the microprocessor has disconnected itself, an external device, usually a DMA controller, can extract from or store information directly into the memory.

To signal the controller that the processor has relinquished control of the buses, the microprocessor sends out a signal that indicates that the buses are indeed at their high impedance state. This HLDA, or hold acknowledge, signal is an indicator that signals the DMA controller or external device to begin transferring the information.

Memory Considerations

The memory in the microprocessor-based system is the determining factor on DMA transfer rate. For example, if RAM, which has a cycle time of 500 ns, is used, the memory bandwidth equals 2 MHz. In other words, DMA transfers can be effected at the rate of 2 million bytes of information per second.

Transfers occur a byte at a time or in *bursts* of many bytes. The type of transfer selected also affects the maximum transfer rate. For example, if data are burst into the memory, the effective transfer rate is approximately equal to the memory bandwidth. On the other hand, if data are transferred a byte at a time, the rate may be considerably lower because the microprocessor requires some time to acknowledge each DMA request.

The DMA Controller

The *DMA controller* is almost as complex as a microprocessor, and in fact it could be one. It must provide the memory with a memory address and control signals to accomplish a transfer. In addition to the memory control signals and addressing information, it must also control the external DMA-controlled I/O device.

Figure 10–1 illustrates the internal structure of a very simple DMA controller. Notice that it contains an address register that selects the desired transfer location. It also contains control logic that provides the memory with its control signals and the I/O device with the appropriate control signals.

A COMPARISON OF DMA SCHEMES 10-2

Most microprocessors have some form of DMA control structure. For example, the Intel 8085A uses a HOLD input and a HLDA output, as does the Zilog Z80. The Motorola MC6800 supports direct memory access with the DBE (data bus enable) and TSC (three-state control) connections. The MC6809 supports DMA through a $\overline{\text{DMA}}/\overline{\text{BREQ}}$ input and

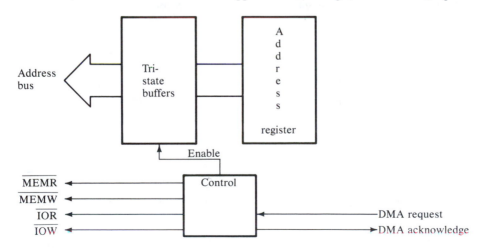

FIGURE 10–1 The block diagram of a simple direct memory access (DMA) controller.

a BA and BS output. The BA and BS output must be decoded to produce a DMA acknowledge signal.

The 8085A DMA Structure

In the 8085A, the user can request a DMA transfer by placing a logic one on the HOLD input. This action causes the 8085A to suspend processing instructions. HOLD is recognized at the end of the current bus cycle, which is usually within three clocking periods, or 1 μs.

Once operations are suspended, the 8085A floats the address, data, and control bus connections $\overline{RD}$, $\overline{WR}$, and IO/$\overline{M}$ and places a logic one on the HLDA output pin. When HLDA becomes a logic one, the external requesting device can begin transferring data. Refer to figure 10–2 for the 8085A HOLD timing.

It is interesting to note that the HOLD input has a higher priority than any of the interrupt inputs, including the TRAP connection. Therefore, care must be taken when using DMA in conjunction with interrupts, since timing may be affected.

The HOLD input is a level-sensitive input and must be held high until it is recognized by the 8085A. This operation may require external synchronization for the proper operation. External synchronization may be accomplished in the same manner used for the level-sensitive interrupt inputs discussed in chapter 8.

The MC6800 DMA Structure

The MC6800 uses three inputs to accomplish a DMA: the TSC input; the DBE input, which is normally the phase-two clock input to the MC6800; and the phase-one clock. Whenever the TSC input and phase-one clock are held high and the DBE input is held low, the MC6800's address, data, and R/$\overline{W}$ pin are held in their impedance state. These conditions occur after a short time delay, as illustrated in figure 10–3. The main problem with DMA in this microprocessor is that it completely stops the phase-one clock pulse. This clock signal is used to refresh the contents of the dynamic register array internally. The number of bytes that can be burst-transferred into or out of the memory during a DMA are thus limited. This clock may only be stopped for 9.5 μs maximum.

The MC6809 DMA Structure

Unlike the MC6800, the MC6809 allows for an unlimited DMA time, making it much

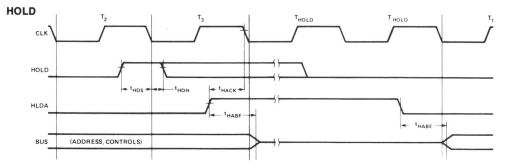

FIGURE 10–2 Intel 8085A microprocessor DMA timing.

SOURCE: Reprinted by permission of Intel Corporation, Copyright 1983.

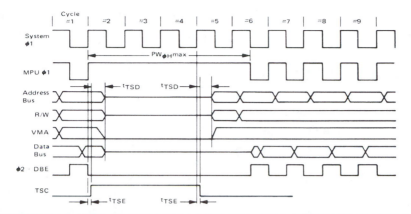

FIGURE 10–3 Motorola MC6800 DMA timing.
SOURCE: Courtesy of Motorola, Inc.

more useful in many applications. This prolonged DMA is accomplished because the microprocessor periodically interrupts the DMA cycle to refresh its internal dynamic register array.

When requesting a DMA cycle, the external device places a logic zero on the $\overline{\text{DMA}/\text{BREQ}}$ connection (illustrated in figure 10–4). The MC6809 then relinquishes control of the memory by floating the address, data, and control buses. This procedure is indicated to the external controller by the BA and BS lines, which must be logically combined to produce a DMA acknowledge signal. When both BA and BS are at their logic one states, the MC6809 is either halted or acknowledging the DMA request.

Comparison of DMA Schemes

It is fairly easy to see that the DMA structure of the MC6800 microprocessor is extremely awkward or impossible to use if DMA bursts of data are to be accomplished. The MC6809 is more widely applied than the MC6800 because it allows DMA bursts. The only disadvantage of the MC6809 is that it requires an external logic gate to generate the acknowledge signal. The 8085A and Z80 are the most efficient DMA controllable devices because

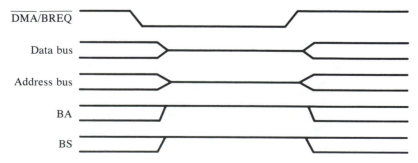

FIGURE 10–4 Motorola MC6809 DMA timing.
SOURCE: Courtesy of Motorola, Inc.

they require no external circuitry and allow unlimited DMA bursting without interrupting the DMA cycle.

10-3 THE 8257-5 DMA CONTROLLER

The 8257-5 DMA controller (Figure 10–5) is a four-channel direct memory access controller compatible with the Intel 8085A and Zilog Z80A microprocessors. This device is capable of single-byte transfers or burst transfers with little or no intervention from the microprocessor. It provides not only the memory address for each of the four channels but also the control signals for the memory and four different DMA I/O devices.

Each DMA Channel

Each of the four DMA channels contains a programmable address register to indicate the location of the DMA transfer. Each channel also contains a 14-bit counter to indicate how many bytes of data are to be transferred at a time. This counter allows a burst of up to 16K

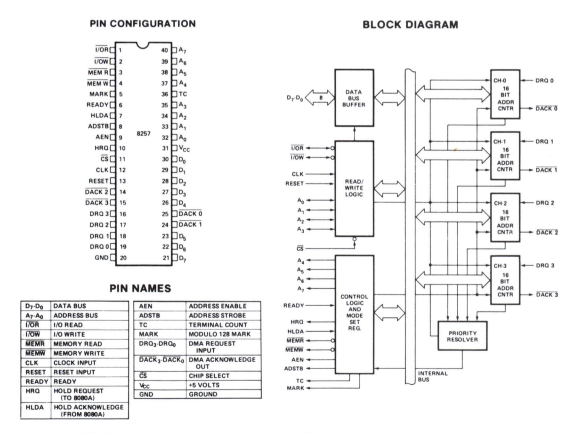

FIGURE 10–5 The 8257-5 programmable DMA controller pinout and block diagram.

SOURCE: Reprinted by permission of Intel Corporation, Copyright 1983.

bytes at a time, which is probably the maximum that would ever be transferred in a DMA for an 8-bit microprocessor.

Each channel contains a request input, DRQ, and an acknowledgment output, $\overline{DACK}$. When the DRQ input becomes active for any channel, the 8257-5 checks whether any other DRQ is active and resolves the priority with a multifunction built-in priority encoder. Either rotating or fixed priority can be selected when the 8257-5 is first programmed. With rotating priority, the most recently accepted DRQ input has the lowest priority. This capacity tends to give all of the DRQ inputs equal priority, if desired. When fixed priority is selected, the DRQ0 input has the highest and the DRQ3 input has the lowest.

Channel two can be used in a special mode of operation that is useful for CRT refreshing. This mode automatically reloads the initial address and count after all bytes are transferred, as is required in a CRT terminal. Reloading is accomplished from the channel three DMA address register and counter.

Microprocessor Connections

Figure 10–6 illustrates the connections from an 8085A to the DMA controller. Notice that this device uses the $\overline{MEMR}$, $\overline{MEMW}$, $\overline{IOR}$, and $\overline{IOW}$ control signals. These have been developed with a 74LS257 quad 2-to-1 line multiplexer. In this circuit, whenever the IO/$\overline{M}$ pin is a logic one, the B inputs to the multiplexer are selected, causing $\overline{WR}$ to be

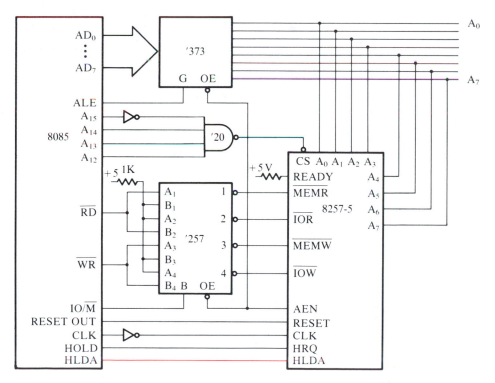

FIGURE 10–6 The 8085A microprocessor portion of the 8257-5 interface.

directed to the $\overline{\text{IOW}}$ output and $\overline{\text{RD}}$ to be directed to the $\overline{\text{IOR}}$ output. If IO/$\overline{\text{M}}$ is a logic zero then $\overline{\text{RD}}$ and $\overline{\text{WR}}$ are directed to the $\overline{\text{MEMR}}$ and $\overline{\text{MEMW}}$ pins. During a hold, the AEN signal from the 8257-5 is a logic one, disabling the control signals generated by the 74LS257. This allows the DMA controller to gain access to the control bus and provide these control signals. The only connection that has not been made is the READY connection, which is sometimes used when slow memory is accessed. Slow memory is virtually nonexistent today because devices are available with access times as low as 80 ns.

The $\overline{\text{CS}}$ pin is connected to a simple port decoder so that this 8257-5 is selected for I/O location 7XH.

Unfortunately, Intel failed to include the ALE signal input and accompanying internal address latch; so an 8085A system using this device must include an external address latch. This is also illustrated in figure 10–6.

Memory Connections

Figure 10–7 illustrates the memory side connections of the 8257-5. Notice that an external memory address register is required because the address output from the 8257-5 is multiplexed in order to reduce its pin count. The controller sends out the most significant address bits on data bus connections D0 through D7, where it must be latched into some form of external address latch. Demultiplexing is accomplished in much the same fashion that the 8085A multiplexes its low-order address.

The address latch is controlled by the ADSTB and AEN control signals. AEN enables the outputs of this address latch during the DMA transfer, providing the memory with A8 through A15 during the transfer. Address bits A0 through A7 are provided on the pins labeled A0 through A7. The ADSTB signal is identical to ALE, except that it is used to clock the A8 through A15 into the address latch.

AEN serves one other function in this system; it disables the normal A0 through A7 address latch and the 74LS257 multiplexer. The least significant address is provided by the DMA controller during a DMA cycle, as are the control signals.

I/O Connections

Figure 10–8 pictures the I/O side connections of the DMA controller. Notice that the I/O

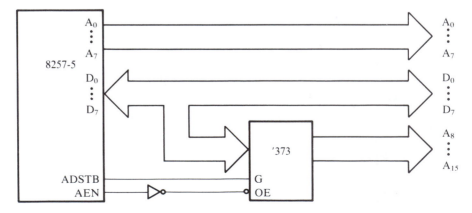

FIGURE 10–7   The memory portion of the 8257-5 DMA controller interface.

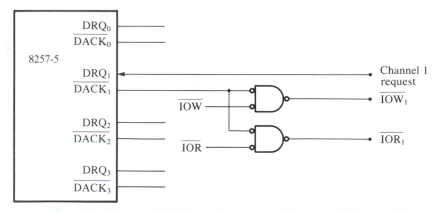

FIGURE 10–8 The I/O portion of the 8257-5 DMA controller interface.

strobes are developed by logically combining the $\overline{\text{IOR}}$ and $\overline{\text{IOW}}$ signals with the $\overline{\text{DACK}}$ output for a particular channel. The $\overline{\text{DACK}}$ output replaces the device selection logic or port selection logic discussed in previous chapters.

In the drawing in figure 10–8, a channel one request is eventually honored by the microprocessor; when it is, the $\overline{\text{DACK1}}$ output becomes a logic zero. This procedure allows the $\overline{\text{IOR}}$ or $\overline{\text{IOW}}$ to be passed on to the DMA-controlled device for activation.

Programming the 8257-5

Programming this device is less difficult than it first appears. Table 10–1 illustrates the port assignments for the 8257-5. When programming this device, the mode set register is programmed first, followed by each active channel's DMA address and the terminal count register. Note that it is important that this order is strictly followed or the programming will be incorrect. Also note that programmed count is one less than the actual count.

Mode Set Programming

The mode set register, which is depicted in table 10–2, directs the operation of the DMA controller, and it must be programmed. The function of each bit of this register is outlined below:

AL Auto load selects the auto load feature for DMA channel two. The channel two count and address registers are loaded from the channel three count and address registers at a terminal count. This mode therefore reduces the number of channels available from four to three if it is activated.

TCS This terminal count stop bit stops a DMA burst at the terminal count. If TCS is not active, the external DMA device must stop the transfer.

EW The extended write bit extends the length of the $\overline{\text{MEMW}}$ and $\overline{\text{IOW}}$ signals as required by some slower I/O and memory devices.

RP This rotating priority bit selects a rotating priority scheme. If it is not set, channel zero has the highest priority and channel three the lowest. If rotating priority is selected, then the most recently serviced DRQ input assumes the lowest priority.

TABLE 10–1   8257 register selection.

Register	Byte	Address Inputs					*Bi-Directional Data Bus							
		A_3	A_2	A_1	A_0	F/L	D_7	D_6	D_5	D_4	D_3	D_2	D_1	D_0
CH-0 DMA Address	LSB	0	0	0	0	0	A_7	A_6	A_5	A_4	A_3	A_2	A_1	A_0
	MSB	0	0	0	0	1	A_{15}	A_{14}	A_{13}	A_{12}	A_{11}	A_{10}	A_9	A_8
CH-0 Terminal Count	LSB	0	0	0	1	0	C_7	C_6	C_5	C_4	C_3	C_2	C_1	C_0
	MSB	0	0	0	1	1	Rd	Wr	C_{13}	C_{12}	C_{11}	C_{10}	C_9	C_8
CH-1 DMA Address	LSB	0	0	1	0	0	Same as Channel 0							
	MSB	0	0	1	0	1								
CH-1 Terminal Count	LSB	0	0	1	1	0								
	MSB	0	0	1	1	1								
CH-2 DMA Address	LSB	0	1	0	0	0	Same as Channel 0							
	MSB	0	1	0	0	1								
CH-2 Terminal Count	LSB	0	1	0	1	0								
	MSB	0	1	0	1	1								
CH-3 DMA Address	LSB	0	1	1	0	0	Same as Channel 0							
	MSB	0	1	1	0	1								
CH-3 Terminal Count	LSB	0	1	1	1	0								
	MSB	0	1	1	1	1								
MODE SET (Program only)	—	1	0	0	0	0	AL	TCS	EW	RP	EN3	EN2	EN1	EN0
STATUS (Read only)	—	1	0	0	0	0	0	0	0	UP	TC3	TC2	TC1	TC0

*A_0-A_{15}: DMA Starting Address, C_0-C_{13}: Terminal Count value (N−1), Rd and Wr: DMA Verify (00). Write (01) or Read (10) cycle selection, AL: Auto Load, TCS: TC Stop, EW: Extended Write, RP: Rotating Priority, EN3-EN0: Channel Enable Mask, UP: Update Flag. TC3-TC0: Terminal Count Status Bits.

ENX   The enable DMA bit positions EN0, EN1, EN2, and EN3 enable the respective DMA channels.

Status Register

The status register (table 10–3), which is read by the microprocessor, indicates the condition of the 8257-5. The function of each status bit is characterized in the following list:

UP   The update flag indicates when the channel-two registers have been reloaded from the channel-three registers in the auto load mode of operation.

TC   The four TC, or terminal count, status bits indicate that a terminal count has been reached and will remain active until the status register is read. They are cleared when the status register is read by the microprocessor.

Programming the Address and Terminal Count Registers

The address register, which must be programmed before the terminal count register, holds

TABLE 10–2   The 8257-5 mode set register.

7	6	5	4	3	2	1	0
AL	TCS	EW	RP	EN3	EN2	EN1	EN0

TABLE 10–3 The 8257-5 status register.

7	6	5	4	3	2	1	0
0	0	0	UP	TC3	TC2	TC1	TC0

the address of the first byte of information to be transferred. This address is incremented by the controller after each DMA read or write.

The terminal count register is a 14-bit counter that indicates how many bytes are to be transferred in the DMA cycle. This register must always be loaded with the number of bytes to be transferred minus one. The remaining two bit positions of the terminal count register indicate the type of DMA operation to be performed by the channel, read or write (refer to table 10–1).

A DMA write cycle causes data to be read from an external I/O device and written into the memory. A DMA read cycle causes data to be pulled from the memory and written into some external I/O device.

In both cases the least significant portion of the register must be programmed first, followed by the most significant portion. Notice that the I/O port number is the same for both. The direction of data flow is internally controlled by an F/L (first/last) flip-flop that indicates least and most significant data bits or first and last.

Operation

Figure 10–9 depicts the operation of the 8257-5 through a state transition diagram. A series of clock states, each of which is equal to the clock period of the host 8085A, directs the operation of this device.

After a reset, the 8257-5 enters into state SI (initialization state) and remains there until one of the enabled DRQ inputs becomes a logic one. When a DRQ request occurs, the HRQ signal connected to the HOLD input on the 8085A is placed at a logic one, requesting a HOLD.

State S0 is entered from the SI where the DMA controller waits for the acknowledge signal, HLDA, from the 8085A. If noise on a DRQ input causes the 8257-5 to enter into state S0, it returns to state SI because it is no longer active.

If the DRQ request is still active once the microprocessor acknowledges the request with HLDA, the controller enters clocking state S1. S1 is used by the controller to send out the memory address to the memory system by latching the upper half of the memory address, which is presented on the data bus connections, into an external most significant address latch.

The next state, S2, is used mainly for memory access time; if the controller has been commanded, it issues the advanced $\overline{\text{MEMW}}$ or $\overline{\text{IOW}}$ signals at this time. Some external devices may require more time to write the information so that the advanced memory or I/O write signals are provided.

In state S3, the data transfer occurs; it is here that the appropriate memory and I/O control signals are activated. During this state the ready line is also sampled to determine whether a slow memory or I/O device is connected to the system.

FIGURE 10–9 The 8257-5 Internal State transition diagram.

SOURCE: Reprinted by permission of Intel Corporation, Copyright 1983.

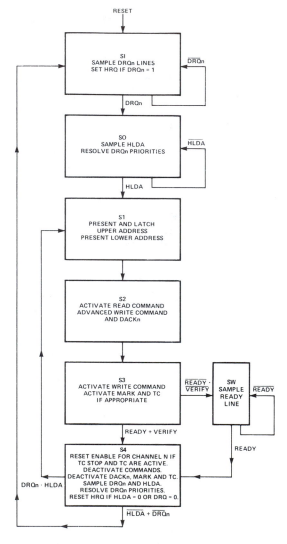

1 DRQn refers to any DRQ line on an enabled DMA channel.

In the last state, the DMA controller decides whether to transfer another byte of information for burst operation or whether to return to state SI. If the DRQ request is still active, there is a branch to state S1; the entire process of presenting a memory address, followed by the control signals, is repeated for the next byte to be transferred.

This controller can transfer one byte of data for every four clock periods in the burst mode and no more than one byte of data for every six clock cycles in the single byte mode. If a 3-MHz clock is used for timing, it is able to burst 750,000 bytes of data per second. That rate is quite a bit faster than the rate of the direct I/O techniques discussed in earlier chapters.

Timing

Figure 10–10 pictures the timing diagram for the 8257-5, which should be compared with the description of the operation of the controller. Beginning with the second waveform, DRQ 0–3, you will notice that it causes the 8257-5 to leave state SI and enter into state S0. It also causes the HRQ output, which is connected to the 8085A hold input, to become a logic one. This procedure requests the HOLD or DMA.

Next the controller enters state S1 if the microprocessor has returned the HLDA signal. At this time a flurry of events occurs: The 8257-5 activates the AEN signal to disable the external bus drivers in the system. It also enables the 8257-5 address latch's output. On the positive edge of the S1 clock pulse, the 8257-5 outputs the 16-bit DMA memory address. Half appears on A0 through A7 and the other half appears on the data bus connections. The most significant half of the address is latched into an external address latch using the ADR STB signal that is also present at this time.

During state S2 the 8257-5 sends out the $\overline{\text{DACK 0–3}}$ signal to acknowledge the DMA request to the I/O device.

Finally the data is transferred in state S3. In a DMA write, the $\overline{\text{IOR}}$ and the $\overline{\text{MEMW}}$ signals activate, causing data to be read from an I/O device onto the data bus. The $\overline{\text{MEMW}}$ signal then causes the contents of the data bus, the I/O data, to be written into the selected memory address. If the operation were a DMA read, the $\overline{\text{IOW}}$ and $\overline{\text{MEMR}}$ signals would be active, causing data from the memory to be written into the external I/O device. In the DMA verify mode of operation, no control signal is issued by the 8257-5. The system merely cycles through the DMA address that can be used by the external device to perform some form of internal verification.

DMA-Controlled Data Communications Example

The DMA-controlled data communications example, whose hardware is depicted in figure 10–11, automatically transmits a block of information from a portion of the memory out through an 8251A communications interface adapter.

Once the area of memory to be transmitted is loaded with data (by a subroutine that is not illustrated here), the DMA controller can be programmed with the starting location of the data and the length of the block of data. Once these registers are programmed, the mode set register is directed to start the transfer by enabling channel one.

Since the transmitter is probably empty at this time, the transmitter ready pin TxRDY, connected to the DRQ1 input, requests a DMA cycle. When the 8085A grants the cycle, a byte of data is read from the memory and transferred or written to the 8251A.

Since it takes some time to transmit a byte of information, the TxRDY pin remains a logic zero for some time to allow the microprocessor to continue processing other information. In this system, the communication takes only six 8085A clock cycles to transfer a byte of information. Normally some form of subroutine is required to check or poll the status bit of the 8251A. This is probably the most efficient data transfer process possible.

When a terminal count (TC) is reached, all bytes have been transferred and the logic circuitry generates a RST 7.5 interrupt request. This interrupt request signals the 8085A that the transmission is complete and that the DMA controller must be disabled on channel one until the next block transfer.

CONSECUTIVE CYCLES AND BURST MODE SEQUENCE

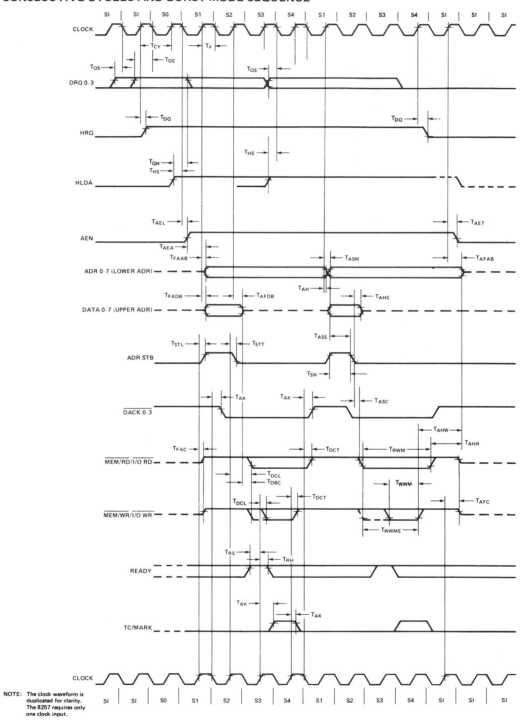

FIGURE 10–10 The timing diagram for the 8257-5 programmable DMA controller.

SOURCE: Reprinted by permission of Intel Corporation, Copyright 1983.

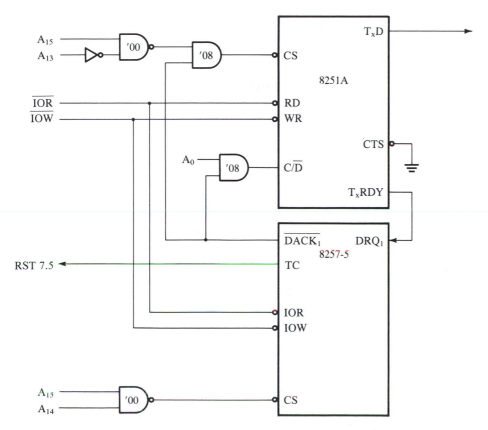

FIGURE 10–11 A DMA-controlled data communications interface.

Software

The software for this example can be broken down into many modules or subroutines for an easier understanding.

A module for the transfer of data into the block of memory to be transmitted is not developed at this time, but all other control software is developed.

Initialization Dialog

The initialization dialog for this example must program both the 8251A and the 8257-5. It must also activate the RST 7.5 interrupt pin used at the end of a transmission. Refer to chapters 7 and 9 for more detailed explanation of some of the initialization dialog that follows:

```
                        ;program the 8257-5 DMA controller
                        ;
0000  97      RESET:    SUB      A              ; clear F/L flip-flop
0001  D3F8              OUT      0F8H
                        ;
                        ;program the 8251A so that it operates in the
                        ;asynchronous mode with 7 data bits, 1 stop,
```

```
                              ;even parity, and divides the clock by 16
                              ;
0003  D381                    OUT       81H              ;reset the 8251A
0005  D381                    OUT       81H
0007  D381                    OUT       81H
0009  3E40                    MVI       A,40H
000B  D381                    OUT       81H
000D  3E7A                    MVI       A,7AH            ;program 8251A
000F  D381                    OUT       81H
0011  3E01                    MVI       A,1              ;condition transmitter
0013  D381                    OUT       81H
0015  3E0B                    MVI       A,0BH            ;unmask RST 7.5
0017  30                      SIM
0018  FB                      EI                         ;enable interrupts
```

The Transmit Subroutine

The transmit subroutine is called after the block of data to be transmitted is loaded with information. Its main function is to program the starting location and length of the block into the DMA controller. Since some parameter must accompany the subroutine CALL, two register pairs are elected to handle this function. The DE pair transfers the block address into the subroutine, and the BC pairs transfers the length of the block.

```
                              ;transmission subroutine
                              ;
                              ;BC = length of data block
                              ;DE = beginning address of data block
                              ;
0200  7B            TRANS:    MOV       A,E              ;load DMA address
0201  D3F2                    OUT       0F2H
0203  7A                      MOV       A,D
0204  D3F2                    OUT       0F2H
0206  0B                      DCX       B                ;adjust count
0207  79                      MOV       A,C              ;program count
0208  D3F3                    OUT       0F3H
020A  78                      MOV       A,B              ;setup DMA read
020B  F680                    ORI       80H
020D  D3F3                    OUT       0F3H
020F  3EFF                    MVI       A,0FFH           ;set transmit busy flag
0211  320003                  STA       TFLAG
0214  3E02                    MVI       A,2              ;enable DMA
0216  D3F8                    OUT       0F8H
0218  C9                      RET
```

The busy flag, or TFLAG, is tested by the system software to determine whether the transmitter is busy. A logic zero indicates not busy, and an FFH indicates a busy condition.

Interrupt Service Subroutine

The interrupt service subroutine has the responsibility of deactivating the channel one DMA and clearing the TFLAG bit to zero.

```
0219  F5            RST75:    PUSH      PSW              ;save registers
021A  97                      SUB       A                ;turn channel 1 off
021B  D3F8                    OUT       0F8H
021D  320003                  STA       TFLAG            ;clear transmit busy flag
0220  F1                      POP       PSW              ;restore registers
0221  FB                      EI                         ;enable future interrupts
0222  C9                      RET
```

VIDEO TECHNOLOGY 10-4

This section provides an overview of the terminology and the basics of video so that *CRT* (cathode ray tube) terminals and monitors may be understood. The basic types of CRT terminals are described so that the study of interfacing the CRT terminal to the microprocessor can be conducted in the next section of this chapter.

Basic Types of CRT terminals

There are two basic types of CRT terminals in use today: the raster-scanned and the graphics display terminals. Raster-scanned terminals are very similar to commercial television sets because the information is displayed in the same manner. The monitor portion of the raster-scanned CRT terminal itself is often a commercial television set. Graphics display terminals, which have extremely high resolution, use a technique that is different from commercial television and far more expensive than raster scanning.

Raster-Scanned Display

A *raster* is a series of lines that are drawn on the face of the picture tube by the electron beam from an electron gun. Figure 10–12 illustrates the internal construction of a monochrome (often called black and white) picture tube. (This could also be an amber or green picture tube; both types are monochromatic.)

The electron gun is a device that emits electrons from its heated cathode connection. Heat applied to the cathode causes electrons to boil off and become free to be attracted toward the screen of the CRT by the high-positive voltage applied to the screen. The

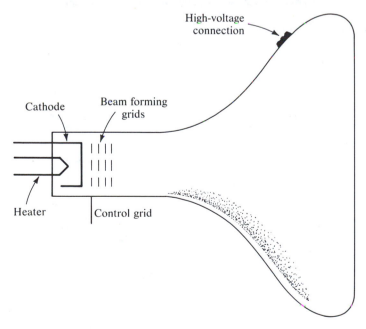

FIGURE 10–12 The construction of a monochrome picture tube.

action of boiling electrons from the cathode is called thermonic emission and is used in most vacuum tube devices.

As the electrons are attracted to the face of the screen by a high-positive voltage, they are controlled by the next element in the tube, the control grid. The control grid controls the amount of electrons that pass through it to the face of the tube so that bright and dark areas are displayed. A negative voltage with respect to the cathode controls the amount of electrons that pass the control grid.

After electrons pass through the control grid, they are formed into a narrow circular beam that strikes a small spot on the screen. This focusing is accomplished by an electrostatic lens constructed from several additional elements in the tube.

After leaving the electrostatic lens, the electrons are traveling at high speed, due to the high-positive voltage applied to the face of the tube, and strike the tube with enough force to cause significant secondary emission. In the process, photons of light are emitted from the phosphorus coating on the inside of the face of the picture tube. The type of phosphor determines whether the light that is emitted is white, green, or amber in a monochrome picture tube. A color picture tube contains three electron gun assemblies and has three different phosphors. These phosphors emit three different colors of light: red, green, and blue. Color picture tubes will be discussed later in this section.

Generating the Raster   The raster is generated with a group of four electromagnets placed around the neck of the picture tube. The placement of these are illustrated in Figure 10–13. This assembly of coils, two for vertical electron beam deflection, and two for horizontal deflection, is called the yoke. The two *vertical deflection* coils allow the electron beam to be scanned vertically on the face of the tube and the two *horizontal deflection* coils allow it to be scanned horizontally. The electron beam is deflected by the magnetic

FIGURE 10–13   The placement of the yoke on the neck of a picture tube.

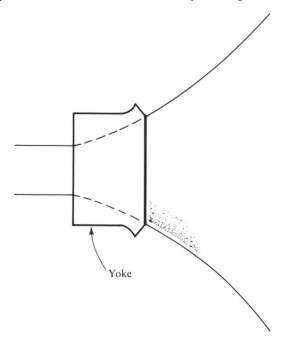

Yoke

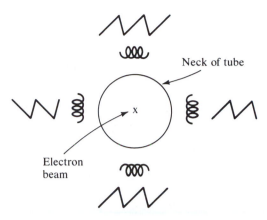

Neck of tube

Electron beam

fields generated in these coils so it can be positioned anywhere on the face of the tube.

Figure 10–14 shows the four deflection coils in the yoke and also the currents that are commonly applied to generate a raster. The frequency of the vertical sawtooth is typically 60 Hz; the frequency of the horizontal sawtooth is 15,600 Hz. (In commercial television these frequencies are 60 Hz and 15,750 Hz.) If 60 Hz are divided into 15,600 Hz, the number of lines displayed on the face of the tube is determined (260 raster lines in this case). These raster lines are used to display the characters found on a CRT terminal screen in computer systems.

Not all of the 260 lines are used. Some of them, usually 20, are lost in *retracing* the electron beam. The electron beam sweeps the face of the screen from the upper left corner to the lower right corner and as it does so, it draws horizontal lines. After displaying 240 lines, the electron beam is turned off and moved back to the upper-left corner. This requires about 20 lines of time to do before the next raster is displayed. Figure 10–15 illustrates the raster found on a CRT terminal screen.

Block Diagram of a Monochrome Monitor

In order to understand the signals required to control a monitor, the block diagram of the

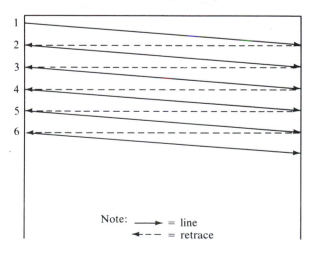

FIGURE 10–15 Raster lines 1 through 6. Note that the slant on the lines has been exaggerated for the illustration.

Note: ──→ = line
──← – – = retrace

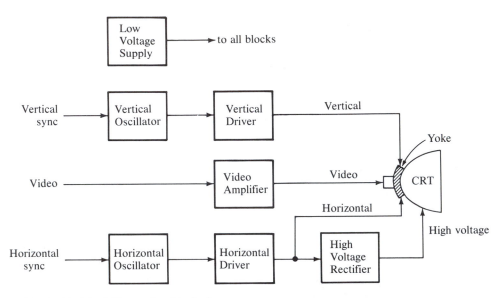

FIGURE 10–16   TTL monitor block diagram.

monitor must be understood. Figure 10–16 illustrates the block diagram of the monitor. Notice that there are three input signals to the monitor: video, vertical sync, and horizontal sync. The video signal is passed through a video amplifier and to the electron gun assembly where it controls the conduction of the electron beam. The vertical and horizontal sync signals are connected to vertical and horizontal oscillators that produce sawtooth current waveforms for the deflection yoke.

The vertical oscillator's output is connected to the vertical deflection amplifier and the horizontal oscillator's output is connected to the horizontal deflection amplifier. The horizontal amplifier provides power for the horizontal deflection coils and also for the high-voltage power supply. The high-voltage power supply consists of a step-up transformer and rectifier, which produce a high-positive voltage equal to approximately 1,000 V per inch of diagonal measurement of the picture tube. For example, a 12-inch monochrome picture tube requires 12 KV.

Effect of Sync

The sync inputs are used to start the retrace of the electron beam. In fact they are used to cause the sawtooth generator to discharge and begin producing a new ramp of current. The effect of the sync signal and the resultant sawtooth waveform that is generated by the sweep oscillator is illustrated in Figure 10–17.

Notice how the sync pulse causes the sawtooth to go from its peak level back to zero. The vertical sync pulse causes the retrace of the electron beam from the lower-right corner to the upper-left corner, and the horizontal sync pulse causes the retrace from the right side of the screen to the left side.

Video Signal and Sync Pulses

With the monitor, there are three distinct inputs: two sync signals and a video signal. This

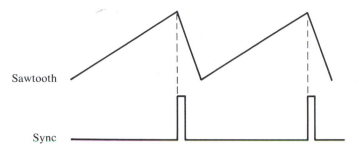

FIGURE 10–17 Sync and its effect on the sawtooth deflection voltage.

type of monitor is called a TTL monitor because it expects these three signals at TTL logic levels. TTL monitors are becoming much more popular. Figure 10–18 shows the video signal and the two sync signals as they would appear in an actual system. Notice that the video signal is a logic one during the time that the sync pulse appears and slightly before and after it appears. This is because the electron beam is shut off during this time; thus, the retrace is not seen on the screen. The logic one level in a positive video system is the black level, and the logic zero level is the white level.

Some monitors require a composite video signal, which is a signal that contains the combination of the sync signals and the video signals on one wire. Figure 10–19 shows the composite video signal required for the composite video monitor. With the composite video signal, there are three signal levels: (1) white (10%), (2) black (75%), and (3) blacker than black (75%–100%). The video information lies between or at white and black, while the sync pulses are in the blacker-than-black region. This is done so that it is easy to strip the sync pulse from the top of the composite video waveform inside of the monitor. The composite video signal is typically 1 V p-p. Notice that the white level is slightly above the 0% point so that noise, which rides at this level, will not appear in the picture.

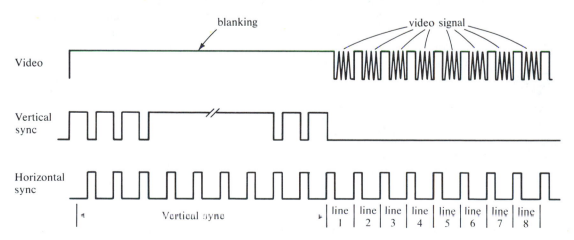

FIGURE 10–18 TTL sync and video signals.

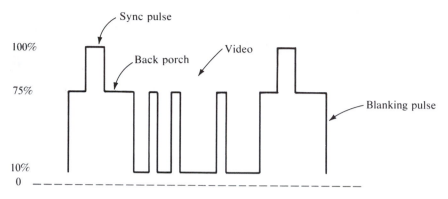

FIGURE 10–19   The composite video signal illustrating horizontal blanking and sync pulses and one line of video.

Color Displays

Today, color displays are becoming very popular because of their attractiveness in home and business presentations. The main difference between the color and monochrome picture tube is that the color tube has three electron guns instead of one. The face of the tube is composed of three different phosphors that display red, green, and blue light, which can be combined to generate any color. Figure 10–20 shows the two common arrangements of phosphors on the face of color picture tubes. Figure 10–20(a) shows the triad pattern which was common until recently, and figure 10–20(b) shows the stripe pattern that is used on most new tubes. If you look closely at the face of your color TV set you will see one of these patterns.

Most monitors display at least 16 colors, including: red, green, blue, black, (which is when the electron beam is off), white (which is a combination of 59% green, 11% blue, and 30% red), magenta (which is red and blue), cyan (which is blue and green), and yellow (which is green and red). Other colors are obtained by other mixes. Some colors, such as pink, are obtained by changing the color saturation level.

There are two basic types of color monitors available. One, the RGB, requires three TTL video signals (red, green, and blue), vertical sync, and horizontal sync. The other type requires one signal—a composite color signal containing the video signal, the sync signals, and color information.

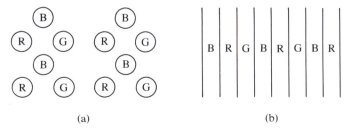

FIGURE 10–20   Patterns found on the face of a color CRT: (a) triad dot pattern, (b) stripe pattern.

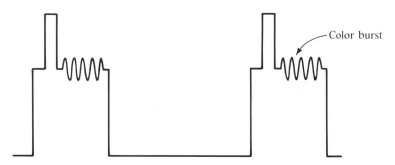

FIGURE 10–21 Color composite video signal depicting the color burst signal.

Figure 10–21 shows a composite color video signal. Notice that there is one main difference between it and the monochrome composite signal presented earlier: the backporch, the last part of the horizontal blanking pulse, contains a sinewave signal at 3.58 MHz. This is the color sync signal and is typically from 8 to 14 cycles in duration. The color sync signal is used to remove the color video, which is amplitude and phase modulated on a 3.58-MHz suppressed subcarrier.

Figure 10–22 shows the frequency spectrum of the color video signal, including the luminance (Y or brightness) information and the color information illustrated as the I and Q signals. With these three signals it is possible to reconstruct the red, green, and blue video signals for the color picture tube. The Y signal is composed of color information in the following percentages (white light): 30% red, 59% green, and 11% blue. The I and Q signals contain the color information that, when combined with the Y signal, produces color saturation on the screen.

Developing the Video

Each character that is displayed on the screen is composed of a dot pattern. Figure 10–23 illustrates the dot pattern that is often used for a CRT display and it shows the word *High* so that the quality can be observed. A 5 × 9 pattern is used in figure 10–23 to display each character. Each character exists in a 7 × 10 matrix, resulting in one line between character lines and two spaces between characters on a line. Notice that the base line of the display is line 6. A character without a descender appears on and above this base line;

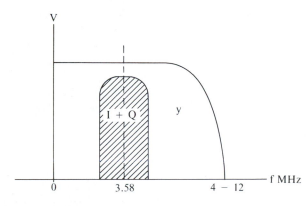

FIGURE 10–22 Bandwidth of the color video signal. Notice the color information surrounding the color subcarrier at 3.58 MHz. The maximum frequency can be anywhere from 4 to 12 MHz, depending upon the resolution of the video signal.

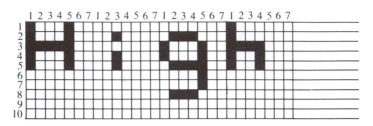

FIGURE 10–23   Raster scan showing the word "High" displayed.

characters with descenders extend two lines below the base line and five lines above it.

We already know that if the monitor is given vertical and horizontal sync pulses it will generate the raster-scanning lines. What must be developed is the video signal that turns the electron beam on and off to display the dot matrix characters and the sync pulses themselves. To accomplish this, the position of the electron beam must be known at all times. This is typically accomplished with counters and a high-frequency dot clock. The *dot clock* is used to time the duration of each dot on the CRT screen and also to generate, through the counters, the sync signals.

We know that there are 260 lines displayed 60 times per second. We also know that 20 of these are lost in retrace. The remaining 240 lines allow the display of 24 character lines on the screen. The duration of each of these lines is 1/15,600 or 64.1 μs. Some of this time is lost during retracing the electron beam from the right back to the left side of the screen. Suppose that after retrace there are 56 μs remaining for the displayed line. Because 80 characters are displayed on each line, and each character has 7 dot times across a line, the number of dots per line is 7 × 80, or 560 dots. This means that the time required to display one dot is 0.1 μs. A dot time of 0.1 μs requires a dot clock frequency of 10 MHz. From this 10-MHz dot clock, all of the timing for the CRT display is obtained. In the example that follows, the dot clock is increased slightly to 10.0464 MHz so that the circuit can be constructed. This means that the dot time is slightly less than 0.1 μs.

Generating Sync   Figure 10–24 illustrates the circuit required to generate the timing and video for this type of display. Notice that this circuit is a series of counters that are used to generate the various waveforms that drive the monitor. The first counter connected to the dot clock is a divide-by-7 counter that is used to time the length of each character position of a raster line. Its output feeds another counter which counts characters on each raster line. This character counter is a divide-by-92 counter that counts from 0 to 91. The character counter counts out the 80 characters and then allows 12 character times for the retrace to occur. Counts 80 to 91 are decoded to produce the TTL-level horizontal sync pulse, which is fed to a delay circuit (explained later in the text).

The output of the character counter feeds the raster line counter, which is divided into two parts. One part, a divide-by-10 counter, counts out each line in a character; the other, a divide-by-26 (0 to 25) counter, counts out each character line. Twenty-six character lines are available, of which 24 are used for displaying characters and 2 are used for retrace. The outputs of the line counter are decoded so that counts 24 and 25 produce the TTL-level vertical sync pulse. Figure 10–25 shows the resulting vertical and horizontal pulse produced by these counters.

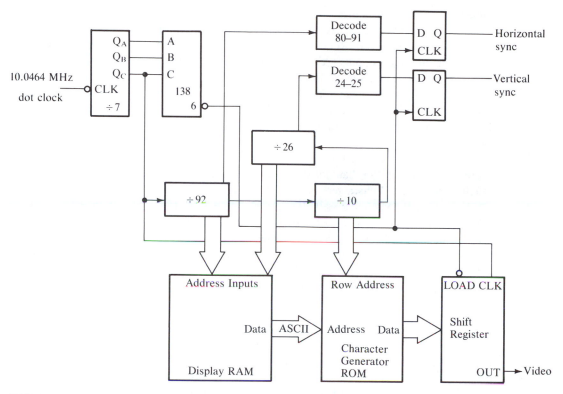

FIGURE 10–24   Timing for a video display terminal.

Generating Video   The video is generated using the same counters along with a shift register, a display RAM, and a *character-generator* ROM as illustrated in Figure 10–23. The 5-bit serial shift register is loaded with the outputs of the character-generator ROM each time the first counter (divide-by-7) goes from a count of 6 to 0. This allows the memory 700 ns to access a character and pass it through the character-generator ROM. This is enough time in most systems to access the data from the RAM and pass it through the ROM. This 6-to-0 transition is also used to delay the sync signals so that the last character on each line is not lost. (See the D-type flip-flops used to delay the sync

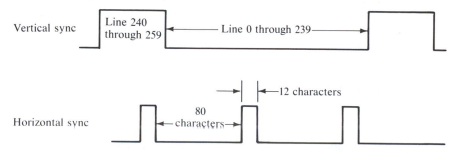

FIGURE 10–25   Vertical and horizontal sync pulses generated by the circuit of figure 10–24.

signals.) Once the shift register is loaded with a line of a character from the ROM, it shifts it out as serial video, which is applied to the video amplifier in the monitor.

The character-generator ROM has 5 output pins (00–04), 4 row address pins (R0–R3), and 7 character address pins (A0–A6). Because the ROM has 11 address inputs, 4 row and 7 character, it contains 2048 different 5-bit memory locations. Any 2K ROM will function in this circuit; for example, a 2K- × -8 2716 can be used for the character-generator ROM, provided its access time plus the RAM memory access time is below 700 ns. The row address inputs are supplied by the divide-by-10 counter that is used to produce the vertical sync pulse and also count the raster lines. This counter changes for each change in a raster line selecting the correct line to be displayed by the ROM. The character address inputs to the ROM are the data output connections of the display RAM. These are usually ASCII-coded characters that are stored in the display RAM for the CRT screen.

The display RAM contains all 1920 character positions (24 × 80) on the display. The RAM obtains its address from the divide-by-92 counter and the divide-by-26 counter. These counters determine which line is being addressed (26) and which character position (92) in a line is being addressed. Because of this configuration, some of the memory locations in the RAM are not used. The display RAM is a 4K- × -8 memory constructed with two TMS4016 2K- × -8 RAMs.

Graphics Display Terminal

The graphics display terminal is different from the raster-scanned terminal because it does not use scanning circuitry to generate lines on the CRT screen. Instead, the electron beam is positioned to any point on the screen by two digital-to-analog converters, one for the horizontal beam position and one for the vertical. This allows the electron beam to be moved to any position on the screen to draw any required pattern on the screen. Figure 10–26 illustrates these DACs and the block diagram of a monochrome graphics display terminal.

Notice that two 12-bit DACs are used so that the resolution is 4096 dots in both the vertical and the horizontal directions, for a 4096 × 4096 display. This is a far superior resolution than the 560 dots per line obtained in the raster-scanned display.

The display is generated by sending out strings of numbers that move the electron beam from place to place on the screen. For example, a byte and a half is used to represent each value sent to each DAC. It requires three bytes of memory for each dot position. The program sends coordinates to the display memory, which then proceeds to scan continually through these coordinates to generate the display. One of the coordinates, a zero-in-three bytes, is used to indicate the end of the display data. Notice that software to draw intricate shapes requires a great deal of time to develop. It is also important to notice that the more intricate the drawing, the longer it takes to scan the beam on the screen.

10-5 CRT REFRESHING USING DMA

A CRT terminal requires that data be periodically moved from the memory to the screen through character-generation circuitry. This process is most often accomplished through DMA techniques because they allow more time for the microprocessor to process other data.

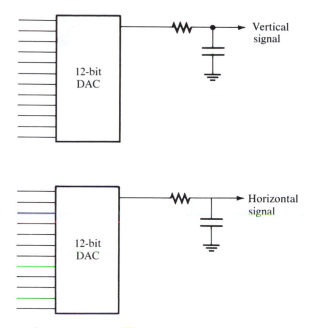

FIGURE 10–26 DAC used to generate the vertical and horizontal drive signals for a graphics display terminal.

In an 80-column display, the refresh rate is one character in every 617 ns, a rate that cannot be directly supported by the DMA controller described earlier. This problem can be circumvented by using an external buffer memory to hold one complete line of display information. The display-generating circuitry then scans this external memory for displayed data. This technique is fine until it is time to begin displaying the next line of information. Here you find that the horizontal retrace time is too short to load the external buffer with the next 80 characters.

This difficulty can also be overcome if two external 80-character buffers are used in the system: one for the display circuitry to scan and the other to be loaded from the DMA controller. This technique is often referred to as *double buffering*.

Since we are talking about extensive external circuitry, it would be best to search for a microprocessor peripheral component that can handle most of this task. Intel provides a CRT controller that contains the necessary buffering for the CRT terminal plus a few additional enhancements.

The 8275 CRT Controller

The 8275 CRT controller is illustrated in figure 10–27 with its pinout diagram. This device is very flexible, since it supports graphic character attributes, cursor control, and the light pen screen address.

Figure 10–28 illustrates the 8085A microprocessor interfaced to this component, indicating that little external circuitry is required for this connection. In this example, port number 8XH is decoded for use with the CRT controller.

Internal Registers

Internally the 8275 is a rather simple device containing command, parameter, and status registers. The command register is the means through which the control of this device can

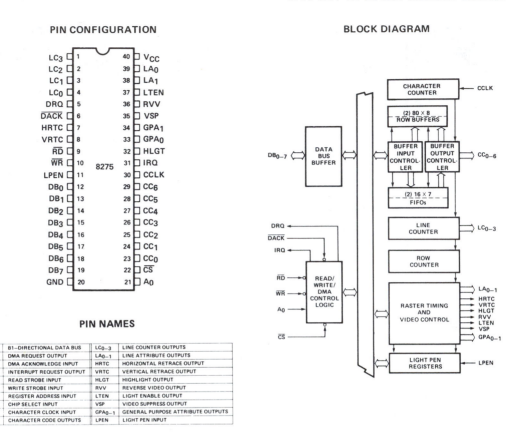

FIGURE 10–27 The pinout and block diagram of the Intel 8275 programmable CRT controller.

SOURCE: Reprinted by permission of Intel Corporation, Copyright 1983.

be accomplished. There are eight different commands that the 8275 will respond to, and each must be followed by a sequence of between zero and four parameters of information for proper device function.

8275 Commands

START DISPLAY (0   0   1   S   S   S   B   B) This command is followed by zero or no parameters and directs the controller to begin displaying data. The DMA requests begin to occur through the DRQ and $\overline{\text{DACK}}$ connections, the interrupts are enabled, and the video is enabled.

Bits SSS direct the 8275 DMA request circuitry and indicate how many clocks are to occur minimally between DMA requests. The exact number is illustrated in table 10–4. Bits BB indicate how many bytes are to be transferred per DMA burst cycle.

STOP DISPLAY (0   1   0   0   0   0   0   0) This command terminates displaying information by disabling the video signal.

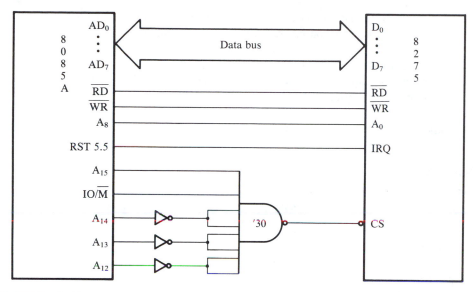

FIGURE 10–28 The 8085A microprocessor interfaced to the 8275 CRT controller.

ENABLE INTERRUPT (1 0 1 0   0 0 0 0) This command enables interrupts and sets the enable interrupt status bit.

DISABLE INTERRUPT (1 1 0 0   0 0 0 0) Interrupts are disabled and the interrupt enable status bit is cleared.

PRESET COUNTERS (1 1 1 0   0 0 0 0) Internal counters are preset to the home, or upper-left-hand corner, position. These counters remain in this state until another command is issued. This command is usually followed by the START DISPLAY command.

READ LIGHT PEN POSITION (0 1 1 0   0 0 0 0) The position of the light pen is returned on the next two read cycles of the parameter register. The character column is returned on the first read, and the line or row number is returned on the

TABLE 10–4 8275 burst codes.

SSS Burst Space Code				BB Burst Count Code		
S	S	S	Character Clocks between DMA Requests	B	B	DMA Cycles per Burst
0	0	0	0	0	0	1
0	0	1	7	0	1	2
0	1	0	15	1	0	4
0	1	1	23	1	1	8
1	0	0	31			
1	0	1	39			
1	1	0	47			
1	1	1	55			

second read. Note that software must be used to supply the correct position because there is a bias of three to four character positions due to internal and external circuitry delays.

LOAD CURSOR POSITION (1 0 0 0   0 0 0 0) The cursor can be directed to any position on the CRT screen by loading the parameter register with the column and row position following this command.

RESET (0 0 0 0   0 0 0 0) The reset command must be followed by four parameters, pictured in figure 10–29, that direct the overall function of the CRT controller.

Status Register

The status indicates the operating condition of the CRT controller. Table 10–5 illustrates this register, and the function of each status bit position is described below:

IE The interrupt enable bit indicates whether or not the last row interrupt will occur.

IR Interrupt request reflects the condition of the IRQ line.

LP The light pen flag bit indicates that the LPEN input pin is activated and the internal light pen registers are loaded with an address.

IC An improper command is received.

VE The video has been enabled.

DU DMA underrun is set whenever a DMA underrun occurs. A DMA underrun occurs whenever the DMA circuitry fails to keep up with the CRT controller. When this happens, the controller has been programmed for the wrong number of DMA characters per burst or the wrong number of clocks between bursts.

FO The FIFO overrun occurs when the internal attributes FIFO is overrun. This occurs whenever more than sixteen attributes per line are attempted.

Attributes

The CRT controller allows six different field attributes: blink, highlight, reverse video, underline, and two general-purpose attributes. The general-purpose attributes can be tailored to individual needs because they control two external hardware pins, GPA0 and GPA1.

Interrupt Request

The interrupt request output, or IRQ, becomes active at the beginning of the last row of display data. It is used with the autoload feature in a system that does not contain a DMA controller to reset the DMA address. Since the auto load mode is available in the DMA controller, it is not needed with this example.

CRT Connections

Figure 10–30 illustrates the circuitry required to connect a CRT to the CRT controller.

TABLE 10–5 The 8275 status register.

7	6	5	4	3	2	1	0
0	IE	IR	LP	IC	VE	OU	FO

1. Reset Command:

	OPERATION	A$_0$	DESCRIPTION	DATA BUS MSB							LSB
Command	Write	1	Reset Command	0	0	0	0	0	0	0	0
Parameters	Write	0	Screen Comp Byte 1	S	H	H	H	H	H	H	H
	Write	0	Screen Comp Byte 2	V	V	R	R	R	R	R	R
	Write	0	Screen Comp Byte 3	U	U	U	U	L	L	L	L
	Write	0	Screen Comp Byte 4	M	F	C	C	Z	Z	Z	Z

Action — After the reset command is written, DMA requests stop, 8275 interrupts are disabled, and the VSP output is used to blank the screen. HRTC and VRTC continue to run. HRTC and VRTC timing are random on power-up.

As parameters are written, the screen composition is defined.

Parameter — S Spaced Rows

S	FUNCTIONS
0	Normal Rows
1	Spaced Rows

Parameter — HHHHHHH Horizontal Characters/Row

H	H	H	H	H	H	H	NO. OF CHARACTERS PER ROW
0	0	0	0	0	0	0	1
0	0	0	0	0	0	1	2
0	0	0	0	0	1	0	3
			.				.
			.				.
			.				.
1	0	0	1	1	1	1	80
1	0	1	0	0	0	0	Undefined
			.				.
			.				.
			.				.
1	1	1	1	1	1	1	Undefined

Parameter — VV Vertical Retrace Row Count

V	V	NO. OF ROW COUNTS PER VRTC
0	0	1
0	1	2
1	0	3
1	1	4

Parameter — RRRRRR Vertical Rows/Frame

R	R	R	R	R	R	NO. OF ROWS/FRAME
0	0	0	0	0	0	1
0	0	0	0	0	1	2
0	0	0	0	1	0	3
			.			.
			.			.
			.			.
1	1	1	1	1	1	64

Parameter — UUUU Underline Placement

U	U	U	U	LINE NUMBER OF UNDERLINE
0	0	0	0	1
0	0	0	1	2
0	0	1	0	3
.				.
.				.
.				.
1	1	1	1	16

Parameter — LLLL Number of Lines per Character

L	L	L	L	NO. OF LINES/ROW
0	0	0	0	1
0	0	0	1	2
0	0	1	0	3
.				.
.				.
.				.
1	1	1	1	16

Parameter — M Line Counter Mode

M	LINE COUNTER MODE
0	Mode 0 (Non-Offset)
1	Mode 1 (Offset by 1 Count)

Parameter — F Field Attribute Mode

F	FIELD ATTRIBUTE MODE
0	Transparent
1	Non-Transparent

Parameter — CC Cursor Format

C	C	CURSOR FORMAT
0	0	Blinking reverse video block
0	1	Blinking underline
1	0	Nonblinking reverse video block
1	1	Nonblinking underling

Parameter — ZZZZ Horizontal Retrace Count

Z	Z	Z	Z	NO. OF CHARACTER COUNTS PER HRTC
0	0	0	0	2
0	0	0	1	4
0	0	1	0	6
.				.
.				.
1	1	1	1	32

Note: uuuu MSB determines blanking of top and bottom lines (1 = blanked, 0 = not blanked).

FIGURE 10–29 The 8275 RESET command.

SOURCE: Reprinted by permission of Intel Corporation, Copyright 1983.

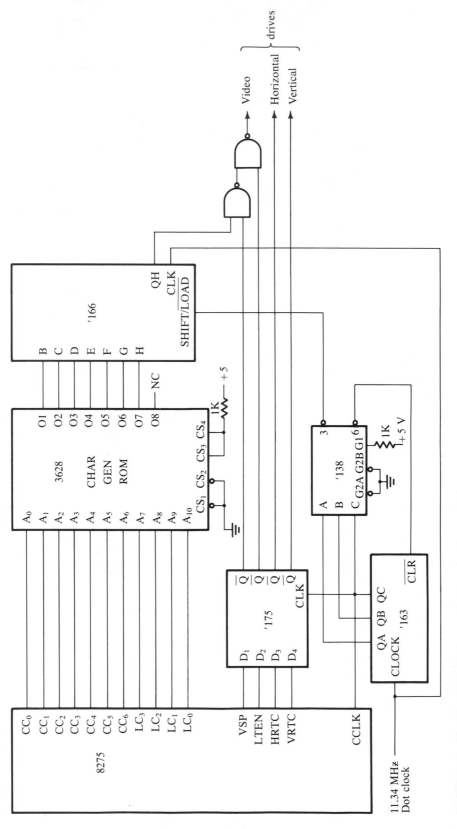

FIGURE 10–30 The 8275 CRT controller interfaced to a CRT.

TABLE 10–6 8275 Attribute codes.

7	6	5	4	3	2	1	0
1	0	U	R	G1	G2	B	H

Bit Name	Function
H	Highlight
B	Blinking
G1, G2	General purpose
R	Reverse
U	Underline

The system consists of only a handful of components; five years ago, there would have been approximately fifty SSI, MSI, and LSI components.

The oscillator shown develops an 11.34-MHz dot clock to shift data through the 74166 serial shift register to the screen. It also clocks a modulus six counter that controls the shifting and loading of the 74166. The video signal is a combination of the output of the shift register, VSP, and LTEN. The LTEN signal turns the video signal on and off for certain video attributes, and the VSP signal blanks the video during normal horizontal and vertical retracing and for a blinking character.

The horizontal and vertical retrace drive signals are developed by the circuitry. The control signal circuitry generates the vertical retrace drive pulse; the horizontal drive pulse is developed by a one-shot multivibrator.

Timing

The timing diagram for the circuit in figure 10–30 is illustrated in figure 10–31. The character clock, or output QC, from the divider is a reference signal to the 8275. It must also be used to latch a character into the shift register on the positive transition, as

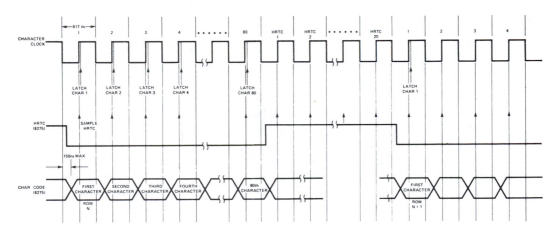

FIGURE 10–31 The timing diagram of the CRT interface illustrated in figure 10–30.

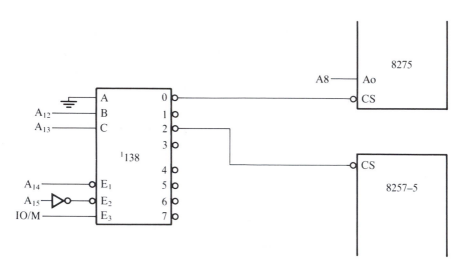

FIGURE 10–32   Decoder used to select the 8275 for I/O ports 80H and 81H and the 8257-5 for ports 90H–98H.

illustrated in the diagram. This edge occurs in coincidence with the decoded state three output of the counter, which latches a character into the shift register.

Interfacing the 8275 to the 8085 with the 8257-5 DMA Controller

In order for the 8275 to be functional in a system, it must be used along with the DMA controller. The DMA controller is used to send bursts of data from a portion of the memory to the 8275 as requested by the 8275 DRQ output. The memory used for CRT data is called the display RAM and it contains the ASCII characters to be displayed.

Figure 10–32 illustrates the 8257 and the 8275 connected to the 8085A. The 8275 is selected for I/O addresses 80H (parameter) and 81H (command/status) and the 8257 is selected for I/O addresses 90H–98H.

The software that follows initializes both the DMA controller and the CRT controller so that 24 lines of 80 characters are displayed on the CRT screen. This type of display is the standard display today, with a few terminals displaying 25 lines. Each character displayed is in a 5-$\times$-7 matrix with the underline occurring in row 8; the cursor type selected is a nonblinking inverted video block.

The DMA controller displays the contents of memory beginning at location 2000H and extending for 1920 characters. Note that to display 1920 characters (80 by 24) the character count programmed into the DMA controller is 1919, which is one less than the total. Once the DMA controller is started, it uses the autoload feature to continually scan the same block of memory beginning at location 2000H. Each DMA transfer consists of a burst of eight bytes that are loaded into the internal FIFO of the 8275 CRT controller. By using the burst mode, time is left to the remaining 8085A-based system for software execution.

```
                              ;initialization dialog for the 8275 and 8257
                              ;
0000  97          RESET:  SUB     A           ;reset and stop display
0001  D381                OUT     81H
0003  3E4F                MVI     A,4FH       ;setup 80 columns
0005  D380                OUT     80H
0007  3E57                MVI     A,57H       ;2 retrace rows, 24 lines
0009  D380                OUT     80H
000B  3E78                MVI     A,78H       ;underline row 8, 9 total
000D  D380                OUT     80H
000F  3E68                MVI     A,68H       ;program cursor and retrace
0011  D380                OUT     80H
0013  3E80                MVI     A,80H       ;cursor position command
0015  D381                OUT     81H
0017  97                  SUB     A
0018  D380                OUT     80H         ; column 0
001A  D380                OUT     80H         ;row 0
001C  3EE0                MVI     A,0E0H      ;preset counters
001E  D381                OUT     81H

                              ;
                              ; initialize the 8257 DMA controller
                              ;
0020  3E80                MVI     A,80H       ;clear F/L flip-flop
0022  D398                OUT     98H         ;and select autoload mode
0024  3E00                MVI     A,0         ;program DMA address CH2
0026  D394                OUT     94H
0028  3E20                MVI     A,20H
002A  D394                OUT     94H
002C  3E7F                MVI     A,7FH       ;count of 1919 CH2
002E  D395                OUT     95H
0030  3E87                MVI     A,87H
0032  D395                OUT     95H
0034  3E84                MVI     A,84H       ;start DMA controller
0036  D398                OUT     98H
0038  3E23                MVI     A,23H       ;start CRT controller
003A  D381                OUT     81H
                              ;
                              ;system program follows
```

Notice that when the 8275 is programmed it is first reset with the reset command. (The reset command is a 00H sent to the command port 81H.) After the reset command is sent to the 8275 it must be sent four parameters that specify how the 8275 is to function. After the reset instruction and the parameters, the cursor is moved back to the home position which is the upper-left-hand corner of the screen. This is accomplished by sending out the cursor position command and then the column and row addresses.

The 8257 DMA controller is programmed by selecting the autoload mode with no channels enabled. This causes whatever is loaded into the channel 2 count and address registers to be automatically loaded into both the channel 2 and 3 count and address registers.

After both the 8257 and 8275 are initialized they are then enabled. The 8257 is enabled in the autoload mode with channel 2 on; the 8275 is enabled with the start display command. The start display command selects 15 character clocks between DMAs and eight bytes transferred per DMA cycle.

Software to Control the CRT Terminal

Software for the CRT terminal amounts to subroutines that clear the screen and position the cursor. Other needed software are subroutines that scroll the display as data are entered into the display memory.

A subroutine to clear the screen and home the cursor appears in the program listing that follows.

```
                                  ;subroutine to clear the screen and home
                                  ;the cursor
                                  ;
3000                              ORG      3000H
3000  3E20        CLEAR:  MVI     A,' '       ;ASCII space
3002  210020              LXI     H,2000H     ;address display RAM
3005  012019              LXI     B,1920H     ;load count
3008  77          LOOP:   MOV     M,A         ;save space
3009  23                  INX     H
300A  0B                  DCX     B           ;decrement count
300B  78                  MOV     A,B
300C  B1                  ORA     C
300D  C20830              JNZ     LOOP        ;repeat 1920 times
3010  3E80                MVI     A,80H       ;home cursor
3012  D381                OUT     81H
3014  97                  SUB     A
3015  D380                OUT     80H         ;column = 0
3017  D380                OUT     80H         ;row = 0
3019  C9                  RET
```

Another subroutine that is found in CRT terminals scrolls the line up, erases the bottom line, and positions the cursor at the bottom line of the display. The subroutine to accomplish this is listed next.

```
                                  ;subroutine that scrolls the display
                                  ;
301A  0617        SCROLL: MVI     B,23        ;load count
301C  215020              LXI     H,2050H     ;address line 1
301F  110020              LXI     D,2000H     ;address line 0
3022  0E50        SC1:    MVI     C,80        ;load character count
3024  7E          SC2:    MOV     A,M         ;move a character
3025  12                  STAX    D
3026  23                  INX     H
3027  13                  INX     D
3028  0D                  DCR     C
3029  C22430              JNZ     SC2         ;repeat until line moved
302C  05                  DCR     B
302D  C22230              JNZ     SC1         ;repeat for 23 lines
3030  0E50                MVI     C,80        ;load count
3032  3E20                MVI     A,' '       ;clear bottom line
3034  12          SC3:    STAX    D
3035  13                  INX     D
3036  0D                  DCR     C
3037  C23430              JNZ     SC3         ;repeat for the line
303A  3E80                MVI     A,80H       ;move cursor to bottom line
303C  D381                OUT     81H
303E  3E00                MVI     A,0         ;column = 0
3040  D380                OUT     80H
3042  3E17                MVI     A,23        ;row = 23
3044  D380                OUT     80H
3046  C9                  RET
```

SPECIAL DMA TECHNIQUES 10–6

Up until this point, DMA transfer has consisted of single byte or burst transfers, but there are other and sometimes more efficient methods of transferring the data. One such method is *cycle stealing*, or *hidden DMA*.

Hidden DMA

Hidden DMA is accomplished during the normal execution of the instructions. For example, in the 8085A microprocessor during an op-code fetch there is at least one clocking period in which the system bus is unused or idle. Unfortunately this is not enough time in most memory systems to accomplish a read or write. In some instructions, though, there are actually two or three clocking periods at this time that allow the bus to be used for external events. It is during these longer instructions and the accompanying idle bus time that a DMA can take place.

In the 8085A the best instruction to use for this purpose is either the DCX or INX; each instruction has three unused clock cycles during execution. These three cycles can be used for a completely hidden or transparent DMA.

To signal when either of these instructions is occurring, it is necessary to decode the instruction as it is being pulled out of the memory. This is possible because the 8085A indicates an op-code fetch with status bits S0 and S1. This operation is illustrated in figure 10–33, along with a circuit for decoding any DCX or INX instruction.

The output of this circuit signals an external device that can access the 8085A memory directly.

The $\overline{RD}$ signal is used as a clock pulse to the flip-flop to capture the output of the NOR gate. The NOR gate's output can become a logic one only when its inputs are all logic zero. This condition occurs when D7, D6, and D2 are low and D0, D1, S1, and S0 are high. S1 and S0 are high only for an op-code fetch, so we are decoding op-codes. In this case the op-code must have the bit pattern 00XX X011. This bit pattern is unique to the eight INX and DCX instructions in the 8085A.

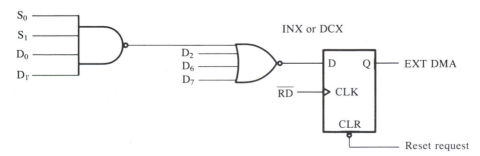

FIGURE 10–33 A circuit that will implement a hidden DMA request for any INX or DCX instruction.

SUMMARY

1   DMA (direct memory access) is a data transfer technique that bypasses the microprocessor and accesses the memory and I/O directly.

2   Two pins are found on the 8085A for DMA: HOLD and HLDA. The HOLD pin is an input that is used to request a DMA and the HLDA is an output that acknowledges the DMA.

3   During a DMA the microprocessor suspends program execution and open-circuits its address, data, and control buses. This allows the DMA controller to gain access to the memory and I/O space of the microprocessor.

4   The speed of the DMA transfer is limited to the speed of the memory and/or the speed of the DMA controller. If the memory can access 2 million bytes per second but the DMA controller can transfer only 1 million bytes per second, then the DMA controller limits the speed to 1 million bytes per second.

5   The DMA controller is a device that provides the memory with an address and the memory and I/O control signals during a DMA. It also can transfer one or more bytes per DMA access.

6   The DMA structure of all microprocessors is very similar. The only exception is the MC6800 which is limited to DMA transfers that last no longer than 9.5 μs.

7   The 8257-5 DMA controller is a four-channel device that can transfer from 1 to 16K bytes of data at one programming.

8   A DMA read occurs when data are transferred from a memory location to an I/O device. A DMA write occurs when data are transferred from an I/O device to a memory location.

9   DMA actions require four control signals to be accomplished. Two are for memory control ($\overline{\text{MEMR}}$ and $\overline{\text{MEMW}}$) and two are for I/O control ($\overline{\text{IOR}}$ and $\overline{\text{IOW}}$).

10 The F/L (first/last) flip-flop is used inside of the 8257-5 to keep track of the least or most significant byte of a channel address or terminal count. If F/L = 0, then the next output to the 8257-5 is a least-significant byte; if F/L = 1, it is a most-significant byte.

11 Each channel of the 8257-5 contains an address register and a terminal count register. The address register is programmed with the starting address of the DMA transfer and the terminal count register is programmed with one less than the number of bytes to be transferred during the DMA.

12 Two types of CRT terminals and monitors are in use today: the raster-scanned display and the graphics display.

13 A raster is a series of lines that are drawn on the face of the CRT screen.

14 A raster is generated by sweeping the electron beam in both the vertical and horizontal directions using magnetic deflection and sawtooths of current. Common raster scanning rates are 60 Hz for the vertical signal and 15,600 Hz for the horizontal signal. These frequencies generate 260 raster lines with 240 usable.

15 The composite video signal is composed of video and vertical and horizontal sync pulses; if color, it also includes color sync and the I and Q phase modulated color information.

16 The 8275 CRT controller develops the sync pulses, controls the cursor, reads a light pen, and transfers memory data to a character-generator ROM that develops the video signal.

17 When the 8275 is reset with the RESET instruction, it expects to receive four parameters that define how it is to operate. Once these parameters have been received, the 8275 functions as a CRT controller.

GLOSSARY

Character generator   A ROM that contains information to display each possible character on the CRT. Usually the characters are in ASCII code.

Color burst   A synchronization signal that lies on the backporch of the horizontal synchronization pulse, which is used to synchronize the color information.

Composite video   A signal that contains the video information and also both the vertical and horizontal synchronization pulses. If it is a composite color signal, it also contains the color synchronization and I and Q color signals.

CRT   Cathode Ray Tube. A device that displays information visually. The picture tube in a television is a cathode ray tube. This abbreviation is sometimes used to indicate a cathode ray tube terminal or tube, as it is sometimes known in the field.

CRT controller   A programmable device that develops and maintains all of the signals related to a CRT terminal, such as video, vertical synchronization, horizontal synchronization, and light pen position.

Cursor   An indicator on a video terminal that depicts the current character entry position.

Deflection coil   A coil that develops a magnetic field which is used to move the electron beam on the screen of a CRT.

DMA   Direct Memory Access. A technique used to store or retrieve information directly from the memory without the intervention of the microprocessor.

DMA burst   A multiple byte direct memory access, as opposed to a single byte transfer.

DMA controller   A device that is dedicated to the management of the DMA system.

Dot clock   A timing signal that is used to time the duration of the dots in a raster-scanned video display.

Frame   In video, a frame is one complete sweep of the screen with the electron beam. In commercial television, a frame is two complete sweeps of the screen.

Hidden DMA   DMA that occurs while the microprocessor is processing other data. Also referred to as cycle stealing.

Horizontal deflection   The act of moving the electron beam in a CRT screen horizontally. The horizontal deflection rate is typically 15,600 Hz for a 24-character line display.

Inverse video   Black characters on a white background. Normal video is white characters on a black background.

Raster   A series of horizontal lines drawn on the face of the picture tube. The raster is modulated to generate characters in a monitor or CRT terminal.

Retrace   The act of moving the electron beam from the bottom-right to the upper-left corner of the CRT screen or from the right back to the left.

Screen refresh   The act of periodically redisplaying information on the screen of a CRT. This normally occurs at the rate of 60 times per second.

Terminal count   The final or terminating count of any counter.

Vertical deflection   The act of moving the electron beam in the vertical direction on a CRT screen. The vertical deflection rate is typically 60 Hz.

Questions and Problems

1   Define DMA.

2   List two applications that would benefit from DMA-processed I/O.

3   What occurs when a microprocessor is forced into its DMA or hold state?

4   Which has higher priority in a microprocessor, the DMA input or the interrupt input?

5   What is the maximum number of bytes that can be transferred by the 8257 DMA controller without reloading its counter?

6   Describe the way the auto load feature in the 8257 DMA controller functions.

7   What does the F/L flip-flop do in the 8257 DMA controller?

8   Write the software to program the channel zero address register with memory location 1000H and the channel zero counter with a read command and a count of 100 decimal. (The initial state of the F/L flip-flop is unknown.)

9   If the terminal count (TC) pin connection is connected to an interrupt pin, is it possible to use more than one of the DMA channels? Explain.

10   Connect an 8155 to an 8257 DMA controller so that a DMA cycle will be requested whenever data are strobed into the port A input port.

11   For the hardware in question 10, develop software that will program the controller and I/O device to store the information at memory location 2000H. Only one byte will be transferred before the controller must be reinitialized.

12   Develop a subroutine to test the status of the 8257 to determine whether or not any channel has reached its terminal count. For a terminal count on channel zero, jump to the program that begins at location 1100H; for channel one, at location 1130H; for channel two, at location 1190H; and for channel three, at location 12A0H.

13   What is a raster-scanned display?

14   Describe how the electron beam is created with the electron gun in a CRT.

15   Describe the operation of the deflection coils in a raster-scanned CRT display.

16   If a raster is developed with a 60-Hz vertical rate and a 16,200-Hz horizontal rate, how many raster lines are developed?

17   The composite video signal is composed of what parts?

18   How is the high voltage developed in a monitor?

19   What is a TTL monitor?

20   If red and blue light are mixed, what color results?

21 If green and red light are mixed, what color results?

22 What percentages of red, green, and blue light generate white light?

23 Explain how the CRT controller is programmed to display an inverse video cursor.

24 Would it be possible to connect the 8275 CRT controller to the 8085A without the use of a DMA controller? Explain.

25 Using the CRT cursor registers, develop a subroutine that will allow the cursor to be moved to any screen position. The D register should contain the X coordinate, and the E register should contain the Y coordinate when the subroutine is called.

11

Disk Memory Systems

Upon completion of this chapter, you will be able to

1 Describe how data are recorded and read from magnetic memory devices using the NRZ (nonreturn to zero) recording technique.
2 Explain how FM (frequency modulation) and MFM (modified frequency modulation) are used to encode disk memory data.
3 Explain how a CRC (cyclic redundancy check) is used to ensure the integrity of recorded data.
4 Select the type of magnetic memory that best fits a particular application.
5 Describe the difference between a standard, mini-, and micro-floppy disk.
6 Interface a disk memory to the 8085A via the 8272A single/double-density floppy disk controller.

Today many modern microprocessor applications require a vast amount of data storage. In order to accommodate this with the lowest possible cost, the disk drive was developed and marketed. Today modern forms of the disk, which store vast amounts of data, are the floppy disk, hard disk, and optical disk memories. Floppy disks and hard disks store data magnetically; optical disks store data optically. In addition to these main types of memory is the magnetic bubble memory, which at times replaces the floppy or hard disk memory. This chapter discusses these memory types and also discusses how data are placed onto and read from these media.

11–1 FLOPPY DISK MEMORY

The floppy disk, or *flexible disk* as it is sometimes called, is by far the most popular form of magnetic storage media in use today. The main advantages of this type of memory are its nonvolatility, the vast amount of data that can be stored on each disk, and its low cost. A *nonvolatile memory* is a memory that retains data for extended periods without power applied and that cannot easily be erased. RAM (random access memory) is a form of volatile memory because data are retained only for as long as power is applied to the memory device. Magnetic memory retains data after power is disconnected and is erased only when new data are written.

Floppy disk memory is currently found in three sizes: (1) the 8-inch standard floppy disk, (2) the $5\frac{1}{4}$-inch mini-floppy disk, and (3) the $3\frac{1}{2}$-inch micro-floppy disk. The 8-inch version of the floppy disk was the first type introduced and today has fallen from popular use. The $5\frac{1}{4}$-inch mini-floppy disk is the most common type and it appears that it will remain so for quite some time. Newer designs use the $3\frac{1}{2}$-inch micro-floppy disk, which is more compact and more durable than the other forms of the floppy disk. This text will use the $5\frac{1}{4}$-inch mini-floppy disk in most examples because of its current popularity.

$5\frac{1}{4}$-Inch Mini-Floppy Disk

Figure 11–1 illustrates the $5\frac{1}{4}$-inch mini-floppy disk. The disk itself is constructed from a circular piece of mylar plastic that is coated with a magnetizable compound and housed in a square, flexible plastic jacket for protection. The disk itself is visible through the head slot and also through the center hub of the jacket. Exercise care when handling the disk so that the surface of the disk is not contaminated through these openings in the jacket. Even a piece of dust or dirt can cause a scratch on the surface of the disk, rendering it useless. For this reason it is recommended that the disk be returned to its protective envelope after each use. The components parts of the disk and its jacket are:

Drive hub   The center hole in the jacket and the center hole in the disk are used by the disk drive to spin the disk at 300 RPM. The disk spins only when data are written or read. A spinning disk is indicated by the red drive activity light on the disk drive.

Head slot   A hole in the jacket where the head and pressure pad or heads touch the surface of the disk through the jacket.

Index hole   A small hole just to the left of the center hub that allows the disk drive to find the beginning of the information on the disk. This hole is in both the jacket and the

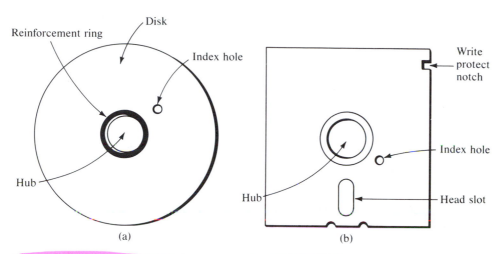

FIGURE 11–1 a) Mini-floppy disk and b) mini-floppy disk jacket.

disk so that when the disk spins they align once per revolution. Each time these holes align, they produce an index mark that is detected by the disk drive.

Write protect notch The small square opening in the jacket of the disk that is used to inhibit writing to the disk. When the hole is covered, data cannot be written to the disk.

Mini-floppy disk memories can be either single sided or double sided. The single-sided disk looks exactly like the double-sided disk, except data are recorded only on the bottom surface of the single-sided mini-floppy disk. The double-sided disk has data recorded on both the top and bottom surfaces.

Mini-floppy disks are commonly single density, double density, or quad density. The single-density form has all but disappeared, but the double- and quad-density forms are very common. About 1.2 million bytes of data are stored on the quad-density double-sided mini-floppy disk.

$3\frac{1}{2}$-Inch Micro-Floppy Disk

Figure 11–2 illustrates the $3\frac{1}{2}$-inch micro-floppy disk. The typical micro-floppy disk holds about 720K bytes of data. The component parts of the micro-floppy disk and its jacket include the following:

Drive hub The disk is reinforced at its center with a metal disk that allows the drive to attach to the disk and spin it accurately. The drive is connected to the mini-floppy disk through a friction mechanism that can slip.

Head door A sliding door that covers and protects the disk surface from contamination.

Write protect hole The hole that contains a sliding piece of plastic that is moved into position to cover the hole when the disk is write inhibited.

Some major changes have been made to the design of the micro-floppy disk when it is compared to the mini-floppy disk. The jacket or case of the micro-floppy disk is constructed of hard plastic that prevents damage to the disk. The mini-floppy disk's softer plastic jacket could be bent, which could destroy it. Also, the head slot on the micro-

FIGURE 11–2   The 3½ inch micro-floppy disk.

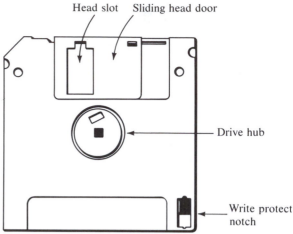

floppy is covered with a sliding door that prevents accidental contamination. Disk surface contamination is a major concern with the mini-floppy disk.

The last major change in the design of the micro-floppy disk, other than size, is the write protect mechanism. On the mini-floppy disk, the write protect notch must be covered with a piece of tape, which can become dislodged. On the micro-floppy, the write protect mechanism is different because a sliding piece of plastic covers the hole when the user wishes to prevent data from being written to the disk. Note that there is no index hole on the micro-floppy disk. This is due to a hub mechanism that includes a pin so that the disk is always perfectly aligned when it is placed into the disk drive.

Disk Data Organization

Data are organized on the surface of the disk as illustrated in figure 11–3. The surface of the disk is divided into concentric rings of data called *tracks*. Although tracks may resemble the grooves on an audio record, they do not spiral inward like on a record. Instead they are circular and the start touches the end of a track. Many disk drives today use as many as 40 tracks per side unless they are quad density, which uses as many as 80 tracks per side.

FIGURE 11–3   Disk data organization showing tracks and sectors of data.

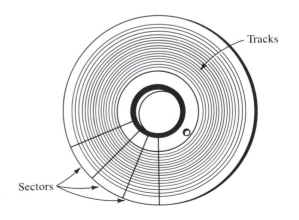

A track is divided into smaller arc-shaped sections (pie-shaped wedges) of data called *sectors*. Typical systems use 8, 9, or 10 sectors per track, but there are other numbers of sectors per track in common use. Each sector most often holds 256 bytes for single density or 512 bytes for double density. If a disk is double sided, then one additional data division is found: the cylinder. A *cylinder* is a pair of tracks, one on the top of the disk and one on the bottom.

Recording Digital Data

Digital data are different from audio data because they are nonsinusoidal data. The record head on a tape recorder is a transformer that can easily convert a sinusoidal waveform into a sinusoidal magnetic field without distortion. Digital data, on the other hand, is nonsinusoidal that is severely distorted by the record head—a transformer. Figure 11–4 illustrates the current flow in the record head for digital data.

Notice from figure 11–4 that head current flows only when the digital data changes logic levels from 1 to 0 or 0 to 1. These changes are hard to distinguish from noise pulses on magnetic media, so this type of direct storage is not typically used to store digital data.

NRZ Recording. A technique called *nonreturn to zero* (NRZ) recording is typically used to store digital data on a magnetic medium such as a disk or even magnetic tape. The term NRZ indicates that the current through the record head never returns to zero while data are recorded. Figure 11–5 illustrates the head current used for an NRZ recording. Notice that when the data are a logic one, head current flows in one direction, and when the data are a logic zero, it flows in the opposite direction.

NRZ offers two major advantages: (1) the disk surface is fully saturated with a magnetic field, and (2) no erase head is required. Because the record head current is always

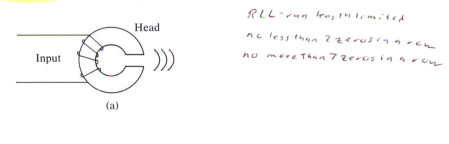

RLL - run length limited
no less than 2 zeros in a row
no more than 7 zeros in a row

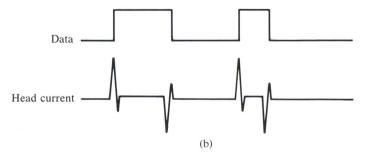

FIGURE 11–4   a) Magnetic head and (b) digital data and the current flow generated in a record head.

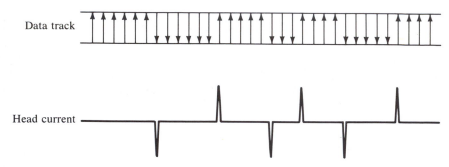

Data track

Head current

FIGURE 11–5 Head current for an NRZ recording.

flowing, the surface of the disk is always fully magnetized, or saturated, in one direction or the other. This means that noise impulses cannot easily exist on the surface of the disk. It also means that a special erase circuit and head is not required because the surface of the disk is always fully remagnetized when new data are written. Audio recording is quite different because the amplitude of the new data is variable and will not erase previous passages. (If audio data are recorded over old data, *sound-on-sound* recording occurs). Audio recording requires a separate erase head that fully saturates the tape with a high-frequency AC signal to erase it.

Figure 11–6 illustrates a circuit that will allow digital data presented at its input to use NRZ recording. Here, four transistors are used to cause current to flow in either direction through the record head. When the data input is at a logic zero level, transistors Q1 and Q3 are turned on and Q2 and Q4 are turned off, which allows current to flow through the head from left to right. When the data input is a logic one, transistors Q2 and Q4 are turned on and Q1 and Q3 are turned off, which allows head current to flow from right to left. The inhibit input ($\overline{I}$) prevents data from being written when it is a logic 0. The inhibit input is a logic one only when new data are written to the disk surface. This input is sometimes also called the write enable input (WE).

FIGURE 11–6 Head driver circuit.

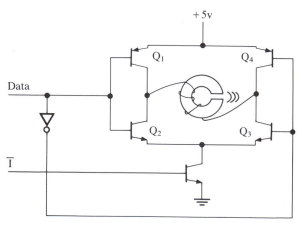

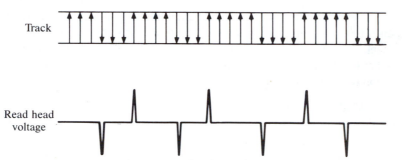

Track

Read head
voltage

FIGURE 11-7 Disk data and the voltage it produces as it passes the read/write head.

Reading Digital Data

Digital data recorded using NRZ recording is read back from the surface of the disk using the same head that was used to record it. Because one head is used to record, read, and erase data, mechanical tracking is made much simpler. Figure 11–7 shows NRZ data on the surface of a disk and the voltage waveform detected by the head when it is read from the disk.

Notice that the output voltage waveform is a series of pulses that indicates changes in the magnetic field on the surface of the disk. These changes must be converted back to a digital waveform that resembles the originally recorded signal. To accomplish this, a simple circuit is used as illustrated in figure 11–8.

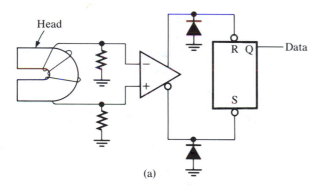

(a)

FIGURE 11-8 (a) Circuit used to reconstruct the digital data and b) waveforms produced from sample data.

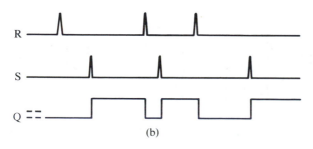

(b)

Figure 11–8(a) illustrates the differential amplifier used to amplify and read back data from a disk. Notice that the amplifier has differential outputs that are used to generate two complementary output voltages. Each of these outputs is rectified to remove the negative pulse so that the positive pulses are applied to the set and reset input of an RS flip-flop. The flip-flop reforms the pulses into a digital waveform, as illustrated in figure 11–8(b).

Frequency Modulation (FM)

In order to detect the data written to a disk, some method must be used to store it in a readily usable form. *Frequency modulation (FM)* is a way of storing digital data on the disk so that it can be easily retrieved. Figure 11–9 illustrates some digital data formatted for storage using FM.

Notice that the data are encoded so that each bit of information is stored with a clock pulse. The standard used in disk memory is a 4 μs frame that contains a clock pulse and a data pulse. Each of these pulses are 1 μs in width and exist in a 2 μs window. FM is used to store single-density data on a disk.

This standard is used mainly so that the bandwidth of the head is known. If digital data are recorded without some format, the bandwidth would be very wide. With FM the bandwidth is fixed because the recorded data will have either a 500 KHz frequency (for a logic one) or a 250 KHz frequency (for a logic zero).

Modified Frequency Modulation (MFM)

Today, most disk systems use *modified frequency modulation (MFM)* to store digital data. MFM allows twice as much data to be stored using the same bandwidth as for FM (250 KHz–500 KHz). MFM is used to store double-density data on a disk.

A frame of double-density data contains a clock time period and also a data time period, but they are used differently than with FM. Each time is only 1 μs in width instead of the 2 μs with FM. Figure 11–10 illustrates a series of data encoded as MFM data. Notice that the clock pulse is never present with logic one data and only present if more than one logic zero is encoded in a row.

If FM and MFM are compared as illustrated in figure 11–11, it is clear that MFM allows twice as much data to be recorded in the same time frame as FM using the same mechanical drive.

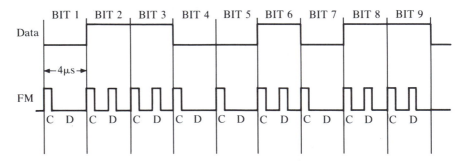

FIGURE 11–9   Data and the FM signal generated. Notice that C = clock and D = data.

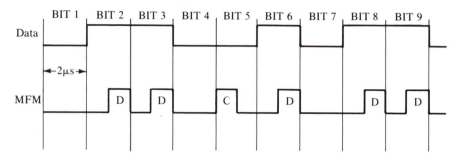

FIGURE 11–10   Data and the MFM signal generated. Note that not all bits have clock or data pulses.

Disk Data Formats

Now that you understand how ones and zeros are stored on a disk, you can investigate the way that digital disk data are formatted in a track. Because the speed of the disk can vary slightly, some room (a gap) must be left in each sector for this speed variation. Also, the disk drive and its associated software must be able to locate the start of a track and the start and address of each sector in the track.

Figure 11–12 illustrates the way that disk data are often stored in a track. Notice that the track illustrated contains eight sectors of data and that the beginning of the first sector is indicated by the index hole in the disk. Also notice that there is a gap before the index. This pre-index gap in the data allows for slight variations in speed when the data are recorded on the disk.

Figure 11–13 illustrates the disk data in more detail. Each sector of data begins with the sector ID field. Each sector ID field contains an ID address mark, track address (00–39), head address, sector address (0–7), sector length (02 for 512 bytes), and two CRC bytes. (The CRC bytes will be explained later in this section of the text). Following the sector ID field is a gap that allows for variations in recording speed. Next is the data field, which contains a data address mark, usually 512 bytes of data (double density) and a two-byte CRC. (Single-density disks usually store data as 256 bytes per sector). This is followed by another gap before the next sector ID field is reached. Each track often

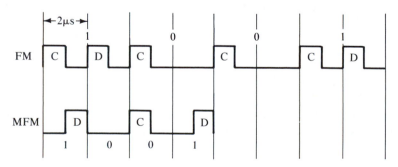

FIGURE 11–11   FM and MFM signals illustrating a 1001.

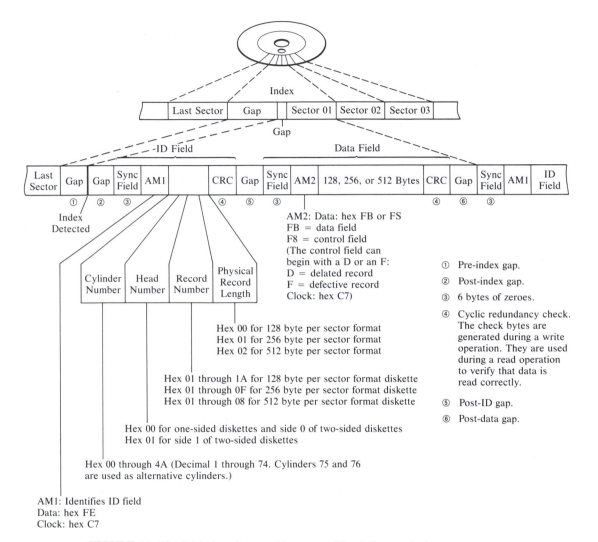

Index

| Last Sector | Gap | Sector 01 | Sector 02 | Sector 03 |

Gap

| Last Sector | Gap | Gap | Sync Field | AM1 | | CRC | Gap | Sync Field | AM2 | 128, 256, or 512 Bytes | CRC | Gap | Sync Field | AM1 | ID Field |

①   ②   ③   ④   ⑤   ③   ④   ⑥   ③

Index
Detected

Cylinder Number   Head Number   Record Number   Physical Record Length

AM2: Data: hex FB or F5
FB = data field
F8 = control field
(The control field can begin with a D or an F:
D = delated record
F = defective record
Clock: hex C7)

① Pre-index gap.

② Post-index gap.

③ 6 bytes of zeroes.

④ Cyclic redundancy check. The check bytes are generated during a write operation. They are used during a read operation to verify that data is read correctly.

⑤ Post-ID gap.

⑥ Post-data gap.

Hex 00 for 128 byte per sector format
Hex 01 for 256 byte per sector format
Hex 02 for 512 byte per sector format

Hex 01 through 1A for 128 byte per sector format diskette
Hex 01 through 0F for 256 byte per sector format diskette
Hex 01 through 08 for 512 byte per sector format diskette

Hex 00 for one-sided diskettes and side 0 of two-sided diskettes
Hex 01 for side 1 of two-sided diskettes

Hex 00 through 4A (Decimal 1 through 74. Cylinders 75 and 76 are used as alternative cylinders.)

AM1: Identifies ID field
Data: hex FE
Clock: hex C7

FIGURE 11–12   Disk data format. (Courtesy of Intel Corporation)

contains eight sectors numbered from 0 to 7. Although not all systems use these values, they are used with the IBM computer and the $5\frac{1}{4}$-inch mini-floppy disk.

Cyclic Redundancy Check (CRC)

The *CRC (cyclic redundancy check)* is a 16-bit number that is used to check the validity of the data in a sector or the information in the sector ID field. CRCs are generated by using a shift register and exclusive-OR gates that generate a unique 16-bit number for each new set of data. Any algorithm may be used to generate a CRC, but the one used most often is $X^{16} + X^{12} + X^5 + 1$. X^{16} is the carry bit and X^{12} and X^5 are data bits in the shift register that are exclusive-ORed with the carry bit. CRC checks rarely miss a bit or multiple bit error in the data as they are read from a disk.

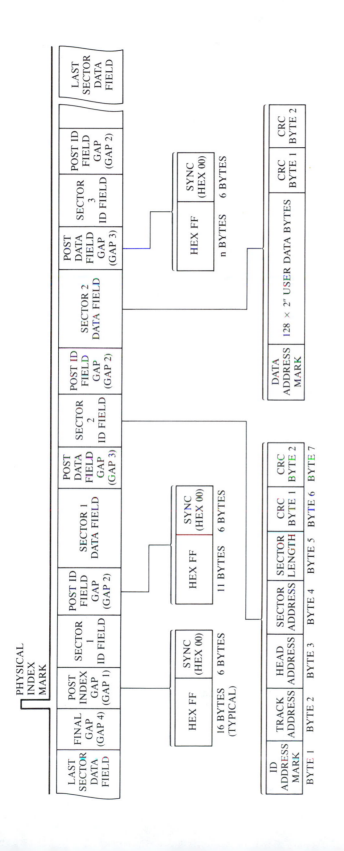

FIGURE 11–13 Single-density FM disk data.

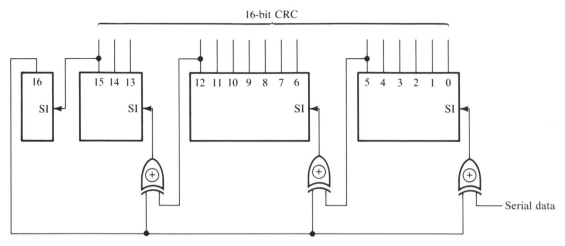

FIGURE 11–14   A circuit that generates the CRC for $X^{16} + X^{12} + X^5 + 1$.

Figure 11–14 illustrates the circuit that is used to generate and check a CRC. In both cases the shift register and carry bit are set to all ones before data are shifted through the circuit to generate or check a CRC. When new data are written to the disk, the number generated by running all of the bits of the data, most significant first, through the circuit is stored on the disk. When the data are read from the disk it is again passed through the CRC circuit, and the outcome is compared with the CRC stored on the disk. If there is a match, the data read from the disk are correct. If no match exists, the data are re-read and the CRCs are again compared. It is not uncommon to have to read a sector of data up to five times before it is finally declared to be a bad sector.

Disk Drive Mechanism

The disk drive consists of two main mechanical systems: (1) a closed-loop servo system that controls the speed of the drive motor, and (2) a stepper motor that positions the head.

The closed-loop servo system uses a DC motor with a built-in generator that indicates the speed of the motor by a voltage produced at the generator's output terminals. Once the motor speed is set, it remains stable because of a servo amplifier connected to the generator. Figure 11–15 illustrates the motor, generator, and servo amplifier used to control the speed of the motor. Notice that as the speed of the motor increases, it generates more voltage, which reduces the amount of current through the armature of the motor. Conversely, as the speed of the motor decreases, the output of the generator decreases, which allows more current to flow through the armature of the motor, increasing its speed.

In order to adjust the speed of the disk drive motor, a timing disk is provided on a flywheel connected to the motor. The timing disk is adjusted under a strobe light as part of the alignment procedure for the disk drive. Figure 11–16 illustrates the timing disk, which has a section for 60 Hz and one for 50 Hz for use in the United States or other parts of the world that use 50 Hz power. The potentiometer in the servo amplifier circuit of figure 11–15 is adjusted until the 60 Hz mark (USA) is stationary.

The head assembly is positioned by a stepper motor that moves the head assembly in

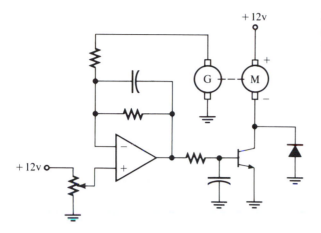

FIGURE 11–15 A motor speed control that controls the speed of the disk in a disk drive.

or out from track 00. Track 00 is called the home position and lies at the outermost edge of the disk surface. No feedback is provided for head position except for a microswitch that closes when the head reaches the track 00 or home position.

Figure 11–17 illustrates the head-positioning mechanism found in many disk drives. Adjustments to the head mechanism are all accomplished mechanically and tested in most cases with a test disk that indicates tracking and head position.

HARD DISK MEMORY 11–2

Hard disk memory has become fairly common for storing vast amounts of data and is currently available in sizes ranging from 10 M bytes to well over 132 M bytes. The first hard disk drive was an IBM drive that stored 30 M bytes of data per side of a disk, and thus eventually became known as a 30–30. Then it became known as a Winchester drive because of the famous early American 30–30 rifle from Winchester.

Hard disk drives use rigid aluminum disks coated with a ferric oxide compound that

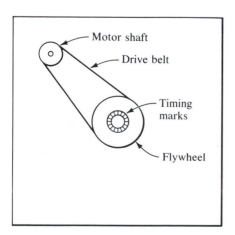

FIGURE 11–16 The underside of a disk drive illustrating the flywheel and timing marks located on it.

FIGURE 11–17 Head assembly.

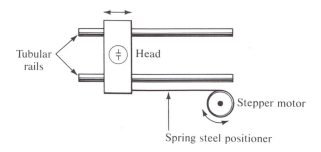

can be magnetized by a head. Most hard disk drives contain at least two disks or platters and some contain many more. Hard disk memory usually uses $3\frac{1}{2}$-, $5\frac{1}{4}$-, 8-, or 14-inch disks. The more modern hard disks are mounted on a printed circuit card and are plugged directly into a computer. This type of drive is usually called an *internal hard disk drive* because it is hidden to the user.

Disk Drive

Figure 11–18 illustrates the internal construction of a hard disk drive. Notice that each platter has a head or series of heads located on both the upper and lower surfaces of each disk. Because more than one head is positioned at a time, the hard disk drive can access many tracks, usually 8 or 16, at one time. This reduces the amount of time required to seek a new track of data. Seek times can take 15–50 ms in a hard disk drive. Also notice that the upper and lower surface of each disk has two heads, so that each disk has four tracks in a cylinder. Some newer drives use four heads on each disk surface. A combination of head number and cylinder number is used to address a particular track in a cylinder.

Figure 11–19 illustrates the way that data are organized on one side of a disk in the hard disk drive. Notice that this surface has two separate sections and actually appears as two separate tracks to the disk drive. Hard disk drives often have 2000 or more tracks, with each track containing 32 sectors of 1K byte each. These numbers vary according to the operating system and also the type of hard disk drive selected.

The hard disk spins whenever power is applied, which is different from the floppy, which spins only when data are written or read. The reason for this is that the hard disk is spun at 1500 RPM, or five times faster than the floppy, making it virtually impossible to start and stop for each access. It often can take over a minute for a hard disk to reach this

FIGURE 11–18 The internal structure of a hard disk drive.

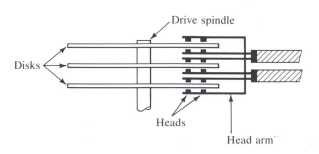

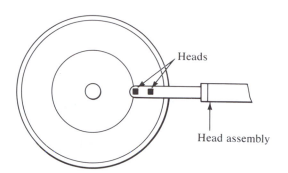

FIGURE 11–19 Hard disk illustrating the two head areas on the surface.

Heads

Head assembly

operating speed. Due to this higher speed, the data transfer rate is much higher on a hard disk. Data are typically transferred at a rate of 5 MHz or higher.

Another difference from the floppy, due to the higher speed of the hard disk, is a special head employed in the hard disk drive called the *flying head*. A flying head is aerodynamically designed to float above the surface of the disk on a cushion of air that travels with the surface of the disk as it spins at 1500 RPM. The flying head glides along the disk at an altitude of about 0.0001 of an inch. Because the flying head never touches the surface of the disk under normal operating conditions, the surface and head do not wear as they do in a floppy disk system. A hard disk typically lasts about 4,000 to 5,000 hours before any wear appears on the disk medium or any other failure occurs.

When the hard disk drive is powered down, the drive moves the head assembly out beyond track 000 to a landing or crash area, where the head comes to rest as the disk speed slows down and stops. The head also takes off from this landing area as the disk picks up speed at the time power is first applied. This protects data stored in the tracks on the disk.

Hard Disk Data

A sector of data on the $5\frac{1}{2}$-inch hard disk drive appears in figure 11–20. Notice that it is organized in much the same manner as on the floppy disk. Before the ID field in the sector, a gap appears that contains 14 bytes of 00H. This gap is used to synchronize the read electronics in the disk drive before the ID field is reached. Next, the ID field appears. The first byte of the ID field is an A1H that signals the electronics that the ID field follows. Located within the ID field are:

Ident   A number that indicates the current cylinder address. (FEH = 0–255, FFH = 256–511, FCH = 512–767, FDH = 768–1023, F6H = 1024–1279, F7H = 1280–1535, F4H = 1536–1791, and F5H = 1792–2048).

Cylinder   Indicates the cylinder address along with Ident. For example, for cylinder address 80H, the Ident = FEH and the Cylinder = 80H. If the address is 180H, then Ident = FFH and Cylinder = 80H.

Head   Indicates the head number (0–7), sector size, (0 = 128, 1 = 256, 2 = 512, and 3 = 1024) and a bad block mark. The bad block mark is used to indicate a bad sector. Hard disk drives often contain bad sectors when first purchased, which are indicated by the bad block mark.

Sector   Contains the sector number.

CRC   A two-byte field that contains the CRC for the ID field.

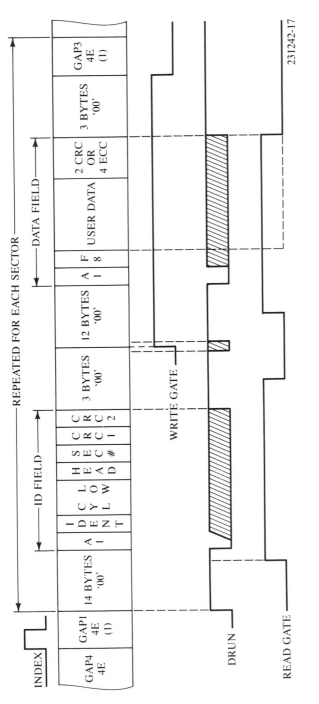

NOTE:
1. GAP 1 and 3 length determined by Sector Number Register contents during formatting.

FIGURE 11–20 Hard disk data for a 5¼-inch disk. (Courtesy of Intel Corporation)

After the ID field, 15 bytes of 00H are recorded as a gap between the ID field and the data field. The data field contains an A1H as its first byte to indicate that the data field follows. The next byte contains an F8H as a data address mark so that the drive knows it has found the data field. The data field follows and can contain from 128 bytes to 1024 bytes as programmed when the disk is formatted. The number of bytes contained in a sector data field is determined by the disk operating system (DOS). Following the data is the 16-bit CRC or 32-bit ECC. The ECC (error correction code) is used to correct a 1-bit error in the data field.

Data are recorded using NRZ techniques and MFM, as with the double-density floppy disk. The main advantage of the hard disk memory over the floppy is the speed and the large volume of data that can be recorded. The main disadvantage of the hard disk memory is the fact that the disk itself cannot be removed from the drive and replaced with a disk containing new data.

MAGNETIC BUBBLE MEMORY 11–3

Magnetic bubble memory is found in relatively few applications because of the size of the currently available bubble memory devices. It takes eight magnetic bubble memory devices to make a 1 M byte magnetic bubble memory that resembles a magnetic disk. The main advantage of the bubble memory is that it is completely electronic with no moving parts, which makes it ideal for use in environments that are subject to vibration or mechanical stress. The main disadvantage, which is major, is that it must be powered up and powered down correctly or the data are lost.

Bubble Memory Device

Figure 11–21 illustrates the structure of the bubble memory device. The bubble memory device is constructed of two layers of yttrium garnet. A substrate of yttrium garnet is coated with a layer of yttrium-iron garnet, which can be magnetized. The bottom surface of the substrate is bonded to a strong permanent magnet that develops magnetic bubbles (or spots) on the surface of the yttrium-iron garnet. These spots are used to represent data and are moved on the surface by a rotating magnetic field generated with field coils that are bonded to the top surface of the device. Structures on the surface of the yttrium-iron garnet called *propagating elements* are thin-film permalloy elements that control and direct the motion of the bubbles as they are moved across the surface of the bubble memory device.

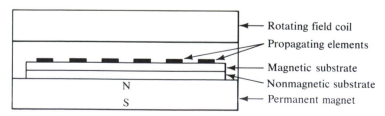

FIGURE 11–21   Structure of a magnetic bubble memory device.

FIGURE 11–22   (a) T-bar propagating element and (b) Chevron
propagating element.

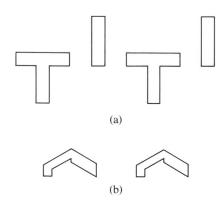

(a)

(b)

Propagating Elements

Figure 11–22 illustrates two commonly used shapes of the permalloy propagating elements found in magnetic bubble memory devices. These shapes are the T-bar and chevron
patterns. Today most bubble memory devices use the chevron pattern for moving the
bubbles across the surface of the bubble memory device.

Figure 11–23 illustrates how bubbles are moved in a bubble memory device using the
chevron propagating elements and the rotating magnetic field. Here, four different directions of the magnetic field are illustrated showing how the bubbles move across the device

FIGURE 11–23   Rotating magnetic field and motion produced on
the bubbles.

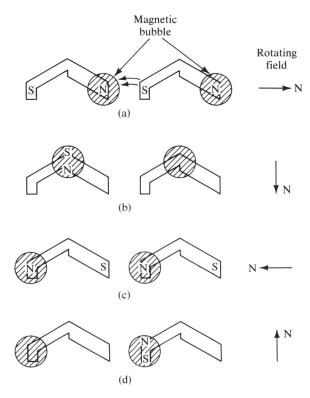

from one propagating element to another. Each full rotation of the magnetic field moves the bubble one bit position. A logic one is represented with a bubble and a logic zero is represented by the absense of a bubble.

Creating and Destroying Bubbles

Bubbles are created on the surface of a bubble memory device by a *generator* and are destroyed with a *replicator/annihilator*. Figure 11–24(a) illustrates the generator. The generator is a loop of wire that creates a magnetic bubble when a large current is passed through it. Once a bubble is created, it is maintained on the surface of the device by the permanent magnetic field. The bubble is then moved away from the generator by the rotating magnetic field.

Figure 11–24(b) illustrates the replicator/annihilator, which is used to split a bubble into two bubbles for replication. Annihilation occurs when the bubble is not replicated and is allowed to pass off the surface of the bubble memory device. Replication occurs if a low-level current is passed through the replicator/annihilator. Replication is accomplished by stretching a bubble enough so that it splits into two new bubbles. One of these new bubbles passes off the surface of the device and the other remains on the surface as a replica if current is passed through the replicator/annihilator.

Bubble Memory Organization

Figure 11–25 shows how the surface of the bubble memory is divided into loops or circular paths for bubble motion. These paths are very similar to the tracks or sectors on a disk memory. Bubble memory is organized so that there are minor loops and a major loop. Suppose that each of these loops is 4 K bits in length. If there are 256 minor loops and one major loop, the device has 1 M byte of memory. A minor loop can be considered a track or sector that can be selected for transfer to the major loop through an addressable transmission gate. If 256 minor loops exist, an 8-bit address is used to select a minor loop.

A *transmission gate* is similar to a replicator/annihilator except that it always replicates the bubbles in the minor loop to the major loop or the major loop to the minor loop. This

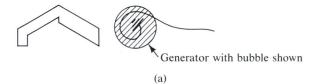

Generator with bubble shown

(a)

FIGURE 11–24   a) bubble generator and b) a replicator/annihilator.

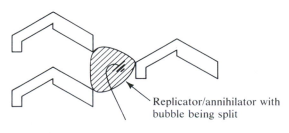

Replicator/annihilator with
bubble being split

(b)

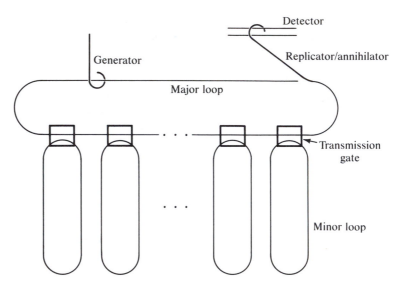

FIGURE 11–25   The internal structure of a bubble memory device illustrating both the major and minor loops.

effectively copies the selected minor loop into the major loop when the transmission gate is activated. The transmission gate never destroys a bubble.

To read data from a minor loop, the transmission gate is activated and the data in the minor loop are copied to the major loop, which contains no bubbles. This effectively removes all the bubbles from the minor loop to the major loop. Once the bubbles from the minor loop are on the major loop, the data can be read and gated back into the minor loop for future access. If new data are written, the data from the minor loop are annihilated and replaced with new data generated by the generator. The new data are then moved into the minor loop for future access.

Sensing a Bubble

In order to read data from a bubble memory, bubbles are passed out of the major loop and off the bubble memory device past a detector. This is called destructive reading. Figure 11–26 illustrates the bridge circuit and sense amplifier used to detect a bubble as it passes the detector. The *detector* is a magneto-resistive element (hall-effect device) that changes in resistance as a magnetic bubble passes by it. This change in resistance is translated into a voltage change at the inputs of the sense amplifier, which produces a logic one output at the sense amplifier output terminal.

11–4 OPTICAL DISK MEMORY

The latest entry into mass data storage is the optical disk memory. Currently available is the write-once optical disk drive. The read-and-write drive will become available in the near future. Write-once optical disk memory has applications in the banking industry for archiving transactions so that an audit trail is established for fraud prevention.

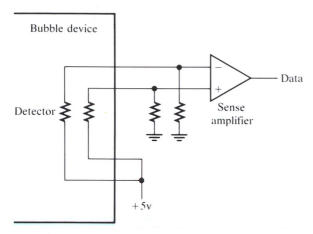

FIGURE 11–26 The detector and sense amplifier in a magnetic bubble memory.

The optical disk itself is constructed from a light-weight plastic that contains a photosensitive layer for data storage. The photosensitive emulsion is covered with a thin plastic coating that protects it from contamination by dust, smoke, and oil. If an optical disk memory becomes soiled, it can be cleaned with a damp cloth.

Optical disk memory uses a laser beam to store and retrieve data placed on the disk. Data are stored by energizing a high-intensity laser beam that causes the photosensitive emulsion to change its ability to reflect light. This allows data to be stored on the surface of the disk for later retrieval. The only disadvantage to storing data in this fashion is that it cannot be erased. Even with this limitation, this type of optical disk memory can still be used to store permanent files. A single 14-inch optical disk can store an astounding 1G bytes of data, or 400,000 typewritten pages of information. Maybe in the near future the entire encyclopedia will be stored on an optical disk memory so that its contents can be viewed on the home computer. The applications for this technology seem incredible. Currently a laser video disk is available with the encyclopedia, but this must be viewed on a TV set with a laser disk playback unit.

Data are read from the disk with a low-intensity laser beam that is focused through the plastic coating onto the photosensitive substrate. The change in reflected light caused by the data originally stored on the disk is sensed by a photosensor and converted back to a digital signal.

Today optical disk memory can store 1 G bytes of data on one 14-inch optical disk. Data are transferred at the rate of 5 M bits per second and stored in 40,000 tracks. Each track contains 25 sectors of data with each sector containing 1 K bytes. The main advantage of the optical disk is its durability; the only way to destroy the data on the disk is to break the disk.

THE 8272A SINGLE/DOUBLE-DENSITY FLOPPY DISK CONTROLLER AND INTERFACE 11-5

The 8272A floppy disk controller contains the circuitry necessary for interfacing up to four floppy disk drives to a microprocessor. The 8272A is capable of using either single-density (FM) or double-density (MFM) data. It also handles double-sided as well as single-sided recording. The 8272A simplifies the interfacing of the floppy disk drive to the microprocessor.

Figure 11–27 illustrates the pinout and internal block diagram of the 8272A. Notice that the 8272A is designed for use with the DMA controller, which handles memory-to-disk and disk-to-memory transfers. If a DMA controller is not available in the system, the 8272A will operate in the nonDMA mode, but nonDMA mode requires a very fast microprocessor because data transfers are required once each 13 μs.

Pinout

The 8272A pin names and description of each pin follow:

Reset The reset pin is an input to the 8272A that places it in the idle state. Reset will not clear the last specify command unless power has been removed from the system.

$\overline{RD}$ A pin that controls reading data from the 8272A and is normally connected to the $\overline{RD}$ pin on the 8085A in the nonDMA mode or the $\overline{IOR}$ pin in the DMA mode.

$\overline{WR}$ Controls writing data to the 8272A. It is connected to $\overline{WR}$ in a nonDMA system and to $\overline{IOW}$ in a DMA system.

$\overline{CS}$ When this pin is a logic zero it allows the $\overline{RD}$ and $\overline{WR}$ pin to function since it selects the 8272A.

AO Selects the data register (AO = 1) or the status register (AO = 0).

DB7–DB0 Bidirectional data bus connections which are normally connected to the system data bus.

DRQ Used to request a DMA when a DMA controller exists in the system.

DACK Acknowledges a DMA action in a DMA-based system.

TC An input to the 8272A that indicates the termination of a DMA action when high. This is normally connected to the TC output of the DMA controller. In nonDMA mode this pin must be activated to terminate a transfer.

IDX Used to input the index signal from the disk drive to the 8272A.

INT An output that requests an interrupt when 8272A reads data from the disk drive. INT becomes a logic one every 13 μs as MFM data are read from a disk.

CLK A 4-MHz clock is used when the 8272A is connected to a mini-floppy disk drive and an 8-MHz clock is used if connected to a standard 8-inch drive.

GND Connected to the system ground bus.

Vcc Connected to the system 5.0 V bus.

RW/SEEK Connected to the floppy-disk drive to select either a seek (1) or read/write (0) operation.

LCT/DIR Determines the direction of the step if $\overline{WR}$/SEEK is a logic one, and lowers the write current for the inner tracks if $\overline{WR}$/SEEK is a 0.

FR/STP Connected to the floppy-disk drive to step the head in the seek mode and to reset faults in the read/write mode.

HDL Loads the head in the floppy disk drive.

RDY A connection to the 8272A indicating that the disk drive is ready.

WP/TS Senses the write protect notch in the read/write mode and senses two-sided disks in the seek mode.

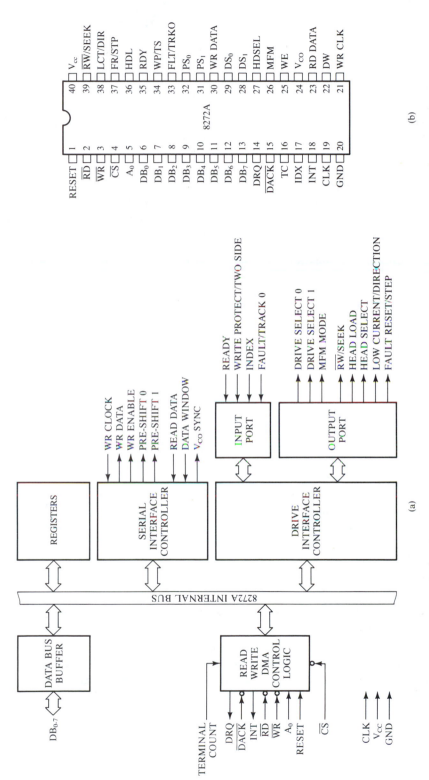

FIGURE 11-27 a) block diagram and b) pinout of the 8272A single/double-density floppy disk controller. (Courtesy of Intel Corporation)

FLT/TRK0   Senses a fault in the read/write mode and senses track 00 in the seek mode.

PS1–PS0   Used for write compensation.

WR DATA   Serial clock and data output from the 8272A to the disk drive.

DS1–DS0   Drive select outputs used to select any of four disk drives.

HDSEL   Used to select the upper or lower head in a two-sided disk drive.

MFM   Selects MFM mode (1) or FM mode (0).

WE   Write enable signal to the floppy disk drive.

VC0   Used to enable and disable the PLL data separator.

RD DATA   Read data input to the 8272A.

DW   Data window input to the 8272A as generated by the PLL.

WR CLOCK   Write clock input must be 500 KHz for FM operation and 1 MHz for MFM operation with a pulse width of 250 ns.

Disk Controller Operation

The 8272A operates in three sequential phases: (1) command, (2) execution, and (3) result.

Command Phase   During the command phase the microprocessor transfers the command and all information required to form a floppy disk controller command to the 8272A. The 8272A executes the following 15 commands:

1   Specify
2   Sense drive status
3   Sense interrupt status
4   Seek
5   Recalibrate
6   Format track
7   Read data
8   Read deleted data
9   Write data
10   Write deleted data
11   Read track
12   Read ID
13   Scan equal
14   Scan high or equal
15   Scan low or equal

The command phase is always entered after a reset or following the completion of the result phase of a previous operation.

Execution Phase   During the execution phase, the 8272A performs the operation specified by the command phase. The execution phase is entered immediately after the last command byte is transferred to the 8272A and ends when the last data byte is transferred to or from the disk or when an error occurs. The end of the execution phase is signaled by an interrupt.

Result Phase   After completion of the execution phase, the 8272A enters the result phase, in which it presents status and other housekeeping information to the microprocessor. After the microprocessor reads this information, the 8272A reenters the command phase where another command may be transferred to it.

8272A Command Instruction Set

Figure 11–28 illustrates the command instruction set for the 8272A. Each command is divided into a command, execution, and result phase, which indicates the action by the microprocessor. For example, the read data command requires that the microprocessor's program send the 8272A nine bytes of data for its command phase. The first byte is the command code, followed by information such as cylinder number, head number, sector number, and other such information. The abbreviations used in Figure 11–28 are defined in Figure 11–29.

Read Data   The read data command causes the disk drive to load the head and search for the sector specified in the current sector register (R). Once the sector is found, the 8272A reads disk data and sends it to the memory through a DMA action or via interrupts (nonDMA). The method used (DMA or nonDMA) is determined by the specify command, which must be sent to the 8272A before reading or writing data. Note that this command does not seek a track.

After the sector of data has been read, the 8272A increments the sector number in the current sector register (R) and begins reading the next sector. The read data command will continue reading disk data until the 8272A receives the terminal count signal (TC) from the microprocessor or DMA controller or until the end of the track is encountered.

Figure 11–30 illustrates the amount of data that can be read by one read data command. Notice that this is a track on a single-sided disk and both upper and lower tracks on a double-sided disk. In many applications data are stored on the disk sequentially so that reading an entire track or cylinder can be advantageous.

At the completion of the read data command, the head remains loaded until after the time specified by the specify command. This allows the software to begin reading another track before the head is unloaded, which saves time for multiple track reads. (Unloading the disk moves the head up from the surface of the disk in double-sided disk drives. Single-sided disk drives usually load the head mechanically when the drive's door is closed.)

The 8272A detects many errors in the read data command mode, which are indicated by bits in the status register. The ND (no data) error occurs if the index hole is detected twice before the selected sector in R is found. The DE (data error) error occurs if the CRC check in the ID field fails for any reason. The DD (data error in the data field) error occurs if the CRC check fails for any data field. The CM (control mark) error is detected if a sector contains a deleted data address mark. The OR (overrun) error is detected if the microprocessor fails to read the data within 13 μs for MFM in the nonDMA mode. This error can occur only in an interrupt-driven system. All of the previous errors terminate the read data command, except the CM error, which skips the deleted sector and continues reading the next sector. A sector is deleted in some systems if it is found to be bad when the disk is initially formatted.

After the read data command completes execution, the results are read from the 8272A. The first three reads yield status registers 0, 1, and 2. This is followed by sector

READ DATA

PHASE	R/W	D7	D6	D5	D4	D3	D2	D1	D0	REMARKS
Command	W	MT	MFM	SK	0	0	0	1	1	0	Command Codes
	W	0	0	0	0	0	HDS	DS1	DS0	Sector ID information prior to Command execution
	W					C				
	W					H				
	W					R				
	W					N				
	W					EOT				
	W					GPL				
	W					DTL				
Execution											Data transfer between the FDD and the main-system
Result	R					ST 0					Status information after Command execution
	R					ST 1					
	R					ST 2					
	R					C					Sector ID information after command execution
	R					H					
	R					R					
	R					N					

READ DELETED DATA

PHASE	R/W	D7	D6	D5	D4	D3	D2	D1	D0	REMARKS
Command	W	MT	MFM	SK	0	0	1	1	0	0	Command Codes
	W	0	0	0	0	0	HDS	DS1	DS0	Sector ID information prior to Command execution
	W					C				
	W					H				
	W					R				
	W					N				
	W				EC 1					
	W					GPL				
	W					DTL				
Execution											Data transfer between the FDD and the main-system
Result	R					ST 0					Status information after Command execution
	R					ST 1					
	R					ST 2					
	R					C					Sector ID information after Command execution
	R					H					
	R					R					
	R					N					

READ A TRACK

PHASE	R/W	D7	D6	D5	D4	D3	D2	D1	D0	REMARKS
Command	W	0	MFM	SK	0	0	0	0	1	0	Command Codes
	W	0	0	0	0	0	HDS	DS1	DS0	Sector ID information prior to Command execution
	W					C				
	W					H				
	W					R				
	W					N				
	W					EOT				
	W					GPL				
	W					DTL				
Execution											Data transfer between the FDD and the main-system. FDC reads the complete track contents from the physical index mark to EOT
Result	R					ST 0					Status information after Command execution
	R					ST 1					
	R					ST 2					
	R					C					Sector ID information after Command execution
	R					H					
	R					R					
	R					N					

READ ID

PHASE	R/W	D7	D6	D5	D4	D3	D2	D1	D0	REMARKS
Command	W	0	MFM	0	0	1	0	1	0	Command Codes
	W	0	0	0	0	0	HDS	DS1	DS0	
Execution											The first correct ID information on the track is stored in Data Register
Result	R					ST 0					Status information after Command execution
	R					ST 1					
	R					ST 2					
	R					C					Sector ID information during Execution Phase
	R					H					
	R					R					
	R					N					

FIGURE 11-28 8272A command summary. (courtesy of Intel Corporation)

FORMAT A TRACK

Phase	R/W	Bits / Byte	Remarks
Command	W	0 MFM 0 0 1 1 0 1	Command Codes
	W	0 0 0 0 0 HDS DS1 DS0	
	W	N	Bytes/Sector
	W	SC	Sectors/Track
	W	GPL	Gap 3
	W	D	Filter Byte
Execution			FDC formats an entire track
Result	R	ST 0	Status information after Command execution
	R	ST 1	
	R	ST 2	
	R	C	In this case, the ID information has no meaning
	R	H	
	R	R	
	R	N	

SCAN EQUAL

Phase	R/W	Bits / Byte	Remarks
Command	W	MT MFM SK 1 0 0 0 1	Command Codes
	W	0 0 0 0 0 HDS DS1 DS0	
	W	C	Sector ID information prior to Command execution
	W	H	
	W	R	
	W	N	
	W	EOT	
	W	GPL	
	W	STP	
Execution			Data compared between the FDD and the main-system
Result	R	ST 0	Status information after Command execution
	R	ST 1	
	R	ST 2	
	R	C	Sector ID information after Command execution
	R	H	
	R	R	
	R	N	

WRITE DATA

Phase	R/W	Bits / Byte	Remarks
Command	W	MT MFM 0 0 0 1 0 1	Command Codes
	W	0 0 0 0 0 HDS DS1 DS0	
	W	C	Sector ID information prior to Command execution
	W	H	
	W	R	
	W	N	
	W	EOT	
	W	GPL	
	W	DTL	
Execution			Data transfer between the main-system and the FDD
Result	R	ST 0	Status information after Command execution
	R	ST 1	
	R	ST 2	
	R	C	Sector ID information after command execution
	R	H	
	R	R	
	R	N	

WRITE DELETED DATA

Phase	R/W	Bits / Byte	Remarks
Command	W	MT MFM 0 0 1 0 0 1	Command Codes
	W	0 0 0 0 0 HDS DS1 DS0	
	W	C	Sector ID information prior to Command execution
	W	H	
	W	R	
	W	N	
	W	EOT	
	W	GPL	
	W	DTL	
Execution			Data transfer between the FDD and the main-system
Result	R	ST 0	Status information after Command execution
	R	ST 1	
	R	ST 2	
	R	C	Sector ID information after command execution
	R	H	
	R	R	
	R	N	

DATA BUS

PHASE	R/W	D7	D6	D5	D4	D3	D2	D1	D0	REMARKS
RECALIBRATE										
Command	W	0	0	0	0	0	1	1	1	Command Codes
Command	W	0	0	0	0	0	0	DS1	DS0	
Execution										Head retracted to Track 0
SENSE INTERRUPT STATUS										
Command	W	0	0	0	0	1	0	0	0	Command Codes
Result	R				— ST 0 —					Status information at the end of each seek operation about the FDC
Result	R				— C —					
SPECIFY										
Command	W	0	0	0	0	0	0	1	1	Command Codes
Command	W		— SPT —				— HUT —			Timer Settings
Command	W		— HLT —						ND	
SENSE DRIVE STATUS										
Command	W	0	0	0	0	0	1	0	0	Command Codes
Command	W	0	0	0	0	0	HDS	DS1	DS0	
Result	R				— ST 3 —					Status information about the FDD
SEEK										
Command	W	0	0	0	0	1	1	1	1	Command Codes
Command	W	0	0	0	0	0	HDS	DS1	DS0	
Command	W				— C —					
Execution										Head is positioned over proper Cylinder on Diskette
INVALID										
Command	W			— Invalid Codes —						Invalid Command Codes (NoOp—FDC goes into Standby State)
Result	R				— ST 0 —					ST 0 = 80 (16)

DATA BUS

PHASE	R/W	D7	D6	D5	D4	D3	D2	D1	D0	REMARKS
SCAN LOW OR EQUAL										
Command	W	MT	MFM	SK	1	1	0	0	1	Command Codes
Command	W	0	0	0	0	0	HDS	DS1	DS0	Sector ID information prior to Command execution
Command	W				— C —					
Command	W				— H —					
Command	W				— R —					
Command	W				— N —					
Command	W				— EOT —					
Command	W				— GPL —					
Command	W				— STP —					
Execution										Data compared between the FDD and the main-system
Result	R				— ST 0 —					Status information after Command execution
Result	R				— ST 1 —					
Result	R				— ST 2 —					
Result	R				— C —					Sector ID information after command execution
Result	R				— H —					
Result	R				— R —					
Result	R				— N —					
SCAN HIGH OR EQUAL										
Command	W	MT	MFM	SK	1	1	1	0	1	Command Codes
Command	W	0	0	0	0	0	HDS	DS1	DS0	Sector ID information prior to Command execution
Command	W				— C —					
Command	W				— H —					
Command	W				— R —					
Command	W				— N —					
Command	W				— EOT —					
Command	W				— GPL —					
Command	W				— STP —					
Execution										Data compared between the FDD and the main-system
Result	R				— ST 0 —					Status information after Command execution
Result	R				— ST 1 —					
Result	R				— ST 2 —					
Result	R				— C —					Sector ID information after command execution
Result	R				— H —					
Result	R				— R —					
Result	R				— N —					

FIGURE 11–28 *continued*

Symbol	Description
EOT	End of Track. The final sector number of the current track.
GPL	Gap Length. The gap 3 size. (Gap 3 is the space between sectors excluding the VCO synchronization field as defined in section 3.)
H	Head Address. Selected head: 0 or 1 (disk side 0 or 1, respectively) as encoded in the sector ID field.
HLT	Head Load Time. Defines the time interval that the FDC waits after loading the head before initiating a read or write operation. Programmable from 2 to 254 milliseconds (in increments of 2 ms).
HUT	Head Unload Time. Defines the time interval from the end of the execution phase (of a read or write command) until the head is unloaded. Programmable from 16 to 240 milliseconds (in increments of 16 ms).
MFM	MFM/FM Mode Selector. Selects MFM double-density recording mode when high, FM single-density mode when low.

Symbol	Description
C	Cylinder Address. The currently selected cylinder address (0 to 76) on the disk.
D	Data Pattern. The pattern to be written in each sector data field during formatting.
DS0,DS1	Disk Drive Select. DS1 DS0 0 0 Drive 0 0 1 Drive 1 1 0 Drive 2 1 1 Drive 3
DTL	Special Sector Size. During the execution of disk read/write commands, this parameter is used to temporarily alter the effective disk sector size. By setting N to zero, DTL may be used to specify a sector size from 1 to 256 bytes in length. If the actual sector (on the diskette) is larger than DTL specifies, the remainder of the actual sector is not passed to the system during read commands; during write commands, the remainder of the actual sector is written with all-zeroes bytes. DTL should be set to FF hexadecimal when N is not zero.

FIGURE 11–29 Command abbreviations for the command summary in figure 11–28. (courtesy Inter Corporation)

Symbol	Description
MT	Multi-Track Selector. When set, this flag selects the multi-track operating mode. In this mode (used only with dual-sided disks), the FDC treats a complete cylinder (under both read/write head 0 and read/write head 1) as a single track. The FDC operates as if this expanded track started at the first sector under head 0 and ended at the last sector under head 1. With this flag set (high), a multi-sector read operation will automatically continue to the first sector under head 1 when the FDC finishes operating on the last sector under head 0.
N	Sector Size. The number of data bytes within a sector. (See Table 9.)
ND	Non-DMA Mode Flag. When set (high), this flag indicates that the FDC is to operate in the non-DMA mode. In this mode, the processor is interrupted for each data transfer. When low, the FDC interfaces to a DMA controller by means of the DRQ and DACK signals.
R	Sector Address. Specifies the sector number to be read or written. In multi-sector transfers, this parameter specifies the sector number of the first sector to be read or written.
SC	Number of Sectors per Track. Specifies the number of sectors per track to be initialized by the Format Track command.

Symbol	Description
SK	Skip Flag. When this flag is set, sectors containing deleted data address marks will automatically be skipped during the execution of multi-sector Read Data or Scan commands. In the same manner, a sector containing a data address mark will automatically be skipped during the execution of a multi-sector Read Deleted Data command.
SRT	Step Rate Interval. Defines the time interval between step pulses issued by the FDC (track-to-track access time). Programmable from 1 to 16 milliseconds (in increments of 1 ms).
ST0 ST1 ST2 ST3	Status Register 0–3. Registers within the FDC that store status information after a command has been executed. This status information is available to the processor during the Result Phase after command execution. These registers may only be read after a command has been executed (in the exact order shown in Table 5 for each command). These registers should not be confused with the Main Status Register.
STP	Scan Sector Increment. During Scan operations, this parameter is added to the current sector number in order to determine the next sector to be scanned.

FIGURE 11–29 *continued*

Multi-Track MT	MFM/FM MFM	Bytes/Sector N	Maximum Transfer Capacity (Bytes/Sector)(Number of Sectors)	Final Sector Read from Diskette
0 0	0 1	00 01	(128)(26) = 3,328 (256)(26) = 6,656	26 at Side 0 or 26 at Side 1
1 1	0 1	00 01	(128)(52) = 6,656 (256)(52) = 13,312	26 at Side 1
0 0	0 1	01 02	(256)(15) = 3,840 (512)(15) = 7,680	15 at Side 0 or 15 at Side 1
1 1	0 1	01 02	(256)(30) = 7,680 (512)(30) = 15,360	15 at Side 1
0 0	0 1	02 03	(512)(8) = 4,096 (1024)(8) = 8,192	8 at Side 0 or 8 at Side 1
1 1	0 1	02 03	(512)(16) = 8,192 (1024)(16) = 16,384	8 at Side 1

FIGURE 11–30   Various data capacity using the 8272A. (courtesy of Intel Corporation)

information. If a read data command is terminated due to an error, then these bytes contain information as defined in figure 11–31.

Write Data   The write data command is very similar to the read data command because it, too, will access the specified sector and then continue to write the remaining sectors in the track, unless the 8272A receives the terminal count signal (TC). If TC is received prior to the end of a sector, the remaining bytes of the sector are automatically filled with 00H. This is useful because the software does not have to keep track of how many bytes are stored in a sector and it does not have to fill a buffer with 00H.

There are only two errors detected by the write data command, and both terminate the write operation. One error is DE, which occurs when the ID field CRC is incorrect. The other is an overrun error (OR), which occurs in an interrupt system if the microprocessor fails to write another byte of data within 15 μs.

Write Deleted Data   The write deleted data command functions exactly as the write data command except a deleted data address mark is written at the start of the data field. This effectively indicates that the sector is bad and the sector will be skipped for normal read data commands.

Read Deleted Data   The read deleted data command functions as the read data command except that when the deleted data address mark is found it reads the data in its data field. It still sets the CM flag in the status register as did the read data command. After reading the sector the command continues reading the next sector, whether deleted or not.

Read a Track   The read a track command is almost identical to the read data command except the data are read beginning at the sector that immediately follows the index mark. Then the 8272A reads all the sectors on the disk. This command also detects the same errors as the read data command except that the ND error flag is set if the R register does not match the sector numbers being read from the disk.

Read ID   The read ID command allows the software to determine the position of the head. This command reads the sector ID field of the first sector that it encounters and

MT	EOT	Final Sector Transferred to Processor	ID Information at Result Phase			
			C	H	R	N
0	1A 0F 08	Sector 1 to 25 at Side 0 Sector 1 to 14 at Side 0 Sector 1 to 7 at Side 0	NC	NC	R + 1	NC
	1A 0F 08	Sector 26 at Side 0 Sector 15 at Side 0 Sector 8 at Side 0	C + 1	NC	R = 01	NC
	1A 0F 08	Sector 1 to 25 at Side 1 Sector 1 to 14 at Side 1 Sector 1 to 7 at Side 1	NC	NC	R + 1	NC
	1A 0F 08	Sector 26 at Side 1 Sector 15 at Side 1 Sector 8 at Side 1	C + 1	NC	R = 01	NC
1	1A 0F 08	Sector 1 to 25 at Side 0 Sector 1 to 14 at Side 0 Sector 1 to 7 at Side 0	NC	NC	R + 1	NC
	1A 0F 08	Sector 26 at Side 0 Sector 15 at Side 0 Sector 8 at Side 0	NC	LSB	R = 01	NC
	1A 0F 08	Sector 1 to 25 at Side 1 Sector 1 to 14 at Side 1 Sector 1 to 7 at Side 1	NC	NC	R + 1	NC
	1A 0F 08	Sector 26 at Side 1 Sector 15 at Side 1 Sector 8 at Side 1	C + 1	LSB	R = 01	NC

NOTES: 1. NC (No Change): The same value as the one at the beginning of command execution.

2. LSB (Least Significant Bit): The least significant bit of H is complemented.

FIGURE 11–31 Result phase data after a read command if termination is due to an error. (Courtesy of Intel Corporation)

returns it in the result phase. If no valid sector ID exists on the disk, the ND flag is set and the command is terminated. This command is normally used after a seek to verify that the disk drive has arrived at the correct track.

Format a Track   The format a track command allows an entire track/cylinder to be formatted. The command specifies the number of bytes per sector (N), number of sectors per cylinder (SC), gap length (GPL), and data pattern (D) to be written in each sector's data field. During formatting, the 8272A requests four bytes of information from the microprocessor for each sector that is formatted. These four bytes are stored in the ID field of each sector as cylinder number (C), head number (H), sector number (R), and number of bytes per sector (N).

Figure 11–32 illustrates the values used for N, SC, and GPL for various sector sizes.

Scan Commands   There are three scan commands, all of which allow memory data to be compared with disk data. The scan equal command is very useful for testing whether data written to the disk match the memory data for verification. Figure 11–33 illustrates

8″ STANDARD FLOPPY

FORMAT	SECTOR SIZE	N	SC	GPL¹	GPL²	REMARKS
FM Mode	128 bytes/Sector	00	1A	07	1B	IBM Diskette 1
	256	01	0F	0E	2A	IBM Diskette 2
	512	02	08	1B	3A	
	1024	03	04	47	8A	
	2048	04	02	C8	FF	
	4096	05	01	C8	FF	
MFM Mode	256	01	1A	0E	36	IBM Diskette 2D
	512	02	0F	1B	54	IBM Diskette 2D
	1024	03	08	35	74	
	2048	04	04	99	FF	
	4096	05	02	C8	FF	
	8192	06	01	C8	FF	

5¼″ MINI FLOPPY

SECTOR SIZE	N	SC	GPL¹	GPL²
128 bytes/Sector	00	12	07	09
128	00	10	10	19
256	01	08	18	30
512	02	04	46	87
1024	03	02	C8	FF
2048	04	01	C8	FF
256	01	12	0A	0C
256	01	10	20	32
512	02	08	2A	50
1024	03	04	80	F0
2048	04	02	C8	FF
4096	05	01	C8	FF

NOTE: 1. Suggested values of GPL in Read or Write Commands to avoid splice point between data field and ID field of contiguous sections.
2. Suggested Values of GPL in format command.

FIGURE 11–32 Sector size relationships. (Courtesy of Intel Corporation)

COMMAND	STATUS REGISTER 2		COMMENTS
	BIT 2 = SN	BIT 3 = SN	
Scan Equal	0	1	$D_{FDD} = D_{Processor}$
	1	0	$D_{FDD} \neq D_{Processor}$
Scan Low or Equal	0	1	$D_{FDD} = D_{Processor}$
	0	0	$D_{FDD} < D_{Processor}$
	1	0	$D_{FDD} \nleqslant D_{Processor}$
Scan High or Equal	0	1	$D_{FDD} = D_{Processor}$
	0	0	$D_{FDD} > D_{Processor}$
	1	0	$D_{FDD} \ngeqslant D_{Processor}$

FIGURE 11–33   Scan status codes. (Courtesy of Intel Corporation)

the status register 2 bits that indicate the outcome of the scans for each of the three scan instructions.

Recalibrate   The recalibrate command causes the head assembly to retract to track 00, the outermost track. If track 00 is not found after the 8272A issues 77 step pulses, the SE (seek end) and EC (equipment check) status bits are set and the command is terminated.

Sense Interrupt Status   An interrupt signal is generated by the 8272A for four reasons: (1) entering the result phase of a command, (2) ready line changes states from the disk drive, (3) end of a seek or recalibrate, and (4) during the execution phase if nonDMA operation is selected. This command is normally used after either reason number (2) or (3). The 8272A polls the four disk drive interfaces and returns their ready conditions between commands. If a disk drive is turned off or fails, or the door is opened during operation, an interrupt is generated. After the interrupt, the sense interrupt instruction is executed to determine the cause. Status register 0 indicates the cause of this interrupt.

Specify   The specify command allows the system software to set values in three internal timers used to control the disk drive. These timers are: (1) head unload timer (HUT), (2) head load timer (HLT), and (3) step rate timer (SRT).

The HUT (head unload time) is programmable in 16 ms intervals from 01H (16 ms) to 0FH (240 ms). Head unload time is the time from the end of a read or write command until the head is unloaded from the disk.

The HLT (head load time) is programmable in 2-ms intervals from 01H (2 ms) to 7FH (254 ms). The load time is the time between the loading of the head until the beginning of a read or write operation. This allows the head to settle.

The SRT (step rate time) is programmed in 1 ms intervals from 0FH (1 ms) to 00H (16 ms). This time should be programmed for 1 ms longer than the step time recommended by the drive manufacturer.

The times indicated are for an 8-MHz clock used with a standard floppy disk drive. If a mini-floppy disk drive is in use, all times are multiplied by 2 because the clock rate is 4 MHz.

The ND bit is used to select DMA or nonDMA operation of the 8272A. If ND = 0, DMA operation is specified; if ND = 1, nonDMA operation is selected.

Sense Drive Status   The sense drive status command is used to obtain the contents of status register 3.

Seek   The seek command is used to move the head from one track or cylinder to another. The head is not moved by the read or write data commands. Because the read and write commands do not seek track, the software should include a seek command, a sense-interrupt status command, and a read-ID field command to verify correct positioning of the head before reading or writing data.

Invalid   Any command not defined is considered an invalid command. This command places the 8272A in a standby mode or no-operation mode.

Status Registers (main, ST0, ST1, ST2, and ST3)

As defined in the description of the commands, the status registers (main, ST0, ST1, ST2, and ST3) are used to convey information about the 8272A and its operation to the microprocessor. Figure 11–34 illustrates the bit patterns of each of five status registers.

The main status register is different from status registers ST0, ST1, ST2, and ST3 because it can be read at any time. Status registers ST0, ST1, ST2, and ST3 may be read only during the result phase of a command.

BIT NO.	NAME	SYMBOL	DESCRIPTION
MAIN STATUS REGISTER BIT DESCRIPTION			
D_0	FDD 0 Busy	D_0B	FDD number 0 is in the Seek mode.
D_1	FDD 1 Busy	D_1B	FDD number 1 is in the Seek mode.
D_2	FDD 2 Busy	D_2B	FDD number 2 is in the Seek mode.
D_3	FDD 3 Busy	D_3B	FDD number 3 is in the Seek mode.
D_4	FDC Busy	CB	A read or write command is in process.
D_5	Non-DMA mode	NDM	The FDC is in the non-DMA mode. This bit is set only during the execution phase in non-DMA mode. Transition to "0" state indicates execution phase has ended.
D_6	Data Input/Output	DIO	Indicates direction of data transfer between FDC and Data Register. If DIO = "1" then transfer is from Data Register to the Processor. If DIO = "0", then transfer is from the Processor to Data Register.
D_7	Request for Master	RQM	Indicates Data Register is ready to send or receive data to or from the Processor. Both bits DIO and RQM should be used to perform the handshaking functions of "ready" and "direction" to the processor.

FIGURE 11–34   The five 8272A status registers. (Courtesy of Intel Corporation)

BIT NO.	NAME	SYMBOL	DESCRIPTION
STATUS REGISTER 0			
D_7	Interrupt Code	IC	$D_7 = 0$ and $D_6 = 0$ Normal Termination of Command, (NT). Command was completed and properly executed.
D_6			$D_7 = 0$ and $D_6 = 1$ Abnormal Termination of Command, (AT). Execution of Command was started, but was not successfully completed.
			$D_7 = 1$ and $D_6 = 0$ Invalid Command Issue, (IC). Command which was issued was never started.
			$D_7 = 1$ and $D_6 = 1$ Abnormal Termination because during command execution the ready signal from FDD changed state.
D_5	Seek End	SE	When the FDC completes the SEEK command, this flag is set to 1 (high).
D_4	Equipment Check	EC	If a fault Signal is received from the FDD, or if the Track 0 Signal fails to occur after 77 Step Pulses (Recalibrate Command) then this flag is set.
D_3	Not Ready	NR	When the FDD is in the not-ready state and a read or write command is issued, this flag is set. If a read or write command is issued to Side 1 of a single sided drive, then this flag is set.
D_2	Head Address	HD	This flag is used to indicate the state of the head at interrupt.
D_1	Unit Select 1	US 1	These flags are used to indicate a Drive Unit Number at interrupt
D_0	Unit Select 0	US 0	
STATUS REGISTER 1			
D_7	End of Cylinder	EN	When the FDC tries to access a Sector beyond the final Sector of a Cylinder, this flag is set.
D_6			Not used. This bit is always 0 (low).
D_5	Data Error	DE	When the FDC detects a CRC error in either the ID field or the data field, this flag is set.

FIGURE 11–34 *continued*

BIT NO.	NAME	SYMBOL	DESCRIPTION
D_4	Over Run	OR	If the FDC is not serviced by the main-systems during data transfers, within a certain time interval, this flag is set.
D_3			Not used. This bit always 0 (low).
D_2	No Data	ND	During execution of READ DATA, WRITE DELETED DATA or SCAN Command, if the FDC cannot find the Sector specified in the IDR Register, this flag is set.
			During executing the READ ID Command, if the FDC cannot read the ID field without an error, then this flag is set.
			During the execution of the READ A Cylinder Command, if the starting sector cannot be found, then this flag is set.
D_1	Not Writable	NW	During execution of WRITE DATA, WRITE DELETED DATA or Format A Cylinder Command, if the FDC detects a write protect signal from the FDD, then this flag is set.
D_0	Missing Address Mark	MA	If the FDC cannot detect the ID Address Mark after encountering the index hole twice, then this flag is set.
			If the FDC cannot detect the Data Address Mark or Deleted Data Address Mark, this flag is set. Also at the same time, the MD (Missing Address Mark in Data Field) of Status Register 2 is set.
STATUS REGISTER 2			
D_7			Not used. This bit is always 0 (low).
D_6	Control Mark	CM	During executing the READ DATA or SCAN Command, if the FDC encounters a Sector which contains a Deleted Data Address Mark, this flag is set.
D_5	Data Error in Data Field	DD	If the FDC detects a CRC error in the data field then this flag is set.
D_4	Wrong Cylinder	WC	This bit is related with the ND bit, and when the contents of C on the medium is different from that stored in the IDR, this flag is set.

FIGURE 11–34 *continued*

BIT NO.	NAME	SYMBOL	DESCRIPTION
D_3	Scan Equal Hit	SH	During execution, the SCAN Command, if the condition of "equal" is satisfied, this flag is set.
D_2	Scan Not Satisfied	SN	During executing the SCAN Command, if the FDC cannot find a Sector on the cylinder which meets the condition, then this flag is set.
D_1	Bad Cylinder	BC	This bit is related with the ND bit, and when the content of C on the medium is different from that stored in the IDR and the content of C is FF, then this flag is set.
D_0	Missing Address Mark in Data Field	MD	When data is read from the medium, if the FDC cannot find a Data Address Mark or Deleted Data Address Mark, then this flag is set.
STATUS REGISTER 3			
D_7	Fault	FT	This bit is used to indicate the status of the Fault signal from the FDD.
D_6	Write Protected	WP	This bit is used to indicate the status of the Write Protected signal from the FDD.
D_5	Ready	RDY	This bit is used to indicate the status of the Ready signal from the FDD.
D_4	Track 0	T0	This bit is used to indicate the status of the Track 0 signal from the FDD.
D_3	Two Side	TS	This bit is used to indicate the status of the Two Side signal from the FDD.
D_2	Head Address	HD	This bit is used to indicate the status of Side Select signal to the FDD.
D_1	Unit Select 1	US 1	This bit is used to indicate the status of the Unit Select 1 signal to the FDD.
D_0	Unit Select 0	US 0	This bit is used to indicate the status of the Unit Select 0 signal to the FDD.

FIGURE 11–34 *continued*

Interfacing the Floppy Disk Drive to the 8085A

The floppy disk drive is interfaced to the 8085A with the aid of the 8272A floppy disk controller and also an 8257-5 programmable DMA controller. Figure 11–35 illustrates this interface to the 8085A microprocessor. This illustration does not include the interface from the 8272A to the disk drive, which is covered later in this section.

The 74LS138 decoder in figure 11–35 is used to decode the address for both the

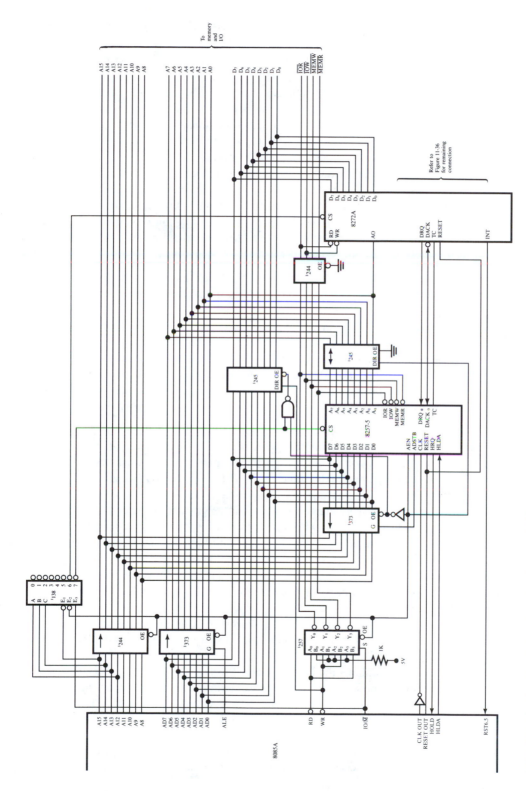

FIGURE 11-35 The 8272A interfaced to the 8085A microprocessor via an 8257-5 DMA controller.

8257-5 and the 8272A. The 8257-5 responds to I/O port number 78H for its command/ status register and I/O ports 70H and 71H for the channel 0 DMA address and terminal count, respectively. The 8272A responds to I/O ports 60H and 61H. Port number 60H is used to read the main status register and port 61H is used in the interrupt service subroutine (RST 6.5) to read the result from an 8272A command or to write commands to the 8272A. Data are not transferred via IN and OUT with the 8272A; data transfer is accomplished with the DMA controller and a DMA action.

Notice in figure 11–35 that all of the buses to the memory and I/O system have been buffered. This is required because in a system with a disk drive, it is likely that the entire memory is populated, and there are also likely to be many different additional I/O devices attached to the buses. This heavy load requires that all of the buses be buffered. Although this system may at first appear rather large, a close examination shows that there are not that many integrated circuits required for the 8272A interface.

The Disk Interface   Figure 11–36 illustrates the block diagram of the interface from the 8272A to the floppy disk drives. Line receivers used to receive signals from the disk drives are 7414 Schmitt trigger circuits whose inputs are pulled up to +5 V to reduce line noise. The outputs to the disk drive are passed through 7438 high-current, open-collector line drivers whose outputs are pulled up to +5 V in the disk drive.

The phase-locked loop data separator is used to generate a data window for the 8272A. The data window must be moved because the data will shift in position slightly as it is read due to speed variations and bit shift on the disk. The PLL accomplishes this by locking onto the data and clock pulses to produce a data window, which is fed to the 8272A.

Interface Software   Software to control the floppy disk controller and transfer data through the DMA controller is simple to write because these two integrated circuits handle most of the chore. Disk control software is often a part of a *DOS* (disk operating system) and is usually part of a set of subroutines in the *BIOS* (binary I/O system). Before we can discuss software, we must discuss the method used to transfer data in a block of memory.

Because a sector of disk data is 1024 bytes in length, the memory buffer used in the software is 1024 bytes in length with a preamble of information transferred for a read or write sector. The preamble need not be stored with the data and is called a *file control block (FCB)*. Figure 11–37 illustrates the organization of the FCB. All operating systems manage the file control block differently, so this system will use yet another form of the FCB. This system is designed for a minimum of disk commands to any of four disk drives.

The first byte (DISK-OP) of the FCB indicates the disk drive number (left-most two bits) and the operation in the right-most two bits. Table 11–1 illustrates the format for this byte and the commands allowed.

The second byte contains the head number (0 or 1), the third byte contains the track number (TRK) (or cylinder number, as it is sometimes called), and the fourth byte contains the sector number (SEC). The fifth and sixth bytes contain the DMA transfer address with the least significant byte first. The FCB can be set up anywhere in the memory, as can the data buffer. When the disk control software (DISK) is called, the contents of the DE register pair must contain the address of the FCB. Upon returning from this subroutine, the contents of the accumulator indicate whether an error has occurred. If the accu-

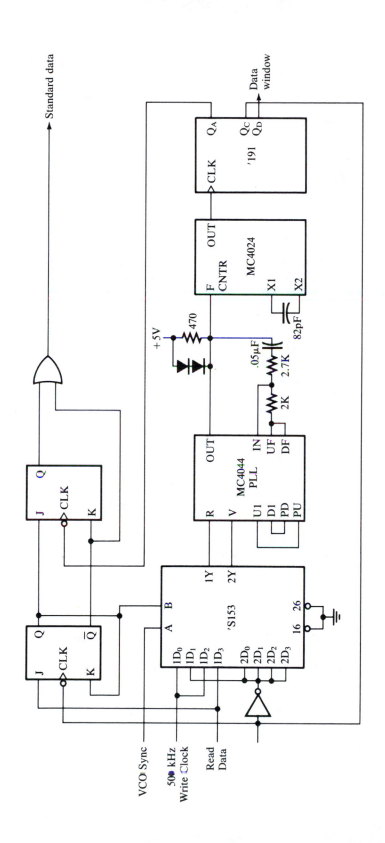

FIGURE 11–37 File control block.

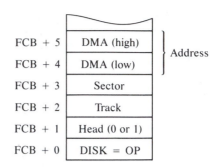

mulator is a 00H upon return, no error is detected and the operation is complete. This organization allows the disk to be managed with the least amount of effort by the programmer using the disk drive.

DISK Subroutine The DISK subroutine is actually a command processor that tests the status of the selected disk drive, determines which operation to perform, and then goes to the subroutine that performs the specified operation. As mentioned earlier, data transfers between the microprocessor and the disk drive are handled by the DMA controller.

The first part of the DISK subroutine tests the DRIVE status to determine if the selected drive door is closed and that power is applied to the selected drive. The DRIVE status word is maintained by the interrupt service subroutine that is called each time drive status changes.

```
                          ;
                          ;Disk control subroutine
                          ;
                          ;DE = address of the disk control block (DCB)
                          ;
                          ;on return Acc = 00 = no errors, operation complete
                          ;               01 = 8272A error
                          ;               02 = drive not ready
                          ;
D000                          ORG   0D000H
                          ;
D000  1A        DISK:       LDAX  D              ;get DISK-OP
D001  07                    RLC
D002  07                    RLC
D003  E603                  ANI   3              ;test drive ready
D005  4F                    MOV   C,A
D006  3242D0                STA   DNUM           ;save drive number
```

TABLE 11–1. DISK-OP byte of the file control block.

| d1 | d0 | X | X | X | X | C1 | C0 |

d1, d0 = select the drive number (0—3)

X = don't care

C1	C0	Function
0	0	Read sector
0	1	Write sector
1	0	Seek track

```
D009  3A41D0                    LDA    DRIVE      ;get drive status byte
D00C  0F            DISK1:      RRC
D00D  3D                        DCR    A
D00E  F20CD0                    JP     DISK1
D011  DA17D0                    JC     DISK2      ;if drive ready
D014  3E02                      MVI    A,2        ;indicate not ready
D016  C9                        RET
```

The second part of the DISK subroutine is a command processor which tests DISK-OP in the FCB to determine which command has been requested. The requested command is then executed by the DISK subroutine.

```
D017  D5            DISK2:      PUSH  D           ;save FCB pointer
D018  1A                        LDAX  D           ;get DISK-OP
D019  E603                      ANI   3           ;get command
D01B  87                        ADD   A           ;jump to correct subprogram
D01C  212BD0                    LXI   H,JTAB
D01F  85                        ADD   L
D020  6F                        MOV   L,A
D021  7C                        MOV   A,H
D022  CE00                      ACI   0
D024  67                        MOV   H,A
D025  5E                        MOV   E,M
D026  23                        INX   H
D027  56                        MOV   D,M
D028  EB                        XCHG
D029  D1                        POP   D           ;get FCB pointer
D02A  E9                        PCHL              ;jump to subprogram
                    ;
D02B  6ED0          JTAB:       DW    READ
D02D  A9D0                      DW    WRITE
D02F  44D0                      DW    SEEK
                    ;
D031                COMM:       DS    9           ;command storage
                    ;
D03A                RESUL:      DS    7           ;result storage
                    ;
D041  00            DRIVE:      DB    0           ;drive status byte
                    ;
D042  00            DNUM:       DB    0           ;drive number
                    ;
D043  00            FLAG:       DB    0           ;interrupt flag
                    ;
```

The SEEK subprogram (part of DISK) seeks the sector for a seek command, read command, or write command. This is accomplished by SEEK because it places the seek command (0FH) in the command block, which is sent to the 8272A by the EXEC subroutine.

```
D044  D5            SEEK:       PUSH  D           ;save FCB pointer
D045  2131D0                    LXI   H,COMM      ;address command buffer
D048  360F                      MVI   M,0FH       ;set seek command
D04A  23                        INX   H
D04B  13                        INX   D
D04C  3A42D0                    LDA   DNUM
D04F  4F                        MOV   C,A
D050  1A                        LDAX  D
D051  07                        RLC
D052  07                        RLC
D053  07                        RLC
```

```
D054  B1                        ORA   C
D055  77                        MOV   M,A
D056  23                        INX   H
D057  13                        INX   D
D058  1A                        LDAX  D
D059  77                        MOV   M,A
D05A  CDB2D0                    CALL  EXEC        ;go seek
D05D  3A3AD0                    LDA   RESUL       ;test for good seek
D060  E6F8                      ANI   0F8H
D062  FE20                      CPI   20H         ;test for good seek
D064  3E00                      MVI   A,0         ;indicate valid seek
D066  CA6CD0                    JZ    SEEK1       ;if good seek
D069  3E01      SEEKE:          MVI   A,1         ;indicate error
D06B  37                        STC               ;set carry
D06C  D1        SEEK1:          POP   D
D06D  C9                        RET
```

The READ subprogram loads the command block and then calls the EXEC subroutine, which executes the read a sector command. Upon the return from EXEC, errors are tested and a return is made with the appropriate error code in the accumulator or a 00H if no error occurred.

```
D06E  CD44D0    READ:           CALL  SEEK        ;seek track
D071  D8                        RC                ;if error on seek
D072  3E46                      MVI   A,46H       ;store read command
D074  3231D0    READ1:          STA   COMM
D077  D5                        PUSH  D           ;save FCB pointer
D078  2134D0                    LXI   H,COMM+3
D07B  23                        INX   H
D07C  1A                        LDAX  D           ;save head address
D07D  77                        MOV   M,A
D07E  23                        INX   H
D07F  13                        INX   D
D080  13                        INX   D
D081  1A                        LDAX  D           ;save sector number
D082  77                        MOV   M,A
D083  23                        INX   H
D084  3603                      MVI   M,3         ;save bytes per sector
D086  23                        INX   H
D087  360F                      MVI   M,0FH       ;save final sector number
D089  23                        INX   H
D08A  3680                      MVI   M,80H       ;save gap length
D08C  D1                        POP   D
D08D  D5                        PUSH  D
D08E  CDB2D0                    CALL  EXEC        ;read sector
D091  3A3AD0                    LDA   RESUL       ;normal command?
D094  E6C0                      ANI   0C0H
D096  C269D0                    JNZ   SEEKE       ;if error
D099  3A3BD0                    LDA   RESUL+1
D09C  B7                        ORA   A
D09D  C269D0                    JNZ   SEEKE       ;if error
D0A0  3A3CD0                    LDA   RESUL+2
D0A3  B7                        ORA   A
D0A4  C269D0                    JNZ   SEEKE       ;if error
D0A7  D1                        POP   D
D0A8  C9                        RET
```

The WRITE subprogram seeks the track and then jumps to the READ subprogram with the write command in the accumulator.

```
D0A9 CD44D0      WRITE:     CALL SEEK        ;seek track
D0AC D8                     RC               ;if seek error
D0AD 3E45                   MVI  A,45H        ;write command
D0AF C374D0                 JMP  READ1        ;go write data
```

The execute subroutine executes the command (seek, read, or write) and returns with the result in the RESUL buffer. If you trace through this subroutine you will notice that after the command is sent to the 8272A and the DMA controller is programmed (read or write), you encounter a HLT instruction. The HLT is used to wait for an interrupt (which signals the end of the command) so that the result can be read from the 8272A.

```
D0B2 1A          EXEC:      LDAX D
D0B3 4F                     MOV  C,A
D0B4 13                     INX  D
D0B5 13                     INX  D
D0B6 13                     INX  D
D0B7 13                     INX  D
D0B8 1A                     LDAX D
D0B9 D370                   OUT  70H          ;program DMA controller
D0BB 13                     INX  D
D0BC D370                   OUT  70H
D0BE 3EFF                   MVI  A,0FFH
D0C0 D371                   OUT  71H
D0C2 79                     MOV  A,C
D0C3 0F                     RRC
D0C4 0F                     RRC
D0C5 E6C0                   ANI  0C0H
D0C7 F603                   ORI  3
D0C9 D371                   OUT  71H
D0CB 2131D0                 LXI  H,COMM
D0CE 73                     MOV  A,M
D0CF FE0F                   CPI  0FH
D0D1 0E03                   MVI  C,3          ;if seek
D0D3 CAD8D0                 JZ   EXEC1
D0D6 0E09                   MVI  C,9
D0D8 DB60      EXEC1:       IN   60H          ;test busy
D0DA E6F8                   ANI  0F8H
D0DC C2D8D0                 JNZ  EXEC1        ;if busy
D0DF CD0FD1   EXEC2:        CALL WRED         ;test ready for command
D0E2 7E                     MOV  A,M
D0E3 23                     INX  H
D0E4 D361                   OUT  61H          ;send command byte
D036 0D                     DCR  C
D0E7 C2DFD0                 JNZ  EXEC2        ;if more command bytes
D0EA 3E41                   MVI  A,41H
D0EC D378                   OUT  78H          ;enable DMA
D0EE 3EFF                   MVI  A,0FFH
D0F0 3243D0                 STA  FLAG
D0F3 76       EXEC3:        HLT               ;wait for 8272A interrupt
D0F4 3A43D0                 LDA  FLAG
D0F7 FEFF                   CPI  0FFH
D0F9 CAF3D0                 JZ   EXEC3        ;if other than RST6.5
D0FC FE02                   CPI  2
D0FE C8                     RZ
D0FF 4F       EXECR:        MOV  C,A          ;save result byte count
D100 213AD0                 LXI  H,RESUL
D103 CD19D1   EXEC4:        CALL RRED
D106 DB61                   IN   61H          ;get result
D108 77                     MOV  M,A
```

```
D109  23                      INX   H
D10A  0D                      DCR   C
D10B  C203D1                  JNZ   EXEC4
D10E  C9                      RET
                     ;
D10F  DB60          WRED:     IN    60H           ;test for ready to
D111  E603                    ANI   3             ;write
D113  FE01                    CPI   1
D115  C219D1                  JNZ   RRED
D118  C9                      RET
                     ;
D119  DB60          RRED:     IN    60H           ;test for ready to
D11B  E603                    ANI   3             ;read
D11D  FE03                    CPI   3
D11F  C219D1                  JNZ   RRED
D122  C9                      RET
```

The interrupt service subroutine, which is vectored to from memory location 34H, follows and contains the software needed to process the 8272A interrupt. Notice that the 8272A is first tested for a busy condition. If it is busy, a result from a read or a write awaits within the 8272A, and a return occurs. If it is not busy, the disk drive has finished a seek, or the ready line from one of the four drives has changed status.

In either of these last two cases, the 8272A is sent a sense interrupt status instruction and the contents of ST0 are read to determine the cause of the interrupt. If a seek has ended, a return from the interrupt service subroutine occurs. If a drive has changed its ready status, the 8272A is sent a sense drive status command so that the status of the drive whose ready line has changed can be determined. The DRIVE byte is then updated to reflect the current condition of the interrupting drive.

```
                     ;
D123  F5            RST65:    PUSH  PSW           ;save registers
D124  DB60                    IN    60H
D126  E608                    ANI   8             ;test 8272A for busy
D128  CA33D1                  JZ    NBUS          ;if not busy
D12B  3E07                    MVI   A,7
D12D  3243D0                  STA   FLAG          ;count for result phase
D130  F1                      POP   PSW
D131  FB                      EI
D132  C9                      RET
D133  CD0FD1        NBUS:     CALL  WRED          ;test status
D136  3E08                    MVI   A,8
D138  D361                    OUT   61H           ;sense interrupt command
D13A  E5                      PUSH  H
D13B  C5                      PUSH  B
D13C  0E02                    MVI   C,2
D13E  213AD0                  LXI   H,RESUL
D141  CD19D1        NBUS1:    CALL  RRED          ;get result
D144  DB61                    IN    61H
D146  77                      MOV   M,A
D147  23                      INX   H
D148  0D                      DCR   C
D149  C241D1                  JNZ   NBUS1
D14C  3A3AD0                  LDA   RESUL
D14F  E6C0                    ANI   0C0H
D151  FEC0                    CPI   0C0H
D153  3E02                    MVI   A,2
D155  3243D0                  STA   FLAG
```

```
D158   CA60D1              JZ     NBUS2
D15B   C1                  POP    B
D15C   E1                  POP    H
D15D   F1                  POP    PSW
D15E   FB                  EI
D15F   C9                  RET
D160   CD0FD1   NBUS2:     CALL   WRED       ;sense drive
D163   3E04                MVI    A,4        ;command
D165   D361                OUT    61H
D167   CD0FD1              CALL   WRED
D16A   3A3AD0              LDA    RESUL
D16D   E603                ANI    3
D16F   D361                OUT    61H
D171   CD19D1              CALL   RRED
D174   DB61                IN     61H        ;get ST3
D176   E620                ANI    20H
D178   07                  RLC
D179   07                  RLC
D17A   07                  RLC
D17B   67                  MOV    H,A
D17C   3A42D0              LDA    DNUM
D17F   4F                  MOV    C,A
D180   0600                MVI    B,0
D182   3A41D0              LDA    DRIVE
D185   1F       NBUS3:     RAR               ;position drive bit
D186   14                  INR    D
D187   0D                  DCR    C
D188   F285D1              JP     NBUS3
D18B   6F                  MOV    L,A
D18C   7C                  MOV    A,H
D18D   0F                  RRC
D18E   7D                  MOV    A,L
D18F   17       NBUS4:     RAL               ;change status
D190   15                  DCR    D
D191   C28FD1              JNZ    NBUS4
D194   3241D0              STA    DRIVE
D197   C1                  POP    B
D198   E1                  POP    H
D199   F1                  POP    PSW
D19A   FB                  EI
D19B   C9                  RET
```

Summary

1   Magnetic media include magnetic disk memories in both flexible and rigid or hard forms, and magnetic bubble memory.

2   Three sizes of floppy disks are available today: (1) the 8-inch standard, (2) the $5\frac{1}{4}$-inch mini, and (3) the $3\frac{1}{2}$-inch micro.

3   A magnetic disk is divided into various groupings: track, sector, and cylinder.

4   Flexible disks are available in single-density, double-density, and quad-density forms with data stored either on one or both sides of the disk.

5   Digital data are normally recorded using the nonreturn-to-zero recording technique (NRZ).

6 Data are stored on the surface of the disk using either FM (frequency modulation) or MFM (modified frequency modulation) techniques.

7 Data are written by the read/write head by passing a current in one direction to store a logic zero and in the opposite direction to store a logic one.

8 The CRC (cyclic redundancy check) is used to indicate the validity of the data as it is read from a sector on the disk.

9 The disk drive mechanism contains two complete control systems. One, closed loop, is used to control the speed of a DC motor. The other, an open loop system, is used to position the head assembly via a stepper motor.

10 Hard disk memory systems, often called Winchester drives, are available in sizes ranging from $3\frac{1}{2}$ inches to 14 inches. Many Winchester hard disk drives contain two or more hard platters or disks.

11 A hard disk drive spins at 1500 RPMs and uses a flying head to read and write information.

12 Magnetic bubble memory devices store data in magnetic bubbles that are maintained on the surface of a substrate by a permanent magnetic field and moved around the surface by a rotating magnetic field.

13 Data are read from the magnetic bubble memory using a hall-effect device.

14 Optical disk memory can store vast amounts of information in a relatively small amount of space. Today the 14-inch optical disk memory can store 1G bytes of data, which is equivalent to 400,000 typewritten pages of information.

15 The 8272A is a single/double-density floppy disk controller that can interface and control up to four floppy disk drives.

16 The 8272A operates in three modes or phases: command, execution, and result. In the command phase, commands are sent to the 8272A via the command port; during the execution phase, data are transferred either by DMA or the data port; and during the result phase, the result and status information are transferred by the data port.

17 The 8272A responds to 15 commands that include read, write, seek, and format a track.

18 Interrupts are requested when the 8272A completes the execution phase, when a ready line changes from a disk drive, at the end of a seek, or during nonDMA operation for the transfer of each byte of data.

19 The 8272A has five status registers: main, ST0, ST1, ST2, and ST3. The main register is read by addressing the status port and the other registers are available during the result phase of certain instructions.

Glossary

BIOS Binary I/O System. A collection of software driver subroutines that control the disk, printer, keyboard, and other I/O devices.

Bubble memory A device that stores data in the form of magnetic bubbles or spots on the surface of a yttrium-garnet substrate.

CRC Cyclic Redundancy Checks. Used to check the validity of the data in a sector and the ID field.

Cylinder A group of tracks that exist under multiple heads such as the top and bottom of the disk.

Detector A magneto-resistive device that detects the motion of a magnetic bubble with a change in its resistance.

DOS Disk Operating System. A collection of subroutines that are used to maintain the files and data stored on the disk.

Drive hub The mechanism used to attach the floppy disk to the disk drive so that it can be rotated to read and write data.

Flexible disk See floppy disk.

Floppy disk A circular piece of mylar plastic that is coated with a magnetizable compound that can store digital data.

Flying head A read/write head that is designed to float on a cushion of air at the surface of a hard disk, which prevents or reduces disk and head wear.

FM Frequency Modulation. Used to store disk data in the single-density format.

Generator A device that generates magnetic bubbles.

Head load time The time required to load or bring the head of a disk drive in contact with the surface of the disk.

Head slot The opening in the jacket that protects the disk and allows the read/write head to make contact with the surface of the disk.

Head unload time The time allowed to the disk drive before the head is unloaded or moved away from the surface of the disk.

Index holes The small holes in the jacket and disk that are used to locate the start of a track of data.

MFM Modified Frequency Modulation. Used to store data on a disk in the double-density format.

Micro-floppy disk A magnetic storage device that is $3\frac{1}{2}$ inches in diameter. The micro-floppy disk can store over 600 K bytes of data.

Mini-floppy disk A magnetic storage device that is $5\frac{1}{4}$ inches in diameter. This type of disk can store up to 1.2 M bytes of data.

Nonvolatile memory A memory device that retains data for an extended period of time, even without the application of power.

NRZ NonReturn-to-Zero. Data that are stored on the disk surface by completely magnetizing it in one polarity for a logic one and the opposite polarity for a logic zero.

Optical disk memory A device that stores binary data that are read with a laser beam.

Propagating element A device on the surface of the magnetic bubble memory device that is used to steer the magnetic bubble around the surface.

Replicator/annihilator An element inside a magnetic bubble device that is used to replicate and annihilate magnetic bubbles.

Sector An arc or pie-shaped portion of a track containing digital data.

Standard floppy disk A storage device that can store 1.2 M bytes of data. It is 8 inches in diameter.

Track A concentric ring of data stored on a surface of a disk drive.

Write protect notch A notch in the disk jacket that prevents data from being written on the disk when the notch is covered.

Questions and Problems

1 What is a volatile memory?
2 List the three types of floppy disk memories in production today.
3 How fast does a $5\frac{1}{4}$-inch floppy disk spin?
4 What is the purpose of the index hole on the mini-floppy disk?
5 Describe the differences between the mini- and micro-floppy disks.
6 Define the following terms: track, sector, and cylinder.
7 What is NRZ recording?
8 Why is NRZ recording used with magnetic disk memory?
9 FM data contains both clock and data times. How long are these times?
10 Draw the FM waveform generated if a 1001111 is stored on the disk.
11 MFM data contains data and clock times. How long are these times?
12 Draw the MFM waveform generated if a 1000011 is stored on the disk.
13 What type of modulation is used to store double-density data?
14 What is a CRC and where is it used?
15 Modify the CRC generator in figure 11–14 so that it generates the following CRC algorithm: $X^{16} + X^{13} + X^7 + X^3 + 1$.
16 Which disk drive control system uses a closed loop system?
17 A hard disk drive uses what type of head?
18 How many heads are found tracking on each side of a typical hard disk memory?
19 What is a hard disk drive that fits inside of a computer system often called?
20 How fast does a typical hard disk spin?
21 What is a crash area?
22 How is a magnetic bubble maintained on the surface of the magnetic bubble memory device?
23 What elements are used to guide a magnetic bubble and what two shapes are commonly found?
24 Explain how a magnetic bubble is created.
25 Explain how a magnetic bubble is sensed.
26 What is the difference between a major and minor loop on a magnetic bubble memory device?
27 How is a magnetic bubble read from the surface of the bubble memory device?
28 How much information can be stored on a 14-inch optical disk memory?
29 What two ways can the 8272A transfer disk data between the microprocessor and the disk drive?
30 What event is caused by activating the TC pin on the 8272A?
31 What is the purpose of the LCT/DIR pin on the 8272A?
32 What is the HDSEL signal used to select?
33 What are three phases in which the 8272A operates?
34 What event occurs at the end of the execution phase in the 8272A?
35 What information is provided during the result portion of an instruction in the 8272A?

36 Explain how to use the read data command in the 8272A.

37 What errors are detected during the execution of a read data command in the 8272A?

38 What information is provided in the result phase of a read ID command for the 8272A?

39 What is the 8272A scan command used for in a disk system?

40 How is the DMA mode of operation selected in the 8272A?

41 How many status registers are found inside the 8272A?

42 Explain when and how the main status register of the 8272A is read.

43 What is the purpose of the phase-locked loop in a disk interface?

44 What is the BIOS?

45 Explain how the DISK subroutine is used to read sector 05H from track 07H into memory locations 2000H–23FFH.

46 What three major errors are detected by the DISK subroutine?

47 Explain how the DISK subroutine jumps to READ, WRITE, or SEEK.

48 Explain how the count and mode are loaded into the DMA controller in the EXEC subroutine.

49 The WRED subroutine tests which main status register bits?

50 Explain how the HLT instruction works in the EXEC subroutine.

12

Printers

Upon completion of this chapter, you will be able to

1   Describe the operation of both a parallel and a serial printer interface.
2   Develop the circuit and software required to interface either a serial or parallel printer to a computer.
3   Describe the advantages and disadvantage of the following printers: dot matrix, daisy wheel, thermal, and laser.
4   Describe the function of each component of a dot matrix printer.
5   Identify the parts of the software used to control a dot matrix printer.

Printers are one of the more common peripheral components connected to computer systems. This chapter presents many of the various types of printers found, as well as a discussion of their operation. It also details the operation of serial and parallel printer interfaces, which are used between the printer and the computer.

To illustrate the operation of a printer, the complete circuit of a typical dot matrix printer is presented along with the software required for it to operate and a description of the operation of the circuitry.

12-1 TYPES OF PRINTERS

This section of the chapter briefly discusses the types of printers that are most often connected to computer systems.

Dot Matrix Printer

One of the most common types of printers available today is the *dot matrix printer*. It is likely popular because of its low cost and extremely high printing speed. Prices range from a low of about $100; speeds range up to 300 cps (characters per second) or higher. The main disadvantage of the low-cost dot matrix printer is that the quality of the print is marginal—good enough for everyday draft usage, but not letter quality. Higher-priced dot matrix printers yield high speeds with letter quality.

Figure 12–1 illustrates the print head of a seven-pin dot matrix print head. This is the type found in most inexpensive nonletter-quality dot matrix printers. Each pin or wire is forced out through the die by a solenoid. Once forced against the ribbon, the pin produces a dot on the paper. After producing the dot, a small spring returns the pin so that the print head may be moved across the paper to the next printing position. The print head illustrated has 7 pins, but print heads are available with up to 24 pins so that letter-quality print can be achieved. Figure 12–2 shows the difference between letter-quality print generated by a 24-pin print head and the draft-quality print generated by a 7-pin print head. Notice the huge difference in the print quality.

In order to increase the speed of the printer, most printers today are bidirectional: as the print head travels from right to left, it prints in the forward direction; as it travels from left to right, it prints in the reverse direction. This effectively increases the speed of the printer

FIGURE 12–1   Dot matrix print head: (a) front view and (b) side view.

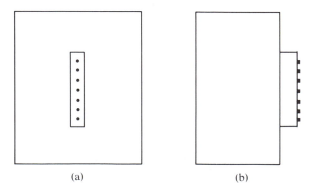

(a)   (b)

FIGURE 12–2 Print quality from a dot matrix printer: (a) 7-pin print head, and (b) 24-pin print head.

(a)   (b)

because the print head doesn't have to be returned to the left margin after each line of information is printed.

Thermal Printer

Another form of dot matrix printer is the *thermal printer*. There are two types of thermal printers available: one type uses a print head that heats up a temperature-sensitive paper that turns black when heated above 100° F, and the other heats a carbon film ribbon that prints on plain paper. The second type is by far the most common available today. The thermal print head resembles the dot matrix print head in that it contains areas in the form of a matrix. These areas are actually heated so that either the paper they are pressed against changes color, or the ribbon is heated, which causes it to leave an ink deposit on the paper. Figure 12–3 illustrates the construction of the thermal print head.

Daisy Wheel Printer

The *daisy wheel printer* is also a very common printer because it offers letter quality at a relatively low cost. A main advantage of this printer is that type fonts (letter sizes and styles) can be changed by changing the print wheel. Its greatest disadvantage is its print speed: most low-cost daisy wheel printers are capable of printing only about 15 cps; most low-cost dot matrix printers will print about 110 cps. The daisy wheel printer is much like a standard typewriter except that the letters are formed on a wheel rather than on type levers. Figure 12–4 illustrates a typical daisy wheel print wheel. The daisy wheel print head usually has 96 print arms with 96 different characters.

Notice that each letter is formed on the end of a short plastic print arm. The wheel is rotated into position in front of a solenoid-fired print hammer that slams the arm against a ribbon where the letter creates a printed character. It is this rotation that limits the speed of this type of printer.

Laser Printer

The *laser printer* is the latest entry into the printer field and it is by far the most expensive and complex of all the printers. Its main advantages are its perfect letter quality, program-

FIGURE 12–3 Front view of a thermal print head illustrating the seven heating elements.

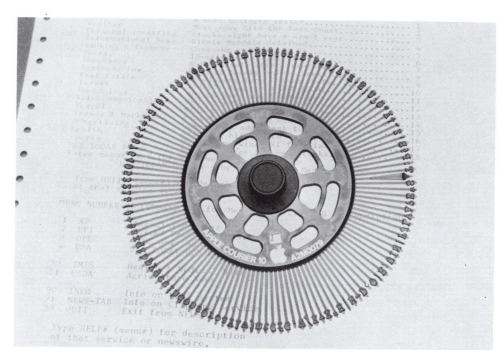

FIGURE 12-4   A daisy wheel print head.

mable fonts, and extremely high speed. Its disadvantage is its cost, which can range up to many thousands of dollars for one containing many different fonts.

The laser printer is basically a photocopier that uses a laser beam to generate characters on a metal transfer drum. The laser actually develops an electrostatic field in the shape of letters on the transfer drum. This electrostatic field is then used to pick up toner (ink in the form of a powder) from a reservoir. The ink that sticks to the surface of the drum is finally transferred to the page that is being printed. Because the laser beam can scan the surface of the drum at a very high rate of speed, a page can be printed in six seconds or less. The low-cost laser printers can print a page in about six seconds and the higher priced versions can do so in about one second. Figure 12-5 illustrates the internal organization of a laser printer.

12-2 PRINTER INTERFACES

A majority of all printers are interfaced to computers using either the *EIA RS-232C serial interface* standard[*] or by the *Centronics parallel interface* standard[†]. This section of the

---

[*] EIA is the Electronic Industries Association, which sets up standards followed by most American and Japanese pheripheral manufacturers.

[†] Centronics is the company that first used this standard, and since that time, many other printer manufacturers have adopted it as their interface.

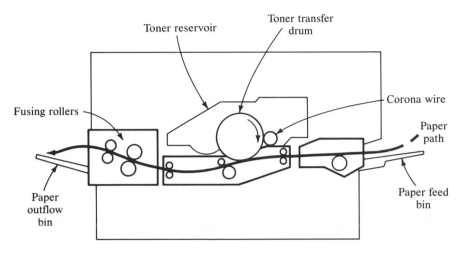

FIGURE 12–5   Internal structure of a laser printer.

text discusses both of these standard interfaces. The serial interface has the advantage of being able to be connected to the computer with only a few wires, but it is rather slow. The parallel standard requires many more wires, but it is extremely fast. Many printer interfaces today use the parallel standard because of its speed and because of the close proximity of the printer to the computer.

Centronics Parallel Interface

The Centronics parallel interface is a TTL interface standard that uses TTL logic levels of 0.0–0.8 V for a logic zero and 2.4–5.0 V for a logic one. This means that no special level shifting is required for connection to a computer system that operates with TTL logic levels. The only limitation with this interface standard is the length of the cable between the computer and the printer: it is recommended that the cable be no longer than 15 feet. Longer cables will cause problems at higher printing speeds in most cases.

The cable between the printer and the computer must be a 36-conductor cable that uses an Amphenol 57-30360 male connector (see figure 12–6) at the printer end. The computer end of the cable varies from computer to computer and is not discussed in this text.

Table 12–1 lists each of the pins and briefly describes the function of each pin. The computer uses the data lines (D1–D8) to transfer ASCII data to the printer, the $\overline{\text{STROBE}}$ signal to indicate to the printer that the data are available, and either the BUSY or $\overline{\text{ACK}}$ signal to determine if the printer has received the ASCII data. Not all printer interfaces use the remaining signals at the printer.

Figure 12–7 illustrates the printer interface timing signals. Notice that the computer sends data (D1–D8) to the printer followed by the $\overline{\text{STROBE}}$ signal. This causes the printer to accept the ASCII data and begin to print a character. The data must be present 0.5 μs before and after the $\overline{\text{STROBE}}$ signal, and the $\overline{\text{STROBE}}$ signal must be at least 0.5 μs in width. When the strobe signal is received by the printer, it begins to print the character and sends the computer the BUSY signal. After the printer completes printing the charac-ter (or accepts it in its buffer) it sends the computer the $\overline{\text{ACK}}$ signal. Once $\overline{\text{ACK}}$ is received, the computer is free to send another character to the printer.

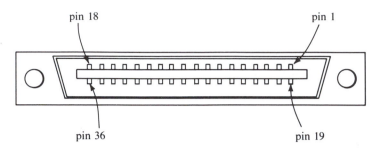

pin 18   pin 1

pin 36   pin 19

FIGURE 12–6   36-pin Centronics-type printer interface connector.

Printer Interface

Figure 12–8 illustrates the 8155 used to interface the 8085A to the Centronics printer. Here the 8155 is decoded at I/O ports F0H–F5H with port A used to transfer the data to the printer and port C used to generate and accept handshaking signals.

Notice that the $\overline{\text{ACK}}$ signal connects to the $\overline{\text{STB}}$ input of port A. When ASCII data are output to port A and the $\overline{\text{STROBE}}$ signal is sent to the printer, the printer responds with $\overline{\text{ACK}}$. The $\overline{\text{ACK}}$ signal pulses $\overline{\text{STB}}$, which clears the internal buffer full (BF) flag. BF is checked by the software to determine whether the printer has printed the data.

Print Subroutine

The PRINT subroutine first checks the BF (buffer full) flag for port A to determine if the printer has printed the previous character. If the previous character is printed, the ASCII contents of the B register are sent to the printer via port A. After the ASCII character is placed on port A, the strobe signal is sent to the printer.

```
                 ;Subroutine to print the character in the B register
                 ;
D300 DBF0        PRINT:    IN      0F0H        ;get 8155 status
D302 E602                  ANI     2           ;test port A buffer full
D304 C200D3                JNZ     PRINT       ;if printer busy
D307 78                    MOV     A,B         ;send ASCII character
D308 D3F1                  OUT     0F1H
D30A 3E00                  MVI     A,0         ;send STROBE
D30C D3F3                  OUT     0F3H
D30E 3EFF                  MVI     A,0FFH
D310 D3F3                  OUT     0F3H
D312 C9                    RET
```

Serial Printer Interface

The EIA RS-232C interface standard is described in the chapter on communications, but is presented again here in brief. The serial interface standard uses +12 V for a logic zero and −12 V for a logic one level with cable lengths of up to approximately 50 feet maximum. Because data are transferred to the printer using a serial format, this interface is somewhat slower than the Centronics parallel interface and therefore used only with low-speed printers.

The interface cable contains a minimum of three conductors and a shield for the interface between the printer and the computer. Figure 12–9 illustrates the 25-pin Cannon-type connector that conforms to the EIA RS-232C standard.

TABLE 12–1 Centronics parallel interface signal description.

Pin	Name	Function
1	STROBE	The STROBE signal is an input to the printer that enters (strobes) the character placed on the data connections (D1–D8) into the printer for printing.
2	D1	Data connection 1 (least significant data line).
3	D2	Data connection 2.
4	D3	Data connection 3.
5	D4	Data connection 4.
6	D5	Data connection 5.
7	D6	Data connection 6.
8	D7	Data connection 7.
9	D8	Data connection 8 (most significant data line).
10	$\overline{\text{ACK}}$	A signal back to the computer that indicates the printer has received the data sent to it via the STROBE signal.
11	BUSY	Indicates that the printer is busy printing data when it is a logic one level.
12	PE	A signal that is a logic one level whenever the printer is out of paper or whenever the ribbon is out.
13	SLCT	A logic one whenever the printer is selected or on line.
14	GND	Ground.
15		No connection.
16	GND	Ground.
17	CHS	Chassis ground.
18	VCC	+5.0 at 20 mA maximum from the printer.
19–30	GND	Ground.
31	$\overline{\text{RESET}}$	This pin is used to reset the printer to its initial state when a logic zero is applied to this pin.
32	$\overline{\text{ERROR}}$	The ERROR pin indicates to the computer that a printer error has occurred.
33–36		No connection.

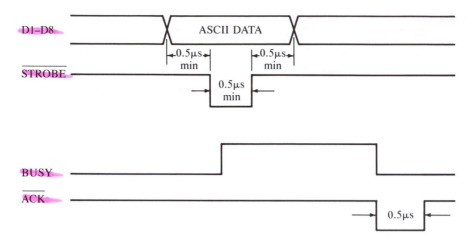

FIGURE 12–7 Centronics printer interface timing signals.

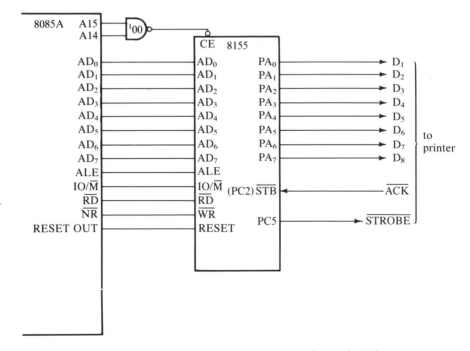

FIGURE 12–8 The 8085A interfaced through an 8155 to a Centronics printer.

Table 12–2 illustrates the name and function of each RS-232C pin that is normally connected between the printer and the computer.

In the simplest of printer interfaces, only the chassis ground (pin 1), signal ground (pin 7), RXD (pin 3) and either DTR (pin 20) or RTS (pin 4) are connected between the computer and the printer. Pin 1 is connected to the shield connection of the cable to prevent stray radiation, as required by the FCC; pin 7 is the ground return signal for the

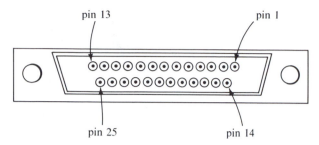

FIGURE 12–9 EIA RS-232C

transmitted data; pin 3 is the ASCII serial data to be printed; and pin 20 or 4 indicates that the printer is busy (logic one). Figure 12–10 illustrates this type of handshake and the signals observed on the RXD connection and also the BUSY connection (pin 20 or 4).

There are two other methods of transferring data between the printer and the computer. One is called XON/XOFF and the other is ETX/ACK. In both systems the printer returns an ASCII character to the computer through the TXD pin (2).

With XON/XOFF, the printer will send the XOFF character (13H) to the computer when its internal buffer is within 32 bytes of becoming full and will send the XON (11H) character when its buffer is within 31 bytes of becoming empty.

With ETX/ACK, the ETX code (03H) is inserted after each block of data that does not exceed the printer's buffer length. At the end of a printed block of data, when the printer reads the ETX code, the printer sends the computer the ACK code (06H), which is used to request more data to be printed. In most applications using ETX/ACK, the ETX code follows a line of printed data.

TABLE 12–2. The serial RS-232C printer interface signal description.

Pin	Name	Function
1	CG	Chassis ground.
2	TXD	Transmitter data sent from the printer to the computer.
3	RXD	Receive data is the data sent to the printer from the computer to be printed.
4	RTS	Request-to-send is used as a signal to the computer in the ready/busy mode of operation explained in the text.
5	CTS	Clear-to-send is used as a signal that indicates the printer is ready to receive data from the computer.
6	DSR	Data set ready indicates that the computer is ready. Most printers ignore this signal input to the printer.
7	GND	Ground.
20	DTR	Data terminal ready indicates that the printer is ready to receive data.

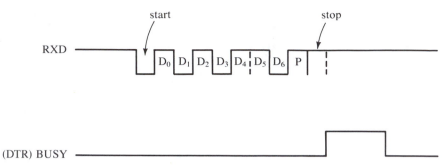

FIGURE 12–10 Timing for RS-232C.

Figure 12–11 illustrates an 8251A USART connected as a serial printer driver. Notice that the USART is interfaced to operate at I/O ports 20H and 21H. Also notice that the $\overline{\text{CTS}}$ input to the USART, which must be grounded for the USART to transmit data, is connected through an inverter to the DTR pin (20) of the printer. If the printer is busy, DTR is a logic zero, which inhibits the USART from transmitting data to the printer. If the printer is ready (pin 20 = 1), then the $\overline{\text{CTS}}$ pin is grounded, allowing the USART to transmit data.

Software to initialize the USART and transmit data follows:

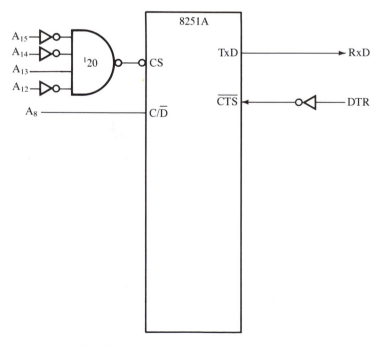

FIGURE 12–11 The 8251A interfaced to a serial printer.

```
                    ;initialize the 8251A for 7 data bits, even parity,
                    ;and 1 stop bit.
                    ;
0055  3E00    INIT:     MVI   A,0              ;reset 8251A
0057  D320              OUT   20H
0059  D320              OUT   20H
005B  D320              OUT   20H
005D  3E40              MVI   A,40H
005F  D320              OUT   20H
0061  3E79              MVI   A,79H            ;program USART
0063  D320              OUT   20H
0065  3E01              MVI   A,01H            ;enable transmitter
0067  D320              OUT   20H

                    ;subroutine to print the contents of the B register
                    ;
D500  DB20    PRINT:    IN    20H              ;get status
D502  E601              ANI   01H              ;test TX ready
D504  CA00D5            JZ    PRINT            ;if not ready
D507  78                MOV   A,B
D508  D321              OUT   21H              ;send data
D50A  C9                RET
```

DOT MATRIX PRINTER 12-3

This section of the chapter presents a complete dot matrix printer, including the hardware and all of the software to operate it. This complete printer system includes stepper motors to move the print head across the page and to move paper up through the machine, a dot matrix print head, and a Centronics-type parallel printer interface. It also contains a 2,048-character buffer memory that is used to hold ASCII data while the printer is printing previous data.

Print Head and Drivers

Figure 12–12 illustrates the nine-pin print head and the drivers used to power each pin solenoid. With a nine-pin print head, fairly good dot matrix quality is attainable because lower-case letters can have descenders. A *descender* is the part of a character that descends below the base line, such as the lower part of the letters *q* or *p*. (see figure 12–13 for a sample of the printed output of a nine-pin print head). The drivers are simple transistor switches that amplify the current at the output of a TTL I/O port (8155) connected to the 8085 microprocessor as illustrated later in this section. In addition to the drivers, a 555 timer is used to fire the print heads for 200 μs each time the 555 timer receives a trigger pulse.

Paper Feed Stepper Motor

The paper feed stepper motor moves the paper up past the print head a fixed distance for each step. In this example the paper is moved one-eighth of a line per step. This printer can print only 66 lines per page and does not have the option to print with different line spacings. Different line spacings are attainable by varying the number of steps between lines and by using more steps per line.

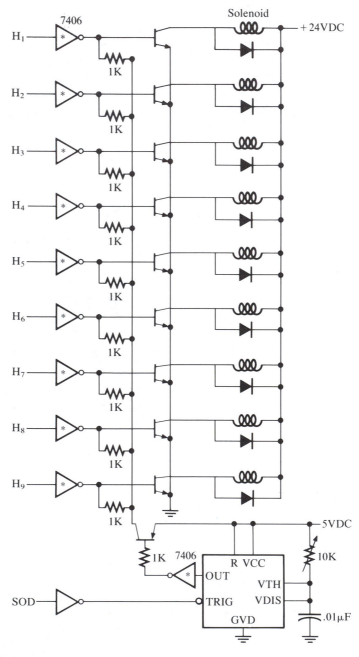

FIGURE 12–12 Print head

FIGURE 12–13 Sample print from a nine-pin print head illustrating descenders.

Figure 12–14 illustrates the stepper motor drive interface used for both the paper feed stepper motor and also for the carriage position stepper motor. The driver circuits require three input signals. Two of the signals are used to energize the four coils in the stepper motor, and the third line is used to hold or step the motor. A small amount of current flows through the coils of the stepper motor to hold them in position when the motor's armature is not being moved.

Carriage Position Stepper Motor

The carriage position stepper motor is used in a closed loop system so that the position of the motor is always known. This is important because this motor positions the print head from one row of dots to another. In order to determine the position of the stepper motor and the print head, a timing disk is added to the shaft of the stepper motor. An optical coupler (LED and phototransistor) is used to sense the timing marks on this timing disk

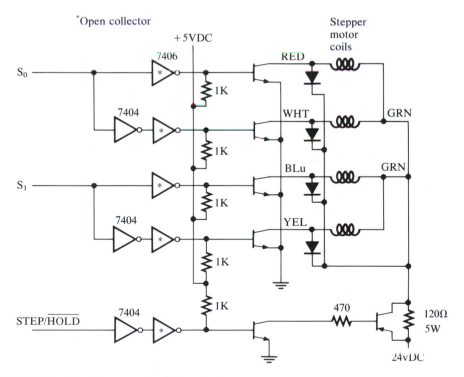

FIGURE 12–14 Stepper motor driver circuit.

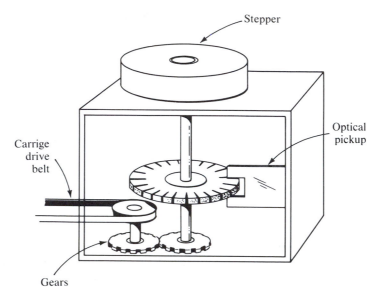

Stepper

Optical
pickup

Carrige
drive
belt

Gears

FIGURE 12–15 Carriage stepper motor assembly.

(refer to figure 12–15). The timing marks are used to time when the print head is fired to produce dots on the page. This assures even spacing for the printed characters.

Printer Schematic

Figure 12–16 illustrates the schematic diagram of the dot matrix printer. This printer in the figure prints in one direction only and has no frills. The 8085A interfaces the printer to the Centronics port via an 8155. It uses a second 8155 to interface to the print head, stepper motors, and both the home and carriage sensors.

The printer's memory consists of the 512 bytes of RAM in the 8155s, 2K bytes of RAM in the 4016, and 4K bytes of EPROM on a 2732. Figure 12–17 illustrates the memory map for the printer.

The EPROM located at address 0000H–0FFFH is used to store the program and a lookup table that contains the dot characters.

The print buffer located in the 4016 RAM (locations 1000H–1FFFH) is used to hold 2,048 ASCII characters for the printer. This memory is organized as a FIFO, with the Centronics interface inputting data and the printer software outputting data.

The scratchpad memory at addresses 2000H–20FFH and 3000H–30FFH is used to hold temporary data and also to hold one line of printed data that is scanned by the print driver. The line buffer allows the printer to print data in the forward or the reverse direction to match carriage motion. (In the example software presented later, only unidirectional printing is supported, which reduces the length of the program.) The scratchpad buffer is loaded from the 2K × 8 RAM that is filled with ASCII data as it enters the printer from the Centronics printer interface.

The 8155 located at I/O ports 20H–25H is used to interface the printer to the computer via a Centronics parallel interface. Port A is used as an input port to accept ASCII data that are strobed into it with the Centronics STROBE signal. The BUSY flag is generated

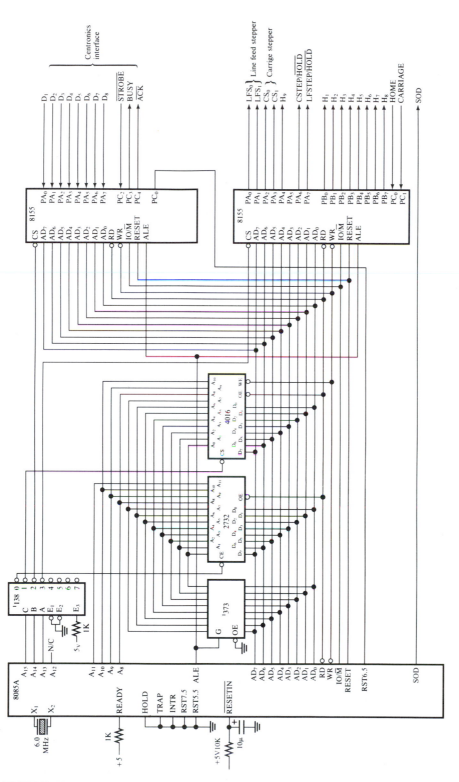

FIGURE 12–16 Circuit for a dot matrix printer.

FIGURE 12–17 Dot matrix
printer memory map.

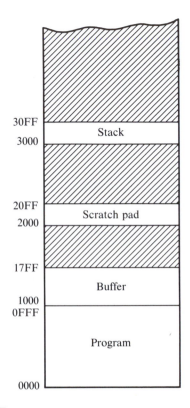

by a port C signal and the $\overline{\text{ACK}}$ signal (5.0 μs in width) is also generated via port C and software.

The 8155 located at I/O ports 30H–35H is used to control the stepper motors, which feed paper and move the carriage, and also to provide the signals to the pin solenoids of the print head. Port B provides eight of the nine bits required to drive the pin solenoids and port A provides the ninth bit and also the signals to the stepper motor. Port C is used to input the data from the home and carriage sensors.

Software to Initialize the Printer

The software to initialize the printer is stored at memory location 0000H so that it executes when power is applied to the printer. The initialization software brings the printer online with its buffer empty and the paper and carriage stepper motors in position to begin printing.

```
                    ;software to initialize the printer
                    ;
0000  3E06    RESET:    MVI   A,06H        ;port A = input
0002  D320              OUT   20H          ;port C = alt3
0004  3E18              MVI   A,18H        ;BUSY = 1, ACK = 1
0006  D323              OUT   23H
                    ;
0008  3E03              MVI   A,3          ;port A & B = output
000A  D330              OUT   30H          ;port C = input
000C  3E00              MVI   A,0          ;clear A & B
```

```
000E  D331                      OUT    31H
0010  D332                      OUT    32H
                      ;
0012  210010                    LXI    H,1000H        ;initialize buffer
0015  220020                    SHLD   INPNT          ;pointer
0018  220220                    SHLD   OUTPNT
                      ;
001B  3E00                      MVI    A,0            ;turn print off
001D  320420                    STA    POS            ;set position
                      ;
0020  310031                    LXI    SP,STACK       ;load stack pointer
                      ;
0023  CD7500                     CALL   LF             ;feed line of paper
                      ;
0026  CDB400                    CALL   HOME           ;home print head
                      ;
0029  3E0B                      MVI    A,0BH          ;enable RST 7.5
002B  30                        SIM
002C  FB                        EI
                      ;
002D  3E16                      MVI    A,16H          ;enable port A interrupt
002F  D320                      OUT    20H
0031  C31B01                    JMP    SYSTEM         ;go print a line
                      ;
                      ;equates
                      ;
2000  =               INPNT:    EQU    2000H          ;input pointer
2002  =               OUTPNT:   EQU    2002H          ;output pointer
3100  =               STACK:    EQU    3100H          ;stack pointer
2004  =               POS:      EQU    2004H          ;motor position
2005  =               LBUF:     EQU    2005H          ;line buffer
```

Interrupt Service Subroutine

The Centronics printer interface is serviced by the RST 6.5 interrupt input to the 8085A microprocessor. Port A of the 8155 is operated in the strobed input mode so that when ASCII data are sent to the printer the $\overline{\text{STROBE}}$ signal activates the $\overline{\text{STB}}$ input to the port. $\overline{\text{STB}}$ causes the 8155 to issue an interrupt request to the 8085A, which calls a subroutine that makes the printer busy by placing a logic one on BUSY. It then reads data from the port and stores the data into an internal FIFO memory buffer and sends out the $\overline{\text{ACK}}$ signal to the computer. If the FIFO is full, the interrupt service subroutine returns with the interrupt disabled. Future interrupts are enabled after the printer prints a line of data.

```
003C                            ORG    3CH
                      ;
                      ;interrupt service subroutine to fill buffer
                      ;
003C  F5              RST75:    PUSH   PSW            ;save registers
003D  3E18                      MVI    A,18H
003F  D323                      OUT    23H            ;BUSY = 1, ACK = 1
0041  E5                        PUSH   H
0042  D5                        PUSH   D
0043  2A0220                    LHLD   OUTPNT         ;get pointers
0046  EB                        XCHG
0047  2A0020                    LHLD   INPNT
004A  23                        INX    H
004B  7C                        MOV    A,H
004C  E607                      ANI    7
```

```
004E  BA                      CMP   D
004F  C26100        ,         JNZ   RST76        ;if not equal
0052  57                      MOV   D,A
0053  7B                      MOV   A,E
0054  BD                      CMP   L
0055  C26100                  JNZ   RST76        ;if not equal
0058  3E06                    MVI   A,06H
005A  D320                    OUT   20H          ;disable 8155 interrupt
005C  D1                      POP   D            ;restore registers
005D  E1                      POP   H
005E  F1                      POP   PSW
005F  FB                      EI
0060  C9                      RET
0061  5F          RST76:      MOV   E,A
0062  DB21                    IN    21H          ;get data
0064  77                      MOV   M,A          ;save data in FIFO
0065  EB                      XCHG
0066  220020                  SHLD  INPNT        ;save incremented pointer
0069  97                      SUB   A
006A  D323                    OUT   23H          ;BUSY = 0, ACK = 0
006C  3E10                    MVI   A,10H
006E  D323                    OUT   23H          ;BUSY = 0, ACK = 1
0070  D1                      POP   D
0071  E1                      POP   H
0072  F1                      POP   PSW
0073  FB                      EI
0074  C9                      RET
```

Line Feed Subroutine

The line feed (LF) subroutine causes the stepper motor connected to the paper platen to move the paper up one line. Since this is a no-frills printer, only one type of line feed is available that will cause the printer to print 66 lines on a standard $8\frac{1}{2} \times 11$ piece of paper. The line feed stepper motor is geared so that eight steps move the paper up exactly one line of paper. Because this is a fairly long step, the stepper motor requires 20 ms between each step.

Notice that the right three bits of memory location POS contain the current position of the stepper motor. In order to spin the motor, the codes 00, 01, 10, and 11 are sent to it. The software sends both stepper motors a code using the same 8-bit I/O port, but the motor doesn't move until it also gets a signal on the hold/step input to the stepper motor circuit. For the line feed stepper motor this step pulse comes from bit position 7 of port A.

```
                  ;
                  ;subroutine to step the paper up one line
                  ;
0075  0608  LF:       MVI   B,8           ;load count
0077  3A0420  LF1:    LDA   POS           ;get position
007A  F680            ORI   80H           ;set step
007C  D331            OUT   31H           ;set line feed motor
007E  CD9A00          CALL  DELAY2        ;wait 20 ms
0081  3A0420          LDA   POS           ;adjust line feed count
0084  E6FC            ANI   0FCH
0086  4F              MOV   C,A
0087  3A0420          LDA   POS
008A  3C              INR   A
008B  E603            ANI   3
008D  B1              ORA   C
```

```
008E  320420            STA   POS
0091  05                DCR   B
0092  C27700            JNZ   LF1            ;repeat 8 times
0095  E67F              ANI   7FH            ;hold line feed motor
0097  D331              OUT   31H
0099  C9                RET
                    ;
                    ;20 ms time delay
                    ;
009A  D5        DELAY2:  PUSH  D
009B  160A               MVI   D,10
009D  CDA600             CALL  DELAY
00A0  15                 DCR   D
00A1  C29D00             JNZ   DELAY2+3
00A4  D1                 POP   D
00A5  C9                 RET
                    ;
                    ;2 ms time delay
                    ;
00A6  C5        DELAY:   PUSH  B
00A7  F5                 PUSH  PSW
00A8  01FA00             LXI   B,250
00AB  0B                 DCX   B
00AC  78                 MOV   A,B
00AD  B1                 ORA   C
00AE  C2AB00             JNZ   DELAY+5
00B1  F1                 POP   PSW
00B2  C1                 POP   B
00B3  C9                 RET
```

Home Subroutine

The HOME subroutine has the responsibility of homing the print head. The home position of the print head, indicated by a photosensor, is the left margin. Homing is accomplished by moving the print head to the left until it is home. If the print head is already in the home position, it is moved to the right off of the home position and then back to the left to the home position for proper alignment.

The stepper motor is sent a 00, 01, 10, and 11 to move the print head to the right and 11, 10, 01, and 00 to move it to the left. Bit position 6 is used to control stepping or holding for the carriage stepper motor.

```
                    ;
                    ;subroutine to home the print head
                    ;
00B4  DB33      HOME:    IN    33H           ;test home
00B6  E601               ANI   1
00B8  CAC400             JZ    HOME1         ;if not home
00BB  0664               MVI   B,100         ;step right 100 pulses
00BD  CDFB00             CALL  RIGHT
00C0  05                 DCR   B
00C1  C2C400             JNZ   HOME1         ;repeat 100 times
00C4  3A0420    HOME1:   LDA   POS
00C7  D331               OUT   31H           ;stop motion
00C9  CD9A00             CALL  DELAY2        ;wait 20 ms
00CC  3A0420    HOME2:   LDA   POS
00CF  E6F3               ANI   0F3H
00D1  4F                 MOV   C,A
00D2  3A0420             LDA   POS
```

```
00D5 D604              SUI    4
00D7 E60C              ANI    0CH
00D9 B1                ORA    C
00DA 320420            STA    POS
00DD F640              ORI    40H              ;step left
00DF D331              OUT    31H
00E1 CDA600            CALL   DELAY            ;wait 2 ms
00E4 DB33      HOME3:  IN     33H              ;wait for carriage pulse
00E6 E602              ANI    2
00E8 CAE400            JZ     HOME3
00EB DB33              IN     33H              ;test for home mark
00ED E601              ANI    1
00EF CACC00            JZ     HOME2            ;keep moving left
00F2 3A0420            LDA    POS              ;stop motor
00F5 D331              OUT    31H
00F7 CD9A00            CALL   DELAY2           ;wait 20 ms
00FA C9                RET
               ;
               ;subroutine to move carriage right until carriage pulse
               ;
00FB 3A0420    RIGHT:  LDA    POS
00FE F640              ORI    40H              ;step motor
0100 D331              OUT    31H
0102 DB33      RIGHT1: IN     33H              ;test for carriage pulse
0104 E602              ANI    2
0106 CA0201            JZ     RIGHT1
0109 3A0420            LDA    POS              ;get next step code
010C E6F3              ANI    0F3H
010E 4F                MOV    C,A
010F 3A0420            LDA    POS
0112 C604              ADI    4
0114 E60C              ANI    0CH
0116 B1                ORA    C
0117 320420            STA    POS
011A C9                RET
```

System Program

The system program is a loop that checks for available data and prints it. As noted before, an interrupt causes data to be input from the printer; software to accomplish this does not appear in the system software.

The system software first checks to see if the FIFO buffer is empty. If it is, it merely loops until an interrupt from the computer begins to fill it. When the FIFO is no longer empty, the system software begins transferring one line from the FIFO into a line buffer. The line buffer is either filled with 80 characters, a complete line, or until the line feed ASCII character (0AH) is encountered.

Once the line buffer is filled with data to be printed, the PRINT subroutine is called to print it. After printing a line, the system program is begun anew, where it once again tests the FIFO for an empty condition.

```
011B CD5A01    SYSTEM: CALL   EMPTY            ;test for empty FIFO
011E CA1B01            JZ     SYSTEM           ;if empty
0121 0650              MVI    B,80             ;load character count
0123 110520            LXI    D,LBUF           ;address line buffer
0126 7E        SYS1:   MOV    A,M              ;fill print buffer
0127 E67F              ANI    7FH              ;strip left-most bit
0129 FE0A              CPI    0AH              ;test for line feed
```

```
012B  CA4B01                JZ    SYS3
012E  12                    STAX  D              ;save it in line buffer
012F  13                    INX   D
0130  23                    INX   H              ;increment OUTPNT
0131  7C                    MOV   A,H
0132  E603                  ANI   3
0134  67                    MOV   H,A
0135  220220                SHLD  OUTPNT
0138  CD5A01        SYS2:   CALL  EMPTY          ;wait for data
013B  CA3801                JZ    SYS2
013E  05                    DCR   B
013F  C22601                JNZ   SYS1           ;get another character
0142  3E0A                  MVI   A,0AH          ;save line feed
0144  12                    STAX  D
0145  CD6B01                CALL  PRINT          ;print line
0148  C31B01                JMP   SYSTEM         ;print another line
014B  12            SYS3:   STAX  D
014C  23                    INX   H
014D  7C                    MOV   A,H
014E  E603                  ANI   3
0150  67                    MOV   H,A
0151  220220                SHLD  OUTPNT
0154  CD6B01                CALL  PRINT          ;print line
0157  C31B01                JMP   SYSTEM         ;print another line
                        ;
                        ;empty subroutine test to see if the FIFO is
                        ;empty
                        ;
                        ;HL = OUTPNT on return
                        ;return zero = empty
                        ;
015A  D5            EMPTY:  PUSH  D
015B  2A0020                LHLD  INPNT          ;data to be printed?
015E  EB                    XCHG
015F  2A0220                LHLD  OUTPNT
0162  7C                    MOV   A,H
0163  BA                    CMP   D
0164  C26901                JNZ   EMPTY1         ;if data
0167  7D                    MOV   A,L
0168  BB                    CMP   E
0169  D1            EMPTY1: POP   D
016A  C9                    RET
```

Print Subroutine

The PRINT subroutine takes the data that are loaded into the line buffer by the system program and prints them on the printer. It accomplishes this by first allowing the print head to reach speed. It takes quite a few pulses to the carriage stepper motor to get the print head to move across the paper at a constant speed. Notice that the print head is first stepped right 20 places before any data are printed to allow it to reach speed. Once speed is reached, the line buffer is emptied a character at a time and the dot pattern for it is looked up in a lookup table. Because each character uses nine bits, the lookup table contains 10 entries per character. In this software, each entry in the lookup table is 16 bytes apart with only the first 10 bytes used for dot data.

As the carriage stepper motor moves the print head across the paper, the pulses coming from the carriage mechanism are used to time the printing of each vertical column of dots. This causes the printed output to have uniform dot spacing across the page.

After each line of data is printed, this no-frills printer does a line feed to a new line of paper and a home to move the print head back to the left margin of the paper. This printer does not print bidirectionally.

Before returning from the PRINT subroutine, the interrupt for the Centronics port is enabled so that it may again begin to accept data from the computer. Recall that the port is disabled if the FIFO becomes full. Printing a line of data leaves room in the FIFO for additional data so the interrupt is enabled at this time.

```
                    ;
                    ;subroutine to print one line of data from the
                    ;line buffer
                    ;
016B  0614          PRINT:   MVI   B,20           ;step right 20 pulses
016D  110520                 LXI   D,LBUF         ;address line buffer
0170  CDFB00        PRIN1:   CALL  RIGHT          ;move head right
0173  05                     DCR   B
0174  C27001                 JNZ   PRIN1          ;repeat 20 times
0177  1A            PRIN2:   LDAX  D
0178  FE0A                   CPI   0AH            ;test for line feed
017A  CAAD01                 JZ    PRIN4
017D  210004                 LXI   H,LOOK         ;address lookup table
0180  6F                     MOV   L,A
0181  29                     DAD   H
0182  29                     DAD   H
0183  29                     DAD   H
0184  29                     DAD   H              ;address dot pattern
0185  0605                   MVI   B,5
0187  CDFB00        PRIN3:   CALL  RIGHT          ;move head right
018A  7E                     MOV   A,M            ;get dots
018B  D332                   OUT   32H
018D  3A0420                 LDA   POS
0190  F640                   ORI   40H
0192  4F                     MOV   C,A
0193  23                     INX   H
0194  7E                     MOV   A,M
0195  B1                     ORA   C
1096  D331                   OUT   31H
0198  3EC0                   MVI   A,0C0H         ;fire head
019A  30                     SIM
019B  3E40                   MVI   A,040H
019D  30                     SIM
019E  23                     INX   H
019F  05                     DCR   B
01A0  C28701                 JNZ   PRIN3
01A3  CDFB00                 CALL  RIGHT
01A6  CDFB00                 CALL  RIGHT
01A9  13                     INX   D
01AA  C37701                 JMP   PRIN2
01AD  CD7500        PRIN4:   CALL  LF             ;get new line
01B0  CDB400                 CALL  HOME           ;home print head
01B3  3E16                   MVI   A,16H          ;enable Centronics interrupt
01B5  D320                   OUT   20H
01B8  C9                     RET
```

FIGURE 12–18 The letter *p* and the lookup table entry to print it. (Note that a logic zero prints a dot and a logic one does not.)

9	00010000	11001111	8
7	00010000	10110111	6
5	00010000	10110111	4
3	00010000	10110111	2
1	00000000	00001111	0

Lookup Table

The lookup table for the printer is stored beginning at memory location 0400H–0BFFH. Each character uses a 16-byte section of the table for the dot patterns to be printed. The first 32 entries contain spaces because it is not normal to print control characters on a printer. Following that, each 16-byte section contains the dot patterns to produce the characters listed in the ASCII code chart. Figure 12–18 illustrates the dot pattern required to print the letter *p* and the contents of the lookup table for that letter.

Summary

1 A dot matrix printer prints via a series of dots that make characters. Most dot matrix printers print with near letter quality at fairly high speeds.

2 A daisy wheel printer uses a plastic disk with arms, each of which has an impression of a print character. The speed of the daisy wheel printer is slow, but its cost and the ability to change the print by changing the print wheel make it desirable.

3 The thermal printer prints either on special paper that turns black when heated, or the printer heats the carbon on a carbon-film ribbon that transfers a character to the paper.

4 The laser printer is by far the quickest printer, but it is also the most expensive. Laser printers can print virtually any type style by changing the software.

5 The Centronics parallel printer interface uses TTL logic levels and parallel data lines for extremely high speeds and also for low cost. The data lines are labeled D1–D8, and the control lines $\overline{BUSY}$, $\overline{STROBE}$, and $\overline{ACK}$. The BUSY line indicates that the printer is busy, the $\overline{STROBE}$ line is used to strobe data into the printer, and the $\overline{ACK}$ line indicates that the printer is ready to receive additional data.

6   The EIA RS-232C serial interface uses $+/-$ 12V for its two logic levels. Data are transmitted via a twisted pair of wires with an additional handshaking signal in most systems.

7   XON/XOFF protocol is used in some systems with RS-232C. The XOFF code is transmitted to the computer when the printer's internal buffer is nearly full; the XON code is sent when the printer's buffer is nearly empty.

8   ETX/ACK protocol is used in some serial interfaces. ETX is appended to the end of the text (usually at the end of a line of data) and the printer sends an ACK back to the computer when it has received the ETX code.

9   Drivers for the pins in a dot matrix print head are current amplifiers that are used to boost the TTL level currents.

10 The stepper motors in the printer require three signals to operate. Two of the three determine the coil currents and the third determines whether the motor steps or holds its position.

11 Feedback is provided to the carriage stepper motor in two forms: (1) the home position at the left margin and (2) a pulse from a sensor each time the print head moves to a new printing position.

12 The printer buffer memory is a FIFO that accepts data from the Centronics printer interface and parts with data as the printer prints.

Glossary

Centronics interface   A printer interface that is used to transfer ASCII data to a printer in parallel.

Daisy wheel printer   A device that prints the characters from a plastic wheel. The print wheel is interchangable, making font changes simple.

Descender   The part of a letter that descends below the base line.

Dot matrix printer   A device that prints each character using 7 to 20 closely spaced pins. Each pin is forced through a die against a ribbon by a solenoid, making dots on paper.

EIA RS-232C interface   A serial interface that is commonly used with printers.

Laser printer   A device that prints with a laser beam to statically charge areas on a metal plate. The charged areas hold powdered ink that is transferred to the paper.

Thermal printer   A device that prints by either heating the paper, which changes color, or by heating the ribbon to transfer ink to the paper.

Questions and Problems

1   How does a dot matrix printer print?
2   Dot matrix print heads may contain up to how many print pins?
3   How many printable characters does the daisy wheel contain?
4   Is a daisy wheel printer faster than a dot matrix printer?

5   Describe the way a thermal printer prints on regular paper.

6   What is toner?

7   Which printer prints the most characters per second?

8   What is the purpose of the $\overline{\text{STROBE}}$ signal in the Centronics printer interface?

9   Which printer interface uses TTL logic signals?

10 What is the purpose of the $\overline{\text{ACK}}$ signal in the Centronics printer interface?

11 How many data lines are used with the Centronic parallel interface?

12 What voltages are used to send and receive signals in the EIA RS-232C serial interface?

13 What is the purpose of the DTR pin in RS-232C as it applies to printers?

14 Describe XON/XOFF protocol.

15 Describe ETX/ACK protocol.

16 Explain the operation of the print head driver circuit of figure 12–12.

17 Which transistors are conducting current in figure 12–14 if a code 11 is applied to the inputs along with a step signal?

18 What is the purpose of the ANI 3 instruction stored at memory location 008B in the LF subroutine?

19 What is the purpose of the ORI 40H instruction at memory location 00DD in the HOME subroutine?

20 Explain how the EMPTY subroutine functions.

13

8085A Application Examples

Upon completion of this chapter, you will be able to:

1 Understand the operation of the 8085A in a complete system, including both the hardware operation and the software.

2 Learn about process control through the dishwasher control circuit.

3 Use an interrupt to drive the display system of a point-of-sales terminal.

Since a thorough understanding of any subject is best fostered by applying one's knowledge, two applications for the 8085A are listed in this chapter. These applications are meant to be used as examples of what can be accomplished with this microprocessor and the interfacing that has been discussed throughout this textbook. These examples can provide new ideas on ways to handle the many different hardware/software interactions illustrated here.

13−1 DISHWASHER CONTROL CIRCUIT

A dishwasher control circuit is simple application of a "real-time" microprocessor-based system. In this example, time delay subroutines develop the proper timing sequence for a simple one-cycle dishwasher.

Figure 13−1 illustrates the circuitry required to control the dishwasher. Included is a 1K-byte ROM, 2K-byte RAM, an address latch to demultiplex the address/data bus of the 8085A, and an output latch for the control of the internal circuitry of the dishwasher.

Looking at the different devices in this circuit, you will notice that the ROM is active whenever address bit A15 is low and therefore will respond to memory addresses 0000H

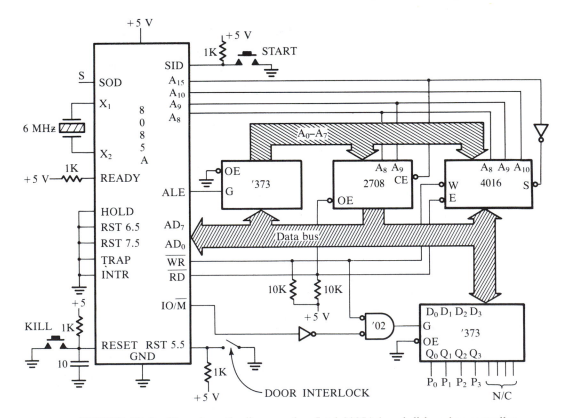

FIGURE 13−1 The schematic diagram of an Intel 8085A-based dishwasher controller.

through 7FFFH. The RAM is active whenever address bit A15 is a logic one, so it has an address range of 8000H through FFFFH. Finally, the output port will respond to any OUT instruction; but you should use only a port number of 00 through 7FH to prevent the writing of output data to the RAM in this system.

Figure 13–2 pictures the interface circuitry required to drive the motor, heating element, drain solenoid, water inlet solenoid, and soap dispenser solenoid. These parts were chosen so that a reliable system could be developed for long-term operation.

The front panel of the dishwasher illustrated in figure 13–3 was chosen so that it contained a minimum number of operator controls for ease of use.

The kill push button resets the microprocessor so that the current sequence can be aborted. Since it is connected to the $\overline{\text{RESET}}$ input of the 8085A, it forces the microprocessor to begin the program over again.

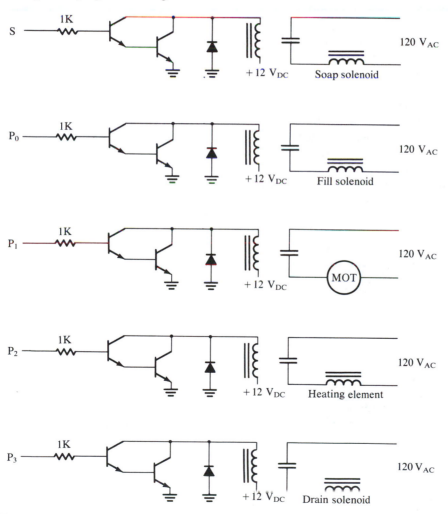

FIGURE 13–2 The solenoid and motor drivers for the dishwasher controller.

FIGURE 13–3 A front view of
the door and control panel of the
dishwasher.

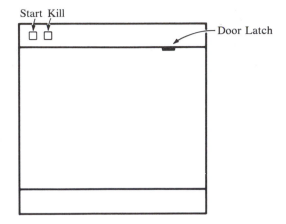

The start push button causes the dishwasher to begin sequencing through its washing cycle. This input is tested by the software by polling the SID pin on the microprocessor.

The only other input signal to the microprocessor is the door interlock switch, which is open circuited whenever the door of the dishwasher is opened. Since this signal is connected to an interrupt input on the microprocessor, it causes the current program to be interrupted, suspending all function until the door is closed.

The basic timing sequence for this machine is depicted in figure 13–4. The entire washing sequence requires 60 minutes to be completed. The first timing event is a prewash, which in theory removes dried food particles from the dishes. This is followed by a heated rinse cycle, heated wash cycle, two rinse cycles, and finally a drying cycle.

The program is depicted in the flowchart of figure 13–5, and the listing follows:

```
                    ;main dishwasher control program
                    ;
8000 =              IOB:    EQU     8000H       ;set up IOB address
                    ;
0000                        ORG     0
                    ;
0000 310084  RESET:  LXI     SP,8400H    ;set stack area
0003 3E0E            MVI     A,0EH       ;enable RST 5.5
0005 30              SIM
0006 20              RIM                 ;read SID pin
0007 07              RLC                 ;start to carry
0008 DA0000          JC      RESET       ;if no start
000B CD2900          CALL    D50         ;wait 50 ms
000E 20              RIM                 ;read SID pin
000F 07              RLC                 ;start to carry
0010 DA0000          JC      RESET       ;if no start
0013 FB              EI                  ;enable door interrupt
0014 CD4F00          CALL    MOTOR       ;type 1 sequence
0017 CD7300          CALL    MOTORH      ;type 2 sequence
001A CD9D00          CALL    MOTORS      ;type 3 sequence
001D CD7300          CALL    MOTORH      ;type 2 sequence
0020 CD4F00          CALL    MOTOR       ;type 1 sequence
0023 CDB400          CALL    HEAT        ;type 4 sequence
0026 C30000          JMP     RESET       ;end of wash
```

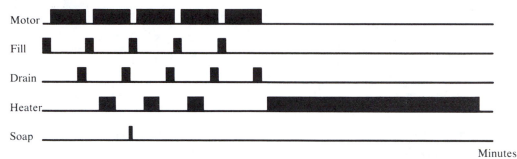

FIGURE 13–4 The timing sequence for the microprocessor-controlled dishwasher.

In the preceding program, if the start button is held down for at least 50 ms, the dishwasher begins its sequence. This, of course, is contingent on the door's being closed.

Once the machine is started, it sequences through four basic modes of operation. The first mode, the type 1 mode, causes the machine to fill with water, run the motor that sprays water on the dishes, and empty the water from the machine. The type 2 mode is identical to type 1, except that the heater is operated to make sure that the water temperature is high enough to kill germs on the dishes and to ensure they are cleaned properly. The type 3 mode is identical to type 2, except that the soap is dispensed in the middle of the cycle. Type 4 is the heater cycle.

The time delay software, which is used in all modes of operation, consists of two subroutines. One delay subroutine causes a 50 ms delay (D50), and the other a one minute delay (D1M).

```
                    ;50 millisecond time delay subroutine
                    ;
0029  016A18  D50:    LXI    B,186AH   ;load count
002C  0B      D50A:   DCX    B         ;decrement count
002D  78              MOV    A,B       ;test count for 0
002E  B1              ORA    C
002F  C22C00          JNZ    D50A      ;if count not 0
0032  C9              RET

                    ;
                    ;one minute time delay
                    ;
0033  11B004  D1M:    LXI    D,04B0H   ;load count
0036  CD2900  D1MA:   CALL   D50       ;waste 50 ms
0039  1B              DCX    D         ;decrement count
003A  7A              MOV    A,D       ;test count for 0
003B  B3              ORA    E
003C  C23600          JNZ    D1MA      ;if count not 0
003F  C9              RET
```

A close examination of the timing chart indicates that the machine must be filled with water for one minute in all types of operations, so a subroutine for filling would be useful. The output condition for each step of the dishwasher sequence is stored in a memory location so that the interrupt, which occurs whenever the door is opened, can suspend the operation until the door is closed. This is illustrated in this subroutine and all subsequent subroutines that control an external event.

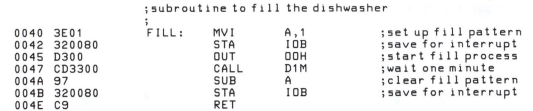

```
;subroutine to fill the dishwasher
;
0040  3E01      FILL:   MVI    A,1      ;set up fill pattern
0042  320080            STA    IOB      ;save for interrupt
0045  D300              OUT    00H      ;start fill process
0047  CD3300            CALL   D1M      ;wait one minute
004A  97                SUB    A        ;clear fill pattern
004B  320080            STA    IOB      ;save for interrupt
004E  C9                RET
```

FIGURE 13–5 The flowchart of the microprocessor-based dishwasher system program.

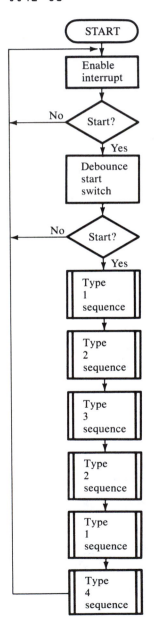

The next routine to be developed will cause the machine to fill with water; run the motor for four minutes; and, during the fifth minute of motor operation, empty the machine of all water. The motor activates a pump that empties the machine when a solenoid is held open for the last minute of operation. This sequence is the type 1 sequence identified in the main program as MOTOR.

```
                     ;subroutine for type-1 sequence
                     ;
004F  CD4000  MOTOR:  CALL    FILL        ;fill dishwasher
0052  3E02            MVI     A,2         ;set motor pattern
0054  320080          STA     IOB         ;save for interrupt
0057  D300            OUT     00H         ;start motor
0059  2604            MVI     H,4         ;load count
005B  CD3300  MOT1:   CALL    D1M         ;wait one minute
005E  25              DCR     H           ;decrement count
005F  C25B00          JNZ     MOT1        ;wait 4 minutes
0062  3E0A    DRAIN:  MVI     A,0AH       ;set motor and drain
0064  320080          STA     IOB         ;save for interrupt
0067  D300            OUT     00H         ;drain dishwasher
0069  CD3300          CALL    D1M         ;wait one minute
006C  97              SUB     A           ;clear pattern
006D  320080          STA     IOB         ;save pattern
0070  D300            OUT     00H         ;stop process
0072  C9              RET
```

The type 2 mode of operation is identical to type 1, except that the heater is turned on for three minutes in the middle of the sequence. In the main program this is identified as subroutine MOTORH, which follows.

```
                     ;subroutine for type-2 sequence
                     ;
0073  CD4000  MOTORH: CALL    FILL        ;fill dishwasher
0076  3E02            MVI     A,2         ;set motor pattern
0078  320080          STA     IOB         ;save for interrupt
007B  D300            OUT     00H         ;start motor
007D  CD3300          CALL    D1M         ;wait one minute
0080  3E06            MVI     A,6         ;motor and heater
0082  320080          STA     IOB         ;save for interrupt
0085  D300            OUT     00H         ;heater and motor on
0087  2603            MVI     H,3         ;load count
0089  CD3300  MOTH1:  CALL    D1M         ;wait one minute
008C  25              DCR     H           ;decrement count
008D  C28900          JNZ     MOTH1       ;wait 3 minutes
0090  3E02            MVI     A,2         ;set motor pattern
0092  320080          STA     IOB         ;save for interrupt
0095  D300            OUT     00H         ;run motor
0097  CD3300          CALL    D1M         ;wait one minute
009A  C36200          JMP     DRAIN       ;drain machine
```

The next subroutine is very short because it uses the MOTORH subroutine to perform all of its tasks except the dispensing of soap.

```
                     ;subroutine for type-3 sequence
                     ;
009D  CD7300  MOTORS: CALL    MOTORH      ;do type-2 sequence
00A0  3EC0            MVI     A,0C0H      ;set soap pattern
00A2  320080          STA     IOB         ;save for interrupt
00A5  30              SIM                 ;set SOD to dispense soap
```

```
00A6   CD2900              CALL    D50             ;wait 100 ms
00A9   CD2900              CALL    D50
00AC   97                  SUB     A               ;clear pattern
00AD   320080              STA     IOB             ;save for interrupt
00B0   3E40                MVI     A,40H           ;set soap pattern
00B2   30                  SIM                     ;soap off
00B3   C9                  RET
```

The next subroutine controls the heating cycle, which lasts for 30 minutes.

```
                           ;subroutine for type-4 sequence
                           ;
00B4   3E04     HEAT:      MVI     A,4             ;set heater pattern
00B6   320080              STA     IOB             ;save for interrupt
00B9   D300                OUT     00H             ;heater on
00BB   3E1E                MVI     A,1EH           ;load count
00BD   CD3300   HEAT1:     CALL    D1M             ;wait one minute
00C0   25                  DCR     H               ;decrement counter
00C1   C2BD00              JNZ     HEAT1           ;wait 30 minutes
00C4   97                  SUB     A               ;clear pattern
00C5   320080              STA     IOB             ;save pattern for interrupt
00C8   D300                OUT     00H             ;heater off
00CA   C9                  RET
```

The last and most important part of the software is the interrupt service subroutine for the door interlock. This routine must be able to turn off all external operations while the door is ajar and must reenable them when the door is closed. This is all handled through the IOB information that is stored in the RAM.

```
                           ;Interrupt service subroutine
                           ;
00CB   F5       RST55:     PUSH    PSW             ;save registers
00CC   C5                  PUSH    B
00CD   CD2900              CALL    D50             ;debounce door sensor
00D0   3E40                MVI     A,40H
00D2   30                  SIM                     ;soap off
00D3   97                  SUB     A               ;clear pattern
00D4   D300                OUT     00H             ;stop everything
00D6   20       RSTA:      RIM                     ;get I5.5
00D7   E610                ANI     10H
00D9   C2D600              JNZ     RSTA            ;wait for closed door
00DC   3A0080              LDA     IOB             ;get IOB pattern
00DF   B7                  ORA     A               ;test for soap
00E0   FAE700              JM      SOAP            ;if soap
00E3   FB       OUTS:      EI                      ;enable interrupts
00E4   C1                  POP     B               ;restore registers
00E5   F1                  POP     PSW
00E6   C9                  RET
00E7   30       SOAP:      SIM                     ;soap on
00E8   C3E300              JMP     OUTS
```

This circuit and its associated software illustrate quite a few principles of the real-time control of a machine. They also illustrate the usefulness of an interrupt in halting or temporarily suspending the control system.

The entire system would have fit on one 8755A combination I/O and EPROM device, but subroutines could not have been incorporated, since no RAM is present in this device. The space required to implement an 8755A-based system in this text is prohibitive because of the length of the program. The industrious student may want to try the suggested problems at the end of this chapter.

POINT-OF-SALES TERMINAL 13–2

Point-of-sales (POS) terminals or cash registers can be simple devices that handle simple entries, or they can be complex devices linked to larger computer systems. The latter type of POS terminal can keep track of inventory and look up the price of any item that the store might sell. To do this, it must contain some form of interface to the larger system and a vast amount of internal data storage. Some newer POS terminals can also verify the credit of the purchaser by contacting the credit department's computer or even a commercial bank's computer system.

This section deals with the simpler form of POS terminal—one that might be found in the corner Mom and Pop food market. Since this type of store cannot afford an inventory computer, and since it has a limited stock of items, it can manage with a simpler POS terminal. The type discussed in this section would cost well under three hundred dollars and maintains an accurate record of tax and sales data for the owners of the market.

Point-of-Sales Terminal Hardware

A basic POS terminal contains a keyboard for data entry, a set of numeric displays, and a cash drawer. The last item is not present in the simplest types of POS terminals but is included in the terminal presented in this discussion.

Figure 13–6 depicts the basic keyboard and display layout of the POS terminal developed in this section. There are the numeric keys 0 through 9 for data entry, a void key to erase erroneous entries, a clear entry key, a taxable department key, a nontaxable department key, a tax key, and a total or final sales key. In addition to the keyboard entry keys, there is also a keyswitch that allows the owner to program the tax table into the machine and another to read the department keys, tax data, and total sales key at the end of each day.

The Display Section

The display section consists of 6 seven-segment numeric displays that allow sales of up to $9999.99 in a single day, large enough for most small stores.

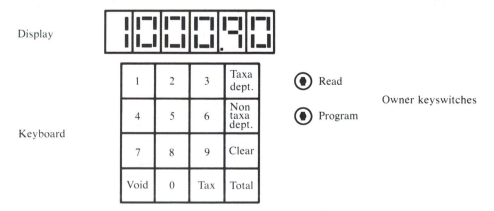

FIGURE 13–6 The keyboard and display layout for the 8085A-based point-of-sales terminal.

Figure 13–7 illustrates the flowchart for the program of this POS terminal. The displaying of data does not appear in this flowchart because display data is handled by a periodic interrupt that appears on a separate flowchart in figure 13–8.

The Memory

The RAM read/write memory is used for the system stack and also to store such information as the display data and the sales totalizers for the register. A complete schematic diagram for the memory and the rest of the hardware is illustrated in figure 13–9. Following is a complete listing of the data locations in the RAM:

```
                        ;memory assignments for Data
                        ;
8000                            ORG        8000H
                        ;
8000            DISP:   DS         3             ;display data
8003            TEMP:   DS         3             ;temporary storage
8006            TAX:    DS         3             ;tax total
8009            NTX:    DS         3             ;nontaxable total
800C            TTAX:   DS         3             ;tax temporary
800F            NTXT:   DS         3             ;nontaxable temporary
8012            TXT:    DS         3             ;taxable temporary
8015            TX:     DS         3             ;taxable total
8018            TOTAL   DS         3             ;total sale
801B            RATE:   DS         1             ;tax rate
801C            LOOK:   DS         20            ;tax lookup table
```

The tax lookup table is used by the program to determine the tax breaks for the cents column below and above one dollar. The tax rate on whole dollars is determined by the value stored at memory location RATE when the machine is programmed by the user. This is necessary because the tax breaks below and above one dollar are not the same, and some states even charge a different percentage tax on amounts of less than one dollar. The tax rate can be programmed in mills so that stores in various states, counties, and cities can adjust the rate to the exact amount of the local tax.

System Initialization Dialog

When power is first applied to this system, the 8156 programmable I/O device must be initialized along with the interrupt structure of the 8085A. In addition to this, the display memory and totalizers must also be cleared to zero. It is assumed that the system power supply is backed up by battery in case of a power failure.

```
                        ;initialization dialog for the POS
                        ;
0000                            ORG        0
                        ;
0000  310081    RESET:  LXI        SP,8100H      ;initialize stack
0003  213080            LXI        H,LOOK+20     ;point to data
0006  97                SUB        A             ;clear Acc
0007  77        RESETA: MOV        M,A           ;clear data
0008  2D                DCR        L             ;decrement count
0009  F20700            JP         RESETA        ;repeat until cleared
000C  3E70              MVI        A,070H        ;program timer to
000E  D384              OUT        84H           ;divide by 6000
0010  3E57              MVI        A,57H
0012  D385              OUT        85H
0014  3ECD              MVI        A,0CDH        ;port A & C = output
```

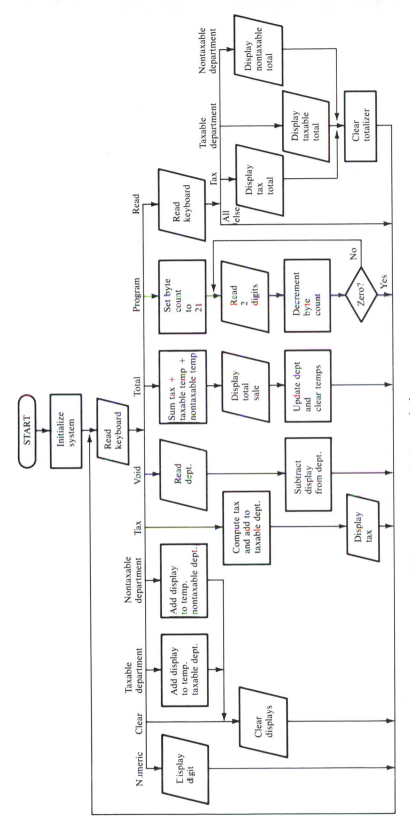

FIGURE 13-7 The system flowchart for the 8085A-based point-of-sales terminal.

FIGURE 13–8 The flowchart of
the interrupt service subroutine
that handles the displaying of data.

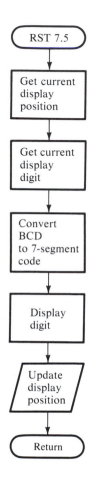

```
0016  D380                    OUT      80H          ;port B = input
0018  3E0B                    MVI      A,0BH        ;enable RST 7.5
001A  30                      SIM
001B  FB                      EI                    ;start display
001C  C37D00                  JMP      SYSTEM       ;enter system software
```

The initialization dialog illustrated has cleared the system memory, intialized the programmable I/O device, enabled the display interrupt, and jumped over the RST 7.5 interrupt service subroutine to the system software. The last step is necessary because the RST
7.5 interrupt service subroutine must be located beginning at memory location 003CH.

System Software

The system software has been implemented directly from the flowchart of figure 13–7.

```
                          ;main system program begins here
                          ;
007D  CDA300     SYSTEM:  CALL     INKEY        ;read keyboard
0080  78                  MOV      A,B          ;get key code
0081  D60A                SUI      10           ;is it a number?
0083  DAA502              JC       NUMB         ;if a number
0086  87                  ADD      A            ;form lookup bias
```

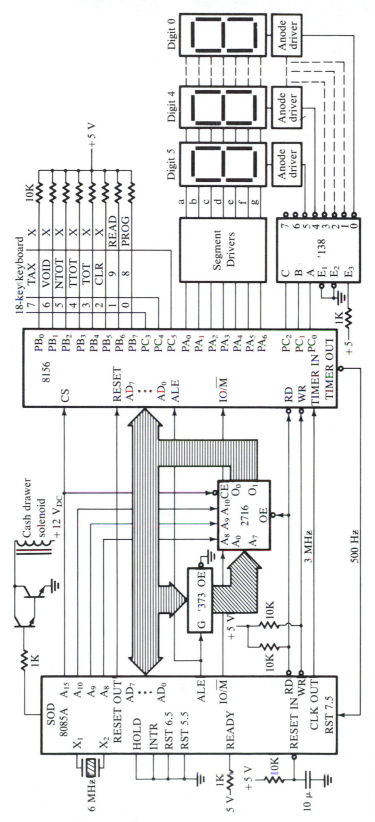

FIGURE 13-9 The 8085A-based point-of-sales terminal schematic diagram.

```
0087  5F            MOV   E,A
0088  1600          MVI   D,0
008A  219300        LXI   H,JTAB     ;address lookup table
008D  19            DAD   D          ;form address
008E  5E            MOV   E,M        ;get jump address
008F  23            INX   H
0090  66            MOV   H,M
0091  6B            MOV   L,E
0092  E9            PCHL             ;jump to routine
                    ;
                    ;lookup table for special keys
                    ;
0093  DB00   JTAB:  DW    CLEAR      ;clear entry key
0095  FE00          DW    TOT        ;total sale key
0097  7801          DW    TTOT       ;taxable entry key
0099  8701          DW    NTOT       ;nontaxable entry key
009B  1402          DW    VOID       ;void key
009D  9601          DW    TAXI       ;tax key
009F  4402          DW    PROG       ;program key
00A1  7902          DW    READ       ;read key
```

The system software is rather simple since its main purpose is to look at the keyboard and sort out the information as it is entered.

Display Interrupt Service Subroutine

The interrupt service subroutine is called once every 2 ms by the timer located inside the 8156. This periodic interrupt displays the next digit on the LED display.

```
                    ;display interrupt service subroutine
                    ;
003C                ORG   3CH
                    ;
003C  F5     RST75: PUSH  PSW        ;save registers
003D  E5            PUSH  H
003E  3A0380        LDA   TEMP       ;get digit address
0041  B7            ORA   A          ;clear carry
0042  1F            RAR              ;divide by 2
0043  6F            MOV   L,A        ;set data address
0044  210080        LXI   H,DISP     ;address display data
0047  6F            MOV   L,A        ;set data address
0048  7E            MOV   A,M        ;get display data
0049  DA5000        JC    RST7A      ;if right half
004C  0F            RRC              ;if not make it
004D  0F            RRC              ;the right half
004E  0F            RRC
004F  0F            RRC
0050  E60F   RST7A: ANI   0FH        ;mask off left half
0052  217300        LXI   H,DTAB     ;address lookup table
0055  85            ADD   L
0056  6F            MOV   L,A
0057  7E            MOV   A,M        ;get data
0058  D381          OUT   81H        ;send data
005A  3A0380        LDA   TEMP       ;get position
005D  67            MOV   H,A        ;save position
005E  3C            INR   A
005F  FE06          CPI   6          ;test for last
0061  C26500        JNZ   RST7B      ;if last
0064  97            SUB   A          ;clear position
0065  320380 RST7B: STA   TEMP       ;save position
```

```
0068  DB83              IN      83H     ;read port C
006A  E6F8              ANI     0F8H    ;mask off position
006C  B4                ORA     H       ;insert new position
006D  D383              OUT     83H     ;select new position
006F  E1                POP     H       ;restore registers
0070  F1                POP     PSW
0071  FB                EI              ;enable interrupts
0072  C9                RET
                 ;
                 ;BCD to 7-segment lookup table
                 ;
0073  7E        DTAB:   DB      01111110B  ;    "0"
0074  30                DB      00110000B  ;    "1"
0075  6D                DB      01101101B  ;    "2"
0076  79                DB      01111001B  ;    "3"
0077  33                DB      00110011B  ;    "4"
0078  5B                DB      01011011B  ;    "5"
0079  5F                DB      01011111B  ;    "6"
007A  70                DB      01110000B  ;    "7"
007B  7F                DB      01111111B  ;    "8"
007C  7B                DB      01111011B  ;    "9"
```

The software illustrated for the display section requires that the code conversion lookup. table be located at a memory location that does not cross a page boundary. If the table does cross a page boundary, the software will require some modification.

The time required to service the displays is approximately 100 μs, which occurs once every 2 ms. This means that the display software uses only about 5 percent of the microprocessor's time, which creates no problem in a point-of-sales terminal.

Keyboard Scanning Software

The keyboard on this particular cash register consists of ten numeric, six exposed function, and two hidden special-function keys. The special-function keys allow data to be entered into the taxable or nontaxable departments and control the outcome of the sale.

The hidden special-purpose keys allow the register to be programmed for the state sales tax and also allow totals for each department to be read at the end of the day or at a change of operators. These keys are often controlled with a locking keyswitch to prevent tampering. See figure 13–10 for a detailed flowchart of this subroutine.

```
                 ;keyboard scanning subroutine
                 ;
00A3  01F003   INKEY:   LXI     B,03F0H   ;set counter and select
00A6  DB83              IN      83H       ;read port C
00A8  E607              ANI     7         ;get digit position
00AA  81                ADD     C         ;select column
00AB  D383              OUT     83H
00AD  DB82              IN      82H       ;read column
00AF  3C                INR     A         ;test for a key
00B0  CABF00            JZ      INKEY1    ;if a key
00B3  05                DCR     B         ;last column?
00B4  CAA300            JZ      INKEY     ;if last column
00B7  79                MOV     A,C       ;get new select code
00B8  87                ADD     A
00B9  F608              ORI     8         ;set bit 3
00BB  4F                MOV     C,A
00BC  C3A600            JMP     INKEY+3   ;next column
00BF  76       INKEY1:  HLT               ;debounce key
```

FIGURE 13–10 The flowchart
of the POS INKEY subroutine.

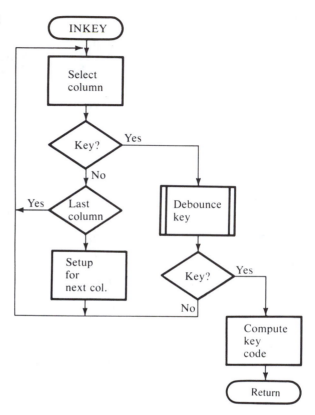

```
00C0  76                          HLT
00C1  76                          HLT
00C2  76                          HLT
00C3  76                          HLT
00C4  76                          HLT
00C5  DB82                        IN      82H         ;read column
00C7  3C                          INR     A           ;test for a key
00C8  CAA300                      JZ      INKEY       ;if noise
00CB  3D                          DCR     A
00CC  4F                          MOV     C,A         ;compute key code
00CD  3E03                        MVI     A,3
00CF  90                          SUB     B
00D0  87                          ADD     A
00D1  87                          ADD     A
00D2  87                          ADD     A
00D3  47                          MOV     B,A
00D4  4F                          MOV     C,A
00D5  07        INKEY2:           RLC
00D6  D0                          RNC
00D7  04                          INR     B
00D8  C3D500                      JMP     INKEY2
```

The INKEY subroutine scans the keyboard until a valid keystroke is detected. Once
detected, the subroutine waits for the key to stop bouncing, since noise could have triggered a response. This procedure is accomplished by a series of six HLT instructions. The

HLT instruction waits until an interrupt occurs before execution continues. Since an interrupt occurs every 2 ms, the amount of time delay caused by the HLT instructions will be 10–12 ms. In general, this is ample time for a keyswitch to be debounced.

Once debouncing is completed, the exact key location is determined, and a return occurs with the code of the keystroke in the B register.

Clear Function Key

Because the clear function is the easiest to understand, it is presented first. This function merely clears the display register in memory locations 8000H through 8002H. Included with the clear function is the return to system point, RETSY, which checks the keyboard for a key release.

```
                      ;clear function key subprogram
                      ;
00DB  CDF300   CLEAR:  CALL    CLRD       ;clear display
00DE  DB82     RETSY:  IN      82H        ;wait for key release
00E0  3C               INR     A
00E1  C2DE00           JNZ     RETSY      ;if not released
00E4  76               HLT                ;debounce release
00E5  76               HLT
00E6  76               HLT
00E7  76               HLT
00E8  76               HLT
00E9  76               HLT
00EA  DB82             IN      82H
00EC  3C               INR     A
00ED  C2DE00           JNZ     RETSY      ;if noise
00F0  C37D00           JMP     SYSTEM     ;return to system
                      ;
                      ;clear display memory subroutine
                      ;
00F3  210000   CLRD:   LXI     H,0        ;clear display memory
00F6  220080           SHLD    DISP
00F9  7C               MOV     A,H
00FA  320280           STA     DISP+2
00FD  C9               RET
```

Total Function Key

The total key, which is used to total a sale, must add the contents of the taxable temp location, the nontaxable temp location, and the tax temp location together to form the total sales price. Once this is accomplished, it must then update the totals of all three items and open the cash drawer.

```
                      ;total function key subprogram
                      ;
00FE  CDF300   TOT:    CALL    CLRD       ;clear display
0101  210080           LXI     H,DISP     ;address display
0104  110C80           LXI     D,TTAX     ;address TTAX
0107  CD6801           CALL    SUM        ;add TTAX to display
010A  110F80           LXI     D,NTXT     ;address NTXT
010D  CD6801           CALL    SUM        ;add NTXT to display
0110  111280           LXI     D,TXT      ;address TXT
0113  CD6801           CALL    SUM        ;add TXT to display
                      ;
                      ;update tax
                      ;
```

```
0116  210680              LXI      H,TAX        ;address TAX
0119  110C80              LXI      D,TTAX       ;address TTAX
011C  CD6801              CALL     SUM          ;add TTAX to TAX
                      ;
                      ;update nontaxable total
                      ;
011F  210980              LXI      H,NTX        ;address NTX
0122  110F80              LXI      D,NTXT       ;point to NTXT
0125  CD6801              CALL     SUM          ;add NTXT to NTX
                      ;
                      ;update taxable total
                      ;
0128  211580              LXI      H,TX         ;address TX
012B  111280              LXI      D,TXT        ;address TXT
012E  CD6801              CALL     SUM          ;add TXT to TX
                      ;
                      ;form new grand total
                      ;
0131  211880              LXI      H,TOTAL      ;address TOTAL
0134  111280              LXI      D,TXT        ;address TXT
0137  CD6801              CALL     SUM          ;add TXT to TOTAL
013A  110F80              LXI      D,NTXT       ;address NTXT
013D  CD6801              CALL     SUM          ;add NTXT to TOTAL
0140  110C80              LXI      D,TTAX       ;address TTAX
0143  CD6801              CALL     SUM          ;add TTAX to TOTAL
                      ;
                      ;clear temporary registers
                      ;
0146  210C80              LXI      H,TTAX       ;address registers
0149  060C                MVI      B,12         ;set count
014B  97                  SUB      A            ;get 0
014C  77         TOTAL1:  MOV      M,A
014D  23                  INX      H
014E  05                  DCR      B
014F  C24C01              JNZ      TOTAL1       ;until cleared
                      ;
                      ;open cash drawer
                      ;
0152  0632                MVI      B,50         ;load count
0154  3EC0                MVI      A,0C0H       ;set SOD
0156  30                  SIM
0157  76         TOTAL2:  HLT                   ;wait 2 ms
0158  05                  DCR      B
0159  C25701              JNZ      TOTAL2
015C  3E40                MVI      A,40H        ;clear SOD
015E  30                  SIM
                      ;
                      ;wait for next sale
                      ;
015F  CDA300              CALL     INKEY        ;get next key
0162  CDF300              CALL     CLRD         ;clear display
0165  C38000              JMP      SYSTEM+3
                      ;
                      ;summation subroutine
                      ;
0168  E5         SUM:     PUSH     H            ;save pointer
0169  0603                MVI      B,3          ;load count
016B  B7                  ORA      A            ;clear carry
016C  1A         SUM1:    LDAX     D            ;get byte
016D  8E                  ADC      M            ;add byte
```

```
016E  27                  DAA                   ;make result BCD
016F  77                  MOV       M,A         ;save result
0170  23                  INX       H           ;increment pointers
0171  13                  INX       D
0172  05                  DCR       B           ;decrement count
0173  C26C01              JNZ       SUM1
0176  E1                  POP       H
0177  C9                  RET
```

Taxable Function Key

The taxable function key stores whatever value is entered into the keyboard into the temporary taxable department. This value is displayed at the same time on the numeric displays.

```
                          ;taxable function key subprogram
                          ;
0178  211280    TTOT:     LXI       H,TXT       ;address TXT
017B  110080              LXI       D,DISP      ;address display
017E  CD6801              CALL      SUM         ;add display to TXT
0181  CDF300              CALL      CLRD        ;clear display
0184  C3DE00              JMP       RETSY       ;return to system
```

Nontaxable Function Key

The nontaxable function key is used whenever the customer purchases nontaxable merchandise. As with the taxable function key, the display is added to the temporary nontaxable total and then cleared.

```
                          ;nontaxable function key subprogram
                          ;
0187  210F80    NTOT:     LXI       H,NTXT      ;address NTXT
018A  110080              LXI       D,DISP      ;address display
018D  CD6801              CALL      SUM         ;add display to NTXT
0190  CDF300              CALL      CLRD        ;clear display
0193  C3DE00              JMP       RETSY       ;return to system
```

Tax Function Key

The tax function key is used just before a sale is complete to compute the sales tax. In other words, to tend the sale, the tax key followed by the total key is the normal sequence.

Whenever the tax function key is depressed, it calculates the amount of sales tax based on programmed tax rate. This is accomplished by looking up the amount of sales tax in a tax table. The table contains the amount of tax on the first dollar, followed by the amount of tax on subsequent pennies of the total amount of the taxable sale.

For example, suppose that a state has a 5 percent sales tax with the rate shown in table 13–1.

The lower cent breaks are stored in the lookup table, beginning with a 10. These amounts are stored in the following BCD order: 10, 20, 35, 65, 85, 00, 00, 00, 00, 00, 10, 30, 50, 70, 90, 00, 00, 00, and 00. The first ten locations contain the breakpoints under one dollar, and the second set of ten locations contains the penny breakpoints over one dollar. Memory location RATE contains the tax rate in mills; in this example, RATE contains a 50H (50 BCD), or 50 mills, for a 5 percent sales tax. Figure 13–11 illustrates the flowchart for the tax function key.

TABLE 13–1 5% sales tax
breakpoints.

Price	Tax
$0.10 to $0.19	$.01
$0.20 to $0.34	$.02
$0.35 to $0.64	$.03
$0.65 to $0.84	$.04
$0.85 to $1.09	$.05
$1.10 to $1.29	$.06
$1.30 to $1.49	$.07
$1.50 to $1.69	$.08
$1.70 to $1.89	$.09
$1.90 to $2.09	$.10

```
                    ;tax function key subprogram
                    ;
0196  2A1380        TAXI:     LHLD      TXT+1       ;get dollar amount
0199  7C                      MOV       A,H         ;check for no dollars
019A  B5                      ORA       L
019B  C2A701                  JNZ       TAX1        ;if one or more
019E  211C80                  LXI       H,LOOK      ;address tax table
01A1  CDE901                  CALL      GETX        ;compute tax on cents
01A4  C3DE00                  JMP       RETSY       ;return to system
```

FIGURE 13–11 The flowchart
of the TAX subprogram.

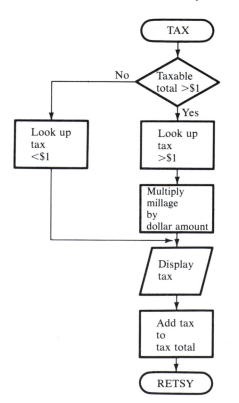

```
01A7  212480      TAX1:   LXI     H,LOOK + 8    ;address tax table
01AA  CDE901              CALL    GETX          ;compute tax on cents
01AD  3A1B80              LDA     RATE          ;get tax rate
01B0  5F                  MOV     E,A
01B1  1600                MVI     D,0
01B3  2A1380              LHLD    TXT + 1       ;get taxable amount
01B6  44                  MOV     B,H           ;copy to BC
01B7  4D                  MOV     C,L
01B8  79          TAX2:   MOV     A,C           ;compute dollar tax
01B9  85                  ADD     L
01BA  27                  DAA
01BB  6F                  MOV     L,A
01BC  D2CB01              JNC     TAX3          ;if no overflow
01BF  78                  MOV     A,B
01C0  8C                  ADC     H
01C1  27                  DAA
01C2  67                  MOV     H,A
01C3  D2CB01              JNC     TAX3          ;if no overflow
01C6  57                  MOV     D,A
01C7  CE00                ACI     0
01C9  27                  DAA
01CA  57                  MOV     D,A
01CB  7B          TAX3:   MOV     A,E           ;decrement millage
01CC  C699                ADI     99H
01CE  27                  DAA
01CF  5F                  MOV     E,A
01D0  C2B801              JNZ     TAX2
01D3  010C80              LXI     B,TTAX        ;address tax
01D6  0A                  LDAX    B
01D7  85                  ADD     L
01D8  27                  DAA
01D9  02                  STAX    B
01DA  03                  INX     B             ;address next
01DB  0A                  LDAX    B
01DC  8C                  ADC     H
01DD  27                  DAA
01DE  02                  STAX    B
01DF  03                  INX     B             ;address last
01E0  8A                  ADC     D
01E1  27                  DAA
01E2  02                  STAX    B
01E3  CD0302              CALL    GETX3         ;display tax
01E6  C3DE00              JMP     RETSY         ;return to system

                  ;
                  ;lookup tax and display it
                  ;
01E9  0600        GETX:   MVI     B,0           ;set cents count
01EB  3A1280      GETX1:  LDA     TXT           ;get cents
01EE  BE                  CMP     M             ;check table
01EF  DAF901              JC      GETX2         ;if found
01F2  23                  INX     H             ;address next entry
01F3  04                  INR     B             ;bump 1 penny
01F4  7E                  MOV     A,M           ;test for last
01F5  B7                  ORA     A
01F6  C2EB01              JNZ     GETX1         ;if not last
01F9  78          GETX2:  MOV     A,B           ;get tax
01FA  320C80              STA     TTAX          ;save tax
01FD  210000              LXI     H,0
0200  220D80              SHLD    TTAX + 1
```

```
0203  210C80      GETX3:    LXI      H,TTAX        ;display tax
0206  110080                LXI      D,DISP
0209  0603                  MVI      B,3
020B  7E          GETX4:    MOV      A,M
020C  12                    STAX     D
020D  23                    INX      H
020E  13                    INX      D
020F  05                    DCR      B
0210  C20B02                JNZ      GETX4
0213  C9                    RET
```

Void Function Key

The void key erases erroneous data from either of the two departments in this register. The void key voids the displayed amount when it is depressed if it is followed by the taxable or nontaxable entry key. The void subprogram is pictured in the flowchart of figure 13–12.

For example, if the display indicates one dollar, and that is the amount to be erased from the taxable department, the void key is depressed and followed by the taxable function key. This procedure erases one dollar from that total.

```
                       ;void function key subprogram
                       ;
0214  CDA300      VOID:     CALL     INKEY         ;get key
0217  78                    MOV      A,B           ;get key code
0218  FE0E                  CPI      14            ;check for void
021A  CA1402                JZ       void          ;if still void
021D  211280                LXI      H,TXT         ;address TXT
0220  FE0C                  CPI      12            ;test for taxable key
0222  CA2D02                JZ       VOID1         ;if taxable
0225  FE0D                  CPI      13            ;test for nontaxable
0227  C2DE00                JNZ      RETSY         ;return on error
```

FIGURE 13–12 The flowchart of the VOID subprogram.

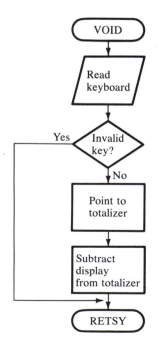

```
022A  210F80            LXI    H,NTXT     ;address NTXT
022D  0E03     VOID1:   MVI    C,3        ;load counter
022F  110080            LXI    D,DISP     ;address display
0232  1A       VOID2:   LDAX   D          ;form difference
0233  47                MOV    B,A
0234  3E9A              MVI    A,9AH
0236  98                SBB    B
0237  86                ADD    M
0238  27                DAA
0239  77                MOV    M,A
023A  3F                CMC
023B  23                INX    H
023C  13                INX    D
023D  0D                DCR    C
023E  C23202            JNZ    VOID2
0241  C3DE00            JMP    RETSY      ;return to system
```

This software will not detect an underflow condition of the targeted department. In practice it is included to prevent voiding too much money from any department.

Special Function Program Tax Rate

The program tax rate function, which is usually controlled by a locking keyswitch, is used only after a massive power failure depletes the energy stored in the batteries used for backup, or if a change in the sales tax is legislated. The flowchart for this subprogram is depicted in figure 13–13.

To program the register, this keyswitch is activated and followed by exactly 42 numeric entries on the keyboard. The first 2 are the tax rate in mills up to 99 mills (or 9.9 cents), followed by the 40 numeric keystrokes for the tax break table. The dealer normally supplies this information to the end user.

```
                        ;special function program tax rate key subprogram
                        ;
0244  211B80   PROG:    LXI    H,RATE     ;address RATE
0247  1615              MVI    D,21       ;set byte count
0249  CD6A02   PROG1:   CALL   INKEYX     ;get digit
024C  78                MOV    A,B        ;get key code
024D  FE0A              CPI    10         ;test for error
024F  D2DE00            JNC    RETSY      ;if error
0252  07                RLC               ;shift to position
0253  07                RLC
0254  07                RLC
0255  07                RLC
0256  5F                MOV    E,A        ;save it
0257  CD6A02            CALL   INKEYX     ;get next digit
025A  78                MOV    A,B        ;get key code
025B  FE0A              CPI    10         ;test for error
025D  D2DE00            JNC    RETSY      ;if error
0260  B3                ORA    E          ;form byte
0261  77                MOV    M,A        ;save byte
0262  23                INX    H
0263  15                DCR    D          ;decrement byte count
0264  C24902            JNZ    PROG1      ;if not done
0267  C3DE00            JMP    RETSY      ;return to system
026A  DB82     INKEYX:  IN     82H        ;wait for key release
026C  B7                ORA    A
026D  C26A02            JNZ    INKEYX     ;if key not released
0270  76                HLT
```

FIGURE 13–13 The flowchart
of the PROG subprogram.

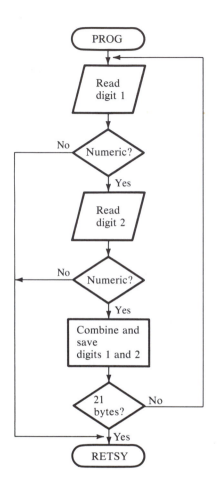

```
0271  76                 HLT
0272  76                 HLT
0273  76                 HLT
0274  76                 HLT
0275  76                 HLT
0276  C3A300             JMP        INKEY        ;go to INKEY
```

Special Function Read Department Totals

The read department totals key allows the operator to read out the daily totals from the
total tax, total taxable, or total nontaxable sales departments. It allows the owner to keep
accurate records of the daily receipts and tax information for the government. See figure
13–14 for a flowchart of this subprogram.

This key displays the totals in each department by striking each department key. After
the amount is displayed, the totalizer is automatically cleared to zero for the next sale day.
A normal sequence of usage is to strike the read key, tax key, taxable key, and nontaxable
key. You would, of course, want to pause between reads to write down the amounts.

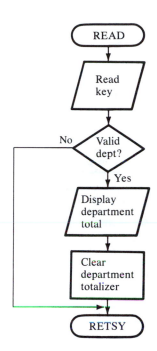

FIGURE 13-14 The flowchart of the READ subprogram.

```
                        ;special function read department totals subprogram
                        ;
0279  CD6A02    READ:   CALL    INKEYX      ;get key
027C  78                MOV     A,B         ;get key code
027D  FE0C              CPI     12          ;test for taxable
027F  211580            LXI     H,TX        ;address TX
0282  CA9502            JZ      READ1       ;if taxable
0285  FE0D              CPI     13          ;test for nontaxable
0287  210980            LXI     H,NTX       ;address NTX
028A  CA9502            JZ      READ1       ;if nontaxable
028D  FE0F              CPI     15          ;test for tax
028F  210680            LXI     H,TAX       ;address TAX
0292  C2DE00            JNZ     RETSY       ;if error
0295  110080    READ1:  LXI     D,DISP      ;address display
0298  0603              MVI     B,3         ;load count
029A  7E        READ2:  MOV     A,M         ;transfer to display
029B  12                STAX    D
029C  23                INX     H
029D  13                INX     D
029E  05                DCR     B
029F  C29A02            JNZ     READ2
02A2  C37902            JMP     READ
```

Numeric Keyboard Data

The numeric data from the keyboard is always moved into the display memory for display and used with the function keys. The display software is written so that numeric data enters the displays from the right-hand side, or by the "right entry method." The flow chart for the numeric keyboard data is pictured in figure 13-15.

FIGURE 13–15 The flowchart
of the NUMB subprogram.

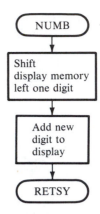

```
                                ;subroutine to process numeric keyboard data
                                ;
02A5  F5              NUMB:     PUSH     PSW              ;save current digit
02A6  2A0180                    LHLD     DISP+1           ;get most significant
02A9  29                        DAD      H                ;shift left 1 digit
02AA  29                        DAD      H
02AB  29                        DAD      H
02AC  29                        DAD      H
02AD  3A0080                    LDA      DISP             ;get least significant
02B0  07                        RLC                       ;shift left
02B1  07                        RLC
02B2  07                        RLC
02B3  07                        RLC
02B4  F5                        PUSH     PSW              ;save it
02B5  E615                      ANI      15H
02B7  B5                        ORA      L
02B8  6F                        MOV      L,A
02B9  220180                    SHLD     DISP+1
02BC  F1                        POP      PSW
02BD  E6F0                      ANI      0F0H
02BF  4F                        MOV      C,A
02C0  F1                        POP      PSW
02C1  B1                        ORA      C
02C2  320080                    STA      DISP
02C5  C3DE00                    JMP      RETSY            ;return to system
```

Software and Hardware Design Highlights

Some important features of this software are BCD arithmetic, interrupt processed display, and interrupt timed delays. These features have led to a very simple hardware configuration and a very structured software.

BCD arithmetic was selected for this application because the information is already in this form as it comes back from the keyboard, and it is required to be in this form for the display. Converting the data from BCD to binary and from binary to BCD would be a waste of effort since no complex arithmetic is performed on the data. This is also the case in many other applications. A general rule of thumb to follow is that if no complex arithmetic is to be performed in a system, it is better to keep the data in BCD form.

Interrupt processing the display frees the programmer from the drudgery of periodically updating the displays. The interrupt service subroutine completely handles this task.

In fact, in this design example, all that is required to change the display information is to change the contents of three memory locations.

Since a periodic interrupt is used in this system, time delays are extremely easy to implement by using the halt (HLT) command. The halt command waits until an interrupt occurs before processing proceeds with the next contiguous instruction. This feature allows a fairly accurate time delay to be created by stringing together a series of halt instructions.

SUMMARY

1 The dishwasher control circuit is an example of a "real-time" microprocessor-based system.
2 The timing in the dishwasher is provided by a 50-ms time delay, which is then used to develop one minute and other time delays.
3 There are four sequences that the dishwasher cycles through to wash the dishes.
4 An 8085A interrupt is used in the dishwasher whenever the door is opened during a wash. The door interlock causes this interrupt, which suspends the operation of the dishwasher until the door is closed.
5 A POS (point-of-sales) terminal, or cash register, is a simple device that contains a keyboard, display, and cash drawer. Although a POS can be much more complicated if it also includes a printer, bar code reader, and a computer interface, it is still the same basic machine.
6 The POS uses BCD arithmetic and stores all data in BCD form.
7 The POS discussed in the text uses an interrupt that occurs once per 2 ms to multiplex a set of six LED displays. Each time that an interrupt occurs, another display digit is selected and a BCD number is displayed.

Suggested Projects

1 Using the 8085A and any other device required, develop a traffic light controller for the intersection pictured in figure 13–16. This traffic light is to run at the times indicated in the example 24 hours per day. The lamp drivers are TTL-compatible and depicted in figure 13–17.

EXAMPLE 13–1

Timing North-South		Timing East-West	
Green	75 seconds	Green	28 seconds
Yellow	2 seconds	Yellow	2 seconds
Red	30 seconds	Red	77 seconds

2 Modify the system developed in question 1 so that the traffic light will flash red in all directions between the hours of 1 AM and 5 AM. The rate of flashing should

FIGURE 13–16 The traffic light intersection.

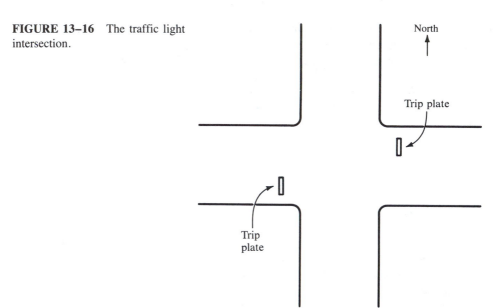

be on for a second and off for a second. To obtain the time of day, develop a real-time clock and interface it to the 8085A.

3 Modify the system in question 1 so that a trip plate can be used to modify the traffic flow pattern from the east or west direction. The trip plate may work only after the light has been red for 15 seconds (s) and then may hold this intersection green only for up to 80 s before turning the light yellow and then red.

  The trip plate section of the software must be able to detect a car and—if another car hits the plate within 5 seconds—extend the green time for up to 80 seconds maximum. Figure 13–18 illustrates a TTL-compatible trip plate with an active high output.

4 Develop the 8085A hardware and software for a coin changer mechanism. It must be able to accept coins in any denomination from 1 cent to 50 cents and dispense change in the fewest number of pennies, nickels, and dimes. The amount of money to be accepted is programmed through a set of switches located inside the vending machine. The programmable amount can be anything from 1 cent to $1.99.

  Your software must accept coins until the amount indicated on the internal switches has either been reached or exceeded; if it has been exceeded, it must

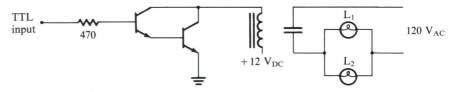

FIGURE 13–17 The traffic light lamp driver circuit.

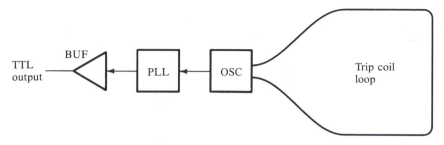

FIGURE 13–18   The block diagram of the trip plate sensor circuit for the traffic light problem.

dispense the fewest number of coins as change and send an active low pulse out the VEND pin for 20 ms.

As coins are inserted, a mechanical assembly that sorts them signals the microprocessor with a pulse indicating the denomination of the coin.

Once your program has detected and remembered the coin, it must drop it into the internal coin box by pulsing the DROP line for 100 ms. There is also a ''bent coin'' signal in case a defective coin is inserted into the machine. If a bent coin is detected, you must pulse the EJECT line for 120 ms to clear the coin slot.

To dispense change, the appropriate CH control line is activated for 100 ms to drop a coin out of the change slot of the vending machine. You must return only one coin at a time with a pause of at least 50 ms between coins for the mechanical ejection mechanism to function properly.

Table 13–2 illustrates all of the TTL input and TTL output connections that are to be interfaced to the 8085A.

Signal	Function
VEND	Used to vend merchandise from the machine attached to this changer
DROP	Used to accept a coin that has been placed into the mechanism
EJECT	Used to return a bent or defective coin
1C	One cent program input switch
2C	Two cents program input switch
5C	Five cents program input switch
10C	Ten cents program input switch
20C	Twenty cents program input switch
50C	Fifty cents program input switch
100C	One dollar program input switch
CH1	Returns a penny as change if pulsed for 100 ms
CH5	Returns a nickel as change if pulsed for 100 ms
CH10	Returns a dime as change if pulsed for 100 ms
CH25	Returns a quarter as change if pulsed for 100 ms

TABLE 13–2   Signal lines for the coin changer.

FIGURE 13–19 The pinout, block diagram, and truth table for the 7490 decade counter.

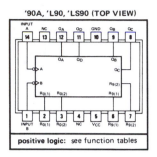

'90A, 'L90, 'LS90 (TOP VIEW)

positive logic: see function tables

'90A, 'L90, 'LS90
BCD COUNT SEQUENCE
(See Note A)

COUNT	OUTPUT			
	Q_D	Q_C	Q_B	Q_A
0	L	L	L	L
1	L	L	L	H
2	L	L	H	L
3	L	L	H	H
4	L	H	L	L
5	L	H	L	H
6	L	H	H	L
7	L	H	H	H
8	H	L	L	L
9	H	L	L	H

'90A, 'L90, 'LS90
BI-QUINARY (5-2)
(See Note B)

COUNT	OUTPUT			
	Q_A	Q_D	Q_C	Q_B
0	L	L	L	L
1	L	L	L	H
2	L	L	H	L
3	L	L	H	H
4	L	H	L	L
5	H	L	L	L
6	H	L	L	H
7	H	L	H	L
8	H	L	H	H
9	H	H	L	L

'90A, 'L90, 'LS90
RESET/COUNT FUNCTION TABLE

RESET INPUTS				OUTPUT			
$R_{0(1)}$	$R_{0(2)}$	$R_{9(1)}$	$R_{9(2)}$	Q_D	Q_C	Q_B	Q_A
H	H	L	X	L	L	L	L
H	H	X	L	L	L	L	L
X	X	H	H	H	L	L	H
X	L	X	L	COUNT			
L	X	L	X	COUNT			
L	X	X	L	COUNT			
X	L	L	X	COUNT			

NOTES: A. Output Q_A is connected to input B for BCD count.
B. Output Q_D is connected to input A for bi-quinary count.

5 Develop an IC test fixture that will automatically test the 7490 TTL decade counter. The pinout of this decade counter is pictured in figure 13–19 with a brief description of its operating characteristics.

Your system must completely test this device; if it is found faulty, the red LED must be lit; if good, the green LED must be lit. This test sequence must test the clear to zero, clear to nine, and count sequence of the counter at least 20 times without failure for a good indication. The test socket and two LED indicators are pictured in figure 13–20.

6 If the system in question 5 is to be able to test any 14-pin integrated TTL circuit, which changes must be made to the hardware?

7 Create a darkroom timer to control the length of time that the enlarger exposes the paper. The timer must be capable of exposing the paper in increments of 0.1 seconds, up to 10 minutes.

Time settings are dialed in on a series of rotary switches labeled in one-tenth seconds, seconds, and minutes (as illustrated in figure 13–21). The push button

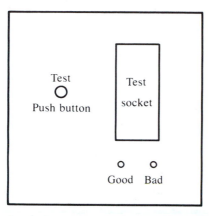

FIGURE 13–20 The control panel of the microprocessor-based TTL integrated circuit tester.

starts the timing sequence that applies AC power to the lamp in the enlarger for the preset amount of time.

8 Redevelop the dishwasher system presented in this chapter, using the 8755A combination EPROM and I/O interface adapter. Data on this device may be found in the Intel 8080A/8085A User's Manual.

You may not use any read/write memory to accomplish this task. Your circuit may include only the 8085A and the 8755A. (Hint: Subroutines can be developed without the use of the stack if the PCHL instruction is used correctly.)

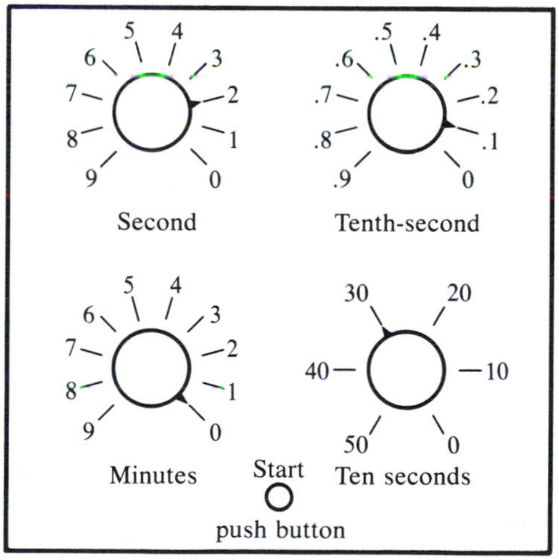

FIGURE 13–21 The control panel of a microprocessor-based darkroom timer.

SOURCE: Courtesy of Texas Instruments

14

MC6800 Application Examples

Upon completion of this chapter, you will be able to

1 Understand the operation of the 6800 in a complete system, including both the hardware operation and the software.

2 Learn about process control through the traffic light controller.

3 Use the 6800 in a data communications environment with the 6850 ACIA.

This chapter collects all of the separate techniques that you have learned throughout this textbook. Example problems that include memory interface, various forms of I/O interface, and digital communications have been illustrated. It is very important that you go through each of the example problems for ideas on hardware and software implementation.

For more examples, see the end of this chapter, which contains a series of projects that illustrate many of the techniques discussed in this text.

14–1 DATA CONCENTRATOR

Data concentrators are used in data communications environments to pack many slow channels of digital data onto one high-speed channel. For example, a department store may have 20 point-of-sales terminals that must be connected to a computer in another city. Instead of leasing 20 telephone lines for the fairly intermittent data from these in-store terminals, a data concentrator can be connected between the POS terminals and the computer in the other city. This connection does not reduce the speed of the system as far as the user is concerned; it only reduces the total system cost by replacing the 20 leased lines with 1.

6800 Data Concentrator Example
The example presented here has two low-speed channels concentrated onto one higher-speed channel for transmission to another system. The data on the low-speed channels are serial asynchronous data transmitted at 300 baud, and the data on the high-speed channel are asynchronous data transmitted at 4800 baud. For this example, we will consider only one-way communications between the two terminals and the remote system.

Figure 14–1 illustrates the protocol between the concentrator and the larger computer system. The data are preceded by an ID byte that indicates which terminal is transmitting the data. The ID byte is always followed by 15 bytes of information, allowing for a fairly efficient means of data transmission between each terminal and the remote computer system.

6800 Data Concentrator Hardware
The hardware for this application is pictured in the schematic of figure 14–2. The 6800 is surrounded by three 6850 ACIAs that receive serial data from the terminals and transmit serial data to the remote computer system. In addition to the ACIAs, there is a 128-byte RAM for data storage and a 1K-byte EPROM for program storage.

The decoder selects the EPROM for memory locations $FXXX, the RAM for locations $0XXX, and the ACIAs for locations $BXXX, $CXXX, and $DXXX. Data channel one uses $BXXX; data channel two uses $CXXX; $DXXX is used as the link between the remote computer and the data concentrator.

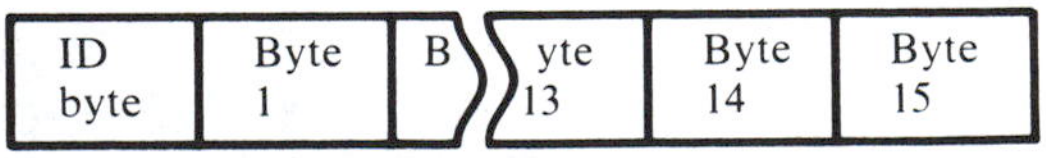

FIGURE 14–1 The protocol for the MC6800-based data concentrator.

ID byte	Byte 1	B	yte 13	Byte 14	Byte 15

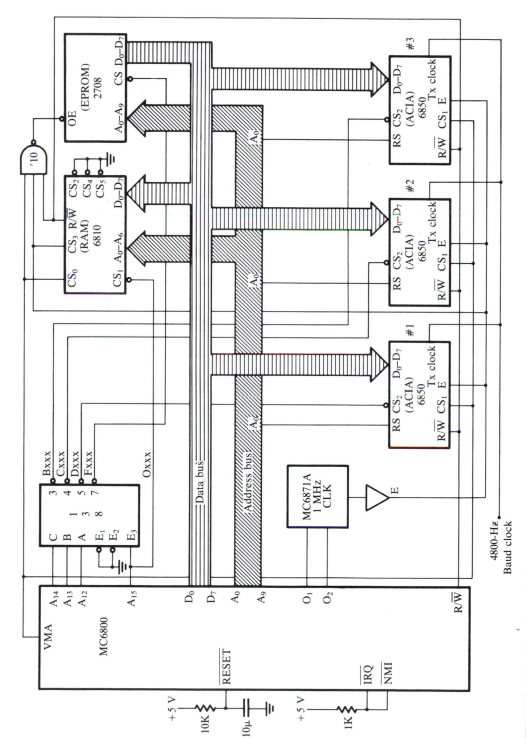

FIGURE 14-2 The schematic diagram of the MC6800 microprocessor-based data concentrator.

445

Data Concentrator Initialization Dialog

In this system the three ACIAs must be initialized to start the communications between the terminals and the remote system. This dialog resides at the location pointed to by the restart vector in locations $FFFE and $FFFF, which in this system is location $F000.

```
                              *data concentrator initialization dialog
                              *
F000                          ORG     $F000
F000  8609      START         LDAA    #$09            setup ACIA
F002  B7B000                  STAA    $B000           program ACIAs
F005  B7C000                  STAA    $C000
F008  7FD000                  CLR     $D000
F00B  8E007F                  LDS     #$007F          setup stack
F00E  CE0049                  LDX     #COUNT          address RAM data
F011  6F00      LOOP          CLR     X               clear memory data
F013  09                      DEX
F014  26FB                    BNE     LOOP
F016  6F00                    CLR     X
F017  8620                    LDAA    #32             setup queue two pointers
F019  9744                    STAA    IPNT2+1
F01B  9746                    STAA    OPNT2+1
```

The terminal ACIAs are programmed to divide the external clock source by 16, to transmit seven data bits with even parity, and to send one stop bit. The high-speed ACIA is programmed with the same data format, except that its internal divider is set up to divide by 1. The resulting transmission speed is 4800 baud.

Data Storage for the Data Concentrator

The data storage consists of two separate buffer areas in the memory. These hold data as they come from the two terminal devices and function as FIFOs, or queue memories.

```
                              *RAM storage
                              *
0000                          ORG     $0
0000            BUF1          RMB     32              terminal one buffer
0020            BUF2          RMB     32              terminal two buffer
0040            IPNT1         RMB     2               queue one pointers
0042            OPNT1         RMB     2
0044            IPNT2         RMB     2               queue two pointers
0046            OPNT2         RMB     2
0048  00        FLAG          FCB     0               Transmit flag
0049  00        COUNT         FCB     0               byte counter
```

The queue pointers are all initialized for the empty condition; that is, both the input and output pointers are equal in value. A full condition is indicated when the IPNT is one less than the OPNT.

ACIA Status Scanning Software

The purpose of ACIA status scanning software is to determine when an ACIA has received information or when it is ready to transmit information. This software immediately follows the system initialization dialog presented earlier. Figure 14–3 illustrates the flowchart of this software, which is the main program for the data concentrator.

FIGURE 14–3 The flowchart of the SYST program for the MC6800-based data concentrator.

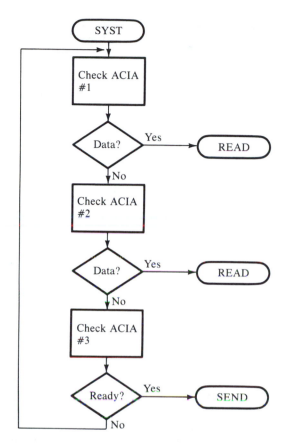

```
              *system scanning software
              *
F01D C601     SYST     LDAB    #1          set ACIA number
F01F B6B000            LDAA    $B000       get status one
F022 8D0D              BSR     CHKI        check ACIA one
F024 5C                INCB
F025 B6C000            LDAA    #C000       get status two
F028 8D07              BSR     CHKI        check ACIA two
F02A B6D000            LDAA    #D000       get status three
F02D 8D22              BSR     CHKO        check ACIA three
F02F 20EC              BRA     SYST        keep checking
```

The software is looped through continually until a ready condition on any receiver is detected or a ready condition in the transmitter is detected. Once detected, data are transmitted or received by subroutines presented later in this text.

```
              *subroutine to check ACIA receiver status
              *
F031 46       CHKI     RORA                RDRF to carry
F032 2501              BCS     READ
F034 39                RTS                 if no data
```

FIGURE 14–4 The flowchart of the READ subroutine.

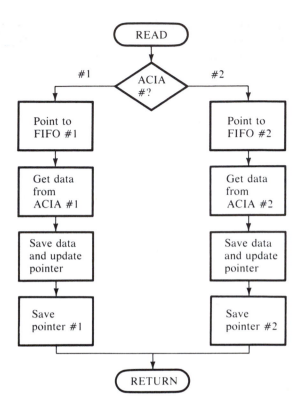

The subroutine illustrated checks the receiver of the selected ACIA to determine if it is ready with data. If it is not ready, a return from the subroutine occurs. If it is ready, the subroutine continues at location READ.

Reception Software

As the data are read from each terminal, they are stored in the terminal's queue, where they are held for later transmission by the high-speed ACIA. No attempt is made to detect a queue full condition, since this can never happen because of the speeds involved. Refer to figure 14–4 for a complete flowchart of this subroutine.

```
                          *subroutine that reads data from an ACIA
                          *
     F035 C102    READ     CMPB    #2        check for ACIA 2
     F037 2707             BEQ     READ2     if ACIA 2
     F039 DE40             LDX     IPNT1     point to queue 1
     F03B B6B000           LDAA    $B000     get data
     F03E A600             STAA    X         save data
     F040 8D6B             BSR     UPDAT
     F042 DF40             STX     IPNT1     save pointer
     F044 200B             BRA     READ3
     F046 DE44    READ2    LDX     IPNT2     point to queue 2
     F048 B6C000           LDAA    $C000     get data
```

```
F04B  A600              STAA    X            save data
F04D  8D5E              BSR     UPDAT
F04F  DF44              STX     IPNT2        save pointer
F051  39       READ3    RTS
```

Transmission Software

```
                        *subroutine that checks the transmitter
                        *
F052  8502    CHK0      BITA    #2           test TDRE
F054  2601              BNE     SEND
F056  39                RTS
```

This short subroutine determines whether the transmitter in the high-speed ACIA is ready for another byte of information. If it is not, a return from the subroutine occurs so that the remaining ACIAs can be tested.

The SEND subroutine transmits data to the remote system through the high-speed ACIA. The flowchart for this routine is pictured in figure 14–5, and the program itself follows.

```
                        *send subroutine for transmitting data
                        *through the high-speed ACIA
                        *
F057  9648    SEND      LDAA    FLAG         get busy flag
F059  261D              BNE     BUSY         if busy
F05B  9641              LDAA    IPNT1+1      get IPNT1
F05D  9143              CMPA    OPNT1+1      compare
F05F  2607              BNE     ST1          if not empty
F061  9645              LDAA    IPNT2+1      get IPNT2
F063  9147              CMPA    OPNT2+1      compare
F065  2605              BNE     ST2          if not empty
F067  39                RTS
```

This portion of the SEND subroutine checks whether the transmitter is currently sending data; if it is not, it continues to check whether data are available to transmit. If no data are present to transmit and the transmitter is not busy, it returns to scanning for input data through the two low-speed data channels.

```
                        *continuation of send when FIFOs are
                        *not empty
                        *
F068  8601    ST1       LDAA    #1           load ID number
F06A  2002              BRA     ST           send it
F06C  8602    ST2       LDAA    #2           load ID number
F06E  B7D001  ST        STAA    $D001        send ID
F071  9748              STAA    FLAG         save in flag
F073  860F              LDAA    #15          load byte count
F075  9749              STAA    COUNT        save count
F077  39                RTS
```

If the transmitter is not busy but data are available to transmit, this portion of the software sends the terminal number through the high-speed ACIA and also sets a byte

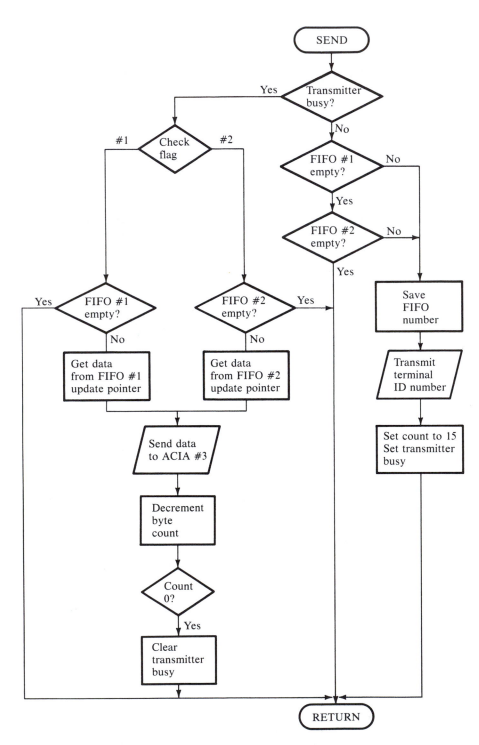

FIGURE 14–5 The flowchart of the SEND subroutine.

counter to 15. The byte counter contains the number of bytes that must follow the ID number. After transmitting the ID number, a return to scanning occurs so that additional data may be received.

```
                         *continuation of send
                         *
      F078 9648   BUSY    LDAA   FLAG      get flag
      F07A 8102           CMPA   #2        test for two
      F07C 2607           BNE    T1        if one
      F07E 9645           LDAA   IPNT2+1   get IPNT2+1
      F080 9147           CMPA   OPNT2+1   compare
      F082 261C           BNE    SEN2      send a byte
      F084 39             RTS
      F085 9641   T1      LDAA   IPNT1+1   get IPNT1+1
      F087 9143           CMPA   OPNT1+1   compare
      F089 2601           BNE    SEN1      send a byte
      F08B 39             RTS
```

If the transmitter has been sending data, it arrives at this section of the software to determine whether any data have been received. If so, a transfer occurs to either SEN1 or SEN2 to send the information. If not, control is returned, and it continues to search for more input data.

```
                     *data transmission portion of send
                     *
F08C DE42   SEN1    LDX    OPNT1      get OPNT1
F08E A600           LDAA   X          get data
F090 B7D001         STAA   $D001      send data
F093 8D18           BSR    UPDAT
F095 DF42           STX    OPNT1      save OPNT1
F097 7A0049 SENX    DEC    COUNT      decrement byte count
F09A 2603           BNE    RETS       if not finished
F09C 7F0048         CLR    FLAG       clear busy flag
F09F 39     RETS    RTS
F0A0 DE46   SEN2    LDX    OPNT2      get OPNT2
F0A2 A600           LDAA   X          get data
F0A4 B7D001         STAA   $D001      send data
F0A7 8D04           BSR    UPDAT
F0A9 DF46           STX    OPNT2      save OPNT2
F0AB 20EA           BRA    SENX       finish up
```

This software sends information through the high-speed ACIA and then decrements the byte counter. If the byte counter reaches zero, which indicates that all 15 bytes have been transferred, the FLAG is cleared so that the transmitter can start transmitting the next 15 bytes of data.

```
                     *increment a pointer and wrap it
                     *
      F0AD DF4A   UPDAT   STX    COUNT+1   save
      F0AF 964B           LDAA   COUNT+2   get pointer
      F0B1 84E0           ANDA   #$E0      strip most significant
      F0B3 36             PSHA             save it
```

```
F0B4  964B          LDAA    COUNT+2    get pointer
F0B6  4C            INCA               increment it
F0B7  841F          ANDA    #$1F       mask
F0B9  974B          STAA    COUNT+2    save it
F0BB  32            PULA               restore A
F0BC  9A4B          ORAA    COUNT+2    combine
F0BE  974B          STAA    COUNT+2    store it
F0C0  DE4A          LDX     COUNT+1    load index
F0C2  39            RTS
```

This subroutine increments the index register and stores the result back into the index register. It is a simple task, except that in this case the number must be a 5-bit cyclic number, which requires all of the special coding listed in the subroutine. Only the least significant five bits are incremented in this subroutine.

System Limitations

This system has one important limitation that should be noted. The low-speed data must continue in increments of 15 bytes. If this does not happen, the system hangs up with no output ever for one of the two channels. If this result is not acceptable, the system can be modified to send a byte at a time, preceded with the terminal number. The only problem with this is that the system's efficiency suffers.

14–2 TRAFFIC LIGHT CONTROLLER

Traffic light control by microprocessors is becoming commonplace in many large cities because these units are easily adjusted for different timing sequences and can be controlled by an external computer system. External computer control has increased traffic flow during peak hours and reduced the number of accidents in the cities where it has been tested.

The system illustrated in this text receives its timing sequence through a keyboard located at the controlled intersection. The keyboard also enters the time of day and other information, such as the times the traffic light should flash. This system also includes a set of trip plates to trip the light for one direction.

Traffic Light Controller Hardware

The hardware for the traffic light controller includes an MC6821, which scans the keyboard and controls the traffic lamps. In addition to the MC6821, an oscillator is included to provide the MC6800 with its clock and to act as a timing source for the nonmaskable interrupt input (NMI). Also included is a trip plate sensor that causes an interrupt to occur whenever a vehicle is in proximity with the trip plate. The trip plate itself is a loop of wire located just below the surface of the roadbed. When a vehicle sits over it, the metal in the vehicle changes the inductance of the loop, which can be sensed by the interface.

Figure 14–6 illustrates the MC6800 controller hardware, including the memory required and the appropriate device selection logic. The outputs of the decoder select the 1K-byte EPROM at address $FXXX, the 128-byte RAM at address $0XXX, and the MC6821 at address $EXXX.

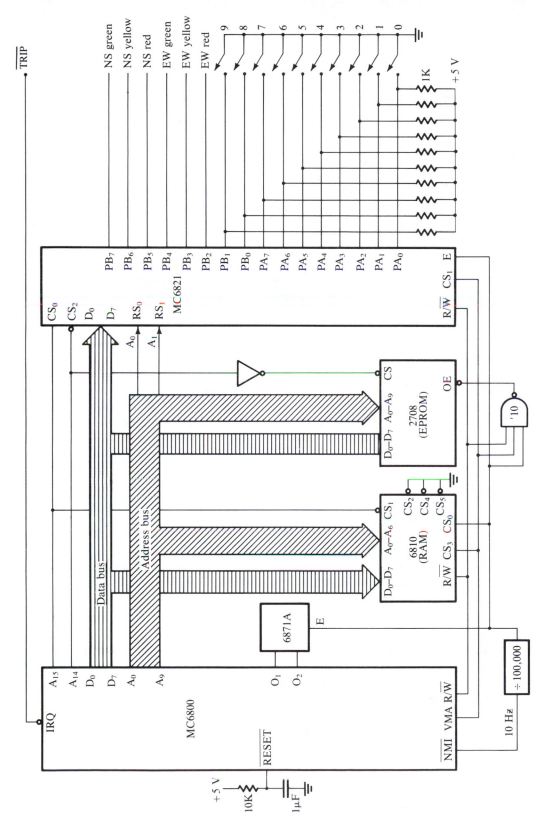

FIGURE 14-6 The schematic diagram of the MC6800-based traffic light controller.

RAM Storage Assignment

```
                    *RAM storage assignments
                    *
0000                          ORG    $0
                    *
0000        CLOCK     RMB    7         clock
0007        TIME      RMB    1         timer
0008        NSRED     RMB    1         north-south red
0009        NSGRE     RMB    1         north-south green
000A        NSYEL     RMB    1         north-south yellow
000B        EWRED     RMB    1         east-west red
000C        EWGRE     RMB    1         east-west green
000D        EWYEL     RMB    1         east-west yellow
000E        MAXTR     RMB    1         maximum trips
000F        MINTR     RMB    1         minimum trips
0010        FLSTR     RMB    6         flash start time
0016        FLEND     RMB    6         flash end time
```

The basic clock timer is allocated seven bytes of memory: six to keep track of the time (in hours, minutes, and seconds) and one to divide the 10-Hz input signal into one-second pulses. The time is kept in unpacked BCD form for ease in software development.

Memory location TIME is used as a down counter that is decremented once per second. TIME is used by the software to time a particular light and is in standard binary form.

The six locations for light timing, NSRED, NSGRE, and so on, are each programmable for times of up to 255 seconds, which should be more than enough time for a lamp in any direction.

Minimum trip time and maximum number of trips indicate how long a light may remain tripped and the minimum amount of time required to cause a trip. A typical minimum time may be 20 seconds, and a typical maximum number of trips may be five. This, of course, depends on the traffic flow pattern at the intersection.

In many cases it is normal to remove a light from service in the early hours of the morning by programming the start and end flash times into the 12 bytes of memory allocated for this purpose.

Initialization Dialog

Since this is a programmable device, it must be initialized whenever power is applied or whenever a change in the sequence of the lights is to be effected. The dialog that follows is executed whenever the microprocessor is restarted. The initialization dialog programs the PIA and branches to the keyboard entry portion of the software.

```
                    *initialization dialog
                    *
F000                          ORG    $F000
                    *
F000  8E007F  RESET   LDS    #$7F       set stack
F003  86FC            LDAA   #$FC       set port B
F005  B7E002          STAA   $E002
```

```
F008 8604         LDAA  #4      select PDR
F00A B7E001       STAA  $E001   send to PIA
F00D B7E003       STAA  $E003   send to PIA
```

Traffic Controller Setup

The controller must be programmed to function after a restart. Programming is accomplished through the keyboard and consists of entering the time of day, the duration of each light, trip times, and flash times.

Each one of these pieces of information must be entered without visual feedback, since this unit contains no display. A display is unnecessary because the sequence is relatively short and can be entered again if an error is detected.

An example of a programming sequence is illustrated in figure 14–7.

```
                  *portion of the system program that sets all
                  *of the programmable features
                  *
F010 CE0001  SETUP  LDX   #CLOCK + 1
F013 8D2E           BSR   INTIM   get time
F015 7F0000         CLR   CLOCK   clear clock
F018 CE0008         LDX   #NSRED  address NSRED
F01B 8D31           BSR   INSEC   seconds for NSRED
F01D 8D2F           BSR   INSEC   seconds for NSGRE
F01F 8D2D           BSR   INSEC   seconds for NSYEL
F021 960A           LDAA  NSYEL   get NSYEL
F023 970D           STAA  EWYEL   save EWYEL
F025 9B09           ADDA  NSGRE   develop EWRED
F027 970B           STAA  EWRED   save EWRED
F029 9608           LDAA  NSRED   get NSRED
F02B 900A           SUBA  NSYEL   develop EWGRE
F02D 970C           STAA  EWGRE   save EWGRE
F02F CE000E         LDX   #MAXTR  address MAXTR
F032 8D1A           BSR   INSEC   seconds for MAXTR
F034 8D18           BSR   INSEC   seconds for MINTR
F036 CE0010         LDX   #FLSTR  address FLSTR
F039 8D08           BSR   INTIM   flash start time
F03B 8D06           BSR   INTIM   flash stop time
F03D 2701           BEQ   SET1    if no trip plate
F03F 0E             CLI           enable trip plate
F040 7EF0F9         JMP   SYST
```

This software accepts all of the programming data from the keyboard and stores it in the appropriate memory locations. See figure 14–8 for a flowchart. It also calculates the

Time of day HH/MM/SS	North south red xxx	North south green xxx	North south yellow xxx	Maximum trip count xxx	Seconds for minimum trip xxx	Start flash time HH/MM/SS	Stop flash time HH/MM/SS

FIGURE 14–7 The setup sequence that programs the traffic light controller.

FIGURE 14–8 The flowchart of the SETUP portion of the traffic light controller system program.

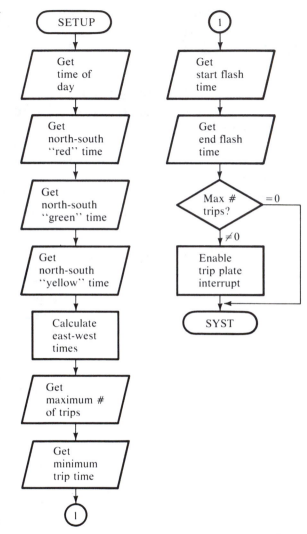

duration of each of the traffic lamps facing east-west and determines whether or not a trip plate is connected to the system. If MAXTR is a zero, it is assumed by the software that no trip plate is connected in the system, and the trip plate interrupt is left disabled.

INTIM Subroutine

The INTIM subroutine reads the time through the keyboard for the time of day, flash starting time, and flash ending time. It stores the time in the format HH/MM/SS. HH is a two-digit number for hours, MM is for minutes, and SS for seconds. This six-digit number is stored in six contiguous memory locations, which are indexed by the X register in unpacked BCD form.

```
                        *subroutine to save the time in
                        *unpacked BCD form
                        *
F043 C606     INTIM     LDAB    #6        count = 6
F045 8D26     INTIS     BSR     INKEY     get a digit
F047 A700               STAA    X         save it
F049 08                 INX               address next byte
F04A 5A                 DECB              decrement count
F04B 26F8               BNE     INTIS     if not finished
F04D 39                 RTS
```

INSEC Subroutine

The INSEC subroutine, illustrated in the flowchart of figure 14–9, accepts a three-digit number from the keyboard and converts it from BCD to binary. It is then stored in the

FIGURE 14–9 The flowchart of the INSEC subroutine.

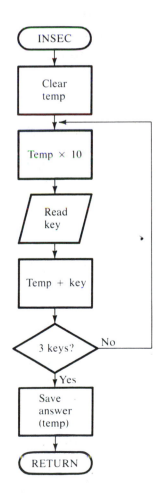

memory location that is indexed by the X register. INSEC is used to get and save data for the timing on the lights and the trip times, if required.

```
                        *inputs data in BCD from the keyboard
                        *and converts it to binary and saves it
                        *
F04E  C603    INSEC     LDAB    #3            count = 3
F050  7F001C            CLR     FLEND+6
F053  961C    INTI1     LDAA    FLEND+6       multiply by 10
F055  48                ASLA                  times 2
F056  971C              STAA    FLEND+6
F058  48                ASLA
F059  48                ASLA
F05A  9B1C              ADDA    FLEND+6
F05C  971C              STAA    FLEND+6
F05E  8D0D              BSR     INKEY         get digit
F060  9B1C              ADDA    FLEND+6       form number
F062  971C              STAA    FLEND+6       save number
F064  5A                DECB                  decrement count
F065  26EC              BNE     INTI1         repeat 3 times
F067  961C              LDAA    FLEND+6       get number
F069  A700              STAA    X             save number
F06B  08                INX                   increment pointer
F06C  39                RTS
```

This subroutine converts from BCD to binary by multiplying the previous binary number by 10 and then adding in the new BCD digit. This will generate a binary number for a BCD number of up to 255. In example 14-1, a 103 is converted to binary using this algorithm.

EXAMPLE 14–1

			FLEND + 6				
	×10	0000	0000	×		0000	1010
First	+1	0000	0000	+		0000	0001
	×10	0000	0001	×		0000	1010
Second	+0	0000	1010	+		0000	0000
	×10	0000	1010	×		0000	1010
Third	+3	0110	0100	+		0000	0011
	RESULT	0110	0111				

INKEY Subroutine

The INKEY subroutine is used to retrieve information from the 10-key numeric keypad interfaced to the MC6800 through an MC6821 PIA. This procedure is accomplished by using the basic INKEY subroutine that was discussed in chapter 7. A flowchart for this subroutine is depicted in figure 14–10.

FIGURE 14–10 The flowchart of the INKEY subroutine.

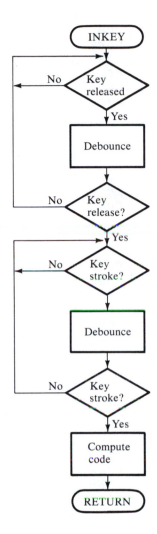

```
*subroutine that reads a character from
*the keyboard
*
F06D  8D27    INKEY   BSR   CHECK     test for keystroke
F06F  26FC            BNE   INKEY     if a keystroke
F071  8D30            BSR   DELAY     debounce
F073  8D21            BSR   .CHECK    test for a keystroke
F075  26F5            BNE   INKEY     if a keystroke
F077  8D1D    INKEY1  BSR   CHECK     test for a keystroke
F079  27FC            BEQ   INKEY1    if no keystroke
F07B  8D28            BSR   DELAY     debounce
F07D  8D19            BSR   CHECK     test for a keystroke
F07F  27F5            BEQ   INKEY1    if no keystroke
```

```
F081  37                    PSHB                  save B
F082  C6FF                  LDAB    #$FF          setup BCD code
F084  B6E000                LDAA    $E000         get 0 to 7
F087  4C                    INCA                  check for any
F088  2605                  BNE     INKEY2        if 0 to 7
F08A  C607                  LDAB    #7            if 8 or 9
F08C  B6E002                LDAA    $E002         get 8 or 9
F08F  5C      INKEY2        INCB
F090  46                    RORA                  rotate
F091  25FC                  BCS     INKEY2        if not found
F093  17                    TBA                   get code
F094  33                    PULB                  restore B
F095  39                    RTS
                *
                *check for any key
                *
F096  B6E000  CHECK         LDAA    $E000         get 0 to 7
F099  4C                    INCA
F09A  2606                  BNE     CHK1
F09C  B6E002                LDAA    $E002         get 8 and 9
F09F  8AFC                  ORAA    #$FC
F0A1  4C                    INCA
F0A2  39      CHK1          RTS
                *
                *10 ms time delay subroutine
                *
F0A3  37      DELAY         PSHB                  save B
F0A4  C614                  LDAB    #$14
F0A6  4F                    CLRA
F0A7  4A      DEL1          DECA
F0A8  26FD                  BNE     DEL1
F0AA  5A                    DECB
F0AB  26FA                  BNE     DEL1
F0AD  33                    PULB
F0AE  39                    RTS
```

Nonmaskable Interrupt Service Subroutine

This subroutine is used for keeping the correct time by modifying CLOCK; it also decrements, once per second, whichever number happens to be in location TIME. This feature provides the traffic light controller with a real-time clock that contains not only the time of day but can also time events. Location TIME is used as a timer and can time events in one-second intervals. See figure 14–11 for a flowchart of the interrupt service subroutine.

```
                *nonmaskable interrupt service subroutine
                *for the real-time clock
                *
F0AF  7C0000  NMI           INC   CLOCK         increment clock
F0B2  C60A                  LDAB  #$0A          test for 10
F0B4  F10000                CMPB  CLOCK
```

FIGURE 14–11 The flowchart of the nonmaskable interrupt service subroutine.

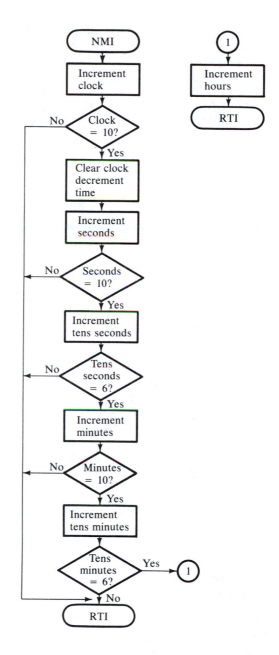

```
F0B7  2633      BNE   NM13      exit
F0B9  7F0000    CLR   CLOCK     clear count
F0BC  CE0007    LDX   #TIME     address time
F0BF  6A00      DEC   X         decrement count
F0C1  09        DEX             decrement address
F0C2  8D29      BSR   INCR      increment seconds
```

```
F0C4  2626              BNE   NMI3          exit
F0C6  C606              LDAB  #6            set wrap
F0C8  8D23              BSR   INCR          increment 10s seconds
F0CA  2620              BNE   NMI3          exit
F0CC  C60A              LDAB  #$0A          set wrap
F0CE  8D1D              BSR   INCR          increment minutes
F0D0  261A              BNE   NMI3          exit
F0D2  C606              LDAB  #6
F0D4  8D17              BSR   INCR
F0D6  2614              BNE   NMI3
F0D8  09                DEX
F0D9  A600              LDAA  X             get 10s of hours
F0DB  C60A              LDAB  #$0A
F0DD  08                INX
F0DE  8102              CMPA  #2            check for 20 hours
F0E0  2602              BNE   NMI2
F0E2  C604              LDAB  #4
F0E4  8D07        NMI2  BSR   INCR          increment hours
F0E6  2604              BNE   NMI3
F0E8  C603              LDAB  #3
F0EA  8D01              BSR   INCR          increment 10s hours
F0EC  38          NMI3  RTI
                  *
                  *increment counter
                  *
F0ED  6C00        INCR  INC   X             increment counter
F0EF  E100              CMPB  X             check for wrap
F0F1  2602              BNE   INCR1         if no wrap
F0F3  6F00              CLR   X             clear count
F0F5  09          INCR1 DEX                 decrement address
F0F6  6D00              TST   X
F0F8  39                RTS
```

The subroutine INCR has been developed to increment the count in the memory location indexed by the X register. If the count equals the number in ACC B, or wrap, the count is cleared. Number wrap indicates the modulus of the counter to the subroutine. A return with the CCR indicating an equal condition means that the next higher order digit of time must be incremented. If a return with the CCR indicating a not equal condition occurs, it means that no further counters need be updated.

Traffic Light System Software

The purpose of this segment of the software is to change the traffic lights. The software scans through the times programmed into the controller and changes the indicator lamps at the appropriate time. You might call this the system software, since most of the controller's time is spent here. Figure 14–12 illustrates the flowchart for the system software.

```
            *system software
            *
F0F9  8601   SYST   LDAA  #1           synchronize with clock
```

FIGURE 14–12 The flowchart of the main traffic light system program.

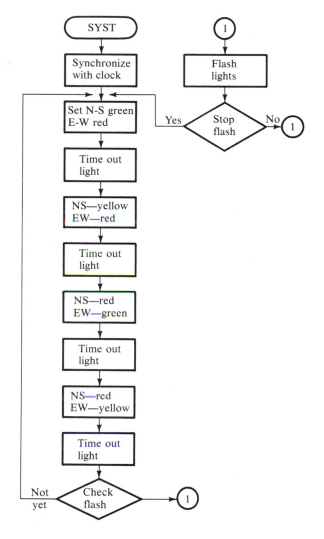

```
F0FB  9707              STAA  TIME
F0FD  7D0007   SYST1    TST   TIME
F100  26FB              BNE   SYST1    wait for sync
F102  8684     SYST2    LDAA  #$84     set NS-green, EW-red
F104  B7E002            STAA  $E002    change lights
F107  9609              LDAA  NSGRE
F109  8D42              BSR   TIMO     time out light
F10B  8644              LDAA  #$44     set NS-yellow, EW-red
F10D  B7E002            STAA  $E002    change lights
F110  960A              LDAA  NSYEL
F112  8D39              BSR   TIMO     time out light
F114  8630              LDAA  #$30     set NS-red, EW-green
F116  B7E002            STAA  $E002    change lights
```

```
F119  960C            LDAA   EWGRE
F11B  8D30            BSR    TIMO        time out light
F11D  8628            LDAA   #$28        set NS-red, EW-yellow
F11F  B7E002          STAA   $E002       change lights
F122  860D            LDAA   EWYEL
F124  8D27            BSR    TIMO        time out light
F126  CE0010          LDX    #FLSTR      address flash start
F129  8D3E            BSR    COMPX       test time
F12B  25D5            BCS    SYST2       continue sequence
F12D  8628     SYST3  LDAA   #$28        set NS-red, EW-yellow
F12F  B7E002          STAA   $E002       change lights
F132  8601            LDAA   #1          get 1 second
F134  8D17            BSR    TIMO        time out light
F136  CE0016          LDX    #FLEND      address flash end
F139  8D1A            BSR    COMP        test for flash end
F13B  24C5            BCC    SYST2
F13D  7FE002          CLR    $E002       change lights
F140  8601            LDAA   #1          get 1 second
F142  8D09            BSR    TIMO        time out light
F144  CE0016          LDX    FLEND       address flash end
F147  8D0A            BSR    COMP        test for flash end
F149  24B7            BCC    SYST2
F14B  20E0            BRA    SYST3       continue flash
                 *
                 *time out light subroutine
                 *
F14D  9707     TIMO   STAA   TIME        save time
F14F  7D0007   TIMOA  TST    TIME        test time
F152  26FB            BNE    TIMOA       if not times out
F154  39              RTS
                 *
                 *subroutine to compare the real-time clock
                 *with the time addressed by X
                 *
F155  9601     COMP   LDAA   CLOCK+1     get clock
F157  A100            CMPA   X           test time (sec)
F159  261C            BNE    COMP1       if not same
F15B  9602            LDAA   CLOCK+2     test time (10s sec)
F15D  A101            CMPA   1,X
F15F  2616            BNE    COMP1       if not same
F161  9603            LDAA   CLOCK+3     test time (min)
F163  A102            CMPA   2,X
F165  2610            BNE    COMP1       if not same
F167  9604     COMPX  LDAA   CLOCK+4     test time (10s min)
F169  A103            CMPA   3,X
F16B  260A            BNE    COMP1       if not same
F16D  9605            LDAA   CLOCK+5     test time (hrs)
F16F  A104            CMPA   4,X
F171  2604            BNE    COMP1       if not same
```

```
F173  9606            LDAA  CLOCK+6   test time (10s hrs)
F175  A105            CMPA  5,X
F177  39      COMP1   RTS
```

The only feature of this software that may be a little difficult to understand is the first portion. The first four statements are used to synchronize the internal interrupt processed clock with the software listed. If this is not accomplished, timing may be inaccurate by one second occasionally.

Trip Plate Software

The trip plate interrupt service subroutine takes effect only if a maximum number of trips is programmed into the controller. If the maximum number is zero, the interrupt remains disabled, and the sequence illustrated in SYST takes complete control. The plate itself produces a pulse on the $\overline{\text{IRQ}}$ pin of the MC6800 every time that a vehicle rests on or crosses the plate.

This interrupt service subroutine must be able to determine if the east-west light is in the red condition; if it is, it must then determine how much time remains before the light changes to green. If this time is equal to or less than the minimum time for tripping, no action is taken.

Once tripped, the software must continue to trip the light for up to the maximum amount of time before changing back to red. This is accomplished by counting how many times the light has been tripped during the on cycle. A flowchart for this interrupt service subroutine is illustrated in figure 14–13.

FIGURE 14–13 The flowchart of the trip plate interrupt service subroutine.

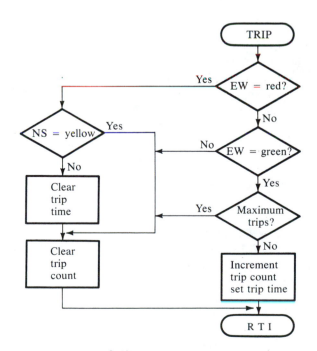

```
                              *trip plate interrupt service subroutine
                              *
        F178  B6E002  TRIP    LDAA   $E002        read lights
        F17B  8504            BITA   #4           test EW-red
        F17D  2612            BNE    TRIP1        if light is red
        F17F  8510            BITA   #$10         test EW-green
        F181  2715            BEQ    TRIP2        if EW-yellow
        F183  961E            LDAA   FLEND+8
        F185  910E            CMPA   MAXTR        check for trips
        F187  270F            BEQ    TRIP2        if done
        F189  7C001E          INC    FLEND+8
        F18C  960F            LDAA   MINTR        get trip time
        F18E  9707            STAA   TIME
        F190  38              RTI
        F191  8540    TRIP1   BITA   #$40         test NS-yellow
        F193  2603            BNE    TRIP2        if yellow
        F195  7F0007          CLR    TIME
        F198  7F001E  TRIP2   CLR    FLEND+8      clear count
        F19B  38              RTI
```

Summary

1 A data concentrator is a microprocessor-based system that takes multiple slow-speed data channels and concentrates them onto one high-speed data line.
2 Data concentrators find application in department stores where transactions on slow-speed point-of-sales terminals are transmitted at high speed to larger mainframe computers in other cities or locations.
3 The traffic light controller in this chapter uses an interrupt-driven real-time clock to time the lights and also to turn the late-night flashing sequence on and off at the appropriate time.
4 The trip plate, located under the roadway, generates a maskable interrupt in the traffic light circuit. When an automobile is detected at the trip plate, the lights are changed so that the vehicle can proceed.

Suggested Projects

1 Develop the MC6800 hardware and software to implement a coin-changer mechanism. It must be able to accept coins in any denomination from 1 cent to 50 cents and dispense change in the fewest number of pennies, nickels, and dimes.

   The amount of money to be accepted is programmed through a set of switches located inside the vending machine. The programmable amount can be anything from $.01 to $1.99.

Your software must accept coins until the amount indicated on the internal switches has been either reached or exceeded. If the amount has been exceeded, dispense the fewest number of coins as change and send an active low pulse out the $\overline{\text{VEND}}$ pin for 20 ms.

As coins are inserted, a mechanical assembly sorts them and signals the microprocessor with a pulse indicating the denomination of the coin. Once your program has detected and remembered the coin, it must drop it into the internal coin box by pulsing the DROP line for 100 ms. There is also a ''bent coin'' signal in case a defective coin is inserted into the machine. If a bent coin is detected, you must pulse the $\overline{\text{EJECT}}$ line for 120 ms to clear the coin slot.

To dispense change, the appropriate $\overline{\text{CH}}$ control line is activated for 100 ms, dropping a coin out of the change slot of the vending machine. You must return only one coin at a time with a pause of at least 50 ms between coins for the mechanical ejection mechanism to function properly. Table 14–1 illustrates all of the TTL input and TTL output connections that are to be interfaced to the MC6800.

Signal	Function
$\overline{\text{VEND}}$	Used to vend merchandise from the machine attached to this changer
$\overline{\text{DROP}}$	Used to accept a coin that has been placed into the mechanism
$\overline{\text{EJECT}}$	Used to return a bent or defective coin
1C	One cent program input switch
2C	Two cents program input switch
5C	Five cents program input switch
10C	Ten cents program input switch
20C	Twenty cents program input switch
50C	Fifty cents program input switch
100C	One dollar program input switch
$\overline{\text{CH1}}$	Returns a penny as change if pulsed for 100 ms
$\overline{\text{CH5}}$	Returns a nickel as change if pulsed for 100 ms
$\overline{\text{CH10}}$	Returns a dime as change if pulsed for 100 ms
$\overline{\text{CH25}}$	Returns a quarter as change if pulsed for 100 ms

TABLE 14–1 Signal lines for the coin changer.

2 Develop an IC test fixture that will automatically test the 7490 TTL decade counter. The pinout of this decade counter is pictured in figure 14–14 with a brief description of its operating characteristics.

Your system must completely test this device. If it is found faulty, the red LED must be lit; if good, the green LED must be lit. The test sequence must test the clear to zero, clear to nine, and count sequence of the counter at least 20 times without failure for a good indication. The test socket and two LED indicators are pictured in figure 14–15.

FIGURE 14–14 The block diagram, pinout, and truth table for the 7490 decade counter.

SOURCE: Courtesy of Texas Instruments, Inc.

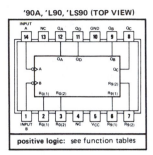

'90A, 'L90, 'LS90 (TOP VIEW)

positive logic: see function tables

'90A, 'L90, 'LS90
BCD COUNT SEQUENCE
(See Note A)

COUNT	OUTPUT			
	Q_D	Q_C	Q_B	Q_A
0	L	L	L	L
1	L	L	L	H
2	L	L	H	L
3	L	L	H	H
4	L	H	L	L
5	L	H	L	H
6	L	H	H	L
7	L	H	H	H
8	H	L	L	L
9	H	L	L	H

'90A, 'L90, 'LS90
BI-QUINARY (5-2)
(See Note B)

COUNT	OUTPUT			
	Q_A	Q_D	Q_C	Q_B
0	L	L	L	L
1	L	L	L	H
2	L	L	H	L
3	L	L	H	H
4	L	H	L	L
5	H	L	L	L
6	H	L	L	H
7	H	L	H	L
8	H	L	H	H
9	H	H	L	L

'90A, 'L90, 'LS90
RESET/COUNT FUNCTION TABLE

RESET INPUTS				OUTPUT			
$R_{0(1)}$	$R_{0(2)}$	$R_{9(1)}$	$R_{9(2)}$	Q_D	Q_C	Q_B	Q_A
H	H	L	X	L	L	L	L
H	H	X	L	L	L	L	L
X	X	H	H	H	L	L	H
X	L	X	L	COUNT			
L	X	L	X	COUNT			
L	X	X	L	COUNT			
X	L	L	X	COUNT			

NOTES: A. Output Q_A is connected to input B for BCD count.
B. Output Q_D is connected to input A for bi-quinary count.

FIGURE 14–15 The control panel of the microprocessor-based TTL-integrated circuit tester.

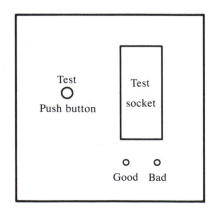

Test
O
Push button

Test socket

O   O
Good   Bad

3 If the above system is to be able to test any 14-pin integrated TTL circuit, which changes would have to be made to the hardware?

4 Create a darkroom timer that will control the length of time that the enlarger exposes the paper. The timer must be capable of exposing the paper in increments of 0.1 second up to 10 minutes.

   Time settings are dialed in on a series of rotary switches that are labeled in one-tenth seconds, seconds, and minutes (as illustrated in figure 14–16). The push button starts the timing sequence that applies AC power to the lamp in the enlarger for the preset amount of time.

FIGURE 14–16 The control panel of the microprocessor-based dark room timer.

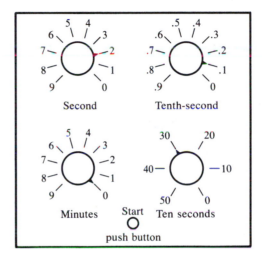

5 Your neighbor's son is a Cub Scout and wants you to build a timer for the annual pinewood derby. This box must be able to determine who wins each heat and to display the winning time on a set of LED numeric readouts.

   Figure 14–17 pictures the ramp, which accommodates two cars at one time, and the location of the beginning and ending trip points.

FIGURE 14–17 The ramp for the pinewood derby.

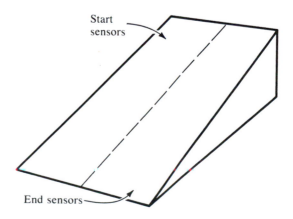

Your software should start timing when either of the first trip points is tripped and continue timing until either of the second trip points is tripped. The hardware should indicate who has won the race and should light up the elapsed time on a set of displays.

Figure 14–18 pictures the layout of the displays and the winner indicator light.

FIGURE 14–18   The display panel on the microprocessor-based pinewood derby.

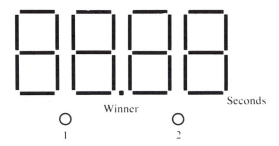

6   Modify the system developed in question 5 so that it can accommodate a four-lane ramp.

Appendices

A   THE ZILOG Z80 MICROPROCESSOR

The Z80 CPU is packaged in an industry-standard 40-pin Dual In-Line Package. The I/O pins and the function of each are shown in the figure below.

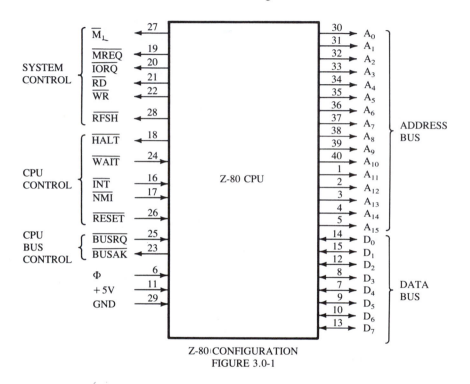

Z-80 CONFIGURATION
FIGURE 3.0-1

A_0-A_{15} **(Address Bus)**   Tri-state output, active high. A_0-A_{15} constitute a 16-bit address bus. The address bus provides the address for memory (up to 64K bytes) data exchanges and for I/O device data exchanges. I/O addressing uses the eight lower address bits to allow the user to directly select up to 256 input or 256 output ports. A_0 is the least significant address bit. During refresh time, the lower seven bits contain a valid refresh address.

D_0-D_7 **(Data Bus)**   Tri-state input/output, active high. D_0-D_7 constitute an 8-bit bidirectional data bus. The data bus is used for data exchanges with memory and I/O devices.

$\overline{M_1}$ **(Machine Cycle one)**   Output, active low. $\overline{M_1}$ indicates that the current machine cycle is the op-code fetch cycle of an instruction execution. Note that during execution of two-byte op-codes, $\overline{M_1}$ is generated as each op-code byte is fetched. These two-byte op-codes always begin with CBH, DDH, EDH, or FDH. $\overline{M_1}$ also occurs with $\overline{IORQ}$ to indicate an interrupt acknowledge cycle.

$\overline{MREQ}$ **(Memory Request)**   Tri-state output, active low. The $\overline{MREQ}$ signal indicates that the address bus holds a valid address for a memory read or memory write operation.

$\overline{IORQ}$ (Input/Output Request) Tri-state output, active low. The $\overline{IORQ}$ signal indicates that the lower half of the address bus holds a valid I/O address for an I/O read or write operation. An $\overline{IORQ}$ signal is also generated with an $\overline{M}_1$ signal when an interrupt is being acknowledged to indicate that an interrupt response vector can be placed on the data bus. Interrupt acknowledge operations occur during M_1 time; I/O operations never occur during M_1 time.

$\overline{RD}$ (Memory Read) Tri-state output, active low. $\overline{RD}$ indicates that the CPU wants to read data from memory or an I/O device. The addressed I/O device or memory should use this signal to gate data onto the CPU data bus.

$\overline{WR}$ (Memory Write) Tri-state output, active low. $\overline{WR}$ indicates that the CPU data bus holds valid data to be stored in the addressed memory or I/O device.

$\overline{RFSH}$ (Refresh) Output, active low. $\overline{RFSH}$ indicates that the lower seven bits of the address bus contain a refresh address for dynamic memories and the current $\overline{MREQ}$ signal should be used to do a refresh read to all dynamic memories.

$\overline{HALT}$ (Halt state) Output, active low. $\overline{HALT}$ indicates that the CPU has executed a HALT software instruction and is awaiting either a nonmaskable or a maskable interrupt (with the mask enabled) before operation can resume. While halted, the CPU executes NOP's to maintain memory refresh activity.

$\overline{WAIT}$ (Wait) Input, active low. $\overline{WAIT}$ indicates to the Z-80 CPU that the addressed memory or I/O devices are not ready for a data transfer. The CPU continues to enter wait states for as long as this signal is active. This signal allows memory or I/O devices of any speed to be synchronized to the CPU.

$\overline{INT}$ (Interrupt Request) Input, active low. The $\overline{INT}$ signal is generated by I/O devices. A request will be honored at the end of the current instruction if the internal software-controlled interrupt enable flip-flop (IEF) is enabled and if the $\overline{BUSRQ}$ signal is not active. When the CPU accepts the interrupt, an acknowledge signal ($\overline{IORQ}$ during M_1 time) is sent out at the beginning of the next instruction cycle. The CPU can respond to an interrupt in three different modes.

$\overline{NMI}$ (Nonmaskable Interrupt) Input, negative edge triggered. The $\overline{NMI}$ request line has a higher priority than $\overline{INT}$ and is always recognized at the end of the current instruction, independent of the status of the interrupt enable flip-flop. $\overline{NMI}$ automatically forces the Z-80 CPU to restart to location 0066_H. The program counter is automatically saved in the external stack so that the user can return to the program that was interrupted. Note that continuous WAIT cycles can prevent the current instruction from ending, and that a $\overline{BUSRQ}$ will override a $\overline{NMI}$.

$\overline{RESET}$ Input, active low. $\overline{RESET}$ forces the program counter to zero and initializes the CPU. The CPU initialization includes:
  1) Disable the interrupt enable flip-flop
  2) Set Register $1 = 00_H$
  3) Set Register $R = 00_H$
  4) Set Interrupt Mode 0

During reset time, the address bus and data bus go to a high-impedance state and all control output signals go to the inactive state.

$\overline{BUSRQ}$ (Bus Request) Input, active low. The $\overline{BUSRQ}$ signal is used to request the CPU address bus, data bus and tri-state output signals to go to a high-impedance state so that other devices can control these buses. When $\overline{\text{BUSRQ}}$ is activated, the CPU will set these buses to a high-impedance state as soon as the current CPU machine cycle is terminated.

$\overline{\text{BUSAK}}$ **(Bus Acknowledge)**   Output, active low. $\overline{\text{BUSAK}}$ is used to indicate to the requesting device that the CPU address bus, data bus, and tri-state control bus signals have been set to their high-impedance state and the external device can now control these signals.

ϕ Single-phase TTL level clock that requires only a 330-ohm pull-up resistor to +5 volts to meet all clock requirements.

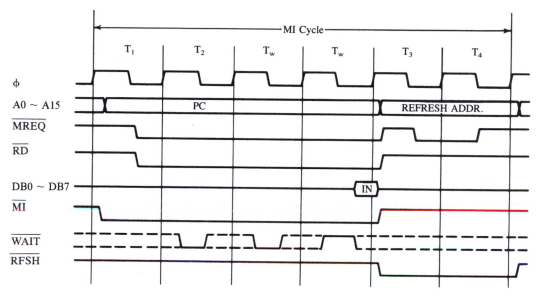

INSTRUCTION OP CODE FETCH WITH WAIT STATES

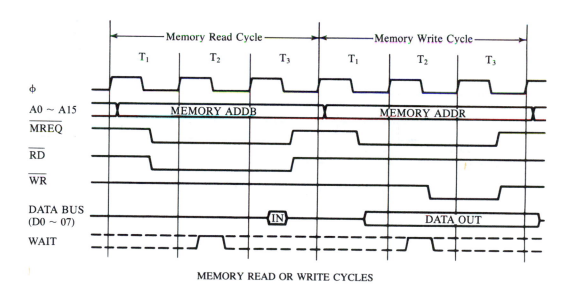

MEMORY READ OR WRITE CYCLES

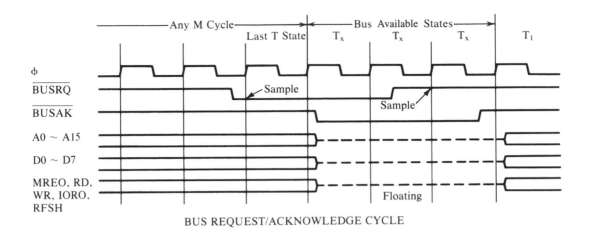

BUS REQUEST/ACKNOWLEDGE CYCLE

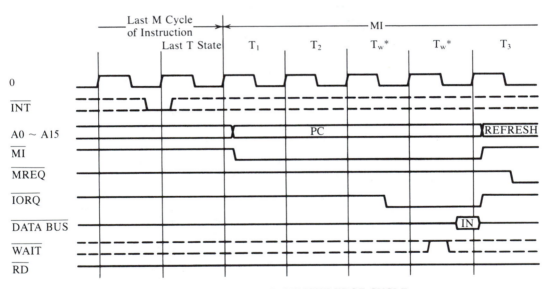

INTERRUPT REQUEST/ACKNOWLEDGE CYCLE

ABSOLUTE MAXIMUM RATINGS

Temperature Under Bias	0°C to 70°C
Storage Temperature	$-65°C$ to $+150°C$
Voltage On Any Pin with Respect to Ground	$-0.3V$ to $+7V$
Power Dissipation	1.4W

● Comment

Stresses above those listed under "Absolute Maximum Rating" may cause permanent damage to the device. This is a stress rating only and functional operation of the device at these or any other condition above those indicated in the operational sections of this specification is not implied. Exposure to absolute maximum rating conditions for extended periods may affect device reliability.

● D.C. CHARACTERISTICS

$T_A = 0°C$ to 70°C, $V_{cc} = 5V \pm 5\%$ unless otherwise specified

Symbol	Parameter	Min.	Typ.	Max.	Unit	Test Condition
V_{ILC}	Clock Input Low Voltage	-0.3		0.45	V	
V_{IHC}	Clock Input High Voltage	V_{cc} [1]		V_{cc}	V	
V_{IL}	Input Low Voltage	-0.3		0.8	V	
V_{IH}	Input High Voltage	2.0		V_{cc}	V	
V_{OL}	Output Low Voltage			0.4	V	$I_{OL} = 1.8mA$
V_{OH}	Output High Voltage	2.4			V	$I_{OH} = 100\mu A$
I_{CC}	Power Supply Current			200	mA	$t_c = 400nsec$
I_{LI}	Input Leakage Current			10	μA	$V_{IN} = 0$ to V_{oc}
I_{LOH}	Tri-State Output Leakage Current in Float			10	μA	$V_{OUT} = 2.4$ to V_{CC}
I_{LOL}	Tri-State Output Leakage Current in Float			-10	μA	$V_{OUT} = 0.4V$
I_{LD}	Data Bus Leakage Current in Input Mode			± 10	μA	$0 \leq V_{IN} \leq V_{cc}$

● CAPACITANCE

$T_A = 25°C$, $f = 1$ MHz

Symbol	Parameter	Typ.	Max.	Unit	Test Condition
$C\phi$	Clock Capacitance		20	pF	
C_{IN}	Input Capacitance		5	pF	Unmeasured Pins Returned to/Ground
C_{OUT}	Output Capacitance		10	pF	

(1) Clock Driver

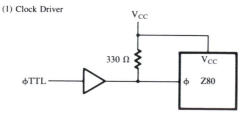

An external clock pull-up resistor of (330Ω) will meet both the A.D. and D.C. clock requirements.

A.C. Characteristics

Z80-CPU

$T_A = 0°C$ to $70°C$, $V_{cc} = +5V \pm 5\%$. Unless Otherwise Noted.

Signal	Symbol	Parameter	Min	Max	Unit	Test Condition
Φ	t_c	Clock Period	.4	[12]	μsec	
	$t_{w(\Phi H)}$	Clock Pulse Width, Clock High	180	∞	nsec	
	$t_{w(\Phi L)}$	Clock Pulse Width, Clock Low	180	2000	nsec	
	$t_{r,f}$	Clock Rise and Fall Time		30	nsec	
A_{0-15}	$t_D(AD)$	Address Output Delay		160	nsec	
	$t_F(AD)$	Delay to Float		110	nsec	
	t_{acm}	Address Stable Prior to $\overline{MRFQ}$ (Memory Cycle)	[1]		nsec	$C_L = 100pF$
	t_{aci}	Address Stable Prior to $\overline{IORQ}$, $\overline{RD}$, or $\overline{WR}$ (I/O Cycle)	[2]		nsec	
	t_{ca}	Address Stable From $\overline{RD}$ or $\overline{WR}$	[3]		nsec	
	t_{caf}	Address Stable From $\overline{RD}$ or $\overline{WR}$ During Float	[4]		nsec	
D_{0-7}	$t_D(D)$	Data Output Delay		260	nsec	
	$t_F(D)$	Delay to Float During Write Cycle		90	nsec	
	$t_{S\Phi}(D)$	Data Setup Time to Rising Edge of Clock During MI Cycle	50		nsec	$C_L = 200\,pF$
	$t_{S\overline{\Phi}}(D)$	Data Setup Time to Falling Edge of Clock During M2 to M5	60		nsec	
	t_{dcm}	Data Stable Prior to $\overline{WR}$ (Memory Cycle)	[5]		nsec	
	t_{dci}	Data Stable Prior to $\overline{WR}$ (I/O Cycle)	[6]		nsec	
	t_{cdf}	Data Stable From $\overline{WR}$	[7]		nsec	
	t_H	Any Hold Time for Setup Time	0		nsec	
$\overline{MREQ}$	$t_{DL\overline{\Phi}}(MR)$	$\overline{MREQ}$ Delay From Falling Edge of Clock, $\overline{MREQ}$ Low		100	nsec	
	$t_{DH\overline{\Phi}}(MR)$	$\overline{MREQ}$ Delay From Rising Edge of Clock, $\overline{MREQ}$ High		100	nsec	
	$t_{DH\Phi}(MR)$	$\overline{MREQ}$ Delay From Falling Edge of Clock, $\overline{MREQ}$ High		100	nsec	$C_L = 50pF$
	$t_{w(\overline{MRL})}$	Pulse Width, $\overline{MREQ}$ Low	[8]		nsec	
	$t_{w(\overline{MRH})}$	Pulse Width, $\overline{MREQ}$ High	[9]		nsec	
$\overline{IORQ}$	$t_{DL\Phi}(IR)$	$\overline{IORQ}$ Delay From Rising Edge of Clock, $\overline{IORQ}$ Low		90	nsec	
	$t_{DL\overline{\Phi}}(IR)$	$\overline{IORQ}$ Delay From Falling Edge of Clock, $\overline{IORQ}$ Low		110	nsec	$C_L = 50\,pF$
	$t_{DH\Phi}(IR)$	$\overline{IORQ}$ Delay From Rising Edge of Clock, $\overline{IORQ}$ High		100	nsec	
	$t_{DH\overline{\Phi}}(IR)$	$\overline{IORQ}$ Delay From Falling Edge of Clock, $\overline{IORQ}$ High		110	nsec	
$\overline{RD}$	$t_{DL\Phi}(RD)$	$\overline{RD}$ Delay From Rising Edge of Clock, $\overline{RD}$ Low		100	nsec	
	$t_{DL\overline{\Phi}}(RD)$	$\overline{RD}$ Delay From Falling Edge of Clock, $\overline{RD}$ Low		130	nsec	$C_L = 50pF$
	$t_{DL\Phi}(RD)$	$\overline{RD}$ Delay From Rising Edge of Clock, $\overline{RD}$ High		100	nsec	
	$t_{DH\overline{\Phi}}(RD)$	$\overline{RD}$ Delay From Falling Edge of Clock, $\overline{RD}$ High		110	nsec	

[1] $t_{acm} = t_{w(\Phi H)} + t_f - 75$

[2] $t_{aci} = t_c - 80$

[3] $t_{ca} = t_{w(\Phi L)} + t_r - 40$

[4] $t_{caf} = t_{w(\Phi L)} + t_r - 60$

[5] $t_{dcm} = t_c - 180$

[6] $t_{dci} = t_{w(\Phi L)} + t_r - 180$

[7] $t_{cdf} = t_{w(\Phi L)} + t_r - 50$

[8] $t_{w(\overline{MRL})} = t_c - 40$

[9] $t_{w(\overline{MRH})} = t_{w(\Phi H)} + t_f - 30$

[12] $t_c = t_{w(\Phi H)} + t_{w(\Phi L)} + t_r + t_f$

Signal	Symbol	Parameter	Min	Max	Unit	Test Condition
$\overline{\text{WR}}$	$t_{DL\Phi}$ (WR)	$\overline{\text{WR}}$ Delay From Rising Edge of Clock, $\overline{\text{WR}}$ Low		80	nsec	
	$t_{DL\overline{\Phi}}$ (WR)	$\overline{\text{WR}}$ Delay From Falling Edge of Clock, $\overline{\text{WR}}$ Low		90	nsec	$C_L = 50$ pF
	$t_{DH\Phi}$ (WR)	$\overline{\text{WR}}$ Delay From Falling Edge of Clock, $\overline{\text{WR}}$ High		100	nsec	
	t_w ($\overline{\text{WRL}}$)	Pulse Width, $\overline{\text{WR}}$ Low	[10]		nsec	
$\overline{\text{M1}}$	t_{DL} ($\overline{\text{M1}}$)	$\overline{\text{M1}}$ Delay From Rising Edge of Clock, $\overline{\text{M1}}$ Low		130	nsec	$C_L = 30$ pF
	t_{DH} ($\overline{\text{M1}}$)	$\overline{\text{M1}}$ Delay From Rising Edge of Clock, $\overline{\text{M1}}$ High		130	nsec	
$\overline{\text{RFSH}}$	t_{DL} (RF)	$\overline{\text{RFSH}}$ Delay From Rising Edge of Clock, $\overline{\text{RFSH}}$ Low		180	nsec	$C_L = 30$ pF
	t_{DH} (RF)	$\overline{\text{RFSH}}$ Delay From Rising Edge of Clock, $\overline{\text{RFSH}}$ High		150	nsec	
$\overline{\text{WAIT}}$	t_s (WT)	$\overline{\text{WAIT}}$ Setup Time to Falling Edge of Clock	70		nsec	
$\overline{\text{HALT}}$	t_D (HT)	$\overline{\text{HALT}}$ Delay Time From Falling Edge of Clock		300	nsec	$C_L = 50$ pF
$\overline{\text{INT}}$	t_s (IT)	$\overline{\text{INT}}$ Setup Time to Rising Edge of Clock	80		nsec	
$\overline{\text{NMI}}$	t_w ($\overline{\text{NML}}$)	Pulse Width, $\overline{\text{NMI}}$ Low	80		nsec	
$\overline{\text{BUSRQ}}$	t_s (BQ)	$\overline{\text{BUSRQ}}$ Setup Time to Rising Edge of Clock	80		nsec	
$\overline{\text{BUSAK}}$	t_{DL} (BA)	$\overline{\text{BUSAK}}$ Delay From Rising Edge of Clock, $\overline{\text{BUSAK}}$ Low		120	nsec	$C_L = 50$ pF
	t_{DH} (BA)	$\overline{\text{BUSAK}}$ Delay From Falling Edge of Clock, $\overline{\text{BUSAK}}$ High		110	nsec	
$\overline{\text{RESET}}$	t_s (RS)	$\overline{\text{RESET}}$ Setup Time to Rising Edge of Clock	90		nsec	
	t_F (C)	Delay to Float ($\overline{\text{MREQ}}$, $\overline{\text{IORQ}}$, $\overline{\text{RD}}$ and $\overline{\text{WR}}$)		100	nsec	
	t_{mr}	$\overline{\text{M1}}$ Stable Prior to $\overline{\text{IORQ}}$ (Interrupt Ack.)	[11]		nsec	

[10] $t_{w(WR)} = t_c - 40$

[11] $t_{mr} = 2t_c + t_{w(\Phi H)} + t_f - 80$

TEST POINT

FROM OUTPUT
UNDER TEST

V_{cc}

$R_1 = 2 1$ KΩ

100μ A

C_L

Load circuit for Output

NOTES:

1. Data should be enabled onto the CPU data bus when $\overline{\text{RD}}$ is active. During interrupt acknowledge data should be enabled when $\overline{\text{M1}}$ and $\overline{\text{IORQ}}$ are both active.

2. All control signals are internally synchronized, so they may be totally asynchronous with respect to the clock.

3. The $\overline{\text{RESET}}$ signal must be active for a minimum of 3 clock cycles.

4. Output Delay vs. Loaded Capacitance.

TA = 70°C $V_{cc} = +5$V $\pm 5\%$

(1) $\Delta C_L = +100$pF ($A_0 - A_{15}$ and Control Signals), add 30 ns to timing shown.

(2) $\Delta C_L = -50$pF ($A_0 - A_{15}$ and Control Signals), subtract 15 ns from timing shown.

479

A.C. Timing Diagram

Timing measurements are made at the following voltages, unless otherwise specified:

	"1"	"0"
CLOCK	4.2V	.8V
OUTPUT	2.0V	.8V
INPUT	2.0V	.8V
FLOAT	ΔV	±0.5V

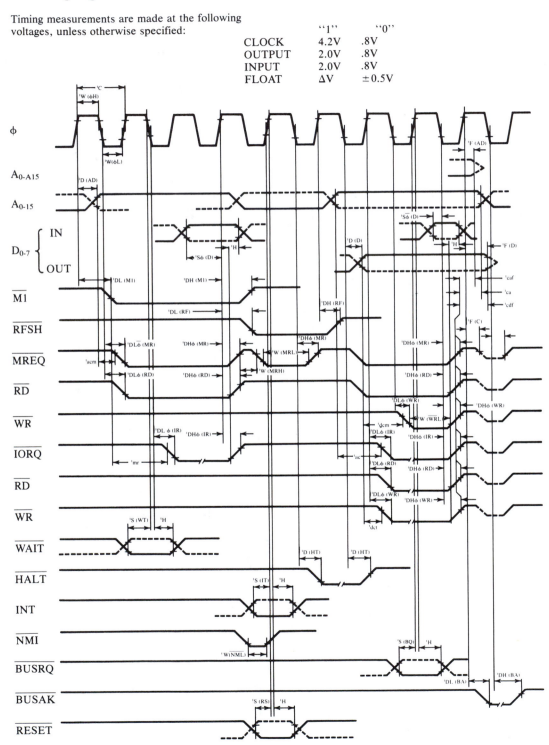

THE 8085A INSTRUCTION SET   B

The 8085A microprocessor executes 246 different instructions. This appendix provides a list of these instructions and also defines the addressing modes allowed by the 8085A microprocessor.

Addressing Modes

The 8085A microprocessor addresses data using four different addressing techniques: (1) register, (2) immediate, (3) direct, and (4) indirect addressing.

Register Addressing   Many of the instructions in the 8085A use register addressing. (see figure B–1 for the internal register set). The allowable 8-bit registers include: A, B, C, D, E, H, and L and the allowable 16-bit registers include: BC, DE, HL, SP, and, in some instructions, PSW (the accumulator and flags).

The MOV instruction is an example of an instruction that uses register addressing. For example, a MOV A,B instruction makes a copy of the contents of the B register and transfers it into the A register. This is an example of 8-bit register addressing.

Sixteen-bit register addressing is used with only a handful of instructions, such as PUSH B. The PUSH B instruction copies the BC register pair to the stack memory. Note that even though a 16-bit register is operated upon, only the letter *B* is used to designate it.

Immediate Addressing   Immediate addressing is a technique in which the data used by the instruction immediately follow the op-code of the instruction in the memory. If an 8-bit immediate operation is executed, then the op-code is followed by a one-byte immediate data. If a 16-bit immediate operation is executed, then the op-code is followed by two bytes of immediate data. With 16-bit immediate data, then the least significant 8 bits preceed the most significant 8 bits. For example, the LXI H,1000H instruction loads the HL register pair with a 1000H. In the machine language version of this instruction, a 21 00 10 is stored in memory. Notice how the least significant byte (00) of immediate data preceeds the most significant byte (10).

This appendix uses a d8 to indicate immediate 8-bit data and a d16 for immediate 16-bit data.

Direct Addressing   Only a few of the 8085A instructions use direct addressing. Direct addressed instructions have an op-code followed by the address of the data. For example, the LDA 2000H instruction loads the accumulator with the contents of memory location 2000H, where 2000H is the address of the data. In machine language this instruction is

8 →	
B	C
D	E
H	L
A	F
SP	
PC	
← 16 →	

FIGURE B–1   The internal register set of the Intel 8085A microprocessor.

coded as 32 00 20, where 32 is the op-code, followed by the address, which is stored with the least significant part first.

This appendix uses an a16 to indicate that the direct addressed mode is used. Direct addressing is also used with the JMP and CALL instructions to indicate the memory address jumped to or called by the instruction.

Indirect Addressing   The last type of memory addressing is indirect addressing. With indirect addressing, a register pair holds the memory address of the data. By far the most common form of indirect addressing occurs when the HL register pair is used to hold the memory address of the data. When HL is used for indirect addressing, the letter M is indicated as a register in the instruction. For example, the MOV A,M instruction copies the contents of the memory location addressed by the HL register pair into the A register.

BC and DE are also used to indirectly address memory if an LDAX or STAX instruction is used in a program. The LDAX B instruction loads the accumulator with a copy of the number stored at the memory location addressed by the BC register pair. If BC contains a 1000H, then the data at 1000H is copied to the A register.

Flag Register

The flag register contains five bits that indicate the outcome of an arithmetic and logic operation. The data transfer and program control instructions do not affect the flag bits in the 8085A microprocessor. Figure B–2 illustrates the bit positions of the flag register. The flag bits are used by the instructions to make decisions. For example, the JZ instruction jumps to another memory address for the next instruction if the zero flag bit is set.

Each flag bit and its purpose are listed as follows:

Sign (S)   The sign flag bit indicates the arithmetic sign of the result from an arithmetic or a logic operation. If it contains a logic one, the result is negative; if it contains a logic zero, the result is positive.

Zero (Z)   The zero flag bit indicates whether or not the outcome of an arithmetic or logic operation was zero. If the zero flag bit contains a logic one, the outcome is zero; if it contains a logic zero, the outcome is not zero.

Carry (Cy)   The carry flag bit indicates whether there was a carry out of the eighth bit with eight-bit addition instructions or a borrow into the eighth bit with subtraction instructions.

Auxilliary Carry (Ac)   The auxilliary carry bit indicates a carry or borrow between the right-most and left-most four bits of the result of an addition or subtraction operation. Only the DAA instruction uses the Ac bit.

Parity (P)   The parity flag bit indicates whether the result from an arithmetic or logic operation has even (P = 1) or odd (P = 0) parity. Parity is a count of the number of bits expressed as an even or an odd number of ones.

FIGURE B–2   The 8085A flag register.

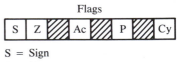

Flags

S = Sign
Z = Zero
Ac = Auxiliary carry
P = Parity
Cy = Carry

8085A Instruction Set

A complete alphabetic listing of all of the 8085A instructions follows, along with a brief description of their operation and also the effect on the flag bits. Note that the change in a flag bit is indicated by an *, and no change is a blank column.

Instruction	Hex Form	Cy	S	Z	P	Ac	Clocks	Description
ACI d8	CE d8	*	*	*	*	*	7	A = A + d8 + Cy
ADC A	8F	*	*	*	*	*	4	A = A + A + Cy
ADC B	88	*	*	*	*	*	4	A = A + B + Cy
ADC C	89	*	*	*	*	*	4	A = A + C + Cy
ADC D	8A	*	*	*	*	*	4	A = A + D + Cy
ADC E	8B	*	*	*	*	*	4	A = A + E + Cy
ADC H	8C	*	*	*	*	*	4	A = A + H + Cy
ADC L	8D	*	*	*	*	*	4	A = A + L + Cy
ADC M	8E	*	*	*	*	*	7	A = A + M + Cy
ADD A	87	*	*	*	*	*	4	A = A + A
ADD B	80	*	*	*	*	*	4	A = A + B
ADD C	81	*	*	*	*	*	4	A = A + C
ADD D	82	*	*	*	*	*	4	A = A + D
ADD E	83	*	*	*	*	*	4	A = A + E
ADD H	84	*	*	*	*	*	4	A = A + H
ADD L	85	*	*	*	*	*	4	A = A + L
ADD M	86	*	*	*	*	*	7	A = A + M
ADI d8	C6 d8	*	*	*	*	*	7	A = A + d8
ANA A	A7	0	*	*	*	1	4	A = A Λ A
ANA B	A0	0	*	*	*	1	4	A = A Λ B
ANA C	A1	0	*	*	*	1	4	A = A Λ C
ANA D	A2	0	*	*	*	1	4	A = A Λ D
ANA E	A3	0	*	*	*	1	4	A = A Λ E
ANA H	A4	0	*	*	*	1	4	A = A Λ H
ANA L	A5	0	*	*	*	1	4	A = A Λ L
ANA M	A6	0	*	*	*	1	7	A = A Λ M
ANI d8	E6 d8	0	*	*	*	1	7	A = A Λ d8
CALL a16	CD ll hh						18	Call subroutine
CC a16	DC ll hh						9/18	Call if carry
CM a16	FC ll hh						9/18	Call if minus
CNC a16	D4 ll hh						9/18	Call if no carry
CNZ a16	C4 ll hh						9/18	Call if not zero
CP a16	F4 ll hh						9/18	Call if positive
CPE a16	EC ll hh						9/18	Call if parity even
CPO a16	E4 ll hh						9/18	Call if parity odd
CZ a16	CC ll hh						9/18	Call if zero
CMA	2F						4	A = $\overline{\text{A}}$
CMC	3F	*					4	Cy = $\overline{\text{Cy}}$
CMP A	BF	*	*	*	*	*	4	A − A
CMP B	B8	*	*	*	*	*	4	A − B

Instruction	Hex Form	Flags		Clocks	Description
		Cy S Z P Ac			
CMP C	B9	* * * * *		4	A − C
CMP D	BA	* * * * *		4	A − D
CMP E	BB	* * * * *		4	A − E
CMP H	BC	* * * * *		4	A − H
CMP L	BD	* * * * *		4	A − L
CMP M	BE	* * * * *		7	A − M
CPI d8	FE d8	* * * * *		7	A − d8
DAA	27	* * * * *		4	Decimal adjust A
DAD B	09	*		10	HL = HL + BC
DAD D	19	*		10	HL = HL + DE
DAD H	29	*		10	HL = HL + HL
DAD SP	39	*		10	HL = HL + SP
DCR A	3D	* * * *		4	A = A − 1
DCR B	05	* * * *		4	B = B − 1
DCR C	0D	* * * *		4	C = C − 1
DCR D	15	* * * *		4	D = D − 1
DCR E	1D	* * * *		4	E = E − 1
DCR H	25	* * * *		4	H = H − 1
DCR L	2D	* * * *		4	L = L − 1
DCR M	35	* * * *		7	M = M − 1
DCX B	0B			6	BC = BC − 1
DCX D	1B			6	DE = DE − 1
DCX H	2B			6	HL = HL − 1
DCX SP	3B			6	SP = SP − 1
DI	F3			4	Disable interrupts
EI	FB			4	Enable interrupts
HLT	76			4	Halt
IN d8	DB d8			10	Input to A
INR A	3C	* * * *		4	A = A + 1
INR B	04	* * * *		4	B + B + 1
INR C	0C	* * * *		4	C = C + 1
INR D	14	* * * *		4	D = D + 1
INR E	1C	* * * *		4	E = E + 1
INR H	24	* * * *		4	H = H + 1
INR L	2C	* * * *		4	L = L + 1
INR M	34	* * * *		10	M = M + 1
INX B	03			6	BC = BC + 1
INX D	13			6	DE = DE + 1
INX H	23			6	HL = HL + 1
INX SP	33			6	SP = SP + 1
JC a16	DA ll hh			7/10	Jump if carry
JM a16	FA ll hh			7/10	Jump if minus
JMP a16	C3 ll hh			10	Jump
JNC a16	D2 ll hh			7/10	Jump if no carry

Instruction	Hex Form	Flags	Clocks	Description
		Cy S Z P Ac		
JNZ a16	C2 ll hh		7/10	Jump if not zero
JP a16	F2 ll hh		7/10	Jump if positive
JPE a16	EA ll hh		7/10	Jump if parity even
JPO a16	E2 ll hh		7/10	Jump if parity odd
JZ a16	CA ll hh		7/10	Jump if zero
LDA a16	3A ll hh		13	Load A from a16
LDAX B	0A		7	Load A from (BC)
LDAX D	1A		7	Load A from (DE)
LHLD a16	2A ll hh		16	Load HL from a16
LXI B,d16	01 ll hh		10	BC = d16
LXI D,d16	11 ll hh		10	DE = d16
LXI H,d16	21 ll hh		10	HL = d16
LXI SP,d16	31 ll hh		10	SP = d16
MOV A,A	7F		4	A = A
MOV A,B	78		4	A = B
MOV A,C	79		4	A = C
MOV A,D	7A		4	A = D
MOV A,E	7B		4	A = E
MOV A,H	7C		4	A = H
MOV A,L	7D		4	A = L
MOV A,M	7E		7	A = M
MOV B,A	47		4	B = A
MOV B,B	40		4	B = B
MOV B,C	41		4	B = C
MOV B,D	42		4	B = D
MOV B,E	43		4	B = E
MOV B,H	44		4	B = H
MOV B,L	45		4	B = L
MOV B,M	46		7	B = M
MOV C,A	4F		4	C = A
MOV C,B	48		4	C = B
MOV C,C	49		4	C = C
MOV C,D	4A		4	C = D
MOV C,E	4B		4	C = E
MOV C,H	4C		4	C = H
MOV C,L	4D		4	C = L
MOV C,M	4E		7	C = M
MOV D,A	57		4	D = A
MOV D,B	50		4	D = B
MOV D,C	51		4	D = C
MOV D,D	52		4	D = D
MOV D,E	53		4	D = E
MOV D,H	54		4	D = H
MOV D,L	55		4	D = L

Instruction	Hex Form	Flags	Clocks	Description
		Cy S Z P Ac		
MOV D,M	56		7	D = M
MOV E,A	5F		4	E = A
MOV E,B	58		4	E = B
MOV E,C	59		4	E = C
MOV E,D	5A		4	E = D
MOV E,E	5B		4	E = E
MOV E,H	5C		4	E = H
MOV E,L	5D		4	E = L
MOV E,M	5E		7	E = M
MOV H,A	67		4	H = A
MOV H,B	60		4	H = B
MOV H,C	61		4	H = C
MOV H,D	62		4	H = D
MOV H,E	63		4	H = E
MOV H,H	64		4	H = H
MOV H,L	65		4	H = L
MOV H,M	66		7	H = M
MOV L,A	6F		4	L = A
MOV L,B	68		4	L = B
MOV L,C	69		4	L = C
MOV L,D	6A		4	L = D
MOV L,E	6B		4	L = E
MOV L,H	6C		4	L = H
MOV L,L	6D		4	L = L
MOV L,M	6E		7	L = M
MOV M,A	77		7	M = A
MOV M,B	70		7	M = B
MOV M,C	71		7	M = C
MOV M,D	72		7	M = D
MOV M,E	73		7	M = E
MOV M,H	74		7	M = H
MOV M,L	75		7	M = L
MVI A,d8	3E d8		7	A = d8
MVI B,d8	06 d8		7	B = d8
MVI C,d8	0E d8		7	C = d8
MVI D,d8	16 d8		7	D = d8
MVI E,d8	1E d8		7	E = d8
MVI H,d8	26 d8		7	H = d8
MVI L,d8	2E d8		7	L = d8
MVI M,d8	36 d8		10	M = d8
NOP	40		4	No operation
ORA A	B7	0 * * * 0	4	A = A V A
ORA B	B0	0 * * * 0	4	A = A V B
ORA C	B1	0 * * * 0	4	A = A V C
ORA D	B2	0 * * * 0	4	A = A V D

Instruction	Hex Form	Flags		Clocks	Description
		Cy S Z P Ac			
ORA E	B3	0 * * * 0		4	A = A V E
ORA H	B4	0 * * * 0		4	A = A V H
ORA L	B5	0 * * * 0		4	A = A V L
ORA M	B6	0 * * * 0		4	A = A V M
ORI d8	F6 d8	0 * * * 0		7	A = A V d8
OUT d8	D3 d8			10	A is output
PCHL	E9			6	PC = HL
POP B	C1			10	BC = stack data
POP D	D1			10	DE = stack data
POP H	E1			10	HL = stack data
POP PSW	F1			10	AF = stack data
PUSH B	C5			12	Stack = BC
PUSH D	D5			12	Stack = DE
PUSH H	E5			12	Stack = HL
PUSH PSW	F5			12	Stack = AF
RAL	17	*		4	Rotate A left through carry
RAR	1F	*		4	Rotate A right through carry
RC	D8			6/12	Return if carry
RET	C9			10	Return
RIM	20			4	Read interrupt masks
RLC	07	*		4	Rotate A left
RM	F8			6/12	Return if minus
RNC	D0			6/12	Return if no carry
RNZ	C0			6/12	Return if not zero
RP	F0			6/12	Return if positive
RPE	E8			6/12	Return if parity even
RPO	E0			6/12	Return if parity odd
RRC	0F	*		4	Rotate A right
RST 0	C7			12	CALL 0000H
RST 1	CF			12	CALL 0008H
RST 2	D7			12	CALL 0010H
RST 3	DF			12	CALL 0018H
RST 4	E7			12	CALL 0020H
RST 5	EF			12	CALL 0028H
RST 6	F7			12	CALL 0030H
RST 7	FF			12	CALL 0038H
RZ	C8			6/12	Return if zero
SBB A	9F	* * * * *		4	A = A − A − Cy
SBB B	98	* * * * *		4	A = A − B − Cy
SBB C	99	* * * * *		4	A = A − C − Cy
SBB D	9A	* * * * *		4	A = A − D − Cy
SBB E	9B	* * * * *		4	A = A − E − Cy
SBB H	9C	* * * * *		4	A = A − H − Cy

Instruction	Hex Form	Flags	Clocks	Description
		Cy S Z P Ac		
SBB L	9D	* * * * *	4	A = A − L − Cy
SBB M	9E	* * * * *	7	A = A − M − Cy
SBI d8	DE d8	* * * * *	7	A = A − d8 − Cy
SHLD a16	22 ll hh		16	HL stored at a16
SIM	30		4	Set interrupt mask
SPHL	F9		6	SP = HL
STA a16	32 ll hh		13	A stored at a16
STAX B	02		7	A stored at (BC)
STAX D	12		7	A stored at (DE)
STC	37	1	4	Cy = 1
SUB A	97	* * * * *	4	A = A − A
SUB B	90	* * * * *	4	A = A − B
SUB C	91	* * * * *	4	A = A − C
SUB D	92	* * * * *	4	A = A − D
SUB E	93	* * * * *	4	A = A − E
SUB H	94	* * * * *	4	A = A − H
SUB L	95	* * * * *	4	A = A − L
SUB M	96	* * * * *	7	A = A − M
SUI d8	D6 d8	* * * * *	7	A = A − d8
XCHG	EB		4	HL exchanged with DE
XRA A	AF	0 * * * 0	4	A = A ∀ A
XRA B	A8	0 * * * 0	4	A = A ∀ B
XRA C	A9	0 * * * 0	4	A = A ∀ C
XRA D	AA	0 * * * 0	4	A = A ∀ D
XRA E	AB	0 * * * 0	4	A = A ∀ E
XRA H	AC	0 * * * 0	4	A = A ∀ H
XRA L	AD	0 * * * 0	4	A = A ∀ L
XRA M	AE	0 * * * 0	7	A = A ∀ M
XTHL	E3		16	HL exchanged with stack

NOTE: d8 = 8 bits of data, d16 = 16 bits of data, a16 = 16-bit memory address, 11 = low-order address or data, and hh = high-order address or data.

C   THE 6800 INSTRUCTION SET

The 6800 microprocessor is capable of executing 197 different instructions using six addressing modes. Data are addressed using immediate, direct, indexed, extended, relative, and implied addressing modes.

Addressing Modes

There are six addressing modes used with most of the 6800 instructions. Before addressing modes can be investigated, the internal 6800 register set must be known. Figure C−1 illustrates the register set of the 6800. The 6800 has two accumulator registers labeled

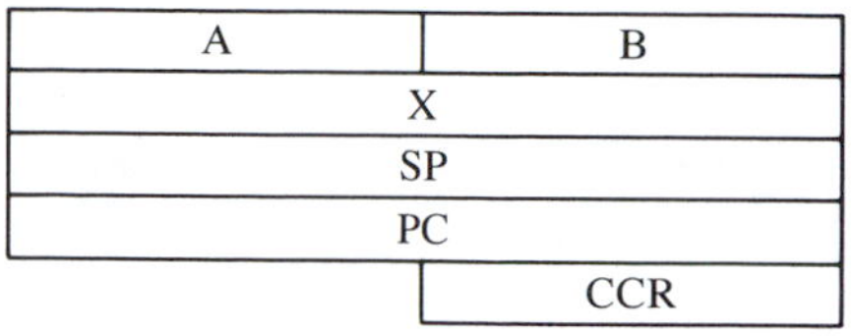

A	B
X	
SP	
PC	
	CCR

FIGURE C–1   The internal register set of the MC6800 microprocessor.

A and B, an index register labeled X, and a stack pointer labeled S. The accumulators are used to hold temporary data, the index register is used to address memory data, and the stack pointer is used to address the stack memory.

Implied Addressing   Instructions that list a register or registers in the op-code are called implied addressed instructions. An example of this type of addressing is the ABA instruction, which adds the contents of register B to A and places the result in A. Many of the 6800 instructions use this mode of addressing.

Immediate Addressing   Immediate addressing is used with many instructions, and in all cases the op-code is followed by one or two bytes of immediate data. If the ADDA #34 instruction (note that # indicates immediate data) is executed it moves a 34 decimal into the A register. In machine language this instruction is coded as an 8B 34. Some immediate addressed instructions use 16 bits of data. An example is the LDX #$1000 instruction (note that $ indicates hexadecimal data) which loads the index register with a 1000 hexadecimal. In machine language this instruction is coded as CE 10 00. Notice how the data follow the op-code.

In the listing of the instructions that follows later in this appendix, immediate data are indicated as either d8 for 8-bit immediate data or as d16 for 16-bit immediate data.

Direct Addressing   Direct addressing uses the first 256 bytes of the memory. This first section of the memory ($0000−$00FF) is called the base page. Base page or direct addressing is available with most instructions and speeds up memory accesses if the data are in the base page. In the instruction listing later in this appendix, a base page address is indicated by a bb.

Extended Addressing   Extended addressing allows most instructions to address any memory location in the memory. The op-code is followed by the 16-bit address of the data for extended addressing. The ADDA $1000 instruction is an example of extended addressing. Here the contents of memory location $1000 are added to the A register. In the instruction listing, extended addressing is indicated by an a16 for a 16-bit memory address in the symbolic version and an hh and ll for the machine language equivalent.

Indexed Addressing   In indexed addressing, the contents of the index register address a memory location. The ADDA X instruction will add the contents of the memory location addressed by the index register to the A register. In addition, a displacement may be listed with the X register. The ADDA 3,X instruction will add the contents of memory location $1003 to A if X = $1000. The displacement is added to the value in X to determine the memory address. In the instruction listing, the displacement is listed as dd.

Relative Addressing   Many of the branch instructions use relative addressing to locate the memory location to be branched to in a program. The displacement (dd) is added to the value in the program counter to determine how far away the branch address is located.

FIGURE C–2   The MC6800
CCR register.

$$CCR$$

| 1 | 1 | H | I | N | Z | V | C |

H = Half carry
I = Interrupt mask
N = Negative
Z = Zero
V = Overflow
C = Carry

Condition Code Register

The condition code register (CCR) (see figure C−2) contains six bits of information that indicate the condition of the most recent instruction. These bits indicate carry (C), overflow (V), zero (Z), negative (N), interrupt mask (I), and half carry (H).

Carry (C)   The carry CCR bit indicates whether a carry has been moved out of the most significant bit after an addition, or a borrow has moved into it after a subtraction.

Overflow (V)   The overflow CCR bit indicates that an addition has caused an arithmetic overflow condition. It also indicates that a subtraction has caused an arithmetic underflow.

Zero (Z)   The zero CCR bit indicates that the most recent operation has resulted in a zero. If the zero CCR bit is a logic one the result is zero.

Negative (N)   The negative CCR bit indicates that the result of the most recent instruction was negative.

Interrupt Mask (I)   The interrupt mask CCR bit is used to indicate the condition of the nonmaskable interrupt input. If I = 1 the interrupts are turned off.

Half Carry (H)   The half carry CCR bit indicates a carry or borrow between the lower- and upper-half of an eight-bit number.

The Instruction Set

The 6800 has 197 different instructions. They are listed in alphabetical order in the following table. Each instruction is listed with the symbolic and machine language versions, the effect on the CCR bits, the number of clock pulses required to execute it, and a comment about the operation of the instruction. Note that the * is used to indicate a change in a CCR bit, and a blank indicates the CCR bit is unaffected.

Instruction	Code	CCR bits						Clocks	Description
		H	**I**	**N**	**Z**	**V**	**C**		
ABA	1B	*		*	*	*	*	2	A = A + B
ADCA #d8	89 d8	*		*	*	*	*	2	A = A + d8 + C
ADCA bb	99 bb	*		*	*	*	*	3	A = A + (BB) + C
ADCA dd,X	A9 dd	*		*	*	*	*	5	A = A + (X+dd) + C
ADCA a16	B9 hh ll	*		*	*	*	*	4	A = A + (a16) + C
ADCB #d8	C9 d8	*		*	*	*	*	2	B = B + d8 + C
ADCB bb	D9 bb	*		*	*	*	*	3	B = B + (bb) + C

Instruction	Code	CCR bits		Clocks	Description
		H I N Z V C			
ADCB dd,X	E9 dd	*	* * * *	5	B = B + (X+dd) + C
ADCB a16	F9 hh ll	*	* * * *	4	B = B + (a16) + C
ADDA #d8	8B d8	*	* * * *	2	A = A + d8
ADDA bb	9B bb	*	* * * *	3	A = A + (bb)
ADDA dd,X	AB dd	*	* * * *	5	A = A + (X+dd)
ADDA a16	B hh ll	*	* * * *	4	A = A + (a16)
ADDB #d8	CB d8	*	* * * *	2	B = B + d8
ADDB bb	DB bb	*	* * * *	3	B = B + (bb)
ADDB dd,X	EB dd	*	* * * *	5	B = B + (X+dd)
ADDB a16	FB hh ll	*	* * * *	4	B = B + (a16)
ANDA #d8	84 d8		* * 0	2	A = A Λ d8
ANDA bb	94 bb		* * 0	3	A = A Λ (bb)
ANDA dd,X	A4 dd		* * 0	5	A = A Λ (X+dd)
ANDA a16	B4 hh ll		* * 0	4	A = A Λ (a16)
ANDB #d8	C4 d8		* * 0	2	B = B Λ d8
ANDB bb	D4 bb		* * 0	3	B = B Λ (bb)
ANDB dd,X	E4 dd		* * 0	5	B = B Λ (X+dd)
ANDB a16	F4 hh ll		* * 0	4	B = B Λ (a16)
ASL dd,X	68 dd		* * * *	7	Shift (X+dd) left
ASL a16	78 hh ll		* * * *	6	Shift (a16) left
ASLA	48		* * * *	2	Shift A left
ASLB	58		* * * *	2	Shift B left
ASR dd,X	67 dd		* * * *	7	Shift (X+dd) right, arithmetic
ASR a16	78 hh ll		* * * *	6	Shift (a16) right, arithmetic
ASRA	47		* * * *	2	Shift A right, arithmetic
ASRB	57		* * * *	2	Shift B right, arithmetic
BITA #d8	85 d8		* * 0	2	A Λ d8
BITA bb	95 bb		* * 0	3	A Λ (bb)
BITA dd,X	A5 dd		* * 0	5	A Λ (x+dd)
BITA a16	B5 hh ll		* * 0	4	A Λ (a16)
BITB #d8	C5 d8		* * 0	2	B Λ d8
BITB bb	D5 bb		* * 0	3	B Λ (bb)
BITB dd,X	E5 dd		* * 0	5	B Λ (X+dd)
BITB a16	F5 hh ll		* * 0	4	B Λ (a16)
BCC dd	24 dd			4	Branch carry clear
BCS dd	25 dd			4	Branch carry set
BEQ dd	27 dd			4	Branch equal
BGE dd	2C dd			4	Branch greater or equal
BGT dd	2E dd			4	Branch greater than
BHI dd	22 dd			4	Branch higher than
BLE dd	2F dd			4	Branch lower or equal
BLS dd	23 dd			4	Branch lower or same
BLT dd	2D dd			4	Branch less than
BMI dd	2B dd			4	Branch minus
BNE dd	26 dd			4	Branch not equal

Instruction	Code	CCR bits						Clocks	Description
		H	I	N	Z	V	C		
BPL dd	2A dd							4	Branch plus
BRA dd	20 dd							4	Branch always
BSR dd	8D dd							8	Branch subroutine
BVC dd	28 dd							4	Branch overflow clear
BVS dd	29 dd							4	Branch overflow set
CBA	11			*	*	*	*	2	A − B
CLC	0C						0	2	Clear carry
CLI	0E		0					2	Clear interrupt
CLR dd,X	6F dd			0	1	0	0	7	(X+dd) = 0
CLR a16	7F hh ll			0	1	0	0	6	(a16) = 0
CLRA	4F			0	1	0	0	2	A = 0
CLRB	5F			0	1	0	0	2	B = 0
CLV	0A					0		2	Clear overflow
CMPA #d8	81 d8			*	*	*	*	2	A − d8
CMPA bb	91 bb			*	*	*	*	3	A − (bb)
CMPA dd,X	A1 dd			*	*	*	*	5	A − (X+dd)
CMPA a16	B1 hh ll			*	*	*	*	4	A − (a16)
CMPB #d8	C1 d8			*	*	*	*	2	B − d8
CMPB bb	D1 bb			*	*	*	*	3	B − (bb)
CMPB dd,X	E1 dd			*	*	*	*	5	B − (X+dd)
CMPB a16	F1 hh ll			*	*	*	*	4	B − (a16)
COM dd,X	63 dd			*	*	0	1	7	$(X+dd) = \overline{(X+dd)}$
COM a16	73 hh ll			*	*	0	1	6	$(a16) = \overline{(a16)}$
COMA	43			*	*	0	1	2	$A = \overline{A}$
COMB	53			*	*	0	1	2	$B = \overline{B}$
CPX #d16	8C hh ll			*	*	*		3	X − d16
CPX bb	9C bb			*	*	*		4	X − (bb)
CPX dd,X	AC dd			*	*	*		6	X − (X+dd)
CPX a16	BC hh ll			*	*	*		5	X − (a16)
DAA	19			*	*	*	*	2	Decimal adjust A
DEC dd,X	6A dd			*	*	*		7	(X+dd) = (X+dd) − 1
DEC a16	7A hh ll			*	*	*		6	(a16) = (a16) − 1
DECA	4A			*	*	*		2	A = A − 1
DECB	5A			*	*	*		2	B = B − 1
DES	34							4	SP = SP − 1
DEX	09				*			4	X = X − 1
EORA #d8	88 d8			*	*	0		2	A = A ∀ d8
EORA bb	98 bb			*	*	0		3	A = A ∀ (bb)
EORA dd,X	A8 dd			*	*	0		5	A = A ∀ (X+dd)
EORA a16	B8 hh ll			*	*	0		4	A = A ∀ (a16)
EORB #d8	C8 d8			*	*	0		2	B = B ∀ d8
EORB bb	D8 bb			*	*	0		3	B = B ∀ (bb)
EORB dd,X	E8 dd			*	*	0		5	B = B ∀ (X+dd)
EORB a16	F8 hh ll			*	*	0		4	B = B ∀ (a16)
INC dd,X	6C dd			*	*	*		7	(X+dd) = (X+dd) + 1

Instruction	Code	CCR bits	Clocks	Description
		H I N Z V C		
INC a16	7C hh ll	* * *	6	(a16) = (a16) + 1
INCA	4C	* * *	2	A = A + 1
INCB	5C	* * *	2	B = B + 1
INS	31		4	SP = SP + 1
INX	08	*	4	X = X + 1
JMP dd,X	6E dd		4	Jump to (X+dd)
JMP a16	7E hh ll		3	Jump to a16
JSR dd,X	AD dd		8	Jump to subroutine (X+dd)
JSR a16	BD hh ll		9	Jump to subroutine a16
LDAA #d8	86 d8	* * 0	2	A = d8
LDAA bb	96 bb	* * 0	3	A = (bb)
LDAA dd,X	A6 dd	* * 0	5	A = (X+dd)
LDAA a16	B6 hh ll	* * 0	4	A = (a16)
LDAB #d8	C6 d8	* * 0	2	B = d8
LDAB bb	D6 bb	* * 0	3	B = (bb)
LDAB dd,X	E6 dd	* * 0	5	B = (X+dd)
LDAB a16	F6 hh ll	* * 0	4	B = (a16)
LDS #d16	8E hh ll	* * 0	3	SP = d16
LDS bb	9E bb	* * 0	4	SP = (bb)
LDS dd,X	AE dd	* * 0	6	SP = (X+dd)
LDS a16	BE hh ll	* * 0	5	SP = (a16)
LDX #d16	CE hh ll	* * 0	3	X = d16
LDX bb	DE bb	* * 0	4	X = (bb)
LDX dd,X	EE dd	* * 0	6	X = (X+dd)
LDX a16	FE hh ll	* * 0	5	X = (a16)
LSR dd,X	64 dd	0 * * *	7	Shift (X+dd) right, logic
LSR a16	74 hh ll	0 * * *	6	Shift (a16) right, logic
LSRA	44	0 * * *	2	Shift A right, logic
LSRB	54	0 * * *	2	Shift B right, logic
NEG dd,X	60 dd	* * * *	7	(X+dd) = 0 − (X+dd)
NEG a16	70 hh ll	* * * *	6	(a16) = 0 − (a16)
NEGA	40	* * * *	2	A = 0 − A
NEGB	50	* * * *	2	B = 0 − B
NOP	01		2	No operation
ORAA #d8	8A d8	* * 0	2	A = A V d8
ORAA bb	9A bb	* * 0	3	A = A V (bb)
ORAA dd,X	AA dd	* * 0	5	A = A V (X+dd)
ORAA a16	BA hh ll	* * 0	4	A = A V (a16)
ORAB #d8	CA d8	* * 0	2	B = B V d8
ORAB bb	DA bb	* * 0	3	B = B V (bb)
ORAB dd,X	EA dd	* * 0	5	B = B V (X+dd)
ORAB a16	FA hh ll	* * 0	4	B = B V (a16)
PSHA	36		4	Stack = A
PSHB	37		4	Stack = B
PULA	32		4	A = stack

Instruction	Code	CCR bits	Clocks	Description
		H I N Z V C		
PULB	33		4	B = stack
ROL dd,X	69 dd	* * * *	7	Rotate (X+dd) left through carry
ROL a16	79 hh ll	* * * *	6	Rotate (a16) left through carry
ROLA	49	* * * *	2	Rotate A left through carry
ROLB	59	* * * *	2	Rotate B left through carry
ROR dd,X	66 dd	* * * *	7	Rotate (X+dd) right through carry
ROR a16	76 hh ll	* * * *	6	Rotate (a16) right through carry
RORA	46	* * * *	2	Rotate A right through carry
RORB	56	* * * *	2	Rotate B right through carry
RTI	3B	* * * * * *	10	Return from interrupt
RTS	39		5	Return from subroutine
SBA	10	* * * *	2	A = A − B
SBCA #d8	82 d8	* * * *	2	A = A − d8 − C
SBCA bb	92 bb	* * * *	3	A = A − (bb) − C
SBCA dd,X	A2 dd	* * * *	5	A = A − (X+dd) − C
SBCA a16	B2 hh ll	* * * *	4	A = A − (a16) − C
SBCB #d8	C2 d8	* * * *	2	B = B − d8 − C
SBCB bb	D2 bb	* * * *	3	B = B − (bb) − C
SBCB dd,X	E2 dd	* * * *	5	B = B − (X+dd) − C
SBCD a16	F2 hh ll	* * * *	4	B = B − (a16) − C
SEC	0D	1	2	Set carry
SEI	0F	1	2	Set interrupt
SEV	0B	1	2	Set overflow
STAA bb	97 bb	* * 0	4	(bb) = A
STAA dd,X	A7 dd	* * 0	6	(X+dd) = A
STAA a16	B7 hh ll	* * 0	5	(a16) = A
STAB bb	D7 bb	* * 0	4	(bb) = B
STAB dd,X	E7 dd	* * 0	6	(X+dd) = B
STAB a16	F7 hh ll	* * 0	5	(a16) = B
STS bb	9F bb	* * 0	5	(bb) = SP
STS dd,X	AF dd	* * 0	7	(X+dd) = SP
STS a16	BF hh ll	* * 0	6	(a16) = SP
STX bb	DF bb	* * 0	5	(bb) = X
STX dd,X	EF dd	* * 0	7	(X+dd) = X
STX a16	FF hh ll	* * 0	6	(a16) = X
SUBA #d8	80 d8	* * * *	2	A = A − d8
SUBA bb	90 bb	* * * *	3	A = A − (bb)

494

Instruction	Code	CCR bits		Clocks	Description
		H I N Z V C			
SUBA dd,X	A0 dd	* * * *		5	A = A − (X+dd)
SUBA a16	B0 hh ll	* * * *		4	A = A − (a16)
SUBB #d8	C0 d8	* * * *		2	B = B − d8
SUBB bb	D0 bb	* * * *		3	B = B − (bb)
SUBB dd,X	E0 dd	* * * *		5	B = B − (X+dd)
SUBB a16	F0 hh ll	* * * *		4	B = B − (a16)
SWI	3F			12	Software interrupt
TAB	16	* * 0		2	B = A
TAP	06	* * * * * *		2	CCR = A
TBA	17	* * 0		2	A = B
TPA	07			2	A = CCR
TST dd,X	6D dd	* * 0 0		7	(X+dd) − 0
TST a16	7D hh ll	* * 0 0		6	(a16) − 0
TSTA	4D	* * 0 0		2	A − 0
TSTB	5D	* * 0 0		2	B − 0
TSX	30			4	X = SP
TXS	35			4	SP = X
WAI	3E			9	Wait for interrupt

NOTES: d8 = 8 bits of data, d16 = 16 bits of data, a16 = 16-bit address, ( ) = contents of, bb = base address, dd = 8-bit displacement, hh = high byte of address or data, and ll = low byte of address or data.

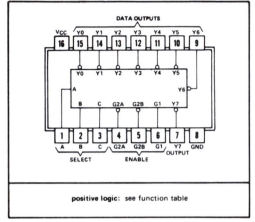

SN54LS138, SN54S138 . . . J OR W PACKAGE
SN74LS138, SN74S138 . . . J OR N PACKAGE
(TOP VIEW)

positive logic: see function table

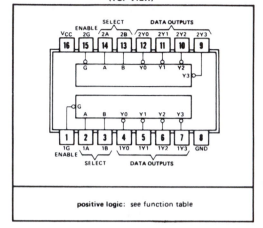

SN54LS139, SN54S139 . . . J OR W PACKAGE
SN74LS139, SN74S139 . . . J OR N PACKAGE
(TOP VIEW)

positive logic: see function table

functional block diagrams and logic

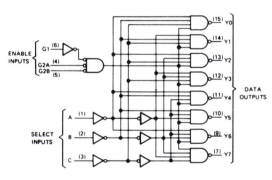

'LS138, 'S138

'LS138, 'S138 FUNCTION TABLE

INPUTS				OUTPUTS							
ENABLE		SELECT									
G1	G2*	C	B	A	Y0	Y1	Y2	Y3	Y4	Y5	Y6	Y7
X	H	X	X	X	H	H	H	H	H	H	H	H
L	X	X	X	X	H	H	H	H	H	H	H	H
H	L	L	L	L	L	H	H	H	H	H	H	H
H	L	L	L	H	H	L	H	H	H	H	H	H
H	L	L	H	L	H	H	L	H	H	H	H	H
H	L	L	H	H	H	H	H	L	H	H	H	H
H	L	H	L	L	H	H	H	H	L	H	H	H
H	L	H	L	H	H	H	H	H	H	L	H	H
H	L	H	H	L	H	H	H	H	H	H	L	H
H	L	H	H	H	H	H	H	H	H	H	H	L

*G2 = G2A + G2B
H = high level, L = low level, X = irrelevant

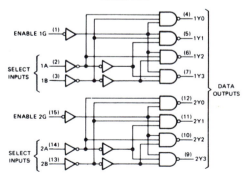

'LS139, 'S139

'LS139, 'S139 (EACH DECODER/DEMULTIPLEXER) FUNCTION TABLE

INPUTS			OUTPUTS			
ENABLE	SELECT					
G	B	A	Y0	Y1	Y2	Y3
H	X	X	H	H	H	H
L	L	L	L	H	H	H
L	L	H	H	L	H	H
L	H	L	H	H	L	H
L	H	H	H	H	H	L

H = high level, L = low level, X = irrelevant

FIGURE D–1 74138 and 74139 data specification.

(SOURCE: Courtesy of Texas Instruments, Inc.)

496

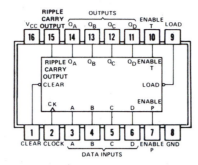

'161, 'LS161A, '163, 'LS163A, 'S163 BINARY COUNTERS

typical clear, preset, count, and inhibit sequences

Illustrated below is the following sequence:

1. Clear outputs to zero ('161 and 'LS161A are asynchronous; '163, 'LS163A, and 'S163 are synchronous)
2. Preset to binary twelve
3. Count to thirteen, fourteen fifteen, zero, one, and two
4. Inhibit

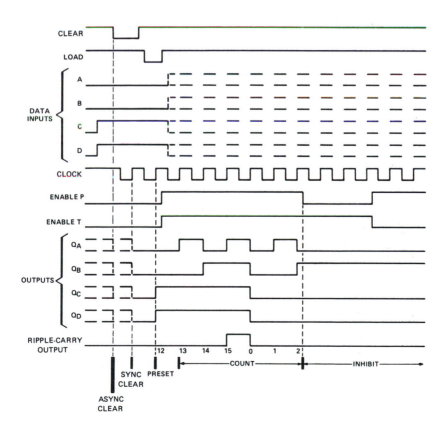

FIGURE D–2 74163 data specifications.

(SOURCE: Courtesy of Texas Instruments, Inc.)

FIGURE D–3 74LS245 data specifications.

(SOURCE: Courtesy of Texas Instruments, Inc.)

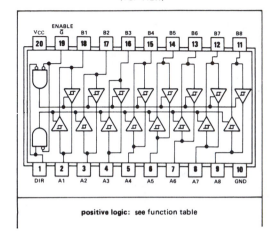

SN54LS245 . . . J PACKAGE
SN74LS245 . . . J OR N PACKAGE
(TOP VIEW)

positive logic: see function table

FUNCTION TABLE

ENABLE $\overline{G}$	DIRECTION CONTROL DIR	OPERATION
L	L	B data to A bus
L	H	A data to B bus
H	X	Isolation

H = high level, L = low level, X = irrelevant

498

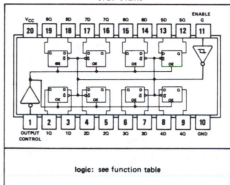

'LS373, 'S373 FUNCTION TABLE

OUTPUT CONTROL	ENABLE G	D	OUTPUT
L	H	H	H
L	H	L	L
L	L	X	Q_0
H	X	X	Z

'LS374, 'S374 FUNCTION TABLE

OUTPUT CONTROL	CLOCK	D	OUTPUT
L	↑	H	H
L	↑	L	L
L	L	X	Q_0
H	X	X	Z

See explanation of function tables on page 3-8.

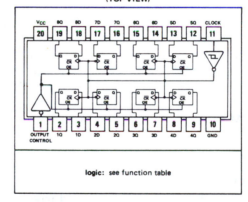

FIGURE D–4 74LS373 and 74LS374 data specifications.

(SOURCE: Courtesy of Texas Instruments, Inc.)

SELECTED ANSWERS TO THE ODD-NUMBERED PROBLEMS E

Chapter 1

1 **Memory size** This is probably the most significant difference between a mainframe and a micro, because the micro normally can address 64K to about 16M bytes of memory, while the mainframe can often address billions of bytes of memory.

Word size The microprocessor can normally manipulate either 8 or 16 bits of data; the mainframe can manipulate 32 or more bits.

Speed The mainframe is many times faster than the microprocessor. (The CRAY computer reputedly can execute an instruction in a few nanoseconds.)

3 If arithmetic operations are being developed for a particular application, a compiler would be much more useful than an assembler, because it already contains all of the arithmetic routines.

5 The text lists PL/M and PASCAL, which are currently found in many places where microprocessor software is being developed. These languages are ideally suited to microprocessor software development.

7 The software module allows a system program to be divided or structured into more manageable segments, enabling programmers to develop systems more efficiently.

9 The software development task begins when the engineering department sends a new product specification to the software development manager. The manager develops an estimate of the amount of memory required to implement the system and the number and type of I/O devices required. This information is returned to engineering for development.

   The manager now develops a system flowchart and assigns programming tasks or modules to the people in the department. At this point, the software for each module is developed. When all of the modules are debugged, the manager links them together and tests the system with software drivers and/or an emulator.

11 Sewing machine, washing machine, microwave oven, printer, CRT terminal, and various other simple digitalized devices.

13 Word processing systems would be ideal since they handle ASCII characters, which are 8-bit numbers if you include parity.

15 Millions of instructions per second.

Chapter 2

1 The CPU or MPU, memory, and input/output comprise all digital computer systems.

3 The memory stores the instructions and data for a program.

5 Programs are normally stored in one of the read-only types of memory.

7 A transparent latch is a device constructed with gated D-type flip-flops. The term *transparent* is derived from the fact that gated D-type flip-flops appear transparent whenever the gate input is at its active level.

9 Propagation delay times are usually short enough that they can be ignored, but not always. It is important that these times be checked if a memory device or external I/O device functions at a speed approaching the upper limit of the microprocessor's operating speed.

11 In a system that uses memory-mapped I/O, the I/O devices are treated exactly as if they were memory.

13 The microprocessor disconnects itself from its address, data, and control buses, allowing an external device to gain access to the microprocessor's memory and I/O equipment.

15 The main differences between these two buses are:

S100	STD-BUS
Local regulation	Remote regulation
16-bit data bus	8-bit data bus
24-bit address bus	16-bit address bus
Vectored interrupts	Single interrupt
Multiple-channel DMA	Single-channel DMA

17 Power supply decoupling is extremely critical in a digital system because digital circuitry generates a tremendous amount of power supply noise. Without adequate decoupling, it is doubtful that a digital system will perform as designed.

Chapter 3

1 The noise immunity of the Intel series of microprocessors is 350 mV.

3 Five lower-power TTL loads may be attached to one output pin. Each load draws a maximum of 0.4 mA of sink current.

5 Since the clock cycle frequency is one-half of the crystal clock frequency, the clock cycle frequency would be 2 MHz for a 4-MHz crystal. This makes the clock cycle time equal to 500 ns.

7 The 8284A clock generator divides the crystal frequency by a factor of three.

9 Since the 8088 contains 20 address pins, it is capable of directly addressing 1M bytes, or 512K 16-bit words of memory.

11 Adding buffering to the data bus decreases the amount of access time allowed for the memory.

13 The $\overline{WR}$ signal is a strobe to the I/O or memory that must be used to cause the write. The data from the data bus is valid only during this strobe; the trailing (or positive, in this case) edge would be used to transfer the data.

15 $DT/\overline{R}$ This signal selects the direction of data flow through an external bus transceiver.
$\overline{DEN}$ This signal enables the bus transceiver.

17 The 8085A always powers up executing instructions beginning at memory location 0000H.

19 The amount of access time allowed the memory by the 8085A is 575 ns at its maximum clock frequency.

21

Pin Name	Vector Location
TRAP	0024H
RST 7.5	003CH
RST 6.5	0034H
RST 5.5	002CH
INTR	*

*This interrupt vector is determined by the hardware (refer to Chapter 8).

FIGURE E–1

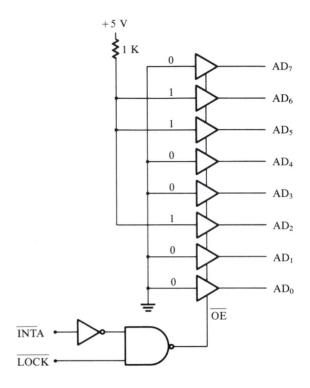

23 See figure E–1
25 During a HOLD condition, the microprocessor floats (or open-circuits) the address, data, and control bus connections $\overline{RD}$, $\overline{WR}$ and $IO/\overline{M}$.
27 The READY input can be used for the implementation of the RUN/STOP or the single-step functions.
29 Since the clock cycle time is equal to 1 μs, it would take 231 μs to execute the sequence in problem 28.
31 The logic analyzer can grab onto op-codes from the system data bus as they are actually executed in a system. This would test the system software under normal operating conditions.

Chapter 4

1

Device	Number of Pins
6800	40
6809	40
68000	64

3 It depends on which pins: some of the pins can supply 3.0 mA of sink current, and some can supply 5.0 mA. The 3.0 mA pins can drive 2 standard or 8 low-power TTL loads. The 5.0 mA pins can drive 3 standard or 13 low-power loads.

5 A 1-MHz input clock frequency would operate the MC6800 at a 1-MHz rate.

7 Either of these microprocessors can directly address 64K bytes of memory.

9 The MC68000 handles data transfers either 8 bits or 16 bits at a time through its 16-pin data bus.

11 The $\overline{AS}$ connection on the MC68000 indicates that the address bus contains a valid memory address.

13 The $\overline{BERR}$ signal indicates to the MC68000 that a bus error has occurred. It is usually developed by a memory error in order to request a repeat of the current bus cycle.

15 BREQ requests a DMA cycle, and a combination of BA and BS acknowledges it.

17 The reset vector is stored in the first eight memory locations in the MC68000-based system.

19 The MC68000 allows 290 ns of time for memory access.

21 The $\overline{DTACK}$ signal indicates that the memory or I/O has received a request for an operation.

23 The $\overline{FIRQ}$, $\overline{IRQ}$, and $\overline{NMI}$ interrupt inputs are present on the MC6809.

25 The main difference between these two inputs is the data that is automatically stacked by the processor whenever either request is honored.
FIRQ This input will stack the contents of the program counter and the condition code register when honored.
IRQ This input will stack all of the internal registers when it is honored.

27 It takes 2–5 μs, depending on the addressing mode.

29
```
*SUBROUTINE TO TEST I/O LOCATION $C000
  *
  TEST  LDAA  $C000      READ LOCATION
        STAA  $C000      WRITE LOCATION
        BRA   TEST
```

Chapter 5

1 **ROM** Mask programmable read-only memory.
PROM Fuse link programmable read-only memory.
EPROM Erasable programmable read-only memory.
EEPROM Electrically erasable read-only memory.
EAROM Electrically alterable read-only memory.
NOVRAM Nonvolatile RAM

3 If such a device could be found, it would contain 14 pins for memory addressing.

5 A bus contention, or conflict, occurs whenever two devices drive a bus line at exactly the same instant in time.

7 In a memory device that has common I/O, the same pin is used to read and write information; in a device that has separate I/O, there is a pin for each function.

9 One reason is that the dynamic cell contains one-half the number of inverters of a static cell. Another, and possibly more important, reason is that the amount of

FIGURE E–2

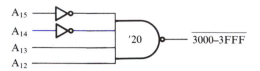

power dissipated in the dynamic cell is much lower than in a static cell. This allows the manufacturer to place the MOSFETS closer together on the IC substrate, thereby increasing the packaging density.

11 See figure E–2.

13 GOOD LUCK!!! (74LS139 sometime)

15 See figure E–3.

17 See figure E–4.

19 See figure E–5.

21 Integrated circuits that contain totem pole outputs, which are constructed of CMOS circuits or dynamic memory elements, must be bypassed because they produce switching transients on the power supply connections that would be coupled to another circuit in a system, causing faults.

23 This input strobes the address from the address pins into an internal row address register. It is also used for refreshing.

25 7FFFFH.

27 The end of the $\overline{RD}$ or $\overline{WR}$ strobe from the microprocessor, which occurs after the counter reaches its terminal count of 1100.

29
```
;8085A TEST ROUTINE
;
TEST-ROM:   LXI    H,0700H     ;POINT TO ROM
            SUB    A           ;CLEAR CHECKSUM
TEST-LOOP:  XRA    M           ;ACCUMULATE CHECKSUM
            INR    L
            JNZ    TEST-LOOP
            DCR    H

            JP     TEST-LOOP
            LXI    H,07FFH
            CMP    M
            JNZ    ERROR       ;IF BAD
            RET                ;IF GOOD
```

Chapter 6

1 If the switch remains at the indicated position, ground is applied to the uppermost input of gate A, which forces its output to a logic one. This one is coupled to the uppermost input of gate B; along with the logic one at the other input, the output becomes a logic zero.

Once the switch is thrown, as it approaches the other contact, the outputs of both gates remain unchanged. Gate A has a zero on its bottom input, so its out-

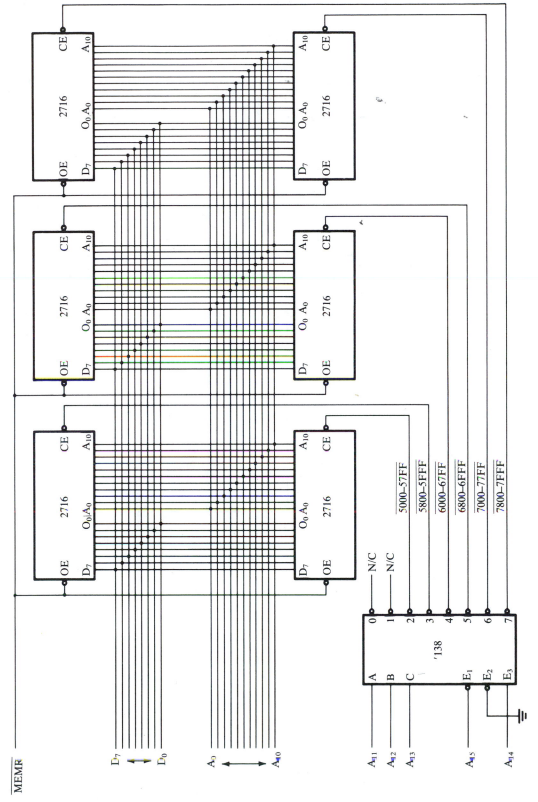

FIGURE E–3

*NOTE: Only the selection and control logic have been illustrated.

FIGURE E–4

NOTE: Only the selection and control logic have been illustrated.

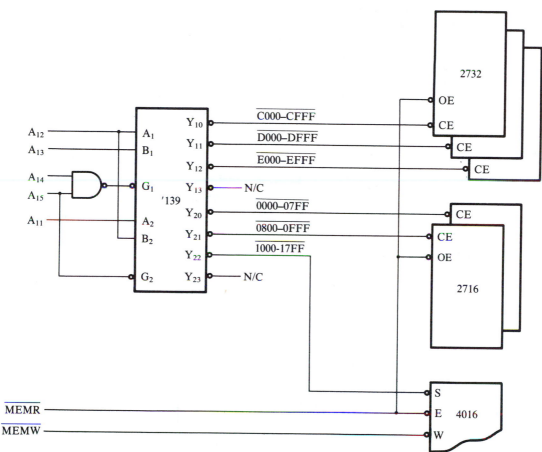

FIGURE E–5

put remains a one; gate B has a one on both inputs and its output remains a logic zero. The instant a connection is made, the logic states of the NAND gates reverse; once they have reversed, they can be changed again only if the contact physically bounces back to the other contact. This, of course, is practically impossible.

3 An input device must use a set of three-state buffers between the TTL-compatible device and the microprocessor data bus.

5 The I/O strobe is produced by combining the read or write signal with the output of either a memory address decoder for memory-mapped I/O or a port decoder for isolated I/O.

7 A page of memory is by definition 256 bytes.

9 All memory reference instructions may be used with memory-mapped I/O.

11 See figure E–6.

13 See figure E–7.
15 See figure E–8.
17 See figure E–9.
191   START: MVI   A,76H   ;LOAD LSB OF TIMER
 2   OUT   0C4H
 3   MVI   A,41H   ;LOAD MSB OF TIMER
 4   OUT   0C5H   ;AND MODE
 5   MVI   A,0C2H   ;START TIMER AND SETUP
 6   OUT   0C0H   ;PORTS A, B AND C
                      +
                      +

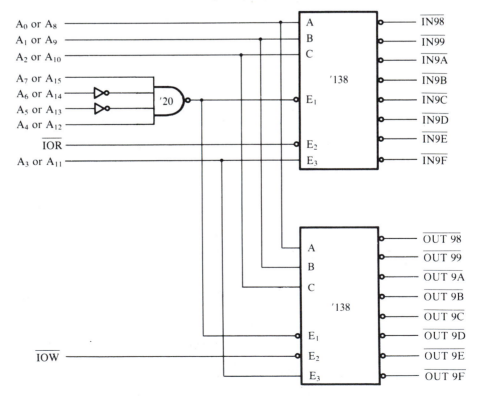

FIGURE E–6

NOTE: This is only one possible configuration.

FIGURE E–7

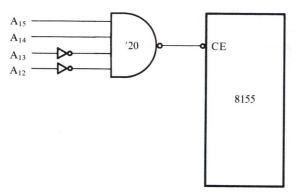

FIGURE E–8

21 See figure E–10.

23 The BF, or buffer full, flag bit indicates that the internal holding register contains data. For an input operation, it indicates that information has been strobed into the port; in an output operation, it indicates that information is available to the external device.

25 HARDWARE: See figure E–11.

INITIALIZATION DIALOG:

```
 1  INIT:   MVI   A,01H        ;PROGRAM PORT A AS AN OUTPUT
 2          OUT   0E0H
 3          SUB   A            ;TURN OFF SOLENOIDS
 4          OUT   0E1H
            +
            +
            +
 5  ;SUBROUTINE TO FIRE THE SOLENOIDS
 6  FIRE:   OUT   0E1H         ;SEND PATTERN TO SOLENOIDS
 7          MVI   A,10         ;WASTE 10 MSEC.
 8  FIRE1:  CALL  DEL1
 9          DCR   A
10          JNZ   FIRE1
11          SUB   A            ;TURN OFF SOLENOIDS
```

FIGURE E–9

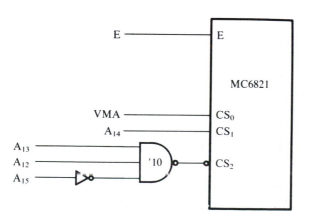

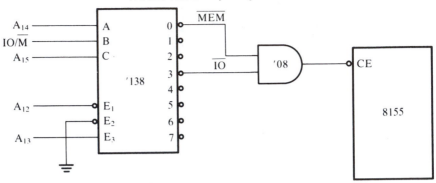

FIGURE E–10

```
12          OUT    0E1H
13          RET
14  ;
15  ;ONE MILLISECOND TIME DELAY (CLOCK CYCLE = 333 NSEC.)
16  ;
17  DEL1:   MVI    B,0CFH         ;LOAD COUNT
18  DEL2:   DCR    B
19          JNZ    DEL2
20          RET
```

Chapter 7

1 HARDWARE: See figure E–12.

3 SOFTWARE:

```
1   ;INITIALIZATION DIALOG
2   ;
3   INIT:  MVI    A,04H    ;SETUP PORT A FOR STROBED INPUT
4          OUT    80H
5   ;DATA TRANSFER SUBROUTINE
```

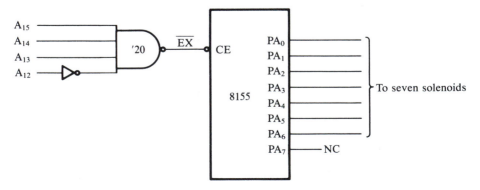

FIGURE E–11

```
6  ;
7  GET:    IN    80H      ;GET ABF
8          ANI   02H      ;ISOLATE ABF
9          JZ    GET      ;IF NO DATA
10         IN    81H      ;GET DATA
11         RET
```

```
5*ACTUAL DELAY TIME = 7.816 MSEC.
   DELAY    LDAB  $#4B    THIS TIME INCLUDES
   DELAY1   LDAA  $#10    THE JSR COMMAND.
   DELAY2   DECA
            BNE   DELAY2
            DECB
            BNE   DELAY1
            RTS
```

```
7;STEPPER MOTOR CONTROL PROGRAM
 ;
RPM:        MVI   A,01H    ;MOVE CLOCKWISE ONE STEP
            CALL  STEP     ;STEP THE MOTOR
            MVI   B,4
LOOP1:      CALL  DELAY    ;WAIT 1 MSEC.
            DCR   B
            JNZ   LOOP1    ;WAIT TOTAL = 4 MSEC.
            JMP   60RPM    ;KEEP STEPPING
```

9 Since the subroutine causes one step in approximately 1 ms, the maximum rotation speed is 300 rpm.

11 Since it takes 4 ms to program a byte, the total programming time is 16.384 s.

13 It would be possible for a program to run wild, possibly causing an erroneous write to the port. This possibility can be prevented by using a key to modify the contents of the bank selection port. This key can be one OUTPUT to enable the

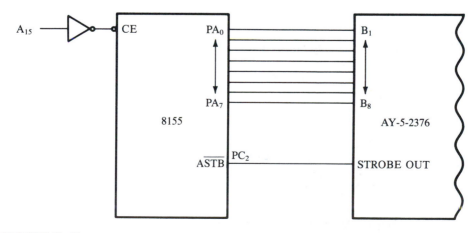

FIGURE E–12

bank latch and a second OUTPUT to send data into the bank latch. The bank latch can then be disabled by a third OUTPUT. This additional protection would make the system almost foolproof.

```
15 ;THIS SUBROUTINE WILL MULTIPLY NUMB1 BY NUMB2
   ;BOTH NUMBERS ARE DOUBLE PRECISION NUMBERS.
                  ;
        DMULT:    SUB    A              ;CLEAR COMMAND
                  OUT    0E1H           ;CLEAR STATUS WORD
                  LXI    H,NUMB1        ;POINT TO NUMBERS
                  CALL   LOAD           ;LOAD MULTIPLICAND
                  CALL   LOAD
                  CALL   LOAD           ;LOAD MULTIPLIER
                  CALL   LOAD
                  MVI    A,2BH          ;DMUL COMMAND
                  OUT    0E1H           ;START TO MULTIPLY
                  CALL   STAT           ;TIME OUT COMMAND
                  PUSH   PSW
                  CALL   UNLOAD         ;GET ANSWER
                  CALL   UNLOAD
                  POP    PSW
                  RET
        NUMB1:    DS     8
        NUMB2:    DS     8
        ANS:      DS     8
```

Chapter 8

1 An interrupt is exactly what the word implies: The program that is currently executing in the microprocessor is interrupted by an external hardware event.

3 If the interrupts are not enabled, there can never be a future interrupt. If the user were to forget to include this instruction, one and only one interrupt could ever occur. The exception is the TRAP interrupt; TRAP interrupt service subroutines should not contain an EI instruction.

5 Real-time clock, queue, printer interface, multiplexing displays, reading keyboards, and so forth.

7 RIM allows the following 8085A information to be read from the internal interrupt register:

> SID – Serial input data
> 17.5 – RST 7.5 input
> 16.5 – RST 6.5 input
> 15.5 – RST 5.5 input
> IE – interrupt enable status
> M7.5 – RST 7.5 mask
> M6.5 – RST 6.5 mask
> M5.5 – RST 5.5 mask

9 In any case in which it is critically important for the interrupt always to remain active. Examples could include power failure detection, display multiplexing and a real time clock.

11
```
        ;TURN RST 6.5 ON
        ;
        ON65:       RIM                 ;GET CURRENT MASKS
                    ANI     00000101B   ;M6.5 ON
                    ORI     00001000B   ;MSE ON
                    SIM                 ;SET MASKS
                      +
                      +
                      +
```

15
```
    ;INITIALIZATION DIALOG
    ;
    INIT:   MVI     A,00010010B     ;ICW1
            OUT     60H             ;SELECT EIGHT
            MVI     A,00010000B     ;ICW2
            OUT     61H             ;ADDRESS 1000H
            MVI     A,00000000B     ;OCW1
            OUT     61H             ;ENABLE ALL INTERRUPTS
            MVI     A,10100000B     ;OCW2
            OUT     60H
              +
              +
              +
```

17 Figure E–13 illustrates a polled interrupt scheme for the MC6800 microprocessor.
```
    *INTERRUPT SERVICE SUBROUTINE
    *
    INTS        LDAA  PORTA         GET INTERRUPT BITS
                ADDA  #$40          CHECK IF BOTH TRUE
                BCS   BOTH          IF BOTH ON
                TST   PORTA         CHECK LEVEL
                BMI   LEVEL1        IF LEVEL ONE
                BRA   LEVEL2        IF NOT LEVEL ONE
    BOTH        LDAA  PRIOR         GET PRIOR INDICATOR
                BMI   LEV1
                ASLA                SELECT OTHER LEVEL
                STAA  PRIOR
                BRA   LEVEL2        DO LEVEL TWO
    LEV1        ASRA                SELECT OTHER LEVEL
                STAA  PRIOR
                BRA   LEVEL1
    *PRIOR WOULD BE INITIALIZED AS A 10000000
```

19 Given the following program, in which ACCB equals the byte count and the index register points to the data, the transfer rate would equal 50,000 bytes per second.
```
            TRANS       LDAA X      ;GET DATA
                        STAA IO     ;SEND DATA
```

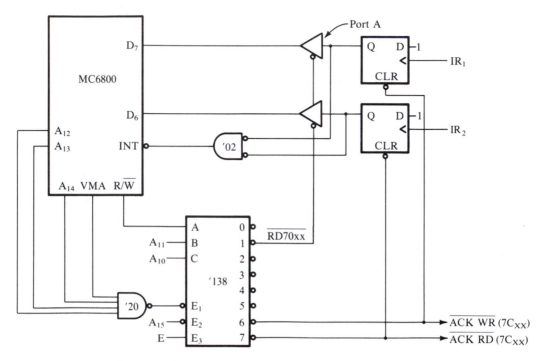

FIGURE E–13

```
INX          ;POINT TO NEXT BYTE
DECB         ;DECREMENT COUNT
BNE          TRANS
+
+
+
```

Chapter 9

1 In asynchronous digital communications, the data is transmitted without a clock and contains synchronization bits with each byte of data. In synchronous digital communications, a clock signal is sent with the data, and a sync character or two is transmitted with each block of data.

3 One.

5 4800 baud is the normal maximum, but data can be transmitted at higher rates, using leased lines.

7
```
    ;INITIALIZE THE 8251A
    ;
    INIT:        MVI   A,11111010B       ;PROGRAM PATTERN
                 OUT   COMMAND
```

9 Twenty-five.

11 2 V, because of the difference between the −5 V level and the −3 V threshold.

13 The main disadvantage of the current loop is its relatively low speed.

15 FSK data are basically generated by steering two different tones: one tone for a logic one condition and the other for a logic zero.

17 PSK.

19 $\overline{\text{CTS}}$ and $\overline{\text{DSR}}$.

21 The synchronous connection uses timing or clock signals and also a sync detect signal; the asynchronous system does not use these signals.

23
```
;CHECK THE MODEM FOR TRANSMISSION
;
CHKT:       MVI   A,00100111B
            OUT   COMMAND
;TURNS TRANSMITTER AND RECEIVER ON AND ALSO
;SETS RTS AND DTR LOW.
            IN    STATUS        ;GET 8251A STATUS
            RLC
            JNC   CHKT          ;WAIT UNTIL DSR = 0
;THE CTS SIGNAL IS CHECKED WITH INTERNAL
;HARDWARE THAT CONDITIONS THE TxRDY OUTPUT PIN
;BUT NOT THE TxRDY STATUS BIT
            +
            +
            +
```

25 The talker checks the NRFD signal to determine whether all of the bus devices are ready to receive data. When they are ready, the talker places the data on the data connections and issues the DAV signal. DAV indicates that data are available to the listeners connected to the bus. The listeners in response to DAV accept the data and respond with the NDAC signal. NDAC indicates that the listeners have all received the information and that it is all right for the talker to continue with its next cycle.

Chapter 10

1 DMA, or direct memory access, is an I/O technique that stops the microprocessor from executing its program so that data can be directly extracted from or stored into the memory.

3 The microprocessor effectively disconnects itself from the address, data, and control buses by floating, or tri-stating, them.

5 16K bytes.

7 The internal F/L, or first/last, flip-flop tracks whichever half of an internal register receives data.

9 More than one DMA channel can use the TC interrupt if the interrupt service subroutine polls the 8257. During the poll the channels that are active can be determined, and the counter can be read to see which one has reached zero or the terminal count.

13 A raster-scanned display is a display generated by sweeping the electron beam across the screen of the CRT. While the beam sweeps the screen it is turned on and off to draw characters.

15 There are two sets of deflection coils in a raster-scanned CRT. One set, the vertical deflection coils, is used to move the electron beam in the vertical direction. The other set, the horizontal deflection coils, is used to move the electron beam in a horizontal direction. By combining these two motions it is possible to sweep the electron beam across the screen and from top to bottom in such a manner as to draw a series of lines on the CRT.

17 The composite video signal contains video information, vertical sync, and horizontal sync. If it is a color composite video signal it also contains color video and a color sync signal.

19 A TTL monitor is a device that accepts video, vertical sync, and horizontal sync on three separate lines at TTL logic levels.

21 Yellow.

23 The field attribute code determines the logic level on the RVV pin connection. This signal, when routed through an external inverter, can cause reverse or inverse video.

Chapter 11

1 Memory that is changed easily is called volatile memory.

3 Three hundred RPM.

5 The mini-floppy disk has some problems that are cured by the micro-floppy disk. The disk is protected on the micro-floppy disk by a sliding door. The write-protect mechanism on the micro-floppy is a sliding piece of plastic that will not dislodge as will the tape used in the mini-floppy disk. The case of the micro-floppy disk is rigid so that the disk is better protected from damage.

7 The term NRZ stands for nonreturn-to-zero. In this recording technique the magnetic flux density never returns to zero.

9 Two microseconds each.

11 One microsecond each.

13 MFM.

17 A flying head.

19 Internal.

21 The area on a hard disk that is designed to receive the flying head during power up or power down is called the crash area.

23 Propagating elements in the shape of a chevron or T-bar are used to move magnetic bubbles on a magnetic bubble memory device.

25 A magnetic bubble is sensed when it passes a hall-effect device. The hall-effect device changes resistance as the bubble passes it.

27 The bubble is gated past the hall-effect sensor to read it.

29 Data transfer can occur using either interrupts or DMA.

31 LCT signals that the head is positioned over cylinders 44–77 and DIR selects the direction of the head travel for a seek.

33 Command, execution, and result.

35 Usually status register information.

37 The data error occurs if the CRC is incorrect, the control mark error if a deleted address mark is detected, and an error if the sector is not found.

39 Scan is used to verify that data are recorded correctly.

41 Five.

43 The PLL is used to generate a data window so that the 8272A can read the data from the disk.

Chapter 12

1 Pins in the print head are forced against the paper through a ribbon to draw characters.

3 Ninety-six.

5 The thermal print head heats carbon on a carbon ribbon that is transferred to the paper.

7 Laser printer.

9 Centronics printer interface.

11 Eight.

13 DTR is used to signal the computer that the printer is busy.

15 With the ETX/ACK protocol, ETX is appended to the end of each line of printed data. When the printer receives the ETX code, it sends the computer the ACK code acknowledging the receipt of the line of data.

19 This instruction causes the carriage stepper motor to step.